HANDBOOK OF TEACHING AND LEARNING AT BUSINESS SCHOOLS

For all involved in teaching in higher education —Annemette and Thyra
For my mum (1938–2021), I will miss you dearly—Adam
For Jon, Noa, and Ifan, with all my love—Eleri
For Yonca and Meryem—Aybars

Handbook of Teaching and Learning at Business Schools

A Practice-Based Approach

Edited by

Thyra Uth Thomsen

Professor, Copenhagen Business School, Denmark

Adam Lindgreen

Professor, Copenhagen Business School, Denmark and Extraordinary Professor, Gordon Institute of Business Science, University of Pretoria, South Africa

Annemette Kjærgaard

Professor, Copenhagen Business School, Denmark

Eleri Rosier

Reader, Cardiff Business School, Cardiff University, UK

Aybars Tuncdogan

Associate Professor, King's College London, UK

EE **Edward Elgar**
PUBLISHING

Cheltenham, UK • Northampton, MA, USA

Published by
Edward Elgar Publishing Limited
The Lypiatts
15 Lansdown Road
Cheltenham
Glos GL50 2JA
UK

Edward Elgar Publishing, Inc.
William Pratt House
9 Dewey Court
Northampton
Massachusetts 01060
USA

Paperback edition 2023

A catalogue record for this book
is available from the British Library

Library of Congress Control Number: 2021946160

This book is available electronically in the **Elgar**online
Business subject collection
http://dx.doi.org/10.4337/9781789907476

ISBN 978 1 78990 746 9 (cased)
ISBN 978 1 78990 747 6 (eBook)
ISBN 978 1 0353 1890 2 (paperback)

Printed and bound by CPI Group (UK) Ltd, Croydon, CR0 4YY

Contents

Figures

Tables

About the editors and authors

EDITORS

Annemette Kjærgaard is Professor (MSO) in Management Learning and Development at Department of Management, Society and Communication at Copenhagen Business School, Denmark. She is also Associate Dean of Technology-Enhanced Learning and leads the project Research in Blended Learning. Kjærgaard teaches leadership development and is a Senior Fellow with the Higher Education Academy. Her research program comprises studies in management learning, with a particular focus on the effects of blended learning on student outcomes, implications for student and teacher identities, and organizational changes due to the adoption of technology-enhanced learning. Her research has been published in journals such as *European Journal of Information Systems*, *Journal of Information Technology*, *Journal of Management Studies* and *Management Learning*.

Adam Lindgreen completed a PhD in marketing from Cranfield University, UK (in 2000), with 18 months spent at the University of Auckland's Business School, New Zealand. Since 2016, Lindgreen has been Professor of Marketing at Copenhagen Business School, Denmark, where he also heads the Department of Marketing. He also is Extraordinary Professor with the University of Pretoria, South Africa's Gordon Institute of Business Science. He serves as co-editor-in-chief for *Industrial Marketing Management*. Lindgreen's publications have appeared in *California Management Review*, *Journal of Business Ethics*, *Journal of the Academy of Marketing Science*, *Journal of Product Innovation Management*, *Journal of World Business* and *Organization Studies*, among others. Furthermore, his 30+ books include *The Emergence and Rise of Relationship Marketing*, *A Stakeholder Approach to Corporate Social Responsibility* (with Kotler, Vanhamme, and Maon; 2012), *Memorable Customer Experiences* (with Vanhamme and Beverland; 2009), *Not All Claps and Cheers* (with Maon, Vanhamme, Angell and Memery; 2018), *Public Value* (with Koenig-Lewis, Kitchener, Brewer, Moore and Meynhardt; 2019), and *Sustainable Value Chain Management* (with Maon, Vanhamme and Sen; 2013). Beyond these academic contributions to marketing, Lindgreen has discovered and excavated settlements from the Stone Age in Denmark, including the only major kitchen midden – Sparregård – in the south-east of Denmark; because of its importance, the kitchen midden was later excavated by the National Museum and then protected as a historical monument for future generations. He is also an avid genealogist, having traced his family back to 1390 and published widely, including eight books and numerous articles in scientific journals (*Personalhistorisk Tidsskrift*, *Genealogist* and *Slægt & Data*), related to methodological issues in genealogy, accounts of population development and particular family lineages.

Eleri Rosier is a Reader in Marketing and Strategy at Cardiff Business School, Cardiff University, UK, as well as a Member of the Chartered Institute of Marketing and a Fellow of the Higher Education Academy. She is also Director of Postgraduate Recruitment and

Admissions and Programme Director for MSc Strategic Marketing. Her main research interests include strategy processes and implementation, mid-level marketing management, blended learning, live case study teaching and bilingual teaching in higher education. Her work has appeared in *European Journal of Marketing, Industrial Marketing Management, Journal of Euromarketing* and *Journal of Strategic Marketing*. Before joining Cardiff Business School, she gained industrial experience in the marketing and event management industry.

Thyra Uth Thomsen is Professor (MSO) of Consumer Research in the Department of Marketing, Copenhagen Business School, Denmark. From 2017 to 2020, she was deputy head of the department, with a special focus on the delivery and development of marketing education. Her research interests lie primarily in consumer transformations and consumption-related individual and societal well-being. In the past, her research has mainly been conducted within the domain of food consumption, particularly related to consumer vulnerabilities and resources. Moreover, she has a keen interest in the scholarship of teaching and learning. She has published in leading journals such as *European Journal of Marketing, Journal of Business Ethics, Journal of Business Research, Management Learning* and *Psychology and Marketing*.

Aybars Tuncdogan is Associate Professor in Marketing and Technology at King's Business School, King's College, London, UK. Previously, he worked as a Lecturer in Marketing and Strategy at Cardiff University. He completed his PhD at the Rotterdam School of Management, Erasmus University, the Netherlands. His research employs psychological constructs to understand ways to explain, predict and shape managers', consumers' and collectives' (e.g., teams, organizations, consumer tribes) strategic decisions. He has published in Industrial Marketing Management, Journal of Business Ethics, Journal of Managerial Psychology, Leadership Quarterly, Long Range Planning, Personality and Individual Differences, R&D Management and Teaching in Higher Education. He has also has co-edited (with Lindgreen, van den Bosch and Volberda) *Strategic Renewal: Core Concepts, Antecedents and Micro-Foundations* (2019).

AUTHORS

Kasper Merling Arendt is a doctoral fellow in the Department of Marketing at Copenhagen Business School, Denmark, where he researches the effects of different pedagogical approaches to entrepreneurship education, with a particular focus on design-based ways of teaching. He also is employed at VIVE, The Danish Center for Social Science Research, where he has conducted both small- and large-scale program evaluations of the Danish school system.

Michael B. Beverland is Professor of Marketing and Head of Department (Strategy and Marketing) at the University of Sussex Business School, UK. He is also an adjunct professor with the Copenhagen Business School, Denmark. Beverland received his doctorate from the University of South Australia. His work has been published in *Journal of the Academy of Marketing Science, Journal of Advertising, Journal of Consumer Research, Journal of Macromarketing, Journal of Management Studies* and *Journal of Product Innovation Management*, among others. He has published a number of teaching cases with the Harvard Business School and the Case Centre, USA.

Roderick J. Brodie is Professor of Marketing in the Department of Marketing at University of Auckland, New Zealand. His 120-plus journal articles have appeared in leading international journals including *Industrial Marketing Management, International Journal of Research in Marketing, Journal of Marketing, Journal of Marketing Research, Journal of Service Research* and *Management Science*, among others. He is an associate editor for *Journal of Service Research* and former associate editor for *Marketing Theory*. He has served on the editorial boards of *Journal of Marketing, International Journal of Research in Marketing* and other leading international journals. He was the first president of the Australian and New Zealand Marketing Academy (ANZMAC), and in 2004 he was made a founding fellow; in 2011, Brodie was made a fellow of the European Marketing Academy (EMAC).

Peter Bryant is an Associate Professor at the University of Sydney Business School, Australia, where he also serves as an Associate Dean (Education). He has worked as an academic and educational leader in several leading UK and Australian institutions, including the London School of Economics and Political Science, University of Greenwich, and Middlesex University, UK. He received his PhD in management from the University of Technology, Sydney, Australia. Bryant is a trustee of the Association for Learning Technology (UK) and the chair of the editorial board for the peer-reviewed open access journal *Research in Learning Technology*.

Leela Cejnar is an interdisciplinary lecturer at the University of Sydney, Australia. She works with the Industry and Community Projects Unit, in the Education Portfolio, Office of the Deputy Vice Chancellor. In this role, Cejnar collaborates with industry, community and government organizations to design and deliver interdisciplinary, experiential learning projects for undergraduate students. She holds a PhD in Law and has published widely in her own discipline, as well as in learning and teaching in higher education. She is a senior fellow of the Higher Education Academy (UK).

Bo T. Christensen is Professor in Creative Cognition at Copenhagen Business School, Denmark. A cognitive psychologist by training, his work centers on cognitive studies of creative, innovative or entrepreneurial practices in the fields of design, business, architecture, engineering and gastronomy. His theoretical focus is on cognitive strategies such as analogy, simulation and incubation, coupled with metacognitive process awareness. He is the Academic Director of CBS Studios, a studio-based learning environment at Copenhagen Business School.

Ad de Jong is Professor of Marketing at Copenhagen Business School, Denmark. He is an expert in the areas of sales management, frontline marketing, service marketing, service innovation and marketing research. In addition to serving on the editorial boards of *Journal of Service Research, Industrial Marketing Management* and *Journal of Personal Selling and Sales Management*, de Jong is a frequently invited speaker and member of a wide variety or international fora, including both highly reputed academic institutions and well-respected professional bodies in marketing.

C. Anthony Di Benedetto is Professor of Marketing and Supply Chain Management and Senior Washburn Research Fellow at the Fox School of Business, Temple University, USA. He has held visiting professorships at Bocconi University and Politecnico di Milano (Italy), Technische Universiteit Eindhoven (Netherlands), Kansai University (Japan), Yonsei

University (Korea), WHU (Germany), St Petersburg State University (Russia), and Edhec Business School and IESEG School of Management (France). In 2010, Di Benedetto was named the Fulbright-Kathryn and Craig Hall Chair in Entrepreneurship and spent a semester at the Wirtschaftsuniversität Wien (Austria). Di Benedetto is co-editor-in-chief of *Industrial Marketing Management* and editor-in-chief of *Journal of International Consumer Marketing*. He served as editor of *Journal of Product Innovation Management* for nine years.

Wim Gijselaers is Full Professor of Educational Research at the School of Business and Economics of Maastricht University, the Netherlands, where he also heads the Educational Research and Development Department. He received his PhD from Maastricht University. Gijselaers has published in *Educational Research Review, Small Group Research, Instructional Science, Studies in Higher Education, Academic Medicine, Medical Teacher* and *European Journal of Psychology of Education*, among others.

Linda Greve is Head of Learning at the Science Museums, Aarhus University, Denmak. She holds a PhD in knowledge communication from Aarhus School of Business and Social Sciences. Greve worked for several years as an educational developer in the fields of entrepreneurship and business administration and is an acknowledged teacher trainer. She has published books and papers on research presentation and higher education teaching; her research mainly focuses on the fields of knowledge creation and knowledge dissemination.

Rachael Hains-Wesson is Director of Work-Integrated Learning and an associate professor at the University of Sydney Business School, Australia. She is responsible for leading the scope and scale expansion of the School's Work-Integrated Learning offerings. A Queen Elizabeth II Silver Jubilee Trust for Young Australians Awardee, Hains-Wesson has extensive senior management and leadership experience in entrepreneurship and creative industries.

Elaine Huber is an associate professor at the University of Sydney Business School, Australia, where she is Academic Director of Business Co-Design. Huber received her PhD in educational evaluation from Macquarie University, Australia and is a leading researcher in the field of educational development and learning technologies, with a teaching philosophy that takes a student-centered approach. She is an active member of the Australasian Society for Computers in Learning in Tertiary Education (ASCILITE) community, reviews for *Australian Journal of Educational Technologies*, and has published in journals such as *Studies in Educational Evaluation, International Journal of Educational Management* and *Evaluation Journal of Australasia*.

Alan Irwin is a professor in the Department of Organization at Copenhagen Business School, Denmark. From 2015 to 2018, he was also the school's Vice-President of Entrepreneurship and Innovation. Between 2007 and 2014, he was Dean of Research and, for a period, served as the Acting President. His PhD is from the University of Manchester, UK, and he has held academic positions at Manchester, Brunel and Liverpool universities, UK. He is currently the principal investigator on a research project examining research and innovation policies in China, Denmark and the United States. He has published in *Environment and Planning A, Minerva, Public Understanding of Science, Science, Technology, and Human Values, Social Studies of Science* and *Sociological Review*, among others.

Marian Iszatt-White is a senior lecturer at Lancaster University Management School, UK, where she also is Director of the School Doctoral Programmes. Iszatt-White received her PhD from Lancaster University, as part of the Centre for Excellence in Leadership. She has published in *International Journal of Management Reviews, Journal of Business Ethics, Management Learning* and *Leadership*, as well as co-authoring a successful postgraduate leadership textbook.

Kaiying Ji is a lecturer in accounting at the University of Sydney Business School, Australia. Ji has a PhD in accounting and is a member of Certified Practising Accountant (CPA) Australia and the Chartered Financial Analyst (CFA) Institute. She has extensive experience teaching accounting, work-integrated learning and business units. Her research areas include work-integrated learning, financial reporting and intangible assets.

David Kember is Professor in Curriculum Methods and Pedagogy in the Education Faculty of University of Tasmania, Australia. Prior to this appointment, he worked in universities in Hong Kong for 25 years, including six years spent running an interinstitutional initiative across the eight universities in Hong Kong, known as the Action Learning Project. It supported 90 action research projects, in which teachers introduced a wide variety of initiatives to improve the quality of student learning. His work in the following areas has been widely cited: student approaches to learning and the influence of teaching and assessment on them; the Chinese and Asian learner; motivation; reflective thinking; teachers' beliefs about and approaches to teaching; action learning and research for teaching quality improvement; and online and distance education.

Rushana Khusainova is a lecturer in marketing at Aston Business School, UK. Her research centers on salesperson motivations and work–life balance, as well as ritualistic consumption. Her teaching-related interests include gamification and game-based learning, infused curricula and student mental health.

Bernadett Koles is an associate professor in the Department of Marketing and Sales Management at IESEG School of Management. Koles received her EdD from Harvard University Graduate School of Education, USA, and her PhD from Durham University Business School, UK. She has published in *Current Opinion in Psychology, Journal of Business Research, Psychology and Marketing, Industrial Marketing Management* and *Journal of Marketing Management*, among others, and she serves as an associate editor for *International Journal of Consumer Studies*.

Carolin Kreber is Professor of Education at Cape Breton University, Canada. From 2015 to 2020, she served as Dean of the School of Education and Health. From 2005 to 2015, she held the Chair of Teaching and Learning in Higher Education at Edinburgh University, UK, where she also directed the Centre for Teaching, Learning and Assessment and led the postgraduate Certificate in Academic Practice. In 2010, she founded the Higher Education Research Group at Edinburgh University and assumed the role of Institute Director of Research two years later. Kreber received her PhD from the University of Toronto, Canada. She taught and developed many courses at Brock University and University of Alberta, Canada, and Edinburgh University. Kreber is the author of many articles and books in the field of education; her most recent book is *Educating for Civic-Mindedness: Nurturing Authentic Professional Identities through Transformative Higher Education* (2017).

Barbara Larson is Executive Professor of Management at the D'Amore-McKim School of Business at Northeastern University, USA. She earned her DBA from Harvard Business School in Management, USA, and her MBA from the Wharton School, University of Pennsylvania, USA, in Finance and Operations Management. She has published in *Management Science, Academy of Management Perspectives, Management Teaching Review* and *Harvard Business Review*, among others.

Sabine Lauer is a postdoctoral researcher at the Chair of Organizational Studies, Continuing Education and Social Management at TU Dortmund University, Germany. Lauer received her PhD from TU Dortmund University in 2019. In her cumulative dissertation, she dealt with "Transformational Governance of Academic Teaching." She has published on higher education in *Studies in Higher Education, Learning Organization* and *Tertiary Education and Management*. In addition, Lauer holds a Master's degree in biostatistics, in which field she also has published in *American Statistician* and *PLOS ONE*.

Catherine Leviten-Reid is an associate professor at Cape Breton University, Canada and teaches in the MBA in Community Economic Development program in the Shannon School of Business. Her research pertains to the social economy, affordable housing and community development, and her articles have appeared in journals including *VOLUNTAS: International Journal of Voluntary and Nonprofit Organizations* and *Nonprofit and Voluntary Sector Quarterly*. Leviten-Reid's research is primarily conducted in partnership with community-based organizations; she currently is leading a five-year, pan-Canadian research initiative on affordable housing for those in greatest need. Her PhD is from the University of Wisconsin-Madison, USA.

Maria Luksich is the Work-Integrated Learning Programs Manager at University of Sydney Business School, Australia. She has postgraduate degrees in education (career development) and communications management from Queensland University of Technology and the University of Technology Sydney, Australia.

Stephanie MacPherson is a senior instructor in the Bachelor of Hospitality and Tourism Management program in the Shannon School of Business at Cape Breton University, Canada. MacPherson joined the faculty at Cape Breton University after more than 15 years' practitioner experience in different sectors and levels of the tourism, hospitality and event management industries, as well as administrative roles in higher education in both Canada and the United States. Her Master's degree in tourism administration reflects a concentration in sustainable destination management, from George Washington University, USA. She also earned a Bachelor of Applied Management in Hospitality and Tourism from the University of New Brunswick, Canada. She has published in the *Journal of Aboriginal Economic Development*.

Lilia Mantai is a lecturer at University of Sydney Business School, Australia and Academic Lead for Course Enhancement, where she currently oversees the assurance of learning and guides curriculum development and assessment design. Mantai graduated with a PhD from Macquarie University, Australia, in 2017, with a thesis on the researcher identity development of PhD students and the role of social support. She has published in higher and doctoral education journals, including *Studies in Higher Education, Teaching in Higher Education, International Journal for Researcher Development, International Journal of Doctoral Studies* and *Australian Educational Researcher*. She is a senior fellow of AdvanceHE and associate editor for *Higher Education Research and Development*.

Stefan Meisiek is an associate professor in the Strategy, Innovation and Entrepreneurship discipline at the University of Sydney Business School, Australia. He received his PhD in Management from the Stockholm School of Economics, Sweden and his MA from the Free University, Berlin, Germany. He researches leadership, strategy, and business innovation. He has a particular interest in how leadership and strategic choices enable or constrain innovation efforts, such as motivating organizational members to inquire into pernicious problems; challenging basic assumptions; and granting licenses for dreaming, imagining and creating. He has worked with many companies, government agencies and non-governmental organizations on innovation projects.

René W.J. Moolenaar is a senior lecturer and associate professor in the Strategy and Marketing Department of the University of Sussex Business School, UK. He is also a board member for multiple creative and technology-led innovative organizations. He has published a video case study within the Pearson Revel compendium to *Global Marketing* (with Hollensen, 2020).

Peter Naudé graduated in marketing from the University of Cape Town, South Africa, and then in operations research from the University of Sussex, UK. After teaching at the Graduate School of Business in Cape Town, he went to Manchester Business School, UK, where after completing his PhD he joined the staff. Between 1999 and 2005, he was Professor of Marketing at the University of Bath's School of Management, UK, before returning to Manchester Business School in 2006. Naudé was Deputy Director of Manchester Business School between 2006 and 2012, and he retired in 2017. He currently holds joint appointments at Manchester Metropolitan University Business School and with the Discipline of Marketing at the University of Sydney, Australia.

Alyson Nicholds is Associate Professor of Business Management at Staffordshire Business School, UK, where she leads programmes in postgraduate research and draws on critical discourse theory to teach about leadership. In her teaching, writing and research, she draws reflexively on this experience, together with her professional background in healthcare and urban development, to make sense of how different actors lead for social purposes in complex times. Nicholds received her PhD from the Institute of Local Government Studies at the University of Birmingham, UK, and her work has been published in high-ranking journals including *Public Management Review*, *International Business Review*, *Management Learning* and *Regional Studies*.

Loïc Plé is Director of Pedagogy and Head of the Center for Educational and Technological Innovation (CETI) at IESEG School of Management. He is also an associate professor in the Department of Innovation, Entrepreneurship, and Information Systems. Plé received his PhD from Paris Dauphine University, France. He has published several papers in *Journal of Business Research*, *Journal of Services Marketing*, *M@n@gement* and *Journal of Business Strategy*, among others, as well as more than 20 case studies. He has also coordinated a book of case studies in strategic management.

Nicola Reimann is an academic developer in the School of Education and Durham Centre for Academic Development at Durham University, UK. She has developed, led and taught a wide range of modules and programs pertaining to learning and teaching in higher education for staff. Reimann received her PhD from Newcastle University, UK. Her research, focused on assessment and feedback in higher education and the development of academics, has been published in journals such as *Assessment and Evaluation in Higher Education* and *International Journal for Academic Development*. She is currently principal investigator of a European Erasmus+ funded project on intercultural reflection on teaching, and a member of the degree standards project team which is responsible for developing and delivering professional development for external examiners across England, Wales and Northern Ireland.

Torsten Ringberg received his MBA, MA (Psychological Anthropology) and PhD in marketing from US universities. He publishes in top-tier international academic business journals, such as *Journal of Marketing*, *Journal of Consumer Research*, *Journal of Management Studies*, *Annals of Tourism Research* and *Research in the Sociology of Organizations*. He teaches masters and PhD courses, as well as courses in the executive and summer programs, and has won several teaching awards in the United States and Denmark. Ringberg also applies academic insights to work for leading US and European organizations.

Ian Sadler is a subject leader in the School of Sport and Exercise Science at Liverpool John Moores University, UK. He has developed, led and taught a wide range of modules and programs related to sport and academic development for staff in higher education. Sadler received his PhD from University of Edinburgh, UK. His research focuses on teacher development, as well as assessment and feedback in higher education. He has published in journals such as *Studies in Higher Education* and *Assessment and Evaluation in Higher Education*. He is currently a member of the degree standards project team which is developing and delivering professional development for external examiners across England, Wales and Northern Ireland.

Yasin Sahhar is a strategic marketing consultant at The Next Organization and a PhD researcher in the research group for Entrepreneurship, Strategy and Innovation Management at University of Twente, the Netherlands. In his consultancy work, he helps industry leaders address strategy and marketing-related challenges. His research interest lies in value creation and value experience, from a service logic perspective, and he has presented and published his work at several conferences.

Kay Sambell is Professor of Higher Education Pedagogy at Edinburgh Napier University, UK. She is also an honorary professor at the University of Cumbria, UK, and president of the internationally acclaimed Assessment in Higher Education conference. She is known for co-leading the ground-breaking Centre for Excellence in Teaching and Learning in Assessment for Learning at Northumbria University, UK. Sambell received her PhD from the University of York, UK. She co-authored the widely cited text on *Assessment for Learning in Higher Education* with Catherine Montgomery and the late Liz McDowell, and has published in *Assessment for Learning in Higher Education*, *Studies in Educational Evaluation*, *Quality in Higher Education* and *Advance HE*, among others. She is a UK National Teaching Fellow (2002) and holds Principal Fellowship in the Higher Education Academy.

Sandra Seno-Alday is a lecturer at the University of Sydney Business School, Australia, where she is also director of the program for high-achieving students. Extending her experience in strategy and organization development consulting, her scholarly and industry research explores global dynamics, international business governance, risk and sustainability. Committed to excellence and innovation in higher education, Seno-Alday is a recipient of an Australian Learning and Teaching Council Citation for Outstanding Contributions to Student Learning.

Maryam Shahbazi is a PhD candidate and research assistant at the University of Sydney Business School, Australia. She has completed her MPhil in social network analysis at the University of Sydney. Her professional background spans international business development, market research and project management experience, and she has led complex projects. Shahbazi also holds a Master's degree in project management from the University of Sydney and an Executive Master's in business administration from Iran. Her research areas include social media and crisis management and influential factors in online social networks.

Michael Sweet is Director of Design and Integration at Northeastern University's Center for Advancing Teaching and Learning through Research, USA. He earned his PhD from the University of Texas, Austin, USA in educational psychology, and has published in *Educational Psychology Review, Journal on Excellence in College Teaching, Decision Sciences, Journal of Innovative Education, To Improve the Academy* and *New Directions for Teaching and Learning*, among others.

Stina Teilmann-Lock is associate professor in the Department of Management, Politics and Philosophy at Copenhagen Business School, Denmark. Her research focuses on intersections of law, design and technology, and she has published widely on intellectual property law, design and digital transformations.

Piet Van den Bossche is Full Professor of Learning in Organizations at the Faculty of Social Sciences, University of Antwerp, Belgium, where he heads the Department of Training and Education Sciences. He is also an associate professor at the School of Business and Economics at Maastricht University, the Netherlands. Van den Bossche received his PhD from Maastricht University. He has published in *European Journal of Psychology of Education, Educational Research Review, Small Group Research, Instructional Science* and *Human Resource Development Quarterly*, among others.

Florence Villesèche is associate professor and Academic Director of the Business in Society platform for Diversity and Difference at Copenhagen Business School, Denmark. She is a Marie Curie alumna and received an Emerald/EFMD Highly Commended Award for outstanding doctoral research. Her published works include books and chapters on diversity, identity and networks, along with contributions to recognized outlets such as *Human Relations, European Management Review, Personnel Review, ephemera* and *Equality, Diversity and Inclusion*. Her main research interests are networks, gender and diversity, identity and the corporate elite.

Sylvia von Wallpach is Professor (MSO) in Branding and Marketing Management at the Department of Marketing at Copenhagen Business School, Denmark. Her main research interests are in the fields of branding, interpretative consumer research and qualitative method development. Von Wallpach is a senior fellow with the Higher Education Academy and has contributed to the development of online and blended learning. Her research has been published in *Tourism Management, Journal of Business Ethics, Journal of Business Research* and *Psychology and Marketing* and she has been awarded international prizes (e.g., SAGE Social Science Space Impact Contest 2020).

Leslie Wardley is Associate Professor of Marketing in the Shannon School of Business and a Social Sciences and Humanities Research Council (SSHRC) Exchange University Research Chair in Social Determinants of Health (2019–2022) at Cape Breton University, Canada. She holds adjunct status in Ryerson University's Department of Mechanical and Industrial Engineering within its Faculty of Engineering and Architectural Science, and in Nipissing University's School of Business, both in Cananda. Wardley began her professional career in small business management and later expanded her expertise to university administration. After shifting from administration to become a faculty member, she continued to concentrate her efforts on higher education policies and administration. Her PhD (Laurentian University, Canada) focused on the co-creation of value and the institutional commitment of students in the post-secondary sector. This work garnered an award for the best doctoral thesis in the field of higher education in Canada (2015), bestowed by the Canadian Society for the Study of Higher Education. The findings were published in *Higher Education: The International Journal of Higher Education Research*.

Uwe Wilkesmann has been a professor at TU Dortmund University, Germany since 2006, where he is also director of the Centre for Higher Education. From 2008 to 2015, he was an adjunct professor at Hong Kong Polytechnic University. Wilkesmann received his doctorate and habilitation at Ruhr University Bochum, Germany. He has published on higher education research, organizational research and knowledge transfer in *Organization Studies, Higher Education, Studies in Higher Education, Tertiary Education and Management, VINE Journal of Information and Knowledge Management Systems, Journal of Knowledge Management* and *Evidence-Based HRM*.

Stephanie Wilson is a senior lecturer at University of Sydney Business School, Australia, where she is Deputy Director of Business Co-Design. Wilson received her PhD from University of New South Wales, Australia, and is a senior fellow of Advance HE. She has published in journals such as *Design Issues, International Journal of Art and Design Education, International Journal of Design Education* and *British Journal of Educational Technology*.

Sonja Zaar is a lecturer and researcher on leadership, learning and development at the School of Business and Economics, Maastricht University, the Netherlands. She received her MBA from TIAS School for Business and Society, the Netherlands, and is currently a PhD candidate at Maastricht University. Her research interests include leadership development, leader identity, cognitive schemas, self-regulation and learning from experiences. She has published in *Academy of Management Learning and Education* and has presented her work at the European Association of Work and Organizational Psychology conferences.

Introduction to the *Handbook of Teaching and Learning at Business Schools*

According to the World Economic Forum (2019), the severe challenges confronting higher education – including the need for lifelong learning, students acting like consumers, technological advances, and an increasing focus on skills rather than degrees – mean that its delivery must change for the future. To this list of challenges we add an increased political and institutional focus on teaching and its impacts, as well as the insufficiencies of the business models currently embraced by mass universities. We consider their implications in turn.

LIFELONG LEARNING

Rapid technological and social changes require people to update their knowledge throughout their careers; in turn, education models must meet this demand for lifelong learning. For workers likely to undertake multiple careers, new skills are prerequisites of remaining relevant in labor markets. Universities must reject a dominant model that suggests they can provide a comprehensive education to younger adults. Their activities and structures instead must reorient toward continuous learning, implying substantial reconsideration of their activities and structures, as well as a novel capacity to adapt to learners with divergent levels of experience and competence.

STUDENTS AS CONSUMERS, WITH SPECIAL NEEDS AND EXPECTATIONS

If governments identify students as consumers, who pay tuition fees and demand a service in return, higher education institutions must address market forces, including competitiveness, efficiency and customer satisfaction. Students embrace this consumer identity too, leading them to demand more from higher education service providers and gauging the value for their money. If students are customers who make their educational decisions on the basis of their economic self-interest, interesting questions emerge about their perceptions of higher education assessment too. But students also call for personalized, collaborative relationships with their university, rather than conventional or superficial consumer transactions. The challenge for universities is to find ways to leverage market competition to enhance the teaching practices they provide and the learning outcomes their "consumers" receive in the long term.

TECHNOLOGICAL ADVANCES

Two key technological trends are particularly relevant for universities. First, developments in robotics, artificial intelligence and machine learning alter the demands of the workforce.

In university settings, machines might grade student assignments, and if artificial intelligence takes responsibility for other human functions, then universities need to rethink what students should learn to be able to contribute to society. They need "robot-proof" human knowledge. Second, new learning technologies, such as online courses, simulation games, virtual learning and online learning platforms, provide new means to promote learning in varied settings. These technologies have attractive benefits, in that they offer a way to transmit knowledge with minimal costs compared with traditional formats, even as they promise to improve students' technological literacy. Rather than solely replacing humans, these technological trends offer opportunities for redefining professions and disciplines, assuming some knowledge transmission can occur through technological platforms and thereby freeing up in-class time for other teaching priorities and learning opportunities.

FOCUS ON SKILLS RATHER THAN DEGREES

Business students traditionally sought a degree. Today, the degree is still important, but the focus is shifting toward the achievement of relevant skills, driven by two main factors. First, university education historically was exclusive, such that relatively few people had access to it. But once-prevalent quotas on how many students may be admitted to universities have been repealed in most nations, and substantial new universities (especially private and online ones) have opened. Thus it has become far easier to find employees with a business degree, but that means a degree is no longer a sufficient condition to ensure a good job. Therefore, business students demand that universities provide them with skills and abilities that differentiate them from other candidates. Second, business research and education suffer a relevance problem. A lot of knowledge is being created and conveyed to the students, but its real-world effectiveness remains poorly documented. Firms do not regard a business degree as proof of necessary skills to do the job. Instead, potential employers turn to various tools to predict the quality of prospective employees (e.g., probation periods, in-house and third-party tests, multi-round interviews). Then, once hired, they provide employees with the skills they want them to have, using on-the-job and in-house training programs. These firms are bringing the functions traditionally outsourced to business schools back in house, which means business schools have a renewed need to demonstrate, to students and potential employers, the value and effectiveness of the education they provide and thereby establish their basic legitimacy.

POLITICAL AND INSTITUTIONAL FOCUS ON TEACHING AND ITS IMPACTS

At a global level, political entities and institutions across societies pay more attention to teaching and its impact on students, manifested in new legislation and accreditation frameworks. For example, in 2019, new Danish legislation required all universities to ensure the continuous professional development of their teachers, regardless of their seniority. Accreditation frameworks for teaching excellence, such as the United Kingdom (UK) Professional Standards Framework, are spreading throughout higher education facilities, such as to Copenhagen Business School, where faculty at all levels are encouraged to seek fellowship awards within this framework. This political and institutional focus on professional development and teaching excellence is not an end unto itself, but it imposes more evidence-based routes toward optimal learning outcomes. As a consequence, virtually all faculty will be forced to reconsider their own *modus operandi* in designing and delivering teaching, such as by embracing student-centered learning designs wholly.

MASS UNIVERSITIES' BUSINESS MODELS

The number of universities distributing business degrees is increasing. With the arrival of new technologies, such as online learning, business schools' abilities to reach students also is increasing. Lockdowns imposed during the COVID-19 pandemic made online education even more legitimate and appealing. Overall, then, business schools are facing unparalleled competition, both within the industry and externally. Because of the lack of knowledge about the actual effectiveness of business education, several alternative service providers (e.g., certification programs by large corporations) have moved into this space. With big data, cheaper, less time-consuming and more effective methods for providing business education also could be developed. To survive, then, business schools must find ways to deal with intra-industry competition (e.g., mergers and alliances) but also anticipate inter-industry competition (e.g., more advanced and effective teaching methods).

CONTRIBUTIONS

The objective of this *Handbook* is therefore to investigate multiple angles from which to consider teaching and learning in business school. Together, the chapters fill gaps in prior research, but they also explore and expand new fields. The *Handbook*'s 25 chapters are divided into seven parts:

Part I: Transformational Perspectives.
Part II: Learning Environments.
Part III: The Use and Value of Learning Technologies.
Part IV: In the Business School Classroom.
Part V: Leadership Education.
Part VI: Continuous Professional Development of Research-Based Teachers.
Part VII: Bridging Teaching, Research and Practice.

PART I: TRANSFORMATIONAL PERSPECTIVES

Rapidly changing societal and workplace requirements necessitate new options for designing and delivering business school programs. In dynamic business landscapes, marked by new opportunities, uncertainty and risk, business schools confront the strategic need to rethink their changing role, reflecting globalization, competition and technological advances. Traditional models and processes, designed to support academically isolated operations, need to be re-evaluated, as should the traditional offering of a fixed degree, such as a flagship MBA. To replace this increasingly irrelevant offer, inventive models of education should focus more on the responsibility to educate responsible leaders. In Part I, the contributions suggest reimagining pedagogical models, building relations, and collaborating with industry and society to provide more impactful educational offerings for a sustainable future.

For example, to meet their responsibility to contribute to the well-being of communities, Kreber, Wardley, Leviten-Reid, and MacPherson (Chapter 1) argue that business schools should offer an intentionally transformative education, such that students develop identities as change agents, capable of achieving a fairer, more sustainable future. In proposing "Community-engaged learning in business schools to effect social change: capabilities perspective," these authors call for a new view of the purpose of business education that reveals a different set of desirable learning outcomes, then defines the pedagogical practices that can produce those outcomes. In illustrating the proposed capabilities development model for higher education, distinct from a human capital development model, this chapter describes how Cape Breton University developed community-engaged experiential learning opportunities. Rather than ideal cases, these examples provide foundations on which to build.

A co-design model offers another alternative for addressing shifts in higher education and achieving strategic pedagogical change, as Wilson, Huber and Bryant (Chapter 2) propose in "Using co-design processes to support strategic pedagogical change in business education." With a focus on the changing roles of educational developers and learning designers, this chapter outlines co-design processes that involve multiple stakeholders, as exemplified by the Connected Learning at Scale initiative at University of Sydney Business School. The analysis reveals some guiding principles and paradoxes that produce a range of impacts and outcomes that can inform efforts by various universities to design methods to meet the challenges and opportunities they face.

In another study set in Australia, Mantai (Chapter 3) investigates the "Benefits and challenges of Assurance of Learning: making the intangible tangible." In an Assurance of Learning (AoL) process, measures of students' achievement of each program goal inform all future program decisions and designs. This reflective account of the benefits and challenges of applying AoL to business schools identifies the need for more effort devoted to operational aspects (i.e., measuring and reporting) rather than to closing the loop. In particular, curriculum design, staff development and genuine stakeholder engagement efforts are what lead to a well-developed AoL system. However, program directors also must recognize that AoL practices constantly evolve, reflecting the constant change and vast complexity of higher education.

PART II: LEARNING ENVIRONMENTS

Environmental variables also inform cognitive processes, such that at both individual and collective (e.g., team) levels of analysis, knowledge acquisition and application depend on the contextual factors. In classrooms, the characteristics of the learning environment determine student motivation, satisfaction and performance. To identify the best classroom designs, such that they facilitate learning by business students, the studies in Part II combine both theoretical and practical insights to delineate several factors that instructors and business schools should include in their learning environments to improve student-related outcomes.

Arendt and Christensen (Chapter 4) propose a studio concept, noting that studios historically provided critical sites for design and architecture learning and increasingly appear in business schools and other institutions of higher learning too. In "The promise of the business studio:

teaching for design and entrepreneurship at business schools," they suggest its relevance as a space in which design pedagogics can inform business and entrepreneurship courses in business schools. A business studio encourages iterative, make-and-reflect processes and hands-on learning, which should enhance student engagement and encourage more active, deeper learning. The resulting skills are clearly in demand in contemporary labor markets. With three examples of teaching in the business studio at Copenhagen Business School, they offer recommendations for developing business studios elsewhere.

With an empirical, grounded theory approach, Kember (Chapter 5) derives a motivational teaching and learning environment framework, based on 36 interviews with undergraduate students, in which they reported on what motivated them to learn. The result, namely, "A framework for motivating business students through teaching, learning and curriculum design," contains eight facets, which this chapter illustrates with verbatim comments from students in business, hospitality and tourism management. It offers a practical guide to teaching and learning to motivate students.

Complimenting the student interviews in the previous chapter, "The challenge of reflexive pedagogy in executive education: a personal case study" reflects the author's perspective as an educator. Iszatt-White (Chapter 6) takes a critical view on reflexive pedagogy, despite a popular view that considers it universally desirable, due to the associated challenges of a sense of "identity undoing" during the shift from content expert to process facilitator. A sense of "unknowability" may also emerge when control for the direction and content of the learning gets assigned to the learner, which upsets the conventional power asymmetry of learning interactions. The author thus recommends that educators carve out their own sense of purpose and ability, which enables them to contribute in conjunction with students' active efforts.

Another popular pedagogical topic, team-based learning (TBL), promises to enhance student engagement by resolving issues associated with traditional group work. But these promises might come in for challenge, as Larson and Sweet (Chapter 7) consider when they seek to determine how and to what extent TBL needs to be adapted to match the individual instructors and their classrooms. In "Team-based learning in the business school classroom: adaptation versus fidelity," they note a tension between adaptation and orthodoxy, then outline some justifications for the variety of adaptations they find in practice. By integrating conceptual discussions of treatment fidelity and the diffusion of innovation, they specify some risks of adaptation too. This nuanced approach identifies essential factors that TBL instructors should be sure to retain.

PART III: THE USE AND VALUE OF LEARNING TECHNOLOGIES

In addition to new approaches, learning technologies strongly influence the way teaching is planned and delivered. Consider a historical example. When chalk was replaced by overhead projectors, a trade-off emerged between the efficiency of reusing teaching slides versus the spontaneous creative content mapping that could happen on the blackboard. More recent technologies continue to revolutionize learning in higher education, as videos, podcasts, simulations, online feedback and online quizzes have broadened the pedagogical toolbox. But as the contributions to Part III highlight, teaching technologies are not just useful tools for content delivery: they change the way teaching gets planned and the way learning outcomes are assessed. Their use and value thus must be carefully assessed before they are adopted in any course design. To this end, the three contributions in Part III discuss the uses and value of learning technologies underlying blended learning, gamified learning in teams, and business school curricula.

For example, Kjærgaard, Thomsen and von Wallpach (Chapter 8) present "Transformations toward blended learning: key issues to address," with a list of assertions that can inform faculty who are considering blended learning. The authors propose that blended learning is not a single pedagogy; rather, it should combine the best practices of multiple domains, which can be achieved if its developers focus on learning rather than technology. In the new learning opportunities created by blended learning, interactions are both facilitated and limited, which creates a powerful need for both organizational and personal adaptation. The authors describe their own experiences with blended learning, as teachers, consultants and administrators, which leads them to assert that addressing these key issues can limit misunderstandings of how blended learning can promote student learning, but also the gaps it cannot address.

Plé and Koles (Chapter 9) offer a different sort of caution, arguing that rather than limiting investigations of the influence of technology to course delivery or course design, researchers also need to address its impact on assessments and course content. Such an approach reflects three pillars of a comprehensive learning experience: pedagogy, assessment and content. Thus "The influence of technology on business schools' curricula: a triple crown perspective" offers a framework that describes which technological solutions can advance student learning journeys. It also acknowledges some challenges linked to technologically infused curricula that, if addressed effectively, can even become opportunities.

The last chapter in Part III deals with "Gamification in education: the case of gamified learning in teams." Concerned that prior literature tends to focus only on how gamified learning informs individual student experiences, not interpersonal or team factors, Khusainova, Sahhar and De Jong (Chapter 10) conduct a study with a real game, available to multiple universities, and gather student and instructor narratives. The results affirm their assertion that interpersonal and team dynamics are critical, so the key dimensions they list can help instructors successfully implement and maintain games for their own courses.

PART IV: IN THE BUSINESS SCHOOL CLASSROOM

Regardless of how much they integrate technology, though, diverse business school classrooms require effective strategies for teaching, delivered by dedicated instructors. In considering demands for high-quality teaching in higher education, the authors in Part IV offer meaningful reflections on multiple aspects of the practice.

Lecturing is one of the oldest methods of teaching, and Greve (Chapter 11) in "Lecturing" provides a comprehensive review of the genre, as well as the affordances and constraints of giving good lectures. To understand this widespread and widely debated teaching format, she investigates large-scale lectures provided by a business school and introduces a taxonomy of lecturing with three archetypes: soundtrack lecture, interaction lecture and engagement lecture. But a successful lecture depends not on its approach or type, but rather on the relation it creates between the lecturer and students, the quality of their interaction, and the added value attained by attending a lecture.

In "the case for cases: using historical and live cases to enhance student learning," Moolenaar and Beverland (Chapter 12) investigate the long history of using case studies for education. Despite some challenges, they continue to offer value for business education, both in class and online. By leveraging their decades of international case development and teaching experiences, these authors introduce several different case types and their purpose. Packed with practical advice for educators, this chapter also provides a compelling argument for traditional paper-based or video-driven cases, as well as live, real-time cases. It contains advice for running cases online or in a blended learning environment.

Rosier (Chapter 13) concurs with Moolenaar and Beverland's perspective, with regard to the use of live projects as a means to encourage students' employability skills. In "Using live business projects to develop graduate employability skills," she gathers students' perceptions of their own skills, using both quantitative and qualitative data, and finds significant changes over time. That is, instructors can help students develop self-management, communication, teamworking, problem-solving and organization skills, as well as enhance their confidence. These insights into a relevant experiential learning approach encourage more learning environments in which students interact with real businesspeople during live projects.

In addition to ensuring students gain employability skills, instructors must offer them direct assessments and feedback, a challenge that appears inherent to higher education. In "Addressing the challenges of assessment and feedback in business schools: developing assessment practices that support learning," Reimann, Sambell, Sadler and Kreber (Chapter 14) cite a paradigm shift, triggered by student dissatisfaction, that altered models of assessment. To support learning, they call for assessment for learning techniques which reflect contemporary concerns and practices of business educators. These techniques prioritize authenticity; they also might be expanded to find innovative assessment and feedback practices. With several vignettes, the authors suggest ways to implement these methods in practice.

Finally, noting that experiments with studio-based inquiry draw inspiration from professional art and design schools, Meisiek (Chapter 15) in "Business studios of practice" argues for a studio approach to bridge traditional divisions in situated learning. That is, it usually refers to either higher education or work and the organization, but a business studio attempts to combine them in a learning space that draws on art, design and craft traditions to encourage innovation in business school settings. The practices it encourages then can enable graduates to participate in communities of practice in their future workplaces. With reference to the Studio at Copenhagen Business School, this chapter leverages activity theory and habits of mind to assert that business studios, as settings for emergent activity, help participants develop necessary practices for future jobs.

PART V: LEADERSHIP EDUCATION

Developing future leaders is a key goal of any business school, both to benefit society by educating students who can accomplish a variety of tasks, and to benefit students themselves. Most well-paid jobs tend to involve leadership, so business students, as consumers, demand that their schools help them prepare to undertake these desirable roles. Among the substantial research devoted to leadership, most of it is rooted in psychology literature, not pedagogy research. In turn, two topic areas tend to focus on who will emerge as successful leaders (trait perspective) or which circumstances help people emerge as successful leaders (social psychology perspective). What is missing is insights into how to encourage people to develop and emerge as successful leaders. The chapters in Part V aim to provide evidence related to how business schools can educate students so that they become successful future leaders.

As Nicholds (Chapter 16) puts it, allegations by management critics that "business schools have lost their way" suggest failures to prepare graduates effectively. She therefore proposes a critical approach to teaching leadership, such that by being critically reflexive about the value and applicability of business theory, business schools can engage in, as the chapter title puts it, "Building a new identity for business schools: learning how to act with authenticity through the critical teaching of leadership." Support for student leaders in the classroom requires helping them understand the contested nature of leadership concepts, so that they can reflect critically on the impacts of their professional practice on organizational outcomes. Embracing this recommended approach, Nicholds offers personal reflections on how this delivery has affected her identity as an academic and practitioner, as well as some unique contributions toward wider societal goals.

Prior literature on leadership development, leader identity and learning from experience offers some notable insights, which Zaar, Van Den Bossche and Gijselaers (Chapter 17) integrate in a guiding framework in "New avenues for leadership education and development: shaping leader identity through meaning-making from experiences." Focused on deeper-level, cognitive elements of leadership, they suggest that meaning-making, derived from experiences, can promote students' leadership development by shaping their leader identities. In turn, leadership education should purposefully leverage classroom experiences to encourage students' identities as leaders, because doing so establishes a foundation for continued leadership development.

Along with such a foundation, business leaders need relevant enterprise skills, capabilities and attributes. In "Equipping students with the attributes needed by business leaders in an era of social and technological change," Kember (Chapter 18) conducts focus group interviews with students to learn which graduate attributes they thought they needed and could develop. Two broad categories emerge: intellectual capabilities and capabilities for working together, which include critical thinking, self-managed learning, problem-solving, adaptability, communication, interpersonal skills and group work. To nurture such attributes, they also believed the teaching and learning environment should provide opportunities to practice using the key capabilities. In turn, the environment should include active learning (to provide practice opportunities), teaching for understanding (to address certain topics in depth), assessment (based on exhibitions of key attributes) and cooperative learning (practice working together).

PART VI: CONTINUOUS PROFESSIONAL DEVELOPMENT OF RESEARCH-BASED TEACHERS

The diverse student populations inhabiting higher education institutions vary widely in their ages, ethnicities and cultures, as well as their prior experience. A student who has been working for several years will want a different education than one who is fresh out of high school. Furthermore, students spending considerable sums on tuition fees, as well as board and accommodation, demand a top-notch education, devoted to their individual needs, not to the average student. Universities also compete for better rankings in (inter)national university assessments, which in turn are based largely on student satisfaction. Thus, universities are reorienting their attention, including developing professional development programs with a view to make academics into better educators. Some programs leverage technological developments that allow teachers to present materials, and students to engage with those materials, in new ways. Other technological developments help universities facing reduced state funding by making it possible for academics to cover larger classes. With Part VI, the contributors consider additional ways to encourage academics to embrace continued professional development.

Setting their contribution in the context of German universities, Wilkesmann and Lauer (Chapter 19) note two key developments: steering instruments introduced on the basis of new public management (transactional governance), and devoted efforts to enhance teaching culture (transformational governance). In "How to motivate professors to teach," they consider these opportunities for universities to exert top-down influences on teaching-related behaviors. According to survey data, transformational governance efforts have positive effects on teaching commitment, but the transactional steering instruments do not. Overall, though, between 2009 and 2016, teaching motivation has changed, such that high-quality teaching informs professors' self-esteem, and guilt arises if they neglect teaching duties.

In relation to associate professors specifically, as a crucial cohort for modern business schools, Irwin (Chapter 20) describes the Associate Professor Development Programme (APDP) at Copenhagen Business School as a pertinent method for enhancing research (including funding), teaching and administrative efforts. This assessment, "Teaching and learning with our colleagues: the Associate Professor Development Programme at Copenhagen Business School," reveals some key lessons. Despite questions and challenges related to the APDP design and operations, it has provided valuable space for reflection and identification of practical career development options. Furthermore, the APDP encourages a sense of identity and academic citizenship throughout the business school.

Many scholars express an interest in diversity; the key is finding ways to ensure they are leveraging diversity in the classroom. Villesèche and Teilmann-Lock (Chapter 21), in "Leveraging Diversity in the Classroom," describe and reflect on the development of such a course, for which they took a design thinking approach. By outlining the class materials, course structure, key features, and exercises and activities they chose, the authors offer an inspirational narrative, but also a model that others can adapt and apply to help ensure consistent considerations of diversity and equality in business schools.

Another key cohort of business schools consists of the next generation of educators, such that guiding them remains a critical consideration. The authors of "Guiding PhD Students," Di Benedetto, Lindgreen and Ringberg (Chapter 22), recall their PhD program experiences, noting their enthusiasm but also their lack of experience with research, insufficient teaching skills, and the incredible amount of time they had to devote to the program. The guidance provided by supervisors was critical, and inspired their own future efforts to emulate those supervisors and provide similar support to current students. Yet the challenges of PhD student supervision require more than simply mimicking others, so this chapter summarizes insights from various colleagues who collectively have supervised scores of PhD students who have gone on to successful academic careers, regarding what makes for effective PhD supervision.

PART VII: BRIDGING TEACHING, RESEARCH AND PRACTICE

Finally, university teaching and supervision comes from academics who actively work to publish their cutting-edge insights, so education inevitably reflects research-related teaching materials, at least to some degree. For example, some research-based courses actually include students in the research process. When academics collaborate with students on projects, the students become co-creators of new research insights. If they adopt a teaching-based research approach, they might discuss research-based issues with students to gain new inspiration for their research. Beyond these efforts, in their attempts to meet societal demands for solutions to global issues, many universities seek collaborations with businesses and other societal actors. Thus, students might work together with practitioners to consider complex, diverse problems that the businesses lack the time or knowledge to resolve on their own. In some cases, such collaborations can lead to full-time positions for the students.

At research-intensive business schools in particular, a core of solid, productive researchers induces recognition and high rankings, as exemplified by the *Financial Times* business school rankings and the *Bloomberg Business Week* Best B-Schools Ranking. In "How to translate research into teaching," Lindgreen, Di Benedetto, Brodie and Naudé (Chapter 23) note that a few business schools (about 1 percent in total) receive accreditations from the Association to Advance Collegiate Schools of Business (AACSB), the Association of MBAs (AMBA) and the European Quality Improvement System (EQUIS), a recognition that attracts undergraduate and postgraduate students seeking to acquire the best capabilities and skills to ensure their career success, along with PhD students eager to function in strong research environments.

Moving away from research-dominant settings, Hains-Wesson, Cejnar, Ji, Shahbazi and Luksich (Chapter 24) detail an evaluation research project for a placement program that aims to encompass undergraduate and postgraduate business school degrees. With a mixed-methods evaluation, in "Work-integrated education: improving placement pedagogy and practice," they suggest options for improving the business school placement program. An online survey that gathered students' and industry partners' impressions of a placement effort revealed several relevant areas. For example, the learning activities, preparation and debrief workshops (integral to the program) needed to be better aligned in time with the work placement activity. Both students and industry respondents believed the assessments should be defined and conducted by the industry partners, which would help align students' efforts with organizational needs. The overall findings thus can be summarized in a set of specific practice recommendations for placement pedagogy.

To close out this *Handbook*, Seno-Alday (Chapter 25) offers a personal reflection: "On the busyness of business schools: harnessing synergy in research, teaching and engagement." Noting the pressures on academic to produce high-impact research, teach innovatively and engage productively with external stakeholders, all in a turbulent, rapidly and radically changing environment, the author offers some ideas for maintaining some balance and moving forward. Further informed by accounts by other scholars regarding how they have found synergy in research, teaching and engagement, she suggests practical tactics to leverage teaching and engagement to expand research, as well as to conduct research in a way that supports teaching and engagement.

CLOSING REMARKS

We extend a special thanks to Edward Elgar Publishing and its staff, who have been most helpful throughout this entire process. Equally, we warmly thank our contributors with whom we have worked. They have exhibited the desire to share their knowledge and experience with the *Handbook*'s readers, and a willingness to put forward their views for possible challenge by their peers. We hope that this *Handbook* of chapters and themes stimulates and contributes to colleagues in their teaching and learning.

REFERENCES

World Economic Forum (2019). The 4 biggest challenges to our higher education model – and what to do about them? https://www.weforum.org/agenda/2019/12/fourth-industrial-revolution-higher-education-challenges/. Accessed January 5, 2021.

PART I

TRANSFORMATION PERSPECTIVES

1. Community-engaged learning in business schools to effect social change: a capabilities perspective

Carolin Kreber, Leslie Wardley, Catherine Leviten-Reid and Stephanie MacPherson

> Education, while by no means the only arena for intervention for the formation of capabilities, might be operationalized to form the kind of human beings who can contribute to shaping the kind of society which values capabilities, who want to contribute to capability building and a society and public culture which can sustain capability for all.
>
> (Walker 2012, p. 392)

PURPOSE AND INTENT

In this chapter we argue that business schools have a responsibility to contribute to the well-being of their communities. Specifically, we propose that business education should be intentionally transformative, encouraging students to develop graduate identities not so much as providers of expert services in return of personal economic rewards, but as change agents for a fairer and more sustainable future. Our goal in this chapter then is threefold: (1) to interrogate and propose a vision of the purpose of business education; (2) to identify desirable learning outcomes associated with this purpose; and (3) to outline curricular and pedagogical practices in business education that make it more likely for these desired outcomes to be achieved.

CONTEXT

In an article published in the *American Journal of Business Education*, Kosnik et al. (2013) made some observations that are of direct relevance to this discussion. In line with the revised accreditation standards for business schools released by the Association to Advance Collegiate Schools of Business (AACSB) in 2013, the authors argued that there was a need for business schools not just to teach about value creation, but to adopt a teaching paradigm of value creation. Business schools operating within a teaching paradigm of value creation would not just help students acquire academic knowledge and professional skills, although these clearly continue to be important in today's world, but also make a contribution to fostering the students' integrity. The latter was essential, Kosnik et al. (2013) observe, given that "unethical or socially unacceptable management conduct continues to be among the root causes of corporate failures and highly publicized scandals" (p. 615), an example of which, we add, the world witnessed in the global financial crisis of 2008. Note in this context that Cortese (2003) had already asserted one decade earlier that "it is the people coming out of the world's best colleges and universities that are leading us down the current unhealthy, inequitable, and unsustainable path," urging institutions of higher education to teach students "the awareness, knowledge, skills and values needed to create a just and sustainable future" (Cortese 2003, p. 17).

Adopting a business education teaching paradigm of value creation, Kosnik et al. (2013) contend, would require business schools to expand their traditional two key stakeholder groups of students and faculty to include employers and society. Through discussion of several examples, the authors then make a case that involving students in experiential learning projects would facilitate the creation of business knowledge (academic value) and skills (professional value), and additionally "offer students opportunities to develop their personal moral character and good judgment when faced with social and ethical dilemmas, as well as cultivate their social responsibility" (Kosnik et al. 2013, p. 615), the latter referring to moral value.

Kosnik et al.'s (2013) article is significant in that it identifies desired learning outcomes of business education (articulated as academic, professional and moral value) and the curricular and pedagogical decisions deemed suitable to achieve these outcomes (namely the employment of experiential learning projects). The authors' reference to social responsibility hints at a certain vision of the purpose of business education, but the purpose is only implied and not articulated in depth. Our contribution in this chapter is to intentionally propose a particular purpose for business education, thereby making our value position explicit. We recognize that the purposes of higher education, and business education, are of necessity multiple and contested (e.g., Simpson 2013); therefore, our intent is not to seek to prescribe purposes, but to make a case for a particular vision and encourage reflection and debate. From our particular vision or proposal of the purpose of business education we derive learning outcomes and then discuss, by drawing from several examples of practice at the Shannon School of Business at Cape Breton University, how the achievement of these outcomes can be supported. Like Kosnik and colleagues, we discuss inquiry-based experiential learning experiences, in particular those that engage students directly with their communities, as these are especially well aligned with the purposes and outcomes we consider to be significant. Specifically, we propose that the purpose of higher education, and business education, is to contribute to capability expansion in society, and that this process is assisted by fostering certain capabilities in students. It is the concept of capabilities, and capability expansion, that we turn to next.

Capabilities and Capability Expansion

In the context of higher education, the term "capabilities" is often employed in reference to a set of skills or competencies that, next to academic knowledge in the chosen discipline, students should develop through their degree program to be adequately prepared for life upon graduation. For a few decades now, the consensus has been that the possession of academic knowledge, even interdisciplinary academic knowledge, is not enough to be successful in a world characterized by rapid changes and increased complexity, and where the ability to engage in adaptive lifelong learning has become an imperative (e.g., Candy 1991; Hager and Holland 2006; Knapper and Cropley 1985; Virtanen and Tynjälä 2019). What is needed to cope and contribute effectively in a rapidly shifting and unstable world and challenging work environments, so goes the argument, are certain capabilities, or skills sets. Spencer et al. (2012), for example, submit that "writing, speaking, inquiry/research, critical thinking, creative problem-solving and team work" are important "graduate capabilities" (p. 217). Similarly, Kember et al. (2007) use the term "capabilities" when they propose that critical thinking, self-managed learning, adaptability, problem-solving, communication skills, interpersonal skills and group work are important "capabilities needed for lifelong learning" (p. 614).

The skills, competencies or outcomes referenced above, called "capabilities" by Spencer et al. (2012) and Kember et al. (2007), are undoubtedly relevant in today's world and important for university students to acquire. However, it is critical that we are explicit early on in this discussion that we mean something slightly different, or rather, something more expansive, by capabilities. When we use the term capabilities in this chapter we do so in reference to the capabilities approach, an approach to social justice pioneered by economist Amartya Sen (1999; Nussbaum and Sen 1993) and further developed by philosopher Martha Nussbaum (2000, 2011).

The capabilities approach is an interdisciplinary framework, drawing on economic as well as philosophical theories, for addressing entrenched social inequalities (Nussbaum and Sen 1993). The framework has inspired much theoretical and empirical research in the social and human sciences and, especially in more recent years, has received considerable attention also in the field of education, including higher education (e.g., Boni and Walker 2013; Otto and Ziegler 2006; Robeyns 2006; Unterhalter 2007; Walker 2012).

The key idea behind the capability approach is that human well-being, or a "good life," is not appropriately defined in terms of individuals' sense of satisfaction, let alone equal distribution of resources, but must be understood in terms of the substantive freedoms (i.e., capabilities) individuals have to actually be or do what they have reason to value. Importantly, then, the capabilities approach (Nussbaum and Sen 1993; Nussbaum 2000, 2011) is grounded in two normative claims: first, the opportunity (or freedom) to achieve well-being is of moral import and hence should be afforded to every human being; and second, well-being can be achieved through capabilities, conceived of as the freedom to do and be what one has reason to value. A key aspiration of proponents of the capabilities approach, therefore, is capability expansion: that is, the roll-out of interventions in our societies that provide more and more people with real chances and substantial freedoms to pursue a good life.

It follows that we understand capabilities as an ethical concept and consequently, like Nussbaum and Sen, are concerned not just with any capabilities, competencies or life skills that might be useful for adapting to new workplace and other challenges (see for instance Kember et al. 2007 and Spencer et al. 2012), but specifically those that facilitate human development and well-being. In her version of the capabilities approach, which differs somewhat from Sen's, American philosopher Martha Nussbaum argues that capabilities need to be informed "by an intuitive idea of a life that is worthy of the dignity of a human being" (Nussbaum 2000, p. 5). She then proposes a list of ten central capabilities, each representing a sphere of life over which individuals must have real choices: (1) life; (2) health; (3) bodily integrity; (4) senses, imagination and thought; (5) emotions; (6) practical reason; (7) affiliation (being able to live with and consider others, and being treated with respect); (8) other species; (9) play; (10) control over one's political and material environment (Nussbaum 2000, pp. 78–80). Only if individuals have real freedom to choose their functioning in these spheres – for example, being able to live a life not threatened by war (in relation to 1), have access to clean water and medicine to facilitate health (in relation to 2), not fearing torture, harassment or physical abuse (in relation to 3), having access to education (in relation to 4), and so forth – according to Nussbaum's contention, can we speak of a life of human dignity, or a life that people have reason to value. By asking "what are individuals actually able to be or do?", the capabilities approach reveals social inequalities treating each person as an end. The purpose of the capabilities approach is to contribute to poverty reduction through capability expansion, whereby poverty is understood broadly, not just in terms of economic deprivation but more generally as deprivation of choice or opportunity (i.e., freedom) in important spheres of life, especially those referred to in Nussbaum's list of ten essential capabilities.

Developing Human Capabilities versus Human Capital

These more expansive capabilities (expansive in the sense that they go beyond skills and competencies related to lifelong learning) are not typically associated with core learning outcomes in higher education, which in the final analysis tend to serve a human capital development model rather than a human capabilities development model (Walker 2012; Wigley and Akkoyunlu-Wigley 2006). The human capital development model assumes a direct link between investment in education, employment, increases in gross domestic product and enhanced global competitiveness. In this model the student or graduate is seen as a contributor or means to economic success, the latter being the valued end. The skills or competencies associated with lifelong learning, such as those relating to problem-solving, communication and team work (e.g., Kember et al. 2007), align directly with the human capital development model and serve to shape a citizenry that is adaptive to change, employable and thus able to contribute to gross domestic product.

By contrast, in a human capabilities development model for higher education the valued end is the well-being of the student, and the well-being of individuals in our society. While for many persons being well will entail participation in the economy, this is not the ultimate purpose or end. The end to be achieved through the distribution of key human capabilities is a society in which all individuals have the opportunity or freedom (i.e., capability) to choose to do and be what they have reason to value. The human capabilities development model for higher education, therefore, can be seen as more expansive than a narrow human capital development model. To be clear, it is not suggested here that economic development is a minor goal of higher education or insignificant; indeed, situated in one of the most economically deprived regions of Canada, our university recognizes and addresses the need for community economic development (Cape Breton University 2020a, 2020b). However, advocates of human capabilities development recognize that economic development in and of itself cannot be the ultimate purpose of education. Stefan Collini (2012), in his widely cited book *What Are Universities For?*, comments on the limitations of the human capital development perspective in higher education in this way:

> one has to make, over and over again, the obvious point that a society does not educate the next generation in order for them to contribute to its economy. It educates them in order that they should extend and deepen their understanding of themselves and the world, acquiring, in the course of this form of growing up, kinds of knowledge and skill which will be useful in their eventual employment, but which will no more be the sum of their education than that employment will be the sum of their lives. And this general point about education takes a particular form in universities, where, whatever level of professional or vocational "training" is also undertaken, the governing purpose involves extending human understanding through open-ended inquiry. (Collini 2012, p. 91)

The types of capabilities to be nurtured in a human capabilities development model for higher education would include a range of knowledge, values and dispositions. Of the ten capabilities Nussbaum (2000) included in her list, there are at least four that have direct relevance to education: practical reason; affiliation; senses, imagination and thought; and emotions. One might argue, therefore, that capability expansion could be achieved simply by enabling greater access to and participation in higher education, owing to the knowledge, skills and practical reason (the latter referring to the ability to think and make decisions about one's own conception of the good) that are cultivated through education. Notable advancements in widening university participation have been observed over the past decade in some countries (e.g., Croxford and Raffe 2012; Haveman and Smeeding 2006; Sutton Trust 2012; Vignoles and Murray 2016). However, as is acknowledged by several authors (e.g., Croxford and Raffe 2012; Haveman and Smeeding 2006), the reality is that universities still tend to attract primarily middle-class students, and few representatives from lower-income groups can access and are afforded adequate supports to succeed, especially in the professional schools. More, then, needs to be done to successfully expand capabilities through widening access. A further question that should be asked though, and one that is at the heart of this chapter, is whether higher education can also work towards capability expansion in other ways. The work of Melanie Walker and Monica McLean (e.g, Walker 2006; Walker and McLean 2013) offers a helpful response to this question. Inspired by both Sen and Nussbaum – that is, by the capabilities approach – the authors identified a set of capabilities to be increased through higher education curricula and pedagogies.

Nurturing Human Capabilities through Higher Education

Upon interviewing a group of students enrolled in a management course in cross-cultural marketing, Walker (2006) observed that the following capabilities were valued by students: (1) critical knowledge generating critical thought; (2) respecting, recognizing, valuing diversity and difference; (3) reflective self-knowledge; (4) participatory and active learning and having a voice which is heard and listened to; and (5) being able to engage a plurality of views in dialogue and debate (as cited in Walker 2006, pp. 82–83). Drawing on the wider and education-specific literature on the capabilities approach (e.g., Boni and Walker 2013; Nussbaum 2000; Nussbaum and Sen 1993; Robeyns 2006; Unterhalter 2007), as well as data from interviews with university students from a range of other fields, Walker then offered her own list of capabilities important to higher education, referring to it as "a draft ideal-theoretical, multi-dimensional education list" that "might offer a starting point for discussion about the capabilities approach and teaching and learning in higher education" (Walker 2006, p. 128).

Capabilities in this list comprise opportunities or freedoms as highlighted by Sen and Nussbaum, but also, interestingly, many of the relevant skills, competencies or capacities highlighted in the lifelong learning literature (e.g., Candy 1991; Kember et al. 2007; Knapper and Cropley 2000; Spencer et al. 2012). The list includes: practical reason; educational resilience; knowledge and imagination; learning dispositions; social relations and social networks; respect, dignity and recognition; emotional integrity, emotions; bodily integrity. A brief outline of each is provided below. Readers interested in a fuller elaboration are referred to Walker's book (Walker 2006).

- Practical reason refers to making well reasoned, informed, independent and socially responsible choices.
- Educational resilience refers to being able to persevere in the face of the various challenges education entails, and have aspirations as well as hopes for the future.

- Knowledge and imagination refer to the ability to acquire complex knowledge, reflect on it critically, be open-minded, imaginative and seek to understand the perspective of others, and to be able to use that knowledge for participation in action in a wide range of spheres.
- Learning dispositions refer to being able to inquire, have curiosity, and a love of learning.
- Social relations and social networks refer to being able to work in and form effective groups and social relations based on mutual trust.
- Respect, dignity and recognition refer to having a voice, being able to have respect for oneself and for others, being respected, being able to show empathy and compassion, act inclusively and being able to respond to human need.
- Emotional integrity and emotions refer to not being stifled by fear and being able to become aware of the situation and standpoint of others through imagination.
- Bodily integrity refers to being able to be free of physical and verbal harassment (Walker 2006, pp. 128–129).

In later work, Walker and McLean focused on students studying on professional programs (e.g., social work, public health, engineering, etc.) to identify those capabilities (i.e., freedoms to function) that professionals need in order to create a better world through their professional practice, a practice which has as its aim to expand basic capabilities in society (see also Kreber 2017). There are clear synergies between the previous list of capabilities for all higher education students and the newer list developed specifically for students on professional programs, the latter including perhaps even more capabilities needed to act as change agents. Examples of the capabilities the authors identified as essential for students on professional programs include: practical reasoning; public reasoning; affiliation; integrity; emotional awareness; informed vision; imagination; empathy; developing relationship and rapport across special groups and status hierarchies; having confidence to act for change; social and collective struggle; resilience; and communicating professional knowledge in an accessible way (see McLean and Walker 2012; Walker and McLean 2009, 2011, 2013).

The authors encourage universities to recognize their potential to help expand capabilities in society, through the curricular and pedagogical decisions they make to prepare future graduates to live a life as social change agents and contributors to the public good (e.g., Walker and McLean 2013, 2011). To be clear, the authors apply the insights of the capabilities approach on two levels. On a first level, following Nussbaum and Sen, they conceive of a fair world as one where people are afforded certain key capabilities that enable them to be and do what they have reason to value (for example, see Nussbaum's list of ten capabilities). On a second level, they then extrapolate from this model to identify the capabilities students need in order to be well supported and prepared to act as change agents. While the authors focus explicitly on programs that educate for specific professions, their argument has broader application and extends to any degree program (Walker 2012) including, we contend, business administration. As noted in the introductory quote to this chapter, the purpose of education, including business education, could be conceived of as an opportunity, through the formation of capabilities, to "form the kind of human beings who can contribute to shaping the kind of society which values capabilities, who want to contribute to capability building and a society and public culture which can sustain capability for all" (Walker 2012, p. 392).

In the next section of this chapter we feature examples of pedagogical practices employed in business education at our own university, and later analyse these for the extent to which they could be seen to promote some of the capabilities identified by Walker and McLean.

These capabilities, as we saw, include, for example: resilience and confidence to act for social change; practical and public reasoning; empathy; integrity; informed vision and imagination; developing partnerships across status hierarchies and communicating professional knowledge in an accessible way. The focus will be on inquiry-based experiential learning opportunities that engage students directly with their communities. The twofold purpose of increasing capability is: (1) to promote in students/graduates those capabilities they need to succeed in higher education and live valuable lives; and (2) to promote in graduates a disposition of wanting to expand capabilities in society (i.e., to act as change agents and work towards greater social justice in their communities).

COMMUNITY-ENGAGED LEARNING IN BUSINESS SCHOOL TO EFFECT SOCIAL CHANGE: EXAMPLES

Below, we provide descriptive accounts of some community-engaged experiential learning opportunities that three of the co-authors, all of whom are instructors in Cape Breton University's business school, build into their courses. Examples are taken from three distinct degree programs offered by the school: the Master of Business Administration in Community Economic Development, the Bachelor of Business Administration and the Bachelor in Hospitality and Tourism programs.

Master of Business Administration in Community Economic Development – Catherine

I teach a Master's level course which introduces MBA students to community economic development. In this course I focus on creating experiential learning partnerships between community organizations and students in order to foster awareness of people living in poverty as well as an understanding of different kinds of organizations, beyond conventional firms, which work to address the well-being of people on the margins and foster and retain community wealth. These social economy organizations include, for example, non-profits, co-operatives, social enterprises and community development corporations. Overall, these partnerships build capabilities which generate not only empathy, but confidence to act for social change.

My classes typically have about 25 students each and are comprised mostly of students from China, although some come from Vietnam, India, Canada and the United States. My students tend to be middle class. While some have experience working in for-profit business, they have little knowledge of what social economy organizations are (although they have surely interacted with many), and little exposure to vulnerable households.

Generally, I create concrete opportunities for students to be involved in projects that support local organizations or initiatives working with low-income people. These include individuals who have low levels of literacy, and people who use substances and who face significant stigma, lack of access to healthcare services, and housing and food insecurity. Partner organizations, in turn, are typically volunteer-driven with a small number of paid staff. Examples of organizations with which I have partnered include the Adult Learning Association of Cape Breton County, which helps adults to improve literacy, numeracy and computer skills; and Northside Rising, an initiative which fosters connections across multiple community constituents and stakeholders (local residents, government, business and the non-profit sector) and focuses on problems related to substance use in the community (Inspiring Communities 2020).

In creating partnerships with local community organizations, I start by having conversations with representatives of these organizations about their needs, their interests in working with university students, and the time constraints they typically have. If there's a match between my course objectives and our timelines, I work with a representative from the organization to devise an applied assignment for students to complete which is useful to the partner organization. Students never collect primary data from the organization's stakeholders (clients, staff, board members or other community stakeholders) because of ethical requirements, time limitations, and because students have not yet completed training in research methods.

Early in the course I invite a staff person (or volunteer) from the organization into my class to give a presentation on the mission of the organization, the organization's budget, staffing and history. The representative also shares stories about the role the organization plays in the community, the individuals who use its services, and potentially about ways that the organization has made a difference in people's lives. During the semester, and in an effort to highlight the international relevance of the project, I'll also share information with students about organizations (or initiatives) with similar mandates but located around the world. Typically, too, there are requests for additional information made to the local organization. Once assignments are completed near the end of the semester, I share them with the community partner, and invite reflections on the content from both the community partner and students, neither of which are part of the final grade. I should add that this is the ideal process I describe here. In reality it varies, depending on the semester and the challenges faced by partner organizations; for example, staff turnover, burnout or community emergencies may mean that students don't receive timely or detailed feedback from the community partner on their work. This too, however, is a lesson in how the community sector works and the challenges it faces.

An example of a partnership is the following. In the province in which our business school is situated, community health boards are mandated to identify priorities related to community health and well-being for their catchment areas every three years (Nova Scotia Health Authority 2018). This means their focus is the social determinants of health, including economic security, housing, social inclusion and access to food. These health boards consist of volunteer members, and they have no staff, although they do receive backbone support from the provincial government. Groups consisting of approximately five students each were matched with the health boards in the local area in order to help these entities establish their priorities, based on local conditions. Specifically, my students conducted community profiles and asset mapping, drawing significantly on the principles of an asset-based approach to community development (García 2020; Kretzmann and McKnight 1993). Community profiles (using census data) drew attention to household income, the percentage of households living in subsidized housing and levels of formal education. Mapping, in turn, allowed students to identify a range of local resources in the geographies they were assigned that were supportive of the social determinants of health, including the presence of local credit unions, social enterprises and non-profit cultural and recreational organizations, as well as local businesses. This project afforded students exposure to socio-demographic characteristics of local populations and increased their understanding of the role organizations beyond conventional firms play in community well-being. They learned the language of community assets, and about the power of a range of local associations and institutions (García 2020) in fostering community well-being. The insights they gained from reflecting on their experiences could then be applied in their work lives, other courses and new volunteer contributions (Kosnik et al. 2013).

Although not project-based experiential learning, I also work to foster empathy and confidence to act for social change by having my students interact with community in a different, but very tangible, way. Although it may seem overwhelming to have large groups of students visit community-based organizations, I hold classes in our university's off-site meeting room (designed to be a community–university research space), which is located in a social economy organization in the largest community on the island. Our first visit includes a tour of the building, which houses many small businesses, a social enterprise café, as well as community organizations involved in food security and arts and culture. This is often the first time that these business school students have knowingly entered this kind of community space, and through the tour students have a chance to interact with a staff member of the organization which owns and manages the building, and with tenants. Beyond exposing students to a diversity of organizations and people, off-site classes also make concrete some of the challenges of the non-profit sector due to, for example, the aging infrastructure in which we are meeting. This is something we reflect upon during our classes, as students are encouraged to discuss what they see and hear and relate this directly to the themes of the course. Using the university off-site meeting room located in a social economy organization is typically a highlight for my business school students.

Bachelor of Business Administration – Leslie

Cape Breton University (CBU) has come to be known as a university that strives to inspire multicultural, creative, innovative and entrepreneurial thinking, personal growth, and a passion for lifelong learning. The university's mission is also to serve the social, cultural and economic needs of the community and our society. If we drill down these goals fit with the previously mentioned examples of the capabilities Walker (2006) identified upon interviewing students on the learning opportunities they valued, and Kosnik et al.'s (2013) description of three sources of educational value (academic, professional, and moral) that an effective business curriculum should help bring about.

Below, I discuss the pedagogical strategies I use in my own courses that I feel encourage Kosnik et al.'s (2013) values and Walker's (2006) student capabilities, such as: (1) getting students interested and involved in the process of learning by giving them a roadmap to follow when conducting tasks (academic value – critical knowledge generating critical thought); (2) providing students with ample opportunities to "learn by doing" through independent work rather than by solely listening to lectures and reading the materials (participatory and active learning, and having a voice which is heard and listened to); (3) offering students sufficient structure and guidance to channel their creativity and develop their independent skills (professional value – reflective self-knowledge); and (4) using group work and in-class sessions for discussions to clarify concepts, ideas, methods, designs and assignments so that meaningful discussions can be initiated by students themselves and among themselves (moral value – being able to engage a plurality of views in dialogue and debate, and respecting, recognizing, valuing diversity and differences).

MRKT 4301 Qualitative Marketing Research and MRKT 4303 Quantitative Marketing Research

Fourth-year students in the BBA program take two marketing courses that build on one another. In the fall semester the focus is on qualitative research methods, and in the winter semester the focus is on quantitative methods. These courses are important components of the curriculum, as marketing students need academic skills in research so they can develop the professional skills needed to promote products and services that fit their target audience's needs and keep ahead of the competition. In an effort to support students in developing experience and expertise in these areas, a large amount of my time is spent interacting with students and offering feedback. Feedback at multiple stages is used to allow students the opportunity to reflect on the course content and relate this knowledge to their own understanding and experiences, so they are able to effectively utilize what they discover during their projects.

My fourth-year students engage in research projects that have helped area businesses (e.g., national parks, local daycare, the international student department at CBU, a local gym, among others) learn more about their clients and start to improve their marketing approaches. The qualitative research course (MRKT 4301) teaches students key aspects of the research process (developing research questions and objectives, performing reviews of the literature, designing data collection frameworks and gaining access to participants, etc.) and students work in self-selected groups of four to collaboratively develop a research proposal which is worth 30 percent of their final mark. In the following semester (MRKT 4303) students implement the group research proposals (40 percent, groups of four) they have developed after gaining ethics approval. Each course typically has 25 students enrolled. There is a diversity in backgrounds with 35 percent being international students from India, China, Egypt and the United Kingdom, and the remaining percentage from Canada (mainly Nova Scotia).

The following examples reflect the 2018/19 school year. Celtic Colours is a cultural festival that has been an important part of the economic development of communities across Cape Breton Island and has helped to solidify Cape Breton's tourism destination image. The annual festival has brought over $130 million into the Cape Breton economy. I had been approached by the organization to help oversee the data collection process, and this invitation sparked the idea to frame the students' course assignment around Celtic Colours. Given that I had already obtained ethics approval, secured research locations and access to participants, it was relatively straightforward for my students to gain access. In the fall semester of 2018, students in my qualitative research course (MRKT 4301) engaged in on-site data collection and later collaborated on marketing reports with the Executive Director of Celtic Colours International Festival. In the winter term these students analysed data collected at the Festival in their quantitative research course (MRKT 4303) to develop research reports used in the Celtic Colours year-end report and financial records.

The Executive Director was invited as a guest speaker to discuss the formation of Celtic Colours International Festival, including the vision of its founders and inspiration of its model, its unique island-wide delivery through intensive community partnerships, the extensive volunteerism required, and its impact on local and regional economic and cultural development. It was important for students to learn about these elements as it meant that there were various cultures to consider, and different economic outcomes for the communities involved. It was also important for students to appreciate that some venue locations were remote, yet each had to be organized by volunteer site managers. These factors represented diverse logistical and infrastructure restrictions to overcome. The information that was shared allowed students to formulate research questions and carry out reviews of literature that were part of their group assignments. There were also class sessions devoted to learning how to approach potential research participants with cultural sensitivity (identifying the influences of their own culture and others) as students were involved in collecting survey responses on site. For many students these community interactions represented a steep learning curve as it was the first time they had to apply the academic skills they had developed.

As a course assignment in MRKT 4301, students had to develop a group research project that would engage community and industry research partners in a way that would empower them to address the consequences of ongoing tourism development, and to create and deliver accurate and ethical tourism images based on multiple perspectives. The assignment was broken down into sections with feedback offered after each component. First, students received feedback on two to three pages that included a topic introduction, a tentative problem statement, research objectives, and ten annotated references. Second, they received feedback on six to eight pages of their beginning proposal including a literature review. Third, they received feedback on four to five pages discussing their qualitative research design, sample research questions and data treatment strategies. Finally, feedback was offered on the completed research. Data were not expected in this course, due to limitations with obtaining additional ethics approval, but details about possible ways to deal with data were required.

In the quantitative methods course offered the following semester (MRKT 4303), students completed the research projects they had developed in the previous semester. The foundational aspects of the prior course's documents could be used after changes were made to the research design and data treatment strategies so quantitative research methods could be utilized. The students were given access to some data obtained during the onsite data collection sessions at the selected venues. These reports examined the practical aspects and benefits of data collection for Cape Breton Island's annual Celtic Colours International Festival, including survey result highlights and themes that have arisen over the years through the use of longitudinal data provided by the festival administrators. This lens allowed students to explore the impact of tourism images, collaboratively develop improved practices which could be applied for tourism site development and offered in-depth insights into the target audiences. This assignment also offered special consideration of participants' views of Cape Breton and the challenges of measuring the economic impact of this festival. A learning outcome associated with these experiences was that students created a better understanding of how to collaboratively incorporate multiple stakeholders' needs and ethical concerns. These insights could then be transferred when attempting to engage in tourism development within their own communities.

Bachelor of Hospitality and Tourism Management – Stephanie

As a self-described "pracademic," I strive to include theory and practice in my classes and stress the importance of "being able to apply what you learn" to enhance critical thinking, quick problem-solving and effective leadership in the workplace. I look back at 15 years of work experience across various sectors and levels within the tourism, events and hospitality management industry, and all my post-secondary education is in this field of study. Now in my role as a senior university instructor this background has proven invaluable in helping students connect theory and practice. Sharing stories from previous work experiences, situations where I needed to problem-solve, lead and make quick decisions, and employing class activities that discuss current world events and their impact on tourism, act as a launch pad for how I prepare students for their assignments and projects. In turn, students have opportunities to reflect on how they would respond in certain situations, act as "consultants" in applied projects, and benefit from industry-related partnerships.

A recent report by the World Economic Forum (2020, p. 5) makes predictions regarding the skills set that will be required by the workforce in 2025, in response to the present pandemic and rapid pace of advancements in technology. The skills discussed as being in high demand by 2025, perhaps not surprisingly, include critical thinking, problem-solving, flexibility, leadership, adapting to changing technology and having social influence, to mention just some examples (World Economic Forum 2020). The list echoes the skills and values proposed by Kosnik et al. (2013, p. 614), which build on the accreditation standards released by the AACSB. As we saw earlier in this chapter, Kosnik and colleagues' model proposes that an effective business school curriculum would deliver three distinct sources of educational value: academic (business knowledge), professional (business skills such as communication, team-work, emotional intelligence and leadership) and moral value (integrity, social responsibility and citizenship). They then suggest that experiential learning approaches are suitable for bringing about value creation in these three domains. Below, I will discuss the experiential learning opportunities I provide for my students in the Bachelor of Tourism and Hospitality Management program.

The third-year course, entitled Meetings and Event Management, is one of three core courses in the program that comprises both a lecture-based and a lab-based component. Prerequisites for the course include completion of the other two core courses: Food Theory and Nutrition, and Restaurant Service Operations. By the time students enroll in my course they are also likely to have completed one of their two required industry internships and thus have some industry experience (even if not in food and beverage).

In the lab classes, the students work in "committees" to plan and execute a special event that is open to the public. Students make decisions on the theme of the event, menu, entertainment, marketing, ticket sales, and so forth, and have a budget to follow. Students not only have the opportunity to learn the importance of timelines, teamwork and collaboration, but also working together in this way allows, and indeed encourages, them to share ideas, act ethically, be creative and experience the reward of their efforts beyond a grade. Students meet twice a week for a lab class of 75 minutes in addition to their two weekly lecture-based classes. The lab classes act as "committee meetings" where students work through the timelines they created (with instructor feedback and evaluation). Lab classes also provide the opportunity to meet with other committees. For instance, the committee responsible for menu planning would meet with the set-up/logistics group to give their set-up requirements based on the menu. Each week the committees submit updates of what has been accomplished and what they plan to work on the following week. This allows me to meet with each group, check whether they are on track, and catch any concerns or issues. The biggest challenge in this class is the class size (59–90 students), and ensuring everyone has a share of responsibility and understands that following and committing to a timeline is critical.

The special event is open to the public and there is a cost to attend. In recent years the event date has coincided with the university's job fairs and prospective employers are invited to attend and offered a complementary ticket sponsored by the university. These events have become a showcase of the Bachelor of Hospitality and Tourism Management program and a networking opportunity for students. Evaluation includes peer and self-evaluation of students' performance in their committees, along with an instructor evaluation of their per-formance working during the event, and a follow-up reflective assignment on the experience.

I also invite tourism industry partners into my classes to talk about issues they are facing. Due to the international make-up of students in the Bachelor of Hospitality and Tourism

Management program, industry partners are interested in hearing ideas from the students who are mainly from two key growth markets for tourism in Canada: China and India. Having students do some research and present ideas or possible solutions to partner organizations can create a win for the university, the students and the organization. For example, in my third-year course entitled Destination Marketing Management, I worked with the local airport authority as it was trying to get ideas on how it could make the airport experience better for visitors and international students. There were almost 80 students in the class, who worked in groups of four. They shared their ideas through poster presentations with representatives from the airport who took the time to attend two classes. Not only did the airport representatives leave feeling excited at some of the ideas generated by the students, but they also took the time to offer feedback in writing for every group presentation, which I then included as part of my evaluation of the students' projects. The students valued and appreciated the feedback the airport representatives had provided, together with the representatives' enthusiasm and questions they asked of the groups. It was especially exciting for the class to hear from representatives that some of their ideas would be discussed further within the organization and potentially implemented in the future.

OBSERVATIONS, DISCUSSION AND CONCLUSION

Prior to offering some observations on the above examples it is helpful to zero in on the key distinctions between skills development and capabilities development, as these are helpful for focusing the discussion. Over the past several decades, observers have noted the need to prepare university students for lifelong learning in a rapidly changing and increasingly complex social world through curricula and pedagogies that should teach key generic learning outcomes, such as communications skills, research skills, creative problem-solving, team work, adaptability and self-managed learning (e.g., Candy 1991; Kember et al. 2007; Knapper and Cropley 2000; Spencer et al. 2012). These learning outcomes are overtly skills-based and, according to the argument presented earlier in this chapter, aligned with a view of higher education as human capital development. As was noted previously, a human capabilities development model for higher education, by contrast, while acknowledging the relevance of skills, places these more firmly in a context of personal and community well-being.

Capabilities such as resilience and confidence to act for social change; practical and public reasoning; empathy; integrity; informed vision and imagination; developing partnerships across status hierarchies; and communicating professional knowledge in an accessible way (see, for example Walker 2006), go beyond mere skills. While, at first glance, skills perhaps appear to be context- or value-neutral and, so it could be judged by some, more appropriate for universities to be concerned with given their tradition of (assumed) impartiality, it is evident from many policy documents (e.g., World Bank 2002) that the agenda behind skills development in higher education is to produce individuals who are flexible, can adapt quickly to changing conditions and contribute to a strong economy. This perspective, represented in many widely read policy documents and institutional mission statements, is manifestly not value-free. Ironically, the capabilities development model for higher education, which is explicitly and intentionally value-based in its language, emphasizing personal and community well-being as the valuable and important end of education, might strike some teachers and policy-makers in higher education as too "political."

There are two further (and related) observations that can made about the skills and capabilities frameworks. First, while the notion of skills, and the importance of skills development in higher education, is readily appreciated by many university teachers, this is not necessarily the case with the expansive notion of capabilities we discussed in this chapter. Second, the fostering of skills is more easily demonstrated in pedagogical practices than the fostering or affordance of capabilities. How would one justify these two assertions? We propose that one reason why the capabilities development model is less intuitive for many instructors in higher education is that the predominant discourse of teaching and learning has been increasingly skills-oriented, a phenomenon that is associated with the gradual process of professionalization of the university that we have witnessed over the past 50 years (Serrano del Pozo and Kreber 2015). When asked to identify learning outcomes, we are conditioned, given our own academic training and these dominant contemporary skills-based discourses in higher education, to think about what is important to know and understand about the subject we are teaching, followed by what skills students may need to be well prepared for work. Much less frequently do we associate learning outcomes with the knowledge, values, skills and dispositions students need to live valuable lives, or those they need to help others live valuable lives. Students in programs that prepare for specific professions, in particular, have a unique opportunity to contribute to capability expansion in society through the professional practice many of them enter into post-graduation.

Basing our pedagogical and curricular decisions in higher education on an expansive or rich notion of capabilities (Walker 2006, 2012) certainly includes recognizing the value that is added through academic knowledge and generic skills such as creative problem-solving, teamwork and communication skills. However, decisions to employ capabilities-oriented curricula and pedagogies also require appreciating that what students need in order to flourish in higher education, and what they need to contribute to a society that respects and seeks to enable well-being for all, is not only relevant academic knowledge and skills but also certain values and dispositions.

Barnett (2007) contends that in the final analysis of what should be learned through higher education, being trumps knowing and doing. At stake here is the student's integrity, resilience and openness to experience (all aspects of the student's being) that are required to not just cope but thrive in a world that is deeply steeped in ambiguity, complexity and constant change. Arguing from an existentialist position, Barnett (2004, 2007) is concerned with complexity and uncertainty in a general postmodern world, including that of higher education, with its multiple (and ever increasing) conflicting explanatory frameworks that make it hard for students to distinguish true from false claims, and find their own position and voice within disputed discourses. Walker (2006, 2012), arguing from the position of the capabilities approach, is concerned with the opportunities or substantial freedoms (i.e., capabilities) students need in order to do and be well in higher education and, by extension, to contribute to the well-being of others in society through their higher education (as they, as graduates, contribute to capability expansion in their communities). While Barnett and Walker represent two distinct ideas on the purposes of higher education, these ideas converge in the acknowledgement that education is not only a matter of knowledge and skills acquisition. Kosnik et al. (2013) also recognized this when they suggested that business education should not only create academic and professional value, but also afford students opportunity "to develop their personal moral character and good judgment when faced with social and ethical dilemmas, as well as cultivate their social responsibility" (Kosnik et al. 2013, p. 615).

In the previous section, we featured examples of inquiry-based experiential learning opportunities that engage students closely with their communities. The decision to focus on these examples was based on three reasons:

- First, we felt that inquiry-based approaches that connect students directly with their communities align well with a human capabilities development model for higher education (Walker, 2006), whose ultimate goal is to effect social change.
- Second, Kosnik et al. (2013) had argued that experiential learning activities in business education would be especially suitable for teaching students academic knowledge, professional skills and social responsibility.
- Third, we agree with Collini (2012) that inquiry and not just skills should be at the centre of higher education (see also Cape Breton University's 2020 academic plan, "Transformation Through Inquiry").

Although, throughout the theoretical part of this chapter, we have taken the position that the human capabilities development model for higher education is superior to the human capital development model, the design phase of the courses we showcased was not guided by either model. In fact, three of the authors have been teaching these courses for several years, and prior to embarking on this collaborative chapter had not been familiar with the capabilities development framework for higher education. All three authors/instructors care deeply about the subject matter they teach, their students' learning and development, and the communities that the university serves. All have observed through their teaching practice that offering business students opportunity to participate in community-engaged learning is associated with valuable learning outcomes and high student satisfaction. It is especially exciting, therefore, to explore the extent to which the experiential approaches they have been employing with enthusiasm and success are aligned with a capabilities development model. We conclude with three observations.

First, involving students in community-engaged experiential learning opportunities is possible across different types of business courses and business degree programs. All examples describe concrete ways of bringing students into close contact with their communities, and encouraging inquiry-based learning. The largest class we discussed had 90 students enrolled. We acknowledge that in really big classes the logistics of organizing community-engaged learning opportunities may be prohibitive without additional assistance for the course organizer and reaching out to groups, organizations or initiatives in a broader geographical area.

Second, some courses, by virtue of the subject matter they deal with, will demonstrate the human capabilities development framework more explicitly than others. For example, the MBA course on community economic development, which offers students opportunity to work with non-profit organizations that seek to enhance the well-being of marginalized groups, evokes more readily some of the central ideas from the capabilities framework than a course, say, on meetings and event management. This is not to suggest, though, that capabilities development was not encouraged in the other courses featured. Leslie, for example, showed how providing students with opportunities to "learn by doing" through independent work encouraged participatory and active learning among students and let them have a voice which is heard and listened to. In addition, using group work and in-class sessions for discussions allowed students to engage a plurality of views in dialogue and debate, and encouraged them to respect, recognize and value diversity and differences. The same can be concluded for Stephanie's classes.

Third, while all featured examples demonstrated that students were provided with opportunities to develop key skills and academic knowledge important for successful participation in the world of work (teaching both academic and professional value, according to the language used by Kosnik et al. 2013), opportunities for the development of moral value (e.g., being able to engage a plurality of views in dialogue and debate; and respecting, recognizing, valuing diversity and differences) and capabilities such as "being able to work in and form effective groups and social relations based on mutual trust" were also given. The fostering of resilience and confidence to act for social change came through most strongly in Catherine's community economic development course; however, Stephanie's students in the hospitality and tourism management program were provided with opportunities to engage in public reasoning with airport representatives on how to make the arrival experience on Cape Breton Island more welcoming; and Leslie's students had opportunity to learn about and navigate different stakeholder perspectives. More broadly speaking, we observe that if the goal is indeed to prepare students to be able to take on the role of change agents for a fairer and more sustainable future, then we may need to consider more deeply how courses could be designed to engage students in developing partnerships across status hierarchies, and engage in deliberation with members of the public.

To conclude, we showed that courses and pedagogical practices employed in our business school provide many opportunities for capabilities development through community-engaged experiential or inquiry-based learning. While opportunities for capability development clearly are not limited to community-engaged learning, it is one way in which capabilities development can be supported. The examples we showcased do not address all of the important capabilities identified by Walker and MacLean (2013), and they were not meant to present ideal cases but possibilities to be built upon. By proposing capabilities development as a vision of the purpose of higher education, we hoped to encourage reflection in the wider business education community on the goals of business education programs, desirable learning outcomes associated with these goals, and the curricular and pedagogical practices required to achieve these.

REFERENCES

Barnett, Ron (2004), "Learning for an Unknown Future," *Higher Education Research and Development*, 23 (3), 247–260.

Barnett, Ron (2007), *A Will to Learn*. Buckingham: Society for Research into Higher Education and Open University Press.

Boni, Alejandra, and Melanie Walker (eds) (2013), *Human Development and Capabilities: Re-imaging the University of the Twenty-First Century*. New York: Routledge.

Candy, Phil (1991), *Self-direction for Lifelong Learning*. San Francisco, CA: Jossey-Bass.

Cape Breton University (2020a), "Transformation Through Inquiry. Academic Plan." https://www.cbu.ca/wp-content/uploads/2020/01/CBU-Academic-Plan.pdf.

Cape Breton University (2020b), "Master of Business Administration in Community Economic Development." https://www.cbu.ca/academics/programs/mba-in-community-economic-development/.

Collini, Stefan (2012), *What Are Universities For?* London: Penguin Books.

Cortese, A. (2003), "The Critical Role of Higher Education in Creating a Sustainable Future," *Planning for Higher Education*, 31 (3), 15–22.

Croxford, Linda, and David Raffe (2012), "Social Class, Ethnicity and Access to Higher Education in the Four Countries of the UK: 1996–2010," *International Journal of Lifelong Education*, 33 (1), 77–95.

García, Ivis (2020), "Asset-Based Community Development (ABCD): Core Principles," in Rhonda Phillips, Eric Trevan and Patsy Kraeger (eds), *Research Handbook on Community Development*. Cheltenham, UK and Northampton, MA, USA: Edward Elgar Publishing, 67–76.

Hager, Paul, and Susan Holland (eds) (2006), *Graduate Attributes, Learning and Employability*. E-book, Springer Link. https://link.springer.com/book/10.1007%2F1-4020-5342-8.

Haveman, Robert, and Timothy Smeeding (2006), "The Role of Higher Education in Social Mobility," *Future of Children*, 16 (2), 125–150. http://www.jstor.org/stable/3844794. Accessed October 25, 2020.

Inspiring Communities (2020), "Northside Rising: What We Do." https://inspiringcommunities.ca/communities/north-sydney-mines/.

Kember, David, Doris Y.P. Leung and Rosa S.F. Ma (2007), "Characterizing Learning Environments Capable of Nurturing Generic Capabilities in Higher Education," *Research in Higher Education*, 48 (5), 609–632.

Kosnik, R. D., Tingle, J. K., and Blanton, E. L. (2013). Transformational Learning in Business Education: The Pivotal Role of Experiential Learning Projects, *American Journal of Business Education*, 6 (6), 613–630.

Knapper, Chris, and Arthur Cropley (1985), *Lifelong Learning in Higher Education*. London: Croom Helm.

Knapper, C.K., and A. Cropley (2000), *Lifelong Learning in Higher Education*. London: Kogan Page.

Kreber, Carolin (2017), "The Idea of a Decent Profession: Implications for Professional Education," *Studies in Higher Education*, 44 (4), 696–707. DOI: 10.1080/03075079.2017.1395405.

Kretzmann, John P., and John McKnight (1993), *Building Communities from the Inside Out*. Evanston, IL: Center for Urban Affairs and Policy Research, Neighborhood Innovations Network.

McLean, Monica, and Melanie Walker (2012), "The Possibilities for University-Based Public-good Professional Education: A Case-study from South Africa Based on the 'Capability Approach'," *Studies in Higher Education*, 37 (5), 585–601.

Nova Scotia Health Authority (2018), "CHB Operations Manual – CHB Overview." https://static1.squarespace.com/static/58d93c67b8a79bb89e7df56c/t/5c1806e870a6adac3b89d584/1545078504891/3+Terms+of+Reference+-+Community+Health+Board+rev+1018.pdf.

Nussbaum, Martha (2000), *Women and Human Development: The Capabilities Approach*. Cambridge, UK and New York, USA: Cambridge University Press.

Nussbaum, Martha (2011), *Developing Capabilities*. Cambridge, UK and New York, USA: Cambridge University Press.

Nussbaum, Martha, and Amartya Sen (eds) (1993), *The Quality of Life*. Oxford: Clarendon Press.

Otto, Han-Uwe, and Holger Ziegler (2006), "Capabilities and Education," *Social Work and Society*, 4 (2). International Online Journal. http://www.socwork.net/sws/article/view/158/549. Accessed October 25, 2020.

Robeyns, Ingrid (2006), "Three Models of Education: Rights, Capabilities and Human Capital," *Theory and Research in Education*, 4, 69–84.

Sen, Amartya (1999), *Development as Freedom*. Oxford: Oxford University Press.

Serrano Del Pozo, Ignazio, and Carolin Kreber (2015), "The Professionalization of the University and the Profession as Macintyrean Practice," *Studies in Philosophy and Education*, 34 (6), 551–564.

Simpson, Timothy, L. (2013), *The Relevance of Higher Education: Exploring a Contested Notion*. Lanham, MD: Lexington Books.

Spencer, David, Matthew Riddle and Bernadette Knewstubb (2012), "Curriculum Mapping to Embed Graduate Capabilities," *Higher Education Research and Development*, 31 (2), 217–231.

Sutton Trust (2012), "Social Mobility and Education Gaps in the Four Major Anglophone Countries," Social Mobility Summit, London. https://www.suttontrust.com/wp-content/uploads/2020/01/social-mobility-summit2012.pdf.

Unterhalter, Elaine (2007), "Gender Equality, Education, and the Capability Approach," in Melanie Walker and Elaine Unterhalter (eds), *Amartya Sen's Capability Approach and Social Justice in Education*. New York: Palgrave Macmillan, 87–108.

Vignoles, Anna, and Neil Murray (2016), "Editorial: Widening Participation in Higher Education," *Education Sciences*, 6 (2) 13. https://doi.org/10.3390/educsci6020013. Accessed October 24, 2020.

Virtanen, Anne, and Päivi Tynjälä (2019), "Factors Explaining the Learning of Generic Skills: A Study of University Students' Experiences," *Teaching in Higher Education*, 24 (7), 880–894. https://doi.org/10.1080/13562517.2018.1515195.
Walker. M. (2006), *Higher Education Pedagogies: A Capabilities Approach*. Maidenhead: Society for Research into Higher Education and Open University Press.
Walker, Melanie (2012), "A Capital or Capabilities Education Narrative in a World of Staggering Inequalities," *International Journal of Educational Development*, 32, 384–393.
Walker, Melanie, and Monica McLean (2009), "A Public Good Professional Capability Index for University-based Professional Education in South Africa," Paper presented at the Annual Meeting of the Society for Research into Higher Education, Newport, Wales, December 8.
Walker, Melanie, and Monica McLean (2011), "Making Lives Go Better: University Education and Professional Capabilities," *South African Journal of Higher Education*, 24 (5), 847–869.
Walker, Melanie, and Monica McLean (2013), *Professional Education, Capabilities and Contributions to the Public Good: The Role of Universities in Promoting Human Development*. London: Routledge.
Wigley, Simon, and Arzu Akkoyunlu-Wigley (2006), "Human Capabilities Versus Human Capital: Guaging the Value of Education in Developing Countries," *Social Indicators Research*, 78, 287–304. https://doi.org/10.1007/s11205-005-0209-7.
World Bank (2002), "Building Knowledge Economies: Opportunities and Challenges for EU Accession Countries. Final Report of the Knowledge Economy Forum 'Using Knowledge for Development in EU Accession Countries', Paris." http://siteresources.worldbank.org/EXTECAREGTOPKNOECO/Resources/Building_Knowledge_Economies_final_final.pdf. Accessed November 14, 2020.
World Economic Forum (2020), "The Future of Jobs Report 2020." http://www3.weforum.org/docs/WEF_Future_of_Jobs_2020.pdf. Accessed November 7, 2020.

2. Using co-design processes to support strategic pedagogical change in business education

Stephanie Wilson, Elaine Huber and Peter Bryant

INTRODUCTION

Co-design is a facilitated, collaborative process in which numerous actors work together to design an educational innovation. As part of this process, prototypes are developed and evaluated based on their effectiveness in addressing an educational need (Roschelle et al. 2006). This chapter explores the potential of co-design to support strategic pedagogical change in business schools in higher education. It begins by highlighting challenges in the higher education environment and recent shifts in business practice, both of which are driving new approaches to learning and teaching in business schools. The chapter reviews ways in which co-design is being used to address such shifts and support educational change. It explores the changing roles of educational developers and learning designers as they increasingly engage in these processes in collaboration with others, and highlights some guiding principles and paradoxes that have been associated with this collaborative approach.

Using the literature as a frame, we demonstrate how co-design is being used to support Connected Learning at Scale (CLaS), a major strategic educational initiative at the University of Sydney Business School, and reflect on its potential impacts and outcomes. While the example presented sits in the context of a business school at an Australian university, the challenges and opportunities the project responds to are common across many business schools internationally; in particular, the shifting landscape of higher education and global changes in business practice.

Challenges in Higher Education and Shifts in Business Practice

Business schools in Australia graduate one-quarter of the country's university students, and almost half of the international university students in Australia (uCube – Higher Education Statistics 2018). Current trends in higher education such as increasing student numbers, significant increases in overseas student enrolments, the growth of alternative higher education providers, university funding cuts, the rate of technological change and the casualization of teaching staff are putting considerable pressure on business schools. As a result, traditional ways of delivering business education are being challenged, and business schools are looking for new ways to deliver quality education to students.

In addition to broader trends in the higher education environment, changes in business education are being driven by changes in business practice. An example is the concept of shared value, which links business strategies with corporate social responsibility (CSR). Porter and Kramer (2011) describe shared value as 'policies and operating practices that enhance the competitiveness of a company while simultaneously advancing the economic and social conditions in the communities in which it operates' (p. 6). Creating shared value involves reframing societal issues as business challenges and requires that business leaders have a greater appreciation of societal needs, a greater understanding of the true basis of company productivity, and the ability to collaborate across profit/non-profit boundaries (Porter and Kramer 2011).

In influencing students with responsible and sustainable business practices, business schools can be guided by the Principles for Responsible Management Education (PRME 2015) and the United Nations Sustainable Development Goals (SDGs). In addressing these goals, business schools are being urged to address the influence, challenges and opportunities of global megatrends in their curricula and research. These include resource security and sustainable development, emerging economies and urbanization, global connectedness, the velocity of technological developments, and demographic changes including the ageing population (Hajkowicz 2015). In addition to influencing the curriculum, we can also reimagine the learning and teaching methods (or approaches) to better align with these goals.

In a report titled *Reimagining Business Education* (Carlile et al. 2016), the authors distilled three actions that require greater attention from business schools based on the changing landscape: (1) enhancing the value of business education, for example by measuring students' contribution to organizations and communities; (2) ensuring real-world relevance that reflects experiences in a 21st century global economy; and (3) providing differentiation in the marketplace by offering technology-driven innovations and new learning formats that meet the needs of industry. Similarly, the Chartered Association of Business Schools (CABS) identified a number of key recommendations for business schools in the United Kingdom in the context of the changing competitive environment. These include for business schools to work with industry partners to create programmes that meet in-demand skills, find ways of using technology to deliver programmes in new environments, and draw on strengths to create differentiation from the competition. In addition to these, CABS recognizes a need for business schools to identify partners in learning and teaching such as corporates, other faculties and international schools.

For business schools to respond to and interrogate these challenging global forces, we also need to leverage innovations as they emerge, and introduce these innovative approaches through strategic pedagogical change mechanisms. Many institutions use the word 'transform' to describe how they wish to change the educational experience for their students (see for example the learning.futures initiative at the University of Technology Sydney: https://www.uts.edu.au/research-and-teaching/learning-and-teaching/learningfutures/how-our-students-learn). There are a number of ways in which pedagogical change is facilitated, but two of the more prominent approaches are through technologies and through community.

Supporting the implementation of a new learning technology platform such as a learning management system (LMS) is one way for schools to influence pedagogical change within an institution (Ryan et al. 2012). However, in actuality, it is often not transformation that is taking place but rather a shift of content from one LMS to a new LMS; that is, a transition rather than a transformation in pedagogical approach. Whilst these two descriptors are similar, the latter has much loftier intent than the former, but the reality of the scale of such change is what limits the original goals of such projects. Bryant (2018) declares that we are long past trying to prove the value of new innovative technologies to transform pedagogy, and encourages us to move towards discussions centred on how our students are learning in this age of information. This message is not new and yet we are still not leveraging technologies to their fullest potential. However, pedagogical change initiated through technology often focuses on the tool, not on the learning actions, with McLoughlin and Lee (2008) privileging the social aspects of learning technology enabling networking, socialization, communication and engagement with communities of learning as ways to introduce pedagogical change.

Another mechanism used to facilitate pedagogical change is through the integration of communities of practice (CoPs) in curriculum design and academic development. Cochrane and Narayan (2017) discuss the benefits of introducing CoPs for academic professional development to upscale from a central learning and teaching model to a faculty-centric one. The aim was then to encourage teaching staff to integrate this model into their own pedagogical practice with their students for learning as a community. One example they highlight is their international student collaboration of mobile video production and sharing. The use of CoPs is a way of building trust and starting conversations which can then lead to incremental change.

An example of developing community engagement to drive pedagogical change is the Macquarie University Professional and Community Engagement (PACE) programme which uses 'teaching models that promote enquiry driven learning, and prepare students for productive professional and civic lives' (Winchester-Seeto et al. 2017, p. 12). The PACE programme combines scaffolded reflection, discussion and experiential learning to empower learners and enable them to confront the pernicious problems of modern society.

One study on pedagogical change also found variation between the needs of the organization and those of the educator (Weinberger 2018). The author found that organizational implementation was successful, yet without adequate professional development, guidance and support the pedagogical transformation was less so. This leads us to consider how we should best ensure faculty can meet both transformational pedagogical and metacognitive goals for our students, and how we can leverage the diverse skills and backgrounds of other actors involved in designing and implementing change.

If a high level of innovation is required by business schools to address changes in both the higher education sector and the changing nature of business, what kinds of educational development processes will best support strategic pedagogical change and avoid the trap of like-for-like replacement and simple technological transition? That is, what processes are appropriate to support the kind of innovation that is needed, and who should be involved, given that what is being called for involves multiple stakeholders: industry, communities and other partners?

CO-DESIGN IN HIGHER EDUCATION

In this section we explore how co-design approaches are being used in higher education to address some of the educational development challenges identified above, and how they are being used to support strategic pedagogical change in business schools.

The Growing Role of Design in Business Practice, Curricula and Research

Design-based methodologies are increasingly being used in the business world to support problem-solving and drive innovation and change. In response, many business schools in higher education have introduced programmes and courses that incorporate design thinking, particularly in the areas of human-centred design (e.g., design innovation courses), integrative thinking, design management and design as strategy (Matthews and Wrigley 2017). Sometimes the learning experiences in these courses involve bringing students from business schools together with students from other disciplines (and industry) to work on real-world problems using design methodologies. A concurrent trend has been the increased attention given to the 'business studio' as both a pedagogical approach and a physical environment in which to conduct studio work. The business studio utilizes processes from art and design and emphasizes 'learning-by-making' (Barry and Meisiek 2015, p. 160). Through this process, some business and design schools have developed closer alliances in recent years.

In addition to an expanding number of business schools embedding design-based methodologies in curricula, there is a growing body of research by business school academics investigating these methodologies and their role in business and management (e.g. Boland and Collopy 2004; Dunne and Martin 2006; Martin 2009; Starkey and Tempest 2009). While the integration of design-based methodologies into business research and curricula is becoming increasingly well documented, what is less clear is how business schools are using design thinking and co-design processes to support strategic educational change in the schools themselves.

Definition and Characteristics

Roschelle et al. (2006) define co-design in education as 'a highly-facilitated, team-based process in which teachers, researchers, and developers work together in defined roles to design an educational innovation, realise the design in one or more prototypes, and evaluate each prototype's significance for addressing a concrete educational need' (p. 606). In this chapter we extend this definition to include a broader range of actors. In addition to teachers, researchers and developers, co-design may also involve students, alumni, industry and other professionals engaged in supporting the educational process. For the purpose of this chapter, we also distinguish between educational design that only involves two actors – an educational developer/designer and a teacher – and more extensive co-design processes which tend to involve more stakeholders over a longer period of time.

Co-design is viewed by Barbera et al. (2017) as having the potential to fulfil unmet needs in the field of learning design. The authors describe the area as underexplored in both research and practice. As a result, there are 'no definitive guidelines for an evolutionary implementation of a co-designed learning scenario that addresses the process of change and thus the collaboration of all agents in the gradual and agreed improvement of the course' (p. 105). Such guidelines would offer practical support to those tasked with educational development and strategic educational change in higher education.

Research suggests that co-design practices in education are often associated with the design and implementation of technological tools to support learning (for example, Hannon et al. 2012; Mor and Winters 2007; Roschelle et al. 2006), but may also be used to address the design of curricula more broadly (Cook et al. 2017; Könings et al. 2011; Shrader et al. 2001; Willness and Bruni-Bossio 2017). Other examples of 'products' resulting from co-design processes reported in the literature include online modules (Barbera et al. 2017), assessments (Deeley and Bovill 2017), specific educational or support resources (Maxwell and Armellini 2019; Petersen et al. 2016), Massive Open Online Courses (MOOCs) (Kennedy and Laurillard 2019) and designs for university infrastructure (Geoffrey 2018).

The co-design approach has close ties to several other design traditions such as participatory design, co-creation and open design processes, and shares assumptions with academics engaged in design-based research (Cobb et al. 2003). For example, co-design processes might be utilized in one or more phases of a broader educational design research framework.

Practical Guidelines

While there are no definitive guidelines for implementing co-design processes in education, some researchers have proposed key characteristics, stages or components to guide practice. For example, Roschelle et al. (2006) propose that co-design processes:

- are based on the design of a concrete and tangible innovation;
- collect information on educational practice and its context;
- have a flexible goal and involve an iterative implementation process;
- involve a shared experience among stakeholders that requires a collaborative effort; and
- are timed to fit with the school calendar and teachers' work schedules. (p. 607)

In terms of those involved in the process, the authors also note that each actor has a role and contributes valuable knowledge, and the team is led by a principal investigator who is responsible for the success of the process.

Cober et al. (2015) reviewed the literature on co-design processes in education to identify a number of typical stages. The authors found that it was common early in the process to share experiences and resources with the aim of building shared understanding in the team. Following this, they found that the co-design process often involves the use of tools (such as concept maps and other prototyping tools) to generate potential designs. The importance of sharing mental representations amongst the actors in the co-design process has also been recognized as characteristic of the process (McKenney et al. 2015).

The practice of co-design between teachers and students is commonly known as 'students as partners', and there is a growing body of research and practice in this area. There are many ways in which students can act as partners in learning and teaching in higher education. In a conceptual model presented by Healy et al. (2014), students as partners is seen as one form of student engagement, and involves high levels of active participation from students. Curriculum design and pedagogic consultancy is one area where students can act as partners. This example of co-design for learning engages students in curriculum design and development processes that are not limited to students participating in course evaluations and committees (a practice often referred to as incorporating the 'student voice'). Rather, it involves students working together with faculty in the process of design and inquiry. This is consistent with the characteristics of co-design more generally, in which 'the person who will eventually be served through the design process is given the position of "expert of his/her experience"' (Sanders and Stappers 2008, p. 12). For students as partners to have the potential to help transform the nature of higher education, the authors argue it needs to go beyond individual initiatives and be embedded in the culture of the institution.

Benefits and Challenges

A number of key benefits and challenges associated with co-design in education have been identified in the literature. In terms of benefits, research suggests that in addition to enhanced motivation and engagement there can be significant learning for those involved (Deeley and Bovill 2017), including notable benefits for teachers engaged in the process in relation to their professional development as teachers (Mor and Craft 2012; Voogt et al. 2015). Students involved in the co-design processes can deepen their understanding of the learning process, and their involvement can offer a diversity of perspectives and lead to more informed peda-gogical practices (Bovill et al. 2011; Cook-Sather 2014). Importantly, the adoption of these practices has also been found to result in an improved sense of belonging for students (Deeley and Bovill 2017).

A number of challenges have been identified in the literature in relation to using co-design processes to support educational change. For example, in situations where the co-design team involves external stakeholders such as industry, challenges may arise when the university and industry have different drivers (Theobald et al. 2019). Time has also been identified in the literature as an important factor, particularly as it is needed to build rapport between team members. As articulated by Gros and López (2016), sustained dialogue between actors in a co-design process helps build trust. The challenge arises because co-design processes are often dependent on academic timetables (e.g., semesters), as noted in Roschelle et al. (2006), and group maturity is difficult to achieve over short time periods (Kvellestad 2017).

After analysing three different co-design processes, Macken-Walsh (2019) identified a number of paradoxes associated with the co-design process: (1) the outputs of the co-design process can be 'orphaned' when they aren't strongly affiliated with specific professional communities outside the co-design team; (2) when diverse participants in the process combine their knowledges in the co-design process the outputs generated can be 'new and strange' (rather than familiar and acceptable) to end-users; and (3) sometimes the interventions that are developed through the co-design process are challenging rather than popular. The author asserts that being aware of these kinds of paradoxes and the dynamics of the co-design process can support 'enhanced facilitation of processes and impacts of outcomes' (p. 247). While the benefits and challenges of co-design are increasingly well documented in the students as partners literature (and the co-design literature in design disciplines outside of education), they appear to be less well documented in relation to co-design processes in higher education involving more diverse actors.

Who Are the Actors?

The literature on co-design in education highlights various combinations of 'actors' in the process. If the co-design work is being carried out by a team within the university this may include combinations such as students and faculty (Gros and López 2016; Rakrouki et al. 2017); students, faculty and developers (Goff and Knorr 2018); teacher and teacher educators (Sewell et al. 2018); or students, researchers and teachers and/or administrators (Barbera et al. 2017; Wagner et al. 2016). Co-design processes focused on pedagogical change can also involve external stakeholders, and include combinations such as the university, business and/ or agencies (Business Higher Education Forum 2018; Motovidlak 2018); the university and science professionals (Rudman et al. 2018); and universities and school students and/or career counsellors (Bown et al. 2016; Holley and Howlett 2015; Shipepe and Peters 2018).

Many of the co-design case studies reported in the literature share a common underlying principle, which is that the actors in the process are considered equal partners. This is artic-ulated particularly in the students as partners literature where establishing shared values between academics and students is an embedded part of the process. Common values cited in the literature include trust, respect, reciprocity, responsibility and openness (Healy et al. 2014,

p. 5). Co-design projects involving interdisciplinary team members may articulate specific shared values to guide their practice, such as 'respecting disciplinary identities and boundaries', or 'extending the understanding beyond the disciplines' (Wagner et al. 2016, p. 47). A more detailed discussion about the changing role of educational developers and designers is included later in this chapter.

Co-Design Processes to Support Educational Development in Business

While there are numerous examples of business school programmes that partner with industry and community groups as part of the learning process (see for example Nikolova and Andersen 2017), a review of the literature reveals a shortage of case studies examining co-design processes to support strategic educational change in business education. A number of studies describe students as partners initiatives where staff and students have co-designed a teaching or research initiative or the use of a particular technology. Examples include Rakrouki et al. (2017), who describe the co-design of a research conference by first-year students and staff; and Stanway et al. (2019), who report on a project that engaged international students as partners to implement WeChat as a communication tool in a postgraduate business school unit.

Some studies describe initiatives where students and other stakeholders have participated in the co-design of a course in both the pre-implementation and implementation phases. For example, Huq and Gilbert (2017) describe how students, industry partners and academic course teams co-designed new modes of delivery and assessment in entrepreneurship education. The authors highlight the capacity for the approach to 'meet the needs of business start-ups, intrapreneurial capacity-building and potentially, enhancement of graduate employability' (p. 155).

A future focus on research investigating co-design processes to support major educational change in business schools is needed to allow business academics and educational developers to share principles and processes that are found to be effective, and to build educational design knowledge specifically in the context of business education.

Changing Roles for Educational Developers and Designers

The roles and responsibilities of educational developers and designers have shifted in recent years and this is due, in part, to a growing need for them to engage in co-design processes. In the field of design practice more broadly, Sanders and Stappers (2008) made a prediction that co-design teams would become increasingly diverse and involve close collaboration between all stakeholders, along with professionals who have a combination of design and research skills. They suggest that such diversity and collaboration is necessary if we want to address complexity and scale, and when we are designing 'the future experiences of people, communities, and cultures who now are connected and informed in ways that were unimaginable even 10 years ago' (p. 49).

New and emerging roles for designers (across different sub-disciplines of design) have been studied, particularly by Inns (2010), and these roles provide insight into the contribution of design practice in current and future contexts. In connection with the Designing for the 21st Century Research Initiative, Inns (2010) identified six emerging roles for designers, including facilitator of thinking, mediator between stakeholders, coordinator of exploration, visualizer of intangibles, navigator of complexity and negotiator of value (p. 41). Wilson and Zamberlan

(2015) conducted a broader review of the literature on the expanding parameters of design to look for additional roles not captured in Inns's framework, and to highlight roles that appear to be underexplored or less well understood in the literature. The review identified a number of additional roles, including the designer as capacity builder, strategist, design lead/interpolator, and driver and translator of innovation. Several other roles were identified as being underexplored in the literature: (1) co-creator – contributor to collaborative and interdisciplinary teams; (2) generator of new design knowledge; and (3) developer of, and contributor to, creative cultures.

Many of these emerging roles are also relevant to educational developers and designers. For example, concerning point 2 above, Reimann (2011) suggests that design-based research in education should focus more on its design methodology (particularly given the challenges of coordinating work with multiple stakeholders). He suggests that the increasing use of information technologies (to support student learning and the design and research process) 'provides many opportunities for innovating (design) methodologies' (p. 46).

Another example is exemplified in a study on the roles of educational designers that finds they 'are professionals with a personal capacity and efficacy for operating in ambiguous, collaborative, and transdisciplinary contexts' (Bisset 2019, p. 15). This study also reports that partnerships between designers and teaching teams give rise to project-based approaches to curriculum development and, in the process, knowledge can be constructed through these temporary networks. This can lead to educational designers performing more of a transformative role by acting as 'agents of social change at the personal, relational and institutional level' (Campbell et al. 2005, cited in Bisset 2019, p. 4).

The Educause Horizon report (higher education edition) is one indicator of the trends and technological developments that will drive educational change on the near, middle and far horizon. In the latest report, Alexander et al. (2019) indicate that there is a growing demand across the higher education (HE) sector for instructional design and digital learning expertise, and that institutions that are leveraging the power of team-based designers working with faculty and using design thinking approaches are growing. In a report for the Gates Foundation (2016), 'Instructional design in higher education', researchers found that instructional designers' activities fall into four broad categories: design, manage, train and support. Furthermore, they found the main challenge experienced by participants was the ability to truly collaborate with faculty. However they were united in proclaiming that their primary goal is student success: 'doing whatever it takes to improve student learning outcomes is their job; they just want the support of administration and faculty to fully realize their capacity to improve the teaching and learning experience' (p. 3).

Mitchell et al. (2017) investigated the differing roles and responsibilities in the area of educational design and development and found a misalignment between role titles and practices. They conjecture that this may be due to a misunderstanding by HE stakeholders of what is encompassed by these roles, which in turn can undermine the value and importance of the collaborative work that they undertake. A scoping review of the literature carried out by Altena et al. (2019) builds on these findings and identifies a range of knowledge, skills and attributes that learning designers espouse. Using a framework of knowing, doing, being (Barnett 2009, cited in Altena et al. 2019), the research suggests that the role of the learning designer is determined by what they do rather than by knowing or being. These 'doing' activities were categorized as course and curriculum design; project management; professional development; stakeholder engagement; and asset production and technical support.

As we begin to understand the changing nature of these roles in context, we suggest that the broader literature on design practice research, which has also addressed role changes, will help us better articulate and understand what is involved in co-design processes in the higher education sector and specifically in business education. In the remainder of this chapter we describe a major strategic initiative at the University of Sydney Business School that is utilizing co-design processes to support large-scale pedagogical change.

CONNECTED LEARNING AT SCALE (CLAS)

Connected Learning at Scale (CLaS) is a strategic priority project at the University of Sydney Business School that aims to transform the teaching and learning experience in our large core units. It is being implemented to allow the school to better manage and then take advantage of the scale of cohort in our undergraduate and pre-experience postgraduate programme.

The aim of the project is to transform the teaching and learning experience for the entire cohort of students, with the key intention being to support, nurture and leverage connections between students, disciplines, industry and society. This represents a paradigm shift around how our students engage in a business school education, and will directly impact on the educational experience of a significant majority of the school's 14 500 students as well as the thousands of students from other faculties that take our units. Connected Learning at Scale (CLaS) is built on three key principles:

- Principle 1 – Information engagement: students both individually and collectively engage with discipline knowledge as opposed to having it 'delivered' to them in a lecture.
- Principle 2 – Connected participation and active learning: face-to-face teaching time, student learning activities and technology are leveraged to build connections and networks to address, debate and solve critical global and local challenges though innovative pedagogical approaches.
- Principle 3 – Relevant and authentic assessment and feed-forward: learning is applied and tested through authentic assessment modes supported by opportunities to receive and share feedback from both academics and peers.

An overarching goal of the project is to generate a series of design blueprints that can be used by other faculties in the university as well as across the sector, to address issues of learning and teaching at scale.

The Co-Design Process in CLaS

As shown in Figure 2.1, the design process being used, documented and tested in the CLaS project involves five key phases. The process is cyclical and may be repeated a number of times during the life of a project. While the figure reflects the broad design process a project might move through, the process is iterative rather than linear. That is, it may contain any number of 'sub-loops' within it, such as repetitions of the designing and building phases before moving to implementation. Like the approach described in Barbera et al. (2017), the co-design process in CLaS is embedded in a design-based research framework. This is to ensure a close connection between theory and practice, and the opportunity to produce reusable design patterns at the end of the project.

For all units of study involved in the CLaS project an educational developer is assigned as the principal investigator (facilitator), and an academic from the unit (usually the current unit coordinator) and a learning designer are also allocated to the project. While these team members are in core roles, a variety of other stakeholders are involved at various stages. Below is a summary of the key activities and actors involved in each phase of the design processes.

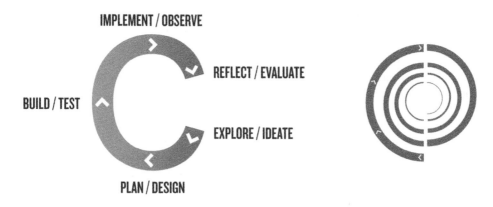

IMPLEMENT / OBSERVE

REFLECT / EVALUATE

BUILD / TEST

EXPLORE / IDEATE

PLAN / DESIGN

Figure 2.1   *The five phases of the design-based research process as applied to the design and development cycles of the Connected Learning at Scale project*

Explore/Ideate

The explore/ideate phase begins with a crowdsourcing exercise called CONNECT:In where students who have completed the unit at some time in the past (for example, over the past six semesters) are invited to rethink how the course could be delivered. This is followed by an ideation workshop involving multiple stakeholders such as the unit coordinator, lecturers, tutors, students, alumni, industry, educational developers and learning designers. The primary goal of the workshop is to identify 'dreams' and 'gripes' with the unit (consistent with IDEO's Design Thinking for Educators toolkit; IDEO 2013). A primary focus of the workshop design is to build rapport between participants, provide processes and tools for design thinking and the development of potential designs, and to promote an environment conducive to creativity.

Consistent with McKenney and Reeves's (2018) model of educational design research, which shares many commonalities with educational co-design processes, the early explore/ideate phase also provides opportunities for 'clarifying the problem and shaping understanding of constraints within which a design will have to operate ... [including] anticipating how the design will align with the needs and wishes of practitioners and other stakeholders, as well as gaining a sense of important system factors related to the problem' (p. 87).

Plan/Design

During the plan/design phase, the unit coordinator and members of the teaching team continue to workshop ideas with educational developers and designers, and act as co-designers in the process. This phase commonly involves one or more additional workshops to plan and design educational developments within the unit. Before building and testing begins, other stake-holders, such as industry members and students, may also be brought back into the process to provide input and feedback on planned developments and to allow further refinements.

Build/Test

While the practitioners involved in the unit are often not directly involved in building and testing the prototypes themselves, they contribute discipline content and engage in feedback and review sessions with educational developers and designers during this phase. These sessions are pivotal in shaping and refining prototypes to be tested. During the plan/design and build/test phases a variety of design 'artefacts' are produced that serve as 'boundary objects' to support communication between the various actors (Reimann 2011).

Implement/Observe

The first stage of implementation commonly involves some level of professional development for the team who will be teaching the unit. Professional development workshops may be co-facilitated by an educational developer in collaboration with members of the teaching team. Once the semester begins, the implement/observe phase continues to require close collaboration between practitioners and educational developers and designers, to address any unexpected issues as they emerge and to track student engagement with the designed prototypes.

Reflect/Evaluate

While focus groups, interviews and surveys with teachers and students are commonly run after the implementation phase, evaluation planning begins much earlier in the process. Existing data from the Unit of Study Survey (USS) is analysed in the early stages to establish key strengths and challenges with the unit from the student perspective. A survey to collect 'baseline data' may also be specifically designed and run prior to the intervention, to allow for a comparison of staff and student experiences after developments have been implemented. Focus groups, interviews and surveys may be conducted immediately after an intervention (during the semester) and/or at the end of the semester. Data is used to assess the effectiveness of the prototype in addressing articulated problems and aspirations, and to make decisions about further developments. As suggested by Goodyear (2015), the design process should also involve '(re-)designing evaluation instruments that are specifically tuned to picking up exactly the right kind of data to feed the next round of design decisions' (p. 32).

DISCUSSION

Our key goal in the CLaS project is to document the co-design process, highlighting not only the benefits and challenges, but also the roles of actors and their interrelationships, the turning points for change to be fully embraced, and the collaborative processes at play. This will help address the paucity of literature on co-design practices in higher education and in our particular context of business education. We have begun the co-design process on our first tranche of units in the CLaS project (our core undergraduate units in the Bachelor of Commerce). Our initial CONNECT:In workshops have been run, with new ideas being co-created and piloted within these units. Across these initial units we have trialled, to varying degrees, the three CLaS principles and are in the process of evaluating their implementation.

We still have some way to go in developing patterns and models of success for delivery of large classes, and we have only just scratched the surface of the possibilities available to us by fully engaging with co-design principles and approaches. What we have found is that the process is iterative and requires constant communication between all members of the co-design team: sharing what is working, what is not, tweaking and adding new ideas throughout the semester rather than leaving it to an evaluative reflection at the end. Summative evaluations have their place but can halt the flow of creativity and extend timelines, whereas taking a formative reflexive perspective is better suited to a co-design approach (Roschelle et al. 2006).

As observed by Goodyear (2015), 'the term "design" does not have much currency in the core practices of higher education' with the exception of disciplines teaching design (p. 31). While this is gradually changing over time, the term is still commonly associated with the 'planning and development' of courses, curricula and assessment, and core characteristics of the design process (such as problem framing) are often not explicitly practised. Goodyear suggests two reasons why educators have a tendency to rush straight to a design solution. The first is that many teachers don't have 'a sense of design as a process' or 'the conceptual tools and skills to work through a design problem in a creative but structured way'; and the second is that often assumptions associated with disciplinary and teaching traditions can make solutions look self-evident (p. 31). The co-design process provides opportunities for teachers and other stakeholders to experience and develop core design skills so that design sits at the centre of educational practices rather than on the sidelines (p. 37), and to support strategic pedagogical change in the discipline.

We concur with Roschelle et al. (2006) that as you increase the number of actors involved in the co-creation process you create tensions through the diversity of their roles and bringing together their points of view. We must also consider 'the context and shared understandings of practice among all agents involved in co-design' (Barbera et al. 2017, p. 120). It takes time to ensure all are abreast of the iterative changes and how the project is progressing. However, this investment in time can pay dividends in terms of depth of ideas and innovations to draw upon. Good project management and communication skills are imperative, not only for effective facilitation of the co-design process but also for explaining the features and functionality of co-designed outputs, as well as the nature of the co-design process itself (Macken-Walsh, 2019). Ensuring certain actors are well versed in these skills will be highly beneficial for the success of any project taking a co-design approach. Furthermore, these skills are indeed those of relevance for our student collaborators and will stand them in good stead in their future careers.

Globally, business schools are facing existential challenges in terms of both the relevance of the ways we teach to a disrupted and fluid global economic, social and political environment, and the relevance of our perspectives and capabilities to the current and future ambitions of students and the community. These are not challenges we can face in isolation or through replicating what every other school does at a curricula or pedagogical level. The early pilot interventions emerging from the co-design approaches taken by the University of Sydney Business School have exposed the dangers of an easy reliance on technology to facilitate change. Co-design represents a fundamental altering of the very structures and principles that inform how we understand higher education, but not necessarily how we deliver it. The CLaS initiative uses a co-design approach to reflect on how we reposition and repurpose our ways of doing by reflecting on and integrating the experiences, expertise and practice of the partners (actors) in the project, whether they be teachers, educational developers and designers, students, industry partners, alumni or management.

Pedagogical transformation is not a process of transition and replication, nor is it a process of redesigning afresh so as to remove the undesirable, as there may well be pedagogically sound approaches already occurring. Authentic transformation is a human skill. It looks at the same set of tools, techniques, knowledges and skills, and sees different and creative patterns and connections in them. Co-design is a process that harnesses these perspectives, supports them with process and capability, and deploys them to teaching and learning. The strength of the CLaS approach is that co-design is also used to ferment and cement connections between the partners in the design and delivery process. It is in the nurturing and leveraging of connection that the potential of transformation can be realized to address, explore and solve critical global, local and personal challenges within and through a business education.

ACKNOWLEDGEMENT

We would like to thank Dr Matthew Taylor for sharing his preliminary scan of the co-design literature. This provided us with initial reading materials to supplement our thinking and experience.

REFERENCES

Alexander, Bryan, Kevin Ashford-Rowe, Noreen Barajas-Murph, Gregory Dobbin, Jessica Knott, et al. (2019), 'EDUCAUSE Horizon Report 2019 Higher Education Edition', EDU19.

Altena, Sharon Lee, Rebecca Ng, Meredith Hinze, Simone Poulson and Dominique Parrish (2019), '"Many hats one heart": a scoping review on the professional identity of learning designers', *Personalised Learning. Diverse Goals. One Heart: Proceedings of ASCILITE 2019*, 359–364.

Barbera, Elena, Iolanda Garcia and Marc Fuertes-Alpiste (2017), 'A co-design process microanalysis: stages and facilitators of an inquiry-based and technology-enhanced learning scenario', *International Review of Research in Open and Distributed Learning: IRRODL*, 18 (6), 104–126.

Barry, Daved and Stefan Meisiek (2015), 'Discovering the business studio', *Journal of Management Education*, 39 (1), 153–175.

Bisset, Donna (2019), 'Role of educational designers in higher education institutions', in *Professional and Support Staff in Higher Education*, C. Bossu and N. Brown (eds), Singapore: Springer, 1–19.

Boland, Richard J. and Fred Collopy (2004), 'Design matters for management', in *Managing as Designing*, R.J. Bolland and F. Collopy (eds), Stanford, CA: Stanford University Press, 3–18.

Bovill, Catherine, Alison Cook-Sather and Peter Felten (2011), 'Students as co-creators of teaching approaches, course design, and curricula: implications for academic developers', *International Journal for Academic Development*, 16 (2), 133–145.

Bown, Oliver, Philip Gough and Martin Tomitsch (2016), 'Learning design through facilitating collaborative design: incorporating service learning into a first year undergraduate design degree course', in *Collaboration and Student Engagement in Design Education*, Hershey, PA: IGI Global, 209–229.

Bryant, Peter (2018), 'Making education better: implementing pedagogical change through technology in a modern institution', in *Higher Education in the Digital Age: Moving Academia Online*, A. Zorn, J. Haywood and J.-M. Glachant (eds), Cheltenham, UK and Northampton, MA, USA: Edward Elgar Publishing, 35–54.

Business Higher Education Forum (2018), 'Building a diverse Cybersecurity Talent Ecosystem to address national security needs'. Accessed 10 April 2020 at https://charteredabs.org/wp-content/uploads/2019/03/CABS41233_2019_Future-Trends-Report_WEB.pdf.

Carlile, Paul R., Steven H. Davidson, Kenneth W. Freeman, Howard Thomas and N. Venkatraman (2016), *Reimagining Business Education: Insights and Actions from the Business Education Jam*, Bingley: Emerald Group Publishing.

Cobb, Paul, Jere Confrey, Andrea DiSessa, Richard Lehrer and Leona Schauble (2003), 'Design experiments in educational research', *Educational Researcher*, 32 (1), 9–13.

Cober, Rebecca, Esther Tan, Jim Slotta, Hyo-Jeong So and Karen D. Könings (2015), 'Teachers as participatory designers: two case studies with technology-enhanced learning environments', *Instructional Science*, 43 (2), 203–28.

Cochrane, Thomas and Vickel Narayan (2017), 'Principles of modeling COPs for pedagogical change: lessons learnt from practice 2006 to 2014', in *Implementing Communities of Practice in Higher Education*, J. McDonald and A. Cater-Steel (eds), Singapore: Springer, 619–643.

Cook, E.J., L.M.W. Mann and Scott A. Daniel (2017), 'Co-designing a new engineering curriculum with industry', in *45th SEFI Annual Conference*, 303–310.

Cook-Sather, Alison (2014), 'Multiplying perspectives and improving practice: what can happen when undergraduate students collaborate with college faculty to explore teaching and learning', *Instructional Science*, 42 (1), 31–46.

Deeley, Susan J. and Catherine Bovill (2017), 'Staff student partnership in assessment: enhancing assessment literacy through democratic practices', *Assessment and Evaluation in Higher Education*, 42 (3), 463–477.

Dunne, David and Roger Martin (2006), 'Design thinking and how it will change management education: An interview and discussion', *Academy of Management Learning and Education*, 5 (4), 512–523.

Gates Foundation (2016), 'Instructional design in higher education', report, Intentional Futures, 16.

Geoffrey, Tabo Olok (2018), 'Application of participatory design in designing infrastructures for learning in resource limiting environments', in Christian Glahn, Loine Dirckinck-Holmfelt (eds), *Proceedings of the 13th EC-TEL Doctoral Consortium co-located with the 13th European Conference on Technology Enhanced Learning*, Leeds, 2294.

Goff, Lori and Kris Knorr (2018), 'Three heads are better than one: students, faculty, and educational developers as co-developers of science curriculum', *International Journal for Students as Partners*, 2 (1), 112–20.

Goodyear, Peter (2015), 'Teaching as design', *HERDSA Review of Higher Education*, 2, 27–50.

Gros, Begoña and Marta López (2016), 'Students as co-creators of technology-rich learning activities in higher education', *International Journal of Educational Technology in Higher Education*, 13 (1), 28.

Hajkowicz, Stefan (2015), *Global Megatrends: Seven Patterns of Change Shaping our Future*, Victoria: CSIRO Publishing.

Hannon, Daniel, Ethan Danahy, Leslie Schneider, Eric Coopey and Gary Garber (2012), 'Encouraging teachers to adopt inquiry-based learning by engaging in participatory design', *IEEE 2nd Integrated STEM Education Conference*, IEEE, 1–4.

Healy, Mick, Abbey Flint and Kathy Harrington (2014), 'Engagement through partnership: students as partners in learning and teaching in higher education', AdvanceHE.

Holley, Debbie and Philip Howlett (2015), 'Engaging our school teachers: An Augmented Reality (AR) approach to continuous professional development', *Second International Conference on E-Learning, E-Education, and Online Training*, Springer, 118–125.

Huq, Afreen and David Gilbert (2017), 'All the world's a stage: transforming entrepreneurship education through design thinking', *Education+ Training*, 59 (2), 155–170.

IDEO (2013), *Design Thinking for Educators Toolkit*, New York: IDEObooks.

Inns, Tom (2010), *Designing for the 21st Century: Interdisciplinary Methods and Findings*, Gower Publishing. Retrieved from www.ashgate.com/pdf/samplepages/designing_for_the_21st_century_intro.pdf.

Kennedy, Eileen and Diana Laurillard (2019), 'The potential of MOOCs for large-scale teacher professional development in contexts of mass displacement', *London Review of Education*, 17 (2), 141–158.

Könings, Karen D., Saskia Brand-Gruwel and Jeroen JG Van Merriënboer (2011), 'Participatory instructional redesign by students and teachers in secondary education: effects on perceptions of instruction', *Instructional Science*, 39 (5), 737–762.

Kvellestad, Randi Veiteberg (2017), 'The Black Thread project: building student communities', Design Society.

Macken-Walsh, Áine (2019), 'Multi-actor co-design of extension interventions: paradoxes arising in three cases in the Republic of Ireland', *Journal of Agricultural Education and Extension*, 25 (3), 245–65.

Martin, Roger L. (2009), *The Design of Business: Why Design Thinking is the Next Competitive Advantage*, Boston, MA: Harvard Business Press.

Matthews, Judy and Cara Wrigley (2017), 'Design and design thinking in business and management higher education', *Journal of Learning Design*, 10 (1), 41–54.

Maxwell, Rachel and Alejandro Armellini (2019), 'Identity, employability and entrepreneurship: the ChANGE framework of graduate attributes', *Higher Education, Skills and Work-Based Learning*, 9 (9), 76–91.

McKenney, Susan, Yael Kali, Lina Markauskaite and Joke Voogt (2015), 'Teacher design knowledge for technology enhanced learning: an ecological framework for investigating assets and needs', *Instructional Science*, 43 (2), 181–202.

McKenney, Susan and T.C. Reeves (2018), *Conducting Educational Design Research*, Boca Raton, FL: Routledge.

McLoughlin, Catherine and Mark Lee (2008), 'Mapping the digital terrain: new media and social software as catalysts for pedagogical change', conference paper, *Hello! Where are You in the Landscape of Educational Technology? Proceedings ascilite Melbourne 2008*. https://www.ascilite.org/conferences/melbourne08/procs/mcloughlin.pdf.

Mitchell, Kate, Colin Simpson and Chie Adachi (2017), 'What's in a name: the ambiguity and complexity of technology enhanced learning roles', *Me, Us, IT! Conference Proceedings*, H. Partridge, K. Davis, and J. Thomas (eds), University of Southern Queensland, 147–151.

Mor, Yishay and Brock Craft (2012), 'Learning design: reflections upon the current landscape', *Research in Learning Technology*, 20 (Sup1), 19196.

Mor, Yishay and Niall Winters (2007), 'Design approaches in technology-enhanced learning', *Interactive Learning Environments*, 15 (1), 61–75.

Motovidlak, David T. (2018), 'Connections, collaboration, and collective knowledge: fostering knowledge sharing community', New Brunswick, NJ: Rutgers University – Graduate School of Education.

Nikolova, Natalia and Lisa Andersen (2017), 'Creating shared value through service-learning in management education', *Journal of Management Education*, 41 (5), 750–780.

Petersen, Lynne, John P. Egan, Elana Curtis and Mark Barrow (2016), 'On the role of "digital learning designer" for non-indigenous designers collaborating within culturally grounded digital design settings', *ascilite 2016: 33rd International Conference of Innovation, Practice and Research in the Use of Educational Technologies in Tertiary Education*, Adelaide, 509.

Porter, Michael E. and Mark R. Kramer (2011), 'Creating shared value: how to reinvent capitalism – and unleash a wave of innovation and growth', *Harvard Business Review*, 89 (1/2), 62–77.

PRME (2015), 'Management education and the sustainable development goals: TRANSFORMING education to act responsibly and find opportunities'. Accessed 16 April 2020 at https://www.unprme.org/resource-docs/SDGBrochurePrint.pdf.

Rakrouki, Zak, Mark Gatenby, Stefan Cantore, Thomas Rowledge and Tom Davidson (2017), 'The Opening Conference: a case study in undergraduate co-design and inquiry-based learning', *International Journal for Students as Partners*, 1 (2). https://doi.org/10.15173/ijsap.v1i2.3092.

Reimann, Peter (2011), 'Design-Based Research', in *Methodological Choice and Design: Scholarship, Policy and Practice in Social and Educational Research*, L. Markauskaite, P. Freebody and J. Irwin (eds), Dordrecht: Springer Netherlands, 37–50. https://doi.org/10.1007/978-90-481-8933-5_3.

Roschelle, Jeremy, William R. Penuel and Nicole Shechtman (2006), 'Co-design of innovations with teachers: definition and dynamics', in *Proceedings of the 7th International Conference on Learning Sciences*, ICLS '06, Bloomington, IN: International Society of the Learning Sciences, 606–612.

Rudman, Hannah, Claire Bailey-Ross, Jeremy Kendal, Zarja Mursic, Andy Lloyd, et al. (2018), 'Multidisciplinary exhibit design in a science centre: a participatory action research approach', *Educational Action Research*, 26 (4), 567–588.

Ryan, Thomas G., Mary Toye, Kyle Charron and Gavin Park (2012), 'Learning management system migration: an analysis of stakeholder perspectives', *International Review of Research in Open and Distributed Learning*, 13 (1), 220–237.

Sanders, Elizabeth B.-N. and Pieter Jan Stappers (2008), 'Co-creation and the new landscapes of design', *CoDesign*, 4 (1), 5–18.

Sewell, Alison, Tracey-Lynne Cody, Kama Weir and Sally Hansen (2018), 'Innovations at the boundary: an exploratory case study of a New Zealand school–university partnership in initial teacher education', *Asia-Pacific Journal of Teacher Education*, 46 (4), 321–339.

Shipepe, Annastasia and Anicia Peters (2018), 'Designing an interactive career guidance learning system using gamification', *Proceedings of the Second African Conference for Human Computer Interaction: Thriving Communities*, 1–4.

Shrader, Gregory, Kimberly Williams, Judith Lachance-Whitcomb, Lou-Ellen Finn and Louis Gomez (2001), 'Participatory design of science curricula: The case for research for practice', *Annual Meeting of the American Educational Research Association, Seattle, WA*.

Stanway, Bonnie Rose, Yiyuan Cao, Tony Cannell and Yihui Gu (2019), 'Tensions and rewards: behind the scenes in a cross-cultural student–staff partnership', *Journal of Studies in International Education*, 23 (1), 30–48.

Starkey, Ken and Sue Tempest (2009), 'The winter of our discontent: the design challenge for business schools', *Academy of Management Learning and Education*, 8 (4), 576–586.

Theobald, Karen A., Alexandra L. McCarthy, Amanda Henderson, Fiona Coyer, Ramon Z. Shaban, et al. (2019), *Academic–Industry Integration in Health: Enhancing Postgraduate Professional Learning [Final report 2019]*, Queensland Government.

uCube – Higher Education Statistics (2018), Australian Government Department of Education, Skills and Employment, Database. Accessed 18 April 2020 at http://highereducationstatistics.education.gov.au/.

Voogt, Joke, Therese Laferrière, Alain Breuleux, Rebecca C. Itow, Daniel T. Hickey and Susan McKenney (2015), 'Collaborative design as a form of professional development', *Instructional Science*, 43 (2), 259–282.

Wagner, Manuela, Fabiana Cardetti and Michael Byram (2016), 'Exploring collaborative work for the creation of interdisciplinary units centered on intercultural citizenship', *Dimension*, 35, 51.

Weinberger, Yehudith (2018), 'Strategies for effecting system-wide pedagogical change: identifying and addressing the gap between organizational and pedagogical implementation', *Professional Development in Education*, 44 (1), 47–61.

Willness, Chelsea and Vincent Bruni-Bossio (2017), 'The curriculum innovation canvas: a design thinking framework for the engaged educational entrepreneur', *Journal of Higher Education Outreach and Engagement (TEST)*, 21 (1), 134–164.

Wilson, Stephanie and Lisa Zamberlan (2015), 'Design for an unknown future: amplified roles for collaboration, new design knowledge, and creativity', *Design Issues*, 31 (2), 3–15.

Winchester-Seeto, Theresa, Kathryn McLachlan, Anna Rowe, Ian Solomonides and Kate Williamson (2017), 'Transformational learning – possibilities, theories, questions and challenges', in *Learning Through Community Engagement*, J. Sachs and L. Clark (eds), Singapore: Springer Singapore, 99–114.

3. Benefits and challenges of Assurance of Learning: making the intangible tangible

Lilia Mantai

ASSURANCE OF LEARNING IN BUSINESS SCHOOLS

The quality and relevance of business education has recently experienced increasing scrutiny by the public, including students, employers, the media and business educators themselves (Alajoutsijärvi et al. 2018; Lawson et al. 2013). With the increasing accessibility of education to larger and more diverse groups of students, paired with the proliferation of private education providers, universities need to provide valid evidence of the quality and relevance their degrees present. In Australia, the Tertiary Education Quality and Standards Agency (TEQSA) has been the body that oversees quality and holds higher education institutions accountable for quality delivery since 2012, following the Australian Universities Quality Agency (AUQA) (Lawson et al. 2013). Assurance of Learning (AoL) is most known to business academics as something business schools engage in to get accreditated, most notably by the Association to Advance Collegiate Schools of Business (AACSB).

What is Assurance of Learning?

AACSB (2019) defines AoL as a systematic process of collecting data about student achievement of programme learning outcomes, reviewing and using it to continuously develop and improve the degree programmes. The systematic process laid out in AACSB (2007) follows the following steps:

1. Establish learning goals and objectives.
2. Align curricula with adopted goals.
3. Identify assessment instruments and measures.
4. Collect, analyse and disseminate assessment information.
5. Use assessment information for continuous improvement, including documentation that the process is being carried out on an ongoing systematic basis.

AoL describes a process which measures how well students achieve the learning goals that the programme sets out to develop. Results help inform programme improvement, including programme resourcing, staffing, design, material development, assessment design, delivery, and so on. In essence, AoL asks the question: Does the programme enable students to achieve the learning goals? And if the answer is 'no', 'not quite' or 'yes but we can do better', then AoL poses the question: How can the programme be improved?

In 2004, AACSB announced that AoL processes need to use direct measures – that is, assessment data – to form an evidence base upon which programme improvements are formulated and actioned. Outcome-based assessment and direct assessment measurements of programme goals are not only recommended but required by AACSB standards to be embedded at unit level (in Gibson 2011). This is based on the premise that there is a close relationship between programme evaluation and evidence of student learning and achievements (Shaftel and Shaftel 2007). Previously, indirect measures such as student evaluation surveys, staff reflections or industry internship host reports were accepted.

Who Leads Assurance of Learning in Business Schools?

Leadership of Assurance of Learning varies amongst business schools, reflecting the historical development of AoL processes, ownership, available support and the value that is assigned to AoL at each individual business school (Lawrence et al. 2011). This is substantially driven by accreditation.

The University of Sydney Business School (USBS) has a dedicated academic role (titled Academic Lead, Course Enhancement) to support departments ('disciplines' at USBS), programme directors, programme managers, and capstone coordinators in curriculum and assessment design and development of each programme as well as coordinating and improving AoL reporting and processes for all programmes. At the time of writing in July 2020, this role is supporting disciplines at USBS in embedding the university's general graduate qualities throughout all business degrees. Equivalent roles in other universities carry the title Director of Assurance of Learning, Quality Assurance Manager/Coordinator/Officer, and are often professional roles located in curriculum management and reporting. Lawson et al. (2013), for instance, found that learning outcome mapping for AoL was overseen by 64 per cent academics and 36 per cent academic managers (*n* = 24 business school Associate Deans of Teaching and Learning). AoL at USBS is currently the responsibility of the Associate Dean of Programs, while assessment-related development is in the portfolio of the Associate Dean of Education. Hence, the two portfolios must work together to streamline AoL practice. The positioning and design of the academic lead role and the skillset required is strategic, and fulfils the purpose of engaging different stakeholders with quality and assurance of learning and teaching. In particular it is set out to:

- promote student engagement in assuring learning;
- design and deliver academic support and development;
- educate school staff in Assurance of Learning;
- consider employer perspectives and involvement.

Hence, knowledge of and experience with learning and teaching best practice, curriculum development and design, academic development and working with students as well as other stakeholders are beneficial to the role.

Language Matters

It might appear trivial, but the terminology of AoL and different use of curriculum terminology at USBS presents the first challenge to engaging with stakeholders. The lack of unanimous terminology across institutions within countries, let alone worldwide, can create quite a bit of confusion and frustration, especially for staff involved in AoL reporting (Gibson 2011). Table 3.1 is a short translation guide in order to aid the comprehension of this chapter.

Table 3.1   Translation guide

AACSB	USBS
Programme	course
Course or subject	unit, unit of study (UoS)
Programme learning outcomes (PLOs)	Graduate qualities or course learning outcomes (CLOs)
Departments	Disciplines

Engaging Stakeholders

Various parties are involved in learning assurance and keeping programmes relevant and competitive. Stakeholder engagement is ongoing, as global economic, societal and cultural changes necessitate regular reviews of educational programmes and outcomes.

Students
There is a large body of literature on student partnerships and genuine student engagement in various learning and teaching activities, including curriculum and assessment design, that evidences various benefits to students and staff. When it comes to Assurance of Learning, student voices are somewhat neglected or only indirectly accounted for. While there is an expectation to design student-centred learning experiences and assessments, and recognition that it would be not only valuable but authentic to involve students (Gilbreath et al. 2016), there is little guidance on how to involve students and at what stage, and more importantly, how to calibrate student and staff expectations and definitions of learning goals. A typical example of where such calibration is valuable is when learning goals are translated into marking criteria, for example a rubric. Rubric development in collaboration with students leads to an agreed understanding of what standard of learning is expected.

Academics (commonly known as 'faculty')
University teaching staff are directly involved with AoL practice as it is primarily their responsibility to help their students achieve the learning outcomes, monitor how their students are tracking on the programme goals, and report on programme improvements. Even if the main directive is compliance with accreditation, academics (ideally) need to engage in curriculum development that is programme-based, student-centred and outcomes-oriented as part of AoL practice. Academics are the only stakeholder group that is overall consistently involved at each step of the AoL cycle and carries full ownership of the process. AACSB AoL seminars target 'faculty, department chairs, deans, associate, and assistant deans who have a thorough working knowledge of AoL procedures' (www.aacsb.edu). There are differences in who does what for AoL amongst programme teams. Programme directors usually carry responsibility for the formalities such as reporting, but also the implementation of improvements, for example closing the loop (Lawson et al. 2013). However, there is no reason why leadership could not be more distributed. At USBS great examples of this already exist and this is due to a long tradition of quality assurance and AoL practice being well established since 2004.

Employers
Engaging employers from industry, government and community in defining quality education and assurance of learning processes helps keep our programmes relevant. Inviting them to collaborate in designing and developing learning activities and assessments – for example

by providing work-integrated and experiential learning opportunities such as placements and internships, pitch events, problem-solving bootcamps, practitioner talks, and so on – helps keep our programmes authentic and engaging for students. With the reinvigorated call for better employability skills, employers' perspectives, on the kinds of skills, attributes and learning experiences graduates should have, gain increased attention. Previous reports state employers want these skills (OECD 2019). The literature on graduate attributes evidently shows that these are well linked to employability and reflected in the educational programme goals (Oliver and Jorre 2018).

BENEFITS OF ASSURANCE OF LEARNING

Although evidence shows most AoL practice is driven by accreditation (Lawson et al. 2013), it affords clear benefits for education and programme management. Because programmes consist of multiple units of study and are often complemented by co-curricular opportunities, the key to achieving programme learning goals is to scaffold them across the programme so students develop the outcomes gradually and attain mastery by the time they graduate. This process is commonly understood as curriculum mapping.

The steps in the AoL process as explained above involve: (1) developing goals; (2) aligning curriculum with goals; (3) identifying measuring instruments (i.e., assessments); (4) collecting and analysing data; and then eventually (5) using insights from analysis to formulate future improvements and actioning them form a rigorous process of programme improvement (AACSB 2007). Each step requires stakeholder collaboration and agreement, hence ideally students, programme teaching staff, programme managing team, programme directors and employers get together, discuss and map how learning goals are scaffolded throughout a programme. Several methodologies and tools are used to facilitate such conversations and the process of curriculum mapping. Having a well-developed AoL system in place has several benefits for any education provider:

1. AoL serves as a clear accountability mechanism at each stage.
2. Changes to learning and teaching are evidence-based, formalized and systematic.
3. AoL guides targeted reflection and prompts behavioural change.
4. AoL presents a value-proposition based quality assurance.

Accountability

On a national and international level, measuring how graduate attributes are achieved (Lawson et al. 2013) is critical to account for the monetary investments made in education and the significant efforts devoted to maintaining the quality of university programmes. Especially business schools accredited by AACSB, and those aspiring to become accredited for the first time, invest significant effort and resources to establish quality procedures for measurement and reporting (Alajoutsijärvi et al. 2018). USBS publicly declares on its web pages its commitment to deliver on its promise of quality education and accountability for its students' achievement of the programme learning goals. USBS has clear AoL principles in place that encapsulate best practice guidelines to develop and assure learning.

Systematic Evidence to Inform Change

Just as assessment drives learning, so compliance drives programme improvement. Where no clear goals might have been stated before, and it was unclear how students develop a skill throughout the degree, AoL prescribes to make these more explicit and visible. The process of curriculum mapping forces the breaking down of big goals into smaller goals that can be achieved as learning outcomes at unit level. As such, seemingly intangible goals such as graduate attributes – for example 'problem-solving' or 'ethical decision-making' – get operationalized at unit level and thereby made tangible (Coy and Adams 2012; Lawrence et al. 2011).

Curriculum tools such as a curriculum map formalize and visualize where students get enough practice and feedback on each graduate quality. If a curriculum map is used as an accountability mechanism and the curriculum is delivered and experienced by students as mapped, assessment at degree exit (e.g., a capstone) provides a reliable measure of student development and at the same time reflects programme effectiveness in supporting student achievement (Porter 2004). Changes can then be implemented where improvement is required, and it may well be that a curriculum map needs to be revisited; for example, expectations are too high and the goals too big, or learning outcomes too vague.

Further, AoL practice drives professional and academic development of business staff involved in AoL processes. Those charged with AoL responsibilities often come to learn about curriculum design and development for the first time. They use pedagogy-based curriculum mapping tools, many of which are freely and publicly available online.[1] USBS, for example, has access to an internal curriculum development online module in the university's learning management system. More recently, a self-guided online learning module on AoL was developed to assist staff new to AoL. Hence, AoL stimulates upskilling of academics in learning and teaching practices of higher education.

Reflection to Change Behaviour

Programme curriculum development as AoL reporting requires a great deal of reflection. Guiding questions at each stage of the AoL process include: Are my learning goals adequate? Which tasks might best develop these? When, how and where should I reliably assess the goal achievement for individual students? And then eventually: What does my data tell me about my program? What can I do to improve the results, the learning experience, and so on? Such reflection arguably occurs to various degrees amongst teaching staff; however, in AoL it is central to programme improvement. In AoL practice at USBS such reflection is formally conducted and evaluated to inform future improvements.

Some scholars of AoL practice go even further by looking at AoL through the research lens. Collecting reliable and valid data on student achievement to then inform changes is conceptualized by Scott et al. (2008) as action research, for instance. They argue that doing AoL and closing the loop is in itself a type of action research. Many papers cited in this chapter support this argument. Stringer (2008) describes action research as very powerful in effecting changes in teachers' behaviours through their engagement in analysis and problem-solving processes in AoL practice, especially where different stakeholders including students are involved in programme improvement. Stringer states: 'This is particularly important in the university context where students frequently do not perceive instructors to have teaching as their priority over research. As Mills indicated, instructors who engage in action research and who overtly involve student perspectives in their work have the 'opportunity to model for their students how knowledge is created' (Mills 2000, p. 11, in Stringer 2008, p. 110). Using indirect measures such as student surveys, teacher reflections (e.g., Scott et al. 2008) are powerful yet underutilized, and now less valid and acknowledged than direct measures. Students' ratings, as we know, are 'influenced by teachers' popularity rather than their effectiveness' (Richardson 2005, p. 407). Nevertheless, the scholarly literature on AoL points to a range of opportunities to treat AoL practice (provided it is well developed and uses research-like rigour) as research in the scholarship of learning and teaching and higher education more broadly.

Value Proposed

Given the wide growth of competing educational programmes, employers want to be reassured that graduates from a particular institution have received quality education. Employers need to know that students' achievements presented in the form of transcripts were based on valid evidence. Now that companies increasingly discount university grades and transcripts, they still want assurance that business educational programmes adequately develop skills for the workplace. This is why we see a rise of work-integrated learning and industry experiences towards the end of business degrees, primarily in capstones where students consolidate and apply their knowledge and skills in solving real-life or near-authentic business problems, often with employer involvement (French et al. 2014, 2015). The fact that a programme regularly undergoes a rigid quality monitoring process – for example, AACSB required AoL – is a solid value proposition. Naturally, accredited business schools enjoy a higher status and superior reputation, particularly with students.

CHALLENGES IN ASSURANCE OF LEARNING

Nature of Graduate Qualities and Skill Development

The recent Organisation for Economic Co-operation and Development (OECD) publication on skills for the future (OECD 2019, p. 61) identifies 'among the knowledge, competencies, attitudes and values that will be increasingly key to success in work and life' these skill groups:

- Foundation skills, including literacy, numeracy and digital literacy.
- Transversal cognitive and meta-cognitive skills such as critical thinking, complex problem solving, creative thinking, learning to learn and self-regulation.
- Social and emotional skills such as conscientiousness, responsibility, empathy, self-efficacy and collaboration.
- Professional, technical and specialized knowledge and skills.

In comparison, AACSB (2018, p. 35) suggests 'contents of the learning experiences provided by programs should be both current and relevant to the needs of business and management positions' and without intending to prescribe, it recommends that the following general skill areas to be developed in business bachelor graduates (2018, p. 35):

- Written and oral communication (able to communicate effectively orally and in writing)

- Ethical understanding and reasoning (able to identify ethical issues and address the issues in a socially responsible manner)
- Analytical thinking (able to analyze and frame problems)
- Interpersonal relations and teamwork (able to work effectively with others and in team environments)
- Diverse and multicultural work environments (able to work effectively in diverse environments)
- Reflective thinking (able to understand oneself in the context of society)
- Application of knowledge (able to translate knowledge of business into practice)
- Integration of real-world business experiences

Business Master's degree programs should provide learning experiences in the following areas according to AACSB (2018, pp. 35–36):

- Leading in organizational situations
- Managing in a diverse global context
- Thinking creatively
- Making sound decisions and exercising good judgment under uncertainty
- Integrating knowledge across fields

The types of skills students need to develop are presumably going to help prepare them for 21st century careers. However, there are a few challenges due to the nature of skills and skill development:

- Skills are interpreted differently between and within business disciplines and are therefore differently translated into varying learning outcomes.
- Students enter our programmes with some degree of these skills already developed.
- Some skills are developed in combination or hierarchical sequence (e.g., critical thinking and problem-solving often go together, while strong communication skills should be developed before students can demonstrate influence and leadership).
- Some skills are developed outside the curriculum.
- Some are easier to measure than others because they are more tangible.

These characteristics of skill development are rarely acknowledged in AoL practice, and present real challenges for adequate assessment of skills and skill development. For instance, Lawrence et al. (2011, p. 929) call out ethical decision-making (EDM) as one of those 'elusive', 'intangible', 'softer' and school 'mission-related' skills, which is difficult to master and measure. Yet, as the authors show, EDM has gained more importance recently, reflecting changing economical and societal foci. An example is the Sustainable Developmental Goals supported by the Principles of Responsible Management Education, which many business schools are pledging to support now. May et al. (2012) present another example that illustrates the challenge of developing and mastering core skills. Employers continuously demand proficient soft skills and emphasize the need for strong writing and communication skills. Corporate executives complain about the lack of effective writing skills of MBA graduates, as exemplified by May et al. based on an MBA program at Clayton State University. Indeed, improving students' skills and achievement of each goal requires extensive effort in scaffolding learning across a programme. Finally, skills are not developed in isolation, but in complementary fashion, and best when developed in the context of disciplinary content (Barrie 2006).

For instance, interdisciplinary effectiveness may only come into play once students have a sufficient amount of knowledge about their own discipline. By taking final measurements near degree exit it is often assumed that skills would have developed continuously and steadily over time. However, a lot of sensemaking and knowledge–skill integration occurs in the final year, perhaps facilitated in a capstone.

In regard to defining skills, Calma and Davies (2020) show, based on the example of critical thinking in an in-depth analysis of 55 articles, how widely this particular and quite common programme learning goal can be understood. The definitions range from 'learning how to think' to 'being more reflective' and 'ability to evaluate and judge' and, more importantly, are conceptualized in terms of skills and attributes. The latter speak to personal characteristics, dispositions, mindsets, values and beliefs, and these are more aspirational in nature. Attributes are potentially less tangible and more difficult to operationalize into learning tasks that would yield measurable results (Pascarella and Terenzini 2005, in Nusche 2008). In addition, there is a risk that measuring these actually measures the student's social and general maturity and dispositions acquired before or outside higher education provisions (Nusche 2008). Curricular measurements, no matter how well developed, cannot exclude the possibility of measuring students' abilities gained elsewhere than curricular activities. Hence, we cannot attribute student achievement entirely to higher education services provided to the student; as Nusche (2008) states: 'learning outcomes are not simply the consequence of an institution's educational quality, but rather a function of students' active engagement with the learning opportunities that the HEI [higher education institution] presents' (p. 11).

The OECD (2019) also draws attention to the difference in developing and measuring cognitive versus non-cognitive outcomes. Cognitive outcomes are comprised of knowledge and skills such as writing, problem-solving, analytical and application skills. These can be measured in the way students solve problems and communicate. Non-cognitive outcomes refer to change in values and personal attributes, such as interpersonal and intercultural skills, autonomy, social responsibility, understanding of diversity, and resilience. Measuring these is more complicated and often done via what AACSB would describe as indirect measures, for example student self-assessment or reflections, or employer's statement (e.g., in placements). Ewell (2005, in Nusche 2008) and others advocate for an integrated development and assessment of cognitive and non-cognitive outcomes based on what students do and how they perform in a performance task, for example that might involve solving a problem.

Today, most universities have graduate attributes or qualities as the overarching learning goals across all their programmes. Some universities treat them as aspirational, others attempt to embed them more explicitly. While for instance Western Sydney University has three overarching holistic attributes – scholarship, lifelong learning, global citizenship – our university states nine qualities that every undergraduate (UG) degree should aim to develop, including our Business UG degree (Table 3.2).

As graduate qualities inform the programme learning goals, business schools aim to embed these explicitly in their curricula, not insignificantly driven by accreditation requirements but also supported by colleagues who value and see the importance of AoL (Lawson et al. 2013). The graduate qualities essentially reflect employability skills, transferable skills or generic skills. The proposition that employability is the ultimate goal of university education has been debated for decades. While the employability agenda seems to have recently regained support, this value proposition of university education still remains a controversial one. A strong view still persists that higher education does not just prepare students to get a job or get them employed, but develops critical and independent individuals who can create their own future and contribute to the society in ways that improve the quality of life for everyone. Employability, in any case, is to be understood as to develop ability for whatever type or definition of employment, rather than actual employment realized by a particular job.

Table 3.2   Nine qualities that every UG degree should aim to develop

Depth of disciplinary expertise	Deep disciplinary expertise is the ability to integrate and rigorously apply the knowledge, understanding and skills of a recognized discipline defined by scholarly activity, as well as familiarity with the evolving practice of the discipline.
Critical thinking and problem-solving	Critical thinking and problem-solving are the questioning of ideas, evidence and assumptions in order to propose and evaluate hypotheses or alternative arguments before formulating a conclusion or a solution to an identified problem.
Communication (oral and written)	Effective communication, in both oral and written form, is the clear exchange of meaning in a manner that is appropriate to the audience and context.
Information and digital literacy	Information and digital literacy is the ability to locate, interpret, evaluate, manage, adapt, integrate, create and convey information using appropriate resources, tools and strategies.
Inventiveness	Inventiveness is generating novel ideas and solutions.
Cultural competence	Cultural competence is the ability to actively, ethically, respectfully and successfully engage across and between cultures. In the Australian context, this includes and celebrates Aboriginal and Torres Strait Islander cultures, knowledge systems, and a mature understanding of contemporary issues.
Interdisciplinary effectiveness	Interdisciplinary effectiveness is the integration and synthesis of multiple viewpoints and practices, working effectively across disciplinary boundaries.
An integrated professional, ethical and personal identity	An integrated professional, ethical and personal identity is understanding the interaction between one's personal and professional selves in an ethical context.
Influence	Influence is engaging others in a process, idea or vision.

Measuring Programme Learning Goals at Scale

Given the complex nature of skills that essentially comprise the programme learning goals of business degrees listed (different disciplinary interpretations, non-linear and complementary development of skills, extracurricular influences, and different skill levels of students at entry), it is not surprising that identifying appropriate measurement instruments and obtaining valid and reliable data present difficulties. In addition, business schools often operate degrees at large scale. For instance, in 2019, USBS had about 5300 students enrolled in the Bachelor of Commerce and about 7600 in the Master of Commerce. Collecting individual achievement data for large cohorts of students has several implications and challenges, for example:

- consistency and transparency in marking and feedback;
- when, where and how data is collected in the programme;
- assessing individual achievement when work is occurring in a group setting;
- providing formative feedback before taking summative measures on students' achievement;
- designing authentic and experiential learning environments and assessments (and subsequent over-reliance on final exam).

In relation to consistency and transparency, our business school uses marking criteria in the form of rubrics, based on which achievement of course learning outcomes are judged. In large degrees, where groups of 30–40 tutors are employed, it is paramount that the teaching team including all tutors share the same understanding of the rubric, and communicate regularly to ensure its validity is preserved while content and assessment tasks change regularly (to uphold academic integrity). This is supported by regular meetings and conversations about AoL where the focus on programme learning goals is a helpful mechanism, and where calibration can occur on the standard that should be expected from students. The team also need to work out assessments that actually measure what they set out to measure. The assessment types need to be valid instruments for a given learning outcome; for example, a final multiple-choice question (MCQ) exam might be less adequate for assessing critical or analytical thinking, but is well suited to test knowledge of disciplinary theories and concepts.

Deciding which units will collect data can also be a challenge if a large degree does not have common core or foundational units or capstones, or lack of resourcing precludes design of experiential learning for large groups. In more developed AoL systems, capstones and other experiential learning units are put in place to meet AoL requirements and provide a common place to measure degree learning goals (French et al. 2015). Capstones are arguably optimal avenues to assess students' goal achievement. Experiential learning, where students learn by doing a work-like task – for example, solving a real business issue – provides suitable settings to collect reliable assessment data. For example, Rexeisen and Al-Khatib (2009) show how study abroad experiences as experiential learning opportunities assist in developing ethical awareness, reasoning and intercultural competencies in students. Capstones, by definition, are designed to integrate knowledge and consolidate students' skills, and offer a demonstration of predominant skills and qualities such as critical and analytical thinking, problem-solving, communication skills, and others (Martell and Calderon 2005). Capstones also employ authentic or experiential learning and assessment activities; firstly, to utilize valid instruments to measure students' achievements; and secondly, to use work-like tasks that will prepare students for the professional business workplace.

At scale, technological solutions are also required to automate data collection, if staff are to engage where academic judgement is required and not spend their time and efforts on the operational or procedural collection of achievement data. Enterprise supported learning management systems (LMSs) do not always support this functionality to the degree necessary for business schools. At our school, staff responsible for AoL assessment data and reporting go to a great degree of effort to collect and record marks manually or outside the LMS. More recently, an in-house developed programme has been successfully applied to collect assessment marks against the course learning outcomes directly via the LMS, while also facilitating increased feedback to students. Future improvements hope to see a well-integrated system of marking, feedback and fully automated data extraction for reporting, to avoid manual handling.

The greatest challenge with AoL, by its definition, is that AoL data primarily serves to inform programme improvement, it does not ensure that each student meets the standard. Although the intention is of course to develop a programme that helps each student to meet the expected standards of each course learning outcome, the primary focus is on improving the programme so it can develop each student's ability. This distinction is critical in understanding what AoL does. To satisfy the requirement of programme improvement, many business programmes collect data near degree end because they are interested in how the programme performs, not the individual student. If AoL was about each student's performance, data would need to be collected at the start of the degree and then regularly thereafter, to ensure that each student at least meets if not exceeds the expectations by the time they graduate. In other words, AoL data collected from current students is used as a proxy to improve the performance of future students. Programmes can naturally do both: ensure each current student's achievement of 'meets standard' while continuing to improve the programme; however, this has resource implications as more frequent measuring is required, and would depend on the degree structure. Lawson et al. (2013) call it a 'progressive approach', where learning outcomes are mapped and measured at different stages (introductory, developing and mastery levels) and provide staff and students with formative feedback.

Mapping Curriculum and Learning Goals

If we review the AACSB definition of AoL given above (a systematic process of collecting data about student achievement of programme learning outcomes, reviewing and using it to continuously develop and improve USBS degree programmes), it becomes apparent that before business educators measure student achievement of learning outcomes, they need to implement sufficient and adequate opportunities to develop these outcomes and be given feedback throughout, so they know how they are tracking and where they need to improve. This means learning goals need to be constructively scaffolded and aligned with learning and teaching activities and assessments across the programme. This is what curriculum mapping does. It essentially facilitates the hidden work behind reported AoL data, including faculty engagement (Gilbreath et al. 2016).

The benefits of curriculum mapping are widely evidenced. It essentially provides a communication tool for discipline and programme teams to develop a shared understanding of the programme aims and the kind of graduates it will develop, and visualizes how each unit in the programme contributes to these aims. It becomes a shared point of reference and a mechanism to keep everyone accountable, while revealing gaps and development needs (Freeman et al. 2008; Oliver 2010). Curriculum mapping, if done well – for example, systematically, programme-based, collaboratively – has clear benefits of providing visibility of learning opportunities towards end goals across the programme and valid evidence of students achieving learning outcomes (Oliver 2010; Taylor et al. 2009).

Furthermore, constructive alignment via curriculum mapping enables an integrated AoL measuring approach and makes separate marking for AoL reporting superfluous. Integrated AoL assessment also avoids a possible scenario where students might pass a unit or module according to one scale, but would not meet the expected standard of a programme learning goal according to the AoL scale.

A curriculum map is also a useful tool to communicate how learning outcomes are structured across to programmes for other stakeholders in AoL: students, employers and accreditors. While it evidences a structured and monitored process to accreditors and employers, which is an indicator of quality, to students it makes visible how, where and when they are expected to develop these outcomes. Students, particularly, need to understand that transferable or employability skills as reflected in the broader programme learning goals or graduate qualities are the focus of learning, not just disciplinary knowledge. Making sure that students actually experience the curriculum as it was intended and mapped (Porter 2004) is key to meeting educational standards.

Seeing the value and necessity for curriculum mapping to ensure good AoL practice might come naturally to educators. Academic teaching staff are often practitioners and disciplinary experts. One cannot assume that all business educators are well trained in curriculum development, savvy with educational technologies, and familiar with contemporary learning and teaching approaches. Naturally, business educators need support and guidance in curriculum development and assessment design (Lawson et al. 2013). Embedding graduate qualities throughout programmes via curriculum mapping is less common in tertiary education, and more common in secondary education in Australia (French et al. 2014). Rigorous versus ad hoc curriculum development and mapping is often driven by central or local reform or restructure and regulation requirements. In fact, in many business degree programmes learning outcomes are assessed separately from the usual coursework assessment using an AoL scale: 'Meets–Not meets–Exceeds expected standard'. Our business school has largely moved to an integrated embedded approach where programme learning goals are clearly reflected in the rubrics, so 'normal' coursework marking provides AoL data and no additional marking is required. In this case the assessment rubric is integrated with AoL standards. This is a result of guided and structured curriculum mapping that occurred at USBS two years ago when the new Bachelor of Commerce was designed.

Given that business experts who teach are not commonly trained in curriculum design, it is unsurprising that they foster varying definitions and perceptions of what it is (Annala et al. 2015). Research (Barrie 2006) has shown that staff engage differently with curriculum and graduate qualities, often being the programme learning goals, because they have different conceptions of both. These conceptions vary greatly within disciplines. Some see graduate qualities as: (1) something to be done outside the curriculum; (2) additional to the curriculum; (3) complimentary to the curriculum; or (4) inherent and 'the actual curriculum'. Knowing where staff stand would benefit those who support and lead AoL practice in business.

According to Bath et al. (2004) there is substantial difference between the teacher's and the students' perceptions of the development of particular graduate attributes. Hence, a shared understanding, or what I call 'calibration', needs to happen at programme level and in collaboration with students, and ideally employers too. In addition, business schools (like universities) employ a range of casual or contract-based staff to deliver programmes. Variation in staff affects student learning because each staff member brings their own perspectives of curriculum, learning goals, and learning and teaching methods. High staff turnover also means the need to train staff in AoL, its purpose and process.

As Gibson (2011, p. 2) states, 'it is well known that the variety of full time and adjunct faculty teaching the course demonstrate considerable variation in what they cover and what they require as student deliverables'. To mitigate the variation in the teaching approaches and delivery, Gibson's university has taken the approach of developing standardized curriculum packages, particularly including grading schemes and rubrics, to be delivered by a team of facilitators. Rubrics are important parts of the package and have been shown to be useful in communicating what's expected to students and staff likewise, to promote consistency and objectivity in assessment. They essentially help achieve calibration and shared meaning. Most AACSB accredited schools realize the value of rubrics and use these to measure learning outcomes (Vitullo and Jones 2010). In Lawson et al. (2013), 80 per cent of the 24 business schools' Associate Deans of Teaching and learning (ADTL) stated using rubrics.

Closing the loop is the most important phase of the AoL process, and yet, the least efforts are devoted at this stage (in Lawson et al. 2013). In Gibson (2011), Kelly et al. (2010) point to a 2010 study with about 420 deans at AACSB accredited business schools showing that only minor modifications and adjustments to programmes were made as part of the closing the loop phase. More importantly, the assessment data results do not always translate back into curriculum changes, pointing to the fact that curriculum maps are perhaps treated as rigid. This finding highlights the need to reinforce the use of curriculum maps. They should not be 'set and forget' documents, rather they should be treated as lived and shared (between stakeholders) documents guiding practice and ongoing programme improvement (in Lawson et al. 2013).

SUMMARY

In 2009, Martell and Caldron claimed that assuring learning was the most frequently discussed topic in tertiary education today. There was and still is much focus on defining learning outcomes, expected standards, appropriate measurement instruments, as well as what data to collect and how (Coy and Adams 2012; Taylor et al. 2009). Yet, curriculum mapping, methods and processes of curriculum development, are less common in tertiary education overall and rarely mentioned in AoL guidelines.

Given the many challenges outlined above, it is without doubt that there is a lot that academics and programme administrators have to work through to move towards establishing optimal processes to evaluate and improve their programmes. Continuous programme improvement, as AoL is defined, is always a work-in-progress as higher education institutions experience constant change, which affects educational learning goals, student and staff profiles, degree structures as well as stakeholder expectations and governmental priorities. Business educators dedicate much energy to defining learning outcomes, expected standards, finding appropriate measurement instruments, as well as determining what data to collect and how (Taylor et al. 2009; Coy and Adams 2012). In most cases, this is not an easy feat as it requires academics to rethink and change their practice. Coates (2010) argues that it requires a total cultural shift. Lawson et al. (2013) suggest a cultural shift might need a policy change also, and a vision that highlights the value of AoL and empowers staff to own the implementation plan of that vision. Rigorous curriculum design and mapping emerges as the key driver to establishing reliable and valid AoL practice.

While a well-developed AoL system and processes have been established at USBS since 2004, more can be done to optimize the outcomes for all stakeholders and to further streamline the process. Future goals include:

- integrate various data available through institutional systems in the AoL reporting to provide business academics with a holistic picture of their programmes;
- automate data collection and simplify reporting to reduce the administrative load on staff;
- provide professional and academic development in curriculum mapping;
- integrate all stakeholder perspectives, especially students at each step of the AoL process;
- continue to optimize and maximize experiential and authentic learning opportunities for students.

This chapter presents a reflective account of the benefits and challenges of AoL practice generally and locally at the University of Sydney Business School. Just as any learning and teaching aspects require ongoing critical reflection, AoL practice too benefits from examining local practices and benchmarking against best practices discussed in the AoL literature. AoL practice in any business school context emerges as ongoing work-in-progress for the benefit of reliable evidence of relevant student learning. This reflective account is by no means comprehensive, but rather presents snippets of local practices where further improvement is desired. Reflecting on best practices helps in realizing where adjustments can and should be made, and where practical examples working well elsewhere do not fit the context. The overall conclusion is that operational and administrative aspects of AoL practice must be made as smooth and seamless as possible and must not compete in time and effort with academic work and judgement that is critical to AoL. Investments made in the background administrative and operational side of AoL would be well justified. The chapter emphasizes the need to focus energy on curriculum design, staff development and genuine engagement with all stakeholders, to achieve a well-developed AoL system.

NOTE

1. Examples include Western Sydney University Curriculum Tools, https://www.westernsydney
.edu.au/learning_futures/home/learning_transformations/re_developing_new_curriculum_courses/
advisors/curriculum_resources/curriculum_tools/curriculum_mapping_tool; and Curriculum
Workbench, https://ltc.uow.edu.au/wop/.

REFERENCES

Alajoutsijärvi, Kimmo, Kerttu Kettunen and Sauli Sohlo (2018), 'Shaking the Status Quo: Business Accreditation and Positional Competition,' *Academy of Management Learning & Education*, 17 (2), 203–225.

Annala, Johanna, Jyri Lindén, and Marita Mäkinen (2015), 'Curriculum in higher education research,' in J. Case & J. Huisman (Eds.) *Researching Higher Education*, International perspectives on theory, policy and practice. SHRE Society for Research into Higher Education and Routledge, 171–189. doi: 10.4324/9781315675404.

Association to Advance Collegiate Schools of Business (AACSB) (2007), *AACSB Assurance of Learning Standards: An Interpretation.* (accessed 20 March 2020) https://naspaaaccreditation.files
.wordpress.com/2014/04/aacsb.pdf

Association to Advance Collegiate Schools of Business (AACSB) (2018), *2013 Eligibility procedures and accreditation standards for business accreditation.* (accessed 20 March 2020) https://www.aacsb
.edu/-/media/aacsb/docs/accreditation/business/standards-and-tables/2018-business-standards.ashx
?la=en&hash=B9AF18F3FA0DF19B352B605CBCE17959E32445D9

Association to Advance Collegiate Schools of Business (AACSB) (2019), *Accreditation Standard 8 (2013 Business Standards): Curricula Management and Assurance of Learning - An Interpretation.* (accessed 15 March 2020) https://www.aacsb.edu/-/media/aacsb/publications/white-papers/aol_white
_paper_standard_8.ashx?la=en&hash=9DF96D5B2A1E0B02E19ACF6984FFFE07D23D45CA

Barrie, Simon C. (2006), 'Understanding what we mean by the generic attributes of graduates', *Higher education*, 51 (2), 215–241.

Bath, Debra, Calvin Smith, Sarah Stein and Richard Swann (2004), 'Beyond mapping and embedding graduate attributes: bringing together quality assurance and action learning to create a validated and living curriculum', *Higher Education Research and Development*, 23 (3), 313–328.

Calma, Angelito and Martin Davies (2020), 'Critical thinking in business education: current outlook and future prospects', *Studies in Higher Education*, 1–17. https://www-tandfonline-com.ezproxy.library
.sydney.edu.au/doi/full/10.1080/03075079.2020.1716324.

Coates, H. (2010), 'Defining and monitoring academic standards in Australian higher education', *Higher Education Management and Policy*, 22 (1), 1–17.

Coy, Steven and Jeffery Adams (2012), 'Walking the talk: continuous improvement of a quality management field exercise', *Decision Sciences Journal of Innovative Education*, 10 (2), 223–244.

Freeman, Mark, Phil Hancock, Lyn Simpson and Chris Sykes (2008), 'Business as usual: a collaborative investigation of existing resources, strengths, gaps and challenges to be addressed for sustainability in teaching and learning in Australian university business faculties', ABDC Scoping Report.

French, Erica, Janis Bailey, Elizabeth van Acker and Leigh Wood (2015), 'From mountaintop to corporate ladder – what new professionals really really want in a capstone experience!', *Teaching in Higher Education*, 20 (8), 767–782.

French, Erica, Jane Summers, Shelley Kinash, Romy Lawson, Tracy Taylor, et al. (2014), 'The practice of quality in assuring learning in higher education', *Quality in Higher Education*, 20 (1), 24–43.

Gibson, Jane Whitney (2011), 'Measuring course competencies in a school of business: the use of standardized curriculum and rubrics', *American Journal of Business Education (AJBE)*, 4 (8), 1–6.

Gilbreath, Brad, S.M. Norman, E.J. Frew, K.L. Fowler and P. Billington (2016), 'Helpful tools for managing the assurance of learning process', *Business Education Innovation Journal*, 8 (1), 111–122.

Kelly, C., P. Tong and B-J. Choi (2010), 'A review of assessment of student learning programs at AACSB schools: a dean's perspective', *Journal of Education for Business*, 85, 299–306.

Lawrence, Katherine E., Kendra L. Reed and William Locander (2011), 'Experiencing and measuring the unteachable: achieving AACSB learning assurance requirements in business ethics', *Journal of Education for Business*, 86 (2), 92–99.

Lawson, Romy, Tracy Taylor, Eveline Fallshaw, J. Summers, S. Kinash, et al. (2013), 'Hunters and gatherers: strategies for curriculum mapping and data collection for assuring learning', ATN Assessment Conference 2011, 35–35. http://otl.curtin.edu.au/atna2011/.

Martell, Kathryn Denise and Thomas G. Calderon (2005), *Assessment of Student Learning in Business Schools: Best Practices each Step of the Way*, Tallahassee, FL: Association for Institutional Research.

May, G.L., M.A. Thompson and J. Hebblethwaite (2012), 'A process for assessing and improving business writing at the MBA level' *Business Communication Quarterly*, 75 (3), 252–270.

Nusche, Deborah (2008), 'Assessment of learning outcomes in higher education: a comparative review of selected practices', OECD Education Working Papers, No. 15, OECD Publishing.

OECD (2019), *OECD Skills Strategy 2019 Skills to Shape a Better Future: Skills to Shape a Better Future*, Paris: OECD Publishing. https://doi.org/10.1787/9789264313835-en.

Oliver, Beverley (2010), 'Teaching fellowship: benchmarking partnerships for graduate employability', Australian Learning and Teaching Council. Final report. https://espace.curtin.edu.au/bitstream/handle/20.500.11937/31598/154904_154904.pdf?sequence=2.

Oliver, Beverley and Trina Jorre de St Jorre (2018), 'Graduate attributes for 2020 and beyond: recommendations for Australian higher education providers', *Higher Education Research and Development*, 37 (4), 821–836.

Porter, A.C. (2004), *Curriculum Assessment (Additional SCALE Research Publications and Products: Goals 1, 2, and 4)*, Nashville, TN: Vanderbilt University. http://www.andyporter.org/papers/CurriculumAssessment.pdf.

Rexeisen, Richard J. and Jamal Al-Khatib (2009), 'Assurance of learning and study abroad: a case study', *Journal of Teaching in International Business*, 20 (3), 192–207.

Richardson, John T.E. (2005), 'Instruments for obtaining student feedback: a review of the literature', *Assessment and Evaluation in Higher Education*, 30 (4), 387–415.

Scott, Shelleyann, Tomayess Issa and Theodora Issa (2008), 'Closing the loop: the relationship between instructor-reflective practice and students' satisfaction and quality outcomes', *International Journal of Learning*, 15 (3), 109–120.

Shaftel, Julia and Timothy L. Shaftel (2007), 'Educational assessment and the AACSB', *Issues in Accounting Education*, 22 (2), 215–232.

Stringer, Ernest T. (2008), *Action Research in Education*, Upper Saddle River, NJ: Pearson Prentice Hall.

Taylor, Tracy, Darrall G. Thompson, Lucille Clements, Lynette Simpson, Andrew Paltridge, et al. (2009), 'Facilitating staff and student engagement with graduate attribute development, assessment and standards in business faculties'. https://ro.uow.edu.au/asdpapers/527.

Vitullo, Elizabeth and Elizabeth A. Jones (2010), 'An exploratory investigation of the assessment practices of selected association to advance collegiate schools of business accredited business programs and linkages with general education outcomes', *JGE: The Journal of General Education*, 59 (2), 85–104.

PART II

LEARNING ENVIRONMENTS

4. The promise of the business studio: teaching for design and entrepreneurship at business schools

Kasper Merling Arendt and Bo T. Christensen

INTRODUCTION

In 2018, the World Economic Forum published a report on the future of jobs in highly advanced societies and on what it believes will be most sought after competences in the labor market in the period 2020–25 (WEF, 2018). The World Economic Forum identified a potential skill gap, and called for a reskilling for about 54 percent of all employees. Some of the skills identified to be in high demand are complex problem-solving, critical thinking, creativity, people management and coordination with others. This has led to the realization that the pedagogical format utilized in most business schools may not be well aligned with these objectives and learning outcomes, given that the standard lecturing format will teach your students very few of these skills.

Studio pedagogy stems from design and architectural education, and offers a potential solution to training skills that closely resemble those identified by the World Economic Forum. Studio pedagogy has recently entered business schools, some of which have set up dedicated business studio spaces.

We argue that the studio environment helps develop cognitive skills, helps train collaborative skills and supports the development of an entrepreneurial mindset. While entrepreneurship is not directly identified as one of the skills in demand, entrepreneurship has been associated with a need for cognitive flexibility (Haynie & Shepherd, 2009; Hjorth, 2011). Training cognitive flexibility in a dynamic environment is precisely what the studio emphasizes, because students have to engage in certain tasks with others over a long duration of time, where in the process they will need to iteratively reformulate or reframe the problem.

Collaborative social skills are also taught in the studio environment, usually because tasks are assigned to groups, but also because outside problems or stakeholders are brought into the studio. Whenever tasks are set by outside stakeholders, students will work trying to solve real-world tasks, possibly involving customers, end users or others in the processes. This helps the training of people management and coordination skills.

This chapter looks at how studio pedagogy transforms the learning experience at business schools, ultimately providing new and exciting ways for teaching 21st century skills through design thinking and entrepreneurship education. Studio pedagogy comes with a promise of increasing the level of student engagement, because it implies a shift in didactics towards learning as an active, participatory, creative and social activity rather than an individual passive activity, also implying a shift from theory-driven learning towards application of theory in practice.

The overall structure of this chapter is as follows. First, we provide a brief introduction to the the history of studio-based pedagogy. We also describe the core characteristics of studio-based pedagogics, that is, formalized critiques as well as the distinct studio culture. Second, we explore the role of the studio in a business school setting, inviting the reader to go on a 'tour' through the business studio. Third, we discuss how studio-based pedagogics might develop students' entrepreneurial mindsets, utilizing certain cognitive strategies as well as elements from design thinking. Fourth, we discuss how and when to conduct teaching in the business studio, introducing practical tools that the educator can use should they be curious about teaching in the studio. Finally, we provide three real-world case-based snapshots of studio-based teaching, ranging from single sessions to whole programs, which might serve as an inspiration to curious educators.

A HISTORY OF THE STUDIO AS A SPACE FOR LEARNING IN DESIGN

Jeffrey Lackney presents the history of the studio-based learning pedagogy in his 1999 article "A History of the Studio-Based Learning Model" (Lackney, 1999). In this, he presents the studio-based learning model as deeply rooted within 19th century architectural education, especially that of the French school Ecole des Beaux Arts in Paris. In this design school for the fine arts, students were – over the course of a term – assigned a specific problem, such as presenting a sketch of a certain building type, or sketches in Gothic, Baroque or Art Nouveau styles, which were to be handed in for critique at the end of term. Throughout the term, individual feedback was given by the teachers, helping students with their work and the specific problems they faced at the specific time in their work process. One key aspect of the learning method was its great focus on learning-by-doing or "learning-by-making." At the end of the term, the students handed in their final products, which were subject to review by professors, guest architects and other masters of the craft for a final assessment of the product. A process that much resembles how a jury or review system might operate today (Lackney, 1999).

Since then, studio-based learning models have developed and been implemented in architecture programs throughout design schools and universities in the Western world, though the basic form of studio-based learning remains the same at its core. The pedagogical approach rests upon the notion that apprentices learn and advance their skills through making and receiving feedback and critique of their works from a master within the field, everything taking place within a specific place, which we term "the studio."

Education in the studio is only partly focused on the actual product that the student produces; rather, the focus is on the student's applied methods and cultures. In a sense, the power of the studio becomes the most clear when compared with laboratories. Laboratories in business schools emphasize processes that resemble those in the laboratories of natural sciences: controlled scientific processes with a focus on models and formulas as well as an emphasis on reducing the accidental and unpredictable (Barry & Meisiek, 2015). The studio, on the other hand, embraces the unpredictable and unscientific, accepting that the studio serves as a place of dealing with "wicked problems," only solvable through creative processes (Buchanan, 1992; Camillus, 2008).

The studio can be considered a physical space where learning happens through making (Barry & Meisiek, 2015). Consequently, the etymological roots of the word "studio" also mean "room for study" in Latin. However, the physical space of the studio does not in itself make students more creative. In order for the studio to also become a space in which you can accomplish educational goals, reflection on how to achieve the distinct studio "feel" is also required.

Hetland et al. (2013) consider how to develop this studio culture, where learning stems from a careful mix of lights and sounds, a social climate, language, as well as providing students with the right assignments and problems that are suited for being solved in the studio. The studio culture is promoted by the decorations, furniture, walls, tools that are used as well as the lighting (Hetland et al., 2013). The room is versatile, functional and able to accommodate both individual and group work. Moreover, it exemplifies authentic, experiential and active learning (Middleton, 2018).

Besides the physical aspects of the studio, another key aspect of the studio experience is the social climate, which is neither formal nor informal. The climate is strongly determined by the interactions between the users of the studio, and especially the teacher–student interactions. Teachers observe when students work, and intervene when necessary. Interactions in the form of interventions may take the form of constructive feedback and shared reflections, but the teacher must also be mindful of the students' need to work and reflect upon their own work, privately (Hetland et al., 2013).

One of the most crucial elements of studio pedagogy is the critique, which can take on many different forms. The critique is central, because it allows students and teachers to reflect – as individuals and in groups – upon their work and process (Hetland et al., 2013). Inspired by critique sessions from a New England design school, Hetland et al. put out four elements of the critique, which we here transform into a business setting (based on Hetland et al., 2013):

- Focus on the work: students must as a group focus their attention on their own and other students' work.
- Reflection: students think about what was successful, what was not, and why.
- Verbal: students must put their reflections into words, describing their work process and result. This also helps in evaluation of their work.
- Forward-looking: a discussion aimed at guiding future work envisioning new possibilities.

The critique must be thought of as an ongoing, heuristic process, that typically takes place at least once within a studio session, though usually towards the end. The main purpose of the critique is for the students and teachers to understand and evaluate both the work and the working process and to look forward. Critiques can take many forms, ranging from just a couple of minutes to several hours, and can take the form of 1-on-1 feedback, or in smaller groups, or something that includes the entire classroom. The critique session is the way of producing learning from working in the studio.

The studio space intends to promote a certain workflow, which requires attention to a range of elements such as time consumption, routines and habits, use of space and a developed language for working creatively. Hetland et al. (2013) consider how to develop a culture defined by "Studio Habits of Mind." These habits are certain competences that are specific for the studio learning culture:

- Engage and persist: learning to embrace problems of relevance and personal importance to develop focus and other mental states conducive to persevering at tasks.

- Envision: learning to picture mentally what cannot be directly observed and to imagine possible next steps in creating something.
- Express: about learning to create works that convey an idea, feeling, or a personal meaning.
- Observe: learning to attend to visual and other contexts more closely. To see things that, otherwise, might not be seen.
- Reflect: learning to think and talk with others about an aspect of one's work and learning to judge one's own work and work process in relation to standards within the field.
- Stretch and explore: reaching beyond one's capacities to explore playfully without a preconceived plan and to embrace opportunities to learn from mistakes

The long tradition of studio pedagogy in design and architecture is seen as a way of developing and enhancing designerly student skills, focusing especially on design as a reflexive practice as well as a problem-solving activity, drawing upon Schön (2017) and Schön and Wiggins (1992). Schön and Wiggins focus on the relationship between creating and reflection upon the created, in such a way that allows for constant re-creation as well as improvement of the product (Johansson-Sköldberg et al., 2013; Schön & Wiggins, 1992). In this sense, design thinking is an ongoing process that implies continuous reflection upon your own work in an almost hermeneutical fashion. Design thinking then refers to methods of employing certain cognitive strategies that are traditionally used by designers in order to learn from experimenting, to create hypotheses and to manage uncertainty (Cross, 2018).

Whilst designerly thinking originates from the ways of thinking within the fields of professional design, the notion of design thinking has found its way beyond the design context, most prominently within management and business contexts. In business contexts, design thinking refers to a way of describing how a designer's methods are integrated into the practices of either academics or business practitioners, in support of organizational creativity and innovation. Often the concepts of "design thinking" and "designerly thinking" are used interchangeably, although they stem from popular management and academic literature, respectively (Johansson-Sköldberg et al., 2013).

Cognitive strategies for design thinking are developed through researching how designers work (Cross, 2018), but are of course not restricted only to the practice of designers. Within business and education settings, design thinking has also been influential (Barry & Meisiek, 2015). The global design company IDEO has become known within the realm of design thinking practice and research for its designerly ways of approaching problem-solving and innovation, and is commonly seen as among the frontrunners in popularizing design thinking. IDEO's work was introduced to managers and social innovators through work stories told by both the company chief executive officer (CEO) Tim Brown, and general manager (GM) Tom Kelley (T. Brown, 2008; Kelley, 2007; Kelley & Littman, 2005).

The development of design thinking as an approach to practices in managerial and business contexts has also resulted in the establishment of studios at business schools, in order to support the educational development of designerly skills.

THE STUDIO IN A BUSINESS SCHOOL SETTING

Studio-based learning is still a fairly uncommon practice within universities and business schools. In recent years, some business schools have adopted the studio-based pedagogy, now offering courses that apply various designerly pedagogical methods or take place in a designated studio space (Barry & Meisiek, 2015; Meisiek, 2017).

Learning spaces in business schools or the university are traditionally auditoriums or classrooms where educators often utilize more traditional lecturing formats (Middleton, 2018). While these formats allow for a strategic use of resources (e.g., one teacher assigned to an auditorium) as well as providing quality learning in some subjects (Biggs & Tang, 2011), they might not provide the best learning environments for creative thinking. Studio-based learning, however, aims at producing atypical results, such as imaginative problem reframing, innovative solutions, promoting synthesis-oriented skill sets, integral learning, and so on (Barry & Meisiek, 2015). It has the potential to support deep learning and creative thinking by challenging the traditional higher learning paradigm of classroom and auditorium teaching in terms of reorganizing the learning dynamics.

According to Meisiek (2017), business schools historically had had more in common with art and design schools than both natural and social sciences, with management, organization and leadership viewed as crafts or an art form, initially founded by trade associations and masters within the field. In this sense, the studio at the business school parallels the studio at the design school, aiming at reintroducing the practical craftsmanship aspects to the practice of teaching for the business disciplines.

The studio in the business school shares some similarities with the studios at design schools. For instance, the ways of teaching might be similar, but business schools are inherently not oriented towards material making, instead focusing on knowledge production. The idea is that if students of business or management learn to think like designers, then they become better equipped to solve a range of problems pertaining to improving products and services (Meisiek, 2017). These are problems that relate to production and distribution, as well as problems such as those relating to power, politics, innovation, sustainability and work–life balance; all problems that are related to each other and constitute the complexity of managing businesses in the 21st century. The interconnectivity of these problems comes into display in the studio, where students are able to feel, work and play with the paradoxes, ambiguities, power differences, cultural sensitivities and organizational identities (Meisiek, 2017). Through casework (often involving stakeholders), role-play, business modelling or creative explorations of change, students (and teachers) are able to work with these problems and attempt to come up with solutions.

A Tour of the Business Studio

Both space and place matter for the potential learning outcomes at the business studio. First, studios at business schools are considered a place "you go." In other words, the studio is a different place than where students normally go; it is a place that attracts and supports creative thinking and learning-by-making.

The studios at Copenhagen Business School are situated in an old porcelain factory and feature whiteboards for brainstorming or conceptualizing on almost every wall, lit mainly by natural light from large windows. The studios also feature high tables, suited for standing discussions in small groups.

If you are familiar with teaching at business schools, but have never visited a business studio before, you may at first experience a mixture of feelings of familiarity and unfamiliarity. In entering a business studio not yet populated with students, it will mainly look like a minimalistic classroom set up for group work, with an excess of furniture that can be rearranged in a variety of ways, that is, as stages mimicking a theatre setting suited for either presentations or role-play. You will also find an excess of available whiteboard space or walls that may be used for writing or putting up visual representations, to encourage an experimental attitude prompting the students' desires to fill out empty spaces. In contrast, design studios often feature renditions of the students' work on the walls for either motivation or inspiration (Hetland et al., 2013).

Once the students enter, you'll notice that they most frequently engage in group work, huddled around a table or whiteboard. When they start working, you may notice that they will continually be attentive to ensuring that the space they are occupying supports their working process by rearranging it, and their processes will often seem obsessed with materials (sketches, Post-it notes, visual representations, Lego, mock-ups) in order to generate, share and develop business models, strategies, products, campaigns or the like. This may appear to you somewhat like a breakout session in a lecture, where the students are given a task, but if you watch across time you'll realize that the session will extend over long periods, and actually constitutes the majority of class time.

Followed over the course of a semester, studio work will resemble long-term student project work, albeit with a strong focus on generative and iterative processes. You may notice that the students are keenly observant on how they work, and that they will continually engage in elaborate discussions and reflections on their process, in groups and with their teachers. Often the project work is initiated by reference to a client or problem-owner who also assists during the process, and receives a student pitch and provides feedback at the end. Frequently, the student group will engage in social encounters in order to develop their projects: with the client, with potential users and customers, with experts and mentors, and with the teachers and fellow students.

On several occasions you'll notice students presenting their work to the entire class, the teacher and/or an external panel, and at first glance this may look like a normal class presentation. But by observing over time, you may notice that there seem to be certain standard formats that are revisited at several timescales (e.g., daily, once per semester): some focusing more on group progress and attendance to learning from the process; and some focusing on the outcomes, critiquing the product or design that has been generated. Unlike in a normal class presentation, extended dialogues between presenting students, fellow students and teachers may ensue.

During most of the class, the teacher will spend time circulating between groups, to engage in observations, discussions and reflections on their process. When you leave you may notice that the students are still there, working, even when the normal class would come to an end. As such, much of what is going on in the business studio will feel familiar to you, but with some unfamiliar twists, and with enhanced attendance to certain elements such as iterative making-and-reflection, and the obsession with physical materials.

These are all elements that support and encourage different types of interactions with the room and the assignments given. Ideally, these elements help promote a studio culture which engages students in experiential problem finding.

FROM DESIGN THINKING TO ENTREPRENEURIAL MINDSETS

Utilizing studio-based pedagogies in business schools serves the purpose of introducing managerially relevant designerly skills into a business context. However, such studio pedagogics may simultaneously help foster entrepreneurial mindsets in students, enabling them to rapidly sense, act and mobilize even under uncertain conditions (Ireland et al., 2003), and venture into establishing new businesses. The skills necessary to excel in such environments have been the subject of research within the field of entrepreneurship education in order to to understand how individuals identify entrepreneurial opportunities and act upon them (McMullen & Shepherd, 2006). It has been suggested that the cognitive strategies deployed in design, design thinking and entrepreneurship bear close resemblance to each other (Garbuio et al., 2018).

Business school teaching increasingly promises to support a range of entrepreneurial outcomes (Nabi et al., 2017; Nabi & Liñán, 2011), from entrepreneurial awareness and intention, to graduate business start-up (Rideout & Gray, 2013) and ultimately economic growth (Bosma, 2013).

Entrepreneurship scholars have sought to understand how individuals identify entrepreneurial opportunities and act flexibly upon them (McMullen & Shepherd, 2006). In this regard, an entrepreneurial mindset may be defined as the ability to be flexible, and self-regulating in one's cognitions given dynamic and uncertain task environments (Haynie et al., 2010). Such self-regulatory behavior relates crucially to student metacognitive capabilities and their cognitive adaptability (Haynie et al., 2010). Metacognition describes a higher-order cognitive process that serves to organize what individuals know about themselves, tasks, situations and their environment in order to promote effective and adaptable cognitive functioning (A. Brown, 1987; Flavell, 1979). Both cognitive strategies (Baron, 2004; DeTienne & Chandler, 2004; Munoz et al., 2011) and metacognition may be enhanced through training (Mevarech, 1999; Schmidt & Ford, 2003), and the learning environment within which student training takes place has been shown to moderate the relation between metacognition and entrepreneurial outcomes (Mann et al., 2009).

As such, it is likely that students who engage in studio-based learning might stand to gain an entrepreneurial mindset from actionable hands-on creativity, and from the reflective elements therein. Thus, employing studio-based pedagogies at business schools promises to promote both design thinking capabilities as well as entrepreneurship mindsets in students.

HOW AND WHEN TO TEACH IN THE STUDIO

In this section, we provide the reader with an introduction to the questions an educator must ask themself when preparing a course in the studio. We also present three snapshots (cases) of studio-based courses, which might serve as an inspiration to educators who want to try out studio teaching. One thing to be aware of as an educator when conducting teaching in the studio is that one would have to give up some control over the classroom situation in order to let students be creative.

One approach to organizing a course in the studio is to use the activity-centered analysis and design framework, developed by Goodyear and Carvalho (2014, 2016). This framework is intended to support both the analysis and design of complex learning environments and is thus well suited for designing the complex learning environment that is the studio.

The framework places activity in its core, because in this framework learning is about what people do. In other words, doing involves thinking, feeling, perceiving, talking, making, moving, and so on. As an educator, you will not be in control of every aspect of what the students do in the studio. This you will have to come to terms with, as acts of co-design and co-creation are not suitable for rigorous planning. However, you will be able to guide students towards the intended learning outcomes using set design, epistemic design and social design.

Set design is about which materials, artefacts, tools and resources students are provided with. Materials, as well as the organization of physical or virtual learning environments, afford certain activities. Visual thinking tools (i.e., pens, paper, Post-its) and devices for research (i.e., computers or smartphones) and writable surfaces such as whiteboards all help students externalize their thoughts. Think about how certain materials and the arrangement of the learning environment will help produce certain types of work.

Epistemic design is about preparing or proposing certain tasks for the students. Many educators with studio experience prefer to act as facilitators in group discussions, rather than providing students with right or wrong answers. Thus, epistemic design is really about suggesting good things for the students to do, which will help them become more epistemically fluent. Epistemic fluency is the capacity to understand, switch between and combine different kinds of knowledge and different ways of knowing. In the business studio one has the opportunity to support the epistemic fluency through the tasks that are given and how they are arranged. One example could be that tasks are given outside the classroom: go learn about the customers and how they purchase these products, or talk to the employees about how they experience certain company policies, or ask companies about problems they haven't yet solved themselves and help them solve them. Helping the students become personally involved in the projects, having them draw upon personal experiences, will usually make them more engaged.

Social design is fundamentally about designing for a certain situation, for example assigning students in dyads, groups or teams, or having them discuss among their work partners which roles they each would like to have in the project. Students will most likely sit in almost the same places in each class, so if you want students to behave differently, it is important to intentionally design around this. Social design could also be about developing simulation games for the students that they have to interact with (or have them design the games themselves). You could also have the groups develop a team charter, since this enables a discussion about their objectives as a team as well as clearing up differences in individual ambitions. Assigning roles to various team members – for example, as a CEO, someone in charge of marketing, finance, customer research, and so on – will provide some interesting dynamics within the group, while also giving each member of the group an important role.

How then do you purposefully combine the set design, epistemic design and social design in your course? If this is your first time planning for teaching in the studio, then take it slow, focus on having a strong alignment between the three types of design, and start asking yourself questions such as these:

- What do learning activities look like in relation to the topic I am teaching?
- What do I want the student to be doing? What task is likely to generate that kind of activity?
- What environment and what tools will best support students with this task?
- What social configuration is likely to facilitate students' learning?

Also consider that being creative or thinking creatively might not be for everyone, and that teaching and learning in the studio requires students to "put themselves out there" or to expose something intimate. Handling this in a professional manner requires great facilitation skills, and phrases such as "let's explore this" or "how might we consider ..." are techniques that help students open up in processes of divergent thinking and explore problems without judgment.

SNAPSHOTS OF TEACHING IN THE BUSINESS STUDIO

For the final section of the chapter, we present three cases that may serve as an inspiration to educators who wish to experiment with introducing studio pedagogics into their teaching. The cases stem from teaching at Copenhagen Business School, and vary in the extent to which they engage with studio pedagogy, from single teaching sessions to entire programs.

The first snapshot illustrates how to implement studio teaching for a single session during a semester-long course. This could inspire teachers to adjust their traditional course and experiment more with studio teaching. The second snapshot shows an intensive week-long workshop conducted in the studio. The final snapshot stems from the MSc in Organizational Innovation and Entrepreneurship. This program focuses on how to design and manage entrepreneurship and innovation processes, with at least 50 percent of the courses using studio pedagogics. We outline the program and describe how one quarter-long course is structured.

Snapshot of a One-Day Studio-Based Single Session

The first snapshot illustrates a singular studio-based session that can fit into a course as a one-time activity for the teacher who may want to try out studio-based work for the first time. The session is lifted from the cross-institution joint Master's program of Strategic Design and Entrepreneurship, which is a joint degree for Copenhagen Business School and the Royal Danish Academy of Fine Arts. The students are enlisted in a course on project management, where they work with design companies in semester-long group projects to strategically (re) design company artifacts and business models. The singular session in question is a one-day studio-based activity where the students work in groups on understanding the company's current business model, and then to try to consider how that business model may be challenged, extended or affected by the group's strategic design ideas.

Epistemic design

The day will initiate with a brief lecture of business models, explicating that they describe organizational designs or architectures (Teece, 2010), whereby their adjustments or improvements require artful iterative processes, along with designerly skills. The common tool, the Business Model Canvas (Osterwalder & Pigneur, 2010) is then introduced. The students are subsequently asked to engage in two tasks. The first is "Understand the company you work with": describe and discuss your company's business model, filling in all aspects of the Business Model Canvas, and focusing especially on the core/crucial elements of their business model, and central relations among elements. The second is "Innovate the company you work with": based on the understanding of the current company business model, how might the group innovate the current business model to create, deliver and capture value in new ways?

Social design
The students work in small groups (4–6) for the session, with class teachers circulating between the groups as they iteratively work in order to offer feedback, and reflect on the process.

Set design
The session is studio-based, with each group working in front of a whiteboard with a template Business Model Canvas drawn on it. Groups utilize sticky notes and whiteboard markers, allowing the entire team to participate in entering information for each element, repositioning, and for color-wise clearly delimitating the existing business model from group proposed innovations. Groups are asked to revisit their visual business model representations a number of times, iteratively refining and getting to the "core" of the business model, while discussing how elements fit together to create configurations and core systems. The process enables theoretical discussions of what business architectures are. At the end of the day, the groups will pitch a presentation for the entire class, with their main findings. At this point, the entire class go around the studio visiting each group's space and business model visualization, and offer a critique.

Snapshot of a One-Week Studio-Based Workshop

The second snapshot concerns a one-week intensive studio-based workshop taking place as part of a Master's-level course on Organizational Creativity and Entrepreneurship in the program of Business Administration and Psychology at Copenhagen Business School (CBS). The workshop is situated in the early part of the course, and serves the purpose of training the approximately 90 students' cognitive and social creative competences by asking them to deliver original and useful value in a short time-frame to a case company. The workshop has mandatory participation, but does not relate directly to the exam of the course. It enforces an intensive hands-on learning experience, where the students enter into the practice of organizational creativity in order for them to try to apply their knowledge of how to structure and engage in organizational processes and deliver conceptual value. The course pedagogy changes with the progression of the course. In the first part of the course, the students mainly engage in standard and blended learning lectures. After a month, the one-week intensive full-time studio-based workshop takes place in order to train students in hands-on skills and reflect on the process. Finally, in the last part of the course, dialogue-based active learning classroom sessions dominate in order to further reflection, and bring in more complex theoretical discussions while the students engage in a group-based project where they set their own topic. Time-wise the workshop is purposefully placed early in the semester, in order to create personal engagement with the topics of the course, at a time and in a way where the students will gain both a sense of competence, and a mass of course-relevant experiences of dilemmas, difficulties, problems and failures that they subsequently try to understand and discuss theoretically in the parts of the course that follow on from the workshop.

Epistemic design
In order to establish a task environment fused with dynamism and uncertainty, the workshop pertains to a purposefully very open and challenging task of delivering conceptual proposals that would reorganize a case company to accelerate its innovation processes (e.g., to focus on 'sustainable innovation'). The case company is a major organization, with complex internal

structures, making it extremely challenging for the students to analyze, and uncertain to redesign for value creation. To create dynamism in the workshop, the structure entails a string of encounters with both managers and employees of the company, as well as ongoing supervision from class teachers who continually circulate amongst student groups, to create opportunities to reflect on their process and progress.

The week is structured in such a way that the students work full-time first (Day 1) to focus on understanding the case and activate relevant theory, then (Day 2) focus on understanding the organization, its customers and employees, then (Days 3–4) Iteratively generate ideas and solutions, and facilitate knowledge production, and then develop a chosen idea into a final concept, and finally (Day 5) pitch their concept to the company board of directors.

The task challenge is purposefully difficult in order to create uncertainty and complexity in the task environment, which allows for a number of course topic-relevant learnings to occur. Framing: entrepreneurship and design typically involve fuzzy problems of significant complexity, and in need of problem framing and reframing (Dorst & Paton, 2011), and effectuation (Sarasvathy, 2001). Feelings: the short timeframe enforces a number of learnings about how it feels to go through complex design or entrepreneurial processes, allowing for moments of frustration, exaltation, flow and demotivation to occur that may later become the subject of theoretical reflections. The students are encouraged to note down their feelings and level of motivation throughout the week, for later reflection and theorizing.

Social design

The workshop is socially configured as a group-based case-competition, with the students organized in cross-functional teams (size: 4–6), who compete with other teams for developing novel and appropriate conceptual solutions. The student groups are the 'social core' of the workshop activities, and the majority of the time these groups work independently and structure their own time, with workshop teachers circulating between teams in order to engage in both assistance with content progression, as well as process reflections.

In addition, planned encounters with other actors ensure progression and dynamism. Case-company employees: on the first day of the workshop, the student groups interview 2–3 employees from the company to get to know the organization. Mentors: each team is assigned a mentor from the case company who works with the students on four occasions (understanding the company; initial ideas; mid-way critique; and final pitch preparation). Twinning teams: to ensure cross-functional diversity, each group is paired with a student group from a technical university who also work on the same challenge, with whom they meet once during the workshop period. Academic domain experts: in one session academic domain experts visit each group to offer feedback and suggestions. Case company Board of Directors: witness and offer feedback on the final pitch.

The complex social orchestration of the workshop serves the course content-relevant experience of engaging with multiple actors to co-create a design solution in a short timeframe, leading to both frustrations of having to figure out how to collaborate, as well as ensuring opportunities to progress with theoretical understanding, creative development and case-specific insights. The mass of social interactions mimic a flux of information where it is time-wise not possible to gain optimal usage of all the available information, while simultaneously creating a situation with substantial and diverse available social and content resources. The social design thus challenges both the students' cognitive flexibility, as well as their capabilities to engage in synergetic social interactions for value creation in organizations.

Set design

The workshop is set in a business studio environment, allowing each student group their own small physical space to iteratively make-and-reflect. The one-week duration does not allow for the establishment of a studio "culture" as such, given it is the first time that the students are present in such an environment. However, the structure of the physical space, as well as the temporal structure and content of the planned activities, ensure that the students can quickly gain an understanding of what is expected of them, and what degree of freedom is offered for their group work in this space. In the business studio, physical materials for making are offered, with the most frequently used being the whiteboards on walls, and tables for visual support of sketches, text, concepts and models. Sticky notes offer a familiar medium for informal conceptual capture and sharing (Christensen et al., 2020), and remain the most frequently used materials. Sticky notes are an excellent and democratic medium for quickly populating and later rearranging walls with concepts than may then serve as a kind of shared mental workspace for the group, affording playful interactions.

Snapshot of a Studio-Based Masters Program (Organizational Innovation and Entrepreneurship at CBS)

Organizational Innovation and Entrepreneurship (OIE) is a two-year international Masters of social science graduate program that focuses on how to design and manage processes of innovation and entrepreneurship at all levels in society and businesses. Students deal with theoretical and practical aspects of managing the processes that lead to the creation, implementation and growth of innovative ventures in a co-creative and case-based learning environment, with a strong focus on user-centric methods and design thinking

Teaching during the first year of the program

Students are provided with the tools and knowledge needed for managing innovation and engaging in entrepreneurial organizations. This includes going through the life cycle model of and organization from business idea to entrepreneurial process, to growth and exit, to impact on society. Students attend two courses each academic quarter – one course with a theoretical perspective in a traditional classroom and one with a practical perspective in the studio.

Table 4.1 shows the link between theoretical and practical perspectives. All studio courses include projects that can be further brought into the real world, or students can bring projects they are working on outside into class. One such example is the course Business Concepts and Prototypes (Q1), which focuses on group projects, where students create and prototype their own businesses, focusing on proof of concept. Experience from this course shows that many students take their projects further after the class is over and begin their own start-ups.

The course Business Concepts and Prototypes is the first course in the studio for students on the OIE program. This course shapes the students' knowledge end experiences with working in the studio, and thus we delve a little deeper into the structure and content of this course.

Table 4.1   First year of Organizational Innovation and Entrepreneurship program

	Perspectives			
Course type	1st quarter	2nd quarter	3rd quarter	4th quarter
Classroom courses – theoretical perspectives	Entrepreneurship and Innovation in Context	Strategic Management and Innovation	The Art of Innovation	Making Social Science Matter
Studio course – practical perspectives	Business Concepts and Prototypes	Entrepreneurial Processes	Organizing Growth: Innovative Communities and Digital Environments	Social Innovation and Entrepreneurship
	Life cycle model of the organization			
Ideas/prototypes → building an organization → growing an organization and exit options				

Epistemic design

The course focuses on theories of value creation and utilizes various frameworks for developing ideas into concrete business concepts and organizational forms. Knowledge is obtained from readings, short lectures and cases, class discussions and group exercises through which the class develops, modifies and refines a series of business concepts and product/service prototypes. Students are graded on the exam as well as a mandatory assignment halfway through the course. The mandatory assignment is graded approved/not approved, while the exam assignment is an analysis of a self-constructed "case" which consists of a diary of all of the activities, experiences and materials gained on a week-to-week basis during the course. The diary is to have daily entries, with at least entries on the following:

- Actions:
  - What kind of activities did I undertake?
  - What went well/what were the challenges?
  - What do I think or how do I feel about this?
- Learning:
  - How do I make sense of what has happened (using course literature)?
  - What did I learn? What will I do differently next time and how?
- Planning:
  - Given what I've learned, what do I plan to do next and why?

Furthermore, students are expected to conduct at least 20 interviews in developing value propositions and engaging in prototyping, in order for the students to gain understanding of customers' and users' life worlds. Interviews are to be made with potential customers, industry experts, competitors, mentors, possible investors or employees.

The mandatory assignment takes on the format of a "trade show." During the trade show, students present the results of their course work – that is, the refined business concepts and (physical) prototypes the students have worked on – to each other as well as to possible stakeholders. The trade show thus serves as critique sessions where masters of the trade as well as students can provide feedback on the students' work, spurring further reflection on their work.

Set design

Students are encouraged to use physical materials when producing prototypes and to seek out help from other students from either CBS or other higher learning institutions with expertise in relevant fields, such as programming or design. Materials – except for whiteboards, Post-its and paper - are not provided, although students are encouraged to use them when prototyping.

Social design

Students are teamed up in pairs in the first lecture. They are assigned with interviewing each other, which leads to sketches of small prototypes. These are pitched at class level where students have a discussion of the analytical patterns used. Value proposition design tools are then introduced.

The Business Concepts and Prototypes course enables students and teachers alike to fully take advantage of the possibilities offered by the business studio; the epistemic, social and set designs support entrepreneurial learning with a strong focus on learning-by-doing. The development of a business prototype that students are personally invested in, and can carry forward into future courses or spend time on outside classes, increases the chance of students engaging in long-term entrepreneurial ventures. Or at least they exit the studio with some experience regarding starting, developing and running businesses.

CONCLUSION

In this chapter, we have showcased the studio pedagogy and illustrated its use in business schools. The business studio offers an exciting and untraditional space for teaching for business in a designerly fashion. In practice, this means approaching tasks experientially, emphasizing problem-solving through processes of learning-by-making coupled with reflection on action through individual and formalized critique sessions. We argue that introducing a studio pedagogy into business teaching may help develop cognitive flexibility, train collaborate skills and support the development of an entrepreneurial mindset, because it fosters a certain studio habit of mind which promotes certain cognitive strategies.

When students are engaged in certain tasks in a changing task environment over time, their cognitive flexibility is trained, which promotes the processes of creative cognition. Doing this in groups trains collaborative skills, teaching the students to balance individual and group concerns, training people management and coordination skills. Employing the studio pedagogy offers a potential solution to training the skills that the 21st century labor market calls for.

Studio work needs careful educational design. As an educator, one practical approach to employing studio pedagogy is to guide students towards intended learning outcomes using epistemic, set and social design, as illustrated in the three snapshots of studio teaching at Copenhagen Business School, ranging from single teaching sessions to entire Master's programs.

REFERENCES

Baron, R.A. (2004). The Cognitive Perspective: A Valuable Tool for Answering Entrepreneurship's Basic "Why" Questions. *Journal of Business Venturing, 19*(2), 221–239. https://doi.org/https://doi.org/10.1016/S0883-9026(03)00008-9.

Barry, D., and Meisiek, S. (2015). Discovering the Business Studio. *Journal of Management Education, 39*(1), 153–175. https://doi.org/10.1177/1052562914532801.

Biggs, J., and Tang, C. (2011). *Teaching For Quality Learning At University*. SRHE and Open University Press Imprint. Retrieved from https://books.google.dk/books?id=XhjRBrDAESkC.

Bosma, N. (2013). The Global Entrepreneurship Monitor (GEM) and Its Impact on Entrepreneurship. *Foundations and Trends in Entrepreneurship, 9*(2), pp 143–248.

Brown, A. (1987). Metacognition and Other Mechanisms. In F.E. Weinert and R.H. Kluwe (eds), *Metacognition, Motivation and Understanding*. Hillsdale, NJ: Lawrence Erlbaum Associates, pp. 65–116.

Brown, T. (2008). Design Thinking. *Harvard Business Review, 86*, 84–96.

Buchanan, R. (1992). Wicked Problems Thinking in Design. *Design Issues, 8*(2), 5–21.

Camillus, J.C. (2008). Strategy as a Wicked Problem. *Harvard Business Review, 86*(5), 1–19.

Christensen, B.T., Halskov, K., and Klokmose, C. (2020). The Properties of Sticky Notes for Collaborative Creativity: An Introduction. In Bo T. Christensen, K. Halskov and C. Klokmose (eds), *Sticky Creativity: Post-It(R) Note Cognition, Computers, and Design*. London: Academic Press, pp. 1–19.

Cross, N. (2018). Expertise in Professional Design. In K.A. Ericsson, R.R. Hoffman, A. Kozbelt and A.M. Williams (eds), *The Cambridge Handbook of Expertise and Expert Performance*. Cambridge: Cambridge University Press, pp. 372–388. Doi: https://doi.org/10.1017/9781316480748.021.

DeTienne, D.R., and Chandler, G.N. (2004). Opportunity Identification and Its Role in the Entrepreneurial Classroom: A Pedagogical Approach and Empirical Test. *Academy of Management Learning and Education, 3*(3), 242–257.

Dorst, K., and Paton, B. (2011). Briefing and Reframing: A Situated Practice. *Design Studies, 32*(6), 573–587.

Flavell, J.H. (1979). Metacognition and Cognitive Monitoring A New Area of Cognitive-Developmental Inquiry. *American Psychologist, 34*(10), 906–911.

Garbuio, M., Dong, A., Lin, N., Tschang, T., and Lovallo, D. (2018). Demystifying the Genius of Entrepreneurship: How Design Cognition Can Help Create the Next Generation of Entrepreneurs. *Academy of Management Learning and Education, 17*(1), 41–61.

Goodyear, P., and Carvalho, L. (2014). *The Architecture of Productive Learning Networks*. New York: Routledge: https://doi.org/10.4324/9780203591093.

Goodyear, P., and Carvalho, L. (2016). Activity Centred Analysis and Design in the Evolution of Learning Networks. *Proceedings of the 10th International Conference on Networked Learning 2016*, 218–225.

Haynie, M., and Shepherd, D.A. (2009). A Measure of Adaptive Cognition for Entrepreneurship Research. *Entrepreneurship Theory and Practice, 315*, 695–714.

Haynie, M., Shepherd, D., Mosakowski, E., and Earley, P.C. (2010). A Situated Metacognitive Model of the Entrepreneurial Mindset. *Journal of Business Venturing, 25*(2), 217–229. https://doi.org/10.1016/j.jbusvent.2008.10.001.

Hetland, L., Winner, E., Veenema, S., and Sheridan, K.M. (2013). *Studio Thinking 2: The Real Benefits of Visual Arts Education*. Teachers College Press. Retrieved from https://books.google.dk/books?id=3-E2018bTKQC.

Hjorth, D. (2011). On Provocation, Education and Entrepreneurship. *Entrepreneurship and Regional Development, 23*(1), 49–63. https://doi.org/10.1080/08985626.2011.540411.

Ireland, R.D., Hitt, M.A., and Sirmon, D.G. (2003). A Model of Strategic Entrepreneurship: The Construct and its Dimensions. *Journal of Management, 29*(6), 963–989. https://doi.org/10.1016/S0149-2063(03)00086-2.

Johansson-Sköldberg, U., Woodilla, J., and Çetinkaya, M. (2013). Design Thinking: Past, Present and Possible Futures. *Creativity and Innovation Management, 22*(2), 121–146. https://doi.org/10.1111/caim.12023.

Kelley, T. (2007). *The Art of Innovation: Lessons in Creativity from IDEO, America's Leading Design Firm*. Currency/Doubleday. Retrieved from https://books.google.dk/books?id=yjgO70g_qbsC.

Kelley, T., and Littman, J. (2005). *The Ten Faces of Innovation: IDEO's Strategies for Beating the Devil's Advocate and Driving Creativity Throughout Your Organization*. Currency/Doubleday. Retrieved from https://books.google.dk/books?id=bmfDeosr40sC.

Lackney, J.A. (1999). A History of the Studio-Based Learning Model. Retrieved from: http://www.edi.msstate.edu/work/pdf/history_studio_based_learning.pdf.

Mann, K., Gordon, J., and Macleod, A. (2009). Reflection and Reflective Practice in Health Professions Education: A Systematic Review. *Advances in Health Sciences Education, 14*, 595–621. https://doi.org/10.1007/s10459-007-9090-2.

McMullen, J.S., and Shepherd, D.A. (2006). Entrepreneurial Action and the Role of Uncertainty in the Theory of the Entrepreneur. *Academy of Management Review, 31*(1), 132–152.

Meisiek, S. (2017). A Studio at a Business School? In S. Junginger and J. Faust (eds), *Designing: Business and Management*. London: Bloomsbury Academic, pp. 159–166. https://doi.org/10.5040/9781474243551.ch-012.

Mevarech, Z.R. (1999). Effects of Metacognitive Training Embedded in Cooperative Settings on Mathematical Problem Solving. *Journal of Educational Research, 92*(4), 195–205.

Middleton, A. (2018). *Reimagining Spaces for Learning in Higher Education*. London: Macmillan International Higher Education.

Munoz, C., Mosey, S., and Binks, M. (2011). Developing Opportunity-Identification Capabilities in the Classroom: Visual Evidence. *Academy of Management Learning and Education, 10*(2), 277–295.

Nabi, G., Fayolle, A., Lyon, E.M., Krueger, N., and Walmsley, A. (2017). The Impact of Entrepreneurship Education in Higher Education: A Systematic Review and Research Agenda. *Academy of Management Learning and Education, 16*(2), 277–299. https://doi.org/10.5465/amle.2015.0026.

Nabi, G., and Liñán, F. (2011). Graduate Entrepreneurship in the Developing World: Intentions , Education and Development. *Education + Training, 53*(5), 325–334.

Osterwalder, A., and Pigneur, Y. (2010). *Business Model Generation: a Handbook for Visionaries, Game Changers, and Challengers*. Hoboken, NJ: John Wiley & Sons.

Rideout, E.C., and Gray, D.O. (2013). Does Entrepreneurship Education Really Work? A Review and Methodological Critique of the Entrepreneurship Education. *Journal of Small Business Management, 51*(3), 329–351. https://doi.org/10.1111/jsbm.12021.

Sarasvathy, S.D. (2001). Causation and Effectuation: Toward a Theoretical Shift from Economic Inevitability to Entrepreneurial Contingency. *Academy of Management Review, 26*(2), 243–263.

Schmidt, A.M., and Ford, J.K. (2003). Learning Within a Learner Control Training Environment: The Interactive Effects of Goal Orientation and Metacognitive Instruction on Learning Outcomes. *Personnel Psychology, 56*, 405–429.

Schön, D.A. (2017). *The Reflective Practitioner: How Professionals Think in Action*. Ashgate. Retrieved from https://books.google.dk/books?id=OT9BDgAAQBAJ.

Schön, D.A., and Wiggins, G. (1992). Kinds of Seeing in Designing. *Creativity and Innovation Management, 1*(2), 68–74. https://doi.org/10.1111/j.1467-8691.1992.tb00031.x.

Teece, D.J. (2010). Business Models, Business Strategy and Innovation. *Long Range Planning, 43*(2–3), 172–194.

WEF (2018). The Future of Jobs Report 2018. World Economic Forum. https://doi.org/10.1177/0891242417690604.

5. A framework for motivating business students through teaching, learning and curriculum design

David Kember

OVERVIEW

This chapter presents a motivational framework derived from interviews with students in a business school and a school of hotel and tourism management. The interviews yielded a large body of data in which the students reported their perceptions of the types of courses and teaching and learning which motivated them to study. This database was analysed to produce a set of themes, which are used to characterize a teaching and learning environment conducive to motivating students to study. This is presented as a motivational teaching and learning environment framework. The elements of the teaching and learning environment are: establishing interest; allowing choice of courses; establishing relevance; learning activities; teaching for understanding; assessment of learning activities; close teacher–student relationships; and sense of belonging between classmates.

This chapter is organized by these elements of the motivational teaching and learning environment framework. It presents detailed descriptions from the interviewees of the types of teaching and learning which motivated or demotivated them. As such, it provides a practical guide to how to design courses and configure teaching and learning so that it will motivate students.

METHOD

There are any number of theories of motivation. Finding one which related, in a practical way, to teaching and learning in higher education was far from straightforward. Many of the theories were based on experiments with young children. Others were focused on the industrial workplace. Still others, such as the intrinsic/extrinsic dichotomy, have been around for so long that the origins are hard to trace in the literature.

The research on which this chapter is based, therefore, took an exploratory grounded theory approach (Charmaz, 2014; Corbin & Strauss, 2015; Glaser & Strauss, 1967; Lincoln & Guber, 1985). The motivational teaching and learning environment framework was derived from interviews with university students.

The motivational orientation framework is presented and explained in this chapter. It is then used as an organizational framework for reporting the analysis of the data on teaching and learning in a way which justifies the framework as research, as well as giving a practical guide to motivating students through teaching and learning.

The study took place in Hong Kong, where there are eight universities funded by the University Grants Council (UGC). The UGC places these universities in three categories, based on their original mission: research-intensive, former polytechnic and former liberal arts college.

As there are only places in undergraduate degrees in these eight universities for about 18 per cent of an age group, Hong Kong can still be interpreted as having an elite university system (Kember, 2010). The very large majority of places in undergraduate degrees go to those who achieve the best results in the external examinations sat at the end of secondary school. Most students go directly from school to university.

Individual interviews were conducted with 36 undergraduate students in the UGC-funded universities. All were conducted in the early part of the third and final year of study. The interviewees were able to discuss how the curriculum and the prevailing teaching and learning environment of the department had influenced their motivation as the course had progressed.

In order to be able to build detailed and verifiable case studies of departmental teaching and learning environments, four students were interviewed from each of nine departments or courses. To make the sample representative of the universities in Hong Kong, and of those in most other countries, three programmes were selected from each of the three types of university. The disciplines or departments selected were chosen to be typical of the type of university and to give a reasonable overall coverage of major discipline areas.

The motivational framework drew upon all 36 interviews. For the purpose of this chapter, quotations are taken from interviews with four students in the business school and four students in the hotel and tourism management school. Quotations from students from the business school are indicated by (BUSS), while those from students in the hotel and tourism management school are indicated by (HTM). More details about the research are given in Kember (2016).

MOTIVATIONAL TEACHING AND LEARNING ENVIRONMENT FRAMEWORK

Analysis of the transcripts by main themes reported as being conducive to motivating student learning resulted in eight main categories or themes. In each case there was a corresponding demotivating element. The complementarity between motivating and demotivating facets of a teaching and learning environment is seen as providing a degree of validating support for the analysis.

The eight themes are presented as a motivational teaching and learning environment framework (Figure 5.1). Each of the themes is represented by a continuum or spectrum with a positive motivating end and a negative demotivating end. This chapter concentrates on the motivating end of the spectrum. Each continuum constitutes a part of a teaching and learning environment. The facets of the environment interact, which is represented by the double-headed vertical arrows.

Taken together, the eight themes of motivating elements can be seen as characterizing a teaching and learning environment conducive to motivating student learning. It appeared necessary to pay attention to all eight elements, to provide a teaching and learning environment conducive to motivating students. The eight elements are listed below:

- Establishing interest.
- Allowing choice of courses so that interests can be followed.
- Establishing relevance.
- Learning activities.
- Teaching for understanding.
- Assessment of learning activities.
- Close teacher–student relationships.
- Sense of belonging between classmates.

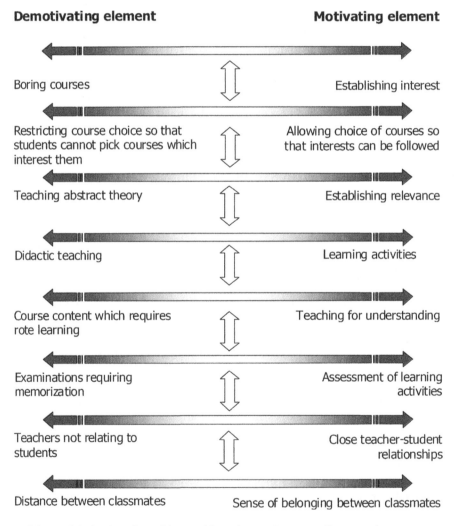

Figure 5.1   Motivational teaching and learning environment framework

The following sections deal with the facets of the teaching and learning environment. Each is illustrated by typical quotations derived from the three studies. Rather than treating the facets evenly, stress is placed on those facets likely to have practical applications for teaching and learning in business schools.

SOCIAL-COGNITIVE MODELS OF MOTIVATION

The framework is consistent with social-cognitive models of motivation (Pintrich, 2003; Pintrich & Schunk, 2002) in that motivation is represented as a multifaceted phenomenon which is dynamic and influenced by the context. The nature of teaching, curriculum design and teacher–student and student–student relationships plays a part in the degree and nature of motivation. Positions on each of the continua change over time and could differ between courses or subjects.

Pintrich (2003) presents five general socio-cognitive principles of what motivates students. These five principles of motivation are:

- Adaptive self-efficacy and competence beliefs.
- Adaptive attributions and control beliefs.
- Higher levels of interest and intrinsic motivation.
- Higher levels of achievement values.
- Achievement goals which motivate and direct.

What is common to the model and the framework is that both represent motivation, as including multiple factors or multiple forms of motivation. Both are also contextual or relational, in that motivation is influenced by the student's perception of the task which has been set and the prevailing teaching and learning environment. Both are also dynamic because they posit that motivation changes over time because of these contextual influences. Both, therefore, reject the notion that motivation is a characteristic of the student or is a stable cognitive style.

Pintrich (2004) went on to develop his model into a conceptual framework for self-regulated learning. The framework included four phases, of planning, monitoring, control and regulation. The planning phase includes goal-setting. Monitoring is through the cognitive or metacognitive processes associated with the task. The control phase involves selecting strategies for managing and engaging with the task. The regulation phase is a reflective one.

ESTABLISHING INTEREST

One of the themes which came through strongly in terms of motivation was interest. Of the 36 undergraduate interviewees, 28 mentioned interest as an element in their motivation.

The level of interest seemed to be partially an expression of individual preferences. There were individual differences between students, expressed as preferences for different types of subject. What they had taken at secondary school had been influenced by these preferences. Their reaction to studying the subject at school influenced their choice of degree to apply for admission to:

> I was an arts student. I studied Chinese history and Computing [at school]. There is no subject related to management. We always needed to recite lots of things. We had to write an essay of more than a thousand words in order to respond to one sentence only. We acted like a typewriter and wrote down everything we had recited in the exam. I didn't take Chinese History or Literature. I am not interested in these subjects. I took these subjects for [secondary school examination] as I had no choice. I love to deal with different kinds of people. I am not interested in pure subjects such as Literature. (BUSS)

The other aspect of the level of interest was that it was partly a function of the nature of the teaching and learning environment. Whether or not students were interested in a subject was dependent upon the curriculum design, the nature of teaching and the way in which content was taught.

Another important factor in establishing interest was related to the degree of relevance discussed in more detail below in the sections on the relevance facet. A common complaint was excessive teaching of abstract theory. Students found it more interesting if the application of the theory could be shown.

ESTABLISHING RELEVANCE IN TEACHING

If teachers wish to motivate their students' learning they need to find ways to show the relevance of topics included in their courses. If relevance was established, students took an interest in the topic. Establishing relevance and stimulating intrinsic interest seemed to be intimately related.

Establishing relevance was related to creating interest, in that demonstrating relevance was a prime way to promote interest. Relevance could be shown by giving an application of a theory. The relevance of material could be shown by relating it to local applications, real-life examples or everyday application or to current topics (Kember & McNaught, 2007).

Relevance to Local Issues

Textbooks normally come from the United States or the United Kingdom. Any examples in them are normally of the country in which they were written. It must seem to Hong Kong students that both theory and applications come from Western countries. It is therefore a good way to establish relevance by showing that theory applies to local issues:

> Maybe it is good to open some new programmes especially related to Asian cities. For example, casinos are famous in Macau but we don't have any courses about it. I think that is better to include some elements peculiar to Asian cities. (HTM)

Relevance to Everyday Applications

Another way of establishing the relevance of topics was to relate them to applications in everyday life. The case below is a negative example of how mathematics can seem to be a theoretical rather than a practical subject if relevance is not established. Unless practical applications are explained, mathematics becomes an exercise in learning procedures for performing seemingly pointless calculations. Some readers may know that logarithms and tangents do have practical applications, but they had not been illustrated to the student quoted below:

Learning is definitely not how many theories that you can memorize. The most important is applying what you have learned in your daily life. In secondary school, we learned something called log and tangent in maths. At the time we were learning that we were able to do the calculations. However, I am sure most of the students who do not pursue their study in maths will soon forget that. We are unable to put them into a real life context. Perhaps we have to learn these things in order to fulfil the requirement of the syllabus. I wonder how important they are to me now. (BUSS)

Applying Theory

Being given the chance to apply theory gives students a chance to see whether they understand it. Application also demonstrates how the theory is relevant:

> For example, financial management involves lots of content related to accounting; like balance sheet or cash flow. After having the lecture, we have to do some practical exercises. If we are unable to work it out, we can raise questions. I think I can learn from this practical way of teaching. (HTM)

The above example is of a small-scale application in the form of an exercise or problem. The quotation below illustrates a larger-scale application in which a body of theory is applied to the type of activity which professionals in the field would engage in:

> We learn lots of marketing theories, and then we have to base on these theories to … How can I explain this? Building up on the top of these theories, we are able to create our views. For example, we are told to run a business through application of the theories. In between, we are allowed room for creativity in doing this particular project. I quite like that. (HTM)

Principles

It should be noted that the ways of showing relevance are consistent with the findings from the interviews with award-winning teachers (Kember & McNaught, 2007, p. 38). The book derived a set of ten principles of good teaching, of which the relevant principle here is to establish the relevance of what is taught, by:

- using real-life examples;
- drawing cases from current issues;
- giving local examples; and
- relating theory to practice.

ESTABLISHING RELEVANCE IN THE CURRICULUM

Curriculum is here interpreted as the design of teaching and learning at the course or degree level. This encompasses the overall philosophy underpinning the design, and the way units fit together to make up the degree. There are major sections for the two most relevant elements of the motivational teaching and learning environment framework: allowing choice versus coherence; establishing relevance versus building theoretical foundations in a basic building blocks curriculum design.

The previous section looked at the impact on relevance of classroom teaching and learning on motivation at the level of the lesson, the individual unit or module, or the teacher. This section moves up a level to consider the curriculum. It therefore considers the design of the collection of units which together make up a degree or programme.

Professional Relevance

The business students' courses were expected to establish relevance to the profession. Expectations were expressed in terms of the applicability of knowledge in the future professional role. This principle applied to other professional fields too. Students entering professional programmes clearly expected themselves to be prepared for their future profession, and therefore expected their courses to be relevant to this need. This was a way in which career expectations could be used as a strong positive motivational influence:

> This course will provide me some understanding on the real business world. I have to learn the operational procedures in the business field. I expect the knowledge I learn here can be used at work in this sense. (BUSS)

Teachers of professional programmes therefore had an opportunity to motivate their students through showing how what was taught could be relevant to a future career in the professional field. When theory was taught there could be an opportunity to establish its relevance by showing how it could be applied in practice by professionals in the field.

This opportunity, however, produced a double-edged sword effect. Students expected professional programmes to prepare them for a career in the profession. If they could not see how material taught in a programme served that purpose, they could easily lose motivation.

Building Block Curriculum

The antithesis of establishing relevance was teaching abstract theory. This seemed to happen all too often, because the most common curriculum design model seemed to be the traditional building block design in which the initial parts of a programme are dedicated to basic theory. This often includes subjects other than that of the subject major. These may be essential prerequisite knowledge related to the major, but if relevance is not established students do not realize this. This seemed to be the case all too often, as the subjects were usually taught as pure theory by specialists in the area without making an attempt to show relevance to the major.

The building block curriculum seemed to be particularly problematic in professional programmes. Students often selected these to escape from the pure subjects studied at school, yet found that much of the initial part of their curriculum consisted of theoretical subjects which in their view did not clearly relate to the professional field they had chosen. The dilemma was not helped by many students in professional programmes having remarkably limited ideas about their intended profession.

There were some suggestions and examples of curriculum designs which could alleviate the problem. Students found it valuable if there was an initial course which provided a road-map showing how constituent knowledge taught in early courses was utilized in later ones. In professional programmes, there was value in having an early period of exposure to professional practice. In these periods the students acted largely as observers to learn what professionals in the field did, and the sorts of knowledge needed to be an effective professional.

ALLOWING CHOICE OF COURSES

This section also applies to the curriculum level. Interest is partly a function of individual preferences and partly a function of the quality of the teaching and curriculum design. As level of interest had quite a strong impact on level of motivation, and interests vary between students, motivation can be boosted if students have a range of courses to choose from, so that they can pick ones which they think they will find interesting:

> I prefer to take the subjects that I want rather than them being assigned ... There are some subjects that I am not interested in. However, it is set in the course so that I have to take them. (HTM)

One of the business students had made a specific programme choice when leaving secondary school to go to university. His interest was to learn more about finance instead of general business knowledge. However, there was no choice of courses for him in the first year of study, which diminished his level of motivation:

> Every BBA student took the same subjects in the first year. I couldn't sense the difference. We only got one subject that was related to our option ... I am more interested in the core subject. I think I can learn the business knowledge from books. (BUSS)

A related issue is courses which are restricted in application. A narrow concentration can exclude subjects which particular students might find interesting:

> Suppose that I am not interested in anything related to the front office. I would like to learn something about conventions. However, there is nothing included on conventions. What I have learned is all about the front office. Can you imagine how annoying it is? It is meaningless to me then. (HTM)

There are, though, reasons to restrict course choice. It is reasonable to argue that students should have breadth as well as depth; so restricting course choice to ensure that students learn about fundamental areas relevant to their discipline is sensible curriculum design. There are also quite legitimate reasons for restricting choice or making a basic core of courses compulsory. It is often important for students to have a sound knowledge of core constituent disciplines before they go on to specialize in their area of interest. This may not be appreciated at the time, but the value can be seen after graduation.

Curriculum design inevitably involves decisions about finding an acceptable balance between opposing tensions. In this case, between providing students with a breadth of knowledge and allowing freedom of choice to maximize interest.

Resource constraints also inevitably place restrictions on the level of course choice. If the level of choice is too high, there will be a tendency for courses to become unviable due to low enrolments.

Another reason for restricting course choice relates to the final facet in the framework. The transcripts suggested that motivation was higher in classes with high levels of cooperative learning or a strong sense of belonging. Programmes with high levels of course options tend to be low on class coherence, because students can have a different group of classmates in each course they take. Ironically, programmes with little or no options have the strongest possibility of developing coherence because the same group of students spend their time together in each class.

LEARNING ACTIVITIES

Motivation also came through being involved in learning activities. Looking across the whole set of interviews, a wide range of types of active learning was mentioned. A distinction came out clearly. Students commonly contrasted sitting passively in lectures, which was generally uninspiring, to being engaged in learning activities. These ranged in the degree of motivation they afforded, but purely didactic courses should clearly be eschewed (McKay & Kember, 1997).

For the business programme, it was common for students to work in groups doing projects or giving presentations. The following quotation from the business student describes his best experience of doing group work. He enjoyed the project in which he was required to work in a group of students majoring in different professional studies. He anticipated that such experiences would be useful for future work, since most businesses function as multidisciplinary teams:

> The subject is called Strategic Management. We form a group with students from different professional studies. Everybody has to contribute what they have got from their professional studies. This is really necessary for us to work in groups. I think this is common for us to work in a similar way in the future. I really appreciate such kinds of group work. (BUSS)

There was a relationship to the facet of relevance. The group project was seen as highly relevant to future career needs, so was highly motivating. In the beginning, though, the business student was not motivated by his individual research project. He regarded the work as meaningless until he talked with his supervisor, who clarified the purpose of the activity:

> To be frank, I don't think it is possible for us to really conduct research individually. What we are doing now is copying from different sources. It is uneasy for us to do a creative or innovative research project. I can't deny that our research is not up to standard. However, my supervisor told me that is a chance for me to practice and learn what research is. This is a trial only. When I view from his perspective, I find it meaningful and useful for me. At least, I have learned how to read journal articles, theses and develop an interest. (BUSS)

TEACHING FOR UNDERSTANDING

Students rated lecturers in terms of their ability to help students understand the constructs they were trying to teach. The worst were those who could not be understood at all. Others gave a mass of materials and left students to work out what were the key constructs. Better teachers provided a road map. This helped in seeing how material fitted together. These better teachers identified the key concepts. Still other teachers restricted their lecturing; they recognized the principle of learning through doing. A more thorough understanding can come through a degree of self-direction in learning.

The students in the business degree thought that promoting understanding was a hallmark of a good teacher. It was also linked to showing relevance:

> Some professors are very skilful in inspiring students with controversial issues or they can explain clearly that enables you to understand the whole mechanism. (BUSS)

The concept of teaching for understanding can be seen as related to encouraging students to employ a deep approach to learning. There is an extensive literature on contextual influences upon approaches to learning, showing that students adopt either deep or surface approaches to learning depending on their perception of the learning task and the prevailing teaching and learning environment (e.g., Marton et al., 2005; Prosser & Trigwell, 1999; Richardson, 2000). This has been very influential, such that aligning curricula to produce teaching and learning environments conducive to a deep approach has become a prominent approach to educational development and quality assurance (e.g., Biggs & Tang, 2007; Ramsden, 1992).

ASSESSMENT OF LEARNING ACTIVITIES

Students are assessment-driven (Biggs & Tang, 2007; Kember and McNaught, 2007). Students concentrate their time and attention on what they perceive will result in marks for them. It is therefore important that the assessment is consistent with the other motivating facets. This means that the assessment needs to test understanding, award marks to learning activities and test the application of theory to relevant practical applications.

If there was a common concern, it was that there was too much emphasis on tests and examinations which tested recall rather than understanding. As many students have recognized, poorly designed examinations can reduce incentives to concentrate on understanding material. Instead, the concentration is upon remembering what is likely to be in the test paper:

> Exam is testing students' learning. If there is over-emphasis on exams, students tend to recite and memorize useful bits in order to fit in the exam requirements. I think that an exam may not be able to show the actual gain and capability of students in different subjects. (BUSS)

Another concern on assessment with a heavy weighting on examinations was that it did not provide feedback. Examinations were at the end, so did not provide feedback during the course. It also seemed common not to return marked papers, so the only feedback was a mark, which did not reveal strengths and weaknesses. Without knowing how well they performed on particular questions, students cannot find how to make improvements.

CLOSE TEACHER–STUDENT RELATIONSHIPS

Generally, three important aspects for the establishment of close teacher–student relationships could be identified from the interviews. They were availability, friendliness and helpfulness. Teachers possessing these three qualities were more successful in establishing close and helpful relationships with students.

Unless the teachers showed that they were approachable, students were reluctant to ask for help with material or tasks they found difficult. Therefore, close teacher–student relationships had a positive influence on the motivation of students in their learning. Teacher–student relationships for the business student were quite good. The business student was willing to contact most of his teachers by going to their offices or sending them emails when he was in need of help:

> I don't find any problems communicating with my professors. We always chat and I am willing to express my view. (BUSS)

Again there was a range, this time in the degree of approachability. Those who showed themselves to be approachable and available were the ones students contacted:

> Some professors are more willing to contact us … We tend to contact or stay with those friendly professors … If the professors are mean and serious, we dare not to go their office for a casual talk. Some professors are always out of office. That's a bit difficult to find them. (BUSS)

There was evidence of good teachers relating well to students and therefore facilitating and motivating their learning. However, teachers who did not make efforts to relate to their students did not help the motivation of their students. The first necessity was to make available time for contact with students. A relationship cannot develop if there is no time in contact:

> In fact, I am not familiar with the teaching staff as they are very busy. Sometimes, we are unable to reach them. (BUSS)

The next level was to develop a rapport with students. Unless students feel comfortable relating with and talking to their teachers, they will not approach them to discuss concepts they have not understood. This leads to frustration and decreased motivation.

The final aspect is the need for teachers to be willing to try to behave in a way towards their students that can facilitate the students' learning. This implies making students feel comfortable to approach teachers when they have problems. It also implies that teachers have developed skills in interaction and question-and-answer techniques, so that they can lead students towards finding their own solutions to problems, rather than feeding them answers to problems all the time.

SENSE OF BELONGING BETWEEN CLASSMATES

Sense of belonging was more likely to develop if students keep together as a class cohort for a substantial part of their degree. This was quite common in the sample of programmes, as it is common in Hong Kong for students to enter specified major streams with a restricted range of options.

This facet could, then, be in tension with stimulating interest through offering a free and wide range of choice of courses. The wider the choice, the less students stay together as a cohort, minimizing the chance of class coherence developing. As with many issues in curriculum design, it is necessary to find an intelligent point of balance between conflicting demands.

The business cohort had established a sense of belonging between classmates. The business student believed this resulted from the small size of the class. This is certainly a helpful factor, but is not the only important variable, as other small class groups did not have such good relationships among the students:

> The class size of my option is not large. There are about 40 students only. As a result, we have quite a close relationship. (BUSS)

A sense of belonging also develops through a class being assigned group activities. These promote relationships among the cohort (Yan & Kember, 2003, 2004a, 2004b):

> A relationship is built up through cooperation rather than having classes together. For example, we have to overcome a common problem which in return ends up with a friendship that lasts. (BUSS)

CONCLUSION

This chapter has presented a motivational framework for teaching and learning in higher education. The motivational framework was derived from empirical qualitative research, using grounded theory, into the student experiences of university students. It is therefore unusual in that the motivational framework is derived from and grounded in research in higher education.

The framework also provides a practical guide to motivating students through teaching and learning. The eight facets of the motivating framework are each presented, with interview quotations, which should enable teachers to configure their own teaching in such a way as to motivate their own students.

There are academics who consider motivation to be a function of the student. While individual differences are important, this study makes it clear that teachers have a major impact on the level of motivation of their students.

The motivation of students was found to be affected by a broadly based teaching and learning environment, characterized by the following eight principal elements:

- Establishing interest.
- Allowing choice of courses so that interests can be followed.
- Establishing relevance.
- Learning activities.
- Teaching for understanding.
- Assessment of learning activities.
- Close teacher–student relationships.
- Sense of belonging between classmates.

The level of interest was strongly linked to motivation. Students choose to study a particular subject because they feel it is consistent with their interests. Therefore, it can help to have a reasonably wide choice of courses to offer so that individuals can select combinations of courses which are of interest to them.

Once courses are selected, the students then expect their teachers to do their best to enhance interest. One of the principal ways this could be accomplished is by establishing the relevance of what was taught. Relevance could be shown by relating theory to practical applications, to local examples, to current issues or to everyday applications. In professional programmes, relevance could be established through courses which prepare students well for their eventual profession. Career preparation was seen by students as a positive motivating force and not as an extrinsic demotivator.

Students reported that motivation could be enhanced through appropriate learning activities. Teaching for understanding was an important component of a motivating environment. As students are assessment driven, it was important for assessment tasks to be consistent with the other elements of the environment.

The final two elements in the motivating teaching and learning environment were the social interaction elements of good teacher–student and student–student relationships. Students wanted to feel that their teachers were approachable so that they could ask for advice and help when necessary. Coherent classes with a strong sense of belonging were a motivating influence. It was possible for teachers to promote coherence through setting activities which encourage discussion and require group work.

The inclusion of the social element in the motivational learning environment meant that the scope was broader than the way curricula are often envisaged in higher education. Using the cases to illustrate the elements of the environment has shown that they act in concert and tend to reinforce each other. To motivate student learning it is therefore necessary to take a holistic view of the teaching and learning environment which students experience.

REFERENCES

Biggs, J. and Tang, C. (2007). *Teaching for Quality Learning at University*, 3rd edition. Buckingham: Society for Research in Higher Education and Open University Press.

Charmaz, K. (2014). *Constructing Grounded Theory*. Thousand Oaks, CA: SAGE.

Corbin, J. and Strauss, A. (2015). *Basics of Qualitative Research*. Thousand Oaks, CA: SAGE.

Glaser, B.G. and Strauss, A.L. (1967). *The Discovery of Grounded Theory*. Chicago, IL: Aldine.

Kember, D. (2010). Opening up the road to nowhere: problems with the path to mass higher education in Hong Kong. *Higher Education*, *59*(2), 167–179.

Kember, D. (2016). *Understanding the Nature of Motivation and Motivating Students through Teaching and Learning in Higher Education*. Singapore: Springer.

Kember, D. and McNaught, C. (2007). *Enhancing University Teaching: Lessons from Research into Award Winning Teachers*. Abingdon: Routledge.

Lincoln, Y. and Guber, E. (1985). *Naturalistic Inquiry*. Newbury Park, CA: SAGE Publications.

Marton, F. Hounsell, D. and Entwistle, N. (eds) (2005). *The Experience of Learning: Implications for Teaching and Studying in Higher Education*, 3rd (Internet) edition. Edinburgh: University of Edinburgh, Centre for Teaching, Learning and Assessment.

McKay, J. and Kember, D. (1997). Spoonfeeding leads to regurgitation: a better diet can result in more digestible learning outcomes. *Higher Education Research and Development*, *16*(1), 55–67.

Pintrich, P. (2003). Multiple goals and multiple pathways in the development of motivation and self-regulation. *Development and Motivation 2*. BJEP Monograph Series II.

Pintrich, P. (2004). A conceptual framework for assessing motivation and self-regulated learning in college students. *Educational Psychology Review*, *16*(4), 385–407.

Pintrich, P. and Schunk, D. (2002). *Motivation in Education*. Upper Saddle River, NJ: Prentice-Hall Merrill.

Prosser, M. and Trigwell, K. (1999). *Understanding Learning and Teaching: The Experience in Higher Education*. Buckingham: SRHE and Open University Press.

Ramsden, P. (1992). *Learning to Teach in Higher Education*. London: Routledge.

Richardson, J.T.E. (2000). *Researching Student Learning: Approaches to Studying in Campus-Based and Distance Education*. Buckingham: Society for Research in Higher Education and Open University Press.

Yan, L. and Kember, D. (2003). The influence of the curriculum and learning environment on the learning approaches of groups of students outside the classroom. *Learning Environments Research*, *6*, 285–307.

Yan, L. and Kember, D. (2004a). Avoider and engager approaches by out-of-class groups: the group equivalent to individual learning approaches. *Learning and Instruction*, *14*(1), 27–49.

Yan, L. and Kember, D. (2004b). Engager and avoider behavior in types of activities performed by out-of-class learning groups. *Higher Education, 48*, 419–438.

6. The challenge of reflexive pedagogy in executive education: a personal case study

Marian Iszatt-White

INTRODUCTION

Adopting a reflexive pedagogy in MBA programmes and executive education more broadly is generally seen as desirable (Hibbert and Cunliffe, 2015) in increasing the level of engagement from students and situating their learning more firmly in their lived experience. It is also seen as beneficial in addressing the perceived power asymmetry between educators and students, by recasting the tutors' power away from that of an instructor delivering expertise, to that of an educator-as-facilitator (Hibbert, 2013) tasked with enabling students to learn rather than with teaching per se. But in a profession where our expertise and intellectual identity are our 'stock in trade', the question arises as to how desirable this shift is for educators who may have to come to terms with the revised (and potentially diminished) sense of identity occasioned by this approach. The need to understand the element of 'identity undoing' (Nicholson and Carroll, 2013) which occurs for academics in this context is an inevitable corollary of the issues of power asymmetry already mentioned above.

Whilst the literature has to some extent explored the implications of reflexive pedagogy from the students' perspective (Hibbert, 2013), little attention has been given to the need to understand the 'subjective experience, tensions and outcomes' (Gagnon and Collinson, 2014: 664) of a reflexive approach from an educator's standpoint. In adopting a reflexive pedagogy, educators are 'dislodged from an implicit position of mastery' (Hibbert and Cunliffe, 2015: 186) and thrust into 'a pedagogy of the unknowable in which we can never fully know ourselves, our experience, others, nor the impact of our actions' (Ellsworth, 1989, cited in Hibbert and Cunliffe, 2015: 186). In exploring the educators' experience of this 'unknowability', this chapter draws on work undertaken by myself and a number of colleagues from Lancaster University Management School in relation to leadership learning interventions which formed part of the school's Executive MBA programme and/or a broader distance learning initiative. The chapter reflects on two personal case studies of the disruption and challenge to the author's taken-for-granted sense of identity and power within an established student–educator relationship. The first relates to the use of a reflexive dialogic 'co-coaching' activity as part of the Executive MBA's leadership module, whilst the second draws on the experience of delivering an online Leadership 'mini-module' to prospective Executive MBA students as part of a school-wide distance learning initiative.

REFLEXIVE PEDAGOGY

Reflexivity has been increasingly recognized as fundamental in enabling learning to take place through the surfacing of our own implicit knowing. Key to reflexivity is its inherent recursiveness in 'translat[ing] something from being used for thinking to being that which we think about' (Hibbert, 2013: 805). That is, it is a process whereby we put our taken-for-granted norms and assumptions under the spotlight and examine them as a source of critical reflection and learning. What occurs in reflexivity is not the 'outside in' (Baker and Kolb, 1993) reflective learning of 'theoretical insights or major intellectual breakthroughs, but moments in which we … "understand something that is already in plain view" (Wittgenstein, 1953: 89) and the difference this new understanding may make to our lives' (Cunliffe, 2002: 57). It is the act of processing past experience such as to generate new understanding and hence new patterns of behaviour.

Reflexivity is not always an easy or pleasurable experience, however. Processes of reflexivity can bring about disturbance and disruption, either to the individual or to the relationships of which they are a part, and may thus be the subject of resistance to limit this disturbance. Such resistance may encompass both the call to explore new identities that is the 'content' of the reflexive process and the handing over of power and agency to the learner which is integral to the process itself. The discomfort encountered is the 'disruptive' (Hibbert et al., 2010: 55) forerunner to the 'clearing out' or 'unlearning' (Antonacopoulou, 2009: 422) of existing knowledge and the questioning of assumptions and perceptions to make room for new insights. Students inhabit a 'liminal space or state of between-ness' (Hawkins and Edwards, 2015: 24) as they transition from one identity to another during the reflexive learning process. The disruption and discomfort experienced by students has been the focus of a growing body of academic writing. That a similar discomfort and requirement to transition from one identity to another may be experienced by us, the designers and educators, is less well documented. The personal case studies which follow are an attempt to address this issue by exploring the disruptive impact associated with a shift in the taken-for-granted identity of teacher-as-expert and the altered power dynamics which result from the adoption of a reflexive pedagogy.

IDENTITY AND 'IDENTITY UNDOING' IN THE CONTEXT OF LEADERSHIP EDUCATION

Identity is a well-established construct in the field of leadership studies and particularly in critical leadership studies (Carroll and Levy, 2010; Ford, 2006), and is also gaining prominence in critically orientated leadership development work (Carroll and Levy, 2010; Gagnon, 2008; Gagnon and Collinson, 2014). Studies in this field tend to build on Alvesson and Wilmott's (2002) 'identity work' framework revolving around an interplay between self-identity, identity work and identity regulation. Within this framework, 'identity' refers to the self as reflexively understood, 'identity work' captures the ongoing struggle to achieve or accomplish self-identity, and 'identity regulation' relates to the adoption of discourses and practices that privileges certain identities above others. Particularly as applied within the critical management/leadership tradition, this framework strongly locates identity within broader organizational themes of power, control and discipline where the subject's sense of self is constantly in tension between a variety of influences and forces at play within an organization. As a result, 'people are continuously engaged in forming, repairing, maintaining, strengthening or revising the constructions that are productive of a precarious sense of coherence and distinctiveness' (Alvesson and Wilmott 2002: 626).

That leadership development requires participants to engage in both identity work and identity regulation is perhaps unsurprising, and reasonably well documented in the literature (Carden and Callahan, 2007; Carroll and Levy, 2010; Gagnon, 2008; Gagnon and Collinson, 2014). Most leadership learning interventions involve at least some presentation of theories and models aimed at shaping the direction of 'desired' learning, and either implicitly or explicitly offer judgements about what counts (or not) as 'good' leadership. As such, leadership learning interventions can be regarded as an 'identity workspace' (Petriglieri, 2011) in which participants process not just the information being presented but also their reflexive response to that information. That educators and facilitators also engage in identity work in the same identity workspace is, however, a very recent field of scholarly interest, although it seems likely that practitioners have long been aware of its occurrence.

Nicholson and Carroll's (2013) work on identity undoing provides a powerful conceptualization of the identity struggle experienced by participants undertaking a leadership development programme. They theorize that beyond the traditional foci of identity formation, construction and regulation, there is a previously overlooked phenomenon of loss, fragmentation and disruption which they term 'identity undoing'. This is presented as a range of processes from reflexive critique (shaking up) to unlearning (letting go), to episodes of 'stuckness' and seeming immobility (floundering), accompanied by a similar range of emotional responses from delight to pain. While the focus of Nicholson and Carroll's (2013) work is primarily on the participants of the programme, they do touch briefly on the parallel experiences of the facilitators/educators. In the early interaction data from their study, facilitators are generally analysed as hierarchical figures with the institutional and pedagogical power to inflict, invite, sanction and moderate identity undoing. In the subsequent analysis of facilitator interviews, however, facilitators reveal their own struggles with identity and their accompanying anxiety and discomfort with holding authority in processes which depend on participants feeling agentic. The insight that 'facilitators too can be subjects and objects in identity processes and that understanding one's impact as facilitator could be assisted by seeing oneself as an object' (Nicholson and Carroll, 2013: 1241) seems both prescient and profound.

POWER AND RESISTANCE AS SHAPERS OF EDUCATOR IDENTITY

Observations on the power asymmetry between teachers and learners in executive education – particularly accredited programmes involving assessed work – have a long history. As long ago as 1999, Reynolds made '[t]he case for rehabilitating less hierarchical approaches to learning' in order to 'achieve a coherence of values between educational content and process' and 'avoid the contradiction between a critically based curriculum and a methodology that reinforces authoritarian relationships' (Reynolds, 1999: 550). Nicholson and Carroll's (2013: 1242) observation of the 'power and authority implicit in facilitators' expertise' and the evident asymmetry felt by their research participants/students even in a more facilitative, less didactic learning environment suggests that things have not changed significantly in the intervening years. Course directors and module leaders continue to personify the 'judgmental gaze' (Ford et al., 2010: s75) of those with the power to award or not award valued outcomes, with this perceived role being internalized by students through the theories presented, the assessment of outputs and the adoption of prescribed managerial discourses. Thus, leadership development programmes – and particularly high-profile, assessed programmes such as Executive MBAs – remain 'technologies of power' (Nicholson and Carroll, 2013: 1227) that shape and dictate the ways in which participants seek to craft and reinvent themselves.

There is, however, an inherent tension in the delivery of such technologies of power, which can result in displays of resistance from students. It is in the nature of the identity shaping intrinsic to leadership development (Gagnon and Collinson, 2014) that participants' identities may not develop in the direction of the 'idealized' (2014: 9) leader identities that are detailed, emphasized and even imposed on participants by the educator. Instead, participants may seek out 'opportunities for oppositional discursive practices and resistance' (2014: 4) and choose to enact alternative and oppositional identities to the idealized ones on offer. Carroll and Nicholson (2014) likewise argue that leadership development spaces are 'steeped in power, resistance and struggle' but go on to recognize that these forces 'entangle facilitators and participants alike' (2014: 1414). They propose a more generative and fluid understanding of 'resisting work' which they argue needs to be understood as a set of relational and situated practices intimately engaged with the exercise of power and leadership. They go on to explore how the facilitators/educators 'consent, cope and resist' (Kondo, 1990: 224) with and in relation to participants, but don't explicitly explore the tensions and struggles with power and identity as experienced by the educator. Elsewhere, it is acknowledged that the 'social, psychological and cultural attributes of the training room' and the performative nature of their 'ritual, scripted and ceremonial behaviours' (Ford and Harding, 2007: 481) significantly inhibit the educator's ability to radically alter or reduce power imbalances in executive education programmes. This is particularly the case where assessment is a central aspect of the learning context.

PERSONAL CASE STUDIES

As a vehicle for reflecting on the 'tensions and struggles with power and identity' experienced by educators adopting a reflexive pedagogy, I want to briefly set out two autoethnographic examples, both of which have been written about in more detail elsewhere (e.g., Iszatt-White et al., 2017).

Example 1: Introducing 'Co-constructed Coaching' as a Leadership Learning Intervention

Drawing on past experience of both co-constructed autoethnography and executive coaching, a colleague and I developed and piloted the idea of 'co-constructed coaching' as a leadership learning intervention for Executive MBA participants. Co-constructed autoethnography (CCAE) has been shown to be useful in leadership learning research (Kempster and Stewart, 2010) and aligns well with the notion of reflexive learning. In the field of leadership development, executive coaching is already popular as a standalone intervention and as a central mechanism within organizational programmes (e.g., Jarvis et al., 2006; Lee, 2003; West and Milan, 2001). In juxtaposing CCAE with executive coaching, we aimed to provide a deeper, more theoretical grounding for coaching conversations within the framework of an accredited leadership development module by encouraging strong engagement in reflexive dialogue within the leadership learning process.

CCAE requires the researcher – the situated individual – to write about themselves and then be open to interrogation by their co-author, creating a co-constructed narrative 'sandwich' (Ellis, 2004: 198). Through this 'dynamic process' (Saldana, 2003: 224) the situated individual researcher becomes highly reflexive of their social experiences – the 'tasty filling' – while the co-researcher probes the emerging narrative, often with related theory, to generate interpretive observations of social practice – the 'bread' (Kempster and Stewart, 2010: 210). Through the infusion of theory and reflexivity associated with CCAE into the executive coaching process the participant derives a critical perspective of their situated practice – rather than more circumscribed performance outcomes common in coaching – whilst the researcher gains deeper understanding of the situated practice under investigation.

The designed intervention that resulted was to place the students/managers into pairs to become co-coaching discussants. The focus of the pair was to help each other examine past influences on their own leadership development and practice and/or current leadership challenges in their working contexts. Each discussant was to interrogate their partner's challenge drawing on relevant theory to enable a critically reflective dialogue. It is inherent in both the 'auto' – that is, self – focus of the process and the co-coaching structure in which the reflexive dialogue is embedded that the educator/facilitator is essentially written out of the process after the initial briefing. When the intervention was piloted, both facilitators expressed a sense of disappointment that the theory that had been presented in the module seemed to operate as a shared language for naming or articulating ideas about leadership practice and experience, but didn't seem to be the driving force behind participant learning. Given that both of us were used to being 'experts' in relation to theory, we shared a sense of identity loss when this potential input was not really valued or required as an ongoing part of the reflexive dialogues which developed. Our 'demotion' from 'sage on the stage' to 'guide on the side' (King, 1993) resulted in a sense of insecurity about what our contribution is or should be in this context and the sense that it may relate to facilitation skills rather than content knowledge. In terms of power dynamics, we had anticipated the empowerment the intervention offered to students – clearly a positive thing – but hadn't really thought about the potential for our 'authority' as experts to become less influential or that their increase in power necessitated that ours decrease. Even when students invited us back into their conversations, the role we were asked to play was that of peer discussant rather than teacher.

Example 2: Introducing Blended Learning in Executive Education

The second example arose not from an explicit intention to adopt a reflexive pedagogy but as a corollary to the aim of introducing blended learning within the MBA programme and more broadly within the school. As part of this wider distance learning initiative, I developed and piloted a five-credit 'mini-module' on authentic leadership (Iszatt-White and Kempster, 2019; Walumbwa et al., 2008) to be utilized as preparatory work for participants joining the Executive MBA programme both in the United Kingdom and elsewhere. The topic area was one with which I was already familiar, having taught it in a face-to-face format and given that it formed a key component within my research profile. The 'content' for the module itself consisted of a variety of media inputs, including PowerPoint slides with an educator voiceover, and a number of YouTube clips and TED talks. This involved significant adaptation of existing teaching resources as well as a much larger component of multimedia resources than I would have used in classroom teaching. In addition, networked activities utilized discussion fora, wikis and online self-tests, with the aim of enhancing engagement and keeping participants connected to me and to each other.

As the educator I had no control over how many of the inputs were viewed by the learners, in what order and with what degree of attention; neither could I have a reliable grasp of what the learners had taken from their viewing of the material and whether this was what I as the educator hoped or intended in making it available. As the online dialogue developed, it also became clear that there was a decreasing need for me to prompt reflection and critical thinking as participants took responsibility for this activity amongst themselves. Thus, in many respects both the topic content and the learning process were out of my control, with learners choosing when, whether and how to engage with the activities on offer. Clearly this is very different from a structured, face-to-face input incorporating direct question-and-answer between the parties involved. This loss of control, and the potential for, say, a carefully crafted PowerPoint presentation to be ditched in favour of – or found less engaging or provocative than – a YouTube clip, was experienced as a source of 'identity undoing' for someone used to having their expertise taken as a valued input to the learning process. Certainly, it was initially an uncomfortable experience for me. The need to explore other roles to play and other contributions to make which I experienced – in particular, ways to develop and utilize online facilitation skills to support the students' own learning processes – felt like a significant change in role and identity that other educators not already familiar with networked learning approaches can be expected to share.

UNPACKING THE CASE STUDIES

The case studies speak to the complex, powerful and largely unforeseen disruption I experienced as a critically informed, committed and experienced educator choosing to adopt a reflexive pedagogy. In unpacking the case studies, I want to not only explore the challenges of such shifts and demands on educators, but also suggest strategies for building capacity and developing tangible practices that will help others negotiate this 'pedagogy of the unknowable'. Both these experiences raised interesting issues of identity and identity work (Alvesson and Wilmott, 2002) for me as the educator. As a result of the decision to adopt a reflexive pedagogy, and through the change to the medium of delivery and engagement that had a similar effect, there is the potential for educators to experience a sense of 'identity undoing' (Nicholson and Carroll, 2013). In both instances, the shift from 'educator as expert' to 'educator as facilitator' – as the identity of 'sage on the stage' gives way to 'guide on the side' (King, 1993) – was an uncomfortable experience as I felt 'dislodged from an implicit position of mastery' (Hibbert and Cunliffe, 2015: 186). As noted above, both reflexive pedagogy and networked learning have the potential to be what Ellsworth (1989, cited in Hibbert and Cunliffe, 2015: 186) calls 'a pedagogy of the unknowable in which we can never fully know ourselves, our experience, others, nor the impact of our actions'. In both instances, unknowability arises from the handing over of control for both direction and content to the learner – the change of emphasis from teaching to learning – and the consequent need for the educator to carve out a sense of purpose and ability to make a contribution in the spaces between what students themselves do.

Power is broadly understood as a complex construct with which to work. An educator's power consists not just in 'power over' students but also as 'power to' achieve educational aims (Huxham and Vangen, 2005) in collaboration with them. This distinction between 'power over' and 'power to' was slow to dawn on me in facilitating the co-constructed coaching learning intervention. I initially experienced both powers as bundled together and didn't consider that I could give up 'power over' (experienced as 'sage on the stage') but keep 'power to' (which seems more compatible with 'guide on the side'). The role of skilled facilitator that I eventually discovered feels like a comfortable example of claiming and holding the 'power to' support, stretch and make visible students' learning without relying on 'an implicit position of mastery' (Hibbert and Cunliffe, 2015: 186) that is the essence of 'power over'. 'Power to' needs to be understood as pedagogically sophisticated; as in the power to frame questions, disrupt assumptions, prompt links to other experiences, draw in other stakeholder perspectives, tease out affective, embodied and aesthetic responses, and model being vulnerable and in doubt. Eventually recognizing that power exists in the space between educator knowledge and student experience in which learning is co-constructed (rather than viewing knowledge as a source of power over students) enabled me to feel less bereft of value to students and the enterprise of reflexive learning.

The entangled nature of different kinds of power points to more fundamental dynamics at a systems and institutional level which can lock in a number of dominant identities at educator and student level. Both educators and students operate in a space which is far from power-neutral and has already carved out lines of institutional, pedagogical and relational power. Malkki and Lindblom-Ylanne (2012) highlight barriers to changing pedagogy in higher education reflected in a desire to be seen as a professional within the student–educator relationship. Hedberg (2009) argues that these power relations are part of what the students are (quite literally) buying into when they enrol on a programme: they have an expectation that they will be 'taught by experts' and may feel short-changed if that doesn't occur. Nicholson and Carroll (2013: 1228) draw on the notion of normalizing judgment from Foucault's (1988) technologies of power to make sense of this set of expectations where 'rules and norms [are] to be followed, respected and preferred, as they represent the "optimum towards which one must move" (Foucault 1977: 183)'. This would suggest that educators need to understand attempts to adopt reflexive pedagogies as a set of see-sawing episodes which move fluidly, if uncomfortably, between traditional and disruptive learning relationships and activities. As a result, educators wishing to move beyond traditional norms will need to develop the ability to map, track and name the experience of power dynamics with their students to build both a capacity and intentionality around shared consenting, coping and resisting.

The educator relationship with theory appears to be at the heart of their sense of identity undoing. Executive MBA participants described themselves as 'dipping into theory' rather than 'driving with theory', with theory thus being demoted from a source of pedagogical power to a more superficial encounter. Set within institutional (higher education) and programme (Executive MBA) norms, the emphasis on theory has historically been largely technical (Miettinen and Virkkunen, 2005) such that it appears to hold value as what it is (rather than what it enables), comes preformed and requiring acquisition rather than adaption, and is the end-game rather than one of a number of ingredients for meaningful learning. In order to achieve new and novel practices, theory needs to be moved from a technical to an epistemic (Miettinen and Virkkunen, 2005) frame where it is seen as relatively undefined, open-ended, historically situated and still experimental, and where learning can occur through a process of bricolage, characterized as 'improvising, imagining, playing and searching for new cultural resources' (Miettinen and Virkkunen, 2005: 451). This distinction between technical and epistemic knowledge and theory helps us to understand that the problem is not theory itself, but how that theory is held and used. This is an identity issue, and the movement from using it in technical to epistemic ways can be viewed as an identity undoing question.

Identity undoing invites us to view the potential loss associated with theory in ways that go beyond simple notions of unlearning and relearning. The distance between being 'masters of theory' and 'a spare part' (a distance I was aware of in both the above case studies) is, after all, a potentially large one. The original work on identity undoing (Nicholson and Carroll, 2013) implied, but didn't specifically explore, that identity undoing might be quite different for educators as opposed to students. From their observational material it could be seen that while educators were committed to co-crafting a learning space with participants, there was still marked asymmetry where the educators in essence held such a space – offering guidance, structure, advice and process facilitation – while students focused on learning how to learn in such a space. In now drawing attention to identity undoing as experienced by educators in the context of a reflexive pedagogy, I would argue that there is an inherent relationality which occurs for both parties: a fluid interplay between the identities of educators and students, invoked through a process of claiming and granting (DeRue and Ashford, 2010) between the parties which allows the educator to fulfil different aspects of the learning process (e.g., supporting learning versus assessing assignments).

It is perhaps ironic that in adopting a reflexive pedagogy with students, neither case study built in space or time for reflexive dialogue between educators and students where educators could openly display their anxiety and doubt and collaboratively frame what needed to occur for the emergence of new educator roles. Thus whilst educators were holding a learning space for students, no one was holding a learning space to support the educator experiencing identity undoing. For reflexive pedagogies to disrupt traditional roles and power relations, then, it is not enough to offer new identities to students. It also requires a shared reflexive space in which educators and students don't just move in relation to each other but make that visible through artefacts, words and actions. 'Spare part', after all, is not the direct opposite of 'master of theory' and there are a wealth of identity options in-between, one of which is that of a 'good facilitator' in which identity is grounded in 'how I work' rather than 'what I know'.

Whilst identity undoing can be an uncomfortable experience, it can also be a productive one, offering opportunities for new and liberating ways of being in the learning space. This came home to me most strongly in relation to my second case study above. In starting to construct a new educator identity for myself within a networked learning space, I can reflect on a number of key takeaways from this experience. In particular, I would highlight the shift to a more student-centred approach as a result of recognizing the affordances of learning mediated by technology, and then working backwards from what I wanted to achieve for the students to understanding how networked learning would allow this to happen. Observation of other educators within the wider distance learning initiative of which my module was a part, together with colleagues who were already experienced in networked learning, allowed me to see that I could usefully go much further in handing over the shaping and leading of activities and responsibility for learning to the students. By letting go of responsibility for learning (though not accountability for module outcomes) I was able to shift my sense of self from 'leader' to 'participant' and from 'teacher' to 'fellow learner'. This shift in identity and sense of comfort with a revised role emerged from the co-coaching intervention as well, albeit at a more tentative level. For me, the overarching realization was that if as educators we can learn to be comfortable with the 'unknowability' (Ellsworth, 1989) of this educator role, then we have the potential to develop a less personally secure but more dynamic and engaging educator practice.

IMPLICATIONS FOR THEORY AND PRACTICE

The parallels between Hanson's (2009) study of the impact of e-learning on academic identity and Iszatt-White et al.'s (2017) exploration of identity undoing arising from the adoption of a reflexive pedagogy are instructive in suggesting recurrent issues facing educators in modern higher education. Drawing out these parallels is likewise suggestive of a number of areas in which educators can be expected to need training and support if they are to remain responsive to student needs. Key amongst such areas are issues relating to identity and power, as outlined below.

Power Relations

Particularly in the early days of adoption, a shift to both reflexive pedagogy and networked learning approaches can highlight an academic's lack of skill with new 'technologies' (where this includes theory as a 'technology of power') when compared with their students, thus breaching their 'protective cocoon' (Giddens, 1991: 3) of being an expert knowledge provider. They can thus come to feel 'de-skilled' and 're-positioned' (Wells, 2005: 17) in ways which threaten their academic identity and shift the balance of power between teacher and student. The desire to engage students in learning interventions which disrupt the power asymmetries and hierarchical dependencies of more traditional educator–student relationships can thus in practice have the effect of highlighting those very asymmetries and dependencies (Iszatt-White et al., 2017). And as Hanson (2009: 557) notes, 'the narrative of this lived reality is frequently ignored by the reflexive pedagogy and e-learning literatures written largely by enthusiastic innovators and early adopters'.

Sources of Knowledge

The growth in electronic sources of knowledge can be felt by academics as resulting in a potential downgrading (Becher and Trowler, 2001) of more traditional academic sources. Networked learning thus threatens academic identity by removing or diminishing the hard-won, sometimes deliberately abstruse intellectual capital on which academics have built their sense of self, and repackaging their knowledge and expertise in freely available, easily consumable, bite-sized chunks (Hanson, 2009). It can be accompanied by the need to 'accede the position as knowledge gatekeeper' (Hanson, 2009: 561) and require educators to 'reconsider the meaning of being an expert' (Conceicao, 2006: 44). In relation to reflexive pedagogy, Iszatt-White et al. (2017) usefully recast this 'downgrading' in power terms as the difference between viewing knowledge as a source of power over students versus seeing it as power to create a space where educator knowledge and student experience come together as a site of learning co-construction. They go on to suggest that academics able to view changes in the educational paradigm in this way are likely to feel 'less bereft of value to students and the enterprise of learning' (Iszatt-White et al., 2017: 591).

New Identities

Along with membership of a discipline, interaction with students has traditionally constituted an important influence on academic identities such that 'anything that threatens the intimacy of that interaction also threatens identity' (Hanson, 2009: 556). The 'loss of presence' occasioned by the shift to networked learning – or to the role of 'guide on the side' – and the need to develop a 'new disembodied identity' (Hanson, 2009: 561) which thus arises require the adoption of new roles by academics. When students become 'discoverers and constructors of knowledge' (Hartman et al., 2007, cited in Hanson, 2009: 556) then academics must become 'co-discoverers' and 'co-constructors' and accept the seeming loss of expert status which this implies. Their expertise comes to rest on facilitation and engagement skills rather than on the delivery of content per se. Iszatt-White et al. (2017: 593) draw attention to the fact that such educational paradigms require both students and educators to 'undo significant aspects of learning and expert identities but, unlike for students, there is no-one to hold and support the identity undoing of educators unless they learn to do so better themselves and/or seek support and input from students'.

Supporting the Development of New Educator Identities

The issues raised above clearly suggest the need for more research into how best to support traditional teachers in making the identity shift to adopting reflexive pedagogies and/or being online educators, and the development of effective sources of continuing professional development in this area. The importance of professional development activities aimed at supporting conceptual change as a necessary precursor to the successful design of digital learning and adoption of educational technologies has been noted by Englund et al. (2017), although writers on reflexive learning have been slower to acknowledge this need. The case studies above suggest that there is a need for academic institutions to ensure the existence of a 'holding environment' (Heifetz and Laurie, 1999: 127) where academics and students alike can 'process and mutually adjust to the changed identities and roles implicit in' (Iszatt-White et al., 2017: 594) changed educational paradigms. Similarly, Hanson (2009: 562) drew attention to the threat to 'ontological security' (Taylor, 1997) arising from the need to learn new skills and practices in making these transitions, and the need for a 'refuge ... [in which to] rehearse new practices before using them with students'.

CONCLUSION

The potential for various forms of reflexive learning to play a significant role in enhancing leadership education has long been mooted (Cunliffe, 2002, 2008), with regular calls for their more frequent adoption. Based on my experiences above, I would agree that the potential exists, but would highlight that such calls do not speak to the issues of educator power and identity which I encountered. It is important to recognize the potential for significant discomfort in the student–educator relationship and to support educators in making the necessary identity transitions required to bring them to a new place of self-worth. The need to 'give up' power and 'let go' of firmly held and valued identities suggests that developing the flexibility to move from 'power over' to 'power to' is likely to be a significant component in educators' ability to reposition themselves and their role. At the same time, they will need to commit to their own reflexivity, both between themselves and with their students, in the moment, in order to surface the educator-with-student reflexive dialogue and to produce the 'holding environment' required to process and mutually adjust to the changed identities and roles implicit in a reflexive context. This in turn will be important in developing the skills and the confidence for educators and students to collectively experiment with a greater identity and pedagogical repertoire around the value and use of theory, such as to engage successfully with it as an 'epistemic frame' upon which to build affordances for mutual learning.

REFERENCES

Alvesson, M. and Willmott, H. (2002) Identity regulation as organizational control: producing the appropriate individual. *Journal of Management Studies*, 39(5): 619–644.

Antonacopoulou, E.P. (2009) Impact and scholarship: unlearning and practicing to co-create actionable knowledge. *Management Learning*, 40(4): 421–430.

Baker, A. and Kolb, D.A. (1993) Diversity, learning and good conversation. In R.R. Sims and R.F. Dennehy (eds), *Diversity and Differences in Organisations*. Westport, CT: Quorum Books, pp. 17–33.

Becher, T. and Trowler, P. (2001) *Academic Tribes and Territories: Intellectual Enquiry and the Cultures of Disciplines*, 2nd edn. Buckingham: SRHE and Open University Press.

Carden, L.L. and Callahan, J.L. (2007) Creating leaders or loyalists? Conflicting identities in a leadership development programme. *Human Resource Development International*, 10: 169–186.

Carroll, B. and Levy, L. (2010) Leadership development as identity construction. *Management Communication Quarterly*, 24: 211–231.

Carroll, B. and Nicholson, H. (2014) Resistance and struggle in leadership development. *Human Relations*, 67(11): 1413–1436.

Conceicao, S.C.O. (2006) Faculty lived experiences in the online environment. *Adult Education Quarterly*, 57(1): 26–45.

Cunliffe, A. (2002) Reflexive dialogical practice in management learning. *Management Learning*, 33(1): 35–61.

Cunliffe, Ann L. (2008) Orientations to social constructionism: relationally responsive social constructionism and its implications for knowledge and learning. *Management Learning*, 39(2): 123–139.

DeRue, D.S. and Ashford, S.J. (2010) Who will lead and who will follow? A social process of leadership identity construction in organizations. *Academy of Management Review*, 35: 627–647.

Ellis, C. (2004) *The Ethnographic I: A Methodological Novel about Autoethnography*. Walnut Creek, CA: Alt Mira.

Ellsworth, E. (1989) Why doesn't this feel empowering? Working through the repressive myths of critical pedagogy. *Harvard Educational Review*, 59: 297–324.

Englund, C., Olofsson, A.D. and Price, L. (2017) Teaching with technology in higher education: understanding conceptual change and development in practice. *Higher Education Research and Development*, 36(1): 73–87.

Ford, J. (2006) Discourses of leadership: gender, identity and contradiction in a UK public sector. *Leadership*, 2(1): 77–99.

Ford, J. and Harding, N. (2007) Move over management: we are all leaders now. *Management Learning*, 38(5): 475–493.

Ford, J., Harding, N. and Learmonth, M. (2010) Who is it that would make business schools more critical? Critical reflections on critical management studies. *British Journal of Management*, 21: s71–s81.

Foucault, M. (1977) *Discipline and Punishment*. London: Allen Lane.

Foucault, M. (1988) Technologies of the self. In L.H. Martin, G. Gutman and P.H. Hutton (eds), *Technologies of the Self: A Seminar with Michael Foucault*. London: Tavistock, pp. 16-49.

Gagnon, S. (2008) Compelling identity: selves and insecurities in global, corporate management development. *Management Learning*, 39: 375–391.

Gagnon, S. and Collinson, D. (2014) Rethinking global leadership development programmes: the interrelated significance of power, context and identity. *Organization Studies*, 35(5): 645–667.

Giddens, A. (1991) *Modernity and Self-Identity*. Cambridge, MA: Polity Press.

Hanson, J. (2009) Displaced but not replaced: the impact of e-learning on academic identities in higher education. *Teaching in Higher Education*, 14(5): 553–564.

Hartman, J.L., Dziuban, C. and Brophy-Ellison, J. (2007) Faculty 2.0. *EDuCAusE Review*, 42(5): 62–77. http://www.educause.edu/EDuCAusE+Review/EduCAusEReviewMagazine Volume42/Faculty20/161909 (accessed 12 August 2009).

Hawkins, B. and Edwards, G. (2015) Managing the monsters of doubt: liminality, threshold concepts and leadership learning. *Management Learning*, 46(1): 24–43.

Hedberg, P. (2009) Learning through reflective classroom practice: applications to educate the reflective manager. *Journal of Management Education*, 33: 10–36.

Heifetz, R.A. and Laurie, D.L. (1999) The work of leadership. *Harvard Business Review*, January–February: 124–134.

Hibbert, P. (2013) Approaching reflexivity through reflection: issues for critical management education. *Journal of Management Education*, 37(6): 803–827.

Hibbert, P., Coupland, C. and MacIntosh, R. (2010) Reflexivity is more than reflection: recursion and relationality in organizational research processes. *Qualitative Research in Organizations and Management*, 5: 47–62.

Hibbert, P. and Cunliffe, A. (2015) Responsible management: engaging moral reflexive practice through threshold concepts. *Journal of Business Ethics*, 127: 177–188.

Huxham, C. and Vangen, S. (2005) *Managing to Collaborate*. London: Routledge.

Iszatt-White, M. and Kempster, S. (2019) Authentic leadership: getting back to the roots of the 'root construct'? *International Journal of Management Reviews*, 21(3): 356–369.

Iszatt-White, M., Kempster, K. and Carroll, B. (2017) An educators' perspective on reflexive pedagogy: identity undoing and issues of power. *Management Learning*, 48(5): 582–596.

Jarvis, J., Lane, D.A. and Fillery-Travis, A. (2006) *The Case for Coaching: Making Evidence-Based Decisions on Coaching*. London: CIPD.

Kempster, S. and Stewart, J. (2010) Becoming a leader: a co-produced autoethnographic exploration of situated learning of leadership practice. *Management Learning*, 41(2): 205–219.

King, Alison (1993) From sage on the stage to guide on the side. *College Teaching*, 41(1): 30–35.

Kondo D.K. (1990) *Crafting Selves: Power, Gender, and Discourses of Identity in a Japanese Workplace*. Chicago, IL: University of Chicago Press.

Lee, G. (2003) *Leadership Coaching: From Personal Insight to Organisational Performance*. London: CIPD.

Malkki, K. and Lindblom-Ylanne, S. (2012) From reflection to action? Barriers and bridges between higher education teachers' thoughts and actions. *Studies in Higher Education*, 37: 33–50.

Miettinen R. and Virkkunen, J. (2005) Epistemic objects, artefacts and organizational change. *Organization*, 12(3): 437–456.

Nicholson, H. and Carroll, B. (2013) Identity undoing and power relations in leadership development. *Human Relations*, 66(9): 1225–1248.

Petriglieri, J.L. (2011) Under threat: responses to and consequences from threats to individuals' identities. *Academy of Management Review*, 36(4): 641–662

Reynolds, M. (1999) Critical reflections and management education: rehabilitating less hierarchical approaches. *Journal of Management Education*, 23(5): 537–553.

Saldana, J. (2003) Dramatising data: a primer. *Qualitative Inquiry*, 9(2): 218–236.

Taylor, P. (1997) Creating environments which nurture development: messages from research into academics' experiences. *International Journal for Academic Development*, 2(2): 42–49.

Walumbwa, F.O., Avolio, B.J., Gardner, W.L., Wernsing, T.S. and Peterson, S.J. (2008) Authentic leadership: development and validation of a theory-based measure. *Journal of Management*, 34(1): 89–126.

Wells, M. (2005) Academics' experience of change. Paper presented at British Educational Research Association Annual Conference, 14–17 September, University of Glamorgan, UK. http://www.leeds.ac.uk/educol/documents/143818.doc (accessed 12 August 2009).

West, L. and Milan, M. (2001) *The Reflecting Glass: Professional Coaching for Leadership Development.* Basingstoke: Palgrave.
Wittgenstein, L. (1953) *Philosophical Investigations.* Oxford: Blackwell.

7. Team-based learning in the business school classroom: adaptation versus fidelity

Barbara Larson and Michael Sweet

Over the past 40 years, team-based learning (TBL) has become a popular framework for enhancing student engagement in many types of classroom. Though the method has its roots in management education, much of the development of TBL in the last 20 years has occurred in the medical and healthcare fields, expanding more recently to many different disciplines. Instructors describe TBL as an approach which solves many of the problems of traditional group work, increasing student engagement, achievement and teamwork skill development.

An interesting debate that has arisen as more instructors adopt TBL is the question of whether, how and the extent to which one should adapt the method to fit the needs of individual instructors and individual classrooms. There are advocates – and arguments – for both sides. On one hand, adapting TBL (or any pedagogical framework) risks the loss of its benefits to students. On the other hand, adaptation can make some of the benefits of TBL attainable in situations where the method otherwise would go completely untapped. The exigencies of the COVID-19 pandemic beginning in early 2020 have raised the question of adaptation to the forefront, as universities were forced to quickly adapt to a dramatically changed set of pedagogical constraints.

In this chapter, we explore the tension between adaptation and orthodoxy for team-based learning, with a focus on the business school context. We briefly summarize the traditional TBL framework for instructors new to the method. We then outline a variety of adaptations of the method that we identified both in the teaching-and-learning literature, and via interviews that we conducted with faculty who are experienced TBL users. We review the potential benefits of and reasons for adaptation that are most often mentioned in both research and our interviews. We then turn to the concept of treatment fidelity (Hulleman & Cordray 2009) as a basis for our discussion of the risks of adaptation, and we illustrate the risks of adaptation with a short case study.

Finally, we suggest a set of essential factors that instructors looking to adapt TBL should be careful to retain. While we do not claim that retaining these factors alone can achieve the same benefits as a robust, unadapted in-classroom version of TBL, we do believe that attention to these factors can help instructors optimize adaptations that they choose to make.

WHAT IS TEAM-BASED LEARNING? A BRIEF HISTORY AND OUTLINE OF THE FRAMEWORK

Team-based learning (TBL) originated in the late 1970s in the classroom of management professor Larry Michaelsen at the University of Oklahoma. Michaelsen learned that his class size was going to increase from 40 to 120, but did not want to give up on highly engaged small-group, case study discussions (Sweet & Michaelsen 2012). In order to retain the benefits

95

of smaller-group discussions in a large class, he began experimenting with the use of in-class teams, gradually developing what is now a widely accepted framework for TBL (Michaelsen et al. 1989; Watson et al. 1991; Michaelsen & Black 1994).

TBL made gradual inroads into higher education but took on greater momentum with a 2000 United States (US) federal grant which funded experimentation with TBL in courses at ten US medical schools (Searle et al. 2003). Collaboration and communication among grant participants resulted in the formation of the Team-Based Learning Collaborative (TBLC), a non-profit organization devoted to cultivating and sharing TBL practices (www .teambasedlearning.org). For historical reasons, the Collaborative had a de facto focus on the allied health professions, but in 2009 made an intentional push toward interdisciplinarity. Today, the TBLC has hundreds of members from around the world, a consultant training program, and an online resource bank. Many continue to implement, investigate and publish about TBL both inside and outside the TBLC.

We present here an abbreviated description of the TBL method, as many other resources are already available with detailed instructions for implementing the framework.[1] It can be helpful to start with a description of what TBL is not. Team-based teaching (in which multiple instructors co-teach a single class) is not TBL. The formation of student teams to complete projects outside of class is not TBL. The use of ad hoc teams in class from time to time, for discussion or problem-solving, is also not TBL.

Team-based learning uses permanent (for the duration of a course), instructor-formed teams in class on a nearly constant basis, to drive student engagement, accountability and learning. The key steps of a TBL-taught course include the following (see Figure 7.1 for illustration of these steps).

Team-Based Learning Sequence
Repeated for each major instructional unit

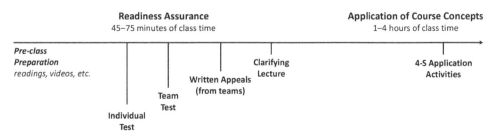

Source: Adapted from Michaelsen and Sweet (2011).

Figure 7.1   Team-based learning sequence

Fundamental content acquisition occurs before, rather than during, the class session.

Students study content in advance of class, which could include readings, online content modules, or even worked examples and problems. This eliminates the need for extensive lecturing by the instructor in class; indeed, one of the key objectives of TBL is to eliminate one-way, instructor-to-student transfer of information.

In class, students are strategically organized by the instructor into teams (of typically 5–7 members). These teams persist through the duration of the course, enabling students to become comfortable with and develop deeper working relationships with their teammates. These teams are the core working unit in the classroom. They are considerably different from much unstructured in-class group work ("get together in pairs and discuss"), and also different from much project-based teamwork, in which the team rarely or never works together as part of the class session.

A hallmark of TBL is the "readiness assurance process" (RAP) that typically begins an instructional unit. The RAP's name comes from its purpose of assuring students are ready to move forward to higher-level application activities once they have completed the relevant instructional unit. The RAP is organized around two sequential readiness assurance tests (RATs), which are typically short multiple-choice (or other objectively evaluated) assessments based on the assigned pre-class preparation content. The RATs are given in two rounds: first, students complete an individual RAT (iRAT), and immediately thereafter, teams take the same test together (tRAT) with the members of each team coming to consensus on their team answers. This second round allows students to compare their understanding of concepts and requires students to advocate their views and answer questions from other students, thus deepening learning.

After the two RAT rounds, student teams discuss any incorrect answers and decide whether they wish to submit a written appeal to the instructor. Appeals must contain a well-reasoned argument for why the team deserve credit for their answer, can only be submitted by an entire team, not by an individual, and can be made due either immediately after the RAT, or by end of the class period, or by end of the day. This step forces students to critically rethink their answers, further developing their understanding of the concepts being taught.

Typically, after the RAT rounds and submission of any appeals, the instructor gives oral feedback to the class, which is tightly focused on the content that tRAT scores indicate has proven challenging to students. This feedback is intended to support students in the areas in which they have struggled, not to serve as a general lecture or other one-way transfer of conceptual material.

The TBL teaching cycle ends with the application of concepts in class-based activities. This step actually consumes the most time, highlighting the emphasis of TBL on application, rather than simply acquisition, of knowledge. Suitable application activities should follow what is commonly known as the "4S" criteria:

- Significance – application activities should demonstrate the taught content's relevance and applicability to real-world problems.
- Specific choice – activities should require student teams to use taught concepts to come to a specific choice, whether a recommended action, specific numerical answer, or otherwise.
- Same problem – in order to leverage the value of simultaneous disclosure (and subsequent comparison) of answers, the same activity or problem should be given to all teams.
- Simultaneous reporting of answers – teams report answers at the same time, whenever possible, to maximize the possible variety of answers, to engage student interest in the answers of others, and to facilitate immediate comparison and discussion of answers.

Indeed, the 4S approach is largely reflected in the other steps of the TBL method as well, including the iRAT and tRAT, in which students – both individually and as a group – are asked to make specific choices relating to the same problem in a simultaneous fashion.

The last component of the TBL method is peer evaluation among team members, which typically occurs more than once across the term, and contributes to students' final grades in the course, thus further establishing accountability during the term. TBL best practices related to peer evaluation include reviewing peer evaluation questions at the beginning of term, so that students are aware of expectations, and conducting a mid-term formative peer assessment (before the summative end-of-term assessment).

RESEARCH ON TBL AND STUDENT OUTCOMES

Team-based learning has received considerable attention over the last two decades from teaching-and-learning researchers, who have documented generally positive outcomes from the method. A recent meta-analysis of research on TBL found a moderately positive effect on academic outcomes (Swanson et al. 2019), with lower-performing students typically experiencing the greatest benefits in knowledge acquisition (Haidet et al. 2014; Koles et al. 2010). Another meta-analysis also found positive effects overall, but noted that there is a wide range of possible outcomes across implementations of the method (Liu & Beaujean 2017).

Individual research studies have identified benefits related to knowledge acquisition (e.g., Rezende et al. 2019; Vaughn et al. 2017), academic performance (e.g., Koles et al. 2010; Zgheib et al. 2010) and student engagement (e.g., Drummond 2012; Seidel & Richards 2001), as well as learning related to team development (e.g., Betta 2016; Oldland et al. 2016). A survey of college and pharmacy school faculty identified student engagement, preparation for class and achievement of course outcomes as perceived benefits of TBL. TBL appeared to these faculty to also perform more effectively than classroom lectures in supporting students' learning in all domains of Bloom's taxonomy of educational objectives (Allen et al. 2013). TBL appears to yield benefits to students across multiple geographic regions, including East Asia (Lang et al. 2019), Europe (Stepanova 2019) and the Middle East (Zgheib et al. 2010).

One area in which there is less agreement is the study of TBL with underrepresented minorities. Macke et al. (2019) found that Black students in the United States achieved course grades similar to those of white students, but received consistently lower peer evaluation scores, supporting earlier research suggesting that underrepresented minorities could also be penalized by the TBL peer-focused structure, especially at predominantly white institutions (Hunn 2014). However, other research suggests that TBL may help to reduce or eliminate the achievement gap experienced by underrepresented minorities in more traditional, lecture-based courses, by giving these students a built-in support network (via the in-class team) and providing a structure for participation that increases their comfort with asking questions and addressing gaps in what may be implicit knowledge to more privileged students (Hettler 2015; McNeil et al. 2019). The use of TBL in a program focused on preparing underrepresented minorities for medical school appeared to level out knowledge disparities within the group (Carrasco et al. 2019). Regardless, it is clear that TBL needs to be managed with attention to the potential for bias in peer evaluations.

Our interviews with experienced faculty anecdotally support the empirical findings, with increased student engagement – even in large classrooms – being the most commonly cited advantage of TBL. Faculty also note that TBL is a good way for students to learn team dynamics (Seltzer 2019), and that student teams have a chance to really develop, because members work continuously together in class through the semester, as opposed to sporadically meeting outside class as is common with traditional team projects (Norris 2019). TBL also teaches students to become more comfortable and skilled at advocating for themselves, as a result of both team discussions and the appeals process (McElligott 2019).

Despite the wealth of TBL research in recent years, there is still a need for more rigorous empirical work. Existing research has typically relied on convenient sampling of students with no random assignment of treatment, and non-standardized measures of outcomes, such as quiz scores and course grades (Sisk 2011; Swanson et al. 2019). Meta-analysis also finds wide variation in effects among studies; variation which is only partly explained by differences in education level and course subject across studies, and which is further complicated by the absence of completed descriptive statistics in many studies (Liu & Beaujean 2017). Clearly, opportunities remain for more robust testing of the effects of TBL.

ADAPTATIONS TO TBL: CAUSES AND BENEFITS

In some ways, team-based learning seems to lend itself to adaptation, given the number of different parts of the method. In this section, we briefly discuss four main categories of adaptation that emerged from our review of the research on TBL along with our interviews with experienced faculty. Adaptation appears to emerge as the result of contextual and institutional constraints, student needs and motivations, instructor needs and preferences, and available technologies.

Contextual or Other Institutional Constraints

Some adaptations occur as result of what Fink (2003) described as the "situational factors" necessary to consider when designing a learning experience. One commonly cited example of these constraints is available classroom layout, such as rooms with a limited number of tables, requiring non-optimal team sizes. Ironically, classrooms that are purpose-built for teamwork, if not flexibly designed, can also result in suboptimal TBL implementations (Michaelsen 2019).

Time is another constraint imposed by institutions on the learning process. Both the duration of a course term (e.g., quarter versus semester) and the duration of a class session can affect the implementation of TBL, and lead to needed adaptations. Some instructors note that they eliminate the student appeals portion of the readiness assurance process, in order to allow more time for an application exercise during the same class period.

Student Needs and Motivations

TBL innovations have also emerged to address gaps in student learning or engagement identified by instructors. One example of this type of adaptation is a novel grading method that was adopted by Carrasco et al. (2019), in which students were required to hit a certain predefined minimum iRAT score in order to share in the benefits of the tRAT score. (Students not meeting the minimum iRAT score had their iRAT score used in place of the tRAT score for that proportion of their grade.) Students under this grading regime showed improvements in overall outcomes, with more poorly performing students demonstrating increased iRAT scores (from increased advance preparation), and better-performing students demonstrating increased tRAT scores (presumably due to improved input from their team members).

Adaptations also emerge sometimes in response to student needs in relation to the course material. Some instructors have found they need to scaffold students' entry into very dense materials by providing input on particularly difficult terms or concepts before students are asked to study for and then take the RATs. For example, in his History of Buddhism classes, DuBois (2012) describes how he gives a "reading orientation" lecture to his students because some of the Sanskrit words and philosophical concepts in the sources his students read are particularly alien to a Western mind. His goal is to help students develop a roadmap of content, determining what to focus most on and how the various parts of the subject matter fit together. Dubois notes that if not given this orientation, students often focus on less important details of complex content, at the expense of core concepts. In this case, the RAT serves as more of an integrating mechanism, as students have already been oriented to content at a more descriptive level. In another example, Goedde (2020) incorporates just-in-time teaching (Novak 2011) in some of his more rigorous case-based modules, asking students to answer a small number of questions online before class begins, so that he is able to make an early assessment of their comprehension of the material and address any significant gaps in knowledge before beginning the readiness assurance process.

Both of these examples not only represent ways in which instructors may choose to scaffold students' learning, but also enable instructors to ask more complex, integrative questions as part of the RAP.

Instructor Needs and Preferences

Other adaptations emerge as a product of instructor readiness for TBL or discomfort with components of the method. One way instructor readiness for TBL can be understood is in terms of Fuller's classic "teacher concerns" developmental stage model (Fuller 1969; Fuller & Bown 1975; Rutherford & Hall 1990; Conway & Clark 2003). In Fuller's model, the things that concern teachers evolve as one gains experience: one begins by being concerned mostly about oneself ("Am I pulling it off? Do I seem like a teacher?"), then one evolves into a concern about the tasks and material ("Am I doing this as well as I could? Am I doing justice to the content?") and those with the most experience focus most on student learning ("Are they getting it? Is there something I could be do more for this student or that one?"). The shorthand for this evolution is that teacher concerns tend to move from "me" to "it" to "them." Many new instructors – or those teaching new content for the first time – may find TBL's activating, engaging effect upon students somewhat overwhelming.

Similarly, instructors may struggle if they are more accustomed to serving as the primary focus of student attention during class time, or if they have a relatively fixed expectation of how every moment of the class will be used. TBL generates highly motivated and deeply engaged students who are aware of what they don't know and can be fairly assertive in their desire for understanding. One "litmus test" question that one of us has come to use to help instructors decide whether they are ready to try TBL is this: "Imagine that you are in class, and a student asks you – in front of everyone – a legitimate, content-based question that in the moment you don't even know how you'd go about answering. How do you feel in that moment?" If the idea of such a moment excites an instructor, then they are likely ready to try TBL. If, on the other hand, the idea of a moment like that is uncomfortable, then they should perhaps take some incremental steps. Experienced TBL faculty echo the author's experience, with Balan (2020) noting that TBL "requires real mastery of content because it's a discussion. Students will come up with questions that relate, say, to content that's coming up in a few sessions – I have to be able to weave it in on the spot."

Available Technology

Certainly, technology has played a role in the evolution of TBL practices. In the early years, Michaelsen would wheel a Scantron machine into his large classes in order to give teams immediate feedback during the RAP. Then the scratch-off "immediate feedback-assessment technique" (IF-AT) cards came along and improved the experience by giving teams immediate feedback for every attempt at every question, not just once per exam. Various computer plat-forms such as InteDashboard and Learning Catalytics have since been developed to facilitate the readiness assurance process and, to a lesser extent, application exercises. Purpose-built TBL classrooms (including several installed at our home institution) feature dedicated moni-tors for each team table, with cables to connect to student computers, with both gallery-walk (table-by-table) and class presentation (table-to-class) presentation capabilities.

In the opposite direction, we found some adaptations that were very low-tech, and yet also effective. For example, Goedde (2020) provides menu card holders (the type often found in restaurants) and large index cards for his student teams to prominently display their answers to application exercises. With simultaneous revealing of answers, the variety of solutions is immediately visible both to the instructor and among teams, and cannot be easily amended by team members.

In summary, there are many reasons given for the adaptation of TBL (and arguably for the adaptation of any teaching method), including contextual constraints, content requirements, as well as student and instructor needs. It is likely that in the absence of these adaptations, many instructors would never attempt the TBL method in the first place. Yet, adaptation is not without its risks. In the next section, we discuss a few of these risks, followed by a brief illustrative case study, and end with recommendations on how to minimize the downsides of adaptation.

RISKS AND DOWNSIDES OF ADAPTATION

Those who have the most extended experience with TBL tend to advocate strongly against significant adaptations to the method. Michaelsen (2019), while allowing that flexibility in implementation of the TBL steps is a benefit of the method, also argues that often instructors who significantly modify the method itself don't realize what they have lost, saying, "most of the time, the process is so robust, people can screw up something and it still goes pretty well. Yet [in doing so] they can miss half the benefit, like filling a tub with the drainplug open. That's the disconcerting thing for me when it's modified." Parmelee (2010), in a critique of two papers presenting TBL research that had used adapted TBL methods, notes that "the TBL strategy is well-developed, and students benefit the most when all components are used."

Smith (2020) notes that new TBL instructors should initially avoid adaptation and focus on "being as pure to the idea as you can be" so as to understand the full impact and benefits of TBL. Faculty also suggest that new TBL instructors may be better served by starting small, such as with one TBL module in a semester at first, rather than attempting an incomplete implementation (Goedde 2020). One of us often suggests that new TBL instructors experiment with the RAT process by using it to help students review for an upcoming high-stakes exam such as a mid-term or a final. In this use, students are motivated to try hard because they want to feel prepared for the upcoming "real" test, but the experimental RAT doesn't have to be worth any "real" points.

Michaelsen and Fink (2008) note that some of the most common problematic adaptations include the overuse of RATs without corresponding application assignments, the absence of peer evaluation leading to reduced individual accountability, insufficient up-front introduction of students to TBL benefits and expectations, and use of inappropriate application exercises, such as lengthy term papers.

A useful concept for thinking about the risks inherent in adapting TBL or any other method is that of treatment fidelity. Treatment (or implementation) fidelity is defined as "the extent to which an intervention is delivered as intended by end users in an authentic education setting" (Roberts 2017). Traditionally used to evaluate the validity of randomized experimental results, the concept of treatment fidelity has more recently been advocated as relevant to the consequences of adapting teaching methods – with controversial results.

A case in point in the US is the No Child Left Behind (NCLB) Act passed in early 2002 (Klein 2015), which used required standardized testing as a way to increase accountability of state and local school systems to the federal government. In response to the Act, many states developed standardized teaching methods to meet the requirements of the standardized tests, and used the notion of treatment fidelity to advocate for a more standardized approach to teaching, suggesting that adaptations of the standardized methods would not yield desired results, and requiring teachers to justify any adaptations that they did make. This has led to one of the biggest debates in K-12 (kindergarten to 12th grade) education today, as many argue that these standards have gone too far in the direction of inhibiting pedagogical innovation (e.g., Meier 2004).

The NCLB example is instructive in the higher education context, in that it points to risks inherent in both adaptation and standardization. On one hand, loss of treatment fidelity resulting from adaptation of a teaching method certainly can put the empirically promised benefits of the method at risk. On the other hand, rigid standardization of the method can result in frustration for both students and instructors, and could lead to a lack of adoption of the method altogether.

Institutional Implementation of TBL and Resulting Adaptations: A Cautionary Tale

Another risk factor inherent in adaptation is the potential for unintended consequences related to the implementation of the adaptation. To illustrate these risks, we briefly describe a case that was related to us in one of our expert interviews. We have anonymized details of the institution in our description below, as they are not relevant; this case is representative of the experience of adopting and adapting teaching methods at many institutions.

Midstate University is a well-regarded public university in a large metropolitan area. Its College of Business was one of the largest faculties in the university, enrolling some 2500 undergraduates and nearly 1000 postgraduate students each year. In the early 2000s, team-based learning was implemented in a single undergraduate course and taught successfully in a tiered lecture hall to about 100 students, largely following the traditional (unadapted)

TBL method. Other faculty were impressed with positive student feedback on the TBL method, and soon a decision was made to use the method for all sections of an Introduction to Business course, taught to all incoming undergraduate students.

The first implementations of TBL across all sections of the large course were acceptable, but not ideal; student evaluations reflected some dissatisfaction with the process. Lead faculty were concerned, but still committed to using TBL. The second implementation was more standardized across sections, and seemed to go a bit better, but lead faculty believed that further improvement was still possible. At this point, the College of Business made a major commitment to TBL, constructing a dedicated TBL classroom for 120 students, outfitted with tables to seat students in groups of six, interactive whiteboards, and projection screens for teams to share their work with each other, and with the rest of the class. Within a few years, the college added two more classrooms of this type, and taught roughly 20 sections of the Introduction to Business course using TBL, mostly staffed with relatively junior faculty who were given a standardized template for teaching.

The introduction of the TBL classrooms, however, resulted in unanticipated consequences. Some instructors, unfamiliar with the technology provided in the specialized classroom, adapted their teaching to avoid using it, sometimes leaving behind critical pieces of the TBL methodology in the process. Furthermore, students, having been introduced to TBL in the purpose-built classroom, complained bitterly when presented with TBL in a regular, tiered classroom, to the point where some instructors of higher-level courses abandoned the method.

Over the next ten years, the Introduction to Business faculty made various adaptations to the TBL method, in an effort to further improve student evaluations. At different points in time, the course was taught with the iRAT as a take-home test, in some cases with no clear deadline. The tRAT was removed altogether from some sections of the course. Instructors were told to give students a mini-lecture on content before the RAP, but struggled to know where to focus these mini-lectures, given that they hadn't been able to assess student readiness. At times, the TBL process would be split across two class sessions, with students not being evaluated until the instructor felt they were "ready." A senior faculty member at Midstate noted that if Larry Michaelsen were to visit the College of Business, it was unlikely that he would recognize the methods being used as TBL; and yet the college still emphasized its commitment to the TBL method. The same faculty member wondered whether the college might have been able to retain more fidelity in the TBL method if junior faculty had been given a bit more time to fully learn the method, with less short-term emphasis on teaching evaluations.

Midstate's experience is instructive in that it reflects the adaptations made by many institutions, albeit at a larger scale than most. Its adaptations were made with the best of intentions, in the hope of improving the student experience. And yet, with the benefit of hindsight and distance, it is possible to see all that was lost through the process of adaptation. In the next section, we turn to the theory of diffusion of innovation to help tease out factors related to the implementation of TBL that led to unintended (and detrimental) adaptations of the method.

Diffusion of Innovation in an Organization: The Anatomy of Midstate's Story

The importance of individuals such as "champions" and "opinion leaders" to the adoption of innovation is understood by anyone who has taken basic marketing or management courses. But there is much more to the success or failure of an innovation's uptake across an organization, especially an innovation as nuanced as TBL, and organizations as complex as college classrooms, departments and divisions.

Greenhalgh et al.'s (2004) meta-analysis on the diffusion of innovations in service organizations offers some illuminating distinctions that help explain the lack of fidelity in the uptake of TBL at Midstate University. Their results show that the likelihood of an innovation's diffusion across an organization can be explained by a model that includes (but is not limited to) aspects of the innovation itself, as well as the approach taken by the organization toward the people choosing to adopt the innovation (or not).

First, addressing TBL as the innovation itself, Midstate engaged in some practices consistent with factors identified as increasing adoption; for example, increasing compatibility with adopters' values and needs, decreasing complexity, and reducing perceived risk to instructors and students. However, in the course of pursuing increased adoption, other decisions were made that ran counter to TBL's successful uptake. For example, theory indicates that if an innovation is presented with a support resource such as a help desk, it is more likely to be adopted. In Midstate's case, support was initially offered in the form of special classrooms and two teachers to ensure success. However, these supports ultimately were viewed as necessary for TBL to succeed, serving as a crutch rather than a support resource, and thereby reducing TBL's perceived relative advantage. Perhaps more important to the tale is Greenhalgh et al.'s (2004, p. 597) notion of "fuzzy boundaries": that is, if an innovation has a "hard core" of irreducible elements but a "soft periphery" of elements that can be adapted to fit into existing systems, it is more likely to be adopted. At Midstate, it appears that in the pursuit of uptake of TBL, adaptations were made that – with the best of intentions – strayed too far from the essential elements of TBL for either effective use or any claim of "treatment fidelity."

With respect to organizational approach, it appears that Midstate could also have benefitted from innovation diffusion best practices, including sharing the "meaning" of the innovation, avoiding top-down decision-making, and continuously sharing information and feedback during adoption of the innovation (Greenhalgh et al. 2004). First, sharing the "meaning," or philosophy of TBL might have helped Midstate avoid some of the less helpful adaptations of the method. If users of an innovation (such as TBL) understand the underlying philosophy of the method, they are more likely to adopt; but we argue that they will also be better equipped to evaluate the effects of possible adaptations. In the case of Midstate, it appeared as though the underlying meaning of TBL was shared less and less over time, as newer faculty were brought on. Lead faculty and college leadership appear to have focused their communications more on how to implement TBL (including its subsequent adaptations), rather than "why" use the method. Second, the TBL method and its subsequent adaptations were decisions made in a top-down fashion and, as such, reduced the sense of ownership and meaning felt among teaching faculty. Finally, according to our interviewee, faculty were given feedback in terms of student evaluations, but were given little time to adjust to that feedback or to learn the overall TBL method before adaptations were introduced. Had there been increased communication of meaning, multi-level ownership of decision-making, and ongoing feedback and communication of the impact of TBL to faculty, it is possible that the method could have been fully implemented in a more effective way, with fewer adaptations and greater retention of the core elements of TBL.

THE ESSENTIAL ELEMENTS OF TBL: SOME CAUTIOUS GUIDANCE

The following four elements have endured as the foundations that make TBL successful (Michaelsen and Sweet, 2008, p. 8):

- Groups. Groups must be properly formed and managed.
- Accountability. Students must be accountable for the quality of their individual and group work.
- Feedback. Students must receive frequent and timely feedback.
- Assignment design. Group assignments must promote both learning and team development.

In the following brief sections, we share what our research and our own experience can offer in terms of adding additional facets to these general principles.

Groups Must be Properly Formed and Managed

According to Michaelsen et al. (2004), groups must be strategically organized to distribute student strengths and challenges, avoid any pre-existing relationships among students, and be permanent across the duration of the learning experience. Across interviews, instructors commented on how positive their TBL group experience was for students, in stark contrast to turbulent and disappointing group project experiences from their past. Some noted that the TBL experience is a more authentic team experience – more like true professional collaboration – because the relationships are enduring across many rounds of interdependent success or failure, like one experiences as part of an ongoing professional team. A few commented on how important it is for the instructors to develop a new set of skills for managing team dynamics without getting too enmeshed in the actual work of any one team.

Our own experience has taught us that learning to reposition team members so they are facing each other, and coaching teams by answering a question with a question, are specific examples of how an instructor can concretely support the social learning experience of team members without monopolizing the thinking that they are doing together (which students are often too willing to let instructors do). While moments of "benevolent neglect" are indeed a feature of the master–apprentice relationship (Lave & Wenger 1991), it is important that – even when they are immersed in their own team discussions – students never perceive the instructor as "checked out." Wandering among the teams and eavesdropping on their conversations not only communicates to them that you are engaged and available, but can also provide invaluable insights into what students are struggling with, how they are navigating those challenges, and even gift you with explanations worded in brilliant ways that would never have occurred to you.

The only adaptation away from the principle of persistent teams that we are comfortable with occurs if the instructor wishes for a student to work meaningfully with many others in the class. For example, if a learning objective is for course participants to begin building professional peer networks, the instructor might reshuffle groups from time to time to accomplish this goal. If this is the case, it would be important for each new group to have several rounds of the full TBL process together, and the RAP to use attempt-level immediate feedback such as the IF-AT (as opposed to whole-test level feedback such as the Scantron) to maximize the team development potency of each experience. It's worth repeating that this reshuffling may come at the expense of ever-deepening relationships within a team, and so would only be reasonable to consider when a broad set of relationships was an explicitly desired outcome of the course.

Students' Accountability for Quality of Individual and Group Work

According to Michaelsen et al. (2004), students must be accountable for their own individual preparation, for team performance and for their contribution to that team performance. Across our interviews and experiences, student-to-student accountability is commonly mentioned as the true heart of the team experience. While we have seen great diversity in how this principle is operationalized, we have seen no reason to believe adaptations that do not include this principle should be entertained; a group only becomes a team when its members feel accountable to one another (Sweet & Pelton-Sweet 2008).

Frequent and Timely Feedback

The immediate feedback of the RAP and 4S application activities triggers powerful learning and social development within teams. When members have argued their way to a position and then gotten immediate feedback on it, they are motivated in the moment by either validation or chagrin to reflect upon their own understanding of the material, and how they contributed to the team's discussion toward a right or wrong answer. One of the authors has also observed that regular feedback helps their business school students gain comfort with the process of learning from failure, and accepting corrective feedback. In this respect, students also learn resiliency, and can take on a learning mindset that is increasingly valued in business (Garvin et al. 2008).

Application Assignment Design Promoting Learning and Team Development

Any TBL instructor will tell you that developing application activities is by far the most difficult aspect of the method, requiring creativity and iteration to envision and refine over time. As a result, this is often where aspiration and lived practice most predictably diverge. One author has advocated, developed and used TBL in his own teaching for more than 20 years – but does every single activity that their teams do together strictly conform to the 4S format? Certainly not. Do his students, nonetheless, do a great many 4S activities? Absolutely. As long as teams have enough experience working toward consensus and getting immediate feedback, there can be room for in-class activities that take other forms.

This necessity for consensus makes 4S "specific choice" activities convergent tasks, as opposed to divergent tasks (Shaw 1971). Divergent tasks are those that drive participants to divide and conquer, thereby working mostly individually and inequitably. Most traditional group project assignments that require groups to produce a complex product such as a team paper or presentation are divergent tasks. This is why group projects have such a checkered history: the underlying task structure drives students apart and into learning experiences that are, by definition, separate and usually unequal.

Instead, convergent tasks require that groups not only produce a decision they can support, but also come to consensus on the decision, thereby driving members together into motivated, analytical conversation. The discussion-stimulating nature of the convergent task is supported by a long and diverse collection of research in the language learning literature (e.g., Duff 1986; Marashi & Tahan-Shizari 2015).

"Specific choice" activities can take many forms, some of which include those previously recommended by Sweet (2017):

- Scenario and multiple-choice question: given a case study, teams must come to consensus on a range of different outcomes (e.g., choosing whether a company in a case should buy, lease, or rent their fleet of trucks).
- Pinpointing: given a map, book, film, graph, image, or other complex artifact, teams must come to consensus on what is the best example of some aspect of it (e.g., the best example of some thematic element in a film, or the best place in a city to open a small dry cleaning business).
- Sorting: given a collection of things, teams must come to consensus on some form of sequencing or categorizing (e.g., sorting images of infants in certain positions by age and by normal or abnormal development, or sorting statements made by authors into philosophical camps).
- Gallery walks: teams produce some other quickly scannable artifact and each team must review the work of the other teams and make specific choices about it (e.g., teams produce a concept map of a fictional character's development or diagram a complex chemical compound, and other teams must each decide which other team's work is most accurate or insightful or curious or "best" in some way).

Though exemplars and templates like this exist, some instructors argue for the traditional group project model because "in the real world" their students will be working in teams to produce complex products such as events, publications, software, various forms of designs, and so on. This is, of course, true. But the motivations, relationships and consequences are entirely different in a professional setting than they are in the classroom. More to the point, the difficulties that humans have working together to produce complex products has itself spawned an entire profession to support it: project management. Armies of trained and certified project managers exist in nearly every industry that does work of this nature. If an instructor wants their students to have a "real-world" experience producing complex products in teams, then they must either provide them project managers or explicitly train them in project management. Short of that, they are setting themself and their students up for the traditionally underwhelming and too often turbulent experience of group projects that many have grown to expect.

ADAPTATION OF TBL TO ONLINE AND HYBRID TEACHING FORMATS

The emergence of the COVID-19 pandemic drove a sudden shift to online teaching in business schools, and in higher education generally. While there had been some discussion of the use of TBL in online teaching before the pandemic (e.g., Clark et al. 2018; Palsole & Awalt 2008), the adaptation of TBL methods to the online environment accelerated dramatically during the writing of this chapter.

Adaptations of TBL for online teaching vary, depending on whether the online course is being taught in a synchronous or asynchronous format. Synchronous web-conferencing enables a nearly perfect replication of the face-to-face experience of the readiness assurance process, for example, whereas the same process can take several days or up to a week to complete in an asynchronous class setting. Furthermore, the lack of social presence and lag-time during asynchronous courses presents some real challenges to the online TBL instructor's ability to activate student engagement (Palsole & Awalt 2008). Below, we briefly discuss some of the key trends and recommendations that we have observed emerging from this period of rapid innovation and adaptation.

Communication Frequency and Detail

Research on virtual and remote work demonstrates that information sharing is a critical challenge in an online setting, with remote co-workers needing to make more intentional efforts to share not only task-related information, but also information about their own work surroundings and context (e.g., Cramton 2001; Makarius & Larson 2017). The same dynamic applies in online learning, in which instructors need to repeatedly and explicitly lay out guidelines and expectations, with more frequency and in more detail than would typically occur in a traditional classroom setting, because of the increased cognitive load demanded by online learning (e.g., Moreno & Mayer 2002). Furthermore, TBL already requires a fair amount of orientation and expectation-setting, even when delivered in the classroom, due to its unique features, such as testing before lecturing (Sibley & Ostafichuk 2014). For all of these reasons, online TBL instruction requires a substantial investment of time and effort in early communication of processes and expectations to students, as well as enablement of a quick start to students' communications with each other.

Use of Technology

While online student-response tools (such as Learning Catalytics) have been available as an alternative to TBL scratch-off IF-AT cards for nearly a decade, they have typically been used in a face-to-face classroom setting, with the technology serving primarily as a means for the organization and automated grading of responses, as well as instructor real-time monitoring of student and team progress. Fully online TBL requires a substantially greater use of technology, typically requiring simultaneous use of at least two platforms: one for communications with and among students (e.g., Zoom), and another for management of the TBL content itself (e.g., iRATs, tRATs, application exercises and peer evaluations). More than two software tools can be used if need be (e.g., Zoom for synchronous sessions, Slack or other chat function for student collaboration, Google docs for application exercises), but each addition brings with it the need for students to implement and learn a separate tool, as well as the challenge of integrating information across tools. For this reason, there are advantages to using a more integrated platform such as InteDashboard to cover all content management. As of the writing of this chapter in late 2020, efforts were under way to use the built-in functionality of learning management systems such as Canvas to replicate the TBL experience as closely as possible without involving an additional software platform (TBLC Listserv 2020).

Perhaps more importantly, students may themselves face technology barriers, such as limited access to a computing device (if sharing with a working family member, for instance), or unreliable internet access or bandwidth (Gonzales et al. 2018). A best practice that has emerged at some universities is a student technology inventory survey, given prior to the start of the term, asking students about their access to hardware, software, wireless access and internet bandwidth. In the case that one or more students in a course indicate that they do not have ready access to computing, the instructor may need to provide increased flexibility, for example in the timing of iRAT and tRATs, or in ensuring that TBL activities can be completed using mobile technology.

RATs and Application Exercises

We find that, when delivered online, RAT questions should fall within a narrower – and more challenging – range than those that might be used in a face-to-face class. Online students will be able to access a wide range of reference resources, barring intensive student test monitoring, which we do not recommend as part of TBL. Instead, we prefer to choose RAT questions that are not easily searchable online, and that go beyond recall of easily available facts, instead asking students to synthesize, integrate and even apply concepts. In terms of Bloom's taxonomy, the RAT questions should reflect a shift from the "remembering" to the "understanding" or "applying" levels of learning (Anderson & Sosniak 1994). Other approaches include asking students to identify an error in a proof or computation, which cannot be easily searched online.[2]

The sequence of the iRAT/tRAT experience can be replicated somewhat by setting up different kinds of quizzes within a learning management system (LMS). For example, in Canvas one can conduct iRATs as "ungraded surveys" to prevent students from getting any feedback at the moment, and after the fact the instructor can retroactively convert those iRAT responses to "graded quizzes" so student iRAT grades flow into the Canvas gradebook. For the tRAT, the instructor can create a "graded quiz" that only one team-member takes while sharing their screen with their team-mates for discussion. Canvas has the capability to give immediate "wrong answer" feedback and let one retake a quiz repeatedly with options for reduced points upon each retake. This "retake with wrong-answer feedback" option somewhat replicates the scratch-off IF-AT card experience.

For application activities, many LMSs have settings on their discussion boards that require students to post something before they are able to see what previous posts there may be. This can simulate a "simultaneous report" structure in which a team's representative needs to take the team's decision public without being able to refer to the thinking of other teams. Beyond the LMS, screen-sharing capabilities mean that teams can work on, for example, diagramming something, and when the time comes for simultaneous report, their representative can share their screen in a form of "hot seat" reporting (Sibley, 2012, p. 43).

Feedback

As discussed earlier in this chapter, immediate feedback is a cornerstone of the TBL method. Without this feedback, student reflection on their understanding of concepts and contribution to the team effort is not naturally triggered; a situation that presents obvious challenges when trying to adapt TBL to an asynchronous online learning format, in which nothing is designed to be "immediate." Palsole and Awalt (2008) resourcefully addressed this challenge in their online TBL courses by stretching the RAP out over the course of a week, designing the RAP questions to be much higher-level and arguable, so they can't simply be looked up, and requiring students to compose a separate reflection statement about their experience of how the conversation unfolded, thereby achieving at least some version of the in-the-moment reflection that truly immediate feedback motivates.

Peer evaluation

More frequent peer evaluations during the class term are desirable in an online setting. Earlier peer evaluations can increase visibility to the instructor of team dynamics and potential problems which the instructor can no longer identify through in-class observation (Clark et al. 2018). Peer evaluation can be a source of increased trust and commitment among team members (Sweet & Pelton-Sweet 2008), which is even more important (and difficult to develop) in an online class setting (Clark et al. 2018).

CONCLUSION

As we finish writing this chapter, faculty around the world are going through intensive adaptation of many teaching methods, TBL included, in response to the COVID-19 pandemic. In our own teaching, we use the concepts of essential elements, treatment fidelity and diffusion of innovation to retain the core values of a given method (TBL or otherwise), while making adaptations required by the exigencies of current circumstances. We hope that these principles can similarly help guide others through their own adaptations, whether in a stable environment, or in times of dynamic change.

NOTES

1. Michaelsen et al. (2008) provides a more detailed, yet still compact, set of instructions and considerations for faculty interested in implementing TBL for the first time. Additional recommended resources for instructors include Michaelsen et al. (2002) and Sibley & Osterfichuck (2014). We draw on these in our description of the TBL method in this section, unless otherwise cited. A video demonstration of TBL can be found at https://vimeo.com/51713733.
2. Additional suggestions offered by Rutgers University can be found at: https://sasoue.rutgers.edu/teaching-learning/remote-exams-assessment#special-advice-for-open-book-assessment-in-quantitative-courses.

REFERENCES

Allen, Rondall, Jeffrey Copeland, Andrea Franks, Reza Karini, Marianne McCollum, et al. (2013), "Team-Based Learning in US Colleges and Schools of Pharmacy," *American Journal of Pharmaceutical Education*, 77 (6), 115.

Anderson, Lorin W. and Lauren A Sosniak (1994), "Bloom's Taxonomy: A Forty-year Retrospective," in *Ninety-Third Yearbook of the National Society for the Study of Education*, Part 2. Chicago, IL: University of Chicago Press.

Balan, Peter (2020), interview by author 1, March 17.

Betta, Michela (2016), "Self and Others in Team-Based Learning: Acquiring Teamwork Skills for Business," *Journal of Education for Business*, 91, 69–74.

Carrasco, Gonzalo, Kathryn Behling and Osvaldo Lopez (2019), "A Novel Grading Strategy for Team-Based Learning Exercises in a Hands-On Course in Molecular Biology for Senior Undergraduate Underrepresented Students in Medicine Resulted in Stronger Student Performance," *Biochemistry and Molecular Biology Education*, 47 (2), 115–123.

Clark, Michele, Laura Merrick, Jennifer Styron, Annetta Dolowitz, Cassandra Dorius, et al. (2018), "Off to On: Best Practices for Online Team-Based Learning," pre-reading document for the Innovations Track workshop at the Team-Based Learning™ Collaborative Conference, San Diego, CA.

Conway, Paul and Christopher Clark (2003), "The Journey Inward and Outward: A Re-Examination of Fuller's Concerns-Based Model of Teacher Development," *Teaching and Teacher Education*, 19 (5), 465–482.

Cramton, Catherine (2001), "The Mutual Knowledge Problem and Its Consequences for Dispersed Collaboration," *Organization Science*, 12 (3), 346–371.

Drummond, Colin (2012), "Team-Based Learning to Enhance Critical Thinking Skills in Entrepreneurship Education," *Journal of Entrepreneurship Education*, 15, 57–63.

Dubois, J. (2012), "Discerning the Elements of Culture: A Team-Based Learning Approach to Asian Religions and Cultures," in *Team-Based Learning in the Social Sciences and Humanities: Group Work that Works to Generate Critical Thinking and Engagement*, Michael Sweet and Larry Michaelsen (eds). Sterling, VA: Stylus Publishing, 181–202.

Duff, Patricia (1986), "Another Look at Interlanguage Talk: Taking Task to Task," in *Talking to Learn: Conversation in Second Language Acquisition*, Richard R. Day (ed.). Cambridge, MA: Newbury House, 147–181.

Fink, L. Dee (2003), *Creating Significant Learning Experiences: An Integrated Approach to Designing College Courses*. San Francisco, CA: Jossey-Bass.

Fuller, Frances (1969), "Concerns of Teachers: A Developmental Characterization," *American Educational Research Journal*, 6, 207–226.

Fuller, Frances and Oliver Bown (1975), "Becoming a teacher," in *Teacher Education*, 74th Yearbook of the National Society of Education, K. Ryan (ed.). Chicago, IL: University of Chicago Press, 25–52.

Garvin, David A., Amy C. Edmondson, and Francesca Gino (2008), "Is Yours a Learning Organization," *Harvard Business Review*, 86 (3), 109–116.

Goedde, Rick (2020), interview by author 1, March 20.

Gonzales, Amy, Jessica Calarco and Teresa Lynch (2018), "Technology Problems and Student Achievement Gaps: A Validation and Extension of the Technology Maintenance Construct," *Communication Research*, 47 (5), 750–770.

Greenhalgh, Trisha, Glenn Robert, Fraser Macfarlane, Paul Bate and Olivia Kyriakidou (2004), "Diffusion of Innovations in Service Organizations: Systematic Review and Recommendations," *Milbank Quarterly*, 82 (4), 581–629.

Haidet, Paul, Karla Kubitz and Wayne McCormack (2014), "Analysis of the Team-Based Learning Literature: TBL Comes of Age," *Journal on Excellence in College Teaching*, 25 (3/4), 303–333.

Hettler, Paul (2015), "Student Demographics and the Impact of Team-Based Learning," *International Advances in Economic Research*, 21 (4), 413–422.

Hulleman, Chris and David Cordray (2009), "Moving From the Lab to the Field: The Role of Fidelity and Achieved Relative Intervention Strength," *Journal of Research on Educational Effectiveness*, 2 (1), 88–110.

Hunn, Vanessa (2014), "African American Students, Retention, and Team Based Learning: A Review of the Literature and Recommendations for Retention at Predominately White Institutions," *Journal of Black Studies*, 45 (4), 301–314.

Klein, Alyson (2015), "No Child Left Behind: An Overview," *Education Week* (accessed August 14, 2020), https://www.edweek.org/ew/section/multimedia/no-child-left-behind-overview-definition-summary.html.

Koles, Paul, Adrienne Stolfi, Nicole Borges, Stuart Nelson and Dean Parmelee (2010), "The Impact of Team-Based Learning on Medical Students' Academic Performance," *Academic Medicine*, 85 (11), 1739–1745.

Lang, Bingchen, Lingli Zhang, Yunzhu Lin, Lu Han, Chuan Zhang and Yan-tao Liu (2019), "Team-Based Learning Pedagogy Enhances the Quality of Chinese Pharmacy Education: A Systematic Review and Meta-Analysis," *BMC Medical Education*, 19, 286.

Lave, Jean and Etienne Wenger (1991), *Situated Learning: Legitimate Peripheral Participation*. Cambridge: Cambridge University Press.

Liu, Sin-Ning and Alexander Beaujean (2017), "The Effectiveness of Team-Based Learning on Academic Outcomes: A Meta-Analysis," *Scholarship of Teaching and Learning in Psychology*, 3 (1), 1–14.

Macke, Caroline, James P. Canfield, Karen Tapp and Vanessa Hunn (2019), "Outcomes for Black Students in Team-Based Learning Courses," *Journal of Black Studies*, 50 (1), 66–86.

Makarius, Erin and Barbara Larson (2017), "Changing the Perspective of Virtual Work: Building Virtual Intelligence at the Individual Level," *Academy of Management Perspectives*, 31 (2), 159–178.

Marashi, Hamid and Parissa Tahan-Shizari (2015), "Using Convergent and Divergent Tasks to Improve Writing and Language Learning Motivation," *Iranian Journal of Language Teaching Research*, 3 (1), 99–117

McElligott, Missy (2019), Interview by author 1, October 22.

McNeil, Jane, Loyin Olotu-Umoren, Michaela Borg, Mike Kerrigan, Sharon Waller, et al. (2019), "Scaling up: Active Collaborative Learning for Student Success," accessed August 14, 2020 at https://aclproject.org.uk/.

Meier, Deborah (2004), *Many Children Left Behind: How the No Child Left Behind Act is Damaging our Children and our Schools*. Boston, MA: Beacon Press.

Michaelsen, Larry (2019), interview by author 1, October 29.

Michaelsen, Larry and Robert Black (1994), "Building Learning Teams: The Key to Harnessing the Power of Small Groups in Higher Education," in *Collaborative Learning: A Sourcebook for Higher Education*, Vol. 2, S. Kadel and J. Keehner (eds). State College, PA: National Center for Teaching, Learning and Assessment, 65–81.

Michaelsen, Larry and L. Dee Fink (2008), "Team-Based Learning: Small Group Learning's Next Big Step," *New Directions for Teaching and Learning*, 116, 1–5. https://doi.org/10.1002/tl.329.

Michaelsen, Larry, Arletta Knight and L. Dee Fink (2002), *Team-Based Learning: A Transformative Use of Small Groups*. Westport, CT: Greenwood Publishing.

Michaelsen, Larry, Arletta Knight and L. Dee Fink (2004), *Team-Based Learning: A Transformative Use of Small Groups in College Teaching*. Sterling, VA: Stylus Publishing.

Michaelsen, Larry and Michael Sweet (2008), The Essential Elements of Team-Based Learning. In L. Michaelsen, M. Sweet and D. Parmelee (eds), *Team-Based Learning: Small-Group Learning's Next Big Step*, 1st edition. New Directions for Teaching and Learning, Vol. 116. San Francisco, CA: Jossey-Bass, 7–27.

Michaelsen, Larry and Michael Sweet (2011), "Team-Based Learning," *New Directions for Teaching and Learning*, 128, 41–51.

Michaelsen, Larry, Michael Sweet and Dean Parmelee (2008), *Team-Based Learning: Small-Group Learning's Next Big Step*, 1st edition. New Directions for Teaching and Learning, Vol. 116. San Francisco, CA: Jossey-Bass.

Michaelsen, Larry, Warren Watson and Robert Black (1989), "A Realistic Test of Individual Versus Group Consensus Decision Making," *Journal of Applied Psychology*, 74 (5), 834–839.

Moreno, Roxana and Richard E. Mayer (2002), "Learning Science in Virtual Reality Multimedia Environments: Role of Methods and Media," *Journal of Educational Psychology*, 94 (3), 598–610.

Norris, Ian (2019), interview by author 1, December 17.

Novak, Gregor M. (2011), "Just-in-Time Teaching," *New Directions for Teaching and Learning*, 128, 63–73.

Oldland, Elizabeth, Josh Allen and Judy Currey (2016), "Students' Perception of the Role of Team-Based Learning in Shaping Individual Learning Style, Team Skills and Clinical Practice," *Australian Critical Care*, 29 (2), 117.

Palsole, Sunay and Carolyn Awalt (2008), "Team-Based Learning in Asynchronous Online Settings," *New Directions for Teaching and Learning*, 116, 87–95.

Parmelee, Dean (2010), "Team-based learning: Moving Forward in Curriculum Innovation: A Commentary," *Medical Teacher*, 32 (2), 105–107. https://www.tandfonline.com/loi/imte20.

Rezende, Alice Belleigoli, André Frutuoso de Oliveira, Thiago Cardoso Vale, Luciana Scapin Teixeira, Alba Regina de Abreu Lima, et al. (2019), "Comparison of Team-Based Learning versus Traditional Lectures in Neuroanatomy: Medical Student Knowledge and Satisfaction," *Anatomical Sciences Education*, 12 (5), 591–601.

Roberts, Greg (2017), "Implementation Fidelity and Educational Science: An Introduction," in *Treatment Fidelity in Studies of Educational Intervention*, Greg Roberts, Sharon Vaughn, S. Natasha Beretvas and Vivian Wong (eds). New York: Routledge, 1–21.

Rutherford, W. and Hall, G. (1990), "Concerns of Teachers: Revisiting the Original Theory After Twenty Years," paper presented at the American Educational Research Association (AERA), Boston, USA.

Searle, Nancy, Paul Hiadet, P. Kelly, Virginia Schneider, Charles Seidel and Boyd Richards (2003), "Team Learning in Medical Education: Initial Experiences at Ten Institutions," *Academic Medicine*, 78 (10), S55–S58.

Seidel, Charles L. and Boyd F. Richards (2001), "Application of Team Learning in a Medical Physiology Course," *Academic Medicine*, 76 (5), 533–534.

Seltzer, Joe (2019), interview by author 1, October 31.

Shaw, Marvin (1971), *Group Dynamics, The Psychology of Small Group Behavior*. New York: McGraw Hill.

Sibley, Jim (2012), "Facilitating Application Activities," in *Team-Based Learning in the Social Sciences and Humanities: Group Work that Works to Generate Critical Thinking and Engagement*, Michael Sweet and Larry Michaelsen (eds). Sterling, VA: Stylus Publishing, 33–50.

Sibley, Jim and Peter Ostafichuk (2014), *Getting Started with Team-Based Learning*. Sterling, VA: Stylus Publishing.

Sisk, Rebecca (2011), "Team-Based Learning: Systematic Research Review," *Journal of Nursing Education*, 50 (12), 665–669.

Smith, Peter (2020), interview by author 1, March 16.

Stepanova, Jelena (2019), "Team-Based Learning in Business English in Latvia and EU," paper presented at the Association for Teacher Education in Europe Spring Conference on Innovations, Technologies and Research in Education, Riga, University of Latvia.

Swanson, Elizabeth, Lisa McCulley, David Osman, Nancy Scammacca Lewis and Michael Solis (2019), "The Effect of Team-based Learning on Content Knowledge: A Meta-Analysis," *Active Learning in Higher Education*, 20 (1), 39–50.

Sweet, Michael (2017), "Structures and Strategies to Help Faculty Design High-Impact Discussion Activities," workshop at the annual meeting of the Professional and Organizational Development Network, Montreal, Canada.

Sweet, Michael and Larry Michaelsen (2012), "Critical Thinking and Engagement: Creating Cognitive Apprenticeships with Team-Based Learning," in *Team-Based Learning in the Social Sciences and Humanities: Group Work That Works to Generate Critical Thinking and Engagement*. Sterling, VA: Stylus Publishing, 5–32.

Sweet, Michael and Laura Pelton-Sweet (2008), "The Social Foundation of Team-Based Learning: Students Accountable to Students," *New Directions for Teaching and* Learning, 116, 29–40.

TBLC Listserv (2020), Multiple e-mail chains accessed from the TBL Collaborative member listserv between April and July 2020.

Vaughn, Sharon, Leticia Martinez, Jeanne Wanzek, Greg Roberts, Elizabeth Swanson and An Fall (2017), "Improving Content Knowledge and Comprehension for English Language Learners: Findings from a Randomized Control Trial," *Journal of Educational Psychology*, 109 (1), 22–34.

Watson, Warren, Larry Michaelsen and Walt Sharp (1991), "Member Competence, Group Interaction and Group Decision-Making: A Longitudinal Study," *Journal of Applied Psychology*, 76 (6), 803–809.

Zgheib, Nathalie, Joseph Simaan and Ramzi Sabra (2010), "Using Team-Based Learning to Teach Pharmacology to Second Year Medical Students Improves Student Performance," *Medical Teacher*, 32 (2), 130–135.

PART III

THE USE AND VALUE OF LEARNING TECHNOLOGIES

8. Transformations towards blended learning: key issues to address

Annemette Kjærgaard, Thyra Uth Thomsen and Sylvia von Wallpach

INTRODUCTION

When supervising teachers transforming their courses into blended learning, we are often asked the following question: "How many minutes of recorded video lectures do I have to produce to replace 45 minutes of face-to-face lecturing?" To the teacher's distress, we may not give a concrete answer (e.g., "Typically, teachers produce 2–3 video lectures of 5–8 minutes"). Instead, we encourage teachers to think about the learning objectives and how they may be best supported through a combination of technology-enhanced (a)synchronous teaching and on-campus classroom teaching. The answer may or may not include pre-recorded videos, and therefore, before beginning to focus on a single multi-media technology, we should discuss what we want the students to do and achieve.

Hopefully, this anecdotal introduction illustrates that blended learning cannot be put to a formula that allows teachers to transform their lectures into blended learning. Instead, we argue that teachers need to learn how to transform their teaching approach to meet their learning objectives in a blended learning context. To help teachers prepare for this transformation, we address the following key issues:

- Blended learning is not a single pedagogy.
- Blended learning should combine the best of both worlds.
- Developers of blended learning should focus on learning rather than technology.
- Blended learning can provide new learning opportunities.
- Interaction is both challenged and supported in a blended learning environment.
- Blended learning calls for organizational and personal adaptation.

We recommend that teachers reflect on these selected issues before they choose specific online tools or activities. Our intention is that teachers will gain some clarity about what blended learning is and what it can and cannot help accomplish. The issues are selected based on the joint experiences of the three authors, two of whom have spearheaded online and blended teaching transformations (both as teachers and as consultants for other teachers) and one who as vice-dean spearheaded the organizational changes and support systems needed to promote blended learning at their institution. Needless to say, the selected issues are linked to a specific context; in this case a business school in which online and blended learning initiatives were considered as strategically important since 2014. The challenges perceived by lecturers as well as the misunderstandings and myths about blended learning encountered by us, the authors, are also tied into this specific background. Having said that, we hear from colleagues at other higher education institutions who have similar concerns, and believe that our experiences will prove useful to lecturers from around the globe.

BLENDED LEARNING IS NOT A SINGLE PEDAGOGY

Rather than a special pedagogy, in this chapter blended learning is defined as a bouquet of different pedagogies that mix online and face-to-face (F2F) teaching and learning activities in a pedagogically valuable manner. So, while the aim is to enhance student learning, there are multiple ways to reach this goal. Well-proven pedagogies of problem-based learning or flipped learning (Akçayır and Akçayır, 2018) can be delivered in a blended format and so can case-based learning (Turk et al., 2019). The key point here is that technology can offer new learning activities or support learning activities in ways that enhance the opportunities for learning. For example, instead of using written cases, one of our colleagues chose to let actors dramatize leadership dilemmas as they would play out in real settings. Using these dramatizations as a starting point for his case-based classes, the case came alive for students when preparing. In total, ten episodes were produced for students to watch prior to class instead of the traditional ten-page written case.

Another example is a class based on problem-based learning, which was transformed by means of blended learning to ensure that time spent together in the classroom was actually spent on collaborative activities on practice-based problems in a room fit for exactly this. Therefore, all task introductions, feedback activities and reflections were moved online as either preparation tasks or post-class reflections.

These examples illustrate that blended learning can support different pedagogies. It should also be mentioned that, while our conceptualization of blended learning as a technology-enhanced approach to teaching and learning is the most common understanding of blended learning, not all definitions of blended learning include technology. They may instead cover other forms of blends such as formal and informal learning, or practice-based and theory-based learning (see for example Collis and Margaryan, 2005).

BLENDED LEARNING SHOULD COMBINE THE BEST OF BOTH WORLDS

Defining blended learning as a combination of online and on-campus teaching and learning, technology often becomes the focus in transformation to blended learning and less attention is paid to in-class teaching and learning activities. This is obviously due to the newness of the use of technology and the perceived need for competence development of teachers to become more fluent in designing and making use of technology in teaching. However, technology is just one of the two components in blended learning, and the face-to-face teaching and learning activities also need to be reconsidered to combine the best of both worlds. Teachers and students have different perceptions of what is actually the best of online and in-class teaching. For online teaching, flexibility in time and place are often emphasized as an advantage, whereas instant feedback and social relations are often emphasized as advantages of in-class teaching.

The recent Covid-19 crisis has been an extreme case to study what activities are difficult to conduct online while keeping the same engagement and learning outcome for students.

Learning from this experience, teachers will be able to point to activities that they prefer to conduct in-class with students, but also to activities which can be conducted equally well online.

In the literature on blended learning, F2F lectures are often the focus of critique as they position students in a passive role as receivers of learning rather than active contributors to learning. Lectures are thus a target for transformation (Fleck, 2012) – typically into shorter videos for students to watch before coming to class – and class time can then be used for more interaction and dialogue. While the ambition for using in-class time for interaction and dialogue is frequently mentioned, teachers are not always sure about what to do in class instead of lecturing, especially if lecturing has been their dominant in-class activity.

An example of innovative F2F teaching in a blended learning context that is worth mentioning is design-based workshops where students conduct project work and produce prototypes of various kinds, including physical products or art productions. Another example is out-of-campus experiences including visits to local businesses or cultural institutions where students are asked to solve tasks that integrate the physical space and context with theoretical reflections. An example of such a class is an elective course on creativity where students immerse themselves in urban life as the context for reflection (Beyes and Mitchels, 2016).

Other examples are the use of simulations or games that may require a different use of time and space, for example consecutive days of teaching in rooms with flexible furniture arrangements. While some teachers thrive as innovators of alternative learning activities, others are less inventive. Transformation to blended learning should therefore be supported by faculty development activities which focus on identifying, designing and implementing all types of activities regardless of the modality of delivery. This is even the case when teachers themselves mostly feel the need to learn about online learning tools. Even when they manage to master online learning tools, they still need to consider how to integrate online and on-campus activities in order to make sure that they are not separate learning experiences but thoughtfully integrated to combine the best of both worlds.

DEVELOPERS OF BLENDED LEARNING SHOULD FOCUS ON LEARNING RATHER THAN TECHNOLOGY

As illustrated above, blended learning is a delivery mode intended to support student learning rather than a specific pedagogy (e.g., case-based teaching) based on a specific technology (e.g., pre-recorded videos). Applying a backwards design approach (Wiggins and McTighe 2001), teachers should therefore consider the intended learning outcome and how this is best achieved, before they choose among the vast variety of technology-enhanced teaching options and F2F activities. A common learning objective, such as "understanding, reflecting upon and contrasting different theoretical approaches," can be achieved by blending different online and F2F teaching and learning activities in various ways. Some teachers at our institution, for instance, use video lectures combined with readings to provide students with basic insights into different theories, thereby freeing up time in class to reflect upon, discuss and apply theories to real-life cases. Other teachers stick to traditional F2F lectures and provide students with online exercises to practice theories or methods.

While teaching situations vary considerably, there is convincing evidence that feedback, student activation and conceptually demanding learning tasks generally support student learning in higher education (Scheider and Preckel, 2017). Further, it is of paramount importance that teachers invest in designing the microstructure of their courses to create a logical, clear and fruitful journey towards fulfilling the learning objectives. This microstructure design allows teachers to weave together feedback, (inter)action and learning tasks to provide the envisioned outcome.

Continuous evaluation allows teachers to identify possibilities for improvement and supports the evidence-based redesign of courses (Allan, 2007). Blended learning supports this evidence-based approach to student learning by enhancing the course microstructure through technology. For example, computer-based peer-grading loops allow teachers to efficiently generate more feedback for the individual student than would have been the case without technology-supported peer grading systems. Even though student peer grading is different from – and often received differently than – teacher feedback, peers are just as able to assess the quality of a contribution (ibid.). Moreover, peer grading processes allow students to see what other students have produced and how assignments can be solved in different ways. Peer feedback can be combined with teacher feedback, for example when a teacher singles out some student contributions (e.g., the top-ranking, or the ones making the most common mistakes, or the ones presenting a brilliant solution to certain parts of the assignment) for discussion in plenum F2F. In this way, technology can support the pedagogical microstructures and help create a close connection between online and on-campus activities.

Technology can help teachers activate students, and as evidenced by several contributions to scholarship in the science of teaching and learning (SoTL), activation greatly supports learning (e.g., Freeman et al., 2014). For example, online discussion boards can help students (even those who are otherwise quiet) to voice their opinions. Quizzes allow students to immediately evaluate their learning after reading a paper or textbook chapter. The same is true for assignments that are to be solved right after processing content, whether delivered through texts, videos, podcasts, or the like. The learning journey built through the microstructure design on the learning management system (LMS) with all its integration of specific learning technologies is of paramount importance. Consequently, the specific role of, for example, video lectures on the learning journey is more important than the actual number and length of the videos; important questions to consider here are, for instance, whether they frame an assignment, recap focal theories or visualize a real-life case. Thereby, video lectures not only add to the bouquet of online learning activities but also constitute a bouquet of options for teachers who need to consider what precedes them, and what follows after the lectures to support students' progress towards the learning objectives.

BLENDED LEARNING CAN PROVIDE NEW LEARNING OPPORTUNITIES

On top of boosting the effectiveness of on-campus learning environments, blended learning can also provide learning opportunities that are different from those pertaining to on-campus learning environments. The ability to "pause" the lecturer in asynchronous videos or podcasts while digesting the theoretical content, or to pay a virtual visit to relevant businesses or organizations in order to understand a teaching case, offers new opportunities for learners. Indeed, when the first fully online electives at Copenhagen Business School (CBS) were evaluated, students pointed to the flexibility of studying when they wanted and where they wanted as the

#1 benefit, whereas better learning of academic content came in second place (Thomsen et al., 2015).

Also, a digital learning environment allows teachers to follow students' progress and to be alerted when individual students get stuck. As the LMS allows for transparency in terms of student activity, teachers will know how students progress and have the opportunity to speed up or slow down the collective learning journey, or to create personalized learning journeys for students who need more or different learning tasks to maximize their learning outcome. Teacher can "see" what students do, even when they are not together in brick and mortar environments.

"Why bother?" some may say. Wasn't this already an option in the good old days, when faculty were actually able to know the names of their students and had the time to deeply engage in students' learning journeys? The answer is 'yes'; however, not without a "but." While technology allows us to compensate for increasing class sizes, increasing time pressure and decreasing resources per student, learning technologies are not only game-reversers: they are also game-changers. The silent student in class might experience opportunities to speak up that are not available in F2F classes, as these usually favor extrovert students who are able to deal with relatively short response times. Therefore, blended learning is important, because it has the potential to change the established ways of teaching through the use of new teaching technologies and resources that open a plethora of learning opportunities to tailor a suitable learning experience for each student. In evidence, a recent CBS study reported significantly higher pass rates in electives based on blended learning than in those of other modalities (Møller Hansen, 2020). Notably, the failure rates were up to 40 percent higher in F2F lecture-based courses than in blended learning courses.

INTERACTION IS BOTH CHALLENGED AND SUPPORTED IN A BLENDED LEARNING ENVIRONMENT

"Then how about interaction?" a lot of teachers new to blended learning rightfully ask. Indeed, online environments can suffer from, for example, students "hiding" from interaction or from temporal distance in asynchronous discussions. If the latest comment was posted a day ago, responding to it will probably seem less urgent than when participating in a F2F debate. This was also evidenced in one of the first online electives at CBS in 2014. As this course was based on asynchronous sessions, students and lecturers never interacted in real time. Consequently, there was always some delay in interactions and they were devoid of body language and facial expressions. Some students missed that sort of interaction and found it "more interesting to be in a classroom than to be alone watching a lecture." Although there are ways to promote interaction in online environments through encouragement or credits, this should be taken very seriously, since past research suggests that student interaction supports learning (Scheider and Preckel, 2017).

This is exactly the reason why an institution such as CBS promotes blended learning rather than online learning. On-campus teaching has many merits, including the opportunity to interact, the opportunity to socialize, and the opportunity to be motivated to think, act, respond and learn right here and right now. Consequently, time spent F2F on courses based on blended learning should be devoted to activities that actually require teachers and students to be together. This means that F2F sessions in blended learning courses should be highly interactive and require physical presence, while mere transmission-oriented lecturing could be offered online. This is probably why many teachers who apply a blended learning framework label their F2F sessions as workshops rather than lectures in the syllabus.

On the other hand, online sections of blended learning courses can be very valuable in terms of preparing students for interaction in F2F sessions. When online activities and processes are crafted towards allowing students to prepare optimally for the F2F sessions, they can intensify and optimize classroom interactions as students come prepared and synchronized knowledge-wise. Instead of only digesting the literature or a preparatory task, an online quiz or question-and-answer forum may address misunderstandings, which means that students are more likely to have a shared understanding of the task at hand and be ready to interact when they meet on campus. Notably, research suggests that a proper design of such course micro-structures has a positive effect on student learning outcome (Schneider and Preckel, 2017).

BLENDED LEARNING CALLS FOR ORGANIZATIONAL AND PERSONAL ADAPTATION

While many teachers and students have been able to adapt to fully online teaching almost overnight as a result of the Covid-19 crisis, this has also made it clear that support for transitions involving technology-enhanced learning is very much needed. To most faculty, making use of online teaching activities (either in a blended learning context or in fully online courses) is completely new, and they need inspiration and support. In fact, blended learning can be more demanding for teachers, as they must navigate various roles from designer to content expert, facilitator and technical supporter. If options for more personalized learning journeys are offered in blended courses to make learning more student-centered (Fleck, 2012), this also puts more responsibility for learning on students. Instead of just showing up for lectures more or less anonymously, in blended formats students are typically asked to complete different tasks and assignments online which can be monitored by the teacher, putting pressure on students to be active, responsible collaborators, and even co-creators of their own learning materials. As in the case of teachers, many students are not used to online learning and have had to learn how to learn online. This points to the need for scaffolding online learning even in the case of more experienced students. If teachers are aware of this and prepare for it they avoid the frustration of students not completing tasks as expected. As many teachers have limited teacher training this needs to be supported by competence development.

These changes and requirements call for organizational responses to support the transitions. If teaching and learning activities are considered to create the most effective mix for enhancing student learning, the administrative context for the activities will need to be adapted as well. Exam forms might no longer be suitable, or schedules originally created to support a specific kind of teaching might not fit new forms. A standard format of 16 two-hour lectures that used to be held as a traditional lecture format might need to change to fewer but longer sessions where students can work on practice-based problems. Finally, the transformation to blended learning might also be an opportunity to reconsider how institutions organize and prepare for teaching and conduct the teaching itself. The classic way of organizing teaching as an individual task, where each teacher is responsible for designing and conducting a course, is challenged in line with new teaching formats which might require a broader set of competences and thereby encourage teachers to collaborate either through inspiration and peer feedback or on the design and actual teaching of the course.

In the pre-coronavirus era, lecturers at CBS were encouraged to experiment with blended learning formats through several different support systems. For example, they were given more teaching hours for developments of new blended learning courses. Also, each department had a liaison consultant from the Teaching and Learning unit, who could both give advice on instructional design and provide help for technological options. Finally, lecturers were offered pedagogical courses and workshops focusing on the design of blended learning courses, and thereby interacted with other lecturers pursuing blended learning. In terms of support systems encouraging organizational change, study boards were able to invite blended learning ambassadors – such as the Vice Dean for Learning and Learning Technologies – to get to know more about blended learning. Likewise, study programs willing to experiment with blended learning were assigned two consultants who would design a series of seminars for faculty teaching in the program, in order to design coherent blended learning microstructures across the courses in the program.

All of these approaches were voluntary for faculty, study boards and study programs. When the coronavirus pandemic forced faculty to engage in online learning, these support systems were in high demand across the business school, even if time pressure did not allow for the development of optimal course design in all cases. Also, due to lockdown, courses needed to be delivered in a fully online version instead of being blended. Therefore, the full potential of combining the best of two worlds could not be unleashed. However, hopefully, one of the positive outcomes of this unfortunate situation will be that a broad range of faculty has been able to experience glimpses of what technology can and cannot do to enhance learning.

FINAL REFLECTIONS AND FUTURE DIRECTIONS

Blended learning is a bouquet of opportunities for constructing learning activities which have the potential to enhance student learning, as we have outlined in this chapter. Extension of the learning space, flexibility, personalized learning and new opportunities for connecting to partners outside the walls of the brick-and-mortar university are just a few examples. For the exact blend to be effective, careful consideration of the online as well as the F2F dimension is needed.

The adoption of blended learning also comes with some challenges, as teachers as well as students are not familiar with the opportunities available and therefore need to develop competence in designing blended learning. This points to the important role of pedagogical and instructional support to help in the transition. Based on our own experiences, we have offered six key issues in this chapter as a starting point for teachers relatively new to blended learning. In our experience, as illustrated in the introduction, teachers new to blended learning are often eager to test online tools and activities, but may skip instructional considerations that could otherwise have informed their choice of tools and activities. Consequently, thinking about the listed issues is not just "nice to have"; in our opinion it is "need to have" if teachers want to construct high-quality courses based on a blended learning design.

The authors hope that this chapter provides encouragement to colleagues to introduce, or continue to use, blended learning design in their courses. However, by making these suggestions we are not making normative judgments about any general superiority of blended learning. Whether or not a course should be blended depends on the specific context and the learning aims and objectives. Through our work with implementing blended learning we have encountered a lot of skepticism of the value of blending the learning, and thereby the need to implement it. While we appreciate critical reflection on the need for change as well as the means for change (read: technology), we also believe that some of our colleagues may resist the changes due to lack of knowledge about the opportunities offered by blended learning, as well as lack of experience, which makes it difficult for them to imagine the potentials. This highlights the need for an institutionally supported strategy supported by resources to help teachers understand the opportunities and, not least, to try out new forms of teaching in close collaboration with teaching support staff or more experienced colleagues.

REFERENCES

Akçayır, G. and Akçayır, M. (2018). The flipped classroom: A review of its advantages and challenges. *Computers and Education* 126: 334–345. DOI: 10.1016/j.compedu.2018.07.021.

Allan, Barbara (2007). *Blended Learning: Tools for Teaching and Training*. London: FacetPublishing.

Beyes, T. and Mitchels, C. (2016). Spaces with a temper: On atmospheres of education. In: Steyaert, C., Beyes, T. and Parker, M. (eds), *The Routledge Companion to Reinventing Management Education*. Abingdon: Routledge, pp. 312–329.

Collis, B. and Margaryan, A. (2005). Design criteria for work-based learning: Merrill's First Principles of Instruction expanded. *British Journal of Educational Technology* 36(5): 725–738. DOI: 10.1111/j.1 467-8535.2005.00507.x.

Fleck, J. (2012). Blended learning and learning communities: Opportunities and challenges. *Journal of Management Development* 31(4): 398–411. DOI: 10.1108/02621711211219059.

Freeman, S., Eddy, S.L., McDonough, M., Smith, M.K., Okoroafor, N., et al. (2014). Active learning increases student performance in science, engineering, and mathematics. *Proceedings of the National Academy of Sciences* 111(23), 8410–8415.

Møller Hansen, M. (2020). Analysis of student performance in electives at CBS with special focus on Blended Learning. Memo from the Teaching and Learning Unit, Copenhagen Business School, February 24.

Schneider, M. and Preckel, F. (2017). Variables associated with achievement in higher education: A systematic review of meta-analyses. *Psychological Bulletin* 143(6), 565.

Thomsen, T.U., Kjærgaard, A., & Møller Nielsen, M. (2015). *Fully Online Courses at CBS: Early Experiences.* Teaching and Learning Report [CBS], No. 2015/1. Frederiksberg: Copenhagen Business School, CBS.

Turk, B., Ertl, S., Wong, G., et al. (2019). Does case-based blended-learning expedite the transfer of declarative knowledge to procedural knowledge in practice? *BMC Medical Education* 19(1): 447. DOI: 10.1186/s12909-019-1884-4.

Wiggins, Grant and McTighe, Jay (2001). What is backward design? In: *Understanding by Design*, 1st edition. Upper Saddle River, NJ: Merrill Prentice Hall, pp. 7–19.

9. The influence of technology on business schools' curricula: a triple crown perspective

Loïc Plé and Bernadett Koles

INTRODUCTION

The Issue

Many academics will remember the spring term of 2020 for a long time to come. In light of the global pandemic that led to border closures and strict confinement measures, schools and universities worldwide were forced to close their campuses to their students, faculty and staff. Consequently, many educational institutions had to discover ways to train their teachers practically overnight to help them move their instruction from predominantly face-to-face to online, using solutions such as Zoom, Microsoft Teams, GoToMeeting, and other virtual collaborative platforms. Even those somewhat uncomfortable with using technology in their instruction had to adapt and cope with the new academic reality. And most of us did; more successfully than we may have thought. At the same time, there is quite a lot of suspicion as to how this mass online or hybrid education may work in the long run, whether the students are learning as much as before, and how institutions, faculty members and students can cope with the new academic reality.

Prior to the health crisis, it had been a minority of early adopter faculty who embraced technological innovations in course design and delivery, leaving others to opt for safer, tried and tested traditional modes of instruction relying heavily on face-to-face practices. This is not surprising, for two reasons. On the one hand, echoing the work of Moore (1991), a chasm often exists when disruptive innovations enter a market, with frequent challenges to move beyond the early adopter group. On the other hand, pedagogical innovations require time, which for faculty is a scarce asset, particularly when combined with the myriad pressures that business school professors are increasingly exposed to, including high workload and expectations across research, teaching and service; lack of institutional recognition for innovative pedagogical activities; and insufficient institutional resources to support potential initiatives. These factors often discourage professors from embarking on a journey of self-driven training, effort and potentially risky experimentation with different technological solutions.

Being exposed to online instructional practices is an important first step in breaking down the barriers to technology. However, a relevant distinction should be made: a technologically infused curriculum is not the same as teaching online. In fact, simply moving lectures from the classroom to a virtual platform falls short in capturing the full promise of technology. It is with this background that we compose the current chapter to demonstrate ways in which technology can assist the important triad of pedagogy, assessment and content. Given the current context and our new reality, it is now a good time to make this move, encouraging institutions and faculty members to establish a climate that nurtures and rewards innovative pedagogical solutions not only in course design and delivery, but also across assessment and content.

The Purpose

The purpose of the current chapter is to explore the impact of technology on business schools' curricula and to provide faculty with a repertoire of simple practices and ideas that enables them to harness different solutions in their course planning and development. We organize the chapter around three core pillars, namely: pedagogical design and delivery, assessment methods, and course content. We argue that such a comprehensive approach can be advantageous to any program determined to foster student engagement and active learning, as it also enables schools to establish a closer alignment between the curriculum, the organization and the image they wish to convey. Although it is not feasible to capture an exhaustive list of all relevant aspects associated with these three areas in a single chapter, we hope to provide food for thought and to initiate exchange amongst interested business school faculty, program directors and administrative support staff.

THE IMPACT OF TECHNOLOGY ON COURSE DESIGN AND DELIVERY

The vast majority of existing research that explores the impact of technology and business school education concerns course design and delivery. Undoubtedly, advancements in computing, cloud storage and software variety enabled us to move from physical to online materials, while collaborative tools and social media sites provided us with alternatives to – at least in part – replace face-to-face interactions. We devote this section to reviewing examples of existing design and delivery approaches, which we organize using certain relevant criteria that are summarized in Figure 9.1. First, we differentiate among design and delivery methods as a function of required institutional resources and support. Second, we account for the necessary faculty input in terms of time commitment as well as technical skills and expertise. Last but not least, in the figure we capture certain important characteristics from the students' standpoint, including personalized engagement and potential for immersion.

Video Communications

For reasons mentioned above, many of us are familiar with tools that allow synchronous video communication such as Zoom or GoToMeeting. These platforms are quite user-friendly as they can be easily downloaded, are normally free of charge (at least to a certain extent) and can be joined from any setting with a device and an internet connection. From an institutional standpoint, video conferencing platforms are simple to implement and manage as they require limited support, concentrated mostly on the initial training period. From the student and the faculty perspectives, the situation can be more complex, with the purpose of usage seeming to have an impact.

Other tools, potentially a bit more complicated yet still very user-friendly, allow professors and students to interact asynchronously. Those tools, such as Flipgrid, Panopto or Kaltura, can be used in different ways: for professors to record course content that they further share with students; for students to record presentations that they share with professors and other students; for professors to deliver feedback, and so on.

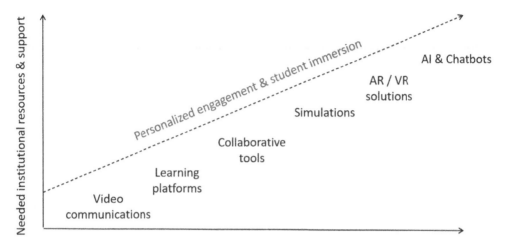

Note: AI = artificial intelligence; AR = augmented reality; VR = virtual reality.

Figure 9.1   Tentative typology of technological resources and activities to favor students' personalized engagement and immersion

Exploiting synchronous or asynchronous video-conferencing tools to replace a teacher-centric lecture that envisions limited interactions in the first place may work quite well. For other classes that embrace a more interactive approach, however, some complications may prevail. While synchronous communication platforms logically seem closer to what can be done in class, their nature implies several differences that may trigger users' apprehension. From the student standpoint, concerns tend to be raised in terms of increased anxiety and stress that originate from having to "appear online," dealing with competing obligations in one's household, and facing other possible concerns associated with privacy or limited financial means (Moses 2020). From the faculty standpoint, these engagements can be quite exhausting given the difficulties recreating the same type of harmonized human conversations that characterize interactive physical classrooms (Blum 2020). Asynchronous video communication tools may raise similar concerns due to the potential sharing of the videos. They also trigger other issues insofar as their usage may be less easy than synchronous platforms. Moreover, their integration in the teaching and learning process necessitates more *ex ante* reflection to make sure that they are used coherently and complementarily to the course's other activities and content (e.g., When should content be recorded and shared with students? How is feedback best delivered to the students?).

Learning Platforms

Engaging learning platforms such as Moodle and Blackboard represent the next step along the continuum, requiring considerably more support and involvement on behalf of the institution as well as the faculty, but also entailing a higher potential for student engagement. Beyond mere content sharing – both by faculty who can distribute learning materials such as slides and readings, and by students who can upload assignments or complete a quiz – these tools provide users with somewhat more advanced options that enable the incorporation of gamification elements, badges, and in general help faculty follow and monitor student progress, performance and learning.

Collaborative Tools

As we progress along Figure 9.1 to the next level, we find a diversified set of collaborative tools such as Asana, Miro, Microsoft Teams (and, more generally, Microsoft 365), or Google apps (docs, sheet, slides) that facilitate online collaboration among virtual – or potentially hybrid – teams. These solutions tend to require more extensive institutional support, in that many of the advanced features are available only by paid subscriptions and, at least when used for instructional purposes, faculty members are also involved to maintain management and oversight. At the same time, these tools can be quite advantageous from the students' perspective.

First, students may feel more encouraged to share their ideas in writing as opposed to through speech, with particular attention to those for whom public speaking may represent a sense of discomfort, driving them to opt for safer outlets. Second, many scholars call for rethinking student roles and participation in order to encourage engagement that works towards developing a participatory culture (Manca et al. 2017). These platforms help encourage a shift in mindset from more passive to more active modes of operation. Third, some of these tools embed game-like features – such as competition and awards – that often characterize these applications, and were shown to be advantageous in further enhancing student engagement and meaningful learning (Alanne 2016). Finally, those tools are increasingly used in firms. Therefore, exposing students to them so that they progressively build online collaborative working routines during their studies will strengthen their professional skills and benefit them when confronted by such situations in companies.

Simulations

Simulations represent an excellent alternative to case studies, exposing students to real-life and hands-on business-related scenarios in a realistic setting. Developing simulations is a rather time-consuming and resource-intensive endeavor, but there are feasible and efficient ways to obtain outsourced alternatives via providers such as Harvard Business Publishing Education (HBPE), CESIM, StratX Simulations, and so on. A rather comprehensive step-by-step guide for developing and managing simulations has been proposed by the Learning and Teaching Centre at Dalhousie University in Canada, connecting simulations to student learning through a series of steps (https://bit.ly/2QCVxnw). According to its framework, the simulation lifecycle proceeds through the following phases: (1) conceptualization; (2) creating an immersive environment; (3) integrating technology; (4) assessment; (5) debrief and reflection; and (5) evaluation of the learning outcomes. To revisit the above continuum, although simulations require substantially greater faculty resources and institutional investment, as long as they fit with the global learning context they can achieve higher student engagement and immersion, and in turn can provide a memorable and impactful learning experience for students.

AR / VR Solutions

Augmented and virtual reality have been gaining traction in a variety of industries and present interesting innovative solutions for the education sector as well. The use of online training, video games and game-based learning have been particularly useful for certain topics such as training statistics skills (Jiang et al. 2019), construction management programs (Oo and Lim 2016; Shanbari and Issa 2019), accounting (Carenys and Moya 2016) and manufacturing (Perini et al. 2018). Importantly, evidence suggests that games can enhance deep learning and student enjoyment particularly in courses that evoke higher levels of anxiety (Crocco et al. 2016). For instance, in a study exploring the efficiency of calculus education, students who participated in the game-based condition demonstrated higher task immersion and greater conceptual understanding in comparison with the control group (Lee et al. 2016). In addition to mastering relevant skills, interactions between the students as facilitated by the game also appeared to be an important factor to enhance learning (Barr 2018). Similarly, enjoyment, effort and quality of the facilitator during the game experience tend to be significant determinants of student learning satisfaction (Mayer et al. 2013). Importantly, although earlier gaming experience may provide users with a slight advantage, non-gamers and females are not necessarily hindered, despite potential concerns (Warden et al. 2016).

AI and Chatbots

With functions such as natural language processing and deep learning, solutions based on artificial intelligence (AI) and machine learning are expected to have a significant impact on the future of education, including different levels from kindergarden to grade 12 (K–12) through higher education. Chatbots are computer programs used to engage in audio- and/or text-based conversations. They represent an innovative form of communication, and have been adopted increasingly in customer service, tech support, training and education. Although more rudimentary forms of chatbot applications have been around since the 1950s, they have become more widely used in recent years in different areas ranging from instant messaging to collection of ethnographic data, teaching subjects such as statistics or accounting, and virtual tutoring (Smutny and Schreiberova 2020). Although research that focuses specifically on the role of chatbots in education is increasing, adoption is in the early stages, leaving a great deal of untapped potential. One of the widely documented benefits derived from AI technology and chatbots lies in their ability to provide individualized learning support for students, which is particularly advantageous in large-scale educational scenarios (Winkler and Söllner 2018). Although these solutions remain relatively complex and resource-intensive to establish, they hold great potential to assist students in a truly personalized fashion and achieve high levels of student engagement.

THE IMPACT OF TECHNOLOGY ON ASSESSMENTS

The previous section concentrated on introducing different tools and technological solutions that can assist institutions and faculty members in their efforts to engage innovative design and delivery methods when developing their courses. Some of the same tools can also be quite advantageous in helping with the management of student assessment, which is the topic of this section. Assessment of student performance in the traditional sense can be a rather time-consuming endeavor, particularly when handling large groups. In fact, the full administrative management of student assessment tends to represent one of the most resource-intensive and burdensome activities for many educational institutions. In fact, many of the tools outlined in the section above can be solicited for assistance and be used as viable alternatives. However, we argue that in order to be effective they should not be used in silos, but instead should be synchronized with the overall curriculum and course content. With this background, our aim in this section is to emphasize three relevant points to consider: the strategic use of remote assessments, the diversification of assessment methods and, last but not least, the use of formative as opposed to summative forms of evaluation. We hope that these ideas will trigger further scholarly and practitioner exchange and encourage faculty members to experiment in their own courses.

The Strategic yet Hazardous Use of Remote Assessments

The issue of remote assessments is one that can easily spark lengthy debates amongst academics and administrative staff alike. And following the recent worldwide closure of academic institutions, this matter became even more immediate and urgent as part of the overall matter of remote teaching and learning. Such a sense of urgency may present a good opportunity for academic institutions to rethink their assessment methods, as for the most part they tend to be outdated. And while technology can help, it has to be considered within a larger conversation. In a rather honest and realistic account concerning educational assessment practices, Stanfield and Strohmayer (2015) emphasized that the methods in use are vastly inefficient, given their reliance on incorrect educational outcomes, and consequently testing the "wrong" thing. The authors critique our continued global reliance on the final exam, an assessment method with initial roots in the 19th and 20th centuries, with an overly heavy emphasis on facts. The authors posit that contemporary assessment should concentrate on the evaluation of 21st century skills, with particular attention to problem-solving and critical thinking. In this sense, without a comprehensive approach to curricular development and review that considers not only content and delivery but also assessment, technology may be insufficient (Higgins 2015).

In situations where the final exam is the primary contributing factor to the final grade, it is not surprising that institutions may feel reluctant to relinquish their power over the administration. And as a result, proposals for change frequently spark controversy and debate initiated by a sense of fear associated with losing control, lack of trust, concerns over student privacy, and lack of sufficient and reliable options available. The fear of losing control and the lack of trust in students assessed online or via technological tools are not novel concerns for faculty and for institutions, with their roots linked to several past issues. Such concerns eventually gave rise to the development of various online anti-plagiarism tools (e.g., Urkund, Turnitin) that have proven to be helpful in preventing students from cheating, or otherwise catching those who cheated and/or plagiarized (Ledwith and Risquez 2008). At the same time, despite its documented benefits, technology can also facilitate cheating behaviors or even work outsourcing that can hardly be uncovered by existing tools (Wolverton 2016).

In response to the surge of demand following the school closures, an increasing number of startups and information technology firms began to introduce new solutions for online proctoring and the digital management of exams, mostly relying on face recognition technology. Given the novelty of these solutions, it may take a while longer until these become mainstream, even though relying on the current emergency may facilitate the implementation and management of changes (Hatch 2009). Consequently, alternative ways need to be identified to be able to manage student assessment. As an alternative, schools can try to counter these challenges by conveying a message to students early on, from orientation onwards, that honesty is a fundamental virtue they uphold, and it is reflected in the value of their degree. Collaborative responsibility for this can be emphasized, with zero tolerance for cheating. Ariely (2012) presents an interesting set of research on cheating and dishonesty, and finds that when students are reminded of the importance of honesty in the form of a moral stature such as recalling the Ten Commandments or the university's moral code, cheating automatically goes down versus the control group. Brief self-administered online training programs are helpful – similar to those used in banks and other firms – to emphasize the importance of honesty. In addition, rethinking and diversifying assessment methods can also help address these issues; with further details on this outlined below.

Diversification of Assessment Methods

A general tendency that characterizes the assessment of student performance concerns the lack of diversity in the employed methods, in turn placing a disproportionate emphasis on a few disconnected deliverables. It is not uncommon, for instance, to assess individual student performance predominantly by mid-term and final exams. The situation is slightly better in business schools, particularly those that manage to attain at least one of the leading international accreditations (e.g., those awarded by Equis or the Association to Advance Collegiate Schools of Business, AACSB), which tend to be more advanced in the sense that as part of the accreditation process they have to demonstrate alignment with the Assurance of Learning (AoL) principles and establish program-level learning goals that are relevant, up-to-date and resonate well with contemporary industry standards. These program-level learning goals are then mapped onto the curriculum to be assessed regularly via specific assignments, projects or activities. While the general idea is great, in reality the implementation can pose a range of challenges to institutions, given the relative complexity, required shift in mindset, and collaborative oversight over the entire curriculum and AoL system. Consequently, faculty members still frequently revert to relying heavily on traditional exams.

As an alternative and more easily implementable solution, faculty members should be encouraged to employ a range of assessment methods that, in combination, may be better suited to guarantee student learning as well as achieve a more reliable view of it. Increased diversity can help faculty members get to know their students better, students be able to affirm their learning and identify potential gaps, and institutions to infuse a culture that is focused on learning as opposed to cramming for an exam. And many of the above-mentioned technological tools can be used quite well in this regard. For instance, students can be given a set of readings or short videos shared on a learning platform, followed by a brief quiz. Faculty members can monitor completion rates, time spent on the platform and other metrics that can ensure students are doing their work and are progressing with the material. For other types of assessment such as papers or case study analyses, learning platforms present a good solution for submission purposes, giving faculty members immediate access and ability to comment or grade. As mentioned above, simulations provide another excellent opportunity to immerse students in a real-life situation, and are often empowered with an embedded assessment tool that can be used easily for grading purposes. And in the case of group projects, the various online collaborative and communication tools can assist faculty members to be able to participate in some of the group discussions and evaluate individual contributions more easily.

The Use of Formative rather than Summative Forms of Assessment

Building on the above discussion concerning assessment diversification, evaluating students on a continuous basis can have a variety of advantages which, in turn, may also resolve some of the issues related to remote assessment and cheating. Taking responsibility for one's education and learning should be at the cornerstone of any program. After all, students who join business schools do so with the aim of becoming the leaders of the future, and that is what most programs promise to do. But then, what happens? With the heavy emphasis on textbooks, exams and periodic assessment, students are often left alone until the final crunch time right before the exam. Such practice is not advantageous from a pedagogical perspective, as students tend to concentrate most of their learning right before the exam and miss a lot of content during the semester; nor from a learning perspective, as much of what is encountered can be more easily forgotten.

Instead, students should be given an opportunity to learn in a continuous fashion, with exercises and deliverables expected throughout each term, where technology can become a great asset. As long as there are measures in place – even simple ones such as an online quiz or documented activity on a learning platform – students may be more likely to complete reading, podcast or video assignments ahead of class, and in turn may also be more likely to actively participate in discussions and get more out of the teacher–class engagements. In addition to getting a more comprehensive understanding of the students' progress, another key purpose of these short checkpoints is to give students the opportunity to stay on target and help them manage their time more effectively. The issues with inadequate classroom performance often originate from inefficient time management practices, which can be worsened by imposing deliverables that not only carry a heavy weight but also concentrate at the end of the term.

As the following section will demonstrate, beyond design and assessment, the type of content covered in courses has a further meaningful contribution to influencing student engagement and learning, and there may be some best practices worthy to contemplate.

THE IMPACT OF TECHNOLOGY ON COURSE CONTENTS

The promise of business schools is to train future leaders who will not only shape markets but also play a fundamental role in society. Traditionally, business school curricula tended to concentrate on providing students with the core technical skills necessary to develop and execute business decisions. Over time, the inclusion of soft skills has become prevalent, recognizing the need for managers to understand their customers and be sensitive to the needs and well-being of their teams. Despite this shift in content, the fundamental premise that faculty are experts in their field and know what to teach to their students continued to prevail. As eluded to above, in recent years faculty members have found themselves faced with another considerable challenge regarding how to teach, including the careful alignment of mode of delivery, assessments and content in a rapidly changing educational landscape. The way students gather information today is strikingly different from a couple of decades ago, when textbooks and lectures were considered the primary source of knowledge. With the availability of Google, blogs, Wikipedia and numerous online applications, books and lectures have become "some of the ways" students could learn, creating a highly different atmosphere from before. Importantly, these experiences give contemporary students an increased sense of choice and control that is likely to make them more demanding in general, and also when they are in the classroom.

Of course, there may always be some teachers who manage to achieve a better overall rapport with their students and in turn secure higher levels of engagement. If we think back to our own education, most of us can probably recall a few particularly memorable teachers – whether in high school or college – who we liked so much that we still recall that special project in great detail we worked so hard for, even if not in our particular area of interest. But these cases tend to be in the minority. At the same time, with the availability of innovative technological tools, we can all create content that is engaging and memorable, and that encourages our students to go the extra mile. In that spirit, in this section we turn to discussing ways in which technology can assist in the development of content that is likely to enhance student engagement and learning. The "right" content can help students understand the value of what they are learning more fully, and in turn encourage them to intrinsically seek out opportunities for contributing to their own education. In particular, we will discuss the benefits of immersive technology, the co-creation of educational content, and adequate preparation for the marketplace.

The Benefits of Immersive Technology

Innovative technologies including simulations and virtual reality can be particularly helpful in recreating real-life situations via interactive platforms that help advance skills such as leadership, perspective-taking and empathy (Chirino-Klevans 2017). Content delivery employing these applications has also been shown to increase student enjoyment and interest (Lee et al. 2016). Hernandez-Pozas and Carreon-Flores (2019) argue that the current generation of students are used to blending virtual and physical realities in their daily existence and expect that to be the case in their education as well. The authors merge experiential learning theory, social cognitive theory, and generational theory to argue that virtual reality (VR), for instance, may serve as an innovative tool to enable students to gain first-hand practical experience in key competencies, including negotiation and intercultural communication.

Immersive experiences are meaningful in that they help students remain focused, and to overcome distractions by becoming "lost" in the task. Good simulation exercises, for instance, require regular participation from students, entail deadlines and periodic reminders, and these all help maintain student control and activity. By mimicking real-life experiences, immersive engagements are able to blur the boundaries between the "real" and "virtual," which have important beneficial consequences for purposes of pedagogy and student learning.

The Use of Video Content: Don't Fight Them, Join Them

Students are exposed to video content on a regular basis on various platforms, including Instagram, Snapchat and LinkedIn. Incorporating this form of media in classrooms is advantageous to diversify the course content, especially when it directly complements the overall learning experience. Interestingly, some research finds that students prefer taking an active role and selecting the media content themselves, as opposed to the instructor, to present to their classmates, giving these activities the potential to enhance student awareness and understanding of core course concepts (Donovan 2016). This suggests that not only can faculty members rely on video content, but also they can benefit from the inputs and interests of students to trigger and facilitate peer learning.

Finally, in addition to engaging students and favoring their own understanding and that of their peers, student-generated content is also a great way to value the work of students differently, whether internally (when shared with other students) or externally (when shared on social media), with potential spillover effects for the institution.

Aligning Contents to the Needs of a Tech-Infused Marketplace

Technology has pervaded all sectors and businesses, to a point where it is hard to identify any job that does not rely on or benefit from it. And technology is likely to impact most if not all activities of a company. For instance, an increasing number of firms rely on chatbots in their recruitment process, whether to convey the right information to the right applicant at the right time, to get more qualified applicants, to manage a large number of applications or to answer recurrent questions (Nawaz and Gomes 2019). The rise of the Internet-of-Things (IoT) has revolutionized business-to-business (B2B) supply chains, business models and services that manufacturers can deliver to their clients (Porter and Heppelmann 2015). Similarly, the growth of blockchain technologies has triggered tremendous change in the banking and financial services industry (Treleaven et al. 2017).

In this context, it is crucial that students are exposed to updated course content that includes technology not just as a dimension of their future job. More and more, students must also learn how technology works, understand how it is used, and become aware of its core building blocks. For instance, recruiters using chatbots need to understand how the algorithm that powers the bot has been elaborated to make sure that it is not biased in favour of specific profiles – something that has happened to Amazon – which could eventually undermine the firm's diversity and performance. Having students (and professors) comprehend how technology works, as well as some technology-related practices, will equip them with the necessary know-how to become more effective when in firms. Combined with their social, organizational or economic knowledge and skills, it will also enable them to understand and guide the tremendous changes that result from and in turn generate this technological pervasiveness.

Therefore, business schools' digital strategies should also consider the content of the courses to guarantee an alignment between firms' practices and the instruction that students receive. However, doing so raises several challenges that we will tackle in the next section.

CHALLENGES RAISED BY TECHNOLOGICALLY INFUSED CURRICULA

Developing technologically infused curricula creates different kinds of often interrelated challenges that business schools and professors must deal with; or, if not already doing so, must learn how to deal with, as some of these challenges are quite new to them. A few of these challenges are listed below, even though this list does not claim to be exhaustive.

Manage, Acknowledge and Measure the Workload of Professors

Recognizing that traditional lectures – at least in isolation – may no longer suffice, faculty members are increasingly encouraged to embrace active learning approaches complemented by innovative technological solutions. However, implementing such a substantial shift is not trivial. In a recent article in the *Chronicle of Higher Education*, Gooblar (2019) emphasized that the incorporation of high-impact practices in classroom instruction can place extensive demands and workload on faculty members that may even risk exposing them to burnout.

Many faculty members may have the interest or motivation to introduce innovative content, pedagogical delivery formats or use technology for assessments, but given their extensive workload and increasing research and/or service expectations, may find it difficult to find "the right time" to redesign their courses. It is important for institutional support teams to provide the right ideas and right kind of support at the right time.

Eventually, teaching online may generate difficulties to assess and monitor professors' teaching loads. In-class teaching can be easily measured thanks to so-called "contact hours," referring to the time spent in class with the students. While synchronous online teaching can be measured in the same way, asynchronous teaching is not so easy. How to measure the time spent by professors to prepare online videos? Should the time spent to find online contents made available to students be counted in their "teaching time"? Answers to such questions are usually institutionally contingent and thus not always easy to comprehend.

Keep Up With (the Pace of) Technology

Developing technologically infused curricula involves large software and hardware invest-ments. The accelerating pace of technological evolution makes it bewildering for professors, educational institutions, firms and even students to remain up-to-date. This is a fundamental issue, as this pace may give individuals and institutions the impression they will never be able to keep up. It also implies being able to understand the relative advantages of education tech-nology products before selecting one of them; yet, with so many of them promising to "rev-olutionize teaching and learning," taking enlightened decisions is not always easy. Finally, it is also crucial to be aware of the changes that occur in firms to make sure that course contents remain up-to-date too.

Train Professors

The recent overnight turn to online teaching due to Covid-19 has made it even more obvious that not all professors had the required digital skills to master the technological tools they would be asked to use. It is crucial that professors develop a digital mindset and tech literacy that would make them much more comfortable with the use of those tools (Allen 2020). This would also help them rethink their teaching with new solutions, and evolve and infuse their course content reflecting a better understanding of business changes resulting from technolog-ical pervasiveness.

Make Sure that Students are Able to Access and Use Technology

Just like professors, not all the students are equally familiar or comfortable with technology, even though this goes against common sense. This may be due to a lack of interest towards technology. It may also result from difficult financial situations that prevent students from accessing costly technological devices or services that other, more affluent students may be more accustomed to. Finally, not all students have internet access, which makes it difficult for them to learn online. In this case, technologically infused curricula may exclude students, even when the level of use of technology is relatively low (e.g., merely online content for students to watch). Again, the Covid-19 crisis has heightened the prevalence of this issue, which business schools must consider when designing online content or virtual or hybrid programs.

Face Massive and Diversified Costs

Implicit in the issues outlined above are the costs associated with the development and adoption of technologically infused curricula. From both an individual and an organizational standpoint, these challenges can be of diverse nature, including time-related, financial, cognitive and other resources. Faculty members need to juggle their time across many tasks, and as teaching excellence often remains insufficiently recognized, they are likely to opt for spending their limited time on research, which counts the most towards their professional advancements; or service tasks, which tend to be the most pressing. Students are often not trained on tools, and the general myth that they must tech-savvy given that they belong to the "online generation" can put many of them at a disadvantage. Finally, institutions often struggle with budgetary allocations and financial resources, coupled with the overabundance of choice in terms of new technological options.

Summing it all up, all parties involved – faculty, students and institutions – tend to face rather complex challenges, which cannot be tackled alone. Instead, it is crucial that institutions develop a long-term collaborative and forward-looking strategy that they stick to. It is likely that success may take a little longer, but there is a need for the enthusiastic and collaborative contributions of faculty, students, staff and some experts in relevant technological solutions.

THE WAY FORWARD

In this final section, we highlight some concrete recommendations that may help institutions tackle the above-mentioned challenges and ultimately turn technology into an opportunity rather than a burden. Figure 9.2 provides a brief summary of the key points.

In terms of design and delivery, it is important for institutions and support teams to provide the right type of training made available in the right form. Faculty members tend to refer to support at the exact moment when they need it. Hence, it may be insufficient to create workshops that are not highly frequented and do not present value. Online resources are much more effective in this regard, and can be accessed at any point. In order to recognize the time commitment on behalf of faculty, it is also useful to develop a reward system that recognizes – as opposed to punishes – pedagogical innovations. These should not be considered in constant competition with research outputs, and should be equally celebrated by using rewards, badges and other forms of recognition. This is mostly possible once institutions manage to instill a digital mindset and create a culture of sharing and peer collaboration.

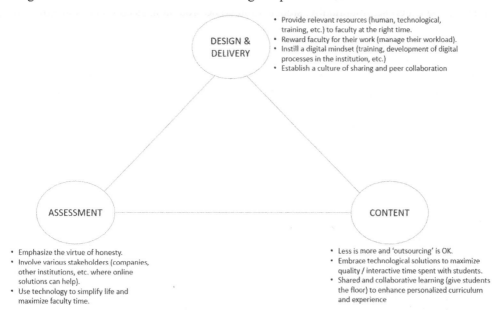

DESIGN & DELIVERY
* Provide relevant resources (human, technological, training, etc.) to faculty at the right time.
* Reward faculty for their work (manage their workload).
* Instill a digital mindset (training, development of digital processes in the institution, etc.)
* Establish a culture of sharing and peer collaboration

ASSESSMENT
* Emphasize the virtue of honesty.
* Involve various stakeholders (companies, other institutions, etc. where online solutions can help).
* Use technology to simplify life and maximize faculty time.

CONTENT
* Less is more and 'outsourcing' is OK.
* Embrace technological solutions to maximize quality / interactive time spent with students.
* Shared and collaborative learning (give students the floor) to enhance personalized curriculum and experience

Figure 9.2   *Turning technology into an opportunity in course design and delivery, assessment and content*

Considering assessment, it is important for institutions to create a culture of trust and encourage their students to behave according to standards that will prevail throughout their careers. Adopting a diversified set of assessments would be a great first step, taking advantage of different sources and options for purposes of evaluation. For instance, many business school students are required to do some form of a practicum, and it would be wise to involve their corporate supervisor in the evaluation process. Taking an approach towards technology as a resource rather than as a risk when it comes to assessment is also important and, if used appropriately, it may have the potential to alleviate faculty workload substantially.

Finally, content should undergo substantial revisions to be aligned with design, delivery and assessment, with an important starting point to allow and encourage faculty members to let go of some of their traditional responsibilities of being the sole expert in the room. Generally speaking, course content is best delivered in relatively small and easily manageable increments or "pods" that include four key areas: (1) reading relevant chapters and articles prior to coming to class to familiarize students with theory and terminology; (2) review, guided by faculty members to emphasize key points; (3) reflection, to enable students to apply and further advance their learning using case studies and individual and group projects; and (4) reinforcement, to help students with their revision using quizzes, multiple-choice questions (MCQs) and short exercises.

Gathering materials that are interesting and relevant for students could be equally as challenging as creating other types of content, and faculty should be encouraged to rely on a variety of resources available. If technological solutions are used effectively, the time spent with students could concentrate on deepening their understanding of the material and equipping them with practical expertise. Importantly, students should be brought in as co-contributors to their learning, which may have valuable consequences in the sense of creating more meaningful associations, relevance and in-depth learning.

Overall, we are confident that business schools have the opportunity to make a valuable contribution to their students' lives and future careers. But they may need to take a step back and re-evaluate their priorities, practices and cultural mindset. Establishing a technologically infused curriculum takes time, effort and meaningful collaboration. But in the end, it may just be the thing that differentiates business schools by creating a meaningful learning journey that all students strive for.

REFERENCES

Alanne, Kari (2016), "An overview of game-based learning in building services engineering education," *European Journal of Engineering Education*, 41 (2), 204–219.

Allen, Scott J. (2020), "On the cutting edge or the chopping block? Fostering a digital mindset and tech literacy in business management education," *Journal of Management Education*, 44 (3), 362–393.

Ariely, Dan (2012), *The Honest Truth about Dishonesty: How We Lie to Everyone – Especially Ourselves*. New York: Harper.

Barr, Matthew (2018), "Student attitudes to games-based skills development: learning from video games in higher education," *Computers in Human Behavior*, 80, 283–294.

Blum, Susan D. (2020), "Why We're Exhausted by Zoom," in *Inside Higher Ed*. https://www.insidehighered.com/advice/2020/04/22/professor-explores-why-zoom-classes-deplete-her-energy-opinion (accessed September 2, 2020).

Carenys, Jordi and Soledad Moya (2016), "Digital game-based learning in accounting and business education," *Accounting Education*, 25 (6), 598–651.

Chirino-Klevans, Ivonne (2017), "Virtual reality in global business: using technology for leadership skills development," *ISM Journal of International Business*, November, 11–15.

Crocco, Francesco, Kathleen Offenholley and Carlos Hernandez (2016), "A proof-of-concept study of game-based learning in higher education," *Simulation and Gaming*, 47 (4), 403–422.

Donovan, Craig Poulenez (2016), "Using media clips with the visual/virtual generation: we are doing it backwards," *Business Education Innovation Journal*, 8 (2), 92–103.

Gooblar, David (2019), "'Is it ever OK to lecture?'," *Chronicle of Higher Education*. https://www.chronicle.com/article/is-it-ever-ok-to-lecture/ (accessed September 2, 2020).

Hatch, Thomas (2009), *Managing to Change: How Schools Can Survive (and Sometimes Thrive) in Turbulent Times*. Series on School Reform. New York: Teachers College Press.

Hernandez-Pozas, Olivia and Horacio Carreon-Flores (2019), "Teaching international business using virtual reality," *Journal of Teaching in International Business*, 30 (2), 196–212.

Higgins, Steve (2015), "Why access to computers won't automatically boost children's grades," *Conversation*. https://theconversation.com/why-access-to-computers-wont-automatically-boost-childrens-grades-47521 (accessed September 2, 2020).

Jiang, Mei, Julia Ballenger and William Holt (2019), "Educational leadership doctoral students' perceptions of the effectiveness of instructional strategies and course design in a fully online graduate statistics course," *Online Learning*, 23 (4), 296–312.

Ledwith, Ann and Angelica Risquez (2008), "Using anti-plagiarism software to promote academic honesty in the context of peer reviewed assignments," *Studies in Higher Education*, 33 (4), 371–384.

Lee, Yu-Hao, Norah Dunbar, Keri Kornelson, Scott Wilson, Ryan Ralston, et al. (2016), "Digital game based learning for undergraduate calculus education: immersion, calculation, and conceptual understanding," *International Journal of Gaming and Computer-Mediated Simulations*, 8 (1), 13–27.

Manca, Stefania, Valentina Grion, Alejandro Armellini and Cristina Devecchi (2017), "Editorial: Student voice. Listening to students to improve education through digital technologies," *British Journal of Educational Technology*, 48 (5), 1075–1080.

Mayer, Igor, Harald Warmelink and Geertje Bekebrede (2013), "Learning in a game-based virtual environment: a comparative evaluation in higher education," *European Journal of Engineering Education*, 38 (1), 85–106.

Moore, Geoffrey (1991), *Crossing the Chasm: Marketing and Selling Technology Products to Mainstream Customers*. New York: Harper Business.

Moses, Tabitha (2020), "5 reasons to let students keep their cameras off during Zoom classes," *Conversation*. https://theconversation.com/5-reasons-to-let-students-keep-their-cameras-off-during -zoom-classes-144111 (accessed September 2, 2020).

Nawaz, Nishad and Anjali Mary Gomes (2019), "Artificial intelligence chabots are new recruiters," *International Journal of Advanced Computer Science and Applications*, 10 (9), 1–5.

Oo, Bee Lan and Benson Teck-Heng Lim (2016), "Game-based learning in construction management courses: a case of bidding game," *Engineering Construction and Architectural Management*, 23 (1), 4–19.

Perini, Stefano, Rossella Luglietti, Maria Margoudi, Manuel Oliveira and Marco Taisch (2018), "Learning and motivational effects of digital game-based learning (DGBL) for manufacturing education – The Life Cycle Assessment (LCA) game," *Computers in Industry*, 102, 40–49.

Porter, Michael E. and James E. Heppelmann (2015), "How smart, connected products are transforming," *Harvard Business Review*, 93 (10), 96-16.

Shanbari, Hamzah and Raja R.A. Issa (2019), "Use of video games to enhance construction management education," *International Journal of Construction Management*, 19 (3), 206–221.

Smutny, Pavel and Petra Schreiberova (2020), "Chatbots for learning: a review of educational chatbots for the Facebook Messenger," *Computers and Education*, 151, 103862.

Stanfield, James and Angelika Strohmayer (2015), "Outdated exams are holding children back – not computers in the classroom," *Conversation*. https://theconversation.com/outdated-exams-are-holding -children-back-not-computers-in-the-classroom-47810 (accessed September 2, 2020).

Treleaven, P., R. Gendal Brown and D. Yang (2017), "Blockchain technology in finance," *Computer*, 50 (9), 14–17.

Warden, Clyde A., James O. Stanworth and Chi-Cheng Chang (2016), "Leveling up: are non-gamers and women disadvantaged in a virtual world classroom?," *Computers in Human Behavior*, 65, 210–219.

Winkler, Rainer and Matthias Söllner (2018), "Unleashing the potential of chatbots in education: a state-of-the-art analysis," *Academy of Management Annual Meeting* (AOM), Chicago, IL.

Wolverton, Brad (2016), "The new cheating economy," *Chronicle of Higher Education*, 63 (1), A40–A45. https://www.chronicle.com/article/the-new-cheating-economy/ (accessed September 2, 2020).

10. Gamification in education: the case of gamified learning in teams

Rushana Khusainova, Yasin Sahhar and Ad de Jong

INTRODUCTION

The trend towards using digital technologies – such as mobile apps, three-dimensional (3D) simulations and online platforms – has encouraged educational institutions to adopt and embrace gamified applications in their pedagogical approaches. Gamification can be defined as the use of game design elements in non-game contexts, such as work environments, industrial settings and educational contexts (Deterding, 2012; Marchand & Hennig-Thurau, 2013). In such settings, gamification involves incorporating one or more game aspects into the nature of the activity or task at hand, in order to increase individual's engagement and performance. For example, various companies have introduced gamified settings in which frontline employees compete against each other based on key service performance indicators.

Gamification is increasingly used in education. Examples are tools such as the Professor Game and Kahoot, which are used to motivate students. In the academic literature, recent studies in teaching and learning have also emphasized the added value of gamification as a facilitator of student engagement (e.g., Buckley & Doyle, 2016; da Rocha Seixas et al., 2016) and the first systematic literature review on gamified learning in higher education (HE) was published in 2018 (by Subhash & Cudney). While an accumulating body of literature pays attention to gamification in teaching and learning settings, little is known about the role of teamwork as an interpersonal process in the context of gamified learning.

Educational settings emphasize the use of teamwork where students can jointly work on projects in order to perform. So far, research in gamification has mainly focused on gamification as a driver of individual student experiences and contributions. However, the interpersonal and team aspect is inherent in gamification as a phenomenon. Recent scholars (e.g., Koivisto & Hamari, 2019) call for research that examines the role of collective and cooperative aspects in gamification approaches. Especially in educational settings, teamwork is relevant, and smooth interpersonal interactions are essential to drive students' intellectual performance and achievements.

Therefore, the purpose of this chapter is to examine team-based gamified learning in an educational context. The structure of the chapter is as follows. First, we provide a short literature review on gamification in education, discussing what it is and why it is of importance in an educational context. Second, we present an example on how a game can be designed based on the case of designing the Marketing and Sales game. Finally, we present and discuss the empirical findings of the study. These are based on a random sample of 50 student reflections. We also provide a set of three instructor reflections, including tips on the successful implementation of a game. We draw some important conclusions, and provide directions for future development of research on gamification in teaching and learning.

GAMIFICATION IN EDUCATION: A LITERATURE REVIEW

What is Gamification?

Gamification is defined as the use of game design elements (also referred to as game elements or game mechanics) in non-game contexts, such as education or the workplace (Deterding et al., 2011). These game elements include such important features of games as, for example, rules, goal, feedback and teams (Reeves & Read, 2009). Specifically, rules help to formalize game elements and tell the player what they can and cannot do, and what they can expect from a game (Vroom 1964; Salen and Zimmerman, 2004). Goals have important motivational power (Locke, 1968). Feedback is concerned with promoting knowledge of the results of performing the task (Hackman & Oldham, 1980). Finally, teamwork encourages cooperation within each team, while providing the fun aspect of competition between teams (Madrid et al., 2007).

The purpose of gamification in education is to make learning more enjoyable and, as such, to increase student engagement (Villagrasa et al., 2014). Simply put, people performing a task labelled as 'play' are more intrinsically motivated and perform better than those working on a task labelled as 'work' (Glynn, 1994). This generally results in a significant positive effect on knowledge attainment and motivation (Connolly et al., 2012). When done in teams, this can also foster student cooperation (Madrid et al., 2007).

Types of Gamification in Education

Gabriele Ferri (2015), presents a detailed discussion of gamification typologies. Some of these classifications are based on the following criteria:

- whether gamification includes win–lose situations or not;
- whether gamification involves technology or is tech-free;
- whether participants play against each other or against an engine.

The main typology though, Ferri (2015) argues, is whether gamification requires participants' full attention (exclusive gamification) or can be played alongside other activities (interstitial gamification). Building on this typology, we propose a specific classification of gamification in education. Based on how gamification is executed or implemented, gamification can be considered as in-learning gamification or for-learning gamification.

The first type is in-learning gamification, whereby game elements are integrated within a course structure or metrics. It can be seen as adding a game layer to the existing systems or processes, as opposed to using an entirely new and separate game (Hamari & Koivisto, 2013). In a broader gamification realm, this is labelled as a classical gamification. In an educational setting this means, for instance, converting module learning metrics into experience or achievement points, utilizing leader boards, badges and levels (Landers, 2014). These can be used on both individual and team levels. With technological advancements, such gamified elements take a more engaging and more enjoyable form. Examples of such classical formats in educational setting are: Kahoot, Quizalize, Blackboard Learn, Venox and Canvas. Most of them are commonly used in academic institutions and have been demonstrated to significantly increase students' engagement.

The second type is for-learning gamification. It concerns so-called gamified learning, which is a form of experiential learning (Subhash & Cudney, 2018). Here, students (usually working in teams) are immersed in a real-life scenario and are free to practice their decision-making and market research, to test knowledge and apply theories in the safety of the simulated environment. Examples of such gamification used at academic institutions are Markstrat, and the Tragedy of the Commons.

This form of gamified learning has been around for a long time. A predecessor of these simulations is a classical business case study where students have to work on a given scenario and solve a case. Indeed, the advent and rapid development of technology has changed the way experiential learning creates engagement as well as the quality of experience a game can offer (McGonigal, 2011). This means that when a good business case meets a smart technology, one can expect that learning becomes a lot more engaging and fun.

The presence of technology and fun aspect of games appear to be especially important in the context of the current student population. It is estimated that currently the majority of HE students fall into the Generation Z and Millennial cohorts. Research shows that these generations prefer environments which are challenging, dynamic, interesting and fun (Gursoy et al., 2008). They are digital natives who prefer the 'hands on', experiential approach to learning where they can practice the skills they will need in their future careers, in the safety of a classroom environment (Seemiller & Clayton, 2019). Both generations value feedback and inclusivity, and enjoy working in teams (although in somewhat different ways).

There is also another example of for-learning gamification in education. This involves the use of simple games which are played alongside learning aimed at adding a layer of fun. Such games do not directly contribute to learning, though they are still often used in a classroom to increase engagement and connection between an instructor and students, or to create a positive learning environment, for example when simple games are used as ice breakers (e.g., Chinese Whispers, Story Cubes or line-ups according to a certain task or criteria).

Gamified Learning in Teams

Research suggests that learning in teams, also known as collaborative learning, can have a positive impact on motivation, performance and the quality of the learning experience (Anderson and Garrison, 1998; Wells and Higgs, 1990). Playing in teams inevitably contributes to creating a positive affective experience by adding a layer of fun inherent in play and games (Mollick & Rothbard, 2013). Tuckman (1965) proposed team formation stages where fun, creativity and harmony become a part of the performing stage of teamwork. This is where the most action happens. Teamwork is 'the willingness and ability of team members to work together in a genuinely cooperative manner toward a common goal' (Lick, 2000, p. 46). Effective teamwork and positive team dynamic are essential parts of the positive experience offered by gamified learning.

Team dynamic, which is defined as the 'interactions among the students and the processes within their groups' (Chapman et al. 2006, p. 562), can be viewed as a function of two categories: (1) interpersonal team processes; and (2) elements of task orientation (Walker et al., 2020). The first category includes such elements as learning how to communicate and enjoy working as a team, managing challenging personalities and conflict resolution. The second category includes coming to the classroom well prepared, task delegation, team members' focus on tasks and readiness to participate. Working through such challenges as building effective communication, managing difficult personalities and learning task delegation become a big part of gamified learning in teams. In this light, playing in teams offers not only an added element of competitive fun, but also an addition layer of valuable learning. An ability to work in teams is one of the top skills graduate recruiters look for (Calanca et al., 2019).

Gamified Learning and Assessment

There are two distinct ways gamified learning in teams can be linked to assessment. The first is when student attainment is directly linked to students' performance in a game. In such cases, in order to receive a certain grade, students must collect a specific amount of points or achieve a certain level, so that their scores in a game are used to form a part of the final module mark (Moccozet et al., 2013).

The second is when students play a game and then produce a separate piece of work (e.g., a report, project or reflective essay) based on an aspect of the game they played. This is usually done as an individual piece of assessment, though it can also be done as a group. This means that students' final marks do not directly depend on how well they did in the game itself, avoiding such problems as fierce competition. And in a case of individual coursework, it also addresses an issue of free-riders (Elliott and Higgins, 2005). Here, playing the game may still remain a fun aspect of the module, and competition will not get fierce. Yet, still, students will benefit from the gamified learning and then can work on producing an assessed piece of work.

THE MAKING OF THE GAME: THE CASE OF THE MARKETING AND SALES GAME

In this section, we present a case of developing and implementing a gamified learning tool for students in HE. This game, called the Marketing and Sales (M&S) Game, was developed as a result of a collaboration between an international business consulting firm and a European university. The aim of the game is to serve as a learning vehicle to increase students' engagement and knowledge in the area of marketing and sales.

The M&S Game Development

At the start of the initiative, initial ideas were jointly generated and screened by the company and the university. The game development team was then formed. It consisted of representatives of the business consultancy firm (professionals in the field of information technology, strategic management and marketing), and representatives of a university (a professor in marketing, and two MSc students who were carefully recruited).

The game development process consisted of several stages. First, ideas were generated and screened. These ideas mainly focused on the game design, including overall goals, game set-up and structure. Subsequently, these ideas were tied to a framework that served as an input for development of the game application. Further to this, the two MSc students, with mixed professional backgrounds of business, design and information technology (IT) experience, helped develop the game into a software tool. The game was then pre-tested with a group of 70 MSc students. Finally, it was launched.

All aforementioned phases contained iterative improvement cycles of designing, developing, testing, evaluating and improving. The consultants and professor were mainly in charge, guiding the process by developing ideas and setting milestones and requirements. The students were involved in the actual making of the game. Since its launch, the game has been played on a regular basis at several academic institutions and companies, with groups ranging from 30 to 150 students.

The Process of Playing the M&S Game

The M&S Game has a dynamic set-up. There are four rounds, where students have to work in teams to make marketing and sales decisions. There are short inspirational lectures at each round, which are used as a vehicle to teach participants about novel theories and concepts, and to introduce a new assignment for each round. Students then apply these theories and concepts in the subsequent rounds of the game.

In between every session the expert hosts provide collective and individual team feedback (qualitatively and quantitatively) to accommodate participants' learning. The game closes with a 'Dragon's Den' wherein each team pitches their ideas and competes on the best possible approach. During the entire game, participants are assessed both on hard and soft skills. Finally, students reflect upon the game, and are invited to provide feedback.

Students play the M&S Game in small teams consisting of 3–6 people. Overall, there may be 4–10 teams competing against each other in the same game. Indeed, teamwork and interpersonal collaboration is an important aspect of game experience. For instance, a positive team dynamic is essential to ensure that participants are able to have fruitful discussions and make informed decisions for each round of the game.

The lively structure effectively contributes to expanding and deepening participants' knowledge. Moreover, it brings advantages for continuously refining and optimizing the game itself. Due to its modular structure with several game rounds, feedback on the game can be processed effectively on specific parts of the game. For example, participants' feedback on a certain session, implying it is not experienced as it should be, can serve as a basis for further refinements. Consequently, beside the core team of the game, participants have a fundamental say in improving the M&S Game.

Future of Gamified Learning in Teams in Higher Education: The Case of the M&S Game

In line with digital and educational developments, gamification in itself is already a trend in several domains. For example, organizations adopt it to train their employees and it has been widely used in education to train students in hard and soft skills. However, gamification itself is also subject to change, and therefore the M&S Game is too.

Continuous optimization will drive the future of the game. For example, as digitalization significantly affects how students are being taught, the game will also play a more dominant role in this. Currently, the game itself is played semi-digitally. Participants play the game on electronic devices and experts host, facilitate and instruct them on the university's premises. Likely in the near future, the M&S Game will be available in a full online version. In other words, participants play where they want, and experts are available online for any questions or necessary instructions. In this way, the game contributes to mobile learning/education.

Moreover, the game will more profoundly play a role in topical themes such as participants' self-development and life-long learning. Also, and especially at universities where a standing challenge is to make education more attractive to students, the game can play an important role to accommodate this. For example, the M&S Game can be a compelling way to make education more joyful and contribute directly to individual and collaborative development; all in all, a more pleasant experience for participants.

EMPIRICAL STUDY: PERSPECTIVES FROM STUDENTS AND INSTRUCTORS

Research Background and Outline

In this section, we present a summary of 50 randomly chosen student reflections from a pool of 200. These reflections were submitted as part of marketing and sales modules taught in two European universities. These modules are at level 6 (final-year undergraduate) and level 7 (MSc). Students wrote these reflective essays within two weeks of playing the game and were encouraged to reflect deeply on their personal experiences of it.

Thematic analysis of the student reflections identified three distinct themes: (1) overall game dynamic; (2) team-related experiences; and (3) individual-level experiences. See Table 10A.1 in the Appendix for the summary. This section summarizes and interprets our findings of the student reflections and presents student quotes in support of these.

Over 80 per cent of the chosen reflections focus solely or partially on participants' team-related experiences with the game. Although we present all three themes, given the positioning of our study the focus is on students' team-related reflections. We also present three instructor reflections, which aim to offer some practical insights, tips and hints on organizing and running such games in an HE setting.

Student Reflections: Overall Game Experience

Students' overall game experience can be grouped into the following themes. We present anonymized student quotes to illustrate each theme.

First, the game is perceived as engaging. It attracts students' attention, causing them to be directly engaged with and throughout the game:

> Overall, I had a great experience of learning through the use of digital technologies and games, as it really engaged my attention throughout.
> The opportunity to present a pitch in the end, even though a bit time-pressured, was also a pleasant experience. Both because it was interesting to see how every group had different solutions and strategies, but also to get a 'real-life experience' and to get immediate feedback.

Secondly, the game offers a safe learning environment, meaning that students can make mistakes and learn from them accordingly. Such an environment stimulates students to come up with creative and innovative ideas and make courageous and rigorous decisions. This may result in an increasing confidence among students and a steeper learning curve:

the game definitely did give a good insight into some of the complications and considerations that arise in this kind of work. I personally really liked the room for creativity, e.g., in the assignment focused on sketching out the customer journey. It was a positive experience that we were able to determine all customer steps ourselves, without too much interference, and evaluate when the value for the customer emerged. It encouraged a lively discussion and underlined that the customer derived value, much fewer times during the entire journey than initially assumed in the group.

Moreover, the physical attributes of the game are a present factor in students' reflections. For example, playing the game in an accessible way through digital technologies such as iPads is part of the overall game experience:

> Overall, I had a great experience of learning through the use of digital technologies and games, as it really engaged my attention throughout. In support to that, effective learning takes place when you are completely engaged in what you are doing. Thus, I would like to conclude that the Marketing and Sales Game is a successful learning experience for me, and I believe that it would be beneficial for organisations to adopt as a training tool.

Finally, students point out that the game offers a real-life replication. Often, students find themselves studying theory in combination with examples from practice. However, they still have scarce knowledge about how 'things happen in real life'. The game offered students such a 'real-life experience' for several reasons. Specifically, students were aware that the game is based on a real-life case (consisting of a market, facts and figures, and a product), professionals from the field host the game, and theory comes together with practice and the game:

> Successfully, the Marketing & Sales Game merged theory and practice by applying key concepts within strategic marketing management on a real-life case revolving around a company offering hearing aids in the British market.

> Training in simulated, safe, and fun environments can thus increase the learning and confidence of the students. Therefore, I think that a simulated reality with a gamification element – such as the marketing and sales game – can prove itself useful in learning situations for salespeople as well as students.

In conclusion, students report that the overall game experience is one which is enjoyable, engaging and provides the real-life replication scenario that students value.

Student Reflections: Team-Related Experience

Our team-level findings are thought-provoking. Since students play in teams, the dynamic among them is an essential part of the learning experience. Students' experience of teamwork may be both facilitating and impeding to the game experience.

Great team dynamic is, for example, open communication where every student's voice can be heard, finding consensus among the group, having a clear task division with trust among one other, and maintaining a positive vibe:

> Straight away I found each member was engaged, excited and willing to put the effort in to try and win. Each of us voiced our opinions and ideas and went through the tasks together as a group. Our personalities matched well and that meant we were able to have fun during the day whilst completing each round.

I explained that everyone needs to be heard in our group. After this our team began to develop an understanding, clear communication and a fun aspect of working together which I believe is key and made me feel confident.

The use of sales game made me grow as an individual and allow me to find my own space within a team of like-minded individuals. I do not feel as if I learnt more about sales but rather more about how to function well as a team.

On the contrary, a poor team dynamic destroys students' collective experience. Examples of such a dynamic are misunderstandings between team members, frustrations among them, and a lack of leadership skills and clear task division:

From the very beginning I could see we had developed very poor team dynamics. This is because we had one individual who jumped to the role of being the leader but in fact came across as an aggressor. This was because she often disagreed with other members and was often inappropriately outspoken. I was quite intimidated which I believe was expressed quite clearly to other members of the team as this incident lead to me not engaging with discussions as much as I should have been. I was consequently afraid of giving my own personal opinion which helped eliminate the fun element this game believed so much in. This led to my team not being able to perform as effectively as we could have as everyone wanted to be seen to agree with the leader. We ultimately became afraid of expressing our own individual opinions. It was evident that the team morale had dropped dramatically and participating in group decisions quickly became awkward and uncomfortable.

Another important construct is how students 'click'. When this happens, students work well together, the process of collaboration seems to flow naturally, confidence increases, and the overall team experience is enhanced. This also accommodates our third example of team experiences, having common goals:

I realised that the disagreements and problems with listening we faced during this phase of the game were a symptom of the team's overall enthusiasm and passion for producing an effective presentation. Despite, the issues myself and the team faced, we were able to produce a presentation which achieved a higher mark than the four other groups.

Lastly, toxic behaviours heavily influenced the team experience. For example, students who obsessively wanted to prove themselves, in front of the other team members or the jury, negatively impacted upon the overall team experience. This creates an environment of battling with each other instead of concentrating on the challenges of the game itself:

At times I felt frustrated because team members were speaking over me when I was trying to present my ideas back to the group. Conversely, at other times I felt pleased to be surrounded with such a lively group that was so enthusiastic about the stimulation. As a result of this, our time management skills were not efficient. Due to speaking over one another, members of the group ended up repeating points which wasted valuable time and made us rush decisions. However, as we were all so enthusiastic, we did not run short of ideas. Everyone in the group contributed and was a valid member of the team.

It could be possible that by having four members of the group that would participate that the other member felt too shy to also contribute. The member who contributed very little was on the end of the row, which may have enabled them to escape discussion without being fully involved in discussion.

To summarize, the team dynamic makes up the most important part of our findings on gamified learning in teams. With a positive team dynamic, effective communication and trust, the game experience becomes much more enjoyable and fun. A poor team dynamic and individual toxic behaviours, on the other hand, contribute to a frustrating experience and increased student disengagement.

Student Reflections: Individual Experience

Finally, students discuss what the game experience meant to them individually, on a personal level. Here, students primarily reflect on their personal development as a result of playing the game. First, this is concerned with overcoming personal anxieties due to operating outside their comfort zone:

> The experience was something out of my comfort zone because it's not something that I am used to, it was working with people I have never worked with before but I relished it as an opportunity to build my confidence as an individual by inputting ideas, discussing and challenging other people's opinions to ensure we clearly got to the right decision.

> Upon completion of the presentation, I was extremely happy with my personal performance and overcoming any anxieties I have. I could have made a little bit more eye contact towards the panellists, but I was clear, it wasn't scripted and I felt confident.

Second, students discuss implications for their future personal and professional development, which often stems from some less successful experience during the game:

> In future, I will try to be more confident in my presenting skills and I intend to take every opportunity which forces me into presenting to practice speaking in front of people. While at university, I will speak to my personal tutor and other lecturers of any tips on presentations as well as look for information online. I would like to improve this skill before I leave my final year as I think this will be crucial in my future career, especially if I want to be in sales.

> I was disappointed when the majority of the team did not agree with my opinion on the final segment. Consequently, in the future I should consider making reference to key statistics to back up my reasoning, as a strategy to influence other members of the group to agree with my point of view.

> In future, when I am placed in a team to complete a project, I hope to open up as soon as I meet everyone, as it also encourages other people to talk as they may perceive me as more friendly. I also hope to not be afraid of taking charge/actively suggesting ideas early on; whilst this may not sit well with some team members, we have a task to complete and shouldn't let nerves sit in the way.

Finally, students discuss the concept of bridging theory with practice, which leads to new insights. This directly contributes to their overall personal learning, making them more confident on both the soft and hard skill level:

> In conclusion, although my team didn't win the game, it was an insightful experience which allowed me to gain an educational insight from practical and relevant experience. It allowed me to prepare for experiences that I'll face within my professional career whilst developing my core and extended skills.

Overall, students find the game experience to be developmental in nature, as it takes them outside their comfort zone. Indeed, playing with a new team, managing the group dynamic, building one's effective communication, working under time pressure and presenting in front of an audience, all contribute to effective personal and professional development inherent in the game design.

Instructor Reflections and Tips

Instructor reflections, which are presented below, provide an overview of the key considerations when organizing a game from a practical, pedagogical perspective. The three reflections below are written by instructors who have been using the game for a number of years.

REFLECTION 1 – YASIN SAHHAR, THE GAME INSTRUCTOR AND HOST

Students 'rule' the game. Even with the best possible preparation from an organizational perspective, the students are the ones that are the key determinant in how the game runs. I know this from my rich experience of three years, running the game three to five times per year, for different groups. The vibe is important, the enthusiasm among students, their ambitions and drive. I personally find it very enjoyable to see students working together in a nice and effective way. They divide tasks, use whiteboards, Post-its and other tools to bring their ideas to life. When individuals click together well, creative ideas can arise. On the other hand, I saw some groups that either had a 'laissez-faire' approach or when individuals were too greedy to have the leading role in their group. This is detrimental to the entire process, which I also experienced being an instructor of the game. In the former, I have the feeling to talk to five people that just do not care. With the latter, I see one individual that tries too much to take the lead while other group members do not use their full potential. That is a pity. In this case, I explicitly point myself towards the other group members too. As a result, they receive attention and might feel better involved. So, speaking in terms of the process and organization, the extent of enjoyment, fun and learning, and the team interdynamic, are crucial for the entire game. So, I would like to return to my first notion: students definitely rule the game. Based on these notions and my experience, I also would like to share some tips.

Plan your structure well. Besides preparing your story content-wise, I have learned that it is imperative to carefully prepare in advance the structure and practicalities of the game. In this, timing is imperative. For example, planning enough breaks during the day in combination with the hours students work consecutively is important, especially in keeping their span of attention at the desired level.

Organize proper material facilities in advance. Material facilities, such as the classroom with possible breakout rooms for extra 'privacy' among groups, and whiteboards or spreadsheets, are also very important to properly run the game. These very straightforward aspects are very important and often underestimated.

Find the right balance in challenging and helping students. The balance between helping students and challenging them to come up with solutions themselves is key. When students approach you with a question or problem, it is important to identify whether they ask you because it is easy, supposing that as a host you have the answer, or whether they have properly thought things through already and are really struggling with the issue at hand. In the first case, I often refer them to specific parts of the game materials in which more information can be found, or ask them a challenging question instead. In the latter, I advise students or ask them triggering questions to think otherwise.

Be aware of the team interdynamic. When students play a game with a group, against other groups, in real life, obviously the team interdynamic plays an important role. It is a natural consequence when putting people together to collaborate, while at the same time competing with others. As a host or organizer of such events, it is important to first of all take this into account, but also accommodate participants in the right manner. Act as a facilitator of group discussions, be a coach to individuals and monitor the overall process.

Have fun, together. When spending time with ambitious students in a competitive, demanding and energetic setting, it is key to maintain and have fun too. So, create a pleasant learning environment where mistakes can be made, give students responsibilities and freedom, and be flexible.

REFLECTION 2 – DR RUSHANA KHUSAINOVA, INSTRUCTOR AND MODULE LEADER

I've been organizing the game for three years in a row now on my final-year undergraduate sales module. It's often a challenge to schedule it, with me working back and forth with our timetabling team to ensure all students have availability for five consecutive hours to play the game, and that there are no timetable clashes. But once it's done, it is a true highlight of the module! Students really enjoy the experience.

I make it clear that their performance on the game is not something they get assessed on. Instead, it's the game experience which matters. Based on that, they write a reflective essay.

Over the years I have learnt that, given that one has a good game to play, there are two important actions that need addressing.

First is encouraging a positive team dynamic. It's huge. As Williams et al. (2006) put it, 'the instructor bears some responsibility for fostering group cohesion and cooperation' (p. 608). This year, I've made it compulsory for the teams to have one 'chemistry' session prior to the game. In addition, I introduced a 'meet the team' exercise where the students were encouraged to memorize each others' names and share one piece of information about themselves (e.g., something they think they are good at or something they enjoy doing in the given context). I also encouraged them to practice active listening, which we discussed in the classroom in one of the seminars. The impact on the student experience and engagement was substantial. Students seemed to have enjoyed the game more, and have exhibited more creativity and efficiency in their work on the game rounds. I also saw an enhanced team dynamic and collaborative learning.

The second factor was predictability. Providing as much information as one can to the students as much in advance as possible, minimizes their stress and anxiety. Talking them through what to expect, sharing the general feedback from the students in previous cohorts, and even sharing images of how the physical game setting looks, have helped a lot. I found that students felt calmer and happier. There were fewer questions and enquiries in regard to what to expect, and students felt well prepared.

Finally, as the game is very interactive, with a 'Dragon's Den' sales pitch as a final round, I found it to be really enjoyable getting to know the students that much more. It contributed to a more positive and a little bit more personal relationship between myself and the students.

REFLECTION 3 – PROF. AD DE JONG, INSTRUCTOR AND MODULE LEADER

Having organized the game for several years, I can reflect upon it with satisfaction. Interestingly, when one comes up with new initiatives, like playing the Marketing and Sales Game, one has to overcome hurdles.

Look beyond the short-term responses and focus on long-term effects. There often is a fair share of initial scepticism among other colleagues, and especially among the ones who are involved in the coordination and management of educational programmes. They don't always get the instructional value of the game and tend to see it as a fun tool only. They sometimes perceive the implementation of games as venturing into uncharted areas which may be risky for teaching evaluations. This implies that the first couple of times you organize and play the game are critical. Mostly, the first year does not always yield the best results, which feeds their scepticism. The first time you play the game, you have to overcome technical issues such as connection issues of the game IT equipment (software and hardware, such as the iPads) with the hosting institution's IT infrastructure, internet access problems when starting up, and recurring internet connection problems during the game.

However, in the year thereafter and subsequent years, it usually turns out to be a great success. Then, those colleagues are also delighted, and sometimes come even up with strong recommendations to use the game as a new template for how teaching should be given body and organized in the future. This is the finest hour that you can achieve as a lecturer.

CONCLUSION

This chapter addresses the use of gamified learning in education, with focus on the driving role of interpersonal processes among students. The chapter discusses the concept of gamification and distinguishes three types of gamification in education: (1) adding a game to existing processes; (2) the use of simple games; and (3) gamified learning. The focus is on gamified learning, as this type of gamification is the most trendy and best addresses the use of gamification in a digital, team-based context. This interpersonal and team-based setting has not received substantive attention.

In addition, the gamified learning format does not come without any development effort. In the context of this study, the development of the gamified learning product started as collaboration between an educational institution and a consultancy company. This development process turned out to be quite a long and expensive process, and several playing rounds were needed to weed out teething problems and come to a full-fledged end-product.

Reflections from students and instructors were then used to evaluate the playing of the game and related processes. To begin with, the student reflections confirm that the interpersonal and team aspect is pivotal to their learning experience in gamified learning. Interestingly, our results also reveal that working in teams goes beyond 'just' collaboration. It stimulates individual students to learn to voice their opinions and communicate, as well as to find their own position in the interpersonal context. Last but not least, the team format motivates students to collaborate and achieve agreement, and even create enthusiasm and passion! One important challenge remains a poor team dynamic, such as an autocratic leader and a situation in which expressing one's opinion is not appreciated. Another challenge concerns the absence of any involvement of some individual members. Especially in educational settings, teamwork and smooth interpersonal interactions are essential to drive students' intellectual performance and achievements.

The instructors' reflections shed light on the use of gamified learning from a somewhat different perspective than the student ones. One important observation was that students rule the game, and thus should be provided with the opportunity to manage playing the game as a sort of project. In addition, as a game organizer, it is essential to ensure a good team spirit as well as providing timely information to reduce unforeseen issues. Finally, the organizing of games in a wider educational context requires optimism and persistence from the organizer, with a high chance for being rewarded for effort in the longer run.

REFERENCES

Anderson, T., and Garrison, D.R. (1998). Learning in a networked world: New roles and responsibilties. In Gibson, Chere Campbell (ed.), *Distance Learners in Higher Education: Institutional Responses for Quality Outcomes*. Madison, WI: Atwood, pp. 97–112.

Buckley, P., and Doyle, E.J.I.l.e. (2016). Gamification and student motivation. *Interactive Learning Environments*, 24(6), 1162–1175.

Calanca, F., Sayfullina, L., Minkus, L., Wagner, C., and Malmi, E. (2019). Responsible team players wanted: an analysis of soft skill requirements in job advertisements. *EPJ Data Science*, 8(1), 13.

Chapman, K.J., Meuter, M., Toy, D., and Wright, L. (2006). Can't we pick our own groups? The influence of group selection method on group dynamics and outcomes. *Journal of Management Education*, 30(4), 557–569.

Connolly, T.M., Boyle, E.A., MacArthur, E., Hainey, T., and Boyle, J.M. (2012). A systematic literature review of empirical evidence on computer games and serious games. *Computers and Education*, 59(2), 661–686.

da Rocha Seixas, L., Gomes, A.S., and de Melo Filho, I.J. (2016). Effectiveness of gamification in the engagement of students. *Computers in Human Behavior*, 58, 48–63.

Deterding, S. (2012). Gamification: designing for motivation. *Interactions*, 19(4), 14–17.

Deterding, S., Dixon, D., Khaled, R., and Nacke, L. (2011). From game design elements to gamefulness: defining gamification. *Proceedings of the 15th International Academic MindTrek Conference: Envisioning Future Media Environments*.

Elliott, N., and Higgins, A. (2005). Self and peer assessment – does it make a difference to student groupwork? *Nurse Education in Practice*, 5(1), 40–48.

Ferri, G. (2015). To play against: describing competition in gamification. In Fuchs, M., Fizek, S., Ruffino, P., and Schrape, N. (eds), *Rethinking Gamification*. Lüneburg: Meson Press, pp. 201–222.

Glynn, M.A. (1994). Effects of work task cues and play task cues on information processing, judgment, and motivation. *Journal of Applied Psychology*, 79(1), 34.

Gursoy, D., Maier, T.A., and Chi, C.G. (2008). Generational differences: an examination of work values and generational gaps in the hospitality workforce. *International Journal of Hospitality Management*, 27(3), 448–458.

Hackman, J.R., and Oldham, G.R. (1980). Work redesign. *Professional Psychology*, 11(3), 445.

Hamari, J., and Koivisto, J. (2013). Social motivations to use gamification: an empirical study of gamifying exercise. *Proceedings of the 21st European Conference in Information Systems*, Utrecht, Netherlands.

Koivisto, J., and Hamari, J. (2019). The rise of motivational information systems: a review of gamification research. *International Journal of Information Management*, 45, 191–210.

Landers, R.N. (2014). Developing a theory of gamified learning: linking serious games and gamification of learning. *Simulation and Gaming*, 45(6), 752–768.

Lick, D.W. (2000). Whole-faculty study groups: facilitating mentoring for school-wide change. *Theory into Practice*, 39(1), 43–49.

Locke, E.A. (1968). Toward a theory of task motivation and incentives. *Organizational Behavior and Human Performance*, 3(2), 157–189.

Madrid, L.D., Canas, M., and Ortega-Medina, M. (2007). Effects of team competition versus team cooperation in classwide peer tutoring. *Journal of Educational Research*, 100(3), 155–160.

Marchand, A., and Hennig-Thurau, T. (2013). Value creation in the video game industry: industry economics, consumer benefits, and research opportunities. *Journal of Interactive Marketing*, 27(3), 141–157.

McGonigal, J. (2011). *Reality is Broken: Why Games Make Us Better and How They Can Change the World*. New York: Penguin.

Mollick, E., and Rothbard, N. (2013). Mandatory fun: gamification and the impact of games at work. Wharton School Research Paper Series, 1.

Moccozet, L., Tardy, C., Opprecht, W., and Léonard, M. (2013, September). Gamification-based assessment of group work. *2013 International Conference on Interactive Collaborative Learning (ICL)*, IEEE, pp. 171–179.

Reeves, B., and Read, L.J. (2009). *Total Engagement: Using Games and Virtual Worlds to Change the Way People Work and Businesses Compete*. Boston, MA: Harvard Business Press.

Salen, K. and Zimmerman, E. (2004). *Rules of Play: Game Design Fundamentals*. Cambridge, MA: MIT Press.

Seemiller, C., and Clayton, J. (2019). Developing the strengths of Generation Z college students. *Journal of College and Character*, 20(3), 268–275.

Subhash, S., and Cudney, E.A. (2018). Gamified learning in higher education: a systematic review of the literature. *Computers in Human Behavior*, 87, 192–206.

Tuckman, B.W. (1965). Developmental sequence in small groups. *Psychological Bulletin*, 63(6), 384.

Villagrasa, S., Fonseca, D., Redondo, E., and Duran, J. (2014). Teaching case of gamification and visual technologies for education. *Journal of Cases on Information Technology (JCIT)*, 16(4), 38–57.

Vroom, V.H. (1964). *Work and Motivation*. New York: Wiley.

Walker, E.R., Lang, D.L., Caruso, B.A., and Salas-Hernández, L. (2020). Role of team dynamics in the learning process: a mixed-methods evaluation of a modified team-based learning approach in a behavioral research methods course. *Advances in Health Sciences Education*, 25(2), 383–399.

Wells, D., and Higgs, Z.R. (1990). Learning styles and learning preferences of first and fourth semester baccalaureate degree nursing students. *Journal of Nursing Education*, 29(9), 385–390.

Williams, E., Duray, R. & Reddy, V. (2006). Teamwork orientation, group cohesiveness, and student learning: a study of the use of teams in online distance education. *Journal of Management Education*, 30, 592–616.

Table 10A.1   Summary of student reflections and comments

Themes	Examples	Quotes
Overall game dynamic	Engaging Safe learning environment Physical attributes of a game Real-life replication	Student quote 1 'Overall, I had a great experience of learning through the use of digital technologies and games, as it really engaged my attention throughout. In support to that, effective learning takes place when you are completely engaged in what you are doing. Thus, I would like to conclude that the Marketing and Sales Game is a successful learning experience for me, and I believe that it would be beneficial for organisations to adopt as a training tool.' Student quote 2 'the game definitely did give a good insight into some of the complications and considerations that arise in this kind of work. I personally really liked the room for creativity, e.g., in the assignment focused on sketching out the customer journey. It was a positive experience that we were able to determine all customer steps ourselves, without too much interference, and evaluate when the value for the customer emerged. It encouraged a lively discussion and underlined that the customer derived value, much fewer times during the entire journey than initially assumed in the group.' Student quote 3 'Pitching is to a great extent a craft that needs to be trained for one to become good at it. Training in simulated, safe, and fun environments can thus increase the learning and confidence of the students. Therefore, I think that a simulated reality with a gamification element – such as the marketing and sales game – can prove itself useful in learning situations for salespeople as well as students.' Student quote 4 'Successfully, the Marketing & Sales Game merged theory and practice by applying key concepts within strategic marketing management on a real-life case revolving around a company offering hearing aids in the British market.'

Themes	Examples	Quotes
		Student quote 5
		'I think the game does a well enough job to replicate the real-life seller–buyer relationship because it does allow us to take the organization, market, and customers into consideration when planning to sell.'
		Student quote 5
		'The way that theory and practice meet is where it becomes interesting and at the same time, it is at this point where it also replicates the real-life seller–buyer relationship the most.'
		Student quote 6
		'The marketing and sales game provided an assignment that included several of the real-life choices marketing managers are met with when creating a marketing and sales strategy for a new product. As a student myself who has worked in a more traditional sales role in a company before, my preconceptions of the sales role were mixed. Having personal experience mostly with the actual sales role myself, it was very interesting to be able to link it together with the overall marketing aspects, such as segmentation and customer journey assessment.'
		Student quote 7
		'The opportunity to present a pitch in the end, even though a bit time-pressured, was also a pleasant experience. Both because it was interesting to see how every group had different solutions and strategies, but also to get a "real-life experience" and to get immediate feedback.'
2. Team-related experiences	Great/poor team dynamic 'Clicking' together Common goals Some toxic behaviours	Student quote 1
		'Straight away I found each member was engaged, excited and willing to put the effort in to try and win. Each of us voiced our opinions and ideas and went through the tasks together as a group. Our personalities matched well and that meant we were able to have fun during the day whilst completing each round.'

Themes	Examples	Quotes
		Student quote 2 'in analysis the reason my team had open communication was due to the Sales Game providing a safe environment to work in. I realised that the disagreements and problems with listening we faced during this phase of the game were a symptom of the team's overall enthusiasm and passion for producing an effective presentation. Despite the issues myself and the team faced, we were able to produce a presentation which achieved a higher mark than the four other groups.' Student quote 3 'from the very beginning I could see we had developed very poor team dynamics. This is because we had one individual who jumped to the role of being the leader but in fact came across as an aggressor. This was because she often disagreed with other members and was often inappropriately outspoken. I was quite intimidated which I believe was expressed quite clearly to other members of the team as this incident lead to me not engaging with discussions as much as I should have been. I was consequently afraid of giving my own personal opinion which helped eliminate the fun element this game believed so much in. This led to my team not being able to perform as effectively as we could have as everyone wanted to be seen to agree with the leader. We ultimately became afraid of expressing our own individual opinions. It was evident that the team morale had dropped dramatically and participating in group decisions quickly became awkward and uncomfortable.'

Themes	Examples	Quotes
		Student quote 4
		'At times I felt frustrated because team members were speaking over me when I was trying to present my ideas back to the group. Conversely, at other times I felt pleased to be surrounded with such a lively group that was so enthusiastic about the stimulation. As a result of this, our time management skills were not efficient. Due to speaking over one another, members of the group ended up repeating points which wasted valuable time and made us rush decisions. However, as we were all so enthusiastic, we did not run short of ideas. Everyone in the group contributed and was a valid member of the team.'
		Student quote 5
		'I explained that everyone needs to be heard in our group. After this our team began to develop an understanding, clear communication and a fun aspect of working together which I believe is key and made me feel confident.'
		Student quote 6
		'It could be possible that by having four members of the group that would participate that the other member felt too shy to also contribute. The member who contributed very little was on the end of the row, which may have enabled them to escape discussion without being fully involved in discussion. To have improved during the simulation, we could have tried to split work more evenly by setting expectations at the start. Furthermore, as a group, the seating arrangements should have been altered to ensure all members feel involved and feel obliged to make contributions.'
		Student quote 7
		'We came 4th which was our worse performance in the game all day. I believe the nerves definitely got the better of all of us. When we saw other teams using PowerPoints and acting, we knew our pitch would look terrible in comparison. We accepted defeat before it had even happened.'

Themes	Examples	Quotes
		Student quote 8
		'The use of sales game made me grow as an individual and allow me to find my own space within a team of like-minded individuals. I do not feel as if I learnt more about sales but rather more about how to function well as a team.'
		Student quote 9
		'The greatest learning curb for me and I believe for the team was how we as a team react to each other and what we do rubs onto each other hence motivation in a team is significantly important.'
		Student quote 10
		'Due to ineffective communication between teammates, we also found ourselves pressed with time while answering all the questions especially for the first stage of the game.'
3. Individual-level experiences	Trying to win Feeling enthusiastic Personal learning	Student quote 1
		'I was very involved in every input the group made, the group naturally ran their decisions past me. It was a good feeling to be in charge for the first time over a large group, winning and controlling the group just certified myself as an effective people's leader as we gained the success we wanted whilst having fun.'
		Student quote 2
		'The experience was also something out of my comfort zone because it's not something that I am use to, it was working with people I have never worked with before but I relished it as an opportunity to build my confidence as an individual by inputing ideas, discussing and challenging other people's opinions to ensure we clearly got to the right decision.'
		Student quote 3
		'Upon completion of the presentation, I was extremely happy with my personal performance and overcoming any anxieties I have. I could have made a little bit more eye contact towards the panellists, but I was clear, it wasn't scripted and I felt confident.'

Themes	Examples	Quotes
		Student quote 4
		'Due to how anxious I was feeling I made a conscious effort to try and show positive body language to other students who I thought were also feeling anxious.'
		Student quote 5
		'I was disappointed when the majority of the team did not agree with my opinion on the final segment. Consequently, in the future I should consider making reference to key statistics to back up my reasoning, as a strategy to influence other members of the group to agree with my point of view.'
		Student quote 6.
		'In future, I will try to be more confident in my presenting skills and I intend to take every opportunity which forces me into presenting to practice speaking in front of people. While at university, I will speak to my personal tutor and other lecturers of any tips on presentations as well as look for information online. I would like to improve this skill before I leave my final year as I think this will be crucial in my future career, especially if I want to be in sales.'
		Student quote 7
		'In future, when I am placed in a team to complete a project, I hope to open up as soon as I meet everyone, as it also encourages other people to talk as they may perceive me as more friendly. I also hope to not be afraid of taking charge/actively suggesting ideas early on; whilst this may not sit well with some team members, we have a task to complete and shouldn't let nerves sit in the way.'
		Student quote 8
		'Moving forward I will also be more confident at speaking up and challenging opinions, which I could improve by joining a debates class.'

Themes	Examples	Quotes
		Student quote 9
		'I learned that if we are really going for a meeting like this, we should gather all the facts needed for an investor to be convinced to invest in our business and that we should have a really good business plan.'
		Student quote 10
		'In conclusion, although my team didn't win the game, it was an insightful experience which allowed me to gain an educational insight from practical and relevant experience. It allowed me to prepare for experiences that I'll face within my professional career whilst developing my core and extended skills.'

PART IV

IN THE BUSINESS SCHOOL CLASSROOM

11. Lecturing

Linda Greve

The genre of lecturing connotes a variety of dichotomies. Active or passive learning (Smith & Cardaciotto, 2011). The educator as authoritarian or facilitator (Grasha, 1994). Students as apprentices or costumers (Guilbault, 2016). Students as empty jars or holistic humans (Gallagher & Lindgren, 2015). Content as information or knowledge (Rowley, 2007). Effective or efficient teaching (Bligh, 1998). Surface or depth learning strategy (Beattie IV et al., 1997). Teaching for learning or evaluation (Macdonald, 2006). Just to mention a few.

The word lecture derives from the Latin word *lectura*, meaning 'to read'. Thus, a lecture in the traditional sense is to read aloud. This chapter serves to move the concept of lectures beyond that definition.

Even though most lecturers know a lot about learning, structure, interaction and use of visuals, there are still habits to be changed and new methods to be employed. The purpose of this chapter is to define and describe the genre of lecturing. Further, a taxonomy of lecturing is introduced on the basis of studies done at a Danish business school, describing different approaches to practising the genre. The taxonomy points to what any lecturer should be able to apply easily in their next lecture, as well as more fundamental changes in habits and style, which would benefit the experience of both educator and students.

My interest in lecturing is personal. I have been lecturing for several years and became curious to better understand why lecturing is still such a big part of higher education when, at least for some years, everyone seemed to agree that small-group classes were much better learning spaces and that active learning was paramount in teaching students. Thus, this chapter unfolds my findings. What is a lecture, what can we say about lecturing from a rhetorical and linguistic perspective, what does research suggest the format to be suitable for and how do lecturers improve their lecture style without necessarily increasing time spent on preparation? What my own research shows is that some lecturers talk all through the lecture with no interaction and succeed in keeping the students' attention, whereas others lose the audience after five minutes. Some lecturers activate, ask questions and bring along assignments and still lose the students, whereas others really succeed in the strategy. It is not black and white. A good lecture comes from having a good structure, making it relevant and making use of the affordances of being in a room together with the students. How that is done is what I have chosen to reveal in this chapter.

THE EYE AND THE HAND

Lecturing is one of the oldest forms of teaching. It is depicted and described back to Ancient Greece, and in that sense is as much a classic as can be. Some would say that the format is outdated and new formats should take over. However, the format also holds significant benefits: lectures makes it possible to gather a large number of students, which is both efficient in the sense of the student per teacher ratio and in terms of creating shared experiences and shared stories for the students. It is like experiencing Red Hot Chili Peppers live in Hyde Park, and knowing I have the experience in common with around 100 000 others who also joined in singing 'Under the Bridge' and also remember a specific political comment. The feeling of being in it together and sharing this moment – even if it is not at the level of a rock concert – is essential in understanding lecturing as a genre. It is a shared event and should be conducted as such.

Criticizing lectures is not reserved for contemporary educators and students. The French philosopher Rousseau wrote in his book *Concerning Education* from 1763 (Rousseau, 1763 [1979]), that 'experience and feeling are our real teachers'. He thought, as did many in his time, the explanatory lecture to be boring and ineffectual. A few decades later in Denmark, natural philosopher Hans Christian Ørsted (1803) wrote that 'These plain, dry lectures, such as they are given in Berlin, without the art of experimenting oneself, do not please me. For surely it is from experimentation that all scientific improvements must emanate.'

In those years of enlightenment and romanticism, we thus see a sharp critique of the genre of lecturing. What Rousseau and Ørsted describe is essentially the split between the epistemology of the ear and eye and the epistemology of the hand: information transformation through watching (and listening) or information transformation through bodily experience. Both Rousseau and Ørsted emphasize the importance of experience as well as feelings. Even though letting all students get hands-on experience in every lecture is a practical and physical impossibility, it is still worth paying attention to the underlying proposition: namely, that lecturing should be an interplay between human beings and thus make use of essential components from interpersonal communication. A lecture without feelings (be that humour, irony, provocation, surprise, frustration …), and a lecture without any activation of experience and active relation to the subject matter, is destined to be plain, dry and ineffectual.

When asked, lecturers describe their lectures as beads on a string and as a train on tracks, indicating that it is already organized and that it is unstoppable (Bager-Elsborg & Greve, 2019). However, as a lecturer you have a huge influence on how you wish to organize the beads and train tracks.

In and Out of Skull

In cognitive linguistics it has long been a recognized fact that cognition, and thus learning, is an interplay between brain, body, environment and sociality (Lakoff & Johnson, 1999; Maturana & Varela, 1980). Thinking and making sense of the world is as much an 'out of skull' activity as an 'in-skull' operation. We make use of brain, body and environment when understanding, thinking, making connections, and so on. Essentially, students gain new understanding and make new connections between theories by making use of brain, body and environment in what is often referred to as 'ecological cognition' (Barsalou, 2010; Jensen & Greve, 2019). Gallagher (2017) states that: 'Saying that cognition is just in the brain is like saying the flight is inside the wing of a bird' (p. 12). He continues:

> [we] should rather think of this [cognitive] process as a kind of ongoing dynamical adjustment in which the brain, as a part of and along with the larger organism, settles into the right kind of attunement with the environment – an environment that is physical but also social and cultural. Neural accommodation occurs in this larger system. (p. 18)

Thus, the lecture hall and everything in it provides that ecological system. The PowerPoint, the students' computers, the peers around them, the temperature and air quality, the expectations, the habits, the level of arousal, the light and the lecturer are all factors in learning from a lecture. The old 'empty jar' metaphor is long dead, imagining the student as an empty container passively being filled with knowledge from the all-knowing lecturer. Students are holistic beings affected by emotions, sensory impulses, words and imagery, and what they understand is highly dependent on what they already know and to what extent they are able to experience the new information in some kind of extension of that prior knowledge. As lecturers, we need to take all this into account to understand the affordances of the rhetorical situation: what is expected, what are the affordances of the lecture hall, what is the opportunity space for providing an experience-evoking and emotional learning opportunity for the student? Turning a lecture into a learning situation is a complex task. Thus, there is no 'one size fits all' or any quick fixes. However, understanding the genre and how to control and use the affordances of a lecture will help make each lecturer a little better.

Before going into the particular observations and the actual taxonomy of lectures, I would like to describe the genre in more detail in order to provide insight into what are the affordances of the lecture. Let us look at the genre traits.

Lecture as Genre and Style

Fundamentally, a lecture can be defined as a live performance of a lecturer holding a higher level of education and knowledge than the audience. To understand the genre and style of lectures, we must tease apart the constituent elements and the traits observed in the practice.

Biber and Conrad (2009) provide a such framework. Lectures are fundamentally a specialized subgenre of speeches, which are a subgenre of public speaking (p. 62). The characteristics of public speaking are that they are interpersonal and preplanned (p. 82). In contrast to textbooks, the lecture has interpersonality and orality as defining factors. Anyone who has ever made a transcription of an interview, speech or conversation knows that what can be perfectly understandable and sound reasonable in oral form will often come across as incoherent and even incomprehensible in writing. Thus, we are aware of oral language being unfit in a written context, unless the purpose is the study of oral language use. That same sensitivity is at play the other way around. When an oral speech is too 'written' in its genre traits, we immediately sense it and it is sensed as a breach of genre. In the context of the lecture, giving a lecture with too many written traits will not be making use of the affordances of interpersonal, oral speech. The elements at play in coming across as orator rather than reader are described in more detail below.

Interpersonality

The form or register of a lecture can ideally be placed midway on a continuum from academic article to everyday conversation. When comparing these two registers, a number of differences stand out. Conversations make use of significantly more modal verbs (which modify the message, such as can, might, will, would, should …) than academic articles (Biber and Conrad, 2009, p. 94). In this regard, lectures lean towards written rather than conversational traits. Modifying the message is a signifier of insecurity. In academia, we use the rebuttal rather than modal verbs to signal that we are not presenting universal truths. That is, rather than saying that this or that theory might suggest a certain tendency, it would be more in line with the genre traits so say that the theory suggests a tendency, with certain exceptions. It makes it easier to understand what the theory is good for, and where it might be less appropriate. In a lecture, this accuracy is useful for the students in terms of understanding how the argument for and against a certain position is formed. Thus, in terms of modal verbs, the academic presentation bears resemblance to the academic article.

However, other language traits set the oral and written language apart. Using verbs as nouns (nominalizations) is a very common trait in written texts. A text would read: 'The analysis shows a failure in respondents' reaction', whereas the oral version would sound more like 'When we analysed the data, it became clear the respondents fail to react'. Nominalizations are extremely common in academic prose and rare in conversations (e.g., investigation instead of investigate, reaction instead of react, failure instead of fail, analysis instead of analyse). This in turn shows another difference between the oral and written academic genres: the use of personal pronouns. In writing they are almost non-existent, and in oral conversation they are very common. In writing, the problem of creating sentences without personal pronouns is solved by use of the passive voice and nominalizations. This language tactic is very detectible in oral language and contributes to a less involving style. Questions are also very common in oral conversation, but extremely rare in written academic texts (Biber and Conrad, 2009, pp. 116–117).

In lectures, refraining from using personal pronouns and questions is a neglect of use of the oral affordances of the shared space with the audience. Other significant language traits of the lecture are repetition, self-correction and the use of lexical bundles, meaning bundles of words which are not as such precise bearers of meaning, but are nevertheless significant in spoken language, such as 'or something like that', 'let's look at the ...', 'as it were', 'we were talking about', and so on.

In sum, the academic oral discourse should be as precise and nuanced as an academic paper, yet personal, self-correcting and as involving as a conversion.

Real time but prepared

The second genre trait is the dichotomy between talking in real time in front of an audience but in a highly prepared and time-limited format. A crucial element of success in lecturing is timing: to keep track of time and not lose yourself in your own words. This calls for a high degree of precision and preparation. Unfortunately, many lecturers prepare by writing down what they want to say, word by word.

Not too surprisingly, humans have been communicating orally for far longer than we have been writing things down (Ong, 2012). However, in academia, written language has been the dominating format for decades, if not centuries. Obviously, you can spread your thoughts wider across geography and time when contained in writing. However, in more recent years formats such as TED talks, YouTube and numerous MOOC platforms (massive open online courses) have opened the doors to a shift in academic orality; such formats have become a road to influence, if you can tell the tale of your research in an appealing and relevant manner.

Oral and written language are profoundly different. Oral language is imperfect but takes place in real time. Written language attempts perfection, but is not interactive and can be read long after the writer is gone, in some cases millennia. This in turn makes lectures important precisely because the students could have downloaded and read your slides or the curriculum at home, or could have seen a video of you presenting it on YouTube. Due to the online video possibilities, attending a lecture and listening to your presentation should add something over and above what watching a video or reading the curriculum could contribute.

Thus, when planning a lecture, plan to be interactive, interpersonal and to give the students a shared experience, providing them with something they could not just as well have got out of reading or following an online course. Not because those formats are not valid and good forms of learning, but because a lecture is a genre in and of itself and should not drift into the written perfection of the textbook or the preplanned TED talk. A good lecture – from a genre perspective – is planned with the purpose of helping the students understand coherence and conflicts between theories and models, and differentiating between relevant and less relevant elements of the curriculum. How to create an engaging and relevant lecture is unfolded below.

LECTURES DEFINED

A vast amount of studies have investigated the effect of lectures in numerous ways. One very thorough account of this is Bligh's (1998) book, *What's the Use of Lectures?* Evidence of what lectures will achieve, according to Bligh, is mainly transmission of information. He concludes that lectures are less effective for teaching values and behavioural skills. That said, the lecture format is well suited for providing an overview, unfolding examples and giving feedback on assignments and levels of understanding.

The account of information transfer in comparison to knowledge generation is interesting in the case of lecturing. Due to the high degree of one-way communication characterizing the genre of lecturing, Bligh's comment does hold some truth. However, if framed and structured right, the lecture can also provide the students with the requisites for turning the information into their own knowledge.

For the purposes of defining lectures, I refer to the data–information–knowledge–wisdom hierarchy (DIKW) (Rowley, 2007). As presented in Figure 11.1, these four concepts can be plotted in a coordinate system spanned by human agency on the x-axis and level of structure on the y-axis. Figure 11.2 is a visualization of the nature of the structure in the four levels. Data is unprocessed and unstructured. To students the data will not make any sense. When we collect data for studies, it is just there as numbers, statements or observations, until we do something about it. Information, in turn, is data provided with categorizations. Nonaka (2007) states that information is everything that can be digitalized. If it goes into a paper, a graph or a text book, it's information. This is what Bligh claims can be transferred in a lecture: the overview, the categories and connections. In order for it to become knowledge, experiences need to be added. This is on the students. They need to add the information presented in the lecture to their experience; they need to reflect upon how this is along the lines of what they already know, or if it is in breach of their prior knowledge. But the lecturer plays a role in making them aware.

C. Otto Scharmer presents three ways of listening to information (Scharmer, 2001): downloading, suspending and pre-sensing. The downloading listener protects their level of knowledge by approaching the information saying 'I knew that' or 'That concurs with my own understandings'. This position entails that we are unable to learn new things, because our self-image is standing in the way. If my attitude to the lecture is that nothing is new to me, I may overlook the elements that are actually not in congruence with my prior knowledge. We are all guilty of this position occasionally.

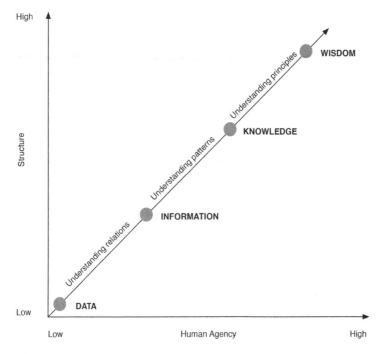

Source: First published in Greve (2016).

Figure 11.1   *The DIKW hierarchy*

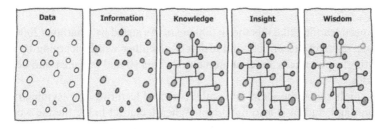

Source: From Data Demystified.

Figure 11.2   *The difference between levels in the DIKW hierarchy*

However, if we wish to transform information into knowledge, it is Scharmer's position that we need to listen more for what we do not know than what we already know. The suspending position of listening is about that: suspending what I think I know, and listening with the purpose of understanding how the presented information adds to my prior understandings. The pre-sensing position of listening is, in Scharmer's framework, the most productive. While attending a lecture, I sense already how this can be put into use and how this will change my ideas, methods or abilities to perform calculations, analyses or whatever the lecture is about.

Having a pre-sensing approach to listening is cognitively the most challenging of the three. Thus, we cannot expect students to attain this position for hours on end. As will be described below, the lecturer must provide the frame for the students to contemplate how their prior knowledge should be suspended, or even for them to pre-sense how the content is usable and applicable to them.

The last level of the DIKW hierarchy is wisdom. This may be the level of the lecturer, but for the students to reach the level of understanding underlying patterns and mechanisms tacitly is expecting too much. Wisdom takes years on end of working within a field. However, the lecture can inspire students to set a such path. This is underpinned by French and Kennedy (2017). They state that:

> Improving lectures is a challenging task that for many academics may require fundamentally rethinking the way they teach and the way that students learn … a stronger statement about the benefits of lectures for both staff and students is needed to ensure they are viewed as having a pedagogical value. (p. 651)

The pedagogical value and how that is embedded into the lecture and communicated to the students will be described in more detail below.

The Role of the Lecturer

The process of tuning the information in a lecture into knowledge is thus mainly the task of the students. Ong dedicated his academic career to understanding the shift from orality to literacy. He writes on the notion of learning in the pre-literary age and in non-literal communities:

> They learn by apprenticeship … by listening, by repeating what they hear, by mastering proverbs, and ways of combining and recombining them, by assimilating other formulary materials, by participation in a kind of corporate retrospection – not by study in the strict sense. (Ong, 2012)

Humans have been learning like this for 40 000 years. As stated by Charlton (2006), 'Literacy and solitude are relatively-recent cultural artifacts'. In other words, learning by talking and in a social setting is potentially much more natural. This should be taken into account when planning lectures.

Apart from emphasizing the social and oral element of lecturing, the asymmetrical relation between lecturer and student is also important. When lecturing in the literate world, the lecturer is the master. Their trustworthiness is paramount for the student's willingness to suspend prior knowledge and venture into admitting to themselves that this is new and rattles what they think they knew about the world. To do that, they need to feel safe. This is ultimately down to the *ethos* of the lecturer. *Ethos* is one of three ways to appeal to an audience, often ascribed to Aristotle around 420 BC. The two other forms of appeal are *logos* (logic, reason) and *pathos* (emotion, state of mind). *Ethos* is a trade of the lecturer and consists of three elements: *phronesis, eunoia* and *areté.*

Phronesis is best translated as 'intelligence'. The lecturer in turn is expected to be intelligent and more knowledgeable in the field of the lecture than the students. Ways to flag *phronesis* are in titles (professor, PhD, etc.) as well as by reference to experience, own writings and examples. Demonstrating *phronesis* is to let students know that the information presented is reliable. If we disregard the lecturer's *phronesis*, we tend to discard the content altogether.

The second element of *ethos* is *eunoia* and could be translated as 'good will'. The lecturer needs to show the students that he or she wishes them well. This can be done by even the smallest recognitions. Recognizing that it's late, that the exam is coming up, that the readings for today were difficult, or thanking the students for attending will increase their focus and attention, simply because the lecturer recognizes that they are there and that wants what is best for them.

Third element of ethos is *areté*. It could be translated as 'level of morality' or 'likeability'. As a lecturer you need to come across as a moral human being and as someone who is sympathetic towards the students. Little comments showing the students that you are interested in them, their education and their understanding of the topics of the lecture, will improve your *areté*. Examples of *ethos* and lack of *ethos* will be elaborated below.

The pragmatist John Dewey makes the distinction in learning between 'copying the world' and 'coping with the world' (Campbell, 1995). In teaching, we should aim for the latter. Students need to be able to act on their own in performing calculation, analysis, and so on. They need to be able to cope with the field of their studies, not just copying what has already been done.

Combining Ong's notion about learning through participation and inclusion in a cultural practice, with the antique thoughts about *ethos* and Dewey's ideas about coping with the world, the lecturer should take on the role of master and emphasize the asymmetrical relation while showing concern for the students and their situation.

Emphasizing the Social Event

Most papers and books on lecturing refrain from actually describing what constitutes a lecture. A lecture could be defined by the size of the audience or the format of the talk. It could be given by the room architecture or the amount of interaction. For the purpose of this chapter, a lecture is defined as: a preplanned, social live performance given in an asymmetrical relation between a lecturer with a higher status and the audience with the purpose of transmitting information and inspiring to know more.

This fleshes out the elements we need to pay attention to as lecturers. It is a live social event for the students. Further, it is an asymmetrical event and this should be used as an asset in the form of making use of *ethos*, transmitting information, but planning for time and space for students to make the information part of their own knowledge.

A TAXONOMY OF LECTURING

The overarching curiosity driving the study presented below was about what's going on in lecture halls. Despite all the knowledge and theories about lecturing and how it should be conducted, little data has been collected and presented. Thus, this study is curiosity-driven and reflects my wish to improve the teacher training in business schools.

I ventured into making a taxonomy of the variety of lectures. The three archetypes I found were: the soundtrack lecture, the interaction lecture and the engagement lecture. The three types are presented in more detail below. What is significant to me is that all three types of lecture were performed both successfully and less so, pointing to the fact that being a good lecturer is about more than just interaction or active learning. This point is exemplified below in order to inspire lecturers to change their habits and approach in order to affect learning and knowledge creation among students in the lecture halls.

Data Collection

The basis of the taxonomy of lecturing presented below is the result of observations made in a Danish business school. The observations were sampled in auditoriums. Over the course of one week, 18 business school lectures took place in three large auditoriums. All 18 lecturers were contacted. One politely declined to participate. Two turned out not to give lectures that week after all, and one was discarded due to overlap with an already planned observation.

In sum, 13 lectures were sampled. All were videotaped. As it is difficult to get consent from all students to film their behaviour, the students' behaviour was observed and noted anonymously by the observer. Two lecturers were female and 11 were male.

All videos were coded and analysed, with special attention given to speed, structure, interaction and students' activities. Below, these four parameters are fleshed out by means of examples. The analyses are summed up at the end of the chapter in a taxonomy containing the three categories of lectures and how they are performed.

I visited the pages in the Learning Management System prior to each lecture. All 13 lecturers put up their slides for the students to download. All lecturers used a projector as a significant part of their lecture: PowerPoint, Keynote, TeXStudio, or similar. Two of 13 used the blackboard. One used the visualizer to draw on a sheet of paper to be broadcast on the screen. None of the 13 observed lecturers used any other kind of information technology solution during their lecture. Thus Padlets, polling or multiple-choice questions (MCQs) were not a part of the repertoire in this sample.

Slow Down!

A common problem of lecturing is the ambition to tell the students everything and to cover all of the curriculum in the lectures. In order to do this, lecturers turn up the speed of the lecture. Then 'at least everything has been said', seems to be the rationale.

The method for calculating speech rate is simple. Record yourself. Transcribe one random minute of the talk. Count the words. This gives you words per minute (WPM). The average conversational speech rate is between 120 and 150 WPM. Podcasts and audiobooks are between 150 and 160 WPM. Sports commentators are 250–400 WPM.

A lecture should ideally be around 130 WPM. Not too slow and not too fast. Mainly, having a good speech rate is about varying your speed. A high speech rate sends signals of engagement and passion. A low speech rate comes across as importance and seriousness, but can also connote confusion or insecurity.

In the study presented here, I transcribed the 15th minute of each lecture, in order to let the lecturer get started. The average speech rate was 160 WPM; the slowest being at 105 WPM and the fastest at 184 WPM. Only one of the 13 observed lectures had a WPM between 120 and 140 (see Figure 11.3).

The general advice thus is: slow down! Take breaks to count to three (in your own head) when you have said something important for the students to understand, for them to finish their notes or for them to have just a few seconds to think. The quiet is much harder for the lecturer than for the students. They need the little spaces between audio stimuli. As lecturers, we may feel that we are wasting time when we are not talking. In fact, we are giving the students a little time to suspend their prior knowledge and maybe even pre-sense the use of the lecture, to use Scharmer's concepts.

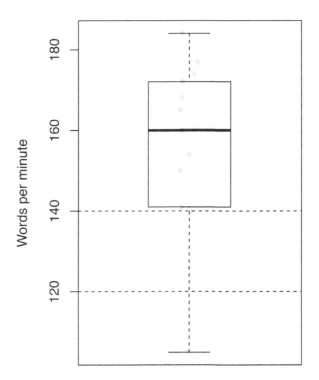

Note: Most lectures are above the recommended 120–140 WPM.

Figure 11.3   Words per minute in dataset

Structure Well

When looking at attention graphs for student attention during a lecture, the students are most aware during the first five and the last five minutes of the lecture. Nevertheless, this valuable time is often spent on practical announcements and framing at the beginning of the lecture, and trying to reach the end of the slide deck before time is up towards the end. The ideal structure is varied. If students feel variation between theory, examples, cases, use of blackboard, use of video-clips, time for questions, time for contemplating, time for trying something themselves, and so on, they will stay alert and engaged for much longer than if the lecture is one-way communication from beginning to end.

In Figures 11.4 and 11.5, you see two different structures of a lecture. The profiles presented in the figures are the result of the lectures being coded with respect to interaction, questions (asked and in some cases answered), time spent on cases, time spent on theory, time spent on other learning activities such as solving problems, talking to peers etc. and lastly time spent on framing the lecture.

Framing

The frame of the lecture should be how this week's lecture fits with the overall structure of the course. In that way, the lectures in a specific course should be like beads on a string: all connected and as part of a whole. Even if you only teach one or two lectures in a course, do not underestimate the value of tying together what you say in one lecture with what happened in the last lecture and what will happen in the next.

A salient example of this in my dataset was a course with two main lecturers. On the day of my observations a third lecturer gave the lecture. He started by criticizing the textbook and the approach to the course chosen by the two main lecturers. He went on to assume what had been said, and his lecture was essentially a rebuttal of what he thought might have been said. The students were unwilling to answers his questions and engage with him, much to his surprise. In the follow-up interview after my observation, I drew his attention to the fact that he undermined the *ethos* of the two other lecturers. Further, he more or less explicitly asked the students to abandon what they had learned already, while making assumptions about what they had learned and never asking for any confirmation of his assumptions. With just a brief 'What do you know about this topic already?' round, either online in a word cloud, or by letting the students talk for a minute and then report back, he would have shown interest in what they knew and found interesting. This in turn could provide the foundations for elaborating and even challenging their knowledge. But it would be done on the basis of interest rather than assumptions.

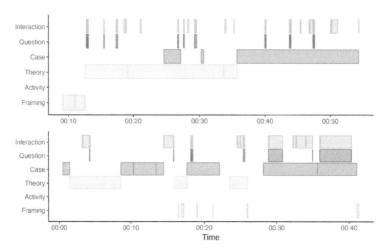

Figure 11.4   *A profile of a lecture with many interactions and changes in topic and approach*

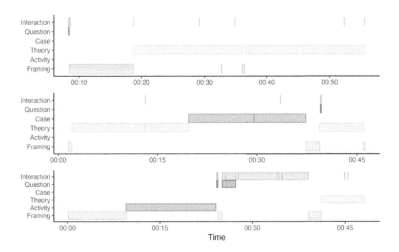

Figure 11.5   A profile of a lecture with very few interactions and shifts

Thus, start by activating the students' knowledge for you to put into use during the lecture. There is a clear tendency that if students get to talk during the first minutes of the lecture, they are more inclined to also ask and answer questions during the lecture. Polling systems and digital word clouds can also serve this purpose. If you do this at the beginning of each lecture, the students will get used to having something to say and you will reinforce the interaction.

Towards the end, the students start to drift. This is thus not the time for them to work on their own, as was the case in many of my observations. Rather, you should have those kinds of activities during the lecture. When put at the end it may feel like they have already finished. Use the end of the lecture to show what was important in this lecture, what they should focus on until next week, and how that is connected to today's themes. Even though it is obvious to you how the chapters in the textbook or the lecture themes are connected, it most likely is less so to them.

The difficult middle
A very established structure is: 'Say what you want to say. Say it. Say what you have just said'. Even though this seems redundant to you as a lecturer, for the students it may prove very helpful. The middle of the lecture should be structured around reflections and assignments, examples and theory. I purposely put reflections and assignments first, because they are often put at the end. This results in lecturers running out of time, or students being so cognitively overheated that they do not have the capacity to do them. Therefore, let students work a little on their own during the lecture. Make shifts between modes (slides, blackboard, just talking, showing something, using the visualizer, showing a movie clip ...) every ten minutes at least, and after the first two rounds, let the students do something on their own. This would give you a structure like this:

- t.0.00-0.03: Thoughts on today's topic and how it relates to last week's and the overall course content.
- t.0.03-0.13: First chunk of theory/case.
- t.0.13-0.23: Second chunk theory/case.

- t.0.23-0.33: Solve task/discuss question and upload answer/do MCQ.
- t.0.33-0.43: Third chunk of theory/case.
- t.0.43-0.45: Sum-up and point forward to next lecture.

A structure like this is more likely to keep students focused and attentive. The attention span of most humans is between 11 and 17 minutes. But providing sufficient changes and interactions makes a 45 minute lecture run by fast and with a high learning outcome.

Besides originating from a too-dense structure, the feeling of information overload can also be triggered by the visuals. In my study, most of the slides were very text-heavy. Since all slides were uploaded prior to the lecture, students had them on their personal computer (PC) screens as well as on the projector. This resulted in very little joint attention towards the lecturer and the projected version of the slides. The students mainly oriented their gaze towards their own screen, thus resulting in the lecturer only being a voiceover for the slides.

One lecture in my sample was significantly different. The course was third-semester statistics and the exam would be solving problems in writing. Thus, the lecturer had instructed the students to practise their handwriting. Of the 130 students present, only three had their PC open during the lecture. When asked in the break how the students felt about taking notes by hand, they told me that it helped them focus on the lecture; and that the distance to Facebook is further when the PC is in the backpack.

Putting less text on slides makes students write more on their own, which in turn potentially makes them process the information better and connect it to their experience and own thoughts (Mueller & Oppenheimer, 2014). Consider having slides which contain more content than the slides the students have on their screen, forcing them to look up; and consider reducing text for your oral lecture to be more significant and important to pay attention to.

Patient Interaction

The difference between an experienced and an inexperienced lecturer can be measured by the time they dare wait for an answer. Inexperienced and insecure lecturers wait on average 3–5 seconds before paraphrasing the question or answering on their own. More experienced lecturers, however, can wait up to 20 seconds.

If students know you will end up answering yourself, then they will not bother to come up with an answer. The awkward silence may pay off: if you teach them that you will wait until an answer is given, they will start answering.

The quality of the question obviously plays an important role in getting good answers and thus giving students feedback on their level of understanding. You should not ask questions just for the sake of it. Further, you should refrain from asking questions that have only one correct answer, turning it into a 'guess what the lecturer thinks' competition. Good questions are open (could not be answered by yes/no), call for reflection and invite a dialogue between student and lecturer.

It can be uncomfortable for students to provide answers in large groups, and I recommend that they are given time to talk in pairs before sharing their answers. It is easier to provide an answer if that answer is checked with someone else, and the peer conversation can also provide important insights for the students. The golden rule of question-and-answer in lecturing is to provide the necessary room for coming up with an answer and to pay attention to students who came up with a different answer, in order for them to have time to correct their potential misunderstandings.

Lecturers in my study did ask questions. However the answers were often not put to good use. Questions such as 'How many are with me conceptually?' or 'Does this make sense to you? Raise your hand' exemplify how questions are not being used for learning. Around one-third did not raise their hand when asked and presumably were either lost or not paying attention. Even if the lecturer thinks it is enough that two-thirds are making sense of the lecture, then it should be considered to provide help for students who apparently feel a little lost, rather than just letting them sit back with that feeling.

Much more recommendable would be to make use of multiple-choice quizzes or think–pair–share exercises during the lecture; not towards the end, but halfway though the lecture when attention is dropping. That would provide students with feedback on their level of understanding, and the lecturer can catch potential misunderstandings and point in the direction of reading materials to improve understanding. The interaction is part of what makes the lecture a social event, and the feedback on the level of understanding is part of what could not be obtained by reading or watching a video at home, thus making use of the people and environment in the room.

What the Students Do While You Talk

A much-cited quote is 'learning is not a spectator sport', by Chickering and Gamson (1987). This quote has been used as a claim against lecturing. But, as presented above, a lecture does not have to be only about spectating, and the value of attending the game/lecture cannot be underestimated.

But what do students do during lectures? As part of the observation I chose ten students in close proximity to where I was sitting and made a note every five minutes about what they were doing.

However, the key to keeping the students focused and on topic is clearly to keep it relevant for them to be present: the more they are noticed and needed, the longer the drift into cyberspace and social media can be postponed. In interaction-heavy lectures students start to drift only after 35–40 minutes. But when the lecturer reads aloud from slides and answers their own questions, the first students start drifting after 10–15 minutes.

A clear tendency is that if a student drifts once, then they keep drifting. Thus, it seems key to postpone the first drift in order for the students to keep focused. Obviously, students in business schools are adults and can do what they want with their time, but if we as lecturers want to be more relevant than life outside the room, we need to emphasize the social and live elements of the lecture throughout the 45 minutes, not just at the beginning and end. From watching the behavior of the students, it seems clear to me that they want to stay present and focused, but are sometimes challenged more than necessary by the use of the room.

A Taxonomy of Lectures

All of the above observations, analyses and literature review lead me to suggest a taxonomy of lectures. My hypothesis at the beginning of the project was that a high degree of interaction would lead to a high degree of attention. That, however, did not prove true in all cases.

The three types in the taxonomy are: soundtrack, interaction and collaboration lectures. A soundtrack lecture is characterized by voiceover slides. The lecturer is interacting very scarcely and the main focus is on visuals and how they are narrated by the lecturer. Lectures in my dataset that are teacher-focused and function as soundtrack lectures, but successfully keep the attention of the students, are characterized by the use of humor and *eunoia*, helping the students see what is difficult, and how elements in curriculum are connected, and meta-communicating about what is important and why. If the lecturer does not pay attention to the students and provides little information other than what is on the slides, the students will drift much faster. In Table 11.1, I exemplify how the soundtrack lecture can be used more or less appropriately.

Table 11.1   Soundtrack lectures

Ill-performed	Well-performed
Reading aloud	Telling a story
Using textbook as structure	Spending time on difficult parts
Not paying attention to students	Making use of cases and eunoia

Another type of lecture is the interaction lecture (Table 11.2). Here the lecturer asks questions, gives assignments and checks the level of understanding during the lecture. On paper, this should provide the basis of a good lecture. However, if the questions are never answered or are always answered by the lecturer, if the assignments are badly framed, and if the test and feedback are not targeted at the weaker students, an entertaining and relevant soundtrack lecture is of much higher learning value.

Table 11.2   Interaction lectures

Ill-performed	Well-performed
Not waiting for answers	Uses questions as dialogue enhancers
Badly framed assignments	Checking levels of understanding
Testing without feedback	Testing and providing feedback

The third type of lecture I observed was the collaboration lecture (Table 11.3). Just as with the two above-mentioned types of lectures, it can swing both ways. A successful collaboration lecture lets the students affect what is on the agenda and collaborate on cases. A conceptual example of the collaboration lecture is the Harvard method (Rebeiz, 2011). In short, the lecturer has prepared a case, and the lecture is then designed for the students to solve the case by use of readings prior to the lecture as well as information and details given by the lecturer during the lecture. The main role of the lecturer is to keep track of the students' answers, and the major part of the lecturing is in the preparation phase: finding a good case, and setting up a framework for the students to work in small groups and put in their results during the lecture, and making timeouts to provide feedback and sum up.

Table 11.3   *Collaboration lectures*

Ill-performed	Well-performed
Ill prepared cases	Relevant and well-prepared cases
Not interacting during group work	Summing up and being accessible
Not making use of results	Using results in discussions and reflections

In my observations, one lecturer tried to make the last of three lectures in a row a collaboration lecture, but he emphasized that the students should only stay if they wanted to talk and discuss the topic of the day. Of the 180 students present in the first two sessions, 22 were left after the break for the collaboration lecture. Those 22 students, however, got a very interesting and relevant session. Had the lecturer emphasized the impact of staying, more would have had that benefit.

In another case the lecturer introduced a collaboration task but did not provide sufficient framing for the students to solve it, gave the students ten minutes to solve it, but left the room and came back after 18 minutes, taking out the seriousness of the task; and ended up spending only a few minutes summing up results and answering questions.

This taxonomy serves to let lecturers decide what kind of lecture they want to give, and then make use of the traits of a well-performed version of that particular type. Good lecturing is first and foremost about providing a social learning opportunity for the students and letting them benefit from your insights and experience in their own work towards mastering the curriculum.

THE TIPS AND TRICKS: IMPROVE AS A LECTURER

I have divided this last section of the chapter on lecturing into the easy tweaks and the more fundamental changes in habits. I recommend focusing on changing only one or two things at a time, letting it become a new habit, and then finding something new to change. If you change everything all at once you may become more insecure and more focused on yourself than on the students.

Four easy and effectful changes:

1. Build in *eunoia* in your lectures: show the students that you care and, if it comes naturally, make use of humour every ten minutes. Talk to them rather than reading to them. This contributes to making the lecture a social event. Make reference to events and observations you share with the students, and do not forget to show your enthusiasm for academia and the topic of the lecture specifically.
2. Count your words per minute. Maybe you talk too fast; find out by recording, transcribing and counting. If you talk too fast, build in little breaks when you change slides, move around or wait for questions. An easy way of slowing down is to take a deep breath when you change topics. That is also good for your own well-being.
3. Ask good questions, and wait for answers. Consider the medium: digital or analogue? Consider the purpose: reflection or test? Consider what the answers can be used for, and teach the students that you will wait for and make good use of their answers.

4. Reduce text on slides. If the students think they will get everything by reading your slides after the lecture, they are less inclined to listen. Provide an opportunity for the students to work with the curriculum on their own.

Four bigger challenges:

1. Choose types of lectures while preparing the whole semester and vary the types throughout the course, for the students to have different experiences with the topics of the class.
2. Build in feedback opportunities for the students to know their level. This can be done in class or online between classes. Use the results to choose what to give attention to in the lecture.
3. Structure well: make 7–10 minute intervals, and let the students work, talk or collaborate in the middle of the lecture rather than in the end. Ask yourself what the students should gain from participating in today's lecture and use that as a guide for choosing material and cases.
4. Make optimal use of the ecological affordances of the lecture – time of day, room, topic, atmosphere and genre – to create a live, social learning opportunity.

REFERENCES

Bager-Elsborg, A., and Greve, L. (2019). Establishing a method for analysing metaphors in higher education teaching: A case from business management teaching. *Higher Education Research and Development*, 38(7), 1329–1342.

Barsalou, L.W. (2010). Grounded cognition: Past, present, and future. *Topics in Cognitive Science*, 2(4), 716–724.

Beattie IV, V., Collins, B., and McInnes, B. (1997). Deep and surface learning: A simple or simplistic dichotomy? *Accounting Education*, 6(1), 1–12. https://doi.org/10.1080/096392897331587.

Biber, D., and Conrad, S. (2009). *Register, Genre, and Style*. Cambridge: Cambridge University Press.

Bligh, D.A. (1998). *What's the Use of Lectures?* Exeter: Intellect Books.

Campbell, J. (1995). *Understanding John Dewey: Nature and Cooperative Intelligence*. Chicago, IL: Open Court Publishing.

Charlton, B.G. (2006). Lectures are such an effective teaching method because they exploit evolved human psychology to improve learning. *Medical Hypotheses*, 67(6), 1261–1265. https://doi.org/10.1016/j.mehy.2006.08.001.

Chickering, A.W and Gamson, Z.F. (1987). Seven Principles for Good Practice, *AAHE Bulletin* 39, 3–7.

French, S., and Kennedy, G. (2017). Reassessing the value of university lectures. *Teaching in Higher Education*, 22(6), 639–654. https://doi.org/10.1080/13562517.2016.1273213.

Gallagher, S. (2017). *Enactivist Interventions: Rethinking the Mind*. Oxford: Oxford University Press.

Gallagher, S., and Lindgren, R. (2015). Enactive metaphors: Learning through full-body engagement. *Educational Psychology Review*, 27(3), 391–404. https://doi.org/10.1007/s10648-015-9327-1.

Grasha, A.F. (1994). A matter of style: The teacher as expert, formal authority, personal model, facilitator, and Delegator. *College Teaching*, 42(4), 142–149. https://doi.org/10.1080/87567555.1994.9926845.

Greve, L. (2016). Metaphors for knowledge in knowledge intensive groups: An inductive investigation of how and which metaphors emerge in conversations. Aarhus BSS, School of Business and Social Sciences, Aarhus University.

Guilbault, M. (2016). Students as customers in higher education: Reframing the debate. *Journal of Marketing for Higher Education*, 26(2), 132–142. https://doi.org/10.1080/08841241.2016.1245234.

Jensen, T.W., and Greve, L. (2019). Ecological cognition and metaphor. *Metaphor and Symbol*, 34(1), 1–16. https://doi.org/10.1080/10926488.2019.1591720.

Lakoff, G., and Johnson, M. (1999). *Philosophy in the Flesh: The Embodied Mind and its Challenge to Western Thought*. New York: Basic Books.

Macdonald, R. (2006). The use of evaluation to improve practice in learning and teaching. *Innovations in Education and Teaching International, 43*(1), 3–13. https://doi.org/10.1080/14703290500472087.

Maturana, H.R., and Varela, F.J. (1980). Embodiments of autopoiesis. In H.R. Maturana and F.J. Varela (eds), *Autopoiesis and Cognition: The Realization of the Living* (pp. 88–95). Springer Netherlands. https://doi.org/10.1007/978-94-009-8947-4_11.

Mueller, P.A., and Oppenheimer, D.M. (2014). The pen is mightier than the keyboard: Advantages of longhand over laptop note taking. *Psychological Science, 25*(6), 1159–1168. https://doi.org/10.1177/0956797614524581.

Nonaka, I. (2007). The knowledge-creating company. *Harvard Business Review, 85*(7/8), 162–171.

Ong, W.J. (2012). *Orality and Literacy* (3rd edition). New York: Routledge.

Ørsted, H.C. (1803). *BREV TIL: Johan Georg Ludvig Manthey FRA: Hans Christian Ørsted (1803-03-06)*, Danmarks Breve. https://danmarksbreve.kb.dk/catalog/%252Fletter_books%252F002053861 %252F002053861_X00-L002053861X000022.

Rebeiz, K.S. (2011). An Insider perspective on implementing the Harvard case study method in business teaching. *US–China Education Review, A5*, 591–601. https://eric.ed.gov/?id=ED527670.

Rousseau, Jean-Jacques (1763 [1979]). *Emilie, or On Education*. New York: Basic Books.

Rowley, J. (2007). The wisdom hierarchy: Representations of the DIKW hierarchy. *Journal of Information Science, 33*(2), 163–180. https://doi.org/10.1177/0165551506070706.

Scharmer, C.O. (2001). Self-transcending knowledge: Sensing and organizing around emerging opportunities. *Journal of Knowledge Management, 5*(2), 137–151. https://doi.org/10.1108/13673270110393185.

Smith, C.V., and Cardaciotto, L. (2011). Is active learning like broccoli? Student perceptions of active learning in large lecture classes. *Journal of the Scholarship of Teaching and Learning, 11*(1), 53–61.

12. The case for cases: using historical and live cases to enhance student learning

René W.J. Moolenaar and Michael B. Beverland

INTRODUCTION

The use of case studies has a long history in business education. Ranging from the famed 'Harvard method' in which entire courses are built around cases, through to the more ancillary use of short case examples to bring theoretical constructs to life, few business courses can engage students without reference to some form of case study. Yet, confusion and even concern exists among even experienced business educators (henceforth, 'educators') about their use. Common concerns relate to how to best use cases, whether cases can be used outside of the executive education environment, the fast obsolescence of written cases, whether students will prepare and engage with such material, and, more recently, how to manage case discussions online. With the second author being active in running seminars on case use and development, it is surprising that even experienced educators approach cases with reluctance, even in the face of student demand for greater exposure to real-life examples and challenges.

The aim of this chapter is to provide guidance on the use of cases in the physical and virtual classroom. By use of cases, we mean courses where cases are designed in as crucial elements of addressing learning objectives, as opposed to the use of examples to illustrate key points, or the use of cases as an assessment tool in exams. In doing so, we focus on two types of cases: the range of traditional paper-based and video-driven historical cases, and so-called 'live' real-time cases. We draw on a combined 30 years of case teaching experience, insights from colleagues along the way, examples and the relevant literature. We explore how to prepare both educators and students for cases, in-class use, course design decisions, and some common concerns and challenges when using different types of teaching cases. Finally, in light of the sudden shift to blended or online learning resulting from the outbreak of COVID-19, we explore challenges arising in case use outside of the traditional classroom.

THE CASE FOR CASES

The use of real-life examples – cases – in study is not new, in fact it goes back thousands of years; in ancient times it was often the only option available to learn. Despite the challenges to effectively use cases in the classroom, as discussed later in this chapter, we start by offering a number of important reasons for their use in business schools.

The first case stems from the criticism which has been voiced at business schools about the gaps in the required knowledge and skills for the real world their students obtain on their programmes (Baldwin et al., 2011). Problem-solving skills, interpersonal skills (goal-directed communication and relationship-building behaviours), self-awareness (understanding one's own capabilities and limitations) are often underdeveloped across sections of the student cohort. The origins of such gaps can often be traced back to the learning outcomes of programmes and related courses or modules, as well as the lack of focus on the development of such knowledge and skills during their delivery. The authors believe that analysing a case and participating in the subsequent critical discussions can make a positive contribution to closing such gaps.

For the next case we ask the following question: is it conceivable that one can graduate with a degree in, say, engineering, arts, nursing or physics without ever having operated a machine, created a work of art, interacted with a patient or conducted an experiment? The answer is, of course, 'unlikely'. In these disciplines it is often an integral part of the course design and related syllabus; again, the interaction with a patient or the application of paint to a canvas adds an additional, and essential, dimension to the learning process. However, it appears to be possible to graduate from a business school without having had an opportunity to apply the theory to a business or organization in a structured and critical manner. Often, much focus is placed on the teaching, and hopefully learning by students, of theory across a wide range of business topics. But its application to an organization seems not to be an integral part of the programme. We suggest that by putting the proverbial 'scalpel' to an organization, to explore and seek to understand the dynamics of its markets, the limitations of its resources and the challenges it faces, is an essential part of the learning journey we should be offering our students.

Increasing diversity, ability and interests of student cohorts makes it increasingly harder to engage students, which leads us to the third case for using the cases. The benefits of experiential learning are well documented (e.g., Kolb and Kolb, 2005) and include higher and wider student attention and attainment levels, deeper learning and improved understanding of limitations. Cases, both historical and real-time, are positioned at the overlap between the traditional lecture and workplace-based learning, combining characteristics of both approaches. Providing students with exposure to, for example, a management team of a local organization, the 'live' case, adds a level of excitement and opportunity for discussion about the challenges it faces in the current economic climate and any specific developments of the markets it serves. It gives students exposure to the characteristics and behaviour of an organization seeking to achieve its objectives in such circumstances. Furthermore, preparing for an interview with, for example, the case management team requires analysis, and the actual interview itself requires being able to ask appropriate questions, and good listening skills to consider the answers given; and all the information gained from the interview requires subsequent synthesis and can fuel critical discussion between students afterwards.

The next case relates to the rising levels of academic misconduct. In particular, plagiarism and the use of 'essay mills' and related writing services are concerns voiced by the academic community. Such services are increasingly sophisticated and affordable as a result of increasing demand and competition. The case study method provides a level of defence against such practices, particularly in situations where case discussions and related reflections thereon are assessed. Live cases in particular provide an additional defence and discouragement to the student to engage in such practices. Interaction with the management of a live case needs preparation and engagement through asking questions and responding to answers given. Such interaction could provide sufficient encouragement and excitement for the student to complete the task at hand, and dissuade them from academic misconduct.

In the context of the rapid shift online following the COVID-19 pandemic, the use of cases in class is more urgent, in light of the need to mix up activities and mimic in-class interactivity. Both authors have had a chance to reflect on the effectiveness of online education, and in discussion with their peers have found that 30–40 minutes of lecturing and discussion is the maximum that can be done in one setting. After that, students start to tire and engagement drops. In this context, shorter cases, video-based material, role plays, live case presentations from experts and indeed students themselves, live case problem-solving, and long cases broken into sessions, are critical to maintain focus. We have both found that the more activities used, the more engaged students are, especially when confronted with intensive block-style teaching.

The final case has an institutional focus. Given the aforementioned operating conditions and challenges for business schools, creating and fostering relationships with industry should continue to be, or become, a priority. Such relationships are notoriously hard to establish and maintain (Garousi et al., 2019) for both schools as well as industry. Lack of understanding about topics of mutual interest and who to contact are typical barriers for such relationships. But once established they can bear fruit in a variety of areas, such as the commercialization of research, funding for research, knowledge exchange, and so forth. Approaching an organization with a straightforward objective of being the subject of a case (historical or live) could be the proverbial low-hanging fruit. Following a successful completion of such a project, this could be the basis for the development of a wider relationship.

OVERVIEW

Compared with lectures, the advantages of using historical and live cases in business education are presented in Table 12.1.

USE OF CASES

Before using cases, it's important to think about positioning. Cases vary in length and difficulty. Drawing on insights from the 2002 North American Case Research Association workshop (see also Naumes and Naumes, 1999), we classify case difficulty on two issues: the problem to be solved and the decision to be made. Figure 12.1 provides details and identifies three levels of case difficulty. The simplest cases are ones where both the problem to be addressed and the decision made are known. 'Simplest' in this case does not mean lacking value; such cases are highly desirable for entry-level courses, for student revision, and for short in-class exercises where educators are focused on describing and exploring new concepts. Since students know the challenge facing the case protagonists and the solution, the focus is typically on bringing constructs to life, applying constructs to a real-life situation, or assisting with revision. The focus of such cases is therefore reinforcement, and it is why such cases, which are usually shorter in length, populate textbooks for undergraduates and, increasingly, taught postgraduate courses.

More typical cases sit in the middle. In these cases, either the business problem or the decision made is provided. Typically, cases published in outlets such as Harvard Business School, the Case Centre or Bloomsbury's recently launched fashion business case series place an emphasis on identifying the key business problem, with the student being required to identify possible solutions. However, some cases, typically those involving mistakes, such as Coca-Cola's infamous 'New Coke' launch, Ford's Edsel or Vegemite's short-lived iSnack

2.0 extension (Keinan et al., 2012) involve understanding the logic for decisions and reflecting on how mistakes could have been avoided (or, in the context of the firm's ethos and culture, perhaps were inevitable). Cases offering a historical perspective – often of the rise, decline and rebirth of brands such as Snapple (Deighton 1999), Burberry (Moon 2003) and the aforementioned Vegemite – also offer opportunities to explore important constructs such as brand equity and brand building, providing a useful way to ease even advanced students into areas where they are less familiar.

Table 12.1   Advantages of using historical and live cases in business education

Lectures	Historical cases	Live, real-time cases
Offer extensive knowledge and concepts	Learn through application of knowledge and concepts	*In addition to the advantages of historical cases:*
Efficient in transferring large number of ideas	Opportunity to learn through knowledge integration	Direct interaction with representatives of the organization
Using common and standardized text	Provide structured environment for team work	Exploration of the situation in the current setting
Learning through listening, reading and memorizing	Provide safe environment to take risk	Increased engagement from students
Learning through acquisition of knowledge and concepts	Opportunity to see management problems and their solutions	Opportunity to foster relationships with external organizations
Relatively easy to convene in online learning environments	Analysis in broad range of controlled settings	Reduced chance for academic misconduct
	Identify and solve problems in controlled settings	More complex to organize in online environments with large class sizes
	Learn sequential analysis of the controlled situation to make appropriate decisions	
	Expose to diversity of decisions contexts for defined problems	
	Learning through active critical thinking, analysis and debates	
	Opportunity to learn interpersonal relations, team work and communication in controlled settings	
	Skill development in controlled and low-risk settings	
	Relatively easy to organize in online learning environments, using breakout rooms to facilitate discussions	

Source: Adapted from Farashahi and Tajeddin (2018).

The most difficult set of cases try to most closely replicate 'real-life' decisions. The many inquiries into why United States law enforcement missed the threats posed by a group of individuals prior to the September 11, 2011 attacks in New York and Washington often identify that all the pieces of the puzzle were available to agents, yet the sheer volume of data, and the variety of sources – some credible, some believed otherwise – made identifying the threat difficult. Academic studies, such as the Mann Gulch disaster (Weick, 1993) or the 1977 Pan Am KLM Tennerife air disaster (Weick, 1990), focus on how difficult it is for actors to make sense of unusual situations, often leading them to repeat learned behaviours when the situation would demand otherwise. Such cases, useful as simulations or even typical of live cases, are challenging for even the best students. Although there was once a trend of writing cases like this, often driven by the ego of those seeking to write the most difficult case possible, the difficulties posed in their use have reduced their popularity.

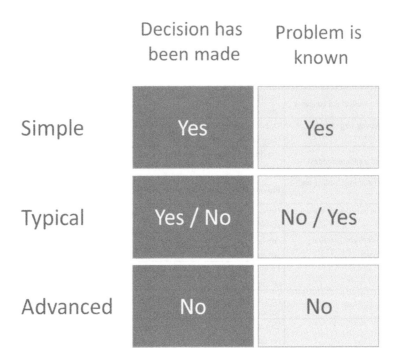

Figure 12.1   Type of case

CHALLENGES OF CASE TEACHING

Teaching with cases is not without challenges. Students and staff must be prepared, or prepare beforehand. In a case-driven course, dominant learning scripts (Schank and Abelson, 1977), including the role of educator and student, shift. Whereas lecturing involves a largely one-way approach to information provision, case-driven teaching involves much more interaction, mutual discovery and less structure. It's important to recognize that these unwritten scripts or norms have often been built up throughout a student's time at university, so deviating from them may trigger a sensemaking crisis, whereby students experience uncertainty, confusion, fear, and even frustration and anger (Marcy, 2015). Therefore, preparing students beforehand for a different learning approach is essential, and something we cover in detail below. Besides this, there are some unique challenges that arise when teaching traditional paper-based cases versus live cases.

CHALLENGES OF USING PAPER-BASED CASES

Leaving aside the need to thoroughly prepare for case teaching (covered below) and selecting the right case (see 'positioning' above), two major challenges arise: (1) pre-class preparation; and (2) in-class engagement. In both cases, we recommend an empathetic approach, whereby one tries to put oneself in the shoes of students and see things from their point of view. In the first instance, students have multiple demands on their time (much as we did when we were at university) and often make trade-offs. In the case of case teaching, widespread staff concern about whether students will engage may reflect the experience of students being poorly prepared, 'winging it', or believing they can coast on the backs of others. With this in mind, it is worth thinking about preparing students for class with some simple tools:

1. Remind students that the case is temporally bound. That is, all the information they need is in the case, no further information is necessary. In fact, information outside of the bounds of the case, gathered through web-based searches, personal insight or others' opinions, is detrimental. The purpose of the case is the focus on making decisions within a real-life, albeit historical, context.
2. Can you cut down on reading time by getting students to focus on only those parts of the case that matter for your learning outcomes? Case writers often include more information in a case to cover multiple uses, so it may be possible to prioritize what students need to read.
3. If you will rely on exhibits or appendices in class, make sure students know this.
4. What knowledge will the case examine? Can they explore this without recourse to set readings, or will the readings help them?
5. Provide key questions. These may not be the one you use in class, but set them 3–4 descriptive questions that ensure they have the basics to engage in discussion.
6. If you are grading participation, explain clearly how this will work. Students may have expectations that they will get marks for 'turning up', or 'saying anything', so be clear what your expectations are. Simple rules, such as 'participate twice a session', may be useful for shy or introverted students to engage initially.

Hopefully this preparation will limit the challenges presented by low student engagement in class. However, it is equally likely that you will need to break the ice, even with MBA students (particularly from cultures where case discussion is unusual). One of the main concerns raised by staff in relation to using cases relates to in-class engagement. Either students are unlikely to participate, or the class will be dominated by a handful of students, not all of whom have actually prepared. From experience, unless students are used to case teaching, you will need to ease them into it. Fortunately this can be done relatively simply:

1. Prior to the session starting, do a quick tour of the room to get a sense of who has prepared. How many students have the cases with them? How many have highlighted passages on the page or, more likely, on a tablet screen? If you get a sense that not many have, you will need to rethink your approach, perhaps allowing for some limited breakout time to start things off (do not overdo this, as it immediately sets expectations for next time).
2. Think about the room layout. Is it conducive to discussion? To working together? To your ability to walk around and interact with students? If you can move furniture about, do so.

3. Can you bring the case to life somehow? In teaching the New Vegemite case, the second author often brings in a jar of the product, hands it around and enables people to smell it (which is usually enough to get the picture) and taste it (if they dare). For the C.W. Dixey case (Keinan and Beverland, 2016), he brings in a prototype of Winston Churchill's glasses to let people feel the quality, try them on and look silly (the second author usually wears these to teach, largely because they do not work on his face, and thus helps breaks the ice), and also provides the packaging and brand logos. These options are not always possible, but where possible – such as investing in a few containers of Pringles to teach the case (Shapiro, 2000) – can break down barriers and also bring to life the brand's 'once you pop you can't stop' tagline. Can you run short videos beforehand, project logos or products, or images of the protagonists on the front screen? All of this helps.

4. Start with a brief overview of the session. This is not a summary of the case per se, rather the focus is on how the session will work in practice. We often broadly outline the board strategy, the purpose of the case vis-à-vis learning outcomes, how it builds on previous material, how it will relate to material to come, and what skills students will gain. Then talk very briefly, one minute or so, about the case in general.

5. Set up the rules of engagement. If you are grading participation, explain how you will do so (and have students make visible name tags so you know who they are). Explain that the purpose of case sessions is not to get the 'right answer' but to engage with material and learn from one another. Thus, while there are wrong answers, it's better to make mistakes in the classroom environment when nothing is at stake, than in an assignment or real life. If you are teaching online, cover practical information such as whether answers are to be in chat, via 'hands up', or general discussion (assuming you are using breakout rooms). Explain what each class member's role is: to be respectful and listen, and be critical in a constructive way. And explain what your role is.

6. Read the audience. Don't give in to the first uncomfortable silence when you've asked a question, but don't let it run forever either (online, don't be surprised if the silent period is a little longer, although our preference is to use chat first, then open up for discussion). If after asking in a couple of different ways you still get little response, switch to a quick group activity, giving people some time to work on a simple list of issues, and then go around the class for input. Be prepared to do this a few times until people feel comfortable engaging on their own. And be prepared to do it again next time (it takes time to build up enough trust).

7. Plan in exercises that help build practical tools. For example, when teaching cases on the rise and fall of brands, we often start with questions that describe how the brand in particular built value. Then we step away from the case and ask: what does this tell us about how brand value is built in general? We repeat the exercise for brand decline and revitalization. Straight away, students have gained useful information that is grounded in an example.

8. Inform students about your assessment of the level of engagement. If you feel it is too little, say so. If it's just right, say so too. If you know some students haven't participated, gently remind 'those of you who didn't participate today' that they may have lost an opportunity to score participation grades or for people to benefit from their insight.

9. When teaching cases online, you will need to adapt to a less spontaneous medium. Our recent experience would indicate that the inability of students to read the room and jump into the conversation makes general discussion harder online. Thus, chat first or hands up is often a really effective way to ensure engagement. Use of polls for either/or starter

questions is also an easy way to trigger engagement, before moving to chat to explore responses. By starting with chat, students can answer quickly without worrying about interrupting, answer without fear of social embarrassment, and then the instructor can invite them to talk about their answer in more detail.

Two final issues with engagement. If you are tempted to use very old (10–20 years), iconic cases, ensure that it is just one, and explain why you've chosen to do this. Students will naturally complain about this, especially since case learning is supposed to bring the real world to the classroom. Cases that require substantive knowledge of the past or of a particular cultural context may be too difficult for students to relate to. If you're stuck with just one option, think of writing an update for yourself. Finally, if teaching in blocks, recognize that student fatigue will set in. At some point, they won't be as engaged with the fourth or fifth case in a week as they were with the first or second. Plan for this to happen, allocate an easy case first, a more difficult one second, then perhaps try video-based materials, or even a breakout option for a third and fourth. Think of ways over a week-long course how you can mix things up to maintain class energy levels. This last point is particularly pertinent for online intensive courses. In a recent four-day MBA block, the second author found two paper cases a day were too much for students, with substantial drop-off in engagement in the second, even with vibrant additional materials. For such situations, try shorter cases, video-based material, live presentations or other forms of engagement.

CHALLENGES USING HISTORICAL AND LIVE CASES

Despite the significant advantages of the case study method over the traditional lecture as shown above, the use of it in higher education is not without challenges. Concerns have been raised about the ability of educators to facilitate constructive discussion between students (Turner, 1981), and the lack of inclusiveness of the discussions, including for students whose first language is not the language in which the course is taught, resulting in discussions taking place between fewer students (Rollag, 2010). The need for educators to spend a significant amount of time preparing and providing feedback is further emphasized by the increase in complexity as a result of the open-ended nature and the inconclusiveness of the subsequent discussions (Klebba and Hamilton, 2007).

Much time needs to be spent on reading about the organization at the time and its historical context, such as the state of the industry and/or markets, the competitor landscape and customer behaviour, the challenges it faces, and more. This is all essential, since the educator in such situations is the 'representative' of the case and the company featured therein; and is particularly pertinent during the class discussions which follow. Equally important is the bridging process between the case situation and the appropriate theory, 'tools', which need to be applied to answer the questions posed. This preparatory work by the educator should lead to an academically solid foundation for the subsequent case analysis and discussions done with and by the students.

Such preparatory work could provide an additional challenge for those schools and universities which have placed a significant emphasis on research and research-led teaching. A result of this focus is the recruitment of research-active academics with research credentials but with no or little teaching and industry experience (Cheit, 1985; Whetten, 2007). This means that more time is likely required in preparing for the presentation and discussion of the case.

For live cases, inviting the management of an organization into the classroom, whilst adding to student experience, should not lead to an abdication of the educator's responsibility to ensure academic rigour and quality. It would be all too easy for the management of an organization to give a presentation about 'some experience' and for the educator to facilitate a discussion about 'some experience'. A vague presentation and an unstructured discussion could in fact hinder the process of learning, and create confusion and misunderstanding. It is therefore essential that a similar, rigorous, process of preparation by the educator and students is adopted for live cases as is needed for historical cases.

A further risk which needs to be considered is the experience of the invited management to present to a potentially large audience of hundreds of students. Keeping such an audience engaged, and to present with the required confidence and clarity, is a challenging task even for an experienced educator, let alone management without such regular exposure. Equally important is the experience of the management in answering questions. Earlier we mentioned the need to provide a bridge between theory and practice; without some knowledge of the relevant theory, the answers provided could in fact be unhelpful or at best not optimal from a learning perspective. Discussion about such linkages, including the question-and-answer (Q&A) process, and practising the presentation beforehand, is essential from all stakeholders' perspectives.

Furthermore, in live cases an additional educational 'audience' is introduced: the management. It is quite reasonable for the presenting management to expect the advancement of their understanding and knowledge too. This needs to be considered by the educator in order to avoid disappointment and potentially compromising the relationship. The conditions and risks for participating in a live case therefore need to be explained clearly and discussed, to ensure understanding and acceptance. Below, we provide guidance on preparing for introducing live case studies.

CASES IN ONLINE DISTANCE LEARNING

Online distance learning (ODL) is a growing feature of higher education, especially in light of the COVID-19 virus. It facilitates engaging with a different audience which seeks to study part-time because of work, financial or family circumstances, and is often international in makeup. It also reduces the need to invest in physical infrastructure in order to meet the growth aspirations of the institution. Particularly in respect of the use of case studies in ODL, there are benefits for students too, given that there is often more time for analysis and subsequent discussion, including discussions over multiple days featuring multiple contributions, building a more complete learning journey comprising multiple perspectives.

However, applying cases to such situations requires three additional considerations, given the unique characteristics of ODL. Firstly, the audience is distributed over many locations, and often countries in different time zones. This reduces the opportunity for real-time discussion between the educator and the students and between the students themselves. Secondly, there are significant varying technological limitations dependent on the virtual learning environment (VLE) and location of the student. The level of internet infrastructure in a country, region, home or office varies greatly across the world, and results in a heterogeneous cohort with differing connection speeds and facilities. Equally, different VLEs have different built-in facilities for facilitating and recording online discussion. All of this needs to be considered when designing the discussion part of the case study. And thirdly, if the student cohort is spread over different time zones, then a live case is virtually not feasible. This means that the presentation by the management of the invited organization needs to be recorded, with the associated requirement for recording equipment, and the subsequent discussions need to be repeated and scheduled to ensure maximum participation.

Finally, the reduced spontaneity arising in the online environment renders general catch-all questions less effective. When teaching brand positioning, for example, it is common to explore the nature of the target segment. In a physical class this is relatively easy, as students throw out information which can easily be written on a whiteboard (for subsequent organization and application). Online, this tends to be more difficult, and directive probes are more necessary to ensure the information necessary to complete the case effectively is elicited. Thus, rather than ask 'What do we know about our customers?' It may be better to break it down into a serious of questions such as 'Where do customers use the product?', 'Do they consume individually or socially?', 'What are their personality characteristics?', 'What do they look for in their consumption experience of this product class?' This tends to more quickly generate information and can also be turned into polls to further speed up responses, capture all the information and encourage greater engagement.

Despite these characteristics and limitations, when considered during the design phase of the course, a case study can also make a positive contribution to student engagement and quality of learning, as described above.

TRANSITIONING FROM LECTURE TO CASE STUDY PEDAGOGY

In addition to the challenges described above, when educators are considering transferring from a lecture mode to a case study form of teaching, then based on the work done by Roy and Banerjee (2012) the following matters should be considered:

If the cohort for which you are introducing the case method is not familiar with this type of pedagogy, for example early-years undergraduate students, then an introductory session(s) to the principles of it must be considered to improve the learning experience and outcome.

Some topics are more suitable than others. For example marketing and human resources management with their applied dimension lend themselves more to case study than more abstract topics such as statistics.

Students with work experience, for example through internships at undergraduate level, or students on an MBA who are in work, more easily adapt to the case method then students without such experience.

There is a potential danger in attributing a grade to the case discussion which is too high in relation to the overall grade, resulting in a heightened reservation by the students to participate for fear of disagreeing with the educator, and a potential reduction in the content which needs to be learned.

As discussed in this chapter, sufficient preparation by both the educator and the student is required to aim for a satisfactory learning experience.

TIPS AND SUGGESTIONS

Preparing Students

When writing a case, authors are often encouraged to write for an overburdened educator who has been given a course at the last minute. This is useful advice for preparing a teaching note, but for academics with more time and forewarning, preparation is key. However, the idea of empathizing with an audience is a good one, and in this case, remember that students must be prepared for case-driven courses or exercises. For students used to lectures, case-based learning can be ambiguous at best, and approached with foreboding. In our experience, even MBA students may not be as comfortable with some styles of case-driven teaching as one would assume. Case-based education often allows for more than one reasonable answer, involves different interpretations, and the 'better' answer may differ heavily from what the protagonists actually did. So, with that in mind, how should we prepare students for case-driven learning?

1. Do some investigation into prior experience. What courses have the students done beforehand, and have any of those exposed them to cases? How were they run? Were they assessed? Case teaching styles can differ widely among educators. The second author prefers a Harvard-driven method, whereby students have prepared in advance and classes are driven primarily by case discussion. In this mode, there is little time (if any) for reading in class: you've either prepared, or you're wasting your time turning up. The last claim is all well and good, but if students are used to time in class to read cases, you may find your carefully planned case session is met with a wall of silence that no amount of probing questions can fix. Remember too that case preparation beforehand represents a significant amount of work in itself, so assessing this via participation may be necessary to drive engagement.
2. Look for resources. There is a wealth of digital information available to help students prepare for case-driven learning. The Case Centre (thecasecentre.org) has a wealth of resources one can use, including videos for educators and students. Make sure you explain to students what case-based learning is, what is its purpose, the benefits, how it links to theory, employability, and adds value to the students' overall experience per se. If you can, introduce this material, or even explain it at an induction for students, or if possible, run a short case to give students a feel for what the experience will be. If your programme has significant numbers of international students who may be unfamiliar with case teaching, work with your colleagues in some of the international induction courses and offer to run a session as an exercise.
3. Place a case as early as possible in your course to set the scene. When teaching strategic brand management, for example, the second author uses a case straight after the introduction to branding. Focusing on brand equity, cases such as Snapple, Burberry, the New Vegemite enable one to explore what makes a brand strong, what causes decline, and how equity is revitalized. At this point in the course, students have done little more than introduce themselves, engage in a (hopefully) fun icebreaker 'how well do you know your global brands' challenge (involving a mash-up of letters from logos), and had a one-hour interactive session discussing definitions of branding. As well as the placement of the case, the choice is also important. Start easy, and then move to more complex cases, requiring detailed analysis and work. A simple exercise involving how the brand grew,

why it faltered and how it came back enables anyone with even a cursory understanding of the material to participate, does not involve a lot of prior knowledge, and overcomes fears about difficulty. Used correctly, these exercises can also help build theory that sets up the course nicely, thereby setting expectations at the very start. And, if students haven't prepared, easy cases can be broken down further into short group discussions, involving five-minute breakouts.

4. Align reading with cases. Try to choose a reading to connect to the case directly. Some providers, such as Harvard Business School, create suggested syllabi or have core readings that link to cases. Even if you don't use these, adopt the logic. If your course is built around cases, use core readings as support. And, don't overdo it! We've lost count of the number of courses we've had to help colleagues with that allocate two textbooks as core and one as suggested, or had extensive reading lists, with extensive redundancies and little coherence. A case-driven course may have no more than 4–6 cases and a similar number of core articles, relevant book chapters, or supportive digital videos.

5. Be careful of the 'famous' case. We're not talking about iconic examples in the field, rather be mindful of what cases or sectors students have been exposed to in prior courses. The second author well remembers teaching on an MBA programme where the Morgan Motor Company was featured in a number of courses. As much as we personally love the story of this iconoclast brand, students made it clear that they had heard enough about a niche motoring firm. Likewise, when teaching fashion branding, we went through prior courses, tapped into students' Instagram feeds, and asked them in inductions what brands inspired them. The result of this exercise was to remove all the icons, bar one, and focus on up-to-date, ethical or sustainable brands, streetwear start-ups, Instagram influencer brands, brands for men (the programme overwhelmingly focused on women's fashion, a highly competitive industry), brands from South East Asia, and brands targeting often-ignored markets, such as plus-size consumers. Suffice to say, the course ran well.

Educator Preparation

It goes without saying that educators need to be sufficiently prepared when using cases. Although teaching notes are written with harried educators in mind, relying on them alone, as a substitute for a close reading of the case, is a recipe for disaster. Winging it may work every now and again, but if students start arguing between different points and you are not across the detail, including that all-important footnote or appendix, students will see through you (and in MBA classes, may call you out for it). So how should educators prepare in advance?

1. Know your material. One well-known educator once told us he took three months to do due diligence on his chosen cases, whittling down a list to the six he needed. It will sound obvious, but read the case, every footnote, every appendix, table, image, as well as the teaching note and suggested readings. Familiarize yourself with the chosen firm, industry and market. Do some due diligence on the main protagonists. All of this helps give you confidence in front of the audience, and when engaging in participation grading, can help you decide if those dominant students have really read the case or not. Case authors are always under pressure to make their material more succinct, so anything left in the published case is there for a reason. In one case used by us, Security Capital Pacific Trust (Fournier, 2000), the first footnote is not only critical for discussing the value branding

can bring to a firm, but it also enables a deeper discussion about financial brand equity. Consumer data, often critical to making informed choices about what to do next, is often located in an exhibit or appendix at the end, and ignored by students (pointing this out in advance is also a good idea).

2. Read the teaching note, but don't be beholden to it. Teaching notes provide a lot of information to educators about how to teach the case, where to place it, suggested questions, and possible answers. In many cases these are useful, but it may not work for you. Think about how best to pitch the case in your context. Sometimes the suggested framework may be obvious, fail to take into account what you've covered before, or be too advanced for your students.

3. Ask around about the case. For popular cases, there will be a number of educators with experience of it, and they can tell you what works and what doesn't. There are numerous cases out there on seemingly great brands that are extremely difficult to use in class, largely because the learning outcomes are unclear and the authors have placed the fame of the case above its sole purpose: to be used by students and educators.

4. Always finish with a 'What happened?' Some teaching notes come with an addendum, but most do not. This is not surprising, the case is focused on 'What should one do next?' and the outcome may not be available at the time of writing. But it is incumbent on educators to have that answer. In cases where the action taken contradicts what you have generated in class, discuss why. This further discussion is helpful in reinforcing the value of cases, and may also introduce some of the wider context that decision-makers operate in, which is often by necessity left out of cases.

5. Set preparation questions. Cases are often detailed, lengthy and designed for multiple purposes. Students are often under time pressure, so give them a set of questions that will enable them to participate in the discussion. These may not be the questions you focus the discussion around, but they will be enough to enable students to engage. They may also differ from the questions listed at the end of the case.

6. Have a plan of action. One critical learning from many of the case teaching workshops is an emphasis on 'boards'. Most case discussions involve use of a whiteboard (for online courses this can be adjusted). The order of development is deliberate. You may start with easy questions that deliberately set students up to fail. We once watched an experience educator do this for the 'Proctor & Gamble in Italy: Pringles' (Shapiro 2000) case, whereby the protagonist seemingly must make quick decisions about an entry strategy, involving the classic '4Ps' (price, promotion, placement and product) of marketing. Students gave rapid-fire answers and it was clear something was amiss, since the educator was uncritically accepting of seemingly contradictory answers. Once the 4Ps had been developed, with alternatives subject to a simple show of hands and quick discussion as to why, the educator gently 'fired' all the students. The point was simple: only by determining the brand's position could one answer these questions. Critically, after developing that position, the case finished with a new vote on the 4Ps, and the answer was often the exact opposite of what was preferred. Having a clear plan in class matters, with each board or question or exercise designed to build on the previous ones and help students explore concepts.

7. Know your audience. Although it's not always possible to get details on your students beforehand, where possible get some background information on where they have worked and what their interests are. When teaching branding on MBA courses, for example, its

virtually guaranteed someone will have worked at P&G or Unilever. Since we use cases involving both, it's good to know someone may have first-hand insight of the firm and decisions in the class. This student can be valuable, and it also means you avoid making comments that make you look silly. In MBA and Master's courses, educators often get details on their students, but if not, a short introduction at the beginning of the session should also include a question on previous employment and experience.

8. Alternate roles for different discussion rounds. Where you are using a case study which features a number of different roles – such as chief executive officer, chief financial officer, chief marketing officer, chief technology officer (CEO, CFO, CMO, CTO), and so on – then the learning journey can be further enhanced with students changing roles in the subsequent rounds of discussion. Equally, students can be given roles which are based on, for example, being a proponent or opponent of scenarios being considered; changing those positions in subsequent rounds. Adopting a different role gives the student the opportunity to consider the case challenges and potential solutions from different perspectives. Experiencing and reflecting on such different viewpoints is an important facet of higher education.

9. Consider whether to use one large, continuing case or a selection of smaller cases. One large case has the advantage of letting students connect one sub-part of the case to the next sub-part, and experiencing the utilization of material gained in earlier parts of the case to the decision-making in subsequent parts. However, it is important to make sure the case is and remains of sufficient interest to the students throughout, otherwise they will lose interest. Using a collection of smaller cases has the advantage of ensuring that each academic topic is supported by an appropriate and most suitable case. However, it may require more preparation time to find the range of suitable cases.

10. When using multiple cases, ensure sufficient diversity with regard to gender, race, ethnicity, country, industry, and so on, in order to create a learning environment which is as inclusive as possible. Case publishers have begun to realize that they are complicit in reaffirming stereotypes or excluding minority voices, and have increased calls for greater representation. The recent Black Lives Matter protests, and calls to decolonize the business school curriculum, provide the momentum to rethink our own representation practices in the classroom (Dar et al., 2020). Are we preparing our students for the realities of a globalized, multicultural world and workplace if all our cases reflect the experience of primarily white, Western, male-run firms? This does not mean adding in a few cases where well-known Western firms enter developing markets; rather, we need to represent fully the diversity of the business world, adding in cases that focus on non-Western markets and different forms of practice.

Specifically for Live Cases

1. Foster relationships with organizations well in advance of the target date to build understanding and appropriateness. It is worth checking the level of experience of the presenter in presenting to larger or large audiences. Not all business managers are equally as comfortable as you might be; despite appearing positive, they might find the presentation quite daunting. Therefore, unless the manager is quite experienced, we recommend you arrange for the manager to practice their presentation as well as the subsequent Q&A. Involving a group of students could facilitate this, giving the manager a more realistic dry run, and the

students an opportunity engage with them and prepare the case from a student perspective. Furthermore, it provides the manager and students with an initial set of questions to kick off the Q&A and discussions. Such questions can be shared in advance or submitted via polling software or other student response software available at your institution.

2. Ensure the presentation of the case has sufficient opportunity for linking with the theory relevant to your course. Checking this beforehand ensures the desired contribution to the learning outcomes is sufficiently achieved.
3. If practical, arrange a site visit with the students to enhance their understanding of the organization and situation to be analysed, and to facilitate engagement with the management.

Specifically for Cases in an Online Distance Learning or Blended Learning Environments

1. For using cases in an ODL environment, consider creating smaller groups of students in the same time zone and use the incumbent features of the VLE to facilitate, record and potentially grade the discussions.
2. In blended learning situations (in this case online and on-campus) an asynchronous approach can be considered. In such situations the initial case presentation and required tasks can take place in the classroom, the subsequent analysis and discussions by the students online and asynchronous, and the summary and closing discussions in the classroom during the next session with all students.

STUDENTS AS AUTHORS

Case teaching involves a form of co-creation between instructors and students. Taking that one step further, is it worth involving students in the writing and running of cases? During a two-year stint at a fashion school in Melbourne, the second author did just that. Responsible for editing a series of fashion business cases, we turned the call into an assessment, trained students to be case authors, and ultimately involved them in running the cases in class. The experience was immensely rewarding, and for students (who were postgraduates), validation of their own experiences and skills. There are some challenges in doing this. Firstly, the brief needs to be fairly tight, and broken down into a standardized template or checklist. Students have often had experience of using cases, but not teaching them, and the two roles require different skills. Since students receive cases in a descriptive form, they often forget that the case is written around a business problem. Spelling this out at the beginning in a training session is critical. Secondly, you need to train students to write cases. The best student cases are usually singular in focus and shorter, around 2000 words. Running them through workshops speeds the whole process up. Thirdly, to run them well, students need training as well, and we spent time working out a lesson plan and whiteboard plan to ensure the case session would work well, even with a very supportive audience of peers. One further benefit of all this is students got to choose brands that reflect their own interests and world, which was often very different from their instructor's.

CONCLUSION

Teaching with cases, historical or live, provides a number of benefits to the learning journey we offer our students, as we have set out in this chapter. Greater opportunity to apply the theory, understanding the resultant rewards and limitations, and the case discussion between students, educator and management team, contribute to more effective learning. Engaging with live cases has further benefits such as reduced opportunity for academic misconduct, and the potential for fostering relationships and collaboration between university and industry, both rising priorities in higher education. The adoption of case studies is not without its challenges, though. For example, without due preparation by the educator and students, or given a lack of focused and respectful critical case discussion as well as a lack of clarity about the pedagogical objectives and type of case to use in a course, a case study could in fact lead to increased confusion, and be a barrier to learning and a waste of valuable time and resources.

Traditional approaches need to be rethought when shifting online, usually involving more planning, greater structure and the use of different types of cases, including shorter and longer, text and video, role playing, and live. With that in mind, it's worth remembering that there are more types of cases than those covered here. For subjects such as negotiation or human resource management, role playing scenarios are better forms of case practice to fully engage students with the reality of difficult situations. In some disciplines, such as fashion (where the second author has taught), performance-based cases are common, with students becoming fully immersed in the performance as a way of reflecting on their own practice. These have much potential in business studies, particularly in issues such as business ethics or behavioural change. The authors hope that this chapter provides encouragement to colleagues to introduce, or continue to use, case studies in their work, and are grateful to receive feedback and any experiences colleagues may have.

REFERENCES

Baldwin, T.T., Pierce, J.R., Joines, R.C. and Farouk, S. (2011) 'The elusiveness of applied management knowledge: A critical challenge for management educators', *Academy of Management Learning and Education*, 10(4), pp. 583–605. doi: 10.5465/amle.2010.0045.

Cheit, E.F. (1985) 'Business schools and their critics', *California Management Review*, 27(3), pp. 43–62. https://doi.org/10.2307/41165141.

Dar, S., Liu H., Martinez, D.A. and Brewis, D.N. (2020) The business school is racist: Act up! *Organization*, July. doi:10.1177/1350508420928521.

Deighton, John (1999) 'Snapple', Harvard Business School Teaching Case 8596-PDF-ENG.

Farashahi, M. and Tajeddin, M. (2018) Effectiveness of teaching methods in business education: A comparison study on the learning outcomes of lectures, case studies and simulations. https://doi.org/10.1016/j.ijme.2018.01.003.

Fournier, Susan (2000) 'Security Capital Pacific Trust', Harvard Business School Teaching Case 500053-PDF-ENG.

Garousi, V., Pfahl, D., Fernandes, J.M., Felderer, M., Mäntylä, M.V., et al. (2019) 'Characterizing industry–academia collaborations in software engineering: Evidence from 101 projects', *Empirical Software Engineering*, 24(4), pp. 2540–2602. doi: 10.1007/s10664-019-09711-y.

Keinan, A. and Beverland, M.B. (2016) 'C.W. Dixey & Son', Harvard Business School Teaching Case 9-517-019.

Keinan, A., Farrelly, F. and Beverland, M.B. (2012) 'Introducing iSnack 2.0: The New Vegemite', Harvard Business School Teaching Case N9-512020.

Klebba, J.M. and Hamilton, J.G. (2007) 'Structured case analysis: Developing critical thinking skills in a marketing case course', *Journal of Marketing Education*, 29(2), pp. 132–139. doi: 10.1177/0273475307302015.

Kolb, A.Y. and Kolb, D.A. (2005) 'Learning Styles and Learning Spaces: Enhancing Experiential Learning in Higher Education, Source: Academy of Management Learning & Education'. https://www.jstor.org/stable/40214287?seq=1&cid=pdf-reference#references_tab_contents.

Marcy, R.T. (2015) 'Breaking mental models as a form of creative destruction: The role of leader cognition in radical social innovations', *Leadership Quarterly*, 26(3), pp. 370–385. doi: 10.1016/j.leaqua.2015.02.004.

Moon, Youngme (2003), 'Burberry', Harvard Business School Teaching Case 504048-PDF-ENG.

Naumes, W. and Naumes, M.J. (1999) *The Art and Craft of Case Writing*. Thousand Oaks, CA: SAGE Publications.

Rollag, K. (2010) 'Teaching business cases online through discussion boards: Strategies and best practices', *Journal of Management Education*, 34(4), pp. 499–526. doi: 10.1177/1052562910368940.

Roy, S. and Banerjee, P. (2012) 'Understanding students' experience of transition from lecture mode to case-based teaching in a management school in India', *Journal of Educational Change*, 13(4), pp. 487–509. doi: 10.1007/s10833-012-9191-4.

Schank, R.C. and Abelson, R.P. (1977) *Scripts, Plans, Goals and Understanding*. New York: John Wiley & Sons.

Shapiro, Roy D. (2000) 'Proctor & Gamble Italy: The Pringles Launch (A)', Harvard Business School Teaching Case 601070-PDF-ENG.

Turner, A.N. (1981) 'The case discussion method revisited', *EXCHANGE: The Organizational Behavior Teaching Journal*, 6(4), pp. 33–38. https://doi.org/10.1177/105256298100600412.

Weick, K.E. (1990) 'The vulnerable system: An analysis of the Tenerife air disaster', *Journal of Management*, 16(3), pp. 571–593.

Weick, K.E. (1993) 'The collapse of sensemaking in organizations: The Mann Gulch disaster', *Administrative Science Quarterly*, 38(4), pp. 628–652. Available at: https://www.jstor.org/stable/2393339?seq=1&cid=pdf-reference#references_tab_contents.

Whetten, D.A. (2007) 'Principles of effective course design: What I wish I had known about learning-centered teaching 30 years ago', *Journal of Management Education*, 31(3), pp. 339–357. doi: 10.1177/1052562906298445.

13. Using live business projects to develop graduate employability skills

Eleri Rosier

INTRODUCTION

Business schools have been accused of concentrating majorly on teaching quantitative and technical abilities (Parker, 2018). However, many other competences are considered crucial and necessary to raise graduate employability levels. Learning outcome should also provide students with interpersonal skills (Bedwell et al., 2014), critical thinking (Živkoviĺ, 2016), workplace readiness (Ritter et al., 2017) and professional confidence (Caza et al., 2015). Oral and written communication, critical thinking and problem-solving, and teamwork skills are in high demand in the contemporary business environment (Clarke, 2017). These skills cannot be gained or developed by studying theory only; in fact, they are the result of the theory application through direct experience (Schlegelmilch, 2020). Moreover, experiential learning contributes to keeping faculty and students connected and updated with the rapidly changing business models and environment, since it creates an intersection between classroom and business learning (Spanjaard et al., 2018).

LITERATURE REVIEW

Employability and Graduate Business Skills

At an institutional level, employability has been a driver of academic policy and a concept that incentivizes resourcing of student services, especially careers services, entrepreneurship activities, and internship and work experience programmes (Quality Assurance Agency for Higher Education, 2019). Academics also seek to embed employability activities into the curriculum and in-course learning experiences (Macfarlane & Roy, 2006). These kinds of initiatives and programmes are becoming more pervasive within higher education institutions, with the embedding of employability programmes increasing greatly in number across higher education institutions in recent years (Artess et al., 2017). Indeed, in the United Kingdom (UK), only 30 per cent of employers look for specific degree types when recruiting (Pollard et al., 2015). This reflects a highly flexible job market, which allows graduates from any discipline to apply for a wide range of jobs not directly related to their degree, as long as they have the required skills (Tomlinson, 2012).

Many higher education institutions have now developed 'graduate attribute' (GA) frameworks, used to describe the qualities and skills they believe students should develop through their studies at their institution (Bowden et al., 2000). There are commonalities across GA frameworks (Artess et al., 2017; Winberg et al., 2018), but graduate attributes are differentiated from graduate skills, in that attributes are defined by individual institutions risking narrow definitions and excluding wider graduate skills (Norton & Dairymple, 2020). Educational researchers, policy-makers and industry bodies have been attempting to define a comprehensive range of graduate skills. These definitions tend to include literacies, soft skills and 'character qualities' such as resilience and autonomy, as well as cognitive skills such as critical thinking (Soffel, 2016; Winberg et al., 2018). This chapter focuses on graduate employability skills, and investigates whether students think they are developing the skills they will need to thrive in the changeable and global graduate labour market (Jones & Killick, 2013).

Students need to develop their own graduate skills, and are equipped to some extent by higher education institutions to enter the graduate labour market but as graduates, do their skills match or mismatch what employers actually need? In the UK, higher education institutions are now evaluated against graduate outcomes with the Teaching Excellence Framework (TEF), which was extended recently to employability programmes (Artess, 2019). These types of drivers to reduce the skills gap are also a response to the increasing set of skills required by employers, and the requirements on graduates to be adaptable in the face of rapid globalization and technological advancement (Burke & Hannaford-Simpson, 2019). Given these developments, a key aim of this study was to investigate ways in which higher education institutions can effectively embed employability skills in the curriculum for graduates.

Studies on students' perceptions of graduate skills demonstrate that levels of awareness and engagement at undergraduate level are often low (Morris et al., 2013), even when higher education institutions explicitly formalize the acquisition of these for students in learning outcomes (Rust & Froud, 2016). Recent findings also suggest that some students are unaware of the importance of graduate skills, and that they underestimate the significance of developing and recording extracurricular achievements (Swingler et al., 2016). This is consistent with previous research suggesting poor use of tools such as the Higher Education Achievements Report (HEAR) to track students' extracurricular achievements (Docherty & Fernandez, 2014). Other work has suggested a mismatch between graduate and employers' expectations, with students overvaluing skills such as creativity and leadership, but undervaluing the importance of flexibility and adaptability, and teamwork, which we know that employers regard highly (Mattis, 2018; QS, 2018).

An integral element in successfully embedding employability in higher education curricula is understanding and incorporating students' perspectives on the skills they are acquiring through their studies. This is important because it helps identify the areas where higher education institutions might need to focus to develop new approaches and practices that better meet the needs of wider society (Vanhercke et al., 2014). Also, graduates' employability is influenced by the way they see themselves as future employees; perceptions likely to be carried through into the labour market and which act as drivers into various career routes (Tomlinson, 2007, 2012).

The Institute of Student Employers identifies nine distinct employability skills, such as commercial and entrepreneurial acumen, and the Higher Education Academy (HEA) has defined many more (HEA, 2006). Despite differences in such skill ranges, employability is seen as a developmental process enabling students to emerge with a valued (by employers) set of skills and qualities. However, based on recent reviews of the literature (Artess et al., 2017; Osmani et al., 2015) and research on student and employer views on the skills gap (Popovic et al., 2010), Table 13.1 lists key employability skills categories, based on literature on general graduate skills (Artess et al., 2017; Hounsell, 2011; Osmani et al., 2015), as well as digital skills based on Jisc (2014) and global skills also emerging from the literature (Morais & Ogden, 2011).

Table 13.1   Key employability skills

Graduate skill	Definition
Critical thinking	Apply a systematic and critical assessment of complex problems and issues and consider issues from a range of perspectives
Problem-solving	Investigate problems and practical situations and formulate, evaluate and apply evidence-based solutions and arguments
Information literacy	Locate, synthesize and analyse information and data from a variety of sources, with attention to detail
Communication	Communicate effectively knowledge, understanding and skills to a variety of audiences in a range of settings and using a variety of media
Curiosity to learn	Search broadly for insights and information across a wide range of situations and to challenge assumptions
Innovative/creative	Examine problems from a fresh perspective and develop innovative solutions
Collaboration	Collaborate, work in teams and groups, and lead where appropriate
Interpersonal/networking	Listen actively, negotiate effectively, be empathetic and develop positive connections with others
Autonomy	Think independently, exercise personal judgement, take the initiative and be enterprising
Self-management	Plan and organize my time, prioritize important tasks, work under pressure and to tight deadlines
Resilience	Respond flexibly and adapt my skills and knowledge when dealing with change, unfamiliar or challenging situations
Reflective/self-awareness	Use feedback productively, identify and articulate my skills in a variety of contexts, and set goals for my continuing personal, professional and career development
Digital skills	Select and fully use appropriate digital tools and software, find, analyse and use credible digital data sources, innovate using digital skills, develop and project a positive digital identity or identities, and manage digital reputation
Global skills	Encompassing knowledge and awareness of global issues, skills in communicating in multicultural settings

Next, different learning styles, such as experiential learning and live case study teaching, are considered as possible methods to better embed graduate employability skills in the curriculum.

Experiential Learning

Experiential learning occurs when students move away from being passive listeners and start to be more active and involved with an experience and the subsequent reflection on that experience (Kolb & Fry, 1975; Hawtrey, 2007). One of the most well-known educational theories in higher education is Kolb and Fry's (1975) experiential learning theory. According to Kolb and Fry (1975, p. 38), 'Learning is the process whereby knowledge is created through the transformation of experience'. An effective learning process, therefore, is a cycle consisting of four stages, all of which learners are expected to experience. The concrete experiences create the foundation for observations and reflections, which in turn are comprehended into abstract concepts and generalizations, producing new implications which can be tested, thus creating new experiences. The process starts with an encounter of a new experience, which is observed for data collection. The data is then analysed to raise new ideas or modifications of an existing concept. The learners, lastly, apply these ideas to the real world and see the results.

Hamer (2000) classified experiential learning into two groups: semi-structured classroom activities and loosely structured experiential activities. The former includes small and focused tasks designed to reinforce course concepts, for students to complete within the class period. Meanwhile, the latter can be computer simulations, role-playing, group projects, debates, and so on. These activities are broader regarding the scope, take longer to complete, are less controlled and more complex.

There is common agreement within the literature that learning can be achieved through practical application and active reflection (e.g., Beard & Wilson, 2002; Hamilton & Cooper, 2001; Kolb, 1984; Meyer, 2003). The active involvement introduces an element of realism within the classroom environment, allowing a significantly richer learning experience, increasing retention of the material and resulting in greater understanding (Culpin & Scott, 2011). Techniques such as computer simulations, field trips, outdoor learning, internships, action learning and structured classroom exercises have all been used to actively engage the learner (Gentry, 1990), and these methods tend to focus on the 'softer' or transferable skills – for example, project management (Darian and Coopersmith, 2001), communication, critical thinking and problem-solving (Kennedy et al., 2001) – often neglected in traditional teaching.

Live Case Study Projects

Gentry (1990) identified a number of critical components that determine the learning success of any experiential learning exercise (which include the current key aspects: active involvement and reflection), and highlighted three methodologies that successfully encapsulated these critical components: internships, computer-assisted instruction and live cases. Case studies have been widely used in education, particularly management education, for a number of years (Shapiro, 1984; Wines et al., 1994) and are claimed to be one of the best techniques for developing generic skills such as communication skills, written skills, interpersonal skills, judgement and analytical skills (Ballantine and McCourt, 2004).

Stewart and Dougherty (1993) identify four types of case study: real-world, incident-based, armchair and descriptive; with real-world cases being 'live', the others based on written material. Within a higher education learning environment the benefit of the live case is particularly pertinent, as a live case enables participants to work on a 'real' business issue facing an organization whilst being immersed in the organizational physical environment, context and culture (Culpin and Scott, 2011). Markulis (1985) notes that live cases are more realistic than written cases as they usually include participation by key decision-makers within the organization, and the business issue is often current and thus 'live'. For Gentry (1990), live cases include the following critical components: the issue to be addressed can be easily related to current business practice for the participant; there is active participation in the process; interactivity is critical; and there is a real and variable situation where information is incomplete.

According to Sara (2011), live projects are a style of learning where 'there is a movement away from notions of individual study, for its own sake, to ideas about working within the community'. There is an enhancement in the engagement between learners and real 'external collaborators' providing learners with opportunities to practice the learned theories, act professionally and locate their work to the real world. At the same time, learners still work in the role of students and continue to receive support from the university. Live projects, therefore, can be seen to sit between the binaries of theory and practice, university and community, designing and making, and ideas about what it is to be a student and what it is to be a professional.

Live Projects and Personal Skill Development

To increase skills such as communication, problem-solving and team-working, classes are suggested to become more 'learner-centred' and collaborative (Cunningham, 1995). Seven guidelines for creating a learner-centred environment in higher education have been compiled in a study sponsored by the American Association of Higher Education, the Education Commission of the States and the Johnson Foundation (Chickering & Gamson, 1987, cited in Gremler et al., 2000). The compilation includes the encouragement of student–faculty contact, cooperation among students and active learning; the giving of prompt feedback, an emphasis of time on task; the communication of high expectations, and a respect of diverse talent and ways of learning.

Live projects, in general, employ some of these principles. For example, experiential learning activities enhance the contact between students and faculties as students seek direction, assistance and insight from supervisors, module leaders, professors, librarians, and so on. Live projects also encourage cooperation and active learning, since students work in groups, learn from each other, and apply theories and materials into practices (Gremler et al., 2000).

According to Kolb and Fry (1975), regardless of various factors such as social environment, educational experiences or the basic cognitive structure of the individual, learning styles are influenced by two elements: the processing continuum (how we approach a task) and the perception continuum (how we think or feel about it). Four learning styles are created: accommodating, diverging, assimilating and converging. Comparing the definitions of each learning style (Kolb & Kolb, 2005) with Belbin team roles explanations (Belbin, 2017), matching areas can be seen. For example, an individual with the converging learning style is best at finding practical uses for ideas and theories. This person has the ability to solve problems and make decisions (Kolb & Kolb, 2005). The converging style of learning matches with the plant role of Belbin (2017) since this role is in charge of solving problems in unconventional ways which requires understandings from various aspects.

Similarly, Kolb and Kolb (2005) describe an assimilating learner as having a favourable understanding of a wide range of information and the ability to put it into concise, logical form. This person serves well as a resource investigator because they are in capable of finding ideas from a significant amount of information and bringing them back to the team (Belbin, 2017). An individual with an accommodating learning style is claimed to enjoy carrying out plans (Kolb and Kolb, 2005), which is an ideal task for teamwork and an implementer (Belbin 2017). Lastly, individuals who are best at viewing concrete situations from many different points of view prefer a diverging learning style (Kolb & Kolb, 2005). They fit in the position of a monitor evaluator, due to the requirements for a logical eye and impartial judgements (Belbin, 2017).

Positive influences of live projects on the improvement in these skills have also been studied and proved by many other researchers (Campbell et al., 2001; Eddleston et al., 2006; Scharf & Bell, 2002; and Thomas & Busby, 2003, cited in Chang & Rieple, 2013).

Live Projects and Participant Emotions

Besides providing students with useful skill improvement, live projects can also be emotionally influential. According to Chang and Rieple (2013), students can experience stress, frustration and anxiety during their live projects, especially due to the lack of the ability to deal with ambiguity and uncertainty when meeting the high expectations from clients. These negative emotions are claimed to be disadvantageous and unfavourable because they inhibit the learning process (Tyson et al., 2009). However, other studies have proved that experiencing negative emotions provides opportunities for self-discovery and growth, encourages further learning and re-engagement with learning processes, and enhances motivation. The learning process from failure is, indeed, emotionally difficult, yet being able to do so will result in ability in regulating emotions, which boosts confidence and professional competence (Finch et al., 2015). According to Finch et al. (2015), students tend to experience more negative emotions when they are mastery goal-oriented rather than performance goal-oriented. Mastery goal-orientation is defined as the goal of personal skill development. Students with this goal intentionally search for more challenging tasks to improve themselves, which results in more frustrations and stress because of the high level of difficulty, whereas performance goal-oriented students are concerned more with looking competent and completing tasks; therefore, they tend to choose easy solutions and less challenging activities. Finch et al. (2015) also indicated that mastery goal-oriented students tend to have better results compared with performance goal-oriented sudents.

Live Projects and Challenges

Live projects also come with some obstacles and challenges. Firstly, courses and modules normally centre on a single specialization, whereas live projects tend to require diversified aspects and knowledge (Chase et al., 2007). This leads to the possibility of students not having enough knowledge and understanding to carry out a live project. Therefore, it is essential that students are prepared with adequate skills and abilities to implement a project. Integrated courses and modules, then, play a significant role in formulating students' abilities (Elam & Spotts, 2004, cited in Camarero et al., 2010).

Another method to assure student abilities to carry out the project is to provide them with feasible cases (ibid.). A further challenge brought up by the clients is the limitation in their provided information (Chase et al., 2007). This restriction can be caused by the confidentiality issue between a company and outsiders, or the unavailability of information due to delays and unmet deadlines. The lack of necessary and useful information and data causes students to become incapable of carrying out some crucial tasks for their projects. Therefore, flexibility is required when assessing student learning. Moreover, the differences between learning styles of students strengthen the requirements for assessing flexibility. Gremler et al. (2000) claimed that evaluating the outcomes of live projects may require a greater level of devotion in terms of time and effort compared with traditional learning.

We considered how HEIs might more effectively embed graduate skills and employability from a student perspective by examining the development of students' employability skills within live business projects. In this study, students worked alongside real organizations to solve business and marketing problems in small groups.

METHODOLOGY

A sample of 31 students studying for a postgraduate module was randomly selected to complete an audit worksheet. As part of their programme, and instead of writing a traditional dissertation, students embark on a three-month live case study in small groups of 3–4 students. Local companies (large, small and medium-sized enterprises, charities and social enterprises) compile a short brief and meet with the student group, presenting a business problem the organization is facing. In recruiting local companies to help design and run experiential learning exercises such as live cases, the students are required to tackle and solve real-world problems. There are no teaching notes and no solutions, so students are tasked with coming up with the solution on their own with some academic supervision over the three-month period. They then present their solutions to their academic supervisor and company representatives in the form of a group presentation, a group formal report and an individual reflective essay.

The questionnaire worksheet consisted of five skills (self-management, communication, team-working, problem-solving and organization) with four assessments for each skill element. Students were asked to grade themselves on a scale of 1 to 4, where 1 means they feel underdeveloped and 4 represents confidence in their excellence at those skills. The questionnaire also included four statements, strongly influenced by Finch et al. (2015), where students were asked to select the extent to which they agree or disagree with each statement. The questionnaire was given to students to complete twice: at the beginning of the live project stage of their module, and again once they had completed their live projects. This method contributes in providing opportunities to recognize the differences, if applicable, in each skill before and after the projects. Accordingly, the effects of live projects on personal skills were studied and analysed. Informal interviews were also conducted with the module leaders and academic supervisors of the live project student groups in order to achieve a holistic view of the live project case study module .

DATA ANALYSIS

According to Gremler et al. (2000), to create a learner-centred study environment, students should be given timely and constructive feedback on their work, as well as areas for improvements. An academic supervisor claimed that:

> feedback will be provided to students as soon as possible via meetings, emails, phone contacts, etc. Although formal and official feedback, for the initial proposal for example, may take a longer time (four weeks) due to university policy and marking process, supervisors and clients tend to provide unofficial feedback within a week, so that students can recognize the strengths and weaknesses in their proposals before creating the final report.

With regard to the improvement in self-management, communication, team-working, problem-solving and organization skills, before the project students showed an acceptable perception towards their skills. After the project, the majority of the indicators rose to above 3. This represents an increase in the confidence of students towards their competence, since they considered their skills 'above average'. Moreover, over 90 per cent of surveyed students agreed or strongly agreed that the live project helped them increase their personal skills. Also worth mentioning, despite the development of these skills in general, some students did not feel that they had developed effective working relations with external stakeholders over the course of the live project. Beside personal skills, students also indicated an increase in the development of specialized skills. More than 90 per cent of the students agreed or strongly agreed when asked whether the live project increased their knowledge in marketing, and whether they are confident in applying it at the workplace.

As observed, students indicated a strong interest in both their engagement in challenging activities and deeper reflective reasoning, and meeting their client's expectations. Therefore, according to Finch et al. (2015), they should experience both negative and positive emotions, but mostly positive. In fact, almost 82 per cent of the surveyed indicated that they felt mostly positive throughout the project. Good communication between the students with their clients and supervisors contributed greatly to their positive emotions. The other 18 per cent felt sometimes positive, sometimes negative. One student-provided reason for negative emotions was the workloads, which caused them to occasionally feel overwhelmed.

One module leader emphasized in an interview that he and the supervisors attach much importance to the feasibility of the live projects. He claimed that apart from agreeing to work with the business school, organizations are only chosen if the provided projects fit with the ability of students. Therefore, not only are students prepared with abilities beforehand through taught modules, but they also have the certainty that their projects are feasible.

CONCLUSIONS

The results indicate that the development of employability skills can be improved by providing a learning environment for all higher education levels in which students interact with real business people on live projects. The adoption of live marketing projects provides the opportunity for students to engage in experiential learning and, according to our results, show that levels of student engagement are higher. Our results also show that student perceptions of the adoption of graduate employability skills are also higher after embarking on live marketing projects as part of the degree programme.

In a traditional classroom environment, students learn about abstract business concepts; however, when a real company is involved and lays out a specific problem, students are suddenly put inside the business. They must develop different solutions and strategies, think about their implications, and then apply real performance and sales numbers to see how their proposed solutions affect salaries and compensation rates. This real-world application helps students achieve a much deeper and more meaningful understanding of the topic (Rapp and Ogilvie, 2019). Live cases also force students to think about how they would explain their solution to a manager or company owner. 'When students know they have to defend their choices to a real client, there is a level of ownership and involvement with the process' (Rapp and Ogilvie, 2019).

However, live projects are mostly limited to postgraduate students at business schools presently. Although there are limited opportunities for undergraduates, there is potential to expand further in this regard. After analysing the positive impacts of live projects on postgradute students' personal and specialized skills, as well as considering their welfare and the implication from the university perspective, the popularization of live projects to more students should now be considered. It is argued that much benefit can be gained by providing opportunities for students to get involved with live projects over a three-year period, covering the entire undergraduate period of a student (Hooper & Minett-Smith, 2015). Also, these opportunities enable students to use the information gathered about the companies' strategies, products and activities as supporting materials for their studies, and provide opportunities for undergraduate students to complete a live project instead of writing a traditional academic dissertation for their final assessment (Derounian, 2011).

Also, embedding graduate, global and digital skills within academic in-course activities was most effective in contributing to skills development, with students frequently mentioning opportunities for reflection on professional skills and personal development planning as crucial for articulating their skills and preparing them for the workplace. Reflection on and articulation of skills and the development of career management skills (for example, reflective writing, portfolios, career planning, opportunity awareness) are essential for navigating a complex and dynamic labour market. Findings suggest that these activities could helpfully be embedded more widely (Artess et al., 2017; Hounsell, 2011; Jackson & Wilton, 2016; Neary et al., 2015; Wadkins & Miller, 2011). In addition, embedding learning activities within the subject discipline that develop students' awareness of their personal strengths and limitations can help prepare students for the workplace (Nicol, 2010). The importance of forming real connections with employers and workplace experience is also well established (Artess et al., 2017; Moores & Reddy, 2012; Shadbolt, 2016; Wakeham, 2016). These experiences include not only formal work placements (which are available only in selected disciplines), but also informal experiences such as part-time, voluntary work and internships, and interacting with employers and alumni in live case study projects (Reibe et al., 2013). The present findings add weight to the recommendations of Artess et al. (2017) for higher education institutions to make more of informal experiences, and help students articulate the value of these experiences in terms of graduate skills.

This study makes a contribution to providing insights into the nature and practice of an experiential learning approach in the form of live case studies at postgraduate level in a business school. The results indicate that the development of skills beneficial to increasing employability can be improved by providing a learning environment in which students interact with real business people on live projects.

REFERENCES

Artess, J. (2019). Learning to be employable. In Burke, C. and Christie, F. (eds), *Graduate Careers in Context: Research, Policy and Practice*. London: Routledge Research in Higher Education, pp. 1–52.

Artess, J., Hooley, T. and Mellors-Bourne, R. (2017). *Employability: A Review of the Literature 2012–16*. York: Higher Education Academy.

Ballantine, J. and McCourt, L.P. (2004). A critical analysis of students' perceptions of the usefulness of the case study method in an advanced management accounting module: The impact of relevant work experience. *Accounting Education*, 13(2): 171–189.

Beard, C. and Wilson, J.P. (2002). *Experiential Learning: A Handbook for Education, Training and Coaching*. London: Kogan Page.

Belbin, M. (2017). The nine Belbin Team Roles. Cambridge: Belbin Associates. http://www.belbin.com/about/belbin-team-roles/.

Bedwell, W.L., Fiore, S.M. and Salas, E. (2014). Developing the future workforce: an approach for integrating interpersonal skills into the MBA classroom. *Academy of Management Learning and Education*, 13(2): 171–186.

Bowden, J., Hart, G., King, B., Trigwell, K. and Watts, O. (2000). *Generic Capabilities of ATN University Graduates*. Canberra: Australian Government Department of Education, Training and Youth Affairs.

Burke, C. and Hannaford-Simpson, S. (2019). 'Investing in your future': the role of capitals in graduate employment pathways. In Burke, C. and Christie, F. (eds), *Graduate Careers in Context: Research, Policy and Practice*. London: Routledge Research in Higher Education, pp. 17–28.

Camarero, C., Rodríguez-Pinto, J. and San Jose, R. (2010). A comparison of learning effectiveness of live cases and classroom projects. *International Journal of Management Education*, 8(3): 83–94.

Campbell, K., Mothersbaugh, D., Brammer, C. and Taylor, T. (2001). Peer versus self assessment of oral business presentation performance. *Business Communication Quarterly*, 64(3): 23–42.

Caza, A., Brower, H.H. and Wayne, J.H. (2015). Effects of a holistic, experiential curriculum on business students' satisfaction and career confidence. *International Journal of Management Education*, 13(1): 75–83.

Chang, J. and Rieple, A. (2013). Assessing students' entrepreneur skills development in live projects. *Journal of Small Business and Entrepreneur Development*, 20(1): 225–241.

Chase, J.D., Oakes, E. and Ramsey, S. (2007). Using live projects without pain. In Ressell, I. et al. *SIGCSE 2007: Proceedings of the Thirty-Eighth SIGCSE Technical Symposium on Computer Science Education: March 7–10, 2007, Covington, Kentucky, USA*. Covington: Association for Computing Machinery, pp. 469–473.

Clarke, M. (2017). Rethinking graduate employability: the role of capital, individual attributes and context. *Studies in Higher Education*, 43(11): 1923–1937.

Culpin, V. and Scott, H. (2011). The effectiveness of a live case study approach: increasing knowledge and understanding of 'hard' versus 'soft' skills in executive education. *Management Learning*, 43(5): 565–577.

Cunningham, L.M. (1995). Involving students in learning through a reading/writing approach. In Safinan, P.T. (ed.), *Focus* (Vol. 12). ERIC Document Reproduction No. ED 384 405. Salt Lake City: University of Utah, pp. 12–16.

Darian, J. and Coopersmith, L. (2001). Integrated marketing and operations team projects: Learning the importance of cross-functional cooperation. *Journal of Marketing Education* 23(2): 128–135.

Derounian, J. (2011). The universities exploring alternatives to undergraduate dissertations. *Guardian*, 23 November.

Docherty, D. and Fernandez, R. (2014). Career portfolios and the labour market for graduates and post-graduates in the UK. http://www.ncub.co.uk/reports/career-portfolios.html.

Eddleston, K.A., Friar, J.H. and Clark, E. (2006). Pitching to the home shopping network: an exercise in opportunity assessment and personal selling. *Organization Management Journal*, 3(3): 257–270.

Finch, D., Peacock, M., Lazdowski, D. and Hwang, M. (2015). Managing emotions: a case study exploring the relationship between experiential learning, emotions, and student performance. *International Journal of Management Education*, 13(1): 23–36.

Gentry J. (1990). What is experiential learning? In Gentry, J. (ed.), *Guide to Business Gaming and Experiential Learning*. London: Kogan Page, pp. 9–20.

Gremler, D.D., Hoffman, K., Keaveney, S. and Wright, L. (2000). Experiential learning exercises in services marketing courses. *Journal of Marketing Education*, 22(1): 35–44.

Hamer, L.O. (2000). The additive effects of semistructured classroom activities on student learning: an application of classroom-based experiential learning techniques. *Journal of Marketing Education*, 22(1): 25–34.

Hamilton, T. and Cooper, C. (2001). The impact of outdoor management development (OMD) programmes. *Leadership and Organisation Development Journal*, 22(7): 330–340.

Hawtrey, K. (2007). Using experiential learning techniques. *Journal of Economic Education* 38(2): 143–152.

HEA (2006). Student employability profiles: a guide for higher education practitioners. Higher Education Authority. https://www.heacademy.ac.uk/knowledge-hub/student-employability-profiles.

Hooper, J. and Minett-Smith, C. (2015). Learning to play the game: delivering a live project to 800 first year business students. Chartered Association of Business Schools. https://charteredabs.org/learning-play-game-delivering-live-project-800-first-year-business-students/ (accessed: 9 October 2017).

Hounsell, D. (2011). Graduates for the 21st century: integrating the enhancement themes. QAA Scotland. https://www.enhancementthemes.ac.uk/completed-enhancement-themes/graduates-for-the-21st-century.

Jackson, D. and Wilton, N. (2016). Developing career management competencies among undergraduates and the role of work-integrated learning. *Teaching in Higher Education*, 21(3): 266–286.

Jisc (2014). Developing digital literacies. 7 October. Northumbria University on behalf of Jisc. http://web.archive.org/web/20141011143516/http://www.jiscinfonet.ac.uk/infokits/digital-literacies/.

Jones, E. and Killick, D. (2013). Graduate attributes and the internationalized curriculum: embedding a global outlook in disciplinary learning outcomes. *Journal of Studies in International Education*, 17(2): 165–182.

Kennedy, E., Lawton, L. and Walker, E. (2001). The case for using live cases: shifting the paradigm in marketing education. *Journal of Marketing Education*, 23(2): 145–151.

Kolb, David A. (1984). *Experiential Learning: Experience as the Source of Learning and Development.* Englewood Cliffs, NJ: Prentice Hall.

Kolb, A.Y. and Kolb, D.A. (2005). *The Kolb Learning Style Inventory – eVersion 3.1: 2005 Technical Specifications.* Boston, MA: Hay Resources Direct.

Kolb, D.A. and Fry, R.E. (1975). Toward an applied theory of experiential learning. In Cooper, C.L. (ed.), *Theories of Group Processes.* New York: John Wiley & Sons, pp. 33–57.

Macfarlane, D. and Roy, A.W.N. (2006). *Enhancing Student Employability: Innovative Projects from Across the Curriculum.* Gloucester: Quality Assurance Agency for Higher Education.

Markulis, P. (1985). The live case study: filling the gap between the case study and the experiential exercise. In Gentry, J. and Burns, A. (eds), *Developments in Business Simulation and Experiential Exercises.* Orlando, FL: Association for Business Simulation and Experiential Learning, pp. 168–171.

Mattis, G. (2018). How can we bridge the graduate skills gap? Institute of Student Employers blog, 14 November.

Meyer, J. (2003). Four territories of experience: a developmental action inquiry approach to outdoor-adventure experiential learning. *Academy of Management Learning and Education*, 2(4): 352–363.

Moores, E. and Reddy, P. (2012). No regrets? Measuring the career benefits of a psychology placement year. *Assessment and Evaluation in Higher Education*, 37(5): 535–554.

Morais, D.B. and Ogden, A.C. (2011). Initial development and validation of the global skills scale. *Journal of Studies in International Education*, 15(5): 445–466.

Morris, S., Cranney, J., Jeong, J.M. and Mellish, L. (2013). Developing psychological literacy: student perceptions of graduate attributes. *Australian Journal of Psychology*, 65(1): 54–62.

Neary, S., Dodd, V. and Hooley, T. (2015). Understanding career management skills: findings from the first phase of the CMS leader project. Derby: International Centre for Guidance Studies, University of Derby.

Nicol, D. (2010). The foundation for graduate attributes: developing self-regulation through self and peer-assessment. https://www.enhancementthemes.ac.uk/docs/ethemes/graduates-for-the-21st-century/the-foundation-for-graduate-attributes-developing-self-regulation-through-self-assessment.pdf?sfvrsn=ab3df981_18.

Norton, S. and Dairymple, R. (2020). Enhancing graduate employability: a case study compendium. Advance HE.

Osmani, M., Weerakkody, V., Hindi, N.M., Al-Esmail, R., Eldabi, T., et al. (2015). Identifying the trends and impact of graduate attributes on employability: a literature review. *Tertiary Education and Management*, 21(4): 367–379

Parker, M. (2018). Why we should bulldoze the business school. *Guardian*, 22 April.

Pollard, E., Hirsh, W., Williams, M. and Ball, C. (2015). Understanding employers' graduate recruitment and selection practices. Department for Business Innovation & Skills

Popovic, C., Lawton, R., Hill, A., Eland, J. and Morton (2010). Creating future proof graduates. Higher Education Authority. https://www.heacademy.ac.uk/knowledge-hub/creating-future-proof-graduates.

QS (2018). QS Applicant Survey: What Drives an International Student Today? QS Intelligence Unit. http://www.iu.qs.com/2018/06/qs-international-student-survey-what-drives-an-international-student-today/.

Quality Assurance Agency for Higher Education (2019). *Focus on Graduate Skills, Views from Students, Graduates and Employers.* August. Glasgow: QAA Scotland.

Rapp, A. and Ogilvie, J. (2019). Live case studies demystified: how two professors bring real-world application to the classroom, *Harvard Business Review*, 7 June.

Reibe, L., Sibson, R., Roepen, D. and Meakins, K. (2013). Impact of industry guest speakers on business students' percepions of employability skills development. *Industry and Higher Education*, 27(1): 55–66.

Ritter, B.A., Small, E.E., Mortimer, J.W. and Doll, J.L. (2017). Designing management curriculum for workplace readiness: developing students' soft skills. *Journal of Management Education*, 42(1): 80–103.

Rust, C. and Froud, L. (2016). Shifting the focus from skills to 'graduateness'. *AGCAS Phoenix*, 148, 8–9 June.

Sara, R. (2011). Learning from life – exploring the potential of live projects in higher education. *Journal for Education in the Built Environment*, 6(2): 8–25.

Scharf, F. and Bell, J. (2002). Developing international management competencies and skills among undergraduate business students. *Journal of European Industrial Training*, 26(6/7): 327–332.

Schlegelmilch, B. (2020). Why business schools need radical innovations: drivers and development trajectories. *Journal of Marketing Education*, 42(2): 93–107.

Shadbolt, N. (2016). *Shadbolt Review of Computer Sciences Degree Accreditation and Graduate Employability*. Department for Business, Innovation and Skills

Shapiro B. (1984). *Hints for Case Teaching*. Boston, MA: Harvard Business School.

Soffel, J. (2016). What are the 21st-century skills every student needs? World Economic Forum. https://www.weforum.org/agenda/2016/03/21st-century-skills-future-jobs-students/

Spanjaard, D., Hall, T. and Stegemann, N. (2018). Experiential learning: helping students to become 'career ready'. *Australasian Marketing Journal*, 26(2): 163–171.

Stewart, J. and Dougherty, T. (1993). Using case studies in teaching accounting: a quasi-experimental study. *Accounting Education*, 2(1): 1–10.

Swingler, M.V., Armour, S., Bohan, J., Cleland-Woods, H., Curry, G.B. and Roy, A.W.N. (2016). Where am I now and where do I want to be? Developing awareness of graduate attributes in pre-honours students. *New Directions in the Teaching of Physical Sciences*. https://journals.le.ac.uk/ojs1/index.php/new-directions.

Tomlinson, M. (2007). Graduate employability and student attitudes and orientations to the labour market. *Journal of Education and Work*, 20(4): 285–304

Tomlinson, M. (2012). Graduate employability: a review of conceptual and empirical themes. *Higher Education Policy*, 25: 407–431

Tyson, D.F., Linnenbrink-Garcia, L. and Hill, N.E. (2009). Regulating debilitating emotions in the context of performance: achievement goal orientations, achievement-elicited emotions, and socialization contexts. *Human Development*, 52(6): 329–356.

Vanhercke, D., De Cuyper, N., Peeters, E. and Witte, H.D. (2014). Defining perceived employability: a psychological approach. *Personnel Review*, 43(4): 592–605.

Wadkins, T.A. and Miller, R.L. (2011). Structuring the capstone experience in psychology. In Miller, R.L., Marsteller Kowalewski, B., Beins, B.C., Keith, K.D. and Peden, B.F. (eds), *Promoting Student Engagement*, Vol. 1: *Programs, Techniques and Opportunities*. Washington, DC: Society for the Teaching of Psychology, US, pp. 95–102.

Wakeham, W. (2016). *Wakeham Review of STEM Degree Provision and Graduate Employability*. Department for Business, Innovation and Skills

Winberg, C., Bester, M., Scholtz, D., Monnapula-Mapesela, M., Ronald, N., et al. (2018). In search of graduate attributes: a survey of six flagship programmes. *South African Journal of Higher Education*, 32(1): 233–251.

Wines, G., Carnegie, G., and Boyce, G. (1994). *Using Case Studies in the Teaching of Accounting*. Melbourne: Australian Society of CPAs.

Živkovił, S. (2016). A model of critical thinking as an important attribute for success in the 21st century. *Procedia – Social and Behavioral Sciences*, 232: 102–108.

14. Addressing the challenges of assessment and feedback in business schools: developing assessment practices which support learning

Nicola Reimann, Kay Sambell, Ian Sadler and Carolin Kreber

INTRODUCTION

The past decade has been characterized by an upsurge of interest in assessment and feedback in higher education. This has been triggered in particular by high levels of student dissatisfaction. In the United Kingdom (UK), for instance, items on assessment and feedback in the annual National Student Survey (NSS) have continuously attracted low satisfaction ratings by students (Bell and Brooks 2018). Not only in the UK but also elsewhere, many institutions have therefore developed policies and guidelines, assessment and feedback principles as well as a plethora of initiatives aimed at improving the student experience of assessment and feedback.

This is also reflected in practice initiatives, research and publications on assessment in business-related subjects. While assessment research of international significance has originated in business schools, such as the studies conducted by Price, O'Donovan, Rust and colleagues (e.g. O'Donovan et al. 2001; Price et al. 2012; Price et al. 2011; Rust et al. 2003), this is complemented by a range of publications about innovative practices in assessment and feedback in business-related disciplines. Many of these publications have been written by practitioners, reporting, evaluating and researching new approaches experimented with in their local contexts, engaging in a practice known as the scholarship of teaching and learning (Kreber 2013). Learning and teaching in business schools has long been underpinned by a desire to incorporate real-world cases, scenarios and tasks, and this has also driven innovations in assessment. This interest in authentic assessment is reflected in publications such as those by, for instance, James and Casidy (2018), Voss (2015) and Neely and Tucker (2012), and it also chimes with current developments in the sector more broadly.

In this chapter we will argue that we need to move away from an exclusive focus on marking and measurement, and think about maximizing the potential of assessment to engender high-quality student learning. We propose that the notion of 'assessment for learning' might offer a way of articulating as well as progressing some of the key contemporary interests, concerns and practices of business educators. The 'signature pedagogies' (Shulman 2005), that is, the forms of teaching and learning that are characteristic for business and management subjects such as the use of real-world case studies, offer considerable opportunities for learning-oriented approaches to assessment. The chapter will first outline the paradigm shift that has characterised debates around assessment in higher education generally. It will then present contemporary models of assessment and discuss the conditions under which assessment supports learning. We argue that these conditions can already be observed in business schools, but also make suggestions for how they can be built on further to advance innovation in assessment practices in business and management contexts. The chapter will conclude with vignettes derived from the published literature on assessment to show real examples of ways in which these conditions have been put into practice. The intention is to inspire our readers to try such practices for themselves.

FROM ASSESSMENT OF LEARNING TO ASSESSMENT FOR LEARNING

Assessment has a strong bearing on how teachers teach and how students learn. It goes well beyond the supposedly simple activity of evaluating the quality of students' performance of tasks and assignments set by their tutors (see, for instance, Brown and Knight 1994; Sambell and McDowell 1998). The fact that assessment drives student learning is well known and referred to as the 'backwash effect'. In other words, 'students will always second-guess the assessment task and then learn what they think will meet those requirements' (Biggs 2003, p. 210). Therefore, carefully crafting assessment can have a positive impact on the nature and quality of student learning.

The Paradigm Shift in Assessment

The way in which assessment has been conceptualized and implemented by researchers, educators and policy-makers has changed fundamentally in recent years. This has been described as a culture change or paradigm shift. Different terms have been used to describe the old and the new models of assessment which underpin these developments: testing versus assessment culture, measurement versus judgement model, scientific measurement versus contextual-qualitative paradigm.

The main aim in the old model of assessment (Gipps 1994) was to differentiate between students and sort them by ability. Discussions of assessment focused on accuracy and objectivity of measurement, to which the reliability of assessment processes and instruments was central. Standardization and technical issues were therefore foregrounded. Corresponding assessment practices privileged simple, discrete tasks remote from the world outside the classroom, and questions with right or wrong answers. These practices predominantly tested the retention of information and were taken under controlled conditions.

In contrast, the new model focuses on validity and the quality and level of learning that is stimulated and assessed. Tasks carried out in the real world, including that of academia and professional practice, tend to be divergent, open-ended and ill-defined – unlike the simplified tasks and tests typically carried out under exam conditions – and assessment of such tasks involves complex judgements informed by evidence from multiple sources. Current assessment practices thus comprise a much wider range of strategies, with an emphasis on holistic tasks, problem-solving and authentic situations from which competence is inferred rather than directly measured. An example of this development is the case-based essay, which is now a standard and well-respected assessment format in business schools.

However, while thinking about assessment has changed fundamentally, in practice both models continue to influence assessment policies and practices. This is a key reason why assessment and feedback in higher education are so full of tensions and dilemmas (Havnes and McDowell 2008).

Multiple Purposes and Multiple Stakeholder

Assessment serves many different purposes and stakeholders, including students, university staff, employers, professional statutory and regulatory bodies (PSRBs), the government and even the general public. In business schools, accreditation by organizations such as the Association of MBAs or the Association of Chartered Certified Accountants (ACCA), to name just two, exerts an important influence on assessment regimes. The tensions arising from this situation have been referred to as assessment doing 'double duty' (Boud 2000):

> Assessment always performs functions other than the ones teachers and examiners normally think about and take account of. It is always about more than judging the achievement of learning outcomes for a given module or course ... Some of the ways in which assessment activities have to do double duty are:
> - [t]hey have to encompass formative assessment for learning and summative for certification[;]
> - [t]hey have to have a focus on the immediate task and on implications for equipping students for lifelong learning in an unknown future[;]
> - [a]nd they have to attend to both the learning process and the substantive content domain.
> Every act of assessment we devise or have a role in implementing has more than one purpose. If we do not pay attention to these multiple purposes we are in danger of inadvertently sabotaging one or more of them. (Boud 2000, p. 160)

Gipps (1994) distinguishes between three purposes of assessment: accountability, which requires quick, manageable and reliable information in order to make judgements about the performance of educational institutions; certification, which relies on detailed and reliable information to enable comparison between individuals' performance; and learning, for which the development of high-level skills and understanding needs to be stimulated. While it is acknowledged that all of them have a role to play, Gipps argues that accountability has dominated and limited, or even damaged, the learning purpose of assessment. This critique has been the starting point of contemporary developments in assessment and feedback.

Many business educators will be familiar with the distinction made between 'summative' and 'formative' assessment. As the name suggests, the purpose of summative assessment is to summarize, grade and certify achievement and learning as it stands at one particular point in time, often at the end of a course. The purpose of formative assessment, on the other hand, is to monitor progress, diagnose problems and improve learning. It is thus inseparable from teaching, and feedback is a key element of formative assessment. Sadler (1989, p. 120) describes formative assessment in terms of 'how judgments about the quality of student responses (performances, pieces, or works) can be used to shape and improve the student's competence by short-circuiting the randomness and inefficiency of trial-and-error learning'.

The Importance of Formative Assessment and Feedback for Learning

Educational research has highlighted the crucial role of formative assessment for student achievement and learning. In 1998 a ground-breaking literature review by Black and Wiliam (1998) demonstrated that formative assessment substantially improves learning, particularly for low achievers. However, this was shown to depend on certain conditions being fulfilled.

Feedback information had to be used in order to be effective; that is, it needed to be analysed, worked with and acted upon, by the student to improve learning and by the teacher to adjust instruction. There was also evidence that a focus on individuals, comparisons and grades had a negative impact on learning. Instead, it was argued that feedback should focus on the qualities of students' work and the ways in which it can be improved, rather than ability and comparisons with others. Similar evidence was provided by Hattie's seminal work which synthesized meta-analyses of educational research in order to identify those factors with the most impact on students. This confirmed that feedback is one of the most significant influences on student achievement (Hattie 2009).

These ideas, initially raised in relation to the school sector, were also taken up in higher education. Since the influential paper by Sadler (1989) on formative assessment in higher education, there has been extensive research and writing about assessment and feedback in terms of how it can be most effectively understood, with an emphasis on formative, learning-oriented assessment (Carless 2007). In line with the new model described above, the social meanings of assessment were redefined: away from viewing it as a means of controlling student learning, and towards framing assessment as a catalyst for student engagement with their chosen disciplinary areas. This cultural shift also required redesigning assessment practices in order to make them tools for learning rather than simply a means of judging and selecting students. Whilst there are variations in terminology to capture the essence of this cultural shift (e.g., assessment for learning, formative assessment, learning-orientated assessment), the new paradigm tends to point to assessment as a constructivist process with the students at its centre as active, self-regulated learners.

Towards Assessment for Learning Practices in Higher Education

The ideas underpinning assessment for learning went hand in hand with the realization that teaching is much more than transmitting information, and needs to support students to construct their own understanding through interactions in communities and cultures. This led to widespread attempts to incorporate assessment as a positive and integral part of teaching and learning, rather than a separate post hoc event (McLean 2018). One important aim of assessment for learning has been to develop and value assessment practices which stimulate students to engage actively with learning activities and subject matter, and support participation and the development of identity (Sambell 2013). Another important goal has been to rethink assessment and feedback practices to ensure they foster student autonomy, so that students learn not to become overly dependent on their teachers to oversee and direct their actions. This entails embedding assessment and feedback processes into the curriculum so that instead of being told what to do, students are supported to exercise increasing levels of control over their own learning by progressively developing their capabilities in self-monitoring and self-regulation (Nicol and MacFarlane-Dick 2006). Strategies which equip students well for the longer term (Boud 2014) and a lifetime of learning in the complex and changing world beyond graduation (Tai et al. 2018), rather than simply focusing on academic success with the immediate piece of work or their programme of study, have been another important characteristic of assessment for learning practices. Although less explicitly defined, assessment for learning contrasts with the notion of assessment of learning, the old model mentioned above which is characterized by a focus on measurement, certification and accountability (Gipps 1994).

The 'assessment for learning movement' (Boud and Falchikov 2007) in higher education has encouraged and supported academics to reconceptualize assessment and feedback by foregrounding learning, and to change their practices accordingly (Sambell et al. 2013; Reimann and Wilson 2012; Reimann 2018). However, the multiple purposes and drivers of assessment often create barriers that resist radical transformation, and conceptual change and change of practices are a slow and gradual process (Sadler and Reimann 2018). There have been a number of large-scale pedagogic initiatives, such as the Re-Engineering Assessment Practices (REAP) project in Scotland, assessment-focused Centres for Excellence in Learning and Teaching at Northumbria University and at Oxford Brookes University in England (based in the Business School), and Carless et al.'s (2006) hugely influential and positive efforts to promote what they termed 'learning-oriented assessment', originating in the University of Hong Kong. These initiatives have largely been driven by establishing evidence-based principles, in an effort to encourage stakeholders – mainly teaching-focused academics – to radically reconfigure their conceptual approaches to assessment design and practices.

Models and Principles of Assessment: The Northumbria Model of Assessment for Learning and Carless's Learning-Oriented Assessment

The large-scale assessment for learning initiative located in the £4.5 million Centre for Excellence in Teaching and Learning in Assessment for Learning at Northumbria University (Reimann and Wilson 2012; Sambell et al. 2013) developed six evidence-informed core conditions to drive conceptual change and a shift in institutional culture. This approach meant rethinking some commonly held assumptions about assessment and feedback, on the part of staff and students alike, changing understandings of assessment as well as practices (Reimann and Sadler 2017), rather than requiring lecturers to simply insert a few new techniques or tactics. This view of assessment for learning aimed to encourage a change in overall thinking, and a reframing of staff–student relationships in terms of shared responsibility and partnership. Seen through this lens, assessment for learning becomes a way of thinking, akin to a philosophy, which thrives in environments where assessment practices are discussed, reflected upon, shared and negotiated, not only in the letter, but in the more radical spirit of assessment for learning (Marshall and Drummond 2006).

We suggest that the readers of this chapter consider this model of assessment for learning as a broad framework to support the development of assessment designs that promote good learning in business schools. The model is based on six conditions, drawn from an extensive review of the literature and evidence-based practice. The six conditions become key questions for practitioners to ask themselves and each other as they (re)design learning environments with integrated and aligned assessment as part of the overall picture. To this end, the model is best seen as a series of interlinking aspects which characterize effective assessment for learning environments, so that ideally all are in play. In other words, it should not be seen as a discrete set of components.

The model of assessment for learning, which two of the authors helped to develop, calls for an overall curriculum design that:

1. Emphasizes authenticity and complexity in the content and methods of assessment rather than reproduction of knowledge and reductive measurement;

2. Uses high-stakes summative assessment rigorously but sparingly rather than as the main driver for learning.
3. Offers students extensive opportunities to engage in the kinds of tasks that develop and demonstrate their learning, thus building their confidence and capabilities before they are summatively assessed.
4. Is rich in feedback derived from formal mechanisms, for example tutor comments on assignments, clickers in class.
5. Is rich in informal feedback, for example peer discussions of work-in-progress, collaborative project work, which provides students with a continuous flow of feedback on how they are doing.
6. Develops students' abilities to direct their own learning, evaluate their own progress and attainments and support the learning of others.

These conditions of assessment for learning in the Northumbria model resonate strongly with the principles of learning-oriented assessment identified by Carless and colleagues. These comprise three core principles or interrelated processes which ensure that the learning potential within the assessment process is maximized (Carless 2007, 2015):

● Principle 1: Learning-oriented assessment tasks.

Assessment tasks should be designed to stimulate sound learning practices amongst students. This involves framing assessment tasks primarily as learning tasks, such that students, when approaching assessment tasks, engage in worthwhile, long-term learning and deep approaches to learning which are aligned with the relevant ways of thinking and practising of the subject domain, rather than short-term cramming and memorization.

● Principle 2: Developing evaluative expertise.

Assessment should involve students actively in engaging with criteria and developing a concept of quality. This can be done through activities in which learners use learning goals, criteria and quality standards in judging their own and their peers' performance.

● Principle 3: Student engagement with feedback.

Feedback should be timely and forward-looking so as to support current and future learning: 'for assessment to promote learning, students need to receive appropriate feedback which they can use to "feedforward" into future work. Feedback in itself may not promote learning, unless students engage with it and act upon it ... Timeliness and promoting student engagement with feedback are thus key aspects' (Carless 2007, p. 13).

When assessment foregrounds learning, 'the ways of thinking, the procedures and practices that are characteristic of particular subjects or disciplines' (Kreber 2009, p. 12) come into view. Such 'ways of thinking and practicing' (McCune and Hounsell 2005) are what set one discipline apart from another in terms of discourse, conventions, truth criteria, values and skills that are specific to the discipline community. Through making these core ideas and ways of functioning explicit, teachers can engender 'authentic conversations' with students (Kreber 2013) which invite them into the discipline's 'community of truth' (Palmer 1998, p. 122). By connecting students with particular issues, problems or scenarios that bring the discipline's core concepts and ways of thinking and practising to life, we exemplify how the discipline works. Due to the backwash effect mentioned earlier, assessment is absolutely critical for socializing students into the discipline's community of truth. Thus, assessment practices in business and management disciplines should be designed in ways that enable students to engage in the academic and professional practices of leaders in marketing, management, accounting, entrepreneurship, and so on, and to think like them. While business and management clearly do not qualify as a single discipline, the notions of ways of thinking and practising (McCune and Hounsell 2005), authentic conversations (Kreber 2013) and communities of truth (Palmer 1998) are nonetheless helpful in shaping assessment tasks in these fields.

As a consequence, in the more recent version of Carless's (2015) model of learning-oriented assessment, an important conceptual addition has been the foregrounding of assessment practice in the subject discipline within which it takes place. Similarly, the Northumbria model emphasizes the importance of opportunities for active participation in disciplinary communities and characteristic ways of 'doing the discipline'. Only through repeated participation in discipline-specific practices and the informal feedback this generates will students be able to develop the tacit know-how which underpins an ability to think, talk, write and act like, say, an accountant, entrepreneur or human resources manager. Engaging with these ways of thinking and practising is much more than simply acquiring subject knowledge. In Carless's (2015) model the specific disciplinary knowledge and skills to be learnt and assessed are particularly central to the design of learning-oriented assessment tasks, that is, principle 1. However, it also bleeds into the other two principles. For example, in developing evaluative expertise, students are developing insight into criteria and exemplars that are accepted within the professional community.

STRATEGIES FOR ASSESSMENT DESIGN THAT SUPPORTS LEARNING

Efforts to instigate change in assessment practices have frequently been framed as diversifying assessment, focused on moving away from conventional formats such as essay assignments, multiple choice or short-answer examinations, and introducing what is often described as more innovative formats. However, while there is clear evidence that different formats produce different levels of and approaches to learning (Biggs 2003), diversification alone is not sufficient for ensuring that assessment supports learning. But what might assessment and feedback situated in the new paradigm look like? How can the principles and conditions of assessment that support learning outlined above be implemented in practice? These questions will be addressed in the subsequent sections of this chapter. By doing so, we aim to stimulate our readers to think about the ways in which assessment practices in business schools already incorporate such assessment for learning practices, or could be developed further to do so.

Authentic Assessment

Authenticity has been a long-standing tradition in the pedagogies typical for business and management and been a feature of learning and teaching in these subjects for a long time. Published almost 20 years ago, Kaye and Hawkridge's (2003) edited volume of case studies of innovation comprises several examples in which the potential of real-world business scenarios for learning is highlighted. Interestingly, at that time relatively little attention was devoted to ways in which such authentic approaches are, or could be, extended to assessment; however, this has changed considerably. Various publications provide accounts and empirical investigations of assessment strategies which make strong links to real-world business and management practices, such as simulations (Farrell 2020; Lohmann et al., 2019; Neely and Tucker 2012; Voss 2015), case studies (Evans 2016; Jones and Kerr 2012; McGreevy et al. 2019; Mihret et al. 2017) and scenarios (James and Casidy 2018). Technologies frequently support such approaches as they allow the world of business and management to be imported into the classroom.

Authenticity is also a key tenet of assessment for learning. Villarroell et al. (2020) define authentic assessment as 'a way to relate learning and work, creating a correspondence between what is assessed in the university and what graduates do in settings in the outside world' (p. 39). However, Burton (2011) cautions against adopting too narrow a definition of authenticity based on workplace knowledge and skills associated directly and literally with 'employability', given the fast pace of change which means specific knowledge and skills soon become outmoded. In addition, as many business lecturers can confirm, vocational relevance alone is not sufficient to ensure student engagement and learning.

Alternative views of authenticity have applied a much broader notion of relevance (National Forum 2017). It has been suggested that developing a sense of self and ownership through personal involvement and personal meaning are crucial for authenticity: 'Personal meaning is best achieved when students are engaged in their own search for knowledge, an activity that offers a degree of self-determination ... Being meaningful in this sense is about an experience that the student determines as significant or worthwhile' (Wald and Harland 2017, p. 757).

In a similar vein, authentic assessment has been linked to tasks whose purpose students buy into, which generate intrinsic interest and enable them to make a genuine and novel contribution, often by resulting in a product or performance (O'Neill 2019). This contrasts with assessed tasks set as hoops to jump through and carried out for the benefit of the assessor. Ashford-Rowe et al. (2014) have identified characteristics of authentic assessment which go beyond an exclusive focus on the 'real world'. These include challenge, a concrete outcome such as a performance or a product, transfer of knowledge, metacognition (i.e., self-monitoring), performance requiring accuracy, authenticity of the environment and the tools (e.g., language) used, opportunities for feedback, and opportunities for collaboration. Business simulation games, for instance, have been shown to embody several of these characteristics. Voss (2015) demonstrates how such games require students to use higher-level thinking and decision-making skills, simulate the real-world business contexts in which such decisions are made, and provide frequent opportunities for practice, feedback and development. However, Voss's research also highlights that implementing simulations poses challenges, both for staff and for students, such as problems arising from group work.

Seen from the viewpoint of immersing learners in the ways of thinking and practising associated with the discipline, authentic tasks in business and management involve students in activities which resonate strongly with the discipline's community of truth. This goes well beyond a narrow emphasis on the vocational, and is particularly important in business schools where tensions can arise from the need to educate students 'for' as well as 'in' business (Warwick 2020). Authentic assessment tasks will need to accommodate both, and to ensure that in addition to being contextualized in the real world of business and management, they have the potential to be personally meaningful. This involves students becoming personally invested in the issues they are learning and assessed on, being encouraged to reflect on what these issues mean to them on a personal level and how they, now and as future graduates, can contribute to society and the world (Kreber 2014). In addition, if the goal is to foster learning that leads to a deeper understanding, both of subject matter and of self, we need pedagogies and assessment practices that provide opportunities for students to experience conceptual shifts (Kreber 2014). Experiential ways of learning that require students to relate abstract academic content to concrete issues of social relevance are therefore a central recommendation, already widely taken up by business schools. However, equally important are ways that provoke students to reflect critically on their own assumptions, beliefs and values, and encourage them to make personal judgements about their learning (Boud 2007). Students also need to learn to take risks. This is facilitated by learning environments of trust where they dare to subject their knowledge claims to the critical assessment of others (Kreber 2014) and which foreground subject mastery, rather than simply a perfunctory quest for marks which can make students risk-adverse (Black and Wiliam 1998).

Student Engagement in Feedback Processes

A considerable body of research has focused on external feedback provided by the teacher or expert (e.g. Hattie and Timperley 2007; Hyland and Hyland 2006). According to Dingyloudi and Strijbos (2018), in a recent review of 195 papers published between 1985 and 2014, Winstone et al. (2017) identified 159 empirical papers out of which 81 per cent focused on expert feedback, predominantly in the context of higher education. This kind of feedback refers to information provided by an expert, as a response to students' performance in a task, to reduce the gap between students' current level of performance and desired level of performance (Hattie and Timperley 2007). In the conventional model, qualities of good feedback are often described as in Table 14.1.

Table 14.1   Good feedback in the conventional model

Good feedback …	Rather than …
Is timely	Provided a long time after producing the work
Is based on criteria and/or learning outcomes (= criterion-referenced)	Based on comparisons between students (= norm-referenced)
Focuses on the task	Focuses on the person
Is specific and refers to concrete examples	Making broad, general statements
Suggests what and how to improve	Justifies grades
Focuses on key points	Is extensive

One issue arising from this kind of teacher feedback, especially if associated with summative tasks, is that it comes too late from students' perspectives, and remains information without any impact and consequences. According to a useful briefing note written by Hounsell (2015) for the WISE Assessment project at Hong Kong University, while teachers may diagnose and suggest remediation, the timing militates against students being able to use it to close the feedback loop. Hounsell therefore suggests strategies to 'flip' feedback, to enhance dialogue and interaction, shifting the focus from 'retrospective feedback to prospective feedforward' (p. 2). This involves rethinking when and how feedback can be provided, such that there is a future horizon in mind. Strategies proposed by Hounsell include: 'draft, comment, revise, resubmit', where comments on a draft impact upon the final submission; 'parts to whole', where comments provided on one or more sections impact upon a longer piece of work developed over time; 'presentation-paper', where an oral presentation generates peer and tutor comments and subsequently results in a written paper; and 'chaining and threading', where students submit coversheets stating how feedback received previously has been addressed. Our own work on feedforward has shown that these ideas are being taken up widely, but that future horizons can vary considerably between improvements made within modules, across modules and into academic and professional practice more broadly (Reimann et al. 2019).

In line with the paradigm shift in assessment, several higher education researchers have recently called for a rethinking or reconceptualization of feedback (e.g., Boud and Molloy 2013; Merry et al. 2013; Sambell 2011) as 'assessment for learning', 'feedback for learning' or 'sustainable feedback'. It is widely accepted that the impact of feedback comments will be restricted if the student is cast in the role of passive recipient (Boud and Molloy 2013). Arguably, the dominant discourse of equating university feedback with comments on summative work poses a particular problem, since it encourages feedback to be conceptualized in a very limited way: as a product and 'provision of information' (Sambell et al. 2013, p. 73), as 'monologue' (Nicol, 2010), as 'an episodic mechanism delivered by teachers' (Boud and Molloy 2013, p. 699), as 'dangling data' (Sadler 1989, p. 121) or as 'telling' (Sadler 2010, p. 539). In response to this restricted view of feedback, there are strong arguments, based on extensive research evidence and views of learning which foreground learning for the longer term, of the developmental benefits of moving towards a much broader definition of feedback, as dialogue 'to support learning in both formal and informal situations' (Askew and Lodge 2000, p. 1). From this viewpoint, learner engagement in formative activity becomes a key driving principle which supports self-regulation and helps bridge the gap between teacher comments and what students do. In the new paradigm, feedback is seen as a process which drives curriculum design.

Active, social and participatory learning and authentic feedback experiences which facilitate self-evaluation through dialogue and involvement all lie at the heart of the Northumbria assessment for learning model outlined above (Sambell et al. 2013). Even with the large classes which are typical for many business contexts, if carefully thought through, this can be enacted by 'flipping feedback' (Hounsell 2015). This kind of feedback is embedded in teaching, based around active-learning exercises where students spend time on a task and generate real-time, authentic feedback during class time, also called 'classroom assessment' (Angelo and Cross 1993). The use of clickers to enable students to have a go at questions and compare their responses to those of their classmates and in discussion with tutors is a prime example of this. In a similar vein Mohrweis and Shinham (2015) show how 'scratch-off' cards have been successfully used to provide instant feedback in a first-year accounting review session, with significant impact on exam results. Other methods of this kind include feedback flowing from peer and self-review exercises, where students generate as well as receive feedback, such as the essay feedback checklist used with first-year management students reported by Mansour (2015).

Developing Evaluative Judgement

Students need to be prepared to function beyond the course 'in a world without marks, grades, rubrics, explicit criteria and markers' (Dawson et al. 2018, p. 1), or in other words, assessment needs to be 'sustainable' (Boud 2000). Preparing for such independence requires the development of students' ability to judge the quality of their own work and that of others. Sadler (1989) points out that this involves an understanding of what constitutes quality in a given domain, the ability to compare one's own work with this standard, and strategies that allow the gap to be closed. Just like teachers who acquire their concept of quality through repeatedly judging students' work, students need to be given opportunities to practise making judgements and making the rationale for their judgements explicit. Since knowledge of standards is tacit and situated (Price et al. 2011), participatory approaches through which students learn to make judgements in collaboration with others help them develop a feel for standards and criteria. The work of Price, O'Donovan and colleagues, which originated in a UK business school, has been highly influential in highlighting the limitations of assessment criteria and rubrics, and the importance of complementary approaches (O'Donovan et al. 2001; Price et al. 2012; Rust et al. 2003). Since standards are socially constructed, providing criteria is not enough: students need to be actively involved in using and discussing them with others and applying them to concrete pieces of work.

Evaluative judgement can be developed through a range of approaches including self-assessment, peer feedback and review, use of rubrics and use of exemplars (Tai et al. 2018). Tai et al. stress that this needs to involve: 'active and iterative engagement with criteria, the enactment of judgements on diverse samples of work, dialogic feedback with peers and tutors oriented towards understanding quality which may not be otherwise explicated, and articulation and justification of judgements with a focus on both immediate and future tasks' (Tai et al. 2018, p. 477).

Approaches intended to develop students' evaluative judgement are increasingly reported in the literature. Nicol's work on peer review (Nicol 2019, 2014; Nicol et al. 2014) has demonstrated that reviewing and commenting on the work of others impacts in particular on students' evaluations of their own work and subsequent attempts to improve its quality. Fraile et al. (2017) developed a structured co-creation process during which students devised, discussed and agreed criteria and then drafted their own definitions of poor and excellent quality based on these criteria. The resulting rubric incorporated students' own words and was subsequently used for summative assessment purposes. In our own work we have frequently used genuine exemplars of varying quality which we ask students to rank-order. The rationale for their rankings is then discussed and compared with our own, with a focus on both students and teachers making the reasons for their judgements explicit, rather than presenting the teacher's as the 'right' answer. Examples for supporting learning from exemplars through scaffolding and dialogue can be found in Carless et al. (2018).

Vignettes of Practice

The vignettes in Boxes 14.1 to 14.5 have been selected to illustrate ways in which contemporary assessment practices in business schools have incorporated some of the ideas outlined above. They are situated in a range of countries (Australia, Canada, South Africa and the UK), at undergraduate and postgraduate level and in different business-related subjects. While each vignette has its own merits, they are not intended as exemplary practices, but rather to demonstrate the intricacies and challenges of attempting to put into practice assessment which supports learning.

BOX 14.1 EXAMPLE PRACTICE 1: FEEDFORWARD EXERCISE ON AN MBA MODULE IN FINANCIAL DECISION MAKING (PARRY AND BAMBER 2010) – UK

This assessment practice was termed 'a structured feedforward exercise', integrated into a course on financial decision-making. Following a six-week taught course, the students had a further three weeks to complete and submit a 2500 word written report, which critically analysed financial problem-solving and decision-making in an area of practice for a chosen organization *[Authenticity]*.

The structured feedforward exercise provided students with guidance and feedback on the assessment development process during the taught course. These activities included:

Development of an assignment planning sheet that guided them through choosing a topic and relevant theory that was then discussed with peers and a tutor (weeks 1–3)

Session to discuss and give examples of what different assessment criteria and terms such as analysis and synthesis may mean and how they could be addressed (week 3) *[Evaluative Judgement]*.

Students used a self-assessment sheet (checklist) to assess their draft report in class and discuss it in small groups. Within this session each student was seen individually by a tutor to discuss the results of the self-assessment exercise. This resulted in generation of feedback from self, peers and the tutor (week 6) *[Evaluative Judgement, Engagement with Feedback]*.

The students were then encouraged to use the outcomes from the structured feedforward exercises to further develop the report prior to submission (week 9).

BOX 14.2 EXAMPLE PRACTICE 2: LEARNING FROM ONE ASSESSMENT TASK TO THE NEXT ON A LARGE FIRST-YEAR BUSINESS UNIT (VARDI 2013) – AUSTRALIA

Two written assignments were designed to enable students to use feedback from their first piece of work to enhance the second. The first assignment was a 1800-word essay to examine a multinational company's performance in society. This second assignment was directly linked to the first, as it required the students to use the research and analysis from the first essay to write a 1000-word critical business report recommending strategies for the company to meet its social responsibility as per the United Nations Global Compact *[Authenticity]*.

This allowed tutors to provide feedback that was highly specific to the first task, which could also be translated to support the work required for the next task. The marks and feedback from the first assignment were provided to students at least a week before submission of the second. To supplement this timely feedback, staff training also took place around a number of feedback principles for markers to ensure that it was forward-looking *[Engagement with Feedback]*.

In addition to the focus on student engagement with feedback, consistent standards of performance were designed for the unit. To support these descriptions, exemplars for the highest level of performance for each assessment task were provided. A workshop activity helped students to deconstruct these exemplars in relation to the assessment task and standards, and these workshops were also videocast *[Evaluative Judgement]*.

BOX 14.3 EXAMPLE PRACTICE 3: AN ASSESSMENT LITERACY-BUILDING INTERVENTION FOR FIRST-YEAR BUSINESS STUDENTS (SMITH ET AL. 2013) – AUSTRALIA

A short (approx. 45 minutes), single workshop activity was used with a large first-year business cohort prior to them submitting a 1500-word literature review. The ability of the students to judge their own and others' work in response to an assessment task was a key aspect focus of the workshop *[Evaluative Judgement]*.

The format of the workshop was as follows. Use of a 'think, pair, and share' exercise where participants considered the quality of two pieces of example work. The students used an assessment rubric, containing the criteria and standards for the assessment, to support their judgements. There were three phases to this activity: individual judgements about the exemplars (think); explanation of the judgement in relation to the criteria to a partner (pair); discussion of judgements with the whole class (share). The outcome from this activity was a list of criteria from the students in their own language.

Identification of the stronger and weaker examples then took place and the students provided the marks they awarded. The tutor then revealed their mark for the work and the reason for it.

The students were then asked to revisit the assessment rubric, and compared the basis for their judgements against the academic standards expressed in it

BOX 14.4 EXAMPLE PRACTICE 4: USING INTERNATIONAL MARKETING SIMULATIONS AS AN AUTHENTIC ASSESSMENT (FARRELL 2020) – CANADA

Computer simulations were used as an authentic assessment of undergraduate business students' capabilities in international marketing. Country Manager was the international marketing simulation used, and the scenario was that a United States-based consumer products company was concerned about the ageing profile and slow growth in its primary markets in North America, Australia and Western Europe. The response to this was that the company was to develop a presence in emerging and fast-growing markets in either Asia or Latin America. The students were required to make a range of strategic decisions to penetrate these markets.

Students worked in self-selected teams of three or four; firstly coming to a decision about the target country that they could justify in terms of social and demographic profile, and then to identify initial strategies for how these markets would be entered, considering the relevant strength and weaknesses of each.

Students attended weekly simulation labs, which provided guidance from tutors. They worked through successive rounds of the simulation where they made strategic marketing decisions in order to achieve profitability. More specifically, students were required to understand consumer buyer behaviour and the factors that motivate purchase decisions *[Authenticity]*.

Students had to submit an online peer evaluation and a ten-page group report at the end of the simulation exercise. Within the report students discussed lessons learned from their experience with the simulation *[Evaluative Judgement]*.

BOX 14.5 EXAMPLE PRACTICE 5: FORMATIVE SELF-ASSESSMENT ON AN UNDERGRADUATE ACCOUNTING PROGRAMME (HILL 2016) – SOUTH AFRICA

For a final-year Taxation module, with 561 accounting students, students completed six class tests that constituted 10 per cent of the overall mark for the module. A self-assessment exercise was conducted for three of the tests. To support engagement in the self-assessment exercises, a self-assessment assignment (worth 5 per cent of the overall mark for the module) was developed where marks were awarded based on the accuracy of the students' judgements about their own work relative to the judgements by the lecturer *[Evaluative Judgement]*.

Self-carbon test answer papers were created with a front-page (white) that students completed the test on and a second copy page (yellow). The white copy was submitted for marking by the tutor, and the yellow page was taken away by the student so they could self-assess. Students were also provided with a model answer and detailed marking plan for the test that they had completed in order that they could undertake the self-assessment.

Once the students had undertaken the self-assessment they were required to submit the mark onto the virtual learning environment for the module. They were also asked reflective questions to encourage them to think about the positive and negative aspects of their performance on the test. Finally they were given the opportunity to compare their mark with that from the lecturer *[Engagement with Feedback]*.

The vignettes illustrate several of the principles and strategies outlined above. They also demonstrate that assessment which supports learning almost always involves close attention to course and curriculum design. Most of the examples do not represent only one-off interventions, but intricate designs consisting of several steps and stages. It is also worthwhile noting the challenges of designing assessment in ways that engender student agency and ownership. In example 1, for instance, the design encourages self- and peer assessment to generate feedback that students need to interpret in order to help them with the current task. Therefore the level of active student involvement and the link for the student to the assessment task in hand appear to be strong. In contrast, in example 2, the feedback on the first assignment is tutor-generated and therefore student agency is lower and students' ability to interpret and use the tutor's comments to inform the task that follows is assumed. In both examples 2 and 3 the workshop activities were designed to support the development of student understanding of the assessment criteria by involving them in making judgements about the work of others. However, while the students are actively involved in this process, the translation of this activity into being able to make judgements about their own work, and take action to improve it, still seems to require quite a large step, which might be difficult for students without additional scaffolding. This demonstrates how complex it is to develop assessment practices that actively address all principles of learning-oriented assessment in an interconnected way

CONCLUSION

This chapter has provided an overview of current debates about assessment and feedback in higher education, and highlighted the opportunities which a focus on assessment for learning can offer to business schools. We have shown that business-related disciplines are already at the forefront of implementing innovative assessment; as is evident, for instance, in the many examples of authentic assessment. We have also pointed the reader towards ideas and debates in the assessment in higher education literature which have the potential to contribute to further enhancements. These include models of authenticity which go beyond an exclusive focus on the world of work, (re)considering feedback as a process rather than a product provided by the 'expert' tutor, and the importance of developing students' evaluative judgement. The latter in particular has received considerable attention in current debates and practice developments, to which business schools may want to contribute. The discussion in this chapter has demonstrated that the multiple stakeholders and purposes of assessment have resulted in a terrain which is full of tensions and challenges, and the examples and vignettes provided have illustrated the complexities of implementing assessment which genuinely supports learning. However, despite these potential difficulties, the principles and conditions of assessment for learning outlined here have already encouraged academics in many countries to have thought-provoking discussions and to develop cutting-edge assessment practices. While there is not one perfect way to teach, there are pedagogies and corresponding assessment practices that are more likely to support meaningful student learning. We hope that this chapter will contribute to sustaining and engendering further dialogue about assessment in business schools, grounded in the above insights gained from theory, research and concrete examples.

REFERENCES

Angelo, Thomas A., and Patricia K. Cross (1993), *Classroom Assessment Techniques: A Handbook for College Teachers*, 2nd edn, San Francisco, CA: Jossey-Bass.
Ashford-Rowe, Kevin, Janice Herrington and Christine Brown (2014), 'Establishing the critical elements that determine authentic assessment', *Assessment and Evaluation in Higher Education*, 39 (2), 205–222.

Askew, Susan, and Caroline Lodge (2000), 'Gifts, ping-pong and loops – linking feedback and learning,' in *Feedback for Learning*, Susan Askew and Caroline Lodge (eds), Routledge: London, UK and New York, USA, 1–17.

Bell, Adrian R., and Chris Brooks (2018), 'What makes students satisfied? A discussion and analysis of the UK's national student survey', *Journal of Further and Higher Education*, 42 (8), 1118–1142.

Black, Paul and Dylan Wiliam (1998), 'Assessment and classroom learning', *Assessment in Education: Principles, Policy and Practice*, 5 (1), 7–74.

Biggs, John B. (2003), *Teaching for Quality Learning at University*, 2nd edn, Buckingham: Open University Press/Society for Research into Higher Education.

Boud, David (2000), 'Sustainable assessment: rethinking assessment for the learning society', *Studies in Continuing Education*, 22 (2), 151–167.

Boud, David (2007), 'Reframing assessment as if learning were important', in *Rethinking Assessment in Higher Education*, David Boud and Nancy Falchikov (eds), London, UK and New York, USA: Routledge, 14–26.

Boud, David (2014), 'Shifting views of assessment: from "Secret Teachers" business to sustaining learning', in *Advances and Innovations in University Assessment and Feedback*, Carolin Kreber, Charles Anderson, Noel Entwistle and Jan MacArthur (eds), Edinburgh: Edinburgh University Press, 13–31.

Boud, David, and Nancy Falchikov (eds) (2007), *Rethinking Assessment in Higher Education: Learning for the Longer Term*, London: Routledge.

Boud, David, and Elizabeth Molloy (2013), 'Rethinking models of feedback for learning: the challenge of design', *Assessment and Evaluation in Higher Education*, 38 (6), 698–712.

Brown, Sally, and Peter Knight (1994), *Assessing Learners in Higher Education*, London: Kogan Page

Burton, Kelley (2011), 'A framework for determining the authenticity of assessment tasks: applied to an example in law', *Journal of Learning Design*, 4 (2), 20–28.

Carless, David (2007), 'Learning-oriented assessment: conceptual bases and practical implications', *Innovations in Education and Teaching International*, 44 (1), 57–66.

Carless, David (2015), 'Exploring learning-oriented assessment processes', *Higher Education*, 69, 963–976.

Carless, David, Gordon Joughlin and Magdalen M.C. Mok (2006), 'Learning-oriented assessment: principles and practice', *Editorial, Assessment and Evaluation in Higher Education*, 31 (4), 395–398.

Carless, David, Kennedy Kam Ho, To Chan, Jessica To, Margaret Lo and Elizabeth Barrett (2018), 'Developing students' capacities for evaluative judgement through analysing exemplars', in *Developing Evaluative Judgement in Higher Education. Assessment for Knowing and Producing Quality Work*, David Boud, Rola Ajjawi, Phillip Dawson and Joanna Tai (eds), Abingdon, UK and New York, USA: Routledge, 108–116.

Dawson, Phillip, Rola Ajjawi, David Boud and Joanna Tai (2018), 'Introduction: what is evaluative judgement? ', in *Developing Evaluative Judgement in Higher Education: Assessment for Knowing and Producing Quality Work*, David Boud, Rola Ajjawi, Phillip Dawson, and Joanna Tai (eds), Abingdon, UK and New York, USA: Routledge, 1–4.

Dingyloudi, Filitsa, and Jan-Willem Strijbos (2018), 'Just plain peers across social networks: Peer-feedback networks nested in personal and academic networks in higher education', *Learning, Culture and Social Interaction*, 18, 86–112.

Evans, Carl (2016), 'Re-thinking case-based assessments in business management education', *International Journal of Management Education*, 14, 161–166.

Farrell, Carlyle (2020), 'Do international marketing simulations provide an authentic assessment of learning? A student perspective', *International Journal of Management Education*, 18. doi: 10.1016/j.ijme2020.100362.

Fraile, Juan, Ernesto Panadero and Rodrigo Pardo (2017), 'Co-creating rubrics: the effects on self-regulated learning, self-efficacy and performance of establishing assessment criteria with students', *Studies In Educational Evaluation*, 53, 69–76.

Gipps, Caroline (1994), *Beyond Testing: Towards a Theory of Educational Assessment*, London, UK and Philadelphia, PA, USA: Falmer Press.

Hattie, John (2009), *Visible Learning*, Abingdon, UK and New York, USA: Routledge.

Hattie, John, and Helen Timperley (2007), 'The power of feedback', *Review of Educational Research*, 77 (1), 81–112.

Havnes, Anton, and Liz McDowell (eds) (2008), *Balancing Dilemmas in Assessment and Learning in Contemporary Education*. New York, USA and Abingdon, UK: Routledge.

Hill, Tany (2016), 'Do accounting students believe in self-assessment?', *Accounting Education*, 25 (4), 291–305.

Hounsell, Dai (2015), 'WISE Assessment Briefing 12', Hong Kong: Centre of Teaching and Learning, University of Hong Kong. https://www.cetl.hku.hk/teaching-learning-cop/wp-content/uploads/2015/08/wise-assessment-briefing12.pdf (accessed 27 March 2020).

Hyland, Ken, and Fiona Hyland (2006), 'Feedback on second language students' writing', *Language Teaching*, 39 (2), 83–101.

James, Lincoln Then, and Riza Casidy (2018), 'Authentic assessment in business education: its effects on student satisfaction and promoting behaviour', *Studies in Higher Education*, 43 (3), 401–415.

Jones, Ollie, and Marie Kerr (2012), 'Refreshment by the case: use of multimedia in case study assessment', *International Journal of Management Education*, 10, 186–200.

Kaye, Roland, and David Hawkridge (eds) (2003), *Learning and Teaching for Business: Case Studies of Successful Innovation*, London, UK, and Stirling, USA: Kogan Page.

Kreber, Carolin (2009), 'Supporting student learning in the context of diversity, complexity and uncertainty', in *The University and Its Disciplines: Teaching and Learning Within and Beyond Disciplinary Boundaries*, Carolin Kreber (ed.), New York: Routledge, 3–18.

Kreber, Carolin (2013), *Authenticity in and Through Teaching in Higher Education: The Transformative Potential of the Scholarship of Teaching*, London, UK and New York, USA: Routledge.

Kreber, C. (2014), 'Flourishing amid strangeness and uncertainty: exploring the meaning of 'graduate-ness' and its challenges for assessment', in *Advances and Innovations* in *University Assessment* and *Feedback*, Carolin Kreber, Charles Anderson, Noel Entwistle and Jan McArthur (eds), Edinburgh: Edinburgh University Press, pp. 32–55.

Lohmann, Gui, Marlene A. Pratt, Pierre Benckendorff, Paul Strickland, Paul Reynolds, and Paul A. Whitelaw (2019), 'Online business simulations: authentic teamwork, learning outcomes and satisfaction,' *Higher Education*, 77, 455–472.

Mansour, Hala F. (2015), 'Enhancing first year management students' engagement: an action research project to explore the use of the Essay Feedback Checklist', *International Journal of Management Education*, 13, 218–226.

Marshall, Bethan, and Mary Jane Drummond (2006), 'How teachers engage with assessment for learning: lessons from the classroom', *Research Papers in Education*, 21 (2), 133–149.

McCune, Velda, and Dai Hounsell (2005), 'The development of students' ways of thinking and practising in three final-year biology courses', *Higher Education*, 49, 255–289.

McGreevy, Sharon, Conor Heagney, and Siobhan Gallagher (2019), 'Authentic assessment in business education – the integrated case study (a capstone project)', in *Inclusive Assessment and Feedback: Universal Design Case Studies from IADT and UCD*, Julie Padden, Julie Tonge, Therese Moylan and Geraldine O'Neill (eds), University College Dublin, Access and Lifelong Learning. https://www.iadt.ie/content/files/Inclusive_Assessment__Feedback-Full_Publication.pdf (accessed 28 March 2020).

McLean, Helen (2018), 'This is the way to teach: insights from academics and students about assessment that supports learning', *Assessment and Evaluation in Higher Education*, 43 (8), 1228–1240.

Merry, Stephen, Margaret Price, David Carless and Maddalena Taras (eds) (2013), *Reconceptualising Feedback in Higher Education: Developing Dialogue with Students*, London: Routledge.

Mihret, Dessalegn Getie, Nadana Abayadeera, Kim Watty and Jade McKay (2017), 'Teaching auditing using cases in an online learning environment: the role of ePortfolio assessment'. *Accounting Education*, 26 (4), 335–357.

Mohrweis, Lawrence C., and Kathe M. Shinham (2015), 'Enhancing students' learning: instant feedback cards', *American Journal of Business Education*, 8 (1), 63–70.

National Forum for the Enhancement of Teaching and Learning in Higher Education (2017), *Authentic Assessment in Irish Higher Education*, Dublin: National Forum for the Enhancement of Teaching and Learning in Higher Education, Forum Insights. https://www.teachingandlearning.ie/publication/authentic-assessment-in-irish-higher-education/ (accessed 28 March 2020).

Neely, Pat, and Jan Tucker (2012), 'Using business simulations as authentic assessment tool', *American Journal of Business Education*, 5 (4), 449–456.

Nicol, David (2010), 'From monologue to dialogue: improving written feedback processes in mass higher education', *Assessment and Evaluation in Higher Education*, 35 (5), 501–517.

Nicol, David (2014), 'Guiding principles for peer review: unlocking learners' evaluative skills', in *Advances and Innovations in University Assessment and Feedback*, Carolin Kreber, Charles Anderson, Noel Entwistle and Jan McArthur (eds), Edinburgh: Edinburgh University, 197–224.

Nicol, David (2019), 'Reconceptualising feedback as an internal not an external process', *Italian Journal of Educational Research*, Special Issue, May. https://ojs.pensamultimedia.it/index.php/sird/article/view/3270/3130 (accessed 30 March 2020).

Nicol, David J., and Debra Macfarlane-Dick (2006), 'Formative assessment and self-regulated learning: a model and seven principles of good feedback practice', *Studies in Higher Education*, 31 (2), 199–218.

Nicol, David, Avril Thomson and Caroline Breslin, Caroline (2014), 'Rethinking feedback practices in higher education: a peer review perspective', *Assessment and Evaluation in Higher Education*, 39 (1), 102–122.

O'Donovan Berry, Margaret Price and Chris Rust Chris (2001), 'The student experience of criterion-referenced assessment (through the introduction of a common criteria assessment grid) ', *Innovations in Education and Training International*, 38, 74–85.

O'Neill, Geraldine (2019), 'Authentic assessment: concept, continuum and contested', Masterclass presented at the Assessment in Higher Education (AHE) Conference, Manchester, June. https://tinyurl.com/AHE2019 (accessed 28 March 2020).

Palmer, Parker J. (1998), *The Courage to Teach*, San Francisco, CA: Josey-Bass.

Parry, Simon, and Matt Bamber (2010), 'Feedforward: the responses of accounting students', *Practitioner Research in Higher Education*, 4 (1), 62–72.

Price, Margaret, Jude Carroll, Jude, Berry O'Donovan and Chris Rust (2011), 'If I was going there I wouldn't start from here: a critical commentary on current assessment practice', *Assessment and Evaluation in Higher Education*, 36 (4), 479–492.

Price, Margaret, Chris Rust, Berry O'Donovan, Karen Handley and Rebecca Bryant (2012), *Assessment Literacy: The Foundation for Improving Student Learning*, Oxford: Oxford Centre for Staff and Learning Development, Oxford Brookes University.

Reimann, Nicola (2018), 'Learning about assessment: the impact of two courses for higher education staff', *International Journal for Academic Development*, 23 (2), 86–97.

Reimann, Nicola, and Ian Sadler (2017), 'Personal understanding of assessment and the link to assessment practice: the perspectives of higher education staff', *Assessment and Evaluation in Higher Education*, 42 (5), 724–736.

Reimann, Nicola, Ian Sadler and Kay Sambell (2019), 'What's in a word? Practices associated with "feedforward" in higher education', *Assessment and Evaluation in Higher Education*, 44 (8), 1279–1290.

Reimann, Nicola, and Angelina Wilson (2012), 'Academic development in "Assessment for Learning": the value of a concept and communities of assessment practice', *International Journal for Academic Development*, 17 (1), 71–83.

Rust, Chris, Margaret Price and Berry O'Donovan (2003), 'Improving students' learning by developing their understanding of assessment criteria and processes', *Assessment and Evaluation in Higher Education*, 28 (2), 147–164.

Sadler, D. Royce (1989), 'Formative assessment and the design of instructional systems', *Instructional Science*, 18 (2), 119–144.

Sadler, D. Royce (2010), 'Beyond feedback: developing student capability in complex appraisal,' *Assessment and Evaluation in Higher Education*, 35 (5), 535–550.

Sadler, Ian, and Nicola Reimann (2018), 'Variation in the development of teachers' understandings of assessment and their assessment practices in higher education', *Higher Education Research and Development*, 37 (1), 131–144.

Sambell, Kay (2011), 'Rethinking feedback in higher education: an assessment for learning perspective', Bristol: University of Bristol, Subject Centre for Education Escalate. http://escalate.ac.uk/downloads/8410.pdf (accessed 29 March 2020).

Sambell, K. (2013), 'Engaging students through assessment', in *The Student Engagement Handbook: Practice in Higher Education*, Elisabeth Dunne and Derfel Owen (eds), Bingley: Emerald Group Publishing, 379–396.

Sambell, Kay, and Liz McDowell (1998), 'The construction of the hidden curriculum: messages and meanings in the assessment of student learning', *Assessment and Evaluation in Higher Education*, 23 (4), 391–402.

Sambell, Kay, Liz McDowell and Catherine Montgomery (2013), *Assessment for Learning in Higher Education*, Abingdon, UK and New York, USA: Routledge.

Shulman, Lee S. (2005), 'Signature pedagogies in the professions', *Daedalus*, 134 (3), 52–59.

Smith, Calvin Douglas, Kate Worsfold, Lynda Davies, Ron Fisher and Ruth McPhail (2013), 'Assessment literacy and student learning: the case for explicitly developing students 'assessment literacy', *Assessment and Evaluation in Higher Education*, 38 (1), 44–60.

Tai, Joanna, Rola Ajjawi, David Boud, Philip Dawson and Ernesto Panadero (2018), 'Developing evaluative judgement: Enabling students to make decisions about the quality of work', *Higher Education*, 76 (3), 467–481.

Vardi, Iris (2013), 'Effectively feeding forward from one written assessment task to the next', *Assessment and Evaluation in Higher Education*, 38 (5), 599–610.

Villarroel, Verónica, David Boud, Susan Bloxham, Daniela Bruna and Carola Bruna (2020), 'Using principles of authentic assessment to redesign written examinations and tests', *Innovations in Education and Teaching International*, 57 (1), 38–49.

Voss, Lynn (2015), 'Simulation in business and marketing education: how educators assess student learning from simulations', *International Journal of Management Education*, 13, 57–74.

Wald, Navé, and Tony Harland (2017), 'A framework for authenticity in designing a research-based curriculum', *Teaching in Higher Education*, 22 (7), 751–765.

Warwick, Philip (2020), personal communication.

Winstone, Naomi E., Robert A. Nash, Michael Parker and James Rowntree (2017), 'Supporting learners' agentic engagement with feedback: a systematic review and a taxonomy of recipience processes', *Educational Psychologist*, 52 (1), 17–37.

15. Business studios of practice
Stefan Meisiek

INTRODUCTION

Business schools are increasingly turning towards situated learning to prepare their students for their first jobs. Turning from lecturing to, for example, working on industry projects and engagements is meant to improve employability. In such projects, authentic activities and experiences take primacy over conveying research-based, generalizable concepts and theories. Learning might still not be exactly like in the next workplace, but it builds a bridge towards it. Authentic activities enable students to participate with their gained knowledge and skills in the communities of practice at their future workplaces (Lave and Wenger 1991).

With the turn to situated learning in business schools, the socio-material side of higher education comes into focus (Brown et al. 1989). This includes the built environment of higher education, learning technology, and at-hand materials such as Post-its, notepads, whiteboards, markers, chairs and tables (Yeoman and Wilson 2019). The materials are considered as enabling and constraining the learner as a member of a learning community. This socio-material side of education has been long subsumed under functional considerations that were meant to enable the time-honoured traditions of education. An ideal outcome of learning is prescribed, and rooms, technology and materials are vetted as to how they help in achieving the predetermined and measurable outcome. In situated learning, however, context matters, and in this context students don't only learn together, but also from one another and with one another. Rather than internalizing predefined knowledge, the participants (a better word than 'students' for this kind of learning) are preparing to join a community of practice in which practices are not only dialogically but also materially constituted (Brown and Duguid 2001).

In order to meet the demands of situated learning, some business schools have changed teaching spaces, technologies and at-hand materials. These steps seem insignificant at first sight, because laboratories in the sciences or studios in architecture embody long traditions of situated learning at universities. For business schools, however, to change their space is part of an ongoing debate about their purpose and responsibility in society (Ghoshal 2005). Should business schools be regarded as scientific institutions researching and teaching general laws, or as applied science schools closely tied to and teaching the ever-evolving practice of management? The Ford and Carnegie reports of the 1950s led schools to aim for the former (Gorden and Howell 1959; Pierson 1959). Recent employers' demands on graduates' qualifications are pulling schools into the latter direction. Today, business schools serve both aims, which inadvertently leads to tensions. Resolving this debate is beyond the scope of this chapter. For our purposes it is sufficient to recognize that business schools are invested in situated learning, often drawing on the traditions and practices from other university faculties.

An example is the Studio at Copenhagen Business School (CBS) (Meisiek 2016). It was created in 2012 to teach business students how to apply creative problem-solving to management and marketing problems. Its inception was inspired by studios in art, design and craft schools. While there are numerous texts on the practices of artists, designers and crafts(wo) men (cf. Sennett 2009; Jacob and Grabner 2010; Melles et al. 2015), there is no such tradition in business schools. The idea to start a studio was driven by a discourse in companies on the need for graduates and professionals to be conversant in creative endeavours, and able to devise and practice relevant approaches. Further, since the 2000s, more and more companies have added design thinking, agile and lean startup methodologies to their problem-solving arsenals. Consequently, they expected business school graduates to learn and extend these practices. The Studio at CBS is an attempt at serving this need by designing educational encounters that make the socio-material aspects of situated learning tangible for students.

There seems to be a divide in conceptions of situated learning. Authors either address the situatedness of learning in a higher education context (Carvalho and Goodyear 2014; Yeoman and Wilson 2019), or the situatedness of learning and participation in an organizational context (Brown et al. 1989; Lave and Wenger 1991). A question remains how the two might be connected, and how participants in higher education might acquire practices that help them join communities of practice in the field (cf. Stein 1998). I will be using the Studio at CBS to illustrate how situated learning, and the accompanying socio-materiality, might play a role in business school education. It offers an opportunity to speculate how studio work in a business school is directly related to the work practices in organizations, and it pinpoints weaknesses of the approach as well.

I look first at business studios to identify place, tasks and community as core aspects of studio education. I then introduce a framework from educational research to show how these aspects lead to situated, emergent activity in the business studio. To fulfil the ambition of business schools, however, the learning needs to be situated not only in a studio, but also towards the communities of practice in the organizations that participants hope to join after their education. The link between studio and workplace lies in the habits of mind, or practices, that arise from the emergent activity in the studio between place, tasks and community. A recast framework, including studio and workplace, allows us to formulate propositions of how business studios might enable and constrain situated learning.

THE BUSINESS STUDIO

The term 'business studio' was introduced to denote a place, a set of tasks to solve problems, and a community of learners. Together, these constitute the environment in which participants develop relevant practices (Barry and Meisiek 2015).

The business studio is a space in a business school that suggests otherness and inspires expectations of creative work (Beckman and Barry 2007). There is no front or back of the room, no rows of chairs, and no seminar table to gather around. Usually, the edges of this place are rough, suggesting something unfinished, and inviting participants to contribute, even to leave traces of their work. Furniture is mobile, encouraging participants to explore patterns of collaboration. There is an abundance of work materials. Colours are more vibrant, suggesting that the important things are happening between participants, rather than at the lectern (Doorley and Witthoft 2012).

Calling it a business studio suggests that it may be connected in space, tasks or output to the educational traditions of art, design and craft studios. Yet, a business studio doesn't require the same tools, furnishings or dimensions. For example, the look or feel of a black box theatre might support role plays, but not other forms of representing business problems. And the tools and resources of a carpenter's shop might benefit making physical models, but those alone would not solve the business issues under consideration. The tasks that participants work on in a business studio are tied to managerial problems, such as competition, strategy, leadership or operations (e.g., Roos and Victor 1999). Tackling these issues in non-traditional ways by completing carefully selected tasks in a studio environment shifts the epistemology of learning. Consequently, the intended output of a business studio is fundamentally different to the artworks, designs and useful items of the traditional studios (Barry and Meisiek 2015).

If it is not space, tasks or output, where is the connection to the studios of art, design and craft? The clue to this connection lies in the word 'studio' itself. It derives from the Latin word *studium* and came to signify a place to study something in great detail and with great care, with the goal to create knowledge and offer practical solutions. Over time, the studio also became the denomination for the place where designers worked. And with the industrial revolution, many of the crafts also found a refuge in the studio, suggesting that they contributed something else or something more than industrial production could (Sennett 2009). As such, the studio is a combination of a room to study and work, offering time for contemplation and materials for discovery (Taylor and Statler 2013). And in this room, practices of mind and hand come into play to inquire into problems with the help of materials (Barry 1997; Sullivan 2005).

The connection between business studios and the educational tradition of art, design and craft studios resides in the practices, more specifically in the practices of inquiry (Csikszentmihalyi and Getzels 1973). It is easy to overlook that a space, however well designed and prepared, will remain a space unless people know, learn or discover how to use it well. Only agency makes a space into a place, which then might inspire a sense of belonging. What makes a space into a place for creative production can be captured in the term 'studio practice'. The space affords the practices, but it doesn't prescribe them. In fact, the more participants master the practices, the less they need a purpose-built space to enact these. Practices, with their tacit and embodied elements, are difficult-to-impossible to learn through a lecture (Meisiek et al. 2016). Consequently, educators in the business studios are not 'sages on stages' but 'guides by your side'. Learning in the business studio means learning by making. Yet, it makes a difference if participants create alone or in groups.

While the common concern with mind and hand connects business studios to the practices of inquiry in art, design and craft studios, the prevailing concern with collaboration does not (Meisiek et al. 2020). This sets business studios apart from their studio cousins. Studios are social places, where groups or teams of participants work on framing problems to inquire, exploring the problems, testing prototypes and preparing solutions. It is the heterogeneity of the participants that is beneficial to the quality of the outcomes. While there are exceptions, artists and designers are often identified in individual terms, ascribing them special vision or abilities that others don't possess. Business studios are a playing field of collective genius, where skills of working in teams and pursuing processes of discovery are central to the educational experience. In an ideal case, the participants form a community of learners, who assemble to learn practices in a place that affords these activities.

EMERGENT ACTIVITY

The three core aspects of business studios – place, task and community – are tied to learning and exercising relevant practices. The three aspects don't work in isolation, however. Each is a means to the others, and together they establish the constraining and enabling environment in a business studio. To describe the dynamic between these three aspects, we can turn to the activity-centred analysis and design (ACAD) framework (Carvalho and Goodyear 2014; Carvalho and Yeoman 2018).

The ACAD framework builds upon Vygotsky's activity theory and was developed to describe situated learning, moving the focus of attention from the individual participant to a learning dynamic that includes material, task and social aspects (Yeoman and Wilson 2019). The framework also highlights that choices entering the design of a learning experience will inadvertently change the dynamic in the classroom or, in our case, the studio. Going into a studio to learn in itself represents a set of learning design choices. There, educators define the studio space, the tasks and the social rules that govern the learning experience. These rules, however, don't define what participants will learn. Learning is situated, but remains largely outside of the direct influence of an educator.

At the core of the ACAD framework is emergent activity. It denotes learners' agency as enabled and constrained by the place, the tasks and the community. Emergent activity might involve material practices such as thinking, feeling, perceiving, talking, making, moving and solving. The relationship to the outcomes is mediated by the emergent activity.

Figure 15.1 depicts how place, task and community lead to emerging activity and the outcome of a studio session. The figure is an adaptation of the ACAD framework to the specific concern with studios. It serves here as a bridge from the aspects of the studio as described, to seeing studios as places for situated learning and, with Vygotsky, the development of relevant practices.

The ACAD framework locates inquiry in the emergent activity at the centre. The framework describes why a business studio is more than a space. It requires material management, carefully chosen tasks and rules for social interaction to function. Together, these lead participants collectively to discover and develop practices that are helpful to address the business problems introduced.

THE STUDIO AT COPENHAGEN BUSINESS SCHOOL

The Studio at CBS exemplifies how a business studio might work and how the ACAD framework helps us describe situated learning there (Meisiek and Barry 2015). The studio was founded in 2012 as an experiment. The purpose was to offer educators an option to break away from the lecture halls and seminar rooms and to develop a more situated learning experience. The studio received funding for two years to prove its concept. After one year, a number of courses had already opted into being taught at the studio, and the occupancy rates started to compare to other educational venues on campus.

In its experimental phase, the studio was housed in a villa. A number of interconnected rooms meant participants had to work in a distributed setup, and educators had limited opportunities to see or speak to all participants at once. In the rooms, there were moveable low and high tables as well as stools and chairs. The walls were covered with whiteboard paint, and there were flipcharts and additional whiteboards on wheels serving as dividers and additional workspace. Paper, pens, scissors, Blue Tack, glue, and other stationery material filled the tables and material carts in the rooms. Cardboard, Styrofoam and other building materials were close at hand as well. A small kitchen provided coffee and a breakout space from the worktables. In the dining hall, a large flatscreen TV could be used to showcase digital prototypes or to give brief presentations. All in all, the physical setup of the studio followed ideas of design thinking and creative spaces, without being specific to a business school context (Doorley and Witthoft 2012). When the studio had proven its concept, it moved to a larger building on campus, effectively doubling in size. The physical setup in the new studio is largely identical to the first, with further breakout spaces and screens to show prototypes.

To stimulate emergent activity, educators define the setup of tables, chairs and workspaces. They bring in or take away work materials. Depending on the topic of a given class, or the problem that participants are to work on, educators introduce products, showcase services, offer videos of leadership scenarios, or bring other items to set the tone and to immerse participants. While participants are not required to use all of them, having these items around usually brings some or most of the participants to consider them and to include them in the emergent activity.

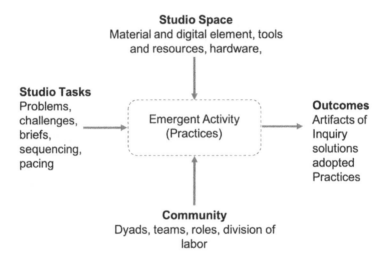

Source: Adapted from Carvalho and Goodyear (2014).

Figure 15.1   How place, task and community lead to emerging activity and the outcome of a studio session

The studio tasks depend on the topic of the course or class in the studio. The most common courses in the studio cover creativity, innovation, entrepreneurship or leadership. In many cases, companies, non-governmental organizations or government organizations provide a brief of an unsolved issue, inviting the participants to cut their teeth on it and to report back with possible solutions. In other cases, students work on problems that they have identified themselves, and that they frame with the help of an educator, now working as a facilitator to make sure the framings relate to the topic of the course.

Educators design the tasks, and define the steps, but they don't present well-defined problems. Framing the problem is a common first step in a studio task (Csikszentmihalyi and Getzels 1973). It frustrates participants who are used to being given neatly defined and well-framed tasks in their higher education experience. The underdefined nature of studio problems, and the tasks that are needed to address these, feed into the emergent activity as participants discover their way forward. Usually, an educator offers a number of steps or sub-tasks to complete to make sure that participants finish the task in the given time.

Finally, participants work in teams on the tasks in the studio. For the time that they work together on problems presented by external organizations, or on problems emerging from their topic of study, the participants form communities of learning. They understand that they can't solve the problem alone, but must make the best use possible of the diversity and resources that they have. Most participants are used to working together on learning tasks, but working in the studio often stretches them because of the ill-defined nature of the problems that they work on and the need to develop new practices through emergent activity.

Depending on the task under consideration, an educator can design the way that participants work together. For example, participants might be asked to work in dyads or teams, to use fish-bowl discussions or to develop role plays. Also, an educator might define how students share the work amongst them. The way participants interact with one another, the degree to which they form a community of learners, and they way that they divide or share labour, influence emergent activity but don't define the outcome.

The Studio at CBS is going into its eighth year at the time of writing in 2020, and it is enjoying a stable followership among educators at CBS. Not everybody likes it or wants to teach in the studio, because not everyone would like to think of design for learning in terms of studio, tasks and community; and for some, giving up control over what is learned seems risky. This notwithstanding, particularly topics of discovery such as entrepreneurship, innovation, leadership, design thinking and creativity have found a new home in the business school. A home that affords the consideration and practices that it wants its participants to develop.

AUTHENTICITY BEYOND THE BUSINESS STUDIO

Up to this point I have considered situated learning in terms of the business studio itself, and the inspiration it drew from art, design and craft studios. I looked at how learning is situated in the studio. For a business studio, however, this is a short-sighted view. While it is essential that participants learn, and it is important how they learn, it is equally as important what they are learning for. A central concern of educators in a business school is how learning in higher education is situated vis-à-vis the communities of practice that graduates encounter on their first jobs, or that MBA and EMBA students return to after their sojourn at the business school (Lave and Wenger 1991). Consequently, the discussion of situated learning in business education addresses also how employees learn for and on the job (Houde 2007). There is agreement that it is possible to learn at a business school in a situated way that is relevant for communities of practice in the workforce, but it is important to pay attention to the relationship to the place, tasks and communities that the learning is for. It is a question of how authentic the learning in a studio is to the work of managers in the field.

A comparison between traditional management practices and studio practices raises doubts over this authenticity relationship. Managers are said to analyse, plan and execute, while people in studios inquire into pernicious problems and seek novel solutions (Sullivan 2005; Jacob and Grabner 2010). Do students learn practices that won't be applicable in organizations, and that they will have to shed as they are growing into their professions and join a community of practice? In this case the business studio would be just a lecture hall in disguise. Learning would be situated in respect to the practices of higher education and not in respect to the practices at workplaces.

Recent changes in the work environment suggest that practices developing through emergent activity in the business studio have become a sought-after qualification for graduates (Colby et al. 2011). Traditional managerial practices regularly fail to provide stable solutions in a world characterized by volatility, uncertainty, complexity and ambiguity. This operating condition is often captured in the acronym 'VUCA' (volatility, uncertainty, complexity, ambiguity), which suggests conditions and situations where it is impossible to predict exact outcomes, and where managers are required to act a lot more tentatively than they might prefer. They have to frame problems, experiment, revisit assumptions, develop prototypes of solutions, test these in limited and time-sensitive contexts, and even when the trial was successful, a rollout can happen only in a staggered fashion, because conditions might change continuously, upending initiatives before they show effect. To find answers to VUCA conditions, organizations have developed a range of approaches over the past years that allow them to act with creativity and agility. The three most prominent ones are design thinking (Martin 2009), lean startup (Ries 2011) and agile (Rigby et al. 2016), but these only stand for a host of other practices that are developing concurrently. Each of these three approaches, although they hail from very different origins, show parallels to the studio practices and links to the ACAD framework.

Design thinking is a case in point here (Martin 2009; Glen et al. 2014). The term was popularized by IDEO as a technique used by product designers to solve problems and develop better products and services. The inspiration for design thinking derived from the participatory design tradition. It suggests that it is not necessary to have a classic design education in order to work in designerly ways on problems. With this, design becomes less the output of a genius individual, and more of a practice of heterogeneous groups under facilitator guidance. This version of design is inherently attractive and adoptable to the workplace of numerous organizations. A classic example is the intention of Proctor & Gamble in the early 2000s to make design thinking a regular part of work and problem-solving across the 140 000 employee company. Since Proctor & Gamble, countless other companies have followed in its tracks, training their managers in design thinking and hiring young graduates to work in the resulting projects (Fraser 2012). From its early use for product and service development, the practices of design thinking have become part of the work culture and practices of the organizations that adopted it (Elsbach and Stigliani 2018).

The stories behind agile and lean startup are similar. The former hails from software development, where ambiguous client requirements made it necessary to move from a waterfall to an iterative development process. The latter hails from entrepreneurship, where uncertainty and ambiguity regarding customer preferences made it necessary to move in more tentative ways to learn 'on the go', instead of planning a venture and its rollout ahead. In fact, lean startup contains elements of design thinking and agile, thus showing how these are cousins in the practices that drive their performance.

With companies placing a premium on graduates who can operate under VUCA conditions and who are able to join their design thinking, agile and lean startup teams, learning at the business studio is situated not only locally in the studio, but also professionally in work practices. A place such as the Studio at CBS, with educators applying the ACAD framework, offers an authentic environment to develop relevant work practices.

STUDIOS OF PRACTICE

From place, tasks and community, to emergent activity, to authentic work practices, I have sketched how business studios serve business schools in their turn towards situated learning: they are studios of practice. Yet, something remains to be explained. How does emergent activity in the business studio lead participants to develop the practices that enable them to join the communities of practice at their future employers? To answer this question, we need to take a brief detour into the art, design and craft studios that inspired the creation of business studios.

When artists or designers learn in a studio to solve particular problems related to their activity, the repetition of this activity forms what Hetland et al. (2007) call habits of mind. These habits of mind, in the way they are involving the material environment of the studio, the tasks at hand and other participants, are practices. Hetland discovered habits of mind while studying students in art studios in the Northeastern United States. She noted that while the material artifacts created in the studio stay behind as the learners move into their professional roles, the habits are carried forward, continuously refined, and allow the learner to join their community of practice. The habits that Hetland describe are surprisingly universal, and it is easy to see how they might also suit business students seeking to join companies working with, for example, design thinking.

The eight habits coming forth from working in a studio, and their relationship to the emerging activity in the ACAD model are:

1. Developing craft: learning to care for and use tools, materials and space. This habit of mind relates to the place aspect in the ACAD model. Craft means that participants not only accept the given environment, tools and materials, but that they also develop their sensibilities and abilities while actively using them. It relates to the tacit and embodied knowledge in situated learning. It allows participants to test their boundaries and follow up on what works and what doesn't.

2. Engage and persist: learning to embrace problems of relevance and persevering at tasks deemed necessary to solve them. Ill-defined problems such as those in business studios require participants to go beyond the surface, to frame and reframe them, and to persist when encountering difficulties that at first might seem insurmountable.

3. Envision: learning to picture mentally what cannot be directly observed and to imagine possible next steps forward. Most problems of creativity, innovation, entrepreneurship or leadership require vision, and sometimes leaps of faith. Participants need the willingness to go beyond what is plainly visible, and to use concepts and images to reach farther.

4. Express: learning to create representations that convey an idea, a feeling or a personal meaning. In a community of learners, it is essential to be able to represent and to lend expression to ideas at multiple levels. Participants expressing their ideas is conducive to and guides the emerging activity.

5. Observe: learning to attend to visual contexts more closely than ordinary looking requires seeing things that otherwise might not be seen. When working with ill-defined problems, being able to observe closely, ask empathetic questions and to be an ethnographer of what is going on is essential for discovering relationships and connections where none were visible before.

6. Reflect: learning to think and work with others about an aspect of one's work or working process. Learning to judge one's own work and working process and the work of others in relation to standards of the field. It goes without saying that reflective practice is an essential part of business studio work (Schön, 1987).
7. Stretch and explore: learning to reach beyond one's capacities, to explore playfully without a preconceived plan, and to embrace the opportunity to learn from mistakes and accidents. Learning from failure is a common element in innovation and entrepreneurship work, and it is also part of the learning process in the business studio.
8. Understand the professional world: learning about current practice and communities, and how to participate in both. This last habit indicates that the learners are aware of a community of practice they seek to join, and that they stay open and curious regarding what their community might value, request and strive for.

CONCLUSION

Pulling the argument of this chapter together, the ACAD model can be extended to reflect the situated learning situation that business schools hope to achieve through business studios. In particular, the role of habits and practices as a bridge between the situated learning in the studio vis-à-vis the application of learned practices in organizations is a contribution of this chapter. The revised model is shown in Figure 15.2.

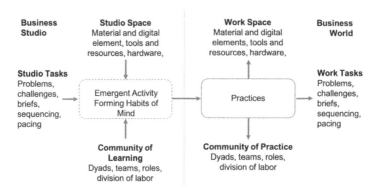

Figure 15.2   Situated learning in the business studio

With the help of the revised model, it is possible to formulate three propositions that might guide future practice in business studios, and that might also inspire future research on business studios and situated learning in business schools:

Proposition 1: Business studio educators can create the circumstances for emergent activity and the forming of habits of mind through designing the place, tasks and the community of learning, but they can't influence the outcome directly.

Proposition 2: The learning activities in the business studio enable participants to form habits of mind through emergent activity, which translate to those workplaces that have already adopted creative forms of problem-solving and where there is a community of practice to join.

Proposition 3: Participants who have developed studio habits of mind are able to draw on and shape their future workplace, tasks and communities of practice in accordance with what works to solve the problems at hand.

I am not entirely sure whether the Studio at CBS has achieved everything that was discussed in this chapter. There is no list of definitive practices that are fostered in a business studio. These habits are likely to be similar or equal to the habits of mind described for art studios, but the differences in place, tasks and community between art studios and business studios suggests that some additional or different habits might be developed. Also, the expectations of companies on the abilities of graduates to join their design thinking, agile or lean startup processes suggest that other practices might be relevant. It will be a task of future research to empirically establish the socio-material practices that are at play in the business studio.

REFERENCES

Barry, Daved (1997), Artful inquiry: A symbolic constructionist framework for social science research, *Qualitative Inquiry*, 2, 411–438.

Barry, Daved and Meisiek, Stefan (2015), Discovering the business studio, *Journal of Management Education*, 39 (1), 153–175.

Beckman, Sara L. and Barry, Michael (2007), Innovation as a learning process: Embedding design thinking, *California Management Review*, 50 (1), 25–57.

Brown, John, Collins, Allan and Duguid, Paul (1989), Situated cognition and the culture of learning, *Educational Researcher*, 18, 32–41.

Brown, John and Duguid, Paul (2001), Knowledge and organization: A social-practice perspective. *Organization Science,* 12 (2), 198–213.

Carvalho, Lucila and Goodyear, Peter (2014), *The Architecture of Productive Learning Networks,* London: Routledge.

Carvalho, Lucila and Yeoman, Pippa (2018), Framing learning entanglement in innovative learning spaces: Connecting theory, design and practice, *British Educational Research Journal*, 44 (6), 1120–1137.

Colby, Anne, Ehrlich, Thomas, Sullivan, William M., and Dolle, Jonathan R. (2011), *Rethinking Undergraduate Business Education: Liberal Learning for the Profession*, San Francisco, CA: Jossey-Bass.

Csikszentmihalyi, Mihaly and Getzels, Jacob (1973), The personality of young artists: An empirical and theoretical exploration, *British Journal of Psychology*, 64 (1), 91–104.

Doorley, Scott and Witthoft, Scott (2012), *Make Space: How to Set the Stage for Creative Collaboration*, New York: Wiley.

Elsbach, Kimberly and Stigliani, Ileana (2018), Design thinking and organizational culture: A review and framework for future research, *Journal of Management*, 44, 2274–2306.

Fraser, Heather (2012), *Design Works: How to Tackle your Toughest Innovation Challenges through Business Design*, Toronto: Rotman-UTP.

Ghoshal, Sumantra (2005), Bad management theories are destroying good management practices, *Academy of Management Learning and Education,* 4, 75–91.

Glen, Roy, Suciu, Christy and Baughn, Christopher (2014), The need for design thinking in business schools, *Academy of Management Learning and Education*, 13, 653–667.

Gorden, Robert A. and Howell, James E. (1959), *Higher Education for Business*, New York: Columbia University Press.

Hetland, Lois, Winner, Ellen, Veenma, Shirley, Sheridan, Kim and Perkins, David (2007), *Studio Thinking: The Real Benefits of Visual Arts Education*, New York: Teachers College Press.

Houde, Joseph (2007), Analogically situated experiences: Creating insight through novel contexts, *Academy of Management Learning and Education,* 6 (3), 321–331.

Jacob, Mary J. and Grabner, Michelle (2010), *The Studio Reader: On the Space of Artists*, Chicago, IL: University of Chicago Press.

Lave, Jean and Wenger, Etienne (1991), *Learning in Doing: Social, Cognitive, and Computational Perspectives. Situated Learning: Legitimate Peripheral Participation*, Cambridge: Cambridge University Press.

Martin, Roger (2009), *The Design of Business: Why Design Thinking is the Next Competitive Advantage*, Cambridge, MA: Harvard Business School Press.

Meisiek, Stefan (2016), A studio at a business school. In Sabine Junginger and Jurgen Faust (eds), *Designing Business and Management*, London: Bloomsbury Publishing, pp. 159–166.

Meisiek, Stefan and Barry, Daved (2015), Creating an organizational studio to enable innovation, in Ulla Johansson Sköldberg, Jill Woodilla and Ariane Berthoin Antal (eds), *Artistic Interventions in Organizations: Current Practice and Theory*, London: Routledge, pp. 183–202.

Meisiek, Stefan, Guillet de Monthoux, Pierre, Barry, Daved and Austin, Robert D. (2016), Four voices: Making a difference with art in management education, in Chris Steyaert, Timon Beyes and Martin Parker (eds), *The Routledge Companion to Reinventing Management Education*, Abingdon: Routledge, pp. 330–341.

Meisiek, Stefan, Wad, Lina and Zubrickaite, Evelina (2020), Design thinking in the business studio, in Gavin Melles (ed.), *Design Thinking in Higher Education*, Singapore: Springer, pp. 183–202.

Melles, Gavin, Anderson, Neil, Barrett, Tom and Thompson-Whiteside, Scott (2015), Problem finding through design thinking in education, in P. Blessinger and J.M. Carfora (eds), *Inquiry-Based Learning for Multidisciplinary Programs: A Conceptual and Practical Resource for Educators*, Bingley: Emerald Group Publishing, pp. 191–209.

Pierson, Frank C. (1959), *The Education of American Businessmen: A Study of University College Programs in Business Administration*, New York: McGraw-Hill.

Ries, Eric (2011), *The Lean Startup: How Today's Entrepreneurs Use Continuous Innovation to Create Radically Successful Businesses*, New York: Crown Business.

Rigby, Darrell, Sutherland, Jeff and Takeushi, Hirotaka (2016), Embracing agile. *Harvard Business Review*, 94 (5), 40–50.

Roos, Johan and Victor, Bart (1999), Towards a model of strategy making as serious play, *European Management Journal*, 17, 348–355.

Schön, Donald (1987), *Educating the Reflective Practitioner*, San Francisco, CA: Jossey-Bass.

Sennett Richard (2009), *The Craftsman*, Princeton, NJ: Yale University Press.

Stein, David (1998), *Situated Learning in Adult Education*, Columbus, OH: ERIC Clearinghouse on Adult, Career, and Vocational Education.

Sullivan, Graeme (2005), *Art Practice as Research: Inquiry in the Visual Arts*, Thousand Oaks, CA: SAGE.

Taylor, Steve and Statler, Matt (2013), Material matters: Increasing emotional engagement in learning, *Journal of Management Education*, 38 (4), 586–607.

Yeoman, Pippa and Wilson, Stephanie (2019), Designing for situated learning: Understanding the relations between material properties, designed form and emergent learning activity, *British Journal of Educational Technology*, 50 (5), 2090–2108.

PART V

LEADERSHIP EDUCATION

16. Building a new identity for business schools: learning how to act with authenticity through the critical teaching of leadership

Alyson Nicholds

INTRODUCTION

The best classroom experiences are those in which professors with broad perspectives and diverse skills analyse cases that have seemingly straightforward technical challenges and then gradually peel away the layers to reveal hidden strategic, economic, competitive, human and political complexities – all of which must be plumbed to reach truly effective business decisions. (Bennis and O'Toole 2005)

As the longstanding guardians of commercial know-how, business schools (BS) have, up until relatively recently, played an important role in training existing and future leaders on how to act in the face of global challenges (Bennis and O'Toole 2005). But cries that 'business schools have lost their way' (ibid.), amidst calls for scholars to reduce the 'theory–practice gap', suggests that BS are failing, not only to prepare graduates but also in explaining how as leaders they come to act on the world they are to encounter (Learmonth et al. 2012). Drawing on critical management studies (CMS), this chapter considers how BS might respond better to the complex social and political terrain by being more 'critically reflexive' about the value and applicability of business theory to practice (Alvesson 1996; Alvesson and Spicer 2012). In doing so, I consider what some of these critically reflexive practices are, and how they have come to shape the institutional conditions for teaching and learning inside the classroom. In keeping with the aims of this *Handbook*, I go on to consider the impact this type of delivery has had on my own identity as an academic and past practitioner, and the unique contribution this makes in supporting future and existing leader learners to act with authenticity outside of the classroom, and the social impact this can have on society (Gibney and Nicholds 2021).

Before beginning, it's worth saying that beyond the usual concern about critical management studies, to say that 'there's something wrong with management' (Fournier and Grey 2000: 16), my enquiry marks a move away, in line with others, from simply 'bridging the theory practice-gap' to considering what 'actually happens' in practice (Learmonth et al. 2012). This is because although CMS is a relatively broad church, ideas tend to unify around an 'anti-performative stance and commitment to some form of denaturalisation and reflexivity' (Fournier and Grey 2000: 14). My own approach is in line with that of Learmonth et al. (2012), to 'destabilize' conventional management theory and practice by challenging its underpinning assumptions. This is solely with a view to highlighting potential 'sources of oppression, exclusion and co-option' (Learmonth et al. 2012: 14). It is this latter goal that leads us to a richer (and arguably more practical) discussion, about how to resolve one of greatest dilemmas that modernday BS face: how to teach about business issues authentically, when 'what business schools do' has been called into question, and when it's clear that these global challenges arise out of a direct consequence of following a market approach.

Hence, one of the first considerations I make in my enquiry is how to engage learners in the (often) discomfiting practice of 'challenging received wisdoms' (Alvesson 1996; Alvesson and Spicer 2012). It is a practice that is central to critique within CMS on the basis that it exists to question the utility (value) of management research to organizational practice. This is because as a largely normative (based on opinion) practice, management studies is reliant on making a value judgement (rather than scientific ones) about whether or not something is useful (Learmonth et al. 2012). This type of critically reflexive enquiry also asks pertinent (often missed) questions about who's doing the asking (i.e., manager versus employee) and the context, time and space in which the business management activity is taking place (i.e., organizational versus non-organizational). By way of an example, the field of critical human resources management (HRM) reveals how managerialist assumptions largely drive the employment relationship (Thompson 2011). This type of critical enquiry not only takes more time (something academics increasingly have less of, in a highly marketized higher education institution context) but is one which also requires real-world experience to decipher (thankfully, something which practitioner-oriented academics as well as learners have in ready supply). But how do we actively use and teach the importance of this critical reflexive enquiry in BS, and what is the hidden value for businesses when doing so?

The second consideration, then, is how to diagnose what is 'actually' happening in practice, not least because this involves much more than a 'rhetoric versus reality' check (Watson 1995), since the suggestion is (rather naively) that those involved in researching practice are divorced from its delivery (Watson 1995). The reality, of course, is that at postgraduate level at least, most learners come already armed with an arsenal of prior knowledge at their disposal; they are often just looking to 'test' it against known theory (at least, they should be!). Hence, being critically reflexive suggests that it's important to address gaps that arise in the implementing of strategy and policy, by bringing to bear one's own personal and professional experience of the different range of meanings that arise through application to practice. How, then, do we get leader-learners to spot the need for where there's apparent 'symbolism' in practice (where things are meant to work in theory, but seemingly do not in practice) (Watson 1995). Doing so positions critical reflexivity in a different line to the goal above, by enabling a fuller consideration of the unintended consequences that occur in practice (Nicholds 2012[1]); the types of tensions and ambiguities experienced by those in management positions (Christophers 2013) and a realization that this can only ever really be achieved through improved dialogue with practitioners (Koss Hartmann 2014: 619). This, as we go on to discuss, has implications for the type of evidence we garner (i.e., not just scientific) and its utility in vouching for the lived experience of organizational life.

The third and final consideration is how to develop the critically reflexive leader-learner to consider how social as well as commercial goals might be met through the enactment of their authentic practice. The benefits of entertaining such critically reflexive enquiry, both inside and outside of the classroom, not only lead to novel insights for those practitioners who dare to try – such as whether 'organizing rather than leading' might be better, or whether 'strategy needs to be set by those in titular leadership positions – but can lead to very rare insights indeed, such as where inequities might start to be challenged by focusing attention on the root causes of problems (Mthethwa-Somers 2013). This requires learners to ask critical questions, such as 'Who is this for?' or 'In what context is this occurring?' It requires consideration of the learner's identity (who they are, what position they hold and what purpose they ultimately seek from their leadership). This is important, since, as I will go on to argue, it is only through the active reflection on one's own practice that such learning is made feasible. This places a huge importance on providing leader-learners with the skills (critical reflexivity) to enable them to challenge their thinking about how processes and practices work, both within and outside of organizations, so that they have the skills to act (performatively) with authenticity to challenge received wisdoms that go against these espoused values. The effects of this not only pave the way for a reconceptualizing of what 'real' business challenges 'actually' look like, but also have the power to transform our thinking about what it's possible to get done in society, through one's own leadership. I now move to consider each of these three considerations about what these critically reflexive practices look like both inside and outside of the classroom.

CONCEPTUALIZING WHAT BUSINESS MEANS IN A GLOBAL CONTEXT

One of the greatest dilemmas that modern-day BS face is in knowing how to teach and facilitate learning about the global challenges that businesses face, when they arise out of a direct consequence of following a globalized market economy. Much like the quotation from Bennis and O'Toole (2005) at the start of this chapter, being critically reflexive means paying close attention to the multiple ways in which political, social (less often) and economic drivers of business are defined and understood. It's why, when I teach about the contested nature of concepts (such as globalization, leadership or strategy, say), I deliberately focus on stimulating debate about their meaning in different contexts, times and spaces, to allow learners to draw their own conclusions about why this might be. This means going beyond describing terms (i.e., through definitions) to considering the multiple ways in which phenomena have come to be understood (conceptualized) over time. This places a high value on mining other disciplines, to see alternative meanings about the same topic (as we discuss below) and the use of conceptual frameworks (thereafter) as they highlight alternative contexts that we may not have considered (as with the term 'business' comprising hidden reference to small, medium-sized and large enterprises as well as organizational and non-organizational forms).

With regard to alternative meanings, for instance, in business management studies, the concept of neoliberalism as an economic driver is often described singularly as the 'primacy of private property', 'free choice in consumption' and a 'night-watchman role for the state' (Harvey 2006). But by turning to other disciplines such as critical geography we can see that Raco (2005: 328) reveals how this occurred more as a process, through an initial 'rolling back' of the frontiers of the welfare state (along with its savage critiques of the capacities and practices of post-war state management), followed by a later 'rolling out' of 'neoliberal state forms (along with its modes of governance and regulatory mechanisms)'. Fuller and Geddes (2008) show the value that separating out these 'processes of neoliberalism' has, in revealing the hidden values that underpin them; with Marxists seeing it as a ruling class strategy to accumulate capital by rolling back the state; whilst Thatcherite views are more about the rolling out of market-based principles through processes of privatization and partnership with the local state. This is important in our quest to challenge assumptions, as Crouch (2012) notes: a failure to conceptualize what is really meant by neoliberalism has led us to a non-critical adoption of it (i.e., hegemony) as a market mechanism, on the basis that it gets uncritically accepted, because there is seemingly no apparent alternative. We can see how these negative effects of liberalization policies (the free market efforts involved in the widespread removal of barriers to trade and the ease of the movement of capital) is largely bound up in the consequences of privatism (the breaking up and selling off of public assets). This ties the most modern meaning of neoliberalism to notions of nativism that have underpinned nationalistic President Trump and Brexit (see article in *The Conversation* by Kean Birch, https://theconversation.com/what -exactly-is-neoliberalism-84755).

Hence, whenever I'm preparing a new topic involving slides that introduce the global context, whilst it's always tempting (not least, for brevity) to select a few quotations about what this constitutes and how different scholars have come to define it, I take the opportunity as educator (and social responsibility as practitioner) to highlight the hidden nuances that reside there. This is with the intention of sparking debate about the range of meanings that exist and the different contexts in which they arise. Traditional critique here would normally focus on pointing out the similarities and differences between the definitions. But being critically reflective means acknowledging the potential for the same term to hold dual (or indeed multiple) meanings. This often means turning detective to see how other disciplines have come to understand the same term (such as the critical geography example above). Doing so rewards one with a much deeper understanding of its temporal dimension (how its meaning has changed over time).

With regard to conceptual frameworks, the same care needs to be taken with seemingly well-known concepts such as leadership: in practice, common parlance, but in theory, a highly contested concept whose meaning has shifted over time, such that there are claims that a 'conceptual confusion' has occurred (Mango 2018). As before, consulting interdisciplinary literature on leadership is absolutely key here, in understanding how the process and practice of leadership has come to be understood in different contexts. For instance, the leadership studies literature tells us that the process can be conceived as 'who leaders are' (their individual character traits), 'what leaders do' (the behaviour and skills they use) and 'the context in which it takes place' (the process used, the atmosphere created), as illustrated in Figure 16.1 (Northouse 2015). Teaching to these broader conceptual frameworks (and making frequent reference to them in the classroom and in assessment) acts as an aide-memoire for learners, enabling them to think more actively about which concept of leadership they are referring to (i.e., trait, behaviour or process), whenever they are using the term. Outside of the classroom in their practice of leading, this is just as important, because hidden within each broad category are different sets of assumptions about what might constitute leadership and how leadership is done, sanctioning opportunities for a learner to adopt a more distributed approach to leadership, irrespective of having a titular leadership role or not.

Helpful though this approach is to teaching about leadership, it is important (and ethical) to remind learners that there still remains a gap in knowledge about how all of these concepts (trait, behaviour, process) seemingly act together to 'make things happen' (Nicholds 2021). Doing so helps to explain the oft-cited lament that 'the more one learns about leadership, the less one knows' (Grint 2005). But it also aids in the development of learner identity, as it builds confidence to know that there are limitations to theory and scope for their (perhaps later) contribution to building this knowledge base, something that may fuel their desire to explore this issue at doctoral level. This is invaluable for BS in promoting learner progression.

Here, whilst it is scholars of critical management who have long been advocating the need for plugging gaps in our understanding about how leadership is really done in practice (Alvesson 1996; Alvesson and Spicer 2012; Alvesson and Deetz 2020), it is my job as an academic to challenge (always) what learners actually mean by it (both in the classroom and in assessment). Doing so not only offers a gentle but constant reminder of the need to be critically reflexive when referring to concepts that are highly contested, but also instils confidence that our understanding of these topics is live, and in constant flux. As I explore in the next section, learners can actively test these meanings in their assessments, but also through application to their workplaces in real life. Teaching conceptual frameworks, like the one above, provides them with the tools to make sense of an otherwise complex and seemingly bloated body of work that might otherwise be difficult to navigate, since it is only through real-life application that the true scope and limitations of these different theories is tested. Whilst learners may not fully appreciate the utility of their efforts until it comes to the assessment, it is the direct application to a real-life case of frameworks which requires the active application of concepts, such as the ones discussed above (such as their own workplace) which has the greatest impact on learning. It is to this more experiential form of learning that the discussion now turns.

Figure 16.1   Conceptualizing leadership

REFLECTING CRITICALLY ON WHAT ACTUALLY HAPPENS IN PRACTICE

When learning how to handle reflection in practice, whether inside or outside the classroom, learners often turn to the literature on a given subject rather than their own direct experience. Hence, bridging this rich enquiry with their own critical reflection on live cases (from their practice experience) allows the learner to directly compare their existing knowledge (from practice) with known theory, in order to test its utility. This process is much more than the types of 'rhetoric versus reality' discussions that often take place in BS, which Watson (1995) suggests (rather naively) assume that those involved in researching practice are divorced from its delivery (Watson 1995). Hence, being critically reflexive here suggests that to address gaps that arise in the implementing of strategy and policy is to bring to bear the range of meanings that concepts can hold for different actors (otherwise known as pluralism). It is also about recognizing (i.e., discursively), that the difference between saying one thing and being critical means being able to spot 'symbolism' (Watson 1995). Exploring symbolism in urban policy formed the focus of my own doctoral research, but it was only possible by asking practitioners what happens when they come to implement policy. This approach tends to be discomfiting because it draws on subjectivist forms of evidence, which have tended to be marginalized in social sciences (Alvesson 1996). But it is the only form of evidence that really counts when it comes to evaluating what works from the practitioner perspective.

This is where the value of direct personal experience through the process of reflection and action comes in (Moon 2004). Theories of reflection are at the heart of such 'informal learning', which place a value on the experience gained from practice and the development of skills to cope with change (Mullins 2010). Rooted pedagogically in so-called experiential learning theory, these approaches have emerged in response to the more traditional 'overly-rationalist' approach to learning which seeks to promote Aristotelian ideas that the only knowledge which counts is that which can be physically observed and measured (McNiff and Whitehead 2012). Historically, these ideas have formed the basis for debate since classical times about the nature of knowledge and whether it exists materially (i.e., in physical form) or ideally (i.e., constructed in the minds of others) (May 2001). But it is in the broader context of business in a post-industrial society that the desire to produce such universal truths remains strong (and therefore worthy of critique). Hence it can be witnessed in any number in fields in education, from science and technology to economics and politics, all of which are driven by an inherent need to know 'what works' in gaining competitive advantage in an increasingly globalized society (Suriñach and Moreno 2012).

Philosophically, then, the informal process of reflection brings with it criticism about its overly subjectivist stance. But from my experience of teaching critically, it is one which avid learners rarely manage to avoid for very long. Such concern is often linked to longstanding debates in the social sciences about the ontological nature of knowledge and whether it has material quality (materialism), or whether it has a more fluid and ambiguous quality which manifests as 'human meaning' (idealism) (May 2001). In business management studies, this historical debate has extended to concerns about what counts as evidence (epistemology) and whether knowledge has an objective quality (empiricism) or is constructed in thought (constructivism).

On the basis that no theory is value-free, there is scope to use critical reflexivity to scrutinize these taken-for-granted assumptions about the nature of knowledge, so that students (as future practitioners) can be more aware of the factors which shape and constrain how the outcomes of strategy and policy are measured. Pedagogically, this fits well with the work of Argyris and Schön's (1974) around 'double-loop learning' (below) which advocates that when goals, values, frameworks and, to a significant extent, strategies are taken for granted a form of 'single-loop learning' seems to be present. Double-loop learning (Figure 16.2), on the other hand, promotes the idea of a 'second-order observation' in which these underlying assumptions are challenged by 'questioning the role of the framing and learning systems which underlie actual goals and strategies' (Argyris and Schön 1974).

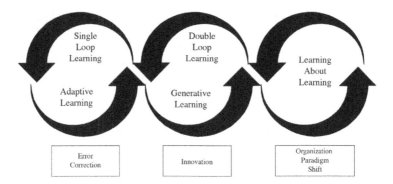

Figure 16.2   Double-loop learning

REFLECTING AUTHENTICALLY ON HOW LEADERS ACT ON THE WORLD

The third and final consideration in this chapter is how to develop the critically reflexive learner to consider how social as well as commercial goals might be met through the enactment of authentic practice (Nicholds et al. 2017). This requires learners to consider how aspects of their own leadership identity (or professional background) might play a part in shaping what is possible. The benefits of making such critical enquiry not only leads to novel insights, such as whether organizing rather than leading might be better, but also leads to rare insights where inequities might start to be challenged by focusing attention on the root causes of problems (Mthethwa-Somers 2013). Interest in this more practice-oriented research better situates the employment relationship in its global, economical political and socio-cultural context (Janssens and Steyaert 2009).

Here, being more critically reflexive (challenging received wisdoms) means being more 'performative' (acting more authentically) by questioning the impact of our and others' actions. In doing so, we are offered an opportunity to reflect on our personal and professional experience about how things might work in practice (in the context of known theory, of course) in the classroom. This provides BS with an opportunity to provide learners with the oft-requested 'toolkit' that they so often request, albeit a conceptual one. One which enables them to incorporate broad elements of their known 'culture' (i.e., by considering how things are 'done around here'), allows them to reflect on how issues 'actually' interact with their own 'personal values' (i.e., intent and purpose) and how this results in a form of identity formation (i.e., how they see themselves and how others see them). It is engaging in this process of critical reflexivity which allows social as well as commercial goals (Nicholds et al. 2017) to be met outside of the classroom too.

Here lies the academic identity work that can take place alongside teaching through critical reflexivity. In my role as associate professor at Staffordshire Business School, I am an academic who teaches across a range of postgraduate programmes involving the development of executive, senior leader apprenticeship and doctoral researcher learners. However, as an ex-practitioner, like my learners, I too share a body of practice knowledge which has been garnered over ten years of working as in healthcare management (as recruiter and nurse) in the NHS and private sector; and in regional development (as a public health and development officer) again in the NHS and third sector. However, whilst this provides me with access to a practical 'toolkit' to facilitate others' learning about their practice, it is only through academic enquiry that this critical enquiry is made possible. I say this because it is only through my late entrance into academia as a mature learner that the critical application of theory to practice has been possible, bringing with it a mechanism for evaluating the utility of management theory through the contribution it makes to improving practice. It is this dialogue between my 'practitioner-self' and 'academic-self' which helps to aid reflection on what these processes are and how they might be applied in practice (in different contexts). This aids the teaching of leadership learning, where authenticity must play an inevitable part. My goal, then, is always to support learners to act with social purpose in their own fields, by sharing with my peers ways of achieving this major feat with learners (just by being critically reflexive about how rather than what you teach) to interrogate the granted assumptions that are inherent within business management theory, that left unchecked result in a deepening of inequality.

For academics delivering such programmes, it is socially responsible to acknowledge that the global context we discussed earlier has impacted equally negatively on the very system which provides this level of higher education. Neoliberalism of higher education institutions has resulted in something of a blending of academic with corporate culture (Alvesson and Spicer 2016), which has had an intensified effect on academics' intellectual enquiry, sense of professionalism and autonomy as scholars (Olssen and Peters 2005). Turning to the literature once again shows how this 'blending of public as well as private learning spaces' (Whitchurch 2010) has led to struggles with the type of academic identity I describe above (Harris 2005), separating 'purist' types of academics (who always sought knowledge for knowledge's sake) from more 'careerist' types (who teach for student satisfaction and write to publish) (Learmonth and Humphreys 2012). This can act (and often does) as a barrier to much-needed 'industry professionals' (recruitment and employability staff) who seek to generate new sources of income through enterprise and business roles (Whitchurch 2010). This represents something of a challenge for business schools (especially in less research-intensive institutions) as it means they not only have a challenging role to play in designing academic provision that's relevant (as I've been describing in this chapter), but also one which provides a supportive enough setting for the important identity work of the (now) very different academic, practitioner and professional services staff that are essential to its delivery. This unique context means paying attention to not just how we have come to understand (conceptualize) business management concepts, but also how to take account of the many different stakeholders that are now seemingly involved. This places greater emphasis not only on the different identities they inhabit (through professional development), but also on the need to pay attention to the different workplace cultures that they require in order to flourish. This simple yet essential tool of critical reflexivity is one way of enabling existing and future leaders to consider the hugely complex terrain that they are working with; and crucially, how this is performed alongside others too. Just asking simple (yet critical) questions, such as 'How are you defining that term?' or 'What context is this taking place in?' or 'Who is this ultimately for?' often sparks huge discussion about the types of values driving their and others' businesses processes and practices, which in turn leads to further discussion about access to resources (and the inherent inequality that goes with it). BS can add value through their civic role by contributing to improving their local communities socio-economically.

CONCLUSION

Critical management studies has long provided BS with the tools to challenge the utility of business management theory to practice, but it has been criticized for claiming the need to revolutionize whilst failing to act (Learmonth et al. 2012). Critical reflection is borne out of this tradition, through the active work of management learning scholars in exploring new ways of researching organizational social life. Classical and contemporary theories in business management have much to offer us in making sense of these changing and complex times. Many of the esteemed practitioners and scholars that I've had the privilege of working with thus far, draw on a wide range of theories in support of 'best practice' (or 'best fit', as my colleagues in human resources would seek to argue). But as an ex-practitioner and interdisciplinary scholar, I am afforded the highly privileged position of being able to draw on and (most importantly) critique these ways of doing (and being), to draw conclusions about their utility and worth for achieving different business (commercial and social) goals.

As the architectures of such enquiry, BS must lend their support to these different 'real-world' campaigns, by working to bring together practitioners and academics inside and outside of the classroom, by openly acknowledging the flaws in different theories, and must 'explore alternatives' (Learmonth et al. 2012: 15). This is what King (2015) refers to as the 'politics of the possible' (Gibson-Graham 2006) in helping to raise awareness of 'what doesn't work' in practice, and of the natural dilemmas faced, by translating meaning. Whatever the context, whether in terms of academic identity or in supporting leader-learners' identity as future leaders, by encouraging those around us to be more critically reflexive of what we see and experience we are better able to build awareness of the rhetoric of theory versus the practical realities of implementation, whilst remaining open to the potential for working collectively with others towards an alternative reality.

Aside from any inherent perils associated with challenging the status quo, the idea of the critically reflexive learner is in knowing personally that it's impossible to have all the answers and that there is greater scope for addressing business issues across the disciplines. This opens up a wonderful space for learning which is not only as empowering for the learner as it is for the academic facilitating it, but which when actively applied, holds the means for questioning the status quo of any business, with the potential for invoking change where perhaps other policies have failed. In teaching about research design, it is this type of critical questioning which always leads me to problematize issues (by acknowledging their inherent complexity), rather than merely stating a problem (as if accepting the reason for its existence as a fait accompli). It is this more critical approach in research that has led to my active use of concepts in my writing about failing policy, 'by putting concepts to work' (Spicer 2009) where they can be actively tested, their flaws revealed and opportunities for a reconceptualization to occur (through a kind of practical politics). It is these efforts that will enable a real dialogue to take place with the actors involved, and questioning of received wisdom about how things are done around here!

NOTE

1.   In my own doctoral research, I explored the contradictions and tensions of implementing urban regeneration by speaking with 50 practitioners who were involved in delivering it, to reveal a deep

commitment to its success whilst being aware of its inherent failure to tackle the root causes of deprivation.

REFERENCES

Alvesson, M. (1996) Leadership studies: from procedure and abstraction to reflexivity and situation. *Leadership Quarterly* 7 (4): 455–485.

Alvesson, M. and Spicer, A. (2012) Critical leadership studies: the case for critical performativity. *Human Relations* 65 (3): 367–390.

Alvesson, M. and Spicer, A. (2016) (Un)Conditional surrender? Why do professionals willingly comply with managerialism? *Journal of Organisational Change Management* 29 (1): 29–45.

Alvesson, M. and Deetz, S. (2020) *Doing Critical Management Research*, London: SAGE.

Argyris, C. and Schön, D. (1974) *Theory in Practice: Increasing Professional Effectiveness*, San Francisco, CA: Jossey-Bass.

Bennis, W. and O'Toole, J. (2005) How business schools lost their way. *Harvard Business Review* 83 (5): 96–104.

Christophers, B. (2013) Wild dragons in the city: urban political economy, affordable housing development and the performative world-making of economic models. *International Journal of Urban and Regional Research*. DOI:10.1111/1468-2427.12037.

Crouch, C. (2012) The strange non-death of neoliberalism. *Journal of Social Policy* 41 (4) 838–840.

Fournier, V. and Grey, C. (2000) At the critical moment: conditions and prospects for critical management studies. *Human Relations* 53 (1): 7–32.

Fuller, C. and Geddes, M. (2008) Urban governance under neo-liberalism: New Labour and the structuring of state-space. *Antipode* 40: 252–282.

Gibney, J. and Nicholds, A. (2021) Re-imagining place leadership as social purpose. In: Sotarauta, M. and Beer, A. (eds), *The Handbook of City and Regional Leadership*, Cheltenham, UK and Northampton, MA, USA: Edward Elgar Publishing.

Gibson-Graham, J.K. (2006) *A Postcapitalist Politics*, Minneapolis, MN: University of Minnesota Press.

Grint, K. (2005) *Leadership: Limits and Possibilities*, Basingstoke: Palgrave Macmillan.

Harris, S. (2005) Rethinking academic identities in neoliberal times. *Teaching in Higher Education* 10 (4): 421–433.

Harvey, D. (2006) *Spaces of Global Capitalism: Towards a Theory of Uneven Geographical Development*. New York: Verso.

Janssens, M. and Steyaert, C. (2009) HRM and performance: a plea for reflexivity in HRM studies. *Journal of Management Studies* 46 (1): 143–155. DOI: 10.1111/j.1467-6486.2008.00812.x.

King, D. (2015) The possibilities and perils of critical performativity: learning from four case studies. *Scandinavian Journal of Management* 31 (2): 225–265.

Koss Hartmann, R. (2014) Subversive functionalism: for a less canonical critique in critical management studies. *Human Relations* 67 (5): 611–632

Learmonth, M. and Humphreys, M. (2012) Autoethnography and academic identity: glimpsing business school doppelgangers. *Organisation* 19 (1): 99–117.

Learmonth, M., Lockett, A. and Dowd, K. (2012) Promoting scholarship that matters: the usefulness of useful research and the usefulness of useless research. *British Journal of Management* 23 (1). DOI: 1 0.1111/j.1467-8551.2011.00754.x.

Mango, E. (2018) Rethinking leadership theories. *Open Journal of Leadership* 7: 57–88. doi: 10.4236/ojl.2018.71005.

May, T. (2001) *Social Research: Issues, Methods and Process*, 3rd edition, Buckingham: Open University Press.

McNiff, J. and Whitehead, J. (2012) *Action Research Living Theory*, London: SAGE.

Moon, J.A. (2004) *A Handbook of Reflective and Experiential Learning: Theory and Practice*, London: RoutledgeFalmer.

Mthethwa-Sommers, S. (2013) Pedagogical possibilities: lessons from social justice educators. *Journal of Transformative Education* 10: 219.

Mullins, L.J. (2010) *Management and Organisational Behaviour*, 9th edition, London: Pearson

Nicholds, A. (2012) Building capacity for regeneration: making sense of ambiguity in urban policy outcomes. PhD thesis, University of Birmingham. https://etheses.bham.ac.uk/id/eprint/3495/1/Nicholds12PhD.pdf.

Nicholds, A. (2021) Old wine in a new bottle: revisiting organisational conceptions of leadership to understand what place leaders 'actually' do to make things happen. In: Sotarauta, M. and Beer, A. (eds), *The Handbook of City and Regional Leadership*, Cheltenham, UK and Northampton, MA, USA: Edward Elgar Publishing.

Nicholds, A., Gibney, J., Mabey, C. and Hart, D. (2017) Making sense of variety in place leadership. *Regional Studies*, 51 (2): 249–259. doi:10.1080/00343404.2016.1232482.

Northouse, P.G. (2015) *Leadership: Theory and Practice*, 7th edition, London: SAGE.

Olssen, M. and Peters. M.A. (2005) Neoliberalism, higher education and the knowledge economy: from the free market to knowledge capitalism. *Journal of Education Policy* 20 (3). DOI: 10.1080/02680930500108718.

Raco, M. (2005) Sustainable development, rolled out neoliberalism and sustainable communities. *Antipode* 37 (2): 324–347.

Suriñach, J. and Moreno, R. (2012) Introduction: intangible assets and regional economic growth. *Regional Studies* 46 (10): 1277–1281.

Thompson, P. (2011) The trouble with HRM. *Human Resource Management Journal* 21 (4): 355–367.

Tomkins, L. and Nicholds, A. (2017) Make me authentic, but not here: reflexive struggles with academic identity and authentic leadership. *Management Learning*, 16 January. https://doi.org/10.1177%2F1350507616684267.

Watson, T. (1995) In search of HRM: beyond the rhetoric and reality distinction or the case of the dog that didn't bark. *Personnel Review* 24 (4): 6–16.

Whitchurch, C. (2010) Some implications of public/private space for professional identities in higher education. *Higher Education* 60: 627–640.

17. New avenues for leadership education and development: shaping leader identity through meaning-making from experiences

Sonja Zaar, Piet Van den Bossche and Wim Gijselaers

INTRODUCTION

Teaching and learning leadership at business schools is a recent trend in higher education (Eich, 2008; Sternberg, 2011). Leadership education is highly in demand, on-campus leadership development initiatives are proliferating, and business schools are increasingly emphasizing the development of leaders and leadership in their mission statements, curricula and programs (DeRue et al., 2011). To develop leaders and leadership, business schools offer a variety of experiences predominantly aimed at sharing knowledge about the traditional trait and behavioral theories of leadership, and at providing opportunities for students to practice a requisite set of leadership skills (Petriglieri & Petriglieri, 2015). Research has demonstrated that these knowledge-driven and skills-based activities serve a valuable purpose in building students' leadership capacity and effectiveness (Dugan, 2011). At the same time, however, research also shows that the effect sizes for these activities actually often remain relatively small (Murphy & Johnson, 2011). This would suggest that the existing knowledge-based and skills-based approach to leadership education at business schools by itself is not enough and that something else is needed to develop leaders and leadership more effectively.

One thing that contemporary research is starting to show is that acquiring a sense of being a leader – a leader identity – is an essential ingredient for leadership development to occur (Day & Dragoni, 2015; Day et al., 2009). Leader identity is a deeper-level cognitive component of leadership that refers to the extent to which a person thinks of themself as a leader rather than a follower (Day & Harrison, 2007). It serves as an organizing force and motivating mechanism for thinking and acting as a leader (Lord & Hall, 2005). Furthermore, it functions as a developmental driver for seeking out and pursuing opportunities to practice and learn leadership (Day et al., 2009). People who identify as a leader are more likely to feel confident and motivated to engage in leadership experiences, to practise leadership and develop leadership knowledge, skills and abilities. This provides the foundation for continuous and ongoing leadership development and future leadership effectiveness. The centrality or importance of the leader identity plays a key role in this (Kwok et al., 2018). A leader identity that is central to a person is more stable and relevant across a wide range of life domains (such as work, community, family and friendship), functions as a cue for activating prior knowledge and skills relevant to leadership, and thereby influences information processing, self-efficacy, motivation and behavior more powerfully (Cross & Markus, 1994; Markus, 1977). Conversely, a leader identity that is not central to a person is less stable and relevant across domains, has a low activation potential, and is thereby less powerful in impacting information processing, self-efficacy, motivation and behavior (Cross & Markus, 1994; Markus, 1977).

In this way, leader identity explains the potential outcomes of leadership education and leadership development activities (Kragt & Guenter, 2018). It explains why students who see themselves as a leader, or at least see being a leader as a possible self, are more likely to seek out opportunities to exhibit leadership (i.e., enact leadership and emerge as leaders) as well as to foster their leadership capabilities (i.e., engage in ongoing leadership development) (Kwok et al., 2018; Miscenko et al., 2017). Their existing knowledge and skills are activated and more readily available for processing new information (Lord & Maher, 1993). This makes them feel more confident about and believe in their ability to practise leadership. It motivates them to engage in activities to further develop leadership (e.g., leadership experiences, taking up leadership roles) (Chan & Drasgow, 2001). Over time, this creates the foundation for continuous and ongoing leadership development and future workplace leadership effectiveness (Day & Sin, 2011; Komives & Dugan, 2014). In contrast, this also explains why students with a leader identity that is not important to them, and who do not view themselves as a leader, are most likely not inclined to demonstrate leadership and will probably shy away from opportunities to further develop leadership capabilities. The prior knowledge and skills activation potential is low, making them feel less confident about their ability to enact leadership. It negatively impacts self-efficacy and provides little incentive or motivation to act or behave as a leader. Over time, this creates the foundation for diminishing engagement in leadership development, and limited workplace leadership effectiveness. Taken together, this research shows that developing leaders and leadership is not only a matter of building knowledge and skills. It is a matter of change in knowledge, skills and identity. Given these research insights, it seems imperative for business schools to include leader identity as part of their leadership education.

What seems to be missing is that we lack substantial understanding of how to pay attention to leader identity development in leadership education (Komives et al., 2006). A rich body of conceptual and empirical work on leadership development shows that experiences are considered as the main driver for learning leadership (McCall, 2004; Van Velsor et al., 2010). Research, however, is unclear about how classroom experiences at business schools contribute to leader identity development and how classroom experiences can be designed to promote and enhance leader identity (Day et al., 2009; Komives, 2011; Petriglieri & Petriglieri, 2010). Existing research lines on how leadership development is influenced by experiences and on leadership development as identity work are quite disconnected. Therefore, it is useful to have a coherent framework that brings together these two lines of research and helps in organizing and synthesizing the existing literature (DeRue & Myers, 2014). This allows leadership educators to acquire a better understanding of the connections between leadership development, leader identity and learning from experiences, thereby showing possibilities for integrating leader identity work into leadership development offerings. Moreover, this would help business schools in strengthening the development of leadership in their programs, and increase the developmental impact of their initiatives.

The present chapter brings together existing research on leadership development, leader identity and learning from experiences. It offers an integrated and theoretically grounded framework, exhibited in Figure 17.1, that can assist business schools in integrating leader identity development into leadership education. In the following sections, we start by introducing our framework and explain its components. We continue by elaborating on the process of leader identity development, and highlight how leadership education can purposefully leverage classroom experiences as so-called holding environments for shaping and developing students' identity as a leader. Last, we describe the developmental features of classroom experiences and the contextual features of the immediate learning environment that promote and enhance students' leader identity development. Here we also provide examples of how these features can be designed into leadership education.

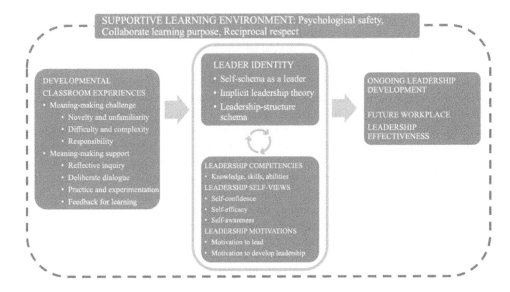

Figure 17.1   *A framework for students' leader identity development through classroom experiences*

AN ORGANIZING FRAMEWORK

Starting at the right-hand side of the model, the box portrays the distal outcome of ongoing leadership development and future workplace leadership effectiveness through engaging in classroom experiences. Leadership development is a process of change that occurs in context and spans an entire lifetime (Day et al., 2009). Experiences are considered the main driver for learning and developing leadership (McCall, 2004; Van Velsor et al., 2010). Development occurs when individuals develop increasingly dynamic and complex ways of conceptualizing and practising leadership (Day & Dragoni, 2015; DeRue & Myers, 2014). Ongoing leadership development then refers to continuous engagement in a wide variety of developmental experiences, that can range across settings and domains, and can occur at all ages and stages of the lifespan (DeRue & Myers, 2014; Hammond et al., 2017; McCauley et al., 2010). Examples of ongoing leadership development experiences could involve formal leadership programs, mentoring and coaching relationships, self-development initiatives or on-the-job assignments (Day et al., 2009; Murphy & Johnson, 2011).

Leadership effectiveness refers to observable, behavioral levels of leadership competencies and the degree to which an individual is considered by others to be successful in enacting leadership within and across specific settings or contexts (Johnson et al., 2012; Kragt & Guenter, 2018). Overall, research has demonstrated that leadership experiences positively influence leadership effectiveness (Avolio et al., 2009; Day & Sin, 2011). More specifically, research shows that leadership experiences at college, university and business school positively impact later workplace leadership effectiveness (Dugan, 2011; Komives & Dugan, 2014). As leadership effectiveness is in the eye of the beholder and contingent on individual differences and context (Engle & Lord, 2011; Hall & Lord, 1995; Martin & Epitropaki, 2001), this could entail various types of leadership (e.g., transformational leadership, servant leadership, leader–member exchange) that could be considered effective.

Continuing to the core of the model, the center box includes leader identity as a proximal outcome of classroom experiences, and as a mediating factor between classroom experiences and ongoing leadership development and leadership effectiveness. Leader identity is the subcomponent of an individual's overall identity that relates to the degree to which a person considers themself to be a leader rather than a follower (Day et al., 2009; Lord & Hall, 2005). Theory suggests, and recent initial empirical evidence confirms, that it includes one's self-schema as a leader ("Who am I as a leader?"), one's perspective on leadership or leadership-structure schema ("What is leadership to me?"), and one's perspective about others as leaders or implicit leadership theory ("Who do I consider to be a leader?") (DeRue & Ashford, 2010; Guillén et al., 2015; Hammond et al., 2017; Zheng & Muir, 2015). Or, in other words, how students view leadership and see others as leaders relates to how they see themselves as a leader. Together these views impact the degree to which they see themselves as a leader, that is, their leader identity.

The center box also depicts leadership competencies (i.e., knowledge, skills and abilities), leadership self-views (i.e., self-awareness, self-confidence, self-efficacy) and leadership motivations (i.e., motivation to lead, motivation to develop leadership) as proximal outcomes of classroom experiences (Murphy & Johnson, 2011). Both theory and empirical evidence indicate that classroom experiences contribute to leadership development of students by building leadership capacity (knowledge, skills and abilities) and leadership self-efficacy (the internalized belief system about one's capacity) (Dugan, 2011). Furthermore, research evidence shows that quantity and quality of leadership experiences impact the level of students' motivation to lead (Chan & Drasgow, 2001). Accumulated experiences over time that enhance self-awareness and self-efficacy, positively impact motivation to lead. Recent theorizing suggests that leader identity interacts with these other proximal outcomes of classroom experiences in a reciprocal fashion, as leader identity functions as a cue for activating and accessing prior knowledge and skills related to leadership, thereby impacting information processing, motivation and self-efficacy (Ashford & DeRue, 2012; Cross & Markus, 1994; Hannah et al., 2009; Ibarra, 1999). In turn, enhanced leadership capacity, motivation and self-efficacy strengthen leader identity (Miscenko et al., 2017; Zaar et al., 2020).

Moving to the left side of the model, the first box shows the classroom experiences that shape leadership development by contributing to leader identity development of students. Classroom experiences refer to the formal leadership interventions that occur in the curriculum, such as in leadership courses, workshops and trainings (Komives & Dugan, 2014). Given that not all experiences are equally developmental (Dewey, 1938; McCall, 2004), the extent to which classroom experiences result in leader identity is dependent on specific developmental features of the experience. It goes without saying that classroom experiences are not the only experiences contributing to students' leadership development during their time at business school. In this chapter, however, we focus on classroom experiences as these are experiences that leadership educators can most directly influence to purposefully design for leadership development. As a side note, although we are cognizant of and fully underwrite the important role that individual factors (e.g., learning orientation, feedback-seeking behavior, self-regulation) also play in the process of learning from experience, our emphasis here is on the developmental features of classroom experiences and their immediate learning environment.

Last, the model includes the contextual factors of the micro learning environment that moderate the extent to which classroom experiences result in leader identity development, and the extent to which leader identity results in ongoing leadership development and future leadership effectiveness. Research is clear that context matters in leadership development, and that particular contextual features of the environment in which learning occurs can be beneficial (or detrimental) for developing leaders and leadership (Van Velsor et al., 2010). The micro learning environment refers to the immediate setting of the learner in which learning is socially constructed (Kolb & Kolb, 2005).

Taken together, the framework depicts: (1) that classroom experiences shape ongoing leadership development and future workplace leadership effectiveness through the mediating factor of leader identity; (2) that leader identity interacts with other proximal outcomes of classroom experiences in a reciprocal fashion; and (3) that these relationships are moderated by the contextual features of the micro learning environment. The extent to which classroom experiences result in leader identity development is contingent on the developmental features of the classroom experience. In the next section, we elaborate on the process of leader identity development and the important role that leadership education can play in this process.

LEADER IDENTITY DEVELOPMENT

Leader identity is a multifaceted construct that is grounded in meaning-making and shaped through a dynamic process of learning from experiences (DeRue & Ashford, 2010; Hammond et al., 2017). It is a multifaceted construct as it includes various cognitive schemas related to leadership and being a leader (Zaar et al., 2020). More precisely, theory suggests, and recent empirical evidence demonstrates, that leader identity is related to one's perspective on how leadership is organized in groups (leadership-structure schema), one's perspective about others as leaders (implicit leadership theory), and one's understanding of oneself as a leader (self-schema as a leader) (DeRue & Ashford, 2010; Guillén et al., 2015; Hammond et al., 2017; Zheng & Muir, 2015). People claim a leader identity based on their understanding of leadership and compared to who they view as leaders. The more alignment there is between these various views, and the broader and more complex an individual's view on leadership and being a leader, the stronger the leader identity (Zaar et al., 2020). These findings indicate that shaping and developing leader identity involves aligning views on leadership and being a leader, as well as broadening and increasing complexity in understandings of leadership.

Leader identity development is a dynamic process in the sense that it involves gains and losses (Freund & Baltes, 1998) and does not develop in a solely linear fashion towards a more positive self-perception as a leader (Kegan, 1982). In fact, longitudinal studies show that leader identity develops in a curvilinear mode, that is, in a J-shaped curve (Day & Sin, 2011; Miscenko et al., 2017). Initially, leader identity changes follow a negative development trend, with an upturn towards the end of the developmental experience. This indicates that leader identity development involves leader identity construction and deconstruction (Miscenko et al., 2017). Leader identity deconstruction – that is, temporary destabilization of the current identity by eliciting and questioning current views on leadership and being a leader – facilitates identity change. It makes room for broadening and increasing complexity in thinking about leadership and leaders, and for a new identity to be constructed. This dynamic process of leader identity construction and deconstruction is prompted by experiences.

Drawing on experiential learning theory (Dewey, 1938; Kolb, 1984), leadership development begins with individuals engaging in concrete experiences that challenge their existing ways of thinking and doing, and elicit the need to learn and develop. The challenge is needed to get people out of their comfort zone and review their habitual ways of thinking and acting (McCauley et al., 2010). Without this challenge, people usually do not feel the need to develop new ways of thinking and acting. Experiences that challenge current ways of meaning-making of leadership and being a leader provide the prompt or trigger for leader identity destabilization by creating uncertainty, confusion or frustration. The challenging experience then creates a disequilibrium, providing the incentive or motivation to stabilize a leader identity rendered fragile, or to transition toward a new one (Petriglieri & Petriglieri, 2010). This involves attempts to reinterpret the experience in ways that allow individuals to maintain their current way of meaning-making of leadership and being a leader, or change to a new way of meaning-making of leadership and being a leader.

Too much challenge, however, can hinder learning from experiences. Experiences that present individuals with demands that far exceed their current capabilities and overly challenge them have been shown to hinder their leadership development (DeRue & Wellman, 2009). Participants found these experiences overwhelming, causing stress and anxiety. This diverts focus, attention and interest away from the experience, and blocks learning from the experience (Boud & Walker, 1998; Fiedler & Garcia, 1987). People then come away from an experience having learned little to contribute to their leader identity development, having learned nothing at all, or even having learned the wrong lessons. The last of these is particularly detrimental for leadership development when people, for example, come away from an experience thinking that being a leader is something that they can never attain.

Receiving adequate support can offset potential negative effects of challenge (DeRue & Wellman, 2009; McCauley et al., 2010). Receiving support is about assisting the learner in reflecting on experiences and engaging in constructive meaning-making of experiences (Schon, 1987). Support in learning from experiences for leader identity development involves facilitating meaning-making of leadership and being a leader, and reducing disturbing emotions such as stress and anxiety that come with being challenged in current ways of meaning-making (Petriglieri & Petriglieri, 2010). It is about providing support in making meaning of new perspectives on leadership and new ways of being a leader, by building on existing perceptions and frameworks and offering new ways of thinking and acting. It is to provide a cognitive bridge for learning by connecting and linking what is new with what already exists (Boud & Walker, 1998). It also involves assistance in providing opportunity to elaborate on, experiment with and consolidate meanings associated to the self as a leader (Ibarra, 1999; Ibarra et al., 2010). This can be achieved by creating collective arrangements, such as work methods or learning structures, and by installing rituals or practices that signal growth and development (Petriglieri & Petriglieri, 2010). With the support of seniors and peers, individuals can then shape and discover who they are as a leader and who they want to become as a leader.

Receiving support also refers to a supportive learning environment. This is the immediate environment in which learning takes place, the micro learning environment. It provides support by promoting feelings of safety and reassurance in the learning process (Kolb & Kolb, 2005; Van Velsor et al., 2010). It offers a formal or informal social arrangement that brings belonging, affiliation and identification to the foreground by providing, for example, recognition and encouragement for attempts at leading (DeRue & Ashford, 2010; Petriglieri & Petriglieri, 2010). This sends the message that a new equilibrium can be found on the other side of change (McCauley et al., 2010). In this way, receiving support turns cognitive and emotional turmoil into meaning (Petriglieri & Petriglieri, 2010).

Taken together, this existing research indicates that shaping and developing students' leader identity requires a social setting in which experiences are offered that challenge current ways of conceptualizing leadership and being a leader, and provide support in meaning-making of new perspectives on leadership and being a leader. These experiences should be embedded in a micro learning environment that offers safety and reassurance in the learning process. Research has conceptualized such settings as 'holding environments' (Kegan & Lahey, 2009; Petriglieri & Petriglieri, 2010). The classroom, as a holding environment for students' leader identity development, assists students in consolidating an existing identity (identity stabilization) or in transitioning to a new one (identity transition) (Petriglieri & Petriglieri, 2010). Leadership education can purposefully leverage the classroom as a holding environment for shaping and developing students' identity by designing specific developmental features in, and particular contextual features around, classroom experiences. We turn to these in the next section.

THE CLASSROOM AS A HOLDING ENVIRONMENT FOR LEADER IDENTITY DEVELOPMENT

We begin by discussing the developmental features of experiences that challenge existing ways of meaning-making of leadership and being a leader, and the developmental features of experiences that support new ways of meaning-making of leadership and being a leader. Next, we discuss the contextual features of the micro learning environment that support the learning process. While in practice these features are closely interconnected, in this chapter we conceptually separate the developmental features of experiences and the contextual features of the learning environment, in order to better discuss them.

Developmental Features of Experiences that Challenge Meaning-Making

From the existing literature, we distinguish three main developmental features of experiences that challenge existing ways of meaning-making of leadership and being a leader. These are: (1) novelty and unfamiliarity; (2) difficulty and complexity; and (3) responsibility. These features of meaning-making challenge push the student out of their comfort zone and into the zone of proximal learning (McCauley et al., 2010).

Novelty and unfamiliarity
The developmental feature of novelty and unfamiliarity refers to the classroom experience being new or unknown to the students. It entails students encountering a situation for the first time ("I have never done that before") or encountering a known situation with different aspects to it ("I have done that before, yet not with such a diverse group of people"). Drawing on activation theory (Scott, 1966), when an individual is unfamiliar with a task or situation, or when a person is exposed to a task or situation that is new to them, a heightened sense of arousal is

created within the individual that is positively linked to behavior and cognition. The novelty and unfamiliarity therefore spark interest and motivation to engage in meaning-making and learning. A relatively straightforward example of a classroom experience that challenges existing ways of meaning-making of leadership, and being a leader through novelty and unfamiliarity, is presenting students with new knowledge and information on how leadership develops. As research shows that the majority of students view leadership as an hierarchical position in an organization and define leadership as what people in positions in authority do (Komives et al., 2005; Wagner, 2011), providing them a perspective of leadership as relational or shared can trigger meaning-making.

Difficulty and complexity
The developmental feature of difficulty and complexity refers to the experience being academically challenging for the students. It includes students encountering a task or situation that they find difficult because it requires thinking beyond their current frames of reference ("I do not understand why people would consider this person a leader") or encountering a task or situation that is too complex to unravel alone ("I understand that I could be a leader, yet I am unable to make sense of it on my own"). It also refers to the experience being ambiguous and open to more than one interpretation, and where a range of views or perspectives should be accounted for. The experience then requires students to process distinct elements simultaneously, deal with multiple demands simultaneously, or manage multiple opposing or seemingly conflicting demands (DeRue & Wellman, 2009). This can be done, for example, by small group projects in which students from various cultures, gender, racial and ethnical background work together on an academic task. The academic task could involve working as a self-organized team in which no one has direct authority, or asking them to reflect on leading–following interactions occurring throughout the group work process.

Responsibility

The developmental feature of responsibility relates to the experience requiring students to take on responsibility, being allocated responsibility, or to manage high levels of responsibility (DeRue & Wellman, 2009). It involves students being allocated responsibility to take on leadership by, for example, allocating them roles and responsibilities to lead small group work or class discussions. It includes students being offered or allocated projects that require high levels of responsibility, such as for example working on and leading a real-life project for an organization. The feature of responsibility challenges current ways of meaning-making of leadership and being a leader by providing assessment data on their attempt at practising leadership (McCauley et al., 2010). These data can come from teachers and peers and can be formal (e.g., examination, assignments, performance evaluations) or informal (e.g., observing others' reactions to one's ideas about leading a group, receiving unsolicited feedback) (McCauley et al., 1994).

Developmental Features of Experiences that Support Meaning-Making

The previously discussed features of classroom experiences trigger and challenge students to review and rethink their current ways of meaning-making of leaders and leadership. Given that challenge alone is not sufficient for individuals to be able to find and establish new ways of meaning-making, support in meaning-making of new ways of thinking about leaders and leadership is needed the facilitate learning from experiences. From the existing literature, we distinguish four main developmental features of meaning-making support. These are: (1) reflective inquiry; (2) deliberate dialogue; (3) practice and application; and (4) feedback for learning. These features of meaning-making support assist students to craft, revise or affirm who they are as a leader; experiment with different leader roles and leadership responsibilities; and decide what to incorporate in their persona (Avolio & Vogelgesang, 2011; Komives & Dugan, 2014). In this way, the meaning-making support facilitates students being in the zone of proximal learning and prevents them from entering the zone of anxiety (McCauley et al., 2010).

Reflective inquiry
The developmental feature of reflective inquiry refers to the posing of critical, open questions about the meaning of leaders and leadership. This is in order to elicit existing knowledge, beliefs and ideas about leaders and leadership, and show variety in existing perspectives on leadership and being a leader, which sets the scene for revisiting these meanings (Schyns et al., 2012). This can be done by asking students to answer three simple, yet foundational questions: "What is leadership?", "Who is a leader?" and "Are you a leader?" These questions prompt students to engage in reflection on what they believe constitutes leadership and being a leader. Sharing the answers to these questions with the entire class or in small groups allows students to gain insight to the variety of perspectives on leaders and leadership, and encourages reflection on the usefulness of currently held views.

Deliberate dialogue
The developmental feature of deliberate dialogue refers to having open discussions and debate about leadership and leaders. Where the reflective inquiry serves to draw out and exchange existing knowledge, beliefs and ideas about leadership from a variety of backgrounds and perspectives, the deliberate dialogue serves to stimulate discussion and debate about varying beliefs about leadership and being a leader. Disagreement and criticism are assets rather than impediments to learning. In addition to input from a reflective inquiry exercise, deliberate dialogue can be further stimulated by, for example, a drawing exercise that asks students to draw what effective leadership looks like (Schyns et al., 2011). This image can be a sketch of people, symbols, diagrams or events, and include followers, metaphors and key words or phrases (Clapp-Smith et al., 2019). It would then serve as a talking point for articulating meanings of leadership held, and sharing interpretations.

Practice and application
The developmental feature of practice and application refers to providing students with the opportunity to transfer knowledge to know-how and apply what they conceptually learned to real-life settings. Put simply, students can shape leader identity by practising leadership. Building on theories of human development, research shows that practice (i.e., experimentation, repetition and reinforcement within and across experiences), and in particular deliberate practice (i.e., dedicated practice on a particular task with appropriate feedback), extends, refines and internalizes new ways of conceptualizing and practising leadership (Ericsson et al., 1993; Kolb, 1984). By practising leadership, individually and collectively, students can experiment with being a leader and taking leadership responsibility, can practise to overcome

challenges and fear, and reinforce and extend lessons learned from prior experiences (DeRue & Myers, 2014).

This can be done in a variety of ways. For example, students can be engaged in practising leadership through allocating them roles and positions of facilitating learning in the classroom and teaching fellow students, through providing opportunities to give individual and group presentations, and by assigning small group projects to experience leading–following interactions. Through small group projects students can learn to practice collaborative leadership by identifying their own ways of being effective as a leader, by taking on various team roles of being leader and follower, and by together finding ways of developing as a team. Repeating these activities within and across courses can be particularly powerful in helping students realize the development of their ways of conceptualizing and practising leadership.

Feedback for learning

The developmental feature of practice and application can be made even more impactful when coupled with feedback for learning. Cognitive theories of learning (Kraiger et al., 1993) posit that feedback availability helps with reducing evaluation uncertainties that arise when presented with challenging situations. It reduces the likelihood that cognitive resources are diverted away from the task and the learning process. Theories and models of learning and leadership development (Avolio, 2004; Ericsson et al., 1993; Kolb, 1984) in particular emphasize the importance of availability of systematic and evaluative feedback, as it provides the student with essential input on the appropriateness and usefulness of thoughts, emotions and behavior for attaining learning goals and objectives. It gives them an evaluative assessment of where they are now: their current strengths as a leader, the level of their current performance or leader effectiveness, and their primary leadership development needs (McCauley et al., 2010).

Feedback for learning can be purposefully designed in classroom experiences by systematically incorporating a feedback moment in the classroom experience set-up. Students are expected to actively engage in feedback moments by asking for feedback as well as by providing feedback in each classroom session that they have together. These feedback moments are timely and given immediately after practice and application has taken place. They are also specific, based on direct observation or received data; and actionable, that is, practical and progress-oriented. In addition, these feedback moments are inclusive, involving all members of the group as feedback givers and feedback receivers, so that all group members participate in and benefit from the feedback. Finally, these feedback moments are mindful in the sense that feedback is delivered in a respectful and empowering way.

Contextual Features of the Micro Learning Environment

The extent to which classroom experiences result in leader identity development, and the extent to which leader identity results in ongoing leadership development and future leadership effectiveness, is likely to differ depending on the contextual features of the micro learning environment. From the existing literature, we distinguish three contextual features of learning environments that have been shown to positively impact leadership development. These are: (1) psychological safety; (2) collaborative learning purpose; and (3) reciprocal respect.

Psychological safety
Research demonstrates that environments which are psychologically safe promote learning and leadership development (Garvin et al., 2008; Kolb & Kolb, 2005). Psychological safety refers to an environment in which people feel confident and safe to express their views and opinions, speak up with ideas and thoughts, experiment and make mistakes, and can do all this without having to fear negative consequences, such as punishment or humiliation, for doing so (Edmondson & Lei, 2014). This reduces potential disturbing emotions such as stress and anxiety that come with being challenged in current ways of meaning-making (Petriglieri & Petriglieri, 2010).

Collaborative learning purpose
Collaborative learning purpose refers to an environment that emphasizes the reasons for why learning is shared, that creates a sense of belonging, and recognizes or validates attempts at learning (Kolb & Kolb, 2005; Petriglieri & Petriglieri, 2010). It highlights that leadership development requires joint intellectual effort and working together so that people can capitalize on each other's resources and skills in order to search for understanding and meanings, solve problems or complete tasks (Kolb & Kolb, 2005). In addition, it emphasizes that developing leadership and a sense of being a leader is a social endeavor that involves interaction between people (DeRue & Ashford, 2010). It includes acts that individuals use to assert leadership (claiming) as well as acts that others use in social interaction to recognize a person's leadership (granting). These claiming and granting acts strengthen leader identity in a spiral fashion (Clapp-Smith et al., 2019).

Reciprocal respect
The contextual feature of respect is about the learning environment reducing status differences and removing barriers between teachers and students. Educators are open and accessible, acknowledge and respect learning efforts, and demonstrate integrity (Eich, 2008). This empowers students and promotes the sharing of knowledge, feelings and thoughts (Kolb & Kolb, 2005). This enables students to learn about leadership and being a leader through observation and role modeling, and enhances holistic development as a leader (Eich, 2008).

CONCLUSION

This chapter draws attention to the deeper-level cognitive components of leadership development, and provides an integrative framework that organizes and synthesizes the existing research on leadership development, leader identity and learning from experiences. The framework demonstrates how business schools and leadership educators can incorporate a cognitive approach to leadership development to complement the existing knowledge-driven and skills-based approach to leadership development. More specifically, the framework shows how classroom experiences can be purposefully leveraged as holding environments for shaping and developing students' identity as a leader through a process of meaning-making, thereby creating a foundation for ongoing leadership development and future workplace leadership effectiveness.

We began this chapter by explaining the role of leader identity in the leadership development process. We offered a framework that places leader identity at the core of the leadership development process, as it serves as an organizing and motivating force for ongoing leadership development, leadership emergence, leadership behavior and effectiveness. Through the framework, we emphasized that leader identity is malleable and develops through a process of meaning-making that is prompted by experiences. Leader identity development occurs when students engage in experiences that challenge the adequacy of their skills, frameworks and approaches, that elicit the need to learn and develop, prompting them to reflect and review and to explore alternatives to extend and refine these. Given that not all experiences are equally developmental, and people do not automatically engage in meaning-making of experiences, developing leader identity requires a so-called holding environment. Holding environments for leader identity work provide experiences that both challenge existing ways of conceptualizing and practising leadership, and support meaning-making of new perspectives of leadership and being a leader. These experiences are embedded in a micro learning environment that offers safety and reassurance in the learning process.

The classroom can serve as a holding environment for students' leader identity work at business school. This requires purposefully designed classroom experiences with specific developmental features and a supportive learning environment. Developmental features of these experiences that challenge existing ways of conceptualizing and practising leadership are novelty and unfamiliarity, difficulty and complexity, and responsibility. These features of challenge can be purposefully designed into classroom experiences by, for example, small group work and real-life projects. Developmental features of experiences that support meaning-making of new perspectives of leadership and being a leader are reflective inquiry, deliberate dialogue, practice and application, and feedback for learning. These features of support can be purposefully designed into classroom experiences by, for example, class discussions, peer teaching, and systematic and evaluative feedback moments. The impact of these developmental classroom experiences can be strengthened when embedded in a supportive learning environment that offers psychological safety, promotes a collaborate learning purpose and demonstrates reciprocal respect. The developmental features of classroom experiences and their immediate context for learning are closely connected and mutually reinforce each other. Classroom experiences that embody and combine the developmental features and contextual features described above positively influence students' leader identity, in turn providing the foundation for ongoing leadership development and future workplace leadership effectiveness.

REFERENCES

Ashford, S.J., and DeRue, D.S. (2012). Developing as a leader: the power of mindful engagement. *Organizational Dynamics, 41*, 146–154. https://doi.org/10.1016/j.orgdyn.2012.01.008

Avolio, B.J. (2004). Examining the full range model of leadership: looking back to transform forward. In D.V. Day, S.J. Zaccaro and S.M. Halpin (eds), *Leader Development for Transforming Organizations: Growing Leaders for Tomorrow* (pp. 71–98). New York: Psychology Press.

Avolio, B.J., and Vogelgesang, G.R. (2011). Beginnings matter in genuine leadership development. In S.E. Murphy and R.J. Reichard (eds), *Early Development and Leadership: Building the Next Generation of Leaders* (pp. 179–204). New York: Routledge.

Avolio, B.J., Walumbwa, F.O., and Weber, T.J. (2009). Leadership: current theories, research, and future directions. *Annual Review of Psychology, 60*, 421–449. https://doi.org/10.1146/annurev.psych.60.110707.163621.

Boud, D., and Walker, D. (1998). Promoting reflection in professional courses: the challenge of context. *Studies in Higher Education*, *23*(2), 191–207. http://web.a.ebscohost.com.ezproxy.ub.unimaas.nl/ ehost/detail/detail?vid=12andsid=37788fa6-895d-4b67-b5c3-17a51ae4bcfb%40sessionmgr40 08andbdata=JnNpdGU9ZWhvc3QtGl2ZSZzY29wZT1zaXRl#AN=823484anddb=pbh.

Chan, K.-Y., and Drasgow, F. (2001). Toward a theory of individual differences and leadership: understanding the motivation to lead. *Journal of Applied Psychology*, *86*(3), 481–498. https://doi.org/10 .1037//0021-9010.86.3.481.

Clapp-Smith, R., Hammond, M.M., Lester, G.V., and Palanski, M. (2019). Promoting identity development in leadership education: a multidomain approach to developing the whole leader. *Journal of Management Education*, *43*(1), 10–34. https://doi.org/10.1177/1052562918813190.

Cross, S.E., and Markus, H.R. (1994). Self-schemas, possible selves, and competent performance. *Journal of Educational Psychology*, *86*(3), 423–438. https://doi.org/10.1037/0022-0663.86.3.423.

Day, D.V., and Dragoni, L. (2015). Leadership development: an outcome-oriented review based on time and levels of analyses. *Annual Review of Organizational Psychology and Organizational Behavior*, *2*(1), 133–156. https://doi.org/10.1146/annurev-orgpsych-032414-111328.

Day, D.V., and Harrison, M.M. (2007). A multilevel, identity-based approach to leadership development. *Human Resource Management Review*, *17*(4), 360–373. https://doi.org/10.1016/j.hrmr.2007.08.007.

Day, D.V., Harrison, M.M., and Halpin, S.M. (2009). *An Integrative Approach to Leader Development: Connecting Adult Development, Identity, and Expertise*. New York: Psychology Press.

Day, D.V., and Sin, H.-P. (2011). Longitudinal tests of an integrative model of leader development: Charting and understanding developmental trajectories. *Leadership Quarterly*, *22*(3), 545–560. https://doi.org/10.1016/j.leaqua.2011.04.011.

DeRue, D.S., and Ashford, S.J. (2010). Who will lead and who will follow? A social process of leadership identity construction in organizations. *Academy of Management Review*, *35*(4), 627–647. https:// doi.org/10.5465/AMR.2010.53503267.

DeRue, D., and Myers, C.G. (2014). Leadership development: a review and agenda for future research. In D.V. Day (ed.), *The Oxford Handbook of Leadership and Organizations* (pp. 832–855). New York: Oxford University Press.

DeRue, D.S., Sitkin, S.B., and Podolny, J.M. (2011). From the Guest Editors: teaching leadership – issues and insights. *Academy of Management Learning and Education*, *10*(3), 369–372. https://doi .org/10.5465/amle.2011.0004.

DeRue, D.S., and Wellman, N. (2009). Developing leaders via experience: the role of developmental challenge, learning orientation, and feedback availability. *Journal of Applied Psychology*, *94*(4), 859–875. https://doi.org/10.1037/a0015317.

Dewey, J. (1938). *Education and Experience*. New York: Simon & Schuster.

Dugan, J.P. (2011). Research on college student leadership development. In S.R. Komives, J.P. Dugan, J.E. Owen, C. Slack, W. Wagner and Associates (eds), *The Handbook for Student Leadership Development* (2nd edn, pp. 59–84). San Francisco, CA: Jossey-Bass.

Edmondson, A.C., and Lei, Z. (2014). Psychological safety: the history, renaissance, and future of an interpersonal construct. *Annual Review of Organizational Psychology and Organizational Behavior*, *1*, 23–43. https://doi.org/10.1146/annurev-orgpsych-031413-091305.

Eich, D. (2008). A grounded theory of high-quality leadership programs. Perspectives from student leadership development programs in higher education. *Journal of Leadership and Organizational Studies*, *15*(2), 176–187. https://doi.org/10.1177/1548051808324099.

Engle, E.M., and Lord, R.G. (2011). Implicit theories, self-schemas, and leader–member exchange. *Academy of Management Review*, *40*(4), 988–1010.

Ericsson, K.A., Krampe, R.T., and Tesch-Romer, C. (1993). The role of deliberate practice in the acquisition of expert performance. *Psychological Review*, *100*(3), 363–406.

Fiedler, F.E., and Garcia, J.E. (1987). *New Approaches to Effective Leadership: Cognitive Resources and Organizational Performance*. New York: Wiley.

Freund, a M., and Baltes, P.B. (1998). Selection, optimization, and compensation as strategies of life management: correlations with subjective indicators of successful aging. *Psychology and Aging*, *13*(4), 531–543. https://doi.org/10.1037/0882-7974.13.4.531.

Garvin, D.A., Edmondson, A.C., and Gino, F. (2008). Is yours a learning organization? *Harvard Business Review*, *86*(3), 109–116. www.hbr.org.

Guillén, L., Mayo, M., and Korotov, K. (2015). Is leadership a part of me? A leader identity approach to understanding the motivation to lead. *Leadership Quarterly*, *26*(5), 802–820. https://doi.org/10.1016/j.leaqua.2015.05.001.

Hall, R.J., and Lord, R.G. (1995). Multi-level information-processing explanations of followers' leadership perceptions. *Leadership Quarterly*, *6*(3), 265–287.

Hammond, M., Clapp-Smith, R., and Palanski, M. (2017). Beyond (just) the workplace: a theory of leader development across multiple domains. *Academy of Management Review*, *42*(3), 481–498. https://doi.org/https://doi.org/10.5465/amr.2014.0431.

Hannah, S.T., Woolfolk, R.L., and Lord, R.G. (2009). Leader self-structure: a framework for positive leadership. *Journal of Organizational Behavior*, *30*, 269–290. https://doi.org/10.1002/job.586.

Ibarra, H. (1999). Provisional selves: experimenting with image and identity in professional adaptation. *Administrative Science Quarterly*, *44*, 764–791. http://journals.sagepub.com/doi/pdf/10.2307/2667055.

Ibarra, H., Snook, S., and Guillén Ramo, L. (2010). Identity-based leader development. In N. Nohria and R. Khurana (eds), *Handbook of Leadership Theory and Practice* (pp. 657–678). Boston, MA: Harvard Business Press.

Johnson, R.E., Venus, M., Lanaj, K., Mao, C., and Chang, C.-H. (2012). Leader identity as an antecedent of the frequency and consistency of transformational, consideration, and abusive leadership behaviors. *Journal of Applied Psychology*, *97*(6), 1262–1272. https://doi.org/10.1037/a0029043.

Kegan, R. (1982). *The Evolving Self: Problem and Process in Human Development*. Cambridge, MA: Harvard University Press.

Kegan, R., and Lahey, L. (2009). *Immunity to Change*. Boston, MA: Harvard University Press.

Kolb, A.Y., and Kolb, D.A. (2005). Learning styles and learning spaces: enhancing experiential learning in higher education experience-based learning systems. *Academy of Management Learning and Education*, *4*(2), 193–2012. http://content.ebscohost.com/ContentServer.asp?T=PandP=ANandK=17268566andS=LandD=bthandEbscoContent=dGJyMNLe80SeprQ4yOvsOLCmr1GeprZSsqq4TbOWxWXSandContentCustomer=dGJyMPGnr0ivr7dPuePfgeyx44Dt6fIA.

Kolb, D.A. (1984). *Experiental Learning: Experience as the Source of Learning and Development*. Upper Saddle River, NJ: Prentice Hall.

Komives, S.R. (2011). College student leadership identity development. In S.E. Murphy and R. J. Reichard (eds), *Early Development and Leadership: Building the Next Generation of Leaders* (pp. 273–292). New York: Routledge.

Komives, S.R., and Dugan, J.P. (2014). Student leadership development: theory, research, and practice. In D.V. Day (ed.), *The Oxford Handbook of Leadership and Organizations* (pp. 805–831). New York: Oxford University Press.

Komives, S.R., Longerbeam, S.D., Owen, J.E., Mainella, F.C., and Osteen, L. (2006). A leadership identity development model: applications from a grounded theory. *Journal of College Student Development*, *47*(4), 401–418. https://doi.org/10.1353/csd.2006.0048.

Komives, S.R., Owen, J.E., Longerbeam, S.D., Mainella, F.C., and Osteen, L. (2005). Developing a leadership identity: a grounded theory. *Journal of College Student Development*, *46*(6), 593–611. https://doi.org/10.1353/csd.2005.0061.

Kragt, D., and Guenter, H. (2018). Why and when leadership training predicts effectiveness: the role of leader identity and leadership experience. *Leadership and Organization Development Journal*, *39*(3), 406–418.

Kraiger, K., Ford, J.K., and Salas, E. (1993). Application of cognitive, skill-based, and affective theories of learning outcomes to new methods of training evaluation. *Journal of Applied Psychology*, *78*(2), 311–328. https://doi.org/10.1037/0021-9010.78.2.311.

Kwok, N., Hanig, S., Brown, D.J., and Shen, W. (2018). How leader role identity influences the process of leader emergence: a social network analysis. *Leadership Quarterly*, *29*(6), 648–662. https://doi.org/10.1016/J.LEAQUA.2018.04.003.

Lord, R.G., and Hall, R.J. (2005). Identity, deep structure and the development of leadership skill. *Leadership Quarterly*, *16*(4), 591–615. https://doi.org/10.1016/j.leaqua.2005.06.003.

Lord, R.G., and Maher, K.J. (1993). *Leadership and Information Processing: Linking Perceptions and Performance*. London: Routledge.

Markus, H. (1977). Self-schemata and processing information about the self. *Journal of Personality and Social Psychology, 35*(2), 63–78. https://doi.org/10.1037/0022-3514.35.2.63.

Martin, R., and Epitropaki, O. (2001). Role of organizational identification on implicit leadership theories (ILTs), transformational leadership and work attitudes. *Group Processes and Intergroup Relations, 4*(3), 247–262.

McCall, M.W. (2004). Leadership development through experience. *Academy of Management Executive, 18*(3), 127–130. http://www.jstor.org/discover/10.2307/4166101?sid=21105710682931anduid=4anduid=3738672anduid=2.

McCauley, C.D., Ruderman, M.N., Ohlott, P.J., and Morrow, J.E. (1994). Assessing the developmental components of managerial jobs. *Journal of Applied Psychology, 79*(4), 544–560. https://doi.org/10.1037/0021-9010.79.4.544.

McCauley, C.D., Van Velsor, E., and Ruderman, M.N. (2010). Our view of leadership development. In E. Van Velsor, C.D. McCauley and M.N. Ruderman (eds), *Handbook of Leadership Development* (3rd edn, pp. 1–26). San Francisco, CA: Jossey-Bass.

Miscenko, D., Guenter, H., and Day, D.V. (2017). Am I a leader? Examining leader identity development over time. *Leadership Quarterly, 28*(4), 605–620. https://doi.org/10.1016/j.leaqua.2017.01.00

Murphy, S.E., and Johnson, S.K. (2011). The benefits of a long-lens approach to leader development: understanding the seeds of leadership. *Leadership Quarterly, 22*, 459–470. https://doi.org/10.1016/j.leaqua.2011.04.004.

Petriglieri, G., and Petriglieri, J.L. (2010). Identity workspaces: the case of business schools. *Academy of Management Learning and Education, 9*(1), 44–60. http://content.ebscohost.com/ContentServer.asp?T=PandP=ANandK=48661190andS=LandD=bthandEbscoContent=dGJyMNLr40Sep7I4v%2BvlOLCmr1CeprdSr664TbCWxWXSandContentCustomer=dGJyMPGnr0ivr7dPuePfgeyx44Dt6flA.

Petriglieri, G., and Petriglieri, J.L. (2015). Can business schools humanize leadership? *Academy of Management Learning and Education, 14*(4), 625–647.

Schon, D.A. (1987). *Educating the Reflective Practitioner*. San Francisco, CA: Jossey-Bass.

Schyns, B., Kiefer, T., Kerschreiter, R., and Tymon, A. (2011). Teaching implicit leadership theories to develop leaders and leadership: how and why it can make a difference. *Academy of Management Learning and Education, 10*(3), 397–408. https://doi.org/10.5465/amle.2010.0015.

Schyns, B., Tymon, A., Kiefer, T., and Kerschreiter, R. (2012). New ways to leadership development: a picture paints a thousand words. *Management Learning, 44*(1), 11–24. https://doi.org/10.1177/1350507612456499.

Scott, W.E. (1966). Activation theory and task design. *Organizational Behavior and Human Performance, 1*, 3–30.

Sternberg, R.J. (2011). The purpose of college education: producing a new generation of positive leaders. In S.E. Murphy and R.J. Reichard (eds), *Early Development and Leadership: Building the Next Generation of Leaders* (pp. 293–308). New York: Routledge.

Van Velsor, E., McCauley, C.D., and Ruderman, M.N. (2010). *Handbook of Leadership Development* (3rd edn). San Francisco, CA: Jossey-Bass.

Wagner, W. (2011). Considerations of student development in leadership. In S.R. Komives, J.P. Dugan, J.E. Owen, C. Slack, W. Wagner and Associates (eds), *The Handbook for Student Leadership Development* (2nd edn, pp. 85–133). San Francisco, CA: Jossey-Bass.

Zaar, S., Van den Bossche, P., and Gijselaers, W. (2020). How business students think about leadership: a qualitative study on leader identity and meaning-making. *Academy of Management Learning and Education, 19*(2), 168–191. https://doi.org/10.5465/amle.2017.0290.

Zheng, W., and Muir, D. (2015). Embracing leadership: a multi-faceted model of leader identity development. *Leadership and Organization Development Journal, 36*(6), 630–656. https://doi.org/https://doi.org/10.1108/LODJ-10-2013-0138.

18. Equipping students with the attributes needed by business leaders in an era of social and technological change

David Kember

INTRODUCTION

Students enrol in business schools with the dream of becoming the next Jeff Bezos, Bill Gates, Steve Jobs, Li Ka Shing, Daniel Zhang or Mark Zuckerburg. Obviously, very few students will achieve the level of success of these outstanding business leaders. However, surely it should be a reasonable dream for fledgling business students that they could become successful entrepreneurs on a more realistic plane.

Giving business students a hope and providing the first few steps down the path requires business schools to reflect upon what the attributes are that empowers business leaders, and whether the curriculum and mode of teaching and learning is geared to provide those attributes. What is clear is that it is not knowledge per se. Often, the most successful business leaders are not the ones who acquired the most theory and knowledge during their time at business school (Jones, 2011). To consider what is needed requires a review of more ill-defined qualities, designated by a variety of terms such as employability skills, enterprise skills, capabilities and graduate attributes.

EMPLOYABILITY SKILLS

The Australian Chamber of Commerce and Industry (ACCI) and Business Council of Australia (BCA) define employability skills as 'skills required not only to gain employment, but also to progress within an enterprise so as to achieve one's potential and contribute successfully to enterprise strategic directions' (2002, p. 3). Their framework identifies eight main employability skills, shown in Table 18.1.

Table 18.1   Main employability skills

Communication	Initiative and enterprise
Teamwork	Problem-solving
Learning	Planning and organizing
Technology	Self-management

These employability skills have been organised into two columns. Those in the left-hand column include the two main social skills of communication and teamwork, together with information technology skills and the cognitive attribute of learning. The employability skills in the right-hand column would enable a graduate to recognize a problematic issue, identify potential novel solutions and take the initiative to implement the alternative practices. In short, these are the attributes needed to display enterprise. The two columns can be distinguished by the employability skills needed for adapting to change, and those for initiating change. Together these skills would be necessary for graduates to adapt to technological and societal changes affecting them in their employment.

These employability skills are also consistent with definitions of employability skills in the United Kingdom (UK) Higher Education Academy report 'Pedagogy for employability' (Pegg et al., 2012), which synthesized its set of employability skills from a wide body of work and consultations with employer groups. The set of employability skills is also similar to Oliver's (2011) review of graduate attributes specified by universities for all disciplines.

The literature reviewed in this section, therefore, suggests a three-category scheme for employability skills:

- Communication skills: for example, communication skills and teamwork.
- Skills for adapting to change: for example, adaptability, problem-solving and critical thinking.
- Skills for initiating change: for example, enterprise skills and creative thinking.

The conceptualization of three overlapping categories is consistent with the Core Skills for Work developmental framework (Commonwealth of Australia, 2013). This envisages skill areas grouped in three overlapping clusters: interact with others, navigate the world of work and get the work done.

Like most category schemes, the three categories are not discrete. They are best envisaged as a set of overlapping and mutually supporting skills. The skills for adapting to change are a prerequisite for the development of enterprise skills. Communication skills are a co-requisite for the effective functioning of the skills needed for adapting to or initiating change.

ENTERPRISE SKILLS

In recent times, the idea of enterprise skills has been gently separated from the notion of entre-preneurial skills. The UK's Quality Assurance Agency (QAA) defines enterprise skills as 'the application of creative ideas and innovations to practical situations. This is a generic concept that can be applied across all areas of education. It combines creativity, ideas development and problem solving with expression, communication and practical action' (QAA, 2012, p.8)

Enterprise education has been defined by the QAA as follows: 'Enterprise education aims to produce graduates with the mindset and skills to come up with original ideas in response to identified needs and shortfalls, and the ability to act on them. In short, having an idea and making it happen' (QAA, 2012, p. 8). This differs from the QAA's definition of entrepre-neurship education that strictly relates to the knowledge and skills required to create a new business. Given the generality of employability skills, this distinction is important. Especially so when the changing nature of the world of work (e.g., freelancing and remote work) is taken into account.

EMPLOYABILITY SKILLS AND GRADUATE ATTRIBUTES

There has been growing interest amongst Australian universities in becoming engaged with employers and industry bodies (e.g., Etzkowitz, 2003; Garlick, 2000; Gunasekara, 2004). This engagement is very important for universities in order to review and address graduate skills needed in professional practice (ACCI, 2007; ACER, 2002; Australian Industry Group, 2006) and confirms the need to involve staff and students in real-world learning experiences (Ostrander, 2004; Ralston, 2006), and better manage competition through attracting students by the relevance of programmes and a perceived expected increase in employability (Nugent et al., 2006; Ralston, 2006).

In a complex and ever-changing world, the major challenge for graduates is not so much about knowing and doing as how to become an authentic being. Jones (2011) emphasizes the socio-cultural aspects of contemporary workplaces. He posits that the ability to engage in situational learning, and the capacity to read situations accurately and sensitively, is likely to be as important as cognitive capacities in contributing to the success or otherwise of graduates seeking and retaining employment. Graduate attributes need to be integrated into the curriculum, particularly if they are to be used by capable people faced with the messiness of problems in the real world (Oliver, 2013).

RESEARCH ON THE DEVELOPMENT OF GRADUATE ATTRIBUTES

There have been a series of studies which address the mechanism by which attributes can be developed (Kember, 2008; Kember et al., 2007; Leung & Kember, 2006, 2013). These studies develop a model for attribute development through a teaching and learning environment including active engagement in learning activities and teacher–student and student–student interaction. This type of learning and teaching environment results in the development of attributes grouped into cognitive, social and affective categories. The research into mechanisms for the nurturing of attributes indicates that attributes develop through interaction, discussion and active engagement of students in activities, which demand the deployment or practice of the attribute in question. For a capability to be developed there needs to be an opportunity to practice its use. Graduate attributes are nurtured if courses and curricula provide learning activities which require the deployment of the attribute in question.

Oliver's (2011) good practice report reinforces this conclusion about the development of attributes by noting that 'Alignment of learning outcomes with experiences and assessment is now regarded as fundamental to sound practice' (p. 12). Curriculum design needs to ensure that there are learning activities of the type which demand the enactment of targeted skills embedded in units through the curriculum. Wide distribution of these activities at all levels of the curriculum is desirable, so that students become accustomed to deploying the skills.

Oliver (2011) reviewed progress on the development of graduate attributes. The most common approach to advancing towards attribute development has advocated the employment of curriculum mapping and curriculum alignment (Biggs & Tang, 2011) as quality assurance mechanisms. However, curriculum mapping will only promote employability skills if the teachers of units adopt pedagogical strategies, activities and assessment tasks consistent with nurturing attributes. Without guidelines for such effective pedagogical strategies, though, it is hard to be confident that units mapped to achieve a particular attribute will do so effectively.

It has not been straightforward to implement the standard quality assurance measure of curriculum mapping to achieve the attainment of graduate attributes, as Oliver (2011, p. 2) observes that 'It would be fair to say that views about graduate demonstration of generic outcomes are often not overly positive.'

Embedding the development of attributes into the curriculum means that all courses and all teachers in a degree need to consider their approach to teaching, teaching activities and assessment. Attributes and competencies develop gradually through a degree, particularly the intellectual capabilities such as critical thinking, problem solving and self-managed learning. Some attributes may be mapped to particular courses. For example, teamwork skills might be nurtured by including group projects in selected courses.

There are specific forms of learning, such as experiential learning or work-integrated learning, which have been demonstrated to have a strong impact on the development of enterprise skills. These are not dealt with in this chapter. They are worthy of inclusion in a business curriculum; however, they must not be seen as all that is needed for the development of enterprise skills. Rather, they should be seen as a capstone to a curriculum in which the development of attributes is embedded throughout. Only then will students be sufficiently prepared through capability development to take full advantage of the capstone.

METHOD

The remainder of this chapter provides examples of how the principles of developing attributes by providing practice in their use can be successfully incorporated into teaching and learning so that students do develop graduate attributes. The examples come from a set of focus group interviews with students in departments in a university in Hong Kong. The students were in departments which were identified as having good records in nurturing graduate attributes. The majority of the departments were not in the business school. This does not mean that the cases are not relevant to business. The principles of how to develop graduate attributes through appropriate learning activities are independent of discipline. Types of activities, such as group projects and solving ill-defined problems, can be common to most if not all disciplines.

The departments with a good record were identified through a survey used to gather feedback from students on the development of capabilities. The survey instrument (Kember, forthcoming; Kember & Leung, 2009) also solicited feedback on aspects of the teaching and learning environment thought to influence capability development. The instrument and the way it is used for quality enhancement purposes is described in Kember and Leung (2009) and Kember (forthcoming). Through the survey it was possible to identify departments which were perceived to be more successful at developing generic capabilities. Accordingly, six departments were selected which had high scores for perceptions of capability development. Focus group interviews were then arranged with four to six students from each of the six departments. The students were generally from the later years of the degree, so that they could comment upon most of the programme.

The interviews had an open format. Prompts were used to seek greater depth and richer descriptions where necessary. Semi-structured questions asked the students to indicate what types of generic capabilities they would need on graduation. They were also asked to describe the approach to teaching, the assessment and the curriculum in their department. Often, this needed little prompting, as when students discussed an attribute they also tended to talk about how it was developed. The six interviews each lasted for approximately 90 minutes. Quotations from the interviews are used for illustration. Letters A to F are used to denote the six departments and each student within the focus group was given a numerical code in addition to the degree identifier.

The findings from the interviews are presented in two stages. The first stage reports what graduate attributes the students thought had been developed during their degree. The second stage reports the principles underlying the teaching and learning activities which help nurture the attributes. The two stages overlap considerably, as when the interviewees commented upon the attributes they thought had been developed, they often at the same time described the learning activities which led to the development of the attribute.

INTELLECTUAL CAPABILITIES

Analysis of the interviews found four categories of attributes, which were closely related and could be grouped together under a higher-order category of intellectual capabilities. The students clearly saw the need for the development of intellectual capabilities. Their comments suggest that these tend to be related rather than discrete. Their comments often discussed two or more capabilities together, which have normally been seen as separate. The formulation of four capabilities under one umbrella is therefore apt.

The following sections look at the four sub-categories of specific intellectual capabilities. Their interrelationship is made apparent. There are also initial suggestions of how they can be nurtured through facets of the teaching and learning environment, which foster their active engagement.

Critical Thinking

The following are successive quotations, from two students in one focus group, which arose as the students were discussing critical thinking in the interview. The essence of their interpretation of critical thinking was the ability to make their own judgements and interpretations and not necessarily accept the perspective of the teacher, which is one of the more challenging notions of critical thinking. (Other definitions of critical thinking are reviewed by Phillips and Bond, 2004).

> Don't blindly agree with what the lecturer says ... When s/he makes a comment or when s/he teaches something, we have to continuously reflect on what s/he says and to relate to our own knowledge, to see whether we truly agree or disagree with what s/he says. (A6)

> I think mostly that relates closely to our ability to analyze ... most of us have our own set of views and are quite subjective, but how are we able to build our views and in addition, able to persuade others by using our views, since we believe that our views are reasonable and rational; and that also includes all the things that she [A6] has just mentioned. (A3)

Accepting this interpretation of critical thinking poses a challenge to many professors in facilitating the development of this form of critical thinking. Professors are appointed because of their expertise in a discipline. Many view teaching as transmitting this expertise to students in lectures (Kember, 1997). This conception of teaching clearly establishes one's position as the authoritative one and leaves little room for students to make their own judgements. Other parts of the interview made it clear that most of the professors in department A discouraged students from reproducing their professors' views, while encouraging personal interpretation. Their conception of teaching appeared to be consistent with a facilitating learning orientation (Kember, 1997).

The interviews suggested that there needs to be a time for discussion of viewpoints if students are to form their own positions. Part of this was in the classes with the professors and a further part was inter-student discussion in tutorials, where the tutors took the role of facilitator. By presenting their own viewpoint and defending it against the challenges of others, the students were engaging in critical debate and discussion. This nurtured their critical thinking capability.

Self-Managed Learning

The need for self-managed learning was amply demonstrated by the following quotation. The pace of change in technology and society is now so rapid that graduates need to be equipped to continue learning by themselves. The faculty thought self-managed learning was an important capability for their students to develop:

> I don't think so, I think 90% of them would remind us that after 5 or 10 years, about 50% of the contents in our books would be changed and updated. Some would tell us that what they had said would not be true anymore and would often remind us to keep updating ourselves. (B5)

The interviews demonstrated that developing self-managed learning skills followed the principle of requiring students to practice the skill they needed to develop. One of the main components of self-managed learning is finding appropriate knowledge and information by oneself. Therefore, the capability was developed by requiring students to search for some material themselves rather than providing them with everything they needed.

> We have to search for our own materials. (C2)

> But I think self learning is very important as well, especially to university students because in the past, we were used to being spoon fed, but now, there are a lot and variety of resources in a university, if you want the lecturers to lecture everything to you, taking 90 credit hours per semester may not even be enough to acquire everything, therefore to motivate oneself to search for information is important for you will at the same time, [be] able to learn something through the process of researching. (B3)

Problem-Solving

Related to self-managed learning was problem-solving ability. Again this was nurtured through practice; in this case by asking the students to do research to solve problems:

> But I would like to stress that university students should also go for researching, shouldn't see university as a place for training them and shouldn't be satisfied with landing a stable job, I think we should make use of our time at university doing research. ... information is forever updating and we don't know everything in our life. If you touch on research, you are truly solving a problem that no one can ever solve in the whole world. If you are to solve a problem, you need to have some kind of an approach, therefore, I think this part is very important. (B1)

Adaptability

Adaptability received less attention than the other intellectual capabilities. It appeared to be seen as something which would develop as a consequence of heightening the other capabilities. This again demonstrates the appropriateness of grouping the four intellectual capabilities under a higher-order category:

> I think […] has touched on an important point, which is to be able to take initiatives. We have to change ourselves in order to adapt to changes; or else, we will be too slow to make reactions. From a personal point of view, I don't think our curriculum has intended to teach us with such an aspect and honestly speaking, it is very difficult to do so and to put it in black-and-white but the ethos of our university, interpersonal skill, emotional quality, etc. are all composite to this issue. If you're able to manipulate well with either one of your skills, you should be able to adapt to changes easily; this is what I think. That is, if you make progress, you won't just progress on one of the skills but will progress and develop on other skills as well. (B1)

WORKING TOGETHER CAPABILITIES

The remaining two capabilities students identified were communication skills, and interpersonal and groupwork skills. These two capabilities were also grouped together under a higher-order category which was given the label 'working together capabilities'.

Communication Skills

Students from each of the disciplines recognized that communication skills were important. Again, these were developed through practice in learning activities. Most commonly this was through discussion in class and by students making presentations. The students in department B had a specific subject to develop communication skills:

> We have a special subject for learning communication skills. There are two aspects here: each individual conveys differently, interacts differently, even their courtesy is different, it all depends on that person. You can't change that person overnight. But our communication skill would stress certain basic rules for us as of how to communicate with others, how to learn listening skill, how to speak with empathy, etc. There is another part where we have to learn how to speak professionally such as how to break the bad news to our patients. (B1)

Interpersonal Skills and Groupwork

Teamwork was recognized by the students as an important capability. There are few professionals nowadays who work as individuals; so the ability to be able to work as part of a team was important:

> I think in university, it is important for us to learn how to work as a team, for our effort are very limited if we choose to work individually. We may not be able to think diversely, therefore able to get along with others and to group our effort together is very important. (B4)

Interpersonal skills were developed through practice in working as part of a team. This occurred in group projects:

Various parts will convey the message to you that good interpersonal skill is a must. Especially from group work; I know that we have a lot of group work, I noticed that our curriculum runs a lot of group work whereas the former curriculum didn't run a lot. (B2)

TEACHING AND LEARNING ENVIRONMENT

This section of the chapter shows how the curriculum and the teaching and learning environment were configured to ensure that practice was provided in the use of the capabilities and hence they were nurtured. The facets of the broad curriculum and the teaching and learning environment were thematically related by the need to exercise the use of the capabilities. Four broad facets were established: active learning, teaching for understanding, assessment and cooperative learning.

Active Learning

One of the most important facets of the teaching and learning environment for promoting the development of capabilities was the provision of active learning experiences. Practice of the capabilities occurred when there was an activity which demanded their application. The capabilities could not be practised through sitting in a lecture theatre listening passively to a lecture.

Perhaps the most common form of learning activity identified by students was discussion. The students judged discussion to be particularly important for developing critical thinking and problem-solving abilities. The quotation below indicates that for discussion to be successful in nurturing capabilities, the professor or tutor needed to take a facilitative and stimulating role. Most of the courses featured student presentations, which required students to research a topic and initiate discussion. The professor could then facilitate in-depth exploration of the topic through searching questions:

> In our programme, we have a lot of tutorials and small group discussion. We have lively interaction with professors. We are engaged in forming and voicing our views and the professor will duly respond to us. They would choose topics which are rather unusual that would shock your system and make you really think. They would have prepared a lot of questions that stimulate our thinking and students are actively engaged in thinking and generating their opinions/answers. (D2)

The interviews were consistent with the conclusion that self-managed learning could be encouraged by setting assignments which required students to find material themselves. This provided practice in learning by themselves, which helped the development of self-managed learning ability:

> Sometimes the notes given do not contain all the information, then we will look up from the references for details of the situation, what is happening and the current thinking abroad. (E1)

The professional programmes needed to ensure that students developed the capabilities necessary for the future performance of the professional role as well as the generic capabilities which are the subject of this chapter. Choosing suitable learning activities meant that both could develop in concert. An example is taken from a programme which featured design projects. Like projects in other courses, these would provide practice in a lot of generic intellectual capabilities in addition to specific design skills:

> In a building technology course, we were asked to build a bridge. You can choose whatever method you want to build this bridge but the length and function is fixed. This is like a small scale design course. The focus is on structure. I discovered that the majority of us directly asked the teacher for comments or feedback. The interaction between teacher and students [is] great. (F5)

Teaching for Understanding

Closely related to the deployment for active learning experiences was the need for teaching to promote an in-depth understanding of a topic. The intellectual capabilities were developed through practice in their use. Courses which aimed to give students a thorough understanding of key concepts could provide that practice. Those which, intentionally or unintentionally, expected students to remember a mass of detail were unlikely to stretch intellectual capacity:

> The reason we have such a course is mainly to prepare us to learn more difficult things in the future. Such as for mechanical properties, we need to have good mathematical foundation in order to apply what we have learnt and to solving problems. That is, you really need to understand, memorizing is just a meaningless act. (C1)

Students suggested that that this meant that topics needed to be explored in depth. As time allocated to courses was finite, this might imply that concentration was on dealing with a restricted number of key concepts in depth, rather than shallow coverage of many topics. Understanding came about through being able to relate to real-life applications, rather than learning abstract theory:

> The good teachers give real life examples, the presentation is informal and yet full of intellectual reflections. They show you how to go in-depth into analysing an issue rather than just touching the surface. (D3)

The interviews indicated that teachers encouraged the process by taking a questioning and facilitative stance. Rather than presenting everything, students were left to explore part of a topic for themselves. When students asked questions they were prompted by questions in return rather than being given answers directly. The aim was to stimulate students to practise the higher-order thinking skills to nurture their development:

> They won't give you a ready-made answer and they expect you to further explore the topic yourself. They use questions to stimulate you to think deeper into the issue or answers. From the point of view of study, some students might prefer teachers to give them a straight answer. (E4)

Assessment

Students tend to be assessment-driven (Biggs & Tang, 2011). The learning approach they adopt is normally consistent with what they perceive the assessment requires (Thomas & Bain, 1984). If students are to develop intellectual capabilities through practising them, the assessment, therefore, should require them to deploy the capabilities to complete the assignments.

The implication of this conclusion is that the assessment needs to be consistent with the aims towards active learning and teaching for understanding argued above. There needs to be compatibility between assessment and teaching approaches in class. If there is inconsistency, such teaching approaches will be undermined:

> I am very satisfied with the assessment practice. Based on my combination, I am free to choose to do a term paper and a presentation. I am given the freedom to concentrate and research in-depth into the topic that I've chosen. I like that very much, to be able to do what I am really interested in. (D4)

Two courses permitted students a significant degree of freedom in choosing an assignment topic. This allowed the students to select an area of interest and explore it in depth. By requiring students to set their own topic they became practised in dealing with ill-defined problems and were required to display self-managed learning:

> I still think it is related to our assessment method. Such as we are to set our own topic, we are responsible for asking questions and solving those questions. We have to do everything on our own. Certainly this process has trained our ability to solving [*sic*] problem. Throughout the whole process, since we have to find out the problem. (F5)

In general, the identified departments used a wide variety of types of assessment. The programmes were aiming to develop a range of capabilities, both professional and generic. For students to practice each of them, the assessment needed to take a variety of forms to provide a genuine assessment of the capabilities:

> Whatever assessment style you can think of, you can find it in our faculty. When I first entered Year 1, I was told by one higher year student that 'just think of all kinds of assessment styles and all these possibilities will exist in our faculty.' Such as oral examination; hands-on examination; written examination. And written examination is divided into multiple choices, matching … no, we only have it during our primary, essays, short questions, so forth. Whatever you can think of. Even to demonstrate or role play. (B1)

Cooperative Learning

The benefit of good student–student relationships comes through the formation of study groups which work together to make sense of difficult concepts. Collaboration was focused towards members of the group trying to reach a better understanding together, so the students worked together out of class using an 'engager' approach (Yan & Kember, 2004a, 2004b):

> Co-operative learning out of class is quite important for me. My academic performance in Year 1 was quite poor and I was lucky to have a few students who could help me out. We would continue our discussion right after class which helped me a great deal in understanding the subject and consolidating my memory. We also discussed how we would tackle the paper assignments and before exams. This has definitely improved the quality of my learning, much better than if I were to do it on my own, going to the library and dig the book out by the author's name. (D5)

Interpersonal skills were practised by requiring students to work together in group projects. The following quotation illustrates graphically the way that group projects can foster teamwork skills as well as academic aims. Groups might not always hit it off from the outset, but the process of establishing a way of working together effectively provides the learning experience which promotes the development of interpersonal skills:

> All of us wanted to be the leader. For I have a way of thinking and I wanted others to agree with me, to write things that goes well with my idea and this is very difficult to achieve. On the contrary I think I have learned the skills of others more … I can remember that I was once partnered with two students, one from journalism whereas the other from geography. The questioning skills of the journalism

student was very different from that of anthropology, I felt s/he was in a stronger position. Another group mate was from geography, all s/he cared about was the environment ... Our approach was to find someone to interview as soon as possible and his/her approach was very different. Nevertheless we worked, each came up with different sources and the outcome was quite pleasurable. (A1)

CONCLUSION

Looking back across the analysis in general, an overarching thematic conclusion becomes apparent. For a capability to be developed there needed to be an opportunity to practise its use. Generic capabilities are nurtured if programmes and curricula provide learning activities which require the deployment of the capability in question.

Arguably, the most important outcomes of business degrees should be graduates equipped with the attributes, capabilities, employability skills and enterprise skills they need to possess to become a successful business leader. For this to happen the nurturing of attributes needs to be embedded and mapped throughout the curriculum. All lecturers need to be aware that the way they teach, the learning activities they design and the assessment playset will impact on the development of attributes. Throughout the curriculum, there need to be activities of the type which will provide practice in the use of the necessary attributes.

REFERENCES

Australian Chamber of Commerce and Industry (ACCI) (2007). *Skills for a Nation: A Blueprint for Improving Education and Training 2007–2017*. Canberra: Australian Chamber of Commerce and Industry.

Australian Chamber of Industry and Commerce and Business Council of Australia (2002). *Employability Skills for the Future*. Canberra: Department of Education Science and Training.

Australian Council for Educational Research (ACER) (2002). *Employability Skills for Australian Industry: Literature Review and Framework Development*. A report to the Business Council of Australia and the Australian Chamber of Commerce and Industry. Canberra: Department of Education, Science and Training.

Australian Industry Group (2006). *World Class Skills for World Class Industries: Employers' Perspectives on Skilling in Australia*. Australian Industry Group, Sydney. http://www.clt.uts.edu.au/ATN.grad.cap.project.index.html.

Biggs, J. and Tang, C. (2011). *Teaching for Quality Learning at University*. Maidenhead: Open University Press.

Commonwealth of Australia (2013). *Core Skills for Work Developmental Framework*. Canberra: Commonwealth of Australia.

Etzkowitz, H. (2003). Innovation on innovation, the triple-helix of university–industry–government relations. *Social Science Innovation*, *42*(3), 293.

Garlick, S. (2000). *Engaging Universities and Regions: Knowledge Contribution to Regional Economic Development in Australia*. Canberra: Department of Education, Training and Youth Affairs.

Gunasekara, C.S. (2004). The third role of Australian universities in human capital formation. *Journal of Higher Education Policy and Management*, *26*(3), 329–343.

Jones, C. (2011). *Teaching Entrepreneurship to Postgraduates*. Cheltenham, UK and Northampton, MA, USA: Edward Elgar Publishing.

Kember, D. (1997). A reconceptualisation of the research into university academics' conceptions of teaching. *Learning and Instruction*, *7*(3), 255–275.

Kember, D. (2008). Nurturing generic capabilities through a teaching and learning environment which provides practise in their use. *Higher Education*, *57*(1), 37–55.

Kember, D. (forthcoming). Implementing an evaluation system to promote student centred learning. In S. Hoidn and M. Klemensic (eds), *Routledge Handbook on Student Centred Learning and Instruction in Higher Education*. New York: Routledge, pp. 528–540.

Kember, D. and Leung, D.Y.P. (2009). Development of a questionnaire for assessing students' perceptions of the teaching and learning environment and its use in quality assurance. *Learning Environments Research, 12*, 15–29.

Kember, D., Leung, D.Y.P. and Ma, R.S.F. (2007). Characterising learning environments capable of nurturing generic capabilities in higher education. *Research in Higher Education, 48*(5), 609–632.

Leung, D.Y.P. and Kember, D. (2006). The influence of teaching approach and teacher–student interaction on the development of graduate capabilities. *Structural Equation Modeling, 13*(2), 264–286.

Leung, D.Y.P. and Kember, D. (2013). Nurturing graduate attributes through a first year student experience which promotes the formation of effective learning communities. *American Journal of Educational Research, 1*(7), 230–239.

Nugent, M., Delaforce, W. and Harding, S. (2006). QUT engagement strategy: journey of discovery and re-discovery. Paper presented at the 2006 Australian Universities Community Engagement Alliance National Conference, Perth, 12–14 July.

Oliver, B. (2011). *Assuring Graduate Outcomes*. Strawberry Hills, NSW: Australian Learning and Teaching Council.

Oliver, B. (2013). Graduate attributes as a focus for institution-wide curriculum renewal: innovations and challenges. *Higher Education Research and Development, 32*(3), 450–463.

Ostrander, S.A. (2004). Democracy, civic participation and the university: a comparative study of civic engagement on five campuses. *Nonprofit and Voluntary Sector Quarterly, 33*(1), 79–93.

Pegg et al. (2012). Pedagogy for employability. UK Higher Education Academy.

Phillips, V. and Bond, C. (2004). Undergraduates experiences of critical thinking. *Higher Education Research and Development, 23*(3), 277–294.

QAA (2012). Quality Assurance Agency for Higher Education – Enterprise and entrepreneurship: a new approach to learning. http://www.qaa.ac.uk/Newsroom/PressReleases/Pages/Enterprise-and-entrepreneurship-a-new-approach-to-learning.aspx.

Ralston, D. (2006). Engagement to build a strategic university. Keynote address given at the 2006 Australasian Association for Institutional Research Forum, Coffs Harbour.

Thomas, P.R. and Bain, J.D. (1984). Contextual differences of learning approaches: the effects of assessments. *Human Learning, 3*, 227–240.

Yan, L. and Kember, D. (2004a). Avoider and engager approaches by out-of-class groups: the group equivalent to individual learning approaches. *Learning and Instruction, 14*(1), 27–49

Yan, L. and Kember, D. (2004b). Engager and avoider behavior in types of activities performed by out-of-class learning groups. *Higher Education, 48*, 419–438.

PART VI

CONTINUOUS PROFESSIONAL DEVELOPMENT OF RESEARCH-BASED TEACHERS

19. How to motivate professors to teach

Uwe Wilkesmann and Sabine Lauer

THE INITIAL CONDITIONS: ACADEMIC TEACHING AS A NEGLECTED STEPCHILD

Academic teaching is assumed to be "the neglected stepchild" (Wilkesmann and Lauer, 2020) of German professors. When being asked how they imagine their ideal working week to be, you will certainly hear a lot: first research, then research, then a bit of administrative work, and if there is still time, then teaching. Considering the fact that the teaching load of 8–9 hours per week at research universities is quite high compared with other countries, the question arises: How can this be, when a considerable amount of working time is taken up by the preparation and follow-up of lectures, seminars and tutorials? To find answers, one has to take a few more steps back on the academic career ladder first.

When a PhD student wants to become a professor, what is the best advice for them? Concentrate on your research and neglect teaching! In the German higher education system, PhDs are no longer students, but employed as research assistants. Depending on their type of fixed-term employment, their teaching load varies between two to four hours per week. Research assistants hired based on an external research grant usually do not teach at all. A PhD thesis is an important milestone of research in any academic biography, where a successful dissertation is judged solely based on research performance. Subsequently, the young researcher must either habilitate after the doctorate (the German professor qualification) or successfully complete an assistant professorship. The habilitation is a second doctoral thesis with an oral examination in which only the research performance is assessed. The same applies – more or less – to the assessment of the assistant professorship (called junior professorship in Germany): here too the main assessment is based on what has been published in high-ranked journals. When the candidate finally applies for a professorship, the appointment committee will again primarily evaluate only the research performance, that is, how many articles have been published in high-ranking scientific journals and how many research projects have already been successfully acquired. In comparison with other countries, such as the United Kingdom or the Netherlands, that already have established teaching-focused career tracks to a professorship, such models do not yet exist in Germany. It is therefore hardly surprising that, even after appointment as a professor, the scientific status is mainly determined by research achievements. According to a recent survey of deans and chairpersons on appointment procedures, only 53 percent of deans and only 50 percent of the chairpersons consider a teaching demonstration to be important or very important. A similar picture emerges for a teaching concept (Kleimann and Klawitter 2017). An nationwide survey of professors at state-controlled research universities conducted by the authors of this chapter in 2016–17 has also shown that a particular commitment to teaching is at the expense of research, that it does not contribute to academic reputation, and that it does little to fertilize one's own research (Figure 19.1).

Nevertheless, the core business of universities is research and teaching. In contrast to research, teaching is organized as a collective action that takes place within the university. Even if seminars and lectures are usually taught by one person, a Bachelor's or Master's program is taught by an entire department. However, this collective thinking is countered by the fact that, according to the German constitution, German professors belong to a species which – in addition to their civil servant status – also enjoys a high degree of autonomy in research and teaching. Accordingly, the direct influence of university management vis-à-vis their professorship how to teach and how to conduct research is considered very low.

In this chapter, we examine what motivates professors to teach, and which opportunities university rectorates have to influence the teaching-related behavior of their professors from the top down. In doing so, we draw primarily on our own research, which has examined the governance of academic teaching at German state-controlled research universities in three externally funded projects between 2008 and 2017. Since two nationwide surveys of full professors were completed within the framework of these research projects, the empirical part will include a comparison of both survey dates.

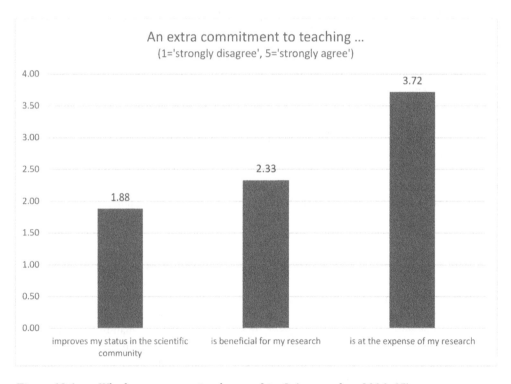

Figure 19.1   Why be extra committed to teaching? (survey data 2016–17)

HIGHER EDUCATION POLICY DEVELOPMENTS TO MAKE TEACHING COUNT MORE IN GERMAN ACADEMIA

To gain a better understanding of the impetus and necessity of our research, we will begin with a brief digression on the higher education policy developments of the last 15 years in the field of academic teaching.

First, with the advent of the new public management (NPM), the "managerial governance" of university rectorates has been strengthened in the form of the so-called "new steering instruments": these are (1) performance bonuses included in the salary of professors; (2) performance-related allocation of funds; and (3) target agreements (management by objectives, MbO). Although most incentives relate to research, in principle they are also used to steer teaching:

1. Performance-related bonuses. Since 2005, all German professors have been automatically assigned to a new salary system with a bonus system. Two-thirds of their salary is a fixed salary and one-third is performance-related, which can be increased by: (a) appointment negotiations (if a professor receives an appointment to another university, they can negotiate a salary increase at the current university); (b) additional management positions (dean or rector); and (c) outstanding achievements in research or teaching. In the last of these cases, a bonus may be granted if, for example, a professor is awarded a high-ranking national teaching prize or if they have developed innovative teaching methods for the entire department or even for the university.
2. Performance-related allocation of funds. In the German higher education system the most frequently used performance criteria include measures such as third-party funding, number of PhD candidates and number of student enrolments. These performance criteria-related funds are passed on to the faculties and departments. The faculties and departments then distribute the funds to the professors, according to the same criteria. In this system, teaching is usually only considered as a "load-dependent factor," whereby a high number of students and examinations are compensated by an additional budget, which is not a performance criterion in the narrower sense, but a measurement of the workload.
3. Management by objectives (MbO). In this case, the rectorate negotiates with the deans or with the professors to agree the single objectives they have to achieve. An example of a teaching objective is a new degree program that has to be developed or introduced within a certain period of time. If the goal is achieved, budgetary funds of professors will be raised.

At the same time, many universities have also introduced teaching awards, at both university and departmental level. However, since usually only one person can win such an award, they are not considered selective incentives in the classical sense.

Second, in addition to these monetary steering instruments, the general upgrade of the status of academic teaching was also the target of further developments in higher education policy. In recent years, the federal government and the states – as well as private funding organizations – have launched numerous funding programs and competitions for teaching which, in addition to improving study conditions, should also lead to a sustainable culture of appreciation and recognition of teaching at German universities. Probably the most important and comprehensive funding program was the Quality Pact for Teaching, which has the support of almost 90 percent of all German universities with a total budget of €2 billion from 2011 to

2020. This nationwide funding opportunity for innovations in university teaching will in future be organized differently in institutional terms, with €150 million per year to be provided on a permanent basis, initially by the federal government alone, and from 2024 with state participation of over €40 million. Among the private funding organizations, the donors' association for the promotion of humanities and sciences in Germany (*Stifterverband für die Deutsche Wissenschaft*) is setting the tone, having already launched the first Competition for Excellence in Teaching in 2009 together with the Conference of Ministers of Education and Cultural Affairs (*Kultusministerkonferenz*) (Schmid and Lauer 2016).

THEORETICAL FRAMEWORK

In order to theoretically grasp these higher education policy developments, Wilkesmann (2013) introduced the distinction between transactional and transformational governance. The terminology is adopted from the "full range leadership model" (Bass and Avolio 1993) and we use it to describe the structural and cultural characteristics of teaching governance. Here, it is important to stress that governance does not mean a formal directive influence, but rather an indirectly mediated influence through a goal-oriented design of the framework conditions under which the members of an organization act (Wilkesmann 2013).

Accordingly, transactional governance is an extrinsic incentive design that is based on contractual exchange processes. Results are monitored, rewarded in the event of compliance and sanctioned in the event of non-compliance. In terms of teaching, the "new steering instruments" previously mentioned are prime examples of this.

In contrast, transformational governance represents the cultural component. This mode thus expands the transactional one through a sense of long-term commitment, common interests and a shared vision within an organization. With regard to teaching, transformational governance refers to all organizational efforts that contribute to a supportive teaching culture in which individual teaching commitment is organizationally valued, supported and rewarded.

We define supportive teaching culture in line with Feldman and Paulsen (1999), as follows:

> In this culture, there is a commitment to, and support of academic teaching from the top of the organization. In addition, the organization offers general conditions that genuinely support teaching, such as: well-equipped classrooms; the establishment of organizational units such as centers of excellence in teaching and learning that offer personal training by professional didactic staff; or other (financial) resources to help improve teaching. In summary, in a supportive teaching culture, teaching is held in high esteem at both the departmental and the university level, which is supported by shared social norms that promote quality teaching. (Wilkesmann and Lauer, 2020, p. 439)

Ultimately, such a supportive teaching culture could thus have a lasting influence on the conditions of socialization in the academic field, in which not only research achievements count, but also teaching achievements.

In light of these theoretical considerations, the following two hypotheses are stated:

H1: Transactional governance increases individual teaching commitment.

H2: Transformational governance increases individual teaching commitment.

How these two modes of teaching governance relate to the individual teaching behavior will be explained in the following.

SELF-DETERMINATION THEORY

One motivation theory that has been used very often in recent years, and which explains motivation behavior very well and, more importantly, explains the relationship between the perceived organization and the working environment and the type of motivation, is self-determination theory (SDT) (Ryan and Deci 2000). As depicted in Figure 19.2, SDT assumes a continuum from heteronomy to self-determination, depending on the perception of the organizational environment in which the person works. It is assumed that the instruments of NPM lead to a perception of heteronomy on the one hand and that a high degree of autonomy in teaching leads to a perception of self-determination on the other hand. According to SDT, the perception of high self-determination is caused by high autonomy, high competence perception and strong social integration (Ryan and Deci 2000). In contrast, the perception of a high degree of heteronomy correlates with external motivation.

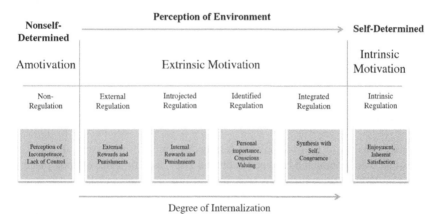

Source: Ryan and Deci (2000, p. 72).

Figure 19.2   Self-determination theory

In extrinsic motivation, actions are performed only for reward or punishment. Applied to teaching, this means for example that they are initially performed only because of contractual obligation or money. Consequently, individual teaching commitment can only be increased if there are appropriate selective (monetary) incentives. This would mean, for example, that a professor will make more effort in teaching if they receive a €500 extra payment. With introjected motivation, external reward and reward mechanisms are already internalized. Typical symptoms are a guilty conscience and incomplete professorial self-esteem when teaching duties are neglected. The identified motivation describes actions that are controlled by social norms. Teaching is based on good academic teaching practice and its standards, which the professors have internalized in their academic education. To teach well has a personal meaning, and is considered a significant contribution to the education of students. Integrated motivation describes an action regulation that corresponds to the self-image and is even stronger than the identified motivation. If one's own self-understanding implies that being a scientist does not only take place in an ivory tower, but also includes teaching in equal parts, then teaching is part of this self-understanding. Finally, an action is intrinsically motivated when it is free of external incentives and constraints and is only performed because it brings fun, joy or satisfaction. Applied to academic teaching, this means that a high level of commitment to teaching results from pure pleasure in the transfer of knowledge and interaction with students. Therefore, in intrinsic action regulation, a rational weighing of advantages or disadvantages in the execution of the action is of no importance for the actors. In empirical studies, however, the integrated type of motivation is difficult to distinguish from intrinsic motivation (Wilkesmann and Schmid 2012, 2014).

Thus, in SDT a continuum is assumed that extends from being externally determined to being self-determined, depending on the actor's perception of the organizational environment. It is now assumed that these two forms of governance have different effects on the individual teaching motivation: transformational governance means a wide scope of action that allows a high degree of self-determination and thus promotes more internalized forms of teaching motivation; however, transactional governance is perceived as external control that does not allow self-determination and instead triggers external motivation.

This leads to the third hypothesis:

H3: The more self-determined the motivation to teach, the higher the commitment to teaching.

DATA BASIS

The data basis consists of two nationwide surveys among full professors at state-controlled universities that were conducted between 2009 and 2017. The first survey took place between May and July 2009. The main focus was to find out whether and how the new steering instruments affect individual teaching motivation and commitment. A disproportionately stratified sample of 8000 professors was drawn from the e-mail distribution list of the German Association of University Professors (DHV), which includes almost all professors at research universities in Germany. All 3244 professors who received performance-related salaries at that time received the e-mail, and the remaining 4756 respondents were randomly selected from all professors who still received salaries based on the seniority principle; 1119 persons completed the questionnaire in full, which represents a net response rate of 14 percent.

As Table 19.1 and Table 19.2 show, it is possible with the help of official data derived from the Federal Statistical Office of Germany to carry out a structural comparison of the most important key features with the population. This good data situation definitely marks a special feature of higher education research.

The second survey took place between November 2016 and June 2017. In this survey, it was of particular interest how the professors perceive the appreciation of teaching at their university on various levels, what teaching and learning support structures and incentives are perceived, how they are used and how effectively they are finally assessed. With regard to the individual teaching practice, teaching motivation as well as the teaching commitment were assessed, as in the previous survey. With regard to sampling, it was a complete survey of the population of all German professors at state-controlled research universities. Here, we have researched a mailing list including 22 405 e-mail addresses, of which 21 089 were successfully delivered; 2663 fully completed questionnaires were included in the data set, which corresponds to a response rate of 12.5 percent. For the subsequent statistical analyses, we only included full professors ($n = 2287$) who had indicated their university affiliation. Again, a detailed sample description is provided in Table 19.2.

Table 19.1   Sample description, 2009

Categories for comparison	Population	Sample
Old C-salary	68.6% ($n = 14\ 388$)	41.5% ($n = 458$)
New W-salary (pay-for-performance)	31.4% ($n = 6569$)	58.5% ($n = 645$)
Male	83.6% ($n = 19\ 109$)	73.1% ($n = 826$)
Female	16.4% ($n = 3914$)	21.2% ($n = 237$)
Age (in years)	49.7 ($n = 23\ 023$)	49.0 ($n = 1030$)
(Pure and applied) soft disciplines		
Humanities	21.4% ($n = 4915$)	27.4% ($n = 292$)
Sports	0.8% ($n = 187$)	0.8% ($n = 9$)
Social science	14.8% ($n = 3413$)	20.2% ($n = 215$)
Arts	11.7% ($n = 2687$)	2.2% ($n = 23$)
Pure hard disciplines		
Mathematics/Natural sciences	24.7% ($n = 5678$)	29.4% ($n = 313$)
Applied hard disciplines		
Human medicine and health science	12.5% ($n = 2836$)	9.1% ($n = 97$)
Forestry, nutritional science and veterinary medicine	2.8% ($n = 635$)	2.4% ($n = 26$)
Engineering	9.9% ($n = 2282$)	8.4% ($n = 89$)

Table 19.2   Sample description, 2016–17

Categories for comparison	Population	Sample
New W-salary (pay-for-performance)	69.8% ($n = 14\ 919$)	62.8% ($n = 1421$)
Old C-salary	30.2% ($n = 6440$)	37.2% ($n = 841$)
Male	78.0% ($n = 16\ 664$)	72.9% ($n = 1638$)
Female	22.0% ($n = 4695$)	27.1% ($n = 608$)
Age (in years)	53.8 ($n = 20\ 229$)	52.6 ($n = 2243$)
(Pure and applied) soft disciplines		
Humanities	15.9% ($n = 3222$)	22.4% ($n = 511$)
Sports	1.0% ($n = 195$)	1.0% ($n = 22$)
Social science	21.3% ($n = 4318$)	21.2% ($n = 483$)
Arts	9.8% ($n = 1989$)	0.8% ($n = 18$)
Pure hard disciplines		
Mathematics/Natural sciences	23.2 ($n = 4710$)	28.6 ($n = 651$)
Pure applied sciences		
Human medicine and health science	11.5% ($n = 2344$)	9.1% ($n = 208$)
Forestry, nutritional science and veterinary medicine	2.5% ($n = 514$)	2.3% ($n = 52$)
Engineering	14.8% ($n = 2994$)	14.6% ($n = 333$)

VALUABLE FEEDBACK FROM THE 2016–17 SURVEY

Especially in the last survey, we received many e-mails from professors who gave us their personal opinion about the status quo of teaching at their university. The following e-mail responses are representative:

> I am a passionate teacher (and researcher, of course) at [the University of X] and I am generally annoyed by the widespread disdain for academic teaching for many, many years. I have set out to do research and teaching, not just research and forced minimal teaching. I know all my students by name and often know many other things about them. This is important to me, because a system like the university cannot be a social one if everything is just serial numbers. I value the personal encounter with people – students and colleagues alike – very highly and am annoyed every time I meet colleagues who, in my opinion, are completely unsuitable as mediators or generally neglect teaching and dispatch students like annoying flies. Unfortunately, I know very, very many colleagues who perform exactly so. (E-mail retrieved October 12, 2016)

> Your research project is highly commendable. Since you wrote to me at my address at [University X], I filled out the survey as if I was still a professor at [University X]. I worked there for 12 years and never got rid of the feeling that I had [bent over backwards] for my students and in return – to put it crudely – only got a slap in the face from the university management. Accordingly, my answers to the questions in your questionnaire, which I have just completed, have been devastating in relation to [University X]. Let me make it quite clear: anyone who, as a university teacher, attaches importance to providing adequate care for the young people entrusted to his care is completely out of place at [University X]. Despite all the soap-box speeches, the rectorate there is interested in teaching and students not at all. At [University X] only third-party funds and the beautiful exterior façade count. Everything else is not important to the university management there. In fact, I have been a professor at [University Y] since October 2015, and if I had filled out your questionnaire in this capacity, my answers would have been much more positive. The working environment here at [University Y] is much more pleasant for professors who are interested in teaching. (E-mail retrieved on November 11, 2016)

Before moving on to the central results, the latent concepts used in the analyses need to be specified more precisely.

HOW TO MEASURE TEACHING COMMITMENT

In a first step, it was initially necessary to develop a measurement inventory that covered the many dimensions of teaching as exhaustively as possible. Accordingly, the original inventory in the first survey covered the following dimensions where the professors had to rate on a five-point Likert scale (1 = very low, 5 = very high) the importance attached and real effort put into: (1) planning and continuous revision of course content; (2) teaching methodology; and (3) examination.

As the results from the 2009 survey data in Figure 19.3 show, overall, the planning and continuous revision of course content is considered to be most important (importance $M = 4.13$, effort $M = 3.46$). In the second place is the examination (importance $M = 3.68$, effort $M = 3.30$), closely followed by teaching methodology (importance $M = 3.46$, effort $M = 3.20$). However, these mean values differ when controlled by gender. This applies above all to the self-assessment of the real effort put into the different dimensions of teaching. It is also noteworthy that the stated importance of the individual dimensions of teaching is always higher than the respective actual effort. Additionally, an above-average commitment to teaching is apparently female-connoted.

INDICATORS OF TRANSACTIONAL AND TRANSFORMATIONAL GOVERNANCE

Although the later survey included more questions regarding the general appreciation of teaching on various levels, in the subsequent analyses only those characteristics of transactional and transformational governance were included that were questioned in both surveys.

The extent of transactional governance was measured as a count variable. Here, the professors were asked for the existence of the following four selective incentives that promote outstanding teaching performance: (1) performance-related pay; (2) teaching awards at the university and/or departmental level; (3) performance-related budgets; and (4) MbO with teaching objectives.

Indicators of a supportive teaching culture in turn were related to transformational governance. This includes the perceived number of didactic support opportunities, which was measured as a count variable asking for the existence of discipline-specific training, personal training or peer coaching. Further indicators were the degree of collegial exchange about teaching (1 = very low, 5 = very high) and the degree of constructive feedback by students (1 = very low, 5 = very high).

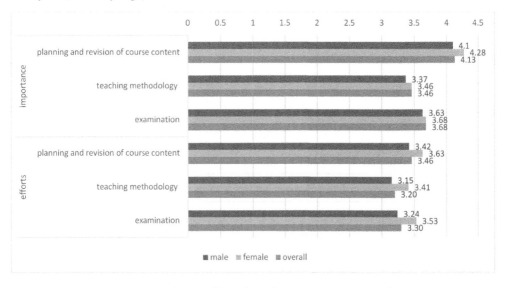

Figure 19.3   Importance and real effort of teaching (survey data 2009)

WHAT THE EMPIRICAL FINDINGS SAY

Although teaching commitment covers several dimensions, only the dimension 'importance attached to teaching methodology' was included in our analyses. The reason for this is statistical in nature, as the explained variance in multivariate testing was comparatively low with the other dimensions (Wilkesmann and Schmid 2012). Therefore, in the later survey the professors were only asked about this dimension. Compared with the 2009 survey, the response behavior has not changed significantly ($M = 3.41$).

To estimate and compare the influence of the assumed factors on the individual teaching commitment, standardization is necessary, since the factors have different units. In Table 19.3, the symbols ++ and -- describe whether there is a positive or a negative effect. For readers interested in statistics, see Table 19A.1 in the Appendix for the regression coefficients.

As Table 19.3 shows, NPM measured by the number of perceived selective incentives has no effect in either survey, which means H1 must be rejected. But if one looks at the signs of the standardized beta coefficients in the Appendix, the association has now become weakly positive.

The supportive teaching culture hypothesis (H2) can only be confirmed for the 2016–17 survey. For example, the number of perceived didactic support structures has a positive influence on the importance attached to teaching methodology. The immediate teaching environment, expressed by a lively collegial exchange on teaching as well as constructive feedback from students, is also positively associated with the importance attached to teaching methodology.

In terms of teaching motivation, the hypothesis on SDT can be confirmed for both survey points, where the importance attached to teaching methodology is mostly associated with intrinsic motivation. One difference that can be noted is that the identified teaching motivation is only significant in the new survey. The introjected and external teaching motivation is not significant in either survey.

Table 19.3   Regression analyses

Variables	2009 ($n = 980$)	2016–17 ($n = 2162$)
H1: Transactional governance (NPM)		
Selective incentives	NE	NE
H2: Transformational governance (Supportive teaching culture)		
Didactic support	NE	++
Collegial exchange about teaching	NE	++
Constructive student feedback	NE	++
H3: SDT (Teaching motivation)		
Intrinsic	++	++
Identified	NE	++
Introjected	NE	NE
External	NE	NE
Control variables		
Female	++	++
Mathematics and natural science	--	--
Age	NE	++

NE = no effect, ++/-- positive/negative significant (p < 0.01)

In addition, we controlled for gender, discipline and age, with gender being the strongest predictor in both regression models. However, age is only significant in the more recent survey; this may have something to do with the fact that a disproportionate sample was drawn in the 2009 survey. Also, professors from mathematics and natural sciences attribute significantly less importance to teaching methodology than professors from other disciplines.

TEACHING MOTIVATION: 2009 VERSUS 2016–17

In a second step, we examined whether anything has changed in the teaching motivation itself. A comparison of means between the two surveys shows that, on average, German professors enjoy their teaching very much and regard it as an interesting activity. Besides that, teaching is also seen as something important both for the development of one's own students and for the academic profession itself.

However, where differences can be observed between the two survey points is in the introjected teaching motivation, where the mean values of the respective items differ by up to 1.6 scale points (see Table 19.4). This is most pronounced in the item 'I have a bad conscience if I have neglected my teaching' and 'I would feel uncomfortable if I have neglected my teaching duties'. But also the motivation to be successful in teaching has increased over the years, as well as the professorial self-esteem, which defines itself even more by good teaching.

Table 19.4   Comparison of means: teaching motivation

Items	2009 M (SD)	2016–17 M (SD)
Introjected teaching motivation		
My aspiration is also to be successful at teaching, otherwise I would feel like a loser.	2.79 (1.26)	3.48 (1.15)
I have a bad conscience if I have neglected my teaching duties.	2.34 (1.14)	3.84 (1.15)
I would feel uncomfortable if I have neglected my teaching duties.	2.99 (1.33)	3.93 (1.01)
My self-concept as a professor is also determined by quality teaching.	3.66 (1.13)	4.21 (0.91)

CONCLUSION

To return to the typical German professor from the introduction, we can conclude from our results that the new steering instruments of the NPM do not change teaching behavior, even if there is a €500 bonus for it. It is therefore not surprising that a considerable number of professors simply do not know about its existence or ignore it, as Table 19.5 shows.

Table 19.5   Comparison: ignorance of NPM instruments (2009 versus 2016–17)

Ignorance – NPM instruments	2009 (n = 1119)	2016–17 (n = 2287)
Performance-based Pay	30.2% (n = 338)	28.5% (n = 655)
Teaching Awards	24.0% (n = 263)	14.1% (n = 318)
Management by Objectives (MbO)	11.8% (n = 132)	23.8% (n = 538)
Performance Related Budget	13.3% (n = 146)	14.1% (n = 319)

While awareness of the existence of performance-based pay and teaching awards has increased between the two survey points, the percentage of those who are unaware of the existence of MbO has decreased significantly.

On the brighter side, it could be shown that transformational governance as supportive teaching culture has gained a positive influence on the individual teaching commitment. Hence, upgrading the status of academic teaching does not occur in a vacuum, but depends on the interaction of many actors at different levels within the university. Here it is especially important to establish a teaching culture in which teaching is understood as a common enterprise, and to foster the dialogue university-wide. In our research we were able to prove that such a teaching culture is still in its infancy. Although university-wide measures such as an annual day for teaching (a one-day event dedicated exclusively to teaching where all university members are welcome) have been implemented at many universities, they have not yet percolated down to the departmental level. When professors were asked in the last survey about the degree of collegial exchange on teaching practice, on a five-point Likert scale, an average value of 2.4 is rather poor: only 17 percent of the respondents stated that this was more or less or fully true (Lauer and Wilkesmann 2019).

However, there is also a strong gender effect: female professors are more involved in teaching than male professors. One reason for this could be gender stereotypes, or the fact that men tend to focus more on research and women more on teaching.

Nonetheless, if professors are intrinsically motivated from the outset, then their commitment to teaching is high, regardless of the gender. As the results indicate, teaching is mostly self-determined, which is good news in terms of SDT. Here, a professor's own intrinsic motivation plays the most important role. When this passion for teaching is not present, then getting motivated all at once through incentive systems is a tough undertaking. After all, a dean cannot say to a professor: "Be intrinsically motivated!" That would be a paradoxical request, because intrinsic motivation must come from within and cannot be forced from outside. Intrinsic motivation can only be encouraged if the work situation is perceived as self-determined.

Fortunately, each university always has some professors who develop innovative teaching concepts and show above-average commitment to teaching. Thus, some management advice for university rectorates would be to be actively on the lookout for such exceptional persons if they wish to make teaching count more at their university. In our own research we have also encountered such "teaching entrepreneurs" (Schmid and Lauer 2016) who significantly influenced their teaching environment for the better. However, these professors had one crucial thing in common: namely, socialization outside of academia. After receiving their doctorates, they spent a notable amount of time in companies, mostly in management positions. Through this "experience of alienation" they developed a cynical picture of the average professor who is mainly interested in their research reputation. Accordingly, this different view caused most of these professors to perceive the prevailing teaching environment as unsatisfactory and dysfunctional when re-entering academia. Such unsatisfactory situations included "no collegial exchange about teaching," a predominant avoidance of confrontation (a "non-aggression pact") among colleagues over teaching issues, or a completely indifferent rectorate. In response, they very consciously confronted their colleagues – some of them in leading positions as dean of studies – with the prevailing grievances in order to optimize their own teaching situation and teaching environment in their own entrepreneurial way.

Thus, as far as the comparison of teaching motivation between 2009 and 2016–17 is concerned, the most exciting result is that only the introjected teaching motivation has changed between the two survey points. This, however, needs further examination due to the lack of longitudinal data. A tentative interpretation could be that due to the developments in higher education policy the issue of "quality teaching" is now simply more on the agenda at German universities than it was perhaps 10–15 years ago. This increased awareness of quality teaching, in turn, may then also be responsible for the changes in the introjected teaching motivation. At this point, it can only be hoped that further national efforts and appropriate university governance will establish a supportive teaching culture at German universities, so that the intrinsic motivation of future professors will be promoted even more.

REFERENCES

Bass, Bernard M. and Bruce Avolio (1993), "Transformational leadership and organizational culture," *Public Administration Quarterly*, 17 (1), 112–121.

Feldman, Kenneth A. and Michael B. Paulsen (1999), "Faculty motivation: The role of a supportive teaching culture," *New Directions for Teaching and Learning*, 78, 69–78.

Kleimann, Bernd and Maren Klawitter (2017), "Berufungsverfahren an deutschen Universitäten aus Sicht organisationaler Akteure" (Appointment procedures at German universities from the perspective of organisational actors), *Beiträge zur Hochschulforschung*, 39, 52–73.

Lauer, Sabine and Uwe Wilkesmann (2019), "How the institutional environment affects collegial exchange about teaching at German research universities: Findings from a nationwide survey," *Tertiary Education and Management*, 25, 131–144.

Ryan, Richard M. and Edward L. Deci (2000), "Self-determination theory and the facilitation of intrinsic motivation, social development and well-being," *American Psychologist*, 55 (1), 68–78.

Schmid, Christian J. and Sabine Lauer (2016), "Institutional (teaching) entrepreneurs wanted! – Considerations on the professoriate's agentic potency to enhance academic teaching in Germany," in *Organizing Academic Work in Higher Education: Teaching, learning and Identities*, L. Leisyte and U. Wilkesmann (eds). London: Routledge, pp. 109–131.

Wilkesmann, Uwe (2013), "Effects of transactional and transformational governance on academic teaching: Empirical evidence from two types of higher education institutions," *Tertiary Education and Management*, 19 (4), 281–300.

Wilkesmann, Uwe and Sabine Lauer (2020), "The influence of teaching motivation and New Public Management on academic teaching," *Studies in Higher Education*, 45 (2), 434–451.

Wilkesmann, Uwe and Christian J. Schmid (2012), "The impacts of new governance on teaching at German universities: Findings from a national survey," *Higher Education*, 63 (1), 33–52.

Wilkesmann, Uwe and Christian J. Schmid (2014), "Intrinsic and internalized modes of teaching motivation," *Evidence-based HRM: A Global Forum for Empirical Scholarship*, 2 (1), 6–27.

APPENDIX

Table 19A.1   Regression analyses

Variable	β (2009)	β (2016–17)
H1: Transactional governance (NPM)		
# Selective incentives	–0.01	0.04
H2: Transformational governance (supportive teaching culture)		
# Didactic support	–0.05	0.07**
Collegial exchange about teaching (1=not at all, 5=to a large extent)	–0.05	0.11**
Constructive student feedback (1=not at all, 5=to a large extent)	0.03	0.06**
H3: SDT (Teaching motivation)		
Intrinsic	0.16**	0.17**
Identified	0.08	0.10**
Introjected	0.01	0.03
External	0.00	0.01
Control variables		
Gender (1=female, 0=male)	0.20**	0.18**
Discipline (1=mathematics and natural sciences, 0 = Rest)	–0.13**	–0.16**
Age	–0.05	0.12**
R^2	0.12	0.19
n	980	2162

**Sig < 0.01; * Sig < 0.05

20. Teaching and learning with our colleagues: the Associate Professor Development Programme at Copenhagen Business School

Alan Irwin

INTRODUCTION

Teaching and learning are usually thought of as activities directed towards students who, one way or another, come 'in' to the university. But what if teaching and learning do not involve students outside the institution but instead colleagues working in the same institution? And what if that teaching and learning are not focused on specific knowledge and skills (how to be a better teacher, how to conduct an examination online, how to store research data) but rather on the more open category of professional development?

In this chapter, I will introduce one short programme targeted at giving support to a particular group of business school academic staff, and reflect upon some of the lessons learnt. How does one create such a programme, get the backing of academic mangers and potential participants, and run it successfully? How does one decide the content of the programme, including the balance between predetermined activities and responsiveness to the expressed needs of participants? Let me say from the beginning (and before this becomes obvious) that I do not approach these issues as an expert in either professional development or educational design. My background is in sociology and in science and technology studies, with an extensive experience in academic management. What follows draws not upon my particular academic expertise but rather upon my own largely practical engagement in developing and teaching the programme in question, and my personal reflections based on this.

The target audience and general thinking behind the educational module in question can be rather clearly stated. Let me try to express this concisely in the kind of terms employed at Copenhagen Business School (CBS) back in 2014–15. When it comes to addressing the needs of different categories of academic staff, quite a lot of attention (although perhaps still not enough) is given to those requiring early-career support as they seek to make the transition to permanent and/or tenured positions. At the same time, one can argue that full professors often get considerable internal and external recognition, and generally form part of extensive international and collegial networks. But, as the CBS discussion went, what about the all-important middle group within the academic career structure?

Associate professors – defined here as mid-career academic staff in relatively secure employment – can find themselves put to service as workhorses responding to many competing demands. Such demands typically include: providing core teaching but also course leadership, taking on key administrative duties, developing a strong set of publications, supervising PhDs, applying for external research funding, and assuming positions of cross-institutional responsibility (including service as members of various committees and working groups). To all this is added the obvious fact that associate professors are at a mid-career level, in many cases expected (or expecting themselves) to develop into full professors. It is not insignificant also that associate professors are often in a period in their lives when family and domestic responsibilities require a particularly high level of care and attention.

Associate and mid-career professors are therefore at a critical but also potentially challenging personal and career stage. At the same time, they are crucial to the development of their institution. Many will remain in the same academic department, often for a considerable period of time. It is from this group that the new leaders, innovators, inspirational teachers and star professors will emerge. It follows that associate professors are absolutely central to the planning, growth and future operation of any academic institution. It is not too much to say that they are the future of the business school. Seen in that way, lack of attention to professional development could lead to a significant loss of potential for the institution as well as for the associate professors themselves.

This argument for increasing the institutional attention on associate professors approximately summarises the logic which led CBS to develop what became known in 2016 as the Associate Professor Development Programme (APDP). The immediate background to the APDP was a general review of professional development needs across all academic and administrative staff at CBS. At that point, support for associate professors was identified as one of several priorities for the institution, with a small budget allocated for this specific purpose. Beginning with 'APDP16', at the time of writing in spring 2021, the programme has run four times (and would already have run five times were it not for COVID-19).

In the following account, I first of all provide some background to the programme and explain something of its practical operation. I then go on to reflect upon some of the main questions and issues which arise as I look back on my experience.

SETTING A DIRECTION

It is hard to say much about the Associate Professor Development Programme without a sense of its institutional context. CBS is a large business university with approximately 20 000 students and 675 full-time academic staff. It is one of the eight universities in the Danish public system. Currently, CBS has 11 academic departments, but this number has been 15 (and more) in recent years. The scale of CBS is particularly relevant here, since it allows both a steady stream of new associate professors and a broad spread of academic staff across different business and management disciplines: from finance to business history, and from law to communications. One key, and specifically appreciated, aspect of the APDP has been its capacity to bring together CBS colleagues at the same career stage who might not otherwise get acquainted.

Having decided that the professional needs of associate professors should be given extra attention across the institution, the next step was for an experienced external consultant to be hired in 2014 to offer a pilot three-day course (simply entitled 'Competence Development Programme'). This was positively rated by those who took it. The emphasis in that initial course was very much on the active and open engagement of participants. This approach, and especially its underlying philosophy of responsiveness to the expressed needs of participants, provided the inspiration for CBS to develop its own programme commencing in 2016. Probably the main difference has been that from 2016 the whole activity has run over two days rather than three. Time is always an issue in contemporary academic life, and this change was designed to make the programme more attractive to the target audience (and their heads of department). At that point also, the author of this chapter, who had overseen the previous process as the dean of research at CBS, resumed his position as a professor and took over the running of the programme. This account is unashamedly written therefore from the perspective of someone who has championed the focus on associate professor development and the creation of the APDP, and has actually been the course leader since 2016. At the time of writing, 37 CBS associate professors have completed the programme.

The focus of the programme was therefore relatively clear in terms of its attention to one specific group of academic staff within CBS and their professional development needs. Based on previous discussions, practical experience of the consultant-run pilot programme, and a series of meetings with academic heads of department, a number of more particular aims and objectives had become clear by 2016.

First of all, the course should bring together associate professors across CBS. It should be built as much as possible around the issues and concerns of associate professors themselves and should be flexible to these needs. Consequently, the idea from the beginning was that one participant per department was a suitable number. It was also decided that the course should not be made compulsory for all associate professors, since this might be seen as an additional burden on that group of staff. Based on the pilot, an intensive programme was chosen rather than a series of shorter meetings. From APDP16 onwards this has run from the morning on day 1 until late afternoon on day 2 at a location outside CBS. Dinner on the first day is an integral part of the programme.

Secondly, and especially given some concerns among heads of department about the relationship between the programme and departmental management and career development processes, it was very important that the aims should be clarified from the start. As the invitation to APDP16 phrased it:

> The intention is not to duplicate individual and academic matters best discussed at departmental level. Instead, the goal will be to bring a group (maximum 15) of associate professors across CBS together in order to focus on common issues and potential solutions. The programme will also create a network across CBS. By discussing shared opportunities and challenges with colleagues from other departments and with CBS's management, the programme goal is that your possibilities for professional development will be improved and positive practical actions identified.

Thirdly, and as is hinted at in the above extract, it was seen to be valuable to involve heads of department and members of senior university management directly in the development programme. One successful idea from the pilot was for participants to prepare a short report to university management, presenting their main views and suggestions. An important role was also given to two heads of department and the two CBS deans (for research and education) in meeting and engaging directly with participants. These meetings are designed to allow an open dialogue: the sessions are chaired by the participants themselves and they set the agenda. Since APDP16, institutional engagement has developed even further to include subsequent meetings involving the APDP participants in order to present their group report to heads of department and the entire senior management team (including the CBS president).

Fourthly, partly in order to deal with the constraint of offering a place to only one associate professor from each department, the decision was taken to focus on recently appointed associate professors (defined as within the five previous years) in order to help them transition to their new role. This rule has gradually relaxed over the years of the programme, and in practice the APDP has generally operated a little below the maximum of one per department (not least due to last-minute cancellations and the inability of some heads to find an appropriate and available participant). However, most of the participants have been relatively recent appoint-ments to an associate professorship, and thus at the younger end of the age spectrum occupying such a position at CBS.

Given these aims and objectives – and also the parameters set out so far – the obvious challenge for the programme leader was to develop a specific module which could satisfy not only a selected group of associate professors but also their immediate managers and senior managers. The support of heads of department is particularly important since it was agreed at the beginning that they should identify candidates who would particularly benefit from the programme. This allows heads to offer the APDP as part of their support to mid-career members of staff; perhaps discussing this within the annual appraisal meeting. It has also created a feedback mechanism where the APDP course leader must in some way be respon-sive to questions and comments from heads (who will no doubt also hear directly from their selected APDP participant after the programme). In the next section, I will turn to questions of course design and operation.

THE APDP IN PRACTICE

> How to survive and thrive as an associate professor at CBS
> What is my role as an associate professor?
> How can I prioritise across the competing demands on my time?
> How should I plan my teaching contribution? And how can I play a part in programme development?
> What is it like to supervise a PhD for the first time – or apply for research funding?
> How can I demonstrate academic leadership or be a good departmental citizen?
> Who can I turn to for advice and support?

This extract from the 2016 APDP invitation captures the general spirit of the two-day module. As the invitation also noted:

> The programme will offer a balance of flexibility to the expressed needs of participants and pre-planned elements. Participants should come prepared to give a short (maximum 10 minute) pres-entation on 'my challenges and opportunities as an associate professor'.

The request to bring at least one challenge/opportunity to the APDP has been central to its operation. This has meant also that it is not possible to know in advance the themes and issues which will be raised during each programme (although certain elements inevitably recur). Instead, one important strand within the APDP begins with each of the 7–12 participants presenting their individual challenge/opportunity. These are then discussed with the whole group. Over the years since 2016, a wide variety of issues have been raised by participants, and at levels ranging from the personal (issues of work–life balance, prioritization, working as a foreigner in a Danish setting), to matters of career development (especially promotion crite-ria, but also PhD supervision and teaching administration), to larger and more generic issues (matters of gender, internationalization and diversity, the societal impact of research, the role of cross-disciplinarity), to questions of overall CBS strategy. This can be a rich mix, but it does offer an intriguing picture of the personal and professional concerns of this group of associate professors in a business school environment.

The next step is to cluster the challenges and opportunities into 3–4 theme groups focused on a specific issue or question. This is done through a collective process of discussion and shared selection. The clustering process can be a little challenging, and at this point some issues are inevitably squeezed out. However, these are noted with the intention that they should be returned to over the coming two days.

Each theme group (for example, on career development or teaching policy) then separately begins to explore its main issue. Very often, a 'this is what we want to share' and 'this is what we think should be done' schema is adopted. Immediate reactions are sought from two pre-invited heads of department as part of a general meeting on the first afternoon. It is usually fascinating to observe this dialogue between heads and the APDP participants (and later between the deans and the participants). Sometimes, of course, questions and issues can be predicted, notably with regard to promotion and performance criteria. But unexpected topics also arise (e.g., student plagiarism). Input from this meeting provides the foundation for each theme group to reflect further on its main focus, sharpen its thinking, and then engage during the second day in a similar (but by this point more focused) discussion with the two deans. Finally, a short PowerPoint presentation is prepared based on the work of all the theme groups. This is subsequently polished in e-mail exchanges after the programme and is then used as the basis for subsequent report-back sessions with department heads and senior management.

The main themes collectively selected by participants inevitably reflect the particular situation of associate professors, but also larger institutional debates. As already noted, discussions during the APDP have often centred on the requirements for future promotion – and especially on the weight given to different kinds of academic contribution. Education – and especially the organization and management of teaching – has been a rather constant theme. Matters of CBS strategy have also featured prominently, often reflecting the international business school debate about the balance between high-level research publications and wider societal impact. Questions and comments which have emerged from the APDP over the years cover a number of areas:

> How should young associate professors prioritise funding applications (small/large grants)?
> Does CBS have a policy and an action plan on social, gender and ethnic diversity in the recruitment of students?
> How much attention should we give to bibliometric indicators/journal rankings early on/later on during our Associate Professorship?
> It is unclear how teaching performance is evaluated, appreciated and factored into various stages of progression (bonuses, promotion etc).
> As we go up the hierarchy, we spend more time on administering teaching rather than doing teaching.

Perhaps as a consequence of the creation of theme groups and the subsequent reporting back to heads of department and senior management, topics defined by APDP cohorts have often had a strategic or policy orientation; usually drawing attention to 'challenges' in the CBS system and making tentative proposals for how to address these. Despite some initial concerns among department heads, these challenges rarely take the form of actual complaints, and the associate professors almost always phrase their questions to university managers in rather constructive and diplomatic terms. In fact, it is hard not to be struck by the obvious sense of identity and indeed loyalty participants exhibit towards their host institution. However, it must be said that this is at least partly a self-selected group of mid-career colleagues, and that the framework of the APDP does encourage the identification of practical solutions and ways forward rather than larger criticisms and disagreements – for which there are other representative bodies within the institution. In that way, the focus has less been on the sustained analysis of long-standing dilemmas and more on how individuals can plan their own professional development in the face of such dilemmas.

The line from individual challenges/opportunities to theme groups to discussions with heads and deans and then finally to a PowerPoint-based report is, however, only one strand through the APDP. A second strand focuses very much on the individual participant and invites each to consider their own wishes and aspirations. This is a quieter exercise which begins with each participant writing down some thoughts purely for their own use (these are not shared and I do not see them myself). By APDP19 this was known as a 'reflective exercise', but back in 2016 was more bluntly labelled 'writing your obituary'. Somewhere between 2016 and 2019, the obituary was reframed as the '80th birthday party'. But the exercise remains essentially the same: how do you wish to be remembered?

> Imagine it is your 80th birthday party. All the most important people in your life are gathered together. Think about the speeches that will be given that day. But what will they say? Lise made every sacrifice for her family, always putting their needs ahead of her own ambitions? Or Lise built a huge international reputation in her field, travelling constantly to participate in important research activities and events? Or perhaps, Lise was a gifted and dedicated teacher – always the first to update her pedagogical skills and to respond to changing student needs?
>
> And who will be at the party? Family only – or colleagues and former students too? Perhaps mainly colleagues and only a few family members? With whom would you like to celebrate your 80th birthday? Who do you want to be the most important people in your life – and what do you hope they will say about you?

Needless to say, this exercise has created both positive and negative reactions. Perhaps the clearest responses have been from those who either felt that their work and personal life were completely separate – why would I invite work colleagues and former students to such an important family occasion? – or else recognized that their work and family time were totally intermingled. Some participants have clearly been surprised that such a personal question should arise in a professional development programme. To this was added a potential split between native Danes and those from outside Denmark whose families might be more distant (at least in physical terms). Such issues obviously have to be handled with care, and only very rarely have discussions become emotionally (over)charged. Participants have also been rather good at paying attention to each other's feelings and reactions. The ethos is collegial and open rather than in any way confrontational. But the intention behind the exercise has been to encourage individuals to take stock of their own personal and professional priorities and to incorporate these within their career goals and planning.

The third strand of the APDP is directly tied to the more spontaneous engagement between associate professors who may never have previously met one another. One recurrent aspect of the programme is for participants to be struck by the contrasts between departments; perhaps especially when it comes to recruitment and promotion requirements. Relatedly, participants often comment on the range of activities within CBS, and even the very existence of colleagues in neighbouring departments who may have overlapping research and teaching interests. One is reminded just how silo-like academic life can be, so that colleagues from different departments even in the same building can be very weakly connected. A regular feedback from the programme is that participants especially appreciate the chance to make personal connections across CBS but also to gain a much broader perspective on the entire institution.

These then are the three main strands of the APDP at CBS: the identification of key themes and issues, personal reflection on one's own priorities and goals, a short but intense interaction with colleagues across different disciplines and departments. As I explain right at the start of the first day, all discussions are under 'Chatham House Rules', meaning that participants are free to make use of any information received – and indeed are encouraged to do so – but such information (including general remarks and the expression of opinions) should not be attributed to any particular person. Of course, this 'rule of the house' applies to the current chapter.

Some more specific and separate activities have additionally taken place following the main programme: for example, a meeting with highly productive researchers at CBS co-organized with previous APDP participants on a topic very much of their choosing: 'How to write a great research paper: planning and writing academic papers – and still keep smiling'. These follow-up meetings have typically brought more than one APDP cohort together. However, what the main two-day programme has deliberately not done is to bring in topic-specific activities. For better or worse, the argument has been that this space should be open to the challenges raised by associate professors themselves, and should not develop into a more conventional staff training or representative group.

Before I finish this section on 'the APDP in practice', let me address two further points. The first relates to participant feedback. A standard evaluation form has been used and it is fair to say that overall feedback has been very positive. The large majority of participants have rated the programme highly, and few have given negative reactions. Perhaps more valuably, individual comments have been collected within the evaluation form. I have incorporated these as appropriate within my discussion in this chapter.

Looking through the more critical evaluation comments, two in particular stand out. Is the 80th birthday exercise appropriate to a programme like this? Could the programme not be shorter: perhaps one day rather than two? In terms of the first comment, this is obviously a matter of judgement. And it needs to be balanced against the fact that other participants find the exercise one of the most valuable parts of the APDP. My own observation is that it raises some key questions in terms of professional development and, furthermore, that it encourages an open, reflective and trusting relationship between participants. I will return to the question of course length in the next section.

The very last point in this section concerns learning objectives. These, as expressed in the APDP16 invitation, have been phrased in rather informal terms: 'the programme goal is that your possibilities for professional development will be improved and positive practical actions identified'. The fact that the programme has run outside the standard education curriculum – there is no course certificate, no European Credit Transfer System (ECTS) allocation and no grade given – has probably allowed learning objectives and goals to be left to develop rather than being more formally stated. Let me also return to this below.

REFLECTIONS

As already acknowledged, I have been closely associated with this programme from the very beginning: helping to identify the needs of associate professors as a priority area, commissioning the pilot from a known and respected British colleague, developing the course itself, and then running it in close association with heads of department and deans. It follows that I can hardly claim to present an objective assessment of its strengths and weaknesses. Let me instead offer some personal reflections based on my experience over the last six or so years.

First of all, I can only report how impressed and refreshed I am every year by the manner in which associate professors at CBS engage in discussions but also with one another. One might expect colleagues at this career stage to be entirely self-focused, concerned mainly with their own career prospects, and reluctant to take on wider responsibilities. That has not at all been my impression through the years of the APDP. The sessions with heads and, separately, deans are run by the participants in a structured but very engaged style; reinforcing the point that these associate professors are very capable of taking leadership and engaging with large institution-wide issues in a responsible and thoughtful manner. For all the legitimate concerns about the future of business schools and the effects of indicators, metrics and new public management on academic career structures, if this group is the future then we should be relatively optimistic.

On reflection, therefore, I am left to wonder why other university meetings do not take place in this serious, friendly but sharply focused fashion. Part of the answer lies in the preparation undertaken by the participants before each meeting with university leaders, and also the level of ownership and control which they themselves assume over what follows. Heads of department and deans are instructed in advance only to introduce themselves, but not to make any opening speeches or to offer their own agenda (unless of course invited to). Their task is to respond and to engage in open discussion, and they nearly always do a good job. This means also that discussions are characterized by a high level of mutual trust and strong sense of collegiality. It has to be acknowledged that there are very often no clear and specific answers to the questions raised. But this has also been a particular learning from the programme. Specifically, not all university managers have the same opinion and not all problems can be solved; but still, practical ways forward need to be found which make sense within one's professional and career development. How can you survive and thrive as an associate professor?

Secondly, it is reasonable to inquire about the form and content of the programme. Why not spread it over a number of shorter sessions? Why not bring in more specific coaching or skills-based sessions such as time management or perhaps an introduction to important CBS-wide initiatives such as diversity action and responsible management? To return to the criticism above, why not make it a one-day rather than a two-day programme?

To be quite honest, I do not have a very coherent response to such entirely fair questions about doing it differently. Yes, the programme could be run in one day, even a half-day. But then it would not be the same programme. It takes time to listen to even a small group of colleagues and to develop a shared agenda. In keeping with discussions through the entire two days, the meetings with heads of department and deans during the programme are not primarily about collecting information but about sharing ideas and opinions, and offering the opportunity for genuine engagement. This means that, possibly for the first time, participants tune in to the legitimately different perspectives of university leaders. The 'reflective exercise' runs through the programme; participants refer to it at different stages as specific observations come to them. The networking aspect almost by definition cannot be rushed.

For this reason also, I have been reluctant to include dedicated sessions on specific, pre-decided topics even though those suggested topics are sometimes rather close to my heart (gender and diversity strategy being an example here). From my side, it would be hard to explain to participants how it is that the programme is open to their needs and challenges and also that I have included (say) a one-hour session on topic X within an already busy couple of days.

My practical compromise has been to offer follow-up sessions on specific topics selected by the group. The session on 'how to write a great paper' was an example of that. Unfortunately, the organization of these one-off sessions has been rather sporadic. This may reflect a lack of activity on my part, or it may be a reflection of the other pressures on this group. It seems easier to clear one's calendar for two days in a setting away from the usual workplace than to find time within the ordinary working week. Having said that, the post-APDP sessions with heads of department and the senior management team have taken more attention than I originally anticipated; and seem to have been beneficial for all parties. I do believe that university leaders can learn (as I have) through listening directly to the views and assessments of associate professors. I also believe that this gives participants a unique opportunity to sit together with heads and senior managers, to be listened to – but also challenged – and to get a glimpse of how things are run at the highest administrative levels of the university.

Thirdly, I would like to return to the question of learning goals and objectives, touched upon briefly at the end of the previous section. As I have already suggested, the fact that the APDP is not linked to a larger educational programme or course structure has probably left these somewhat understated compared with my usual teaching activities. But I have to say that writing this chapter has made me reflect a lot about this point. I think it would be fair to suggest that teaching and learning goals have developed across the different cohorts in just the same way that new ideas about how to run the programme have been incorporated along the way. However, one can also see the APDP as a course in 'good CBS citizenship'. In working closely with colleagues across the business school, reflecting upon one's own and other people's challenges, raising questions with university leaders and gauging the response, exercising power and responsibility, finding practical ways forward in complex situations, making future plans and prioritizations, considering the development of CBS and debating the very purpose of a business school, one is also finding a way of developing an identity as a full member of the academic community. As one previous APDP participant reflected after reading a draft of this chapter: 'I personally enjoyed that the workshop was also very much about transitioning from a narrow focus on one's department (which is very much the case as an assistant professor) to understanding that one is a member of CBS as a whole.'

Fourthly, and having acknowledged my own role in developing and running the programme, I probably have no choice but to reflect a little on this. To some degree, the APDP has developed out of my former position as dean of research at CBS, which involved being line manager for heads of department and with special responsibility for academic recruitment across the university. CBS is a large business school but still small enough for personal connections and some sense of recent history to be important.

One can see my connection to CBS as both an advantage and a disadvantage. The good side is that I have received a lot of local support and I can bring my experience of the institution to the benefit of the participants. The bad side (to put it like that) is that I cannot pretend to be neutral or without opinions. In practice, this means that I have to self-police on the occasions where I am tempted to share my own perspectives too forcefully. It is possible also that my views run ahead of me, so that participants anticipate some of these before even signing on for the programme. In my defence, I would argue that all participants are free, and positively encouraged, to share their opinions; these are indeed colleagues rather than students. However, I am very aware of the challenge of shaping and framing the discussion without imposing my views. Perhaps unavoidably, my own values colour the programme: including the idea of an 'open' academic community which views critical debate as a strength, a commitment to cross-institutional and cross-disciplinary engagement, and a rather pragmatic approach to finding working solutions and making appropriate personal choices.

It is, then, obvious to ask whether such a course would be better taught by an educational consultant or in more standard 'executive training' mode. Given that CBS is a large business school and that the course has run with an average of nine participants over the last four years, this point also links to the possibility that business schools could combine in some way rather than offering such a programme individually and within each institution's own walls.

It is of course true that the pilot programme was developed successfully by an outside consultant, albeit one with very extensive experience of academic life. My view is that there are undoubtedly many people capable of doing a better job than me. But anyone running such a course has to have broad knowledge of the operation of business schools, be open to the ideas and opinions of participants, and have the authority to manage key stakeholders. The discussions during the APDP do not just happen by themselves, but need careful and persistent attention. Going further, and if I now link back to my previous point, then one can see why the APDP as it has been developed at CBS needs to be run by someone with academic authority and who can in some way connect personally to the question of 'being a good academic citizen'. There are different ways of doing this; it seems to be in the very nature of academic citizenship that not everyone will approach the underlying issues in the same way. But without that connection, an essential part of the APDP would be lost.

CONCLUSION: THE LESSONS LEARNT

What would I then do differently if I were starting all this again? Let me express this in three main points.

I would not take responsibility for the programme alone. My institutional standing and experience have (hopefully) been valuable. But such an important teaching and learning activity with a core group of academic staff should not be identified with just one programme leader. If in the end the goal is to encourage the development of good academic citizens and colleagues, then it seems really important to have a core programme team which can reflect upon, and as necessary challenge, the APDP's development.

I would probably put more energy and effort into planning follow-up activities. The fact that the larger 'APDP network' has not fully developed across different cohorts has probably been a consequence of my single-teacher role (although I have always had excellent administrative support). Perhaps also the increased follow-up with heads and deans has diverted from other activities. My hope of course is that all this creativity, energy and engagement has not been lost, but rather has shifted to other, perhaps more important, settings.

I would think from the beginning about the meaning of 'success' in this context. Is this to be judged in terms of the numbers of participants, positive comments on evaluation forms, expressed support from heads of department? Or can it only be measured by the participants themselves when they later look back on the programme? Inevitably, success in this context has to be judged in multidimensional terms. Meanwhile, I tend to rely on my teacher's sense of the classroom rather than on any more transparent or quantifiable measure.

How, in the end, would I describe the APDP? I would present it as a small space for reflection within one's professional development, an opportunity to invest time and attention in a key group of business school colleagues, and as a place to create links with others who share at least some of one's challenges, frustrations, passions and ambitions. It can also be practically helpful in identifying professional challenges and generating workable solutions. To a modest degree, the APDP offers the chance to step outside the usual work setting and to address questions which will in some way guide one's future, but also the future of the business school. In my experience, the effect is to encourage questioning but also understanding of the business school as a whole, and in that way to build a greater sense of identity, ownership and citizenship. In a crowded academic environment, such spaces are hugely important.

ACKNOWLEDGEMENTS

I would like to thank my excellent administrative colleagues for their support with this programme (especially Afrodita Jeftic and Jessie Tvillinggaard). I also thank those CBS colleagues who have chosen to participate in the CBS Associate Professor Development Programme (APDP). I am specifically grateful to the former APDP participants who took the time to comment on a previous draft of this chapter. Thanks also to an anonymous reviewer. Finally, Maja Horst read this chapter at an early stage and was, as always, generous with her creative ideas and suggestions.

21. Leveraging diversity in the classroom

Florence Villesèche and Stina Teilmann-Lock

INTRODUCTION

"Leveraging Diversity in the Classroom": this is the name we gave to a new course in the ped-agogical curriculum offered in the Assistant Professor Programme at Copenhagen Business School (CBS). It is the first course of its kind at CBS and developing it has been a captivating and humbling journey for us. This chapter aims to document and reflect on this journey with the hope of entering a conversation with other trainers and teachers in the business school environment and advancing on our own learning trail.

This adventure started with mixed emotions: excitement as we are both firm advocates of putting diversity-related questions on the (teaching) agenda and are always eager to take on a new challenge in this area, but also fear when we realized that this meant starting from scratch and taking a hard look at our teaching practices. Even if in business schools we teach about the diverse ways in which to approach and work with strategy, marketing, human resources, operations, and more, we (along with large parts of higher education) have many assumptions about a universally proper way to deliver university-level teaching. We may think about the diversity of students in the classroom, but much less about our positionality; we tend to reproduce the way we were taught and the handed-down conceptions of a teacher's duties in the classroom, whether consciously or not. Moreover, in universities and business schools, as in every professional practice, there are dominating institutional logics or norms that lead us to strive for similarity in order to enforce such co-constructed normative expectations (DiMaggio and Powell, 1983). Our peers, as well as our students, assess us (e.g., as part of pedagogical programs or mentoring programs, during hiring and promotion processes), and we want to perform according to (what we believe to be the) expectations. Thus, we do not reflect enough about who we are as a person and teacher, who our students are, and how we can better work together in the classroom to leverage diversity.

We are certainly not the first ones to try to question a universal, homogeneous approach to teaching and to developing a curriculum in higher education. To start with, we take inspiration from previous engagement with awareness-raising and behavioural change through educa-tional practice (see, e.g., Akrivou & Bradbury-Huang, 2015; Christensen et al., n.d.; Semper & Blasco, 2018). Second, we adopt an exploratory approach as the norm, which applies both to the content of the course and to the way we developed it. We will illustrate this exploratory take throughout with vignettes, for example when reflecting on our self-assessment or when presenting some of our course activities such as the production of a 'diversity statement' that teachers can include in their pedagogical portfolio. Third, we think of this chapter as fulfilling the function of storytelling as well as being the presentation of a model. The storytelling element implies that we aim to start a conversation where we shine a light on the characters of diversity (who are the protagonists? who are the narrators? whose perspectives are we taking? and so forth) and on how we enable the telling and retelling of our own and others' stories and shape new and actionable narratives about diversity in the classroom. The aim to develop a model in this chapter is linked to our ambition to present replicable approaches to leveraging diversity in the classroom. In other words, we want to describe things we did in class in a way that makes them adoptable or imitable by readers of this chapter; so, not in the sense of a set of plug-and-play tools, but more in the sense of an invitation to join the exploratory trajectory that we are outlining.

FROM DIVERSITY AS A RESEARCH TOPIC TO DIVERSITY AS A TEACHING PARADIGM

Before we delve into our work in the classroom, it seems fitting to say more about who we are, or rather from which standpoint we speak. We are both associate professors at Copenhagen Business School and work in the same department (Management, Politics and Philosophy). We are also, however, quite different. Florence is Swiss and French, has worked at CBS for about seven years, and teaches diversity management, leadership, strategy and social entrepreneurship. Stina is Danish, has joined CBS recently, and teaches strategic design and intellectual property law. Our collaboration to 'teach the teachers' flows from a previous collaboration to create and carry out the GenderLAB format, a solution-oriented workshop during which participants use tools based on design thinking and norm-critical theory to address gender and diversity-related issues in their organizations.[1] Such a combination of knowledge bases was crucial in ensuring that the GenderLAB would not become a diversity management course for practitioners, and the same line of thought was translated to the development of a pedagogical course about leveraging diversity in the classroom. Indeed, in this course, we aim at understanding diversity not only as referring to the diversity of individuals in the classroom (including the teacher), but rather as an umbrella term that also lets us address course design, learning tools, ethics and institutional environments. Yes, all of that. While this can sound rather ambitious, we aimed, in this first run of our course, to "go broad" rather than focus on only a part of the puzzle, trusting that the junior teachers will then venture further through some of the doors we opened for them, with them.

The first step in the process was for us to reflect on the task at hand and on our own practices with leveraging diversity in the classroom. Vignette 1 offers a narrative summary of how this course came about and its inherent challenges. In this section, we reflect on what we considered to be some of the key challenges: finding and selecting materials to include in our course and grounding the course in our pre-existing teaching approaches and practices.

VIGNETTE 1: "WE WOULD LIKE YOU TO DEVELOP A SPECIALIZED COURSE ABOUT DIVERSITY, BUT IT SHOULD BE FOR EVERYONE"

The whole story started when the colleague who had made the original proposition left our school, but the teaching and learning department still wanted to carry on. The original title of the course was meant to be "Classroom Diversity: Dilemmas and Challenges," and be designed to cater mainly to international, incoming teachers who were little acquainted with Danish culture, and locals who were eager to better engage students with a variety of backgrounds and demographics. At the same time, the first conversation with this colleague clarified that the Teaching and Learning development and support unit worried that the course would attract too few participants. That is the usual worry about courses with the word "diversity" in them, we thought; almost a paradox that there is a will to talk about diversity seriously, but it is perceived as a conversation that will be taken up by people who see themselves as "diverse" compared with a given norm. Also, we were a bit doubtful of the terms "Dilemma and Challenges" that pose diversity as a problem to be solved.

We quickly agreed that we wanted to come across as complementary in this course beyond the fact that one of us is foreign and the other in a Dane. So, we decided to change (almost) everything: the working title and content, and the description of the target audience. We flipped the assumptions and set the target to "all teachers" at CBS, and by putting a positive spin on the course title: "Leveraging Diversity in the Classroom." Yes, that sounds a bit like business lingo, but we wanted something action-oriented and appealing throughout the school. What about the learning objectives, the content? How do we leverage diversity in our other courses? Also, we were asked to develop the course with an online, synchronous part and an offline, asynchronous part. The conversation was much less straightforward than expected. Even if we may be more attuned to such questions, given what we teach and research, we quickly realized that we did not ourselves have a systematic approach to diversity in our classrooms and that we had not confronted our approach to others in that matter. This diagnostic was quite humbling for both of us, and we thus decided to take time to write down what we had done and why, identify blind spots, discuss our self-assessments, and scan practices out there in parallel. What we initially thought would be right down our alley was thus going to be quite some work and a learning experience for us as well!

Taking Stock of our Approaches and Practices

The process of reflecting on our own practices and scanning the environment took several loops and discussions. A Lacanian could analyze our process as attempting to mitigate for a double lack: the lack of a systematic, research-based approach in our practices and (self-) education as teachers on the one hand; and the striking lack of pedagogical work in this area at least on this side of the Atlantic. Having these elements in mind, we nevertheless set out to reach a balance between formalizing and systematizing our practices to share them with the course participants, and supplementing these with new ideas from both sides of the pond. This implied dynamics of inclusion and exclusion, as we had to make choices while aiming to offer a broad overview of possibilities to the course participants. The inclusion and exclusion dynamics do not stop at the choice of materials and contents, however. Another focal point for us was to "walk the talk" and apply our recommendations while teaching about them; this was meant to be constantly reflexive about how we might be including and excluding participants or student groups based on our choices and the way we delivered our teaching in the Assistant Professor Programme at CBS. We now develop on these points with a focus on illustrations rather than the theoretical discussion of our process, and will dive more concretely into teaching situations in the subsequent section.

To start with, we shared the view that rather than seeking to give students an overview of a wide variety of tools and approaches to leveraging diversity – which may very well end up in a superficial, descriptive catalogue – we preferred to explicitly ground the course in our existing practices and materials and then expand from there. In that sense, we envisioned the course more as an introduction to being reflexive around classroom diversity and how this can unfold, rather than as an exhaustive and prescriptive effort. Besides this focus on contextualization and situatedness of ourselves as teachers, we also shared a vision to apply what is known as "design thinking."

While – as mentioned above – it was not our aim to teach tools, we nonetheless let the design thinking toolbox inform our approach. In particular, we wanted our exploratory trajectory to be informed by the ways that designers work with wicked problems, framing and co-creation. The benefits of working with design thinking in relation to diversity in education are that the methods of designers have a long-standing practice for formalizing procedures for the value-making that comes out of developing solutions by working with human-centeredness and by enhancing cognitive diversity as a means for problem-solving (Brown, 2019). In addition, design thinking has an operational character that works as a handy complement to critical theory-oriented approaches to diversity issues that tend to be non-operative (i.e., generally focused on the critique rather than on the development of solutions).

In an article published in 1973, H.W.J. Rittel and M.M. Webber proposed a category of problems that they labelled "wicked problems" or "higher-level" problems (Rittel & Webber, 1973). Wicked problems are, among others, characterized by their having no stopping rule: that is, there is no way of knowing when an optimal solution is found. Solutions to wicked problems are neither good nor bad, true nor false. Moreover, according to Rittel and Webber, "the existence of a discrepancy representing a wicked problem can be explained in numerous ways. The choice of explanation determines the nature of the problem's resolution." The latter point has been rephrased by Richard Buchanan as an assertion in design methodology that "every formulation of a wicked problem corresponds to the formulation of a solution" (Buchanan, 1992). We may add that every solution to a wicked problem is only a solution to a particular manifestation of the problem in question: the way a problem is formulated pre-empts the range of suitable solutions. Issues related to diversity in education are typical wicked problems: the particular formulations of the problems related to diversity will anticipate the way we address them. Similarly, solutions to diversity issues can only ever be more or less good or bad, and there is no way of knowing for certain if one has found an optimal solution.

As a concept in design theory, "framing" is that which enables us to make sense of the world, but also blinds us to prejudices or biases in our perceptions as well as in our attempts at problem-solving. Thus, framing is "a way of selecting, organising, interpreting, and making sense of a complex reality to provide guideposts for knowing, analysing, persuading, and acting. A frame is a perspective from which an amorphous, ill-defined, problematic situation can be made sense of and acted on" (Rein & Schön, 1994: 146). Working reflexively with framing and reframing is useful in the addressing of wicked problems, since a wicked problem cannot be solved by pursuing a true solution; a wicked problem can be resolved by negotiating the multiple truths about it, which is rendered possible by reframing it. Indeed, reframing is what design processes are about, and practising design thinking:

> involves knowing (or at least pretending for a little while) that all frames are fundamentally contestable, incomplete and, therefore, plastic. Thinking like a designer also entails creating new meanings by repositioning and synthesising contending frames. It is also an effective strategy for dealing with the complexity of wicked problems and the attendant ambiguity of knowledge. (Ney & Meinel, 2019: 37)

By reframing the wicked problems of diversity in the classroom, we should be able to discover the blind spots of existing framings and transcend the reductionism of looking for a single objective frame of understanding. This approach saves us from the stifling notion of a "constant interplay of an endless multitude of different frames [that] subvert any attempt of extracting meaning from reality" (ibid.: 35). In other words, what we were aiming at with our course was to leverage diversity in the classroom not as a form of solutionism, but rather as an invitation to an ongoing process through the reframing of issues that came up in dialogue between the two of us, with the Teaching and Learning development and support unit, and with the course participants.

Moreover, co-creation is at the heart of the methodology of design thinking. The inherited wisdom of designers is that the cognitive diversity that goes into the making of a design solution contributes substantially to the value and viability of the solution for the people who it is supposed to be a solution for. It is illustrative of this piece of designerly wisdom that design consultants work with "unfocus groups" where the value of the sample group derives from the fact that the group represents not the average, but rather the boundary cases (Brown, 2019). Accordingly, the innovative abilities of a co-creating group derive from the encounters between different perspectives and between the diverse capabilities, expertise, insights and experiences of group members. As we viewed it and aimed to apply it in the course, co-creation was to serve as the default setting of what takes place in the classroom. In other words, diversity was to be the vehicle of education in any given group with its particular boundary cases, and not a challenge to it. We realize that this places considerable responsibility on the teacher who will be the key person in charge of facilitating the identification and bringing out the value of any group's diversity potential, including what teachers bring to the table themselves. Concretely, the insights of design thinking relative to wicked problems, framing and co-creation meant that we did not want to start class by analytically thinking about questions regarding specific identity groups, such as "How do we get male and female students to work better together in workshops?" Rather, we wanted to start by asking ourselves questions such as "How can we help people with different backgrounds and interest to get something out of a business school course?" To put it even more sharply, by asking ourselves the question "How do we extract educational value out of any given diversity spectrum in the classroom?"

Looking Right, Looking Left: Not Much on the "Diversity in Teaching" Horizon

Although we were not expecting to find a wealth of resources in Denmark and other European countries, we were rather surprised to find very little (publicly available) resources about teaching and diversity, even at leading European business schools. While there is a growing awareness around the question of diversity – in the wake of work about corporate social responsibility (CSR), sustainability and/or the United Nations Sustainable Development Goals – most attention (when there is any) concentrates on academic workplace issues (e.g., women's careers, international mobility, harassment) or student attraction and retention work (e.g., student recruitment, student integration in the job market). When looking to North America, it appears that most universities include the question of teaching into their public discourse about diversity. So: problem solved? One the one hand, this meant that there was indeed quite rich material available to enrich and complement our own practices, make sense of them, and so on. On the other hand, this meant addressing the question of the translation of diversity practices from the United States (US) context, which is not a new discussion. Diversity scholarship has extensively discussed the history of diversity policies, from equal opportunities to diversity management, and the challenges of importing practices into a different historical, political, economic and social context (for translation to the Danish context specifically, see, for example, Boxenbaum, 2006; Risberg and Søderberg, 2008).

The US context, in short, can be characterized as a legislation-heavy and business-centred approach to diversity, and a focus on race and gender. In Denmark – to focus only on our context, the term "diversity" (*mangfoldighed*) is usually understood as referring to ethnic diversity and is linked to a broader CSR agenda, while gender (*køn*) is treated separately, and rather as a business issue since equality is assumed to be achieved (Holck and Muhr, 2017; Kamp and Hagedorn-Rasmussen, 2004). In the higher education context more specifically, this means that all schools observe rules for and report on the intake of students according to race and gender. Moreover, the business case for diversity that is advocated in business life is also promoted in American business schools. In contrast, the assumptions of gender equality on the one hand, and the fact that (im)migrants are not considered explicitly in higher education management in Denmark, explains a quasi-absence of information and tools to address diversity, not least in teaching. In sum, this means that assumptions about why we address the question of diversity and whose identities we have in mind, as well as how we categorize them, will affect how managers and decision-makers – including us as teachers, coordinators, program heads – can and will approach diversity in practice (Villesèche et al., 2018).

With this in mind, and rather than sharing a list-style document for course participants with links to finding resources for leveraging diversity in the classroom, we decided to focus on the "teaching perspective level." We did this, notably, by delving into the example of a European university website that explains its rationale for leveraging diversity and offers a set of ways to do so, and on a practice that has been gaining popularity over the last decade in the United States: the "diversity statement" that candidates include in their application for academic jobs. We delve more into these examples in the next section, in which we will turn our attention to how our course "Leveraging Diversity in the Classroom" was delivered and our reflections on this "first edition."

TEACHING TEACHERS HOW TO LEVERAGE DIVERSITY: A SNEAK-PEEK INTO OUR COURSE

In this section, we focus on discussing some elements about the course structure, how it unfolded, and highlighting some of the activities and exercises we used. Throughout, we will connect these to our design thinking approach.

The first part of the course was asynchronous, and online, through the learning platform we use in our school. This was part of an effort to have diversity as part of the course design, but also to address expectations in our institution to have a blended learning approach. This included an introductory video where we present the course, texts to read, a brief survey (about participants, their experience in the classroom diversity, and to enquire about specific issues they have encountered or want to address), as well as a video we asked them to react to and discuss. We will here focus on this last aspect. The video we shared comes from a European university, as an example of how leveraging diversity in teaching can be understood and communicated about in our region of the world. Freie Universität Berlin has an open access web page (in German and partly available in English) called "Toolbox: Gender and Diversity in Academic Teaching."[2] We shared the three-minutes video Freie Uni Berlin has on the homepage and asked students to comment, in order for them to warm up to the topic, get their analytical skills into motion, and start online interaction between participants before coming to class. This type of approach can, for example, mitigate the anxiety about "Will I be the only XX on the course?" and allow written expression rather than focus on oral interaction only. This way of opening the course was part and parcel of our ambition to launch diversity in the classroom as a wicked problem: we wanted to allow for as broad a spectrum of problem formulations as possible from the beginning,

Moreover, the participants' comments on this video and their engagement with the other online activities allowed for a smooth transition to the classroom environment for the face-to-face component of the course (four hours). After a short physical warm-up to connect bodies and minds across the group, inspired by improvisation techniques, we could thus start with interactions and debates rather than a more traditional lecture component. Starting in this way may give more opportunities for a diversity of voices, values and opinions to manifest, since the teacher has not extensively shared their worldview yet, and creates an open atmosphere than can hopefully be maintained throughout the course session. We shared some of the background research about diversity, design and bias, also sharing some of our practices, and Vignette 2 proposes further illustrations from each of our experiences as educators on how to make diversity part of the course design. Our guest, Maribel Blasco, then took the stage to address the question of the "invisible curriculum," based on the article the course participants read beforehand (Semper and Blasco, 2018). This led to a fruitful discussion not only about diversity among the students, but also about teachers' own biases about what academic teaching and learning is or should be; how we make decisions about readings, teaching formats, examples or cases to work with; and so on. This also raised interesting questions about the possible paradoxes – and the wicked problem character – of trying at the same time to address (include) diversity and diverse needs and keep up with the idea and value of higher education that distinguishes (excludes) who can receive such education and eventually a degree.

VIGNETTE 2: HOW TO MAKE DIVERSITY PART OF THE COURSE DESIGN?

An example from Stina's teaching constituted a model for implementing diversity as an enhancer of educational value. Stina teaches in an MA program which is a collaboration between the Copenhagen Business School and the Royal Danish Academy of Fine Arts, Schools of Design and Architecture. Students enrolled in the program have previous degrees from a range of business schools, design schools and architecture schools around the world. In the program, students are taught about strategic design and entrepreneurship. Importantly, its aim is not to educate one type of candidate. The balanced admission of students from dissimilar backgrounds serves as a vehicle for producing new knowledge, skills and competences in the cross-fields between design, architecture, entrepreneurship and business. This is only possible because the diversity of the student cohort is turned into a positive agenda by actively working with co-creation and reframing mindsets: students bring their different backgrounds, training, habitus, experiences, and more, into play in innovative ways and create a solution space that would not have been possible without the presence of cognitive diversity. Students are encouraged to collaborate, communicate and solve problems across domains; in this way, diversity becomes a lever for educational value. Thus, diversity is treated more like a means – as a generator of value – than as an end in itself.

Another example from Florence's teaching was also discussed regarding the formation of groups, whether these are working groups for exercises, or case studies in class, or groups for project-based exams. While some programs (as the MA above) are diverse by design, there is a diversity of students in any program, not least with regard to demographic dimensions such as gender, nationality/culture or student status (e.g., full-time program student or taking the course as an elective). When free to form their groups, students tend to work repeatedly with the same people, who also tend to be similar to each other. This relates to the homophily principle, the natural tendency that we associate with similar others. Homogeneous groups indeed boast advantages, such as reaching consensus faster, having fewer conflicts, and having lower turnover. However, we also know from a growing body of research that diversity can be a strong asset for groups engaging in knowledge-intensive tasks. While reaping beneficiary effects from diversity depends on positive diversity attitudes on the part of the team members and the organization at large (Lauring & Villesèche, 2019), we should work on making groups diverse by design so that the value of diversity can be leveraged subsequently. Notably, this is also a principle from design thinking for working with co-creation in addressing wicked problems. Florence proposes to follow the rule that groups should have at least one form of diversity along the axis of gender, nationality,[3] or local versus exchange student status when applicable. While such rules are not always immediately popular, the students are usually sensitive to the arguments regarding potential benefits of diverse teams, as well as by the argument that we are rarely able to choose our team members in the workplace, and that leveraging diversity is thus a key skill to develop during their studies.

The last part of the face-to-face element of the course was based on a mapping exercise where students worked together in diverse-designed groups (see Vignette 2) in order to apprehend issues differently but also to co-create solutions, in line with our design thinking approach. In practice, we asked participants to contribute to the co-creation of a mind map using the e-learning tool Mindmeister. Accessible to participants via a shared URL, the mind map served as a vehicle for framing and reframing the diversity issues that had been brought up in the classroom, and in this way to let the mind map function as a form of solution prototyping, as well as a log or record of our joined efforts in exploring new trajectories for leveraging diversity in the classroom.

This was not the end of the course, however. We had planned a follow-up asynchronous, individual written activity on which participants would receive feedback from one of their peers and one of us, and that would act as a reflexive, integrative summary of how they have related to diversity in their teaching and how they would relate to the subject in their future practice. In order to do this, we this time took inspiration outside of our school again, and even from across the Atlantic. While a large part of the North American communication and tools about diversity in the classroom was used for overall inspiration, as we discussed earlier, many of the materials were not easily transferable. However, a more recent type of exercise for higher education teachers and researchers caught our interest: the diversity statement. We can define the diversity statement as a statement in which we (at the individual level, as compared with the more common institutional diversity statements found on websites; see, e.g., Singh and Point, 2006), address our past and future intended engagement with the topic of diversity in teaching, but also in research, academic citizenship or external activities. In the same way as a teaching statement or teaching portfolio, the diversity statement is gaining in popularity as a requirement for academic job applications, in particular in the United States.

While having emerged more than a decade ago, the format and content can vary, and are also discussed in specialized media (Reyes, 2018); also, there are disciplinary differences in how candidates write these statements (Schmaling et al., 2015). Finally, there are heated debates about how important or essential such a statement should be (Flaherty, 2018), which illustrates once more that diversity can be a contentious, political question that has to be addressed carefully. Nevertheless, we found that this would be an interesting way for the course participants to develop an explicit account of their role, practices and considerations in relation to leveraging diversity in the classroom, with both a retrospective and a prospective dimension, regardless of whether they were diversity/gender scholars or teaching about the topic at our school. Furthermore, here is where the storytelling dimension of this chapter intersects with a storytelling element of the course: all participants left the course with a (new) narrative of diversity in the classroom and their own part in this as the protagonist, narrator, spectator, or other. We pointed them to some resources about how to write such a statement; for example, a very detailed guide from Vanderbilt University (Beck, 2018) that also testifies to the level of institutionalization of the practice. The exercise was well received and executed (in a relatively short, 500–800 word format), and reading at least one other person's statement was seen as one more iteration of co-creation, as this can inspire changes in an individual's statement or at least reflection on their take.

CONCLUSION

In this chapter, we have reflected on the topic of leveraging diversity in the classroom, grounded in our experience of designing and teaching an eponymous course targeted at other teachers in our business school. We have shared more detail about the process of taking a design thinking approach to our course, as well as the process of selecting materials both from our own experience and by looking for best practices in Europe and North America. Also, we have given an overview of the course delivery, with some examples of activities, the different parts in the course (including the blended learning aspects); connecting these illustrations back to our design thinking approach. Overall, as mentioned in the introduction, we see this chapter as having a dimension of storytelling as well as being the presentation of a model to be borrowed, stretched and adapted, rather than a normative frame to leverage diversity in the classroom. The development and delivery of this new course was extremely enriching for ourselves, and inspired us to think about our contribution to diversity more holistically and more systematically across teaching, research and service. We hope that the readers will find some inspiration or push to try this themselves, and that those of us who are program leaders or deans can use these starting ideas to inspire their efforts to mainstream diversity and equality in business schools. Finally, while finishing the revision of this chapter, we saw the world changing around us. Following the violent death of George Floyd in the US, the question of race is now on the agenda again, not least in academia,[4] and the Covid-19 crisis has heightened and foregrounded the effects of inequality in the workplace and in education systems. We shall consider these dimensions for our next course, while also striving even more to develop approaches to leverage diversity that can be deployed or flexibly adapted to different contexts and historical circumstances.

NOTES

1. See, for information: https://www.cbs.dk/en/knowledge-society/strategic-areas/business-in-society -platforms/diversity-and-difference-platform/research-and-activities/networks-and-projects/ genderlab-a-research-based-tool.
2. https://www.genderdiversitylehre.fu-berlin.de/en/toolbox/index.html.
3. It is specified that we mean, for example, born and raised in Denmark, rather than the citizenship one is holding.
4. See, for example, the online webinar organized at Cass Business School (which will also change name soon in relation to the racial justice agenda) accessible at: https://www.cass.city.ac.uk/ faculties-and-research/centres/cre/events.

REFERENCES

Akrivou, K., and H. Bradbury-Huang (2015), "Educating Integrated Catalysts: Transforming Business Schools Toward Ethics and Sustainability," *Academy of Management Learning and Education*, 14 (2), 222–240.

Beck, S.L. (2018), "Developing and Writing a Diversity Statement," Vanderbilt University Center for Teaching, retrieved from https://cft.vanderbilt.edu/developing-and-writing-a-diversity-statement.

Boxenbaum, E. (2006), "Lost in Translation," *American Behavioral Scientist*, 49 (7), 939–948.

Brown, T. (2019), *Change by Design, Revised and Updated: How Design Thinking Transforms Organizations and Inspires Innovation*. New York: HarperCollins.

Buchanan, R. (1992), "Wicked problems in design thinking," *Design Issues*, 8 (2), 5–21.

Christensen, J., R. Mahler and S. Teilmann-Lock (n.d.), "GenderLAB: Norm-Critical Design Thinking for Gender Equality and Diversity," working paper.

DiMaggio, P.J., and W.W. Powell (1983), "The Iron Cage Revisited: Institutional Isomorphism and Collective Rationality in Organizational Fields," *American Sociological Review*, 48 (2), 147–160.

Flaherty, Colleen (2018), "Making a statement on diversity statements," *Inside Higher Ed*, November 12, retrieved from https://www.insidehighered.com/news/2018/11/12/former-harvard-deans-tweet -against-required-faculty-diversity-statements-sets-debate.

Holck, L., and S.L. Muhr (2017), "Unequal Solidarity? Towards a Norm-Critical Approach to Welfare Logics," *Scandinavian Journal of Management*, 33 (1), 1–11.

Kamp, A., and P. Hagedorn-Rasmussen (2004), "Diversity Management in a Danish Context: Towards a Multicultural or Segregated Working Life?," *Economic and Industrial Democracy*, 25 (4), 525–554.

Lauring, J., and F. Villesèche (2019), "The Performance of Gender Diverse Teams: What Is the Relation between Diversity Attitudes and Degree of Diversity?," *European Management Review*, 16(2), 243–254.

Ney, S., and C. Meinel (2019), *Putting Design Thinking to Work: How Large Organizations Can Embrace Messy Institutions to Tackle Wicked Problems*. Cham: Springer.

Rein, M., and D. Schön (1994), *Frame Reflection: Towards the Resolution of Intractable Policy Controversies*. New York: Basic Books.

Reyes, Victoria (2018), "Demystifying the Diversity Statement," *Inside Higher Ed*, January 25, retrieved from https://www.insidehighered.com/advice/2018/01/25/how-write-effective-diversity-statement -job-candidate-opinion.

Risberg, A., and A.-M. Søderberg (2008), "Translating a Management Concept: Diversity Management in Denmark," *Gender in Management: An International Journal*, 23 (6), 426–441.

Rittel, H., and M. Webber (1973), "Dilemmas in a General Theory of Planning," *Policy Sciences*, 4, 155–169.
Schmaling, K.B., A.Y. Trevino, J.R. Lind, A.W. Blume and D.L. Baker (2015), "Diversity Statements: How Faculty Applicants Address Diversity," *Journal of Diversity in Higher Education*, 8 (4), 213–224.
Semper, J.V.O., and M. Blasco (2018), "Revealing the Hidden Curriculum in Higher Education," *Studies in Philosophy and Education*, 37 (5), 481–498.
Singh, Val, and Sébastien Point (2006), "(Re) Presentations of Gender and Ethnicity in Diversity Statements on European Company Websites," *Journal of Business Ethics,* 68 (4), 363–379.
Villesèche, F., S.L. Muhr and L. Holck (2018), *Diversity and Identity in the Workplace: Connections and Perspectives.* Cham: Palgrave Pivot.

22. Guiding PhD students

C. Anthony Di Benedetto, Adam Lindgreen and Torsten Ringberg

INTRODUCTION

As business academics, one of our tasks is to train the next generation of educators. We ourselves entered our PhD programs years ago, full of enthusiasm about an academic career, but still in need of training and experience in research, and lacking in teaching skills. Many of us think back to our time in the PhD program, recalling the incredible amount of work that was required, and the guidance provided by our supervisors. In the succeeding years, we have "paid it forward," and have attempted to emulate our supervisors and provide the same kind of support to our own students. In this chapter, we explore the challenges of PhD student supervision. We have turned to several of our colleagues, who have collectively supervised many PhD students who have gone on to successful academic careers, and have asked them to contribute their thoughts on the PhD supervision process.

To focus our presentation, we asked contributors to reflect on the following series of questions:

- Will you share your PhD guidelines with us?
- Is there anything unique about your school/university, or country, regarding the PhD programs?
- What are your expectations of PhD students? Have your expectations changed over the last 5–10 years – and how?
- What kind of challenges/difficulties do PhD students face, and what is your role as supervisor? What are the typical "mistakes" that PhD students make?
- What are PhD students' expectations of you (academics in general, as well as the school/university)? Have their expectations changed over the last 5–10 years?
- Will you share a brief positive story of a PhD student you supervised in terms of what attributed to his/her success?
- Will you share a brief "negative" story of a student you supervised, and how/why the relationship/collaboration deteriorated, and how you handled this situation?

We stated that a few lines for each piece of advice would be sufficient; but also that it would be wonderful if the contributors could share a short story or two to illustrate their points for each of the topics.

This chapter summarizes the collective thoughts of our colleagues. The chapter is structured as follows. We first discuss the tasks of supervision, including how these may need to be adapted depending on student characteristics such as number of years of managerial experience. Next, we explore the challenges faced by PhD students, and discuss how the capabilities of both student and supervisor can be employed to address these challenges. A later section discusses the role of the supervisor in helping build student capabilities in publishing and teaching. We then turn to a reflection on how one can measure the contribution of a PhD thesis, and a discussion of the benefits of taking on supervisory responsibility. In the conclusion, the co-authors of this chapter each provide a personal retrospective on their own experiences as PhD supervisors.

SUPERVISION AND MANAGING THE CAREER TRANSITION

Anyone who has supervised PhD students knows that this is time-consuming work, which requires much flexibility and adaptation to different student capabilities and work styles. Conventional students, entering a PhD program early in their professional careers, have different expectations, expertise and weaknesses relative to mid-career executives seeking a career change. To supervise effectively, one must be ready to adapt to these differences and anticipate the issues that may arise. In any case, a major responsibility of the supervisor is to oversee the student's transition to an academic career. This section explores the challenges in effective supervision.

Meetings and Supervision

Supervision and guidance of a PhD student is a major time commitment for both the PhD student and the supervisor. Business schools will vary in the number or duration of meetings or other requirements, but there is general agreement that close supervision throughout the program is required to get students on track early so that they can reach their thesis goals, and to keep them on track.

Matthew Robson notes that some flexibility is often built into the supervisory task, which is designed to keep the student moving forward incrementally and not lose research momentum:

> In terms of guidelines for supervisory arrangements, this is quite loose. In my previous School, Leeds University, students were meant to upload meetings records every month. This was checked by administrators. At Cardiff Business School, the meetings logs are uploaded to feed into a six-monthly progress review. This system is not so prescriptive in terms of how often supervisors would see their student and for how long. It can flex to suit the circumstances, for example, the evolving nature of the student–supervisor partnership and stage of the work. However, the Leeds system had the advantage of creating record logs that the next meeting can launch off, which gives those involved the sense of incremental forward momentum. (Robson)

The requirements at Copenhagen Business School (CBS) are quite detailed, with several progress milestones along the way. The process requires the PhD student to develop a research proposal very early and receive feedback from PhD supervisors. Updates are required every six months to ensure the student maintains momentum:

> At CBS, the requirements of the PhD students and the PhD supervisors' roles are outlined and continuously monitored in great details. Within the first three months, the student has to present and have approved a research plan for the entire PhD study with tentative courses listed (30 ECTS in all), when to fulfill teaching/advising obligations, and a research plan (in addition, when/where a three-six months stay abroad takes place. Apart from having a primary supervisor from within CBS (minimum associate professor level), a secondary supervisor is required and can be from CBS or from outside of CBS. The research proposal has to be presented at a faculty meeting within the first six months of enrollment. Every six months, the student enters a progress report online, which is signed off by the

primary advisor, the PhD School's department representative, the head of department, and the head of the PhD School in sequential order. Any of aforementioned individuals can request additional information and/or question the entered attained course ECTS, as well as the overall progress of the student's plan. The supervisors meet regularly with the students, who, by the way, are referred to as PhD candidates because they are considered research colleagues and also salaried with a significant pay as a research assistant. There are no requirements in terms of physical meetings, but each six months, the students allocate up to 30 hours to their advisor based on their ongoing engagement (at CBS, all activities are measured in hours). The PhD can be terminated if insufficient progress is evidenced. That is, if the primary supervisor cannot document sufficient academic and/or administrative progress, the six-month progress report is left unsigned. That signals a potential for termination of the enrollment if the student does not rectify the situation within an additional three months. (Ringberg)

Transitioning to a Career in Research and Teaching

An important characteristic of any PhD program is transition: from graduate student to career academic with research and teaching responsibilities. PhD supervisors not only guide PhD students in writing and defending their thesis research, but they also ensure that students leave the program with a wide range of research skills that they can access in the future. Many research skills and capabilities cross disciplinary boundaries, so multidisciplinary classes can be offered efficiently. Often, students also will have teaching opportunities, which allows them to develop teaching skills and also claim teaching experience on their resumes. Audhesh Paswan describes this aspect of supervision, as it is handled at University of North Texas, which is typical of many PhD programs in North America:

> At University of North Texas, we have a single PhD program with seven concentrations. This allows us to combine some of the common skills and knowledge across different concentrations and enhance our efficiency in terms of faculty resources, especially in the domain of research tools and techniques. This is based on an assumption that areas such as marketing, management, IT [information technology] and decision science, and behavioral accounting and finance need a combination of psychometric and econometric skills and capabilities, whereas others like accounting and finance and some from decision science that use more archival data would need more of econometric modeling skills. These integrations, I hope, also help PhD students see some commonality across different concentration areas. I also hope that it helps break down functional silos and barriers, and develop a cross disciplinary approach to business research. I am sure that a lot of schools follow this structure and philosophy. We also try to emphasize the teaching aspect of an academician's life by getting our students to participate in a teaching seminar and actual teaching activities through teaching assistantship and fellowship assignments. (Paswan)

This transition process is handled differently at Copenhagen Business School, where students become accustomed to life as a career researcher at the outset of their program. While details may vary across departments, the objective is to get PhD students involved early in all faculty activities:

> At CBS, PhD students are regarded as research colleagues, which means they participate in academic activities, meetings, outings, and discussions. They also form a PhD union across CBS in which they discuss their general work conditions, their interaction with and support from supervisors, and they take initiatives to useful activities that might advance their academic careers (e.g., invited guest speakers, access to a psychologist, work/life balance, and general course requirements). The PhD life can be stressful, in spite of being well salaried, due to the short duration of the program (i.e., three years) during which the students have to fulfill a number of teaching and course requirements in addition to show research progress and submit the final thesis (typically three publishable academic

manuscripts). Each department sets its own requirements in terms of which courses the students need to take. In some departments, there are cohorts that go through a very structured program while in other departments the students can take courses not only at CBS but across European institutions. Similarly, it varies considerably how many students are enrolled within each department, which also determines their work environment and inter-personal dynamics. (Ringberg)

Supervision of Conventional PhD Students

Most PhD students fall into one of two categories: the conventional student, with strong academic capabilities and possibly some relevant work experience, seeking a career in research and teaching; and the mid-career professional, with years of middle- or senior-level supervisory and managerial experience, who perceives research problems from a practical, decision-making perspective. This section discusses providing guidance for conventional students; the next explores the challenges when supervising experienced professionals.

Ken Peattie provides an interesting starting point, recognizing that conventional students differ in significant ways, and recommending that the supervisor's role can be tailored according to the apparent requirements of the individual student:

> My experience in the role of PhD supervisor could be summarized using the 2x2 matrix beloved of marketers, with 'confidence' and 'capability' (relatively speaking, they are all bright) providing the two axes. For the low confidence/high capability student, your primary role is that of cheerleader to stop insecurity preventing progress. For the high confidence/low capability candidate, you act more as guardrail to counter thoughts like 'Of course, CEOs [chief executive officers] of FTSE companies will want to be interviewed by me!' or 'I'm assuming a 50% response rate for my survey'. For those in the high/high quadrant, you are mostly a sounding board helping them to articulate their ideas and providing a little guidance, whereas in the low/low quadrant you more play the Jedi Master, contributing motivation, direction, philosophy, (sometimes harsh) lessons, hopefully a good example to follow, and even the odd mind-trick! Working out early on which quadrant a student leans towards can be very helpful in getting your supervision style right. (Peattie)

Echoing these sentiments, Peter Naudé stresses the importance of understanding conventional students as individuals, recognizing when to apply pressure and when to back off and allow for student creativity:

> As far as I am concerned, it is largely about getting two things right. The first is the selection process, identifying bright, curious, hard-working students (and I have not always got that right!). And then, once they are on board, it is to walk the middle road of not sitting on their shoulders telling them what to do, but also not leaving them feeling so lost that they do not know which way to turn. It is an important balancing act: providing guidance, while allowing and encouraging, autonomy, creativity, and personal investigation. (Naudé)

Supervision of Experienced Professionals

The professional who decides on a mid-career change carries a different set of tools. Unlike the conventional student, the experienced professional has first-hand knowledge of business decisions developed over many years. To best manage these students, John Nicholson advises focusing on theories that have pragmatic applications, allowing the students' wealth of experience to be channeled effectively into their research process. The supervisor should therefore remain open and pragmatic in the selection of the research paradigm and method:

Supervision of experienced professionals should differ from that of more conventional PhD students. I believe that the ambition of PhD programs for experienced professionals should be to produce theories that are performative in practice, that is, that drive practices to converge with the theory derived during the period of study (Kelly et al., 2020). Accordingly, supervisors should respect the experience of such students and find ways to inculcate that experience into the research process, rather than seeing this as an unhelpful encumbrance to be erased in order to achieve a value-neutral approach to a subject matter that the student may know much better than the supervisor.

Supervisors should not dominate experienced professionals for rigor, but allow them to bring in their vision of relevance as of at least equal importance to rigor. A key element is to allow research questions to emerge from a practical problem rather than from a traditional gap-spotting method grounded in academic literature. Who is to say that academic incrementalism is in step with practice and that taking inspiration from a practical trajectory could be anything but rewarding for our discipline? Is there not the opportunity here for a democratic cocreation of knowledge between the supervisor and the experienced professional in this arrangement?

Experienced professionals should not be inculcated into a paradigm, potentially that of the supervisor, and then working down from that ontological fixed position to the problem. An alternative is to follow a methodological pluralism (Midgley et al., 2017) that allows for a more pragmatic approach to the choice of methods and methodologies, which nonetheless maintains a strong ontological position. (Nicholson)

Another alternative is for the experienced professionals to maintain their position with their company, where company management and academic supervisor may share supervisory duties; an arrangement that presents challenges, but which may benefit both student and company. This is an option offered at the Copenhagen Business School:

At CBS, the industrial PhD students spent half their time at CBS and the other half at their company that contributes financially to their salary (often in a 50/50 arrangement). Supervision of industrial PhD students typically is done by a representative from the company and a CBS researcher (who is the primary supervisor). The academic rigor of the thesis is the same as for normal PhD students, but the industrial students do not have to teach. The focus is to match the academic rigor with an applied and relevant issue that might also benefit the company. At times, the coordination and especially the integration of these students into the daily department environment and activities can be logistically challenging and difficult. (Ringberg)

CAPABILITIES

The PhD program is challenging for both student and supervisor. This section explores the major challenges faced by PhD students, including unclear expectations and lack of research focus. We discuss how some students handle these challenges, and why others seem to have difficulty overcoming the roadblocks. We also reflect on the characteristics of the PhD supervisor that are most appreciated by students in guiding them through the difficult moments.

Challenges that PhD Students Face

Regardless of their academic background or work experience, all PhD students face challenges and enter the PhD program with uncertainties. PhD supervisors should anticipate these issues and be prepared to handle them. Perhaps more now than ever before, supervisors take a more active role, both in guiding students and helping them achieve work–life balance, as the expectations of PhD students have intensified over the years. Markus Reihlen notes that:

> PhD students generally expect to receive insightful and timely feedback on their work. Have the expectations changed over the last decades? I think on average yes, they have. Students increasingly ask for how to balance a demanding research project with private life arrangement. They also demand more guidance, as well as feedback through which they hope to reduce uncertainty of their research venture. Highly independent research of students increasingly is replaced by close collaboration and feedback. They also demand more services and support of their PhD research by the universities. (Reihlen)

Reihlen identifies some of the most common challenges confronting PhD students, as they progress through their program:

- Unrealistic scope of the research project: This could be the case because there is a lack of focus, a lack of a clear academic conversation the PhD research would like to contribute to, or a lack of methodological skills that would not allow a rigorous mixed method approach.
- Unaware how to make a real contribution: Students sometimes envision to make a study, but do not ask themselves under what conditions this study is truly interesting, engaging, and novel.
- Unrealistic expectations of what it means to work on PhD research: Students should be prepared to go on a rollercoaster ride and not a merry-go-round.
- Bad project management: In some instances, students do not plan their research well. For instance, they may start to generate data for a cross-sectional study and then change their mind and jump on the process organization studies bandwagon. Yet, they did not adjust their research design towards a process study design. (Reihlen)

Some students will enter the PhD program with a good idea of what they want to study, but this is not case for other students. They may possess a general thought, but have difficulty developing it into a meaningful research question. The supervisor can play a supporting role in the creation of a worthy research study. Audhesh Paswan often recommends to PhD students to think about their own realities and find inspiration there: he calls it a "slice of life" approach:

> In my mind, the most daunting challenge confronting PhD students is how to imagine, create, and tell a story. In our seminars, we expose our students to a lot of tools and techniques and "so and so said this" from the literature. However, we often do not teach them or have a platform that teaches them how to imagine, create, and tell a story. As a result, most of the students turn into technicians and develop a research question based on "slice of literature", that is, read the literature till the cows come home, and then try to fill a gap in the literature. There is nothing wrong with this approach, except that it often results in a research that may not have much to do with real life. I like to tell my students to develop a research idea based on "slice of life": look at what is going in our lives, society, and focal business context, and then develop a research question that tries to solve a life problem. Personally, I have had fun with this approach, and my students who take to it love it. I also look at this as the exploitation versus exploration approach. While I agree that we need both, I feel that students need more of an exploration mindset. (Paswan)

All PhD students know that they will be facing publish-or-perish pressures in their careers, and some may enter the review process for the first time fearfully. Audhesh Paswan reminds the PhD supervisor of the importance of supporting their PhD students through this challenging task and helping them learn the ropes for future success:

I believe the second biggest challenge for PhD students is to overcome their fear of failure and the nightmarish review process. In our seminars, we expose our students to all the literature, which are the results of several failed attempts and trial and errors. We do not put the students in a situation where they can fail without paying a heavy price. As a PhD supervisor, I see my role as getting my students to take that first step, that is, put their manuscript in the review process, and be supportive when it comes back rejected or gets a revise and resubmit. Most of my students who work with me get their first manuscript through this process. (Paswan)

Like many other schools, Copenhagen Business School places high publishing expectations on their PhD students, whose thesis chapters may be three publishable manuscripts tied together with overall implications. Close supervision is required to guide students through this challenging process for the first time, and to ensure that they are on the right path for producing future research on their own:

At CBS, the challenge is to reframe the PhD students' way of thinking toward producing new research, and not merely consuming, and in addition finding something that contributes significantly to what experienced researchers already are producing in well-regarded journal outlets. That is a task that requires close and continuous interaction between the PhD students and their supervisors. The Danish system is quite demanding on students, as they only get three years to submit their thesis. During this time, they need to take courses (30 ECTS), teach courses (624 working hours), ideally do a research stay abroad, and develop, write, present, and preferably submit three publishable manuscripts for medium- to high-level journals, which are included as part of their thesis, in addition to overarching chapters that tie it all together. It is quite a challenging task given that international PhD students often have four–five years at their disposal. (Ringberg)

Markus Reihlen summarizes many types of challenges faced by PhD students, and outlines the kind of support that can be provided by the PhD supervisors to help students to cope. While some of these challenges pertain specifically to the German university system, many are familiar to academics in PhD programs worldwide. He lists the following categories of challenges and how he personally has dealt with them:

- Committing PhD students to the ethics of science: While in general this is not necessarily an issue, I put clear emphasis on ethical principles as laid out by the German Research Foundation. Among them are clear rules concerning co-authorship, methodological, and citation practices, etc. These are important prevention measures.
- Aligning PhD students' motivation with an interesting topic: Not every hot topic is a good topic for an individual student. Therefore, a key task for me is to find out and guide students in their venture, especially negotiating the right topic that fits for them and their deeper interests.
- Dealing with a lack of scientific skills: This is an issue, but usually less problematic because either I try to skill them by myself – starting with a reading list, meeting to explore interesting topics, etc. – and/or sending [*sic*] them to good PhD courses, conferences, and summer schools.
- Dealing with personal challenging situations: Finishing a PhD thesis can become a rollercoaster ride for students. Going on this ride means that students have to learn how to deal with the lows, rejections, and critical feedback, while enjoying the acceptance and positive feedbacks of their work. However, sometimes stress is unrelated to the PhD research, but rather located in particular contextual conditions such as private relational issues or that the students have decided to found their own start-up venture. Conducting these talks as counsellor goes beyond the normal supervision.
- Dealing with a lack of ambition: A lack of ambition is critical, and this is not always clear from the start. One way of dealing with this is a clear signaling strategy in the beginning and intensive talks before the person is accepted as a PhD student. In the German system, you are not "simply" accepted into a program, but you have to be accepted by a specific supervisor before you can enter

the program. In addition, a lack of ambition will trigger intensive face-to-face talks and more formal feedbacks that document the lack of engagement.

- Dealing with non-collaborating practice partners: Especially students who work in close collaboration with companies, or are financed by their companies, sometimes face challenges. For instance, the company was supposed to be the subject of the empirical study, but in the process is unwilling to do so. As a supervisor, I try to save the topic by arranging talks with the company gatekeeper, which sometimes works, but sometimes, we have to invent a new topic, which does not require company data in order to save the PhD research. (Reihlen)

Characteristics of Capable PhD Students

Experienced PhD supervisors can reflect on their PhD students over the years, and recognize which ones stood out. What do they look for in a student? Perhaps not surprisingly, many contributors favored ambitious students with positive attitudes who successfully made the transition from graduate student to research colleague. Here are some of the thoughts on this topic:

My expectation of the PhD students are usually threefold:
- Individual attitudes and skills: I expect my PhD students to show a great commitment, curious for their field of research, and a high intrinsic motivation. Do they really have the taste for science? In addition, the CV should indicate a high level of commitment to research.
- Ambitious research: I expect the students to work with my help on research that is truly ambitious and can make a real impact to the field. The metaphor "try to reach out for the stars" has been commonly used, although we know that it will not always happen. Yet, this should be the level of ambition.
- Realistic contextual conditions: It is important that the PhD research operates under realistic contextual conditions. For instance, I have had a number of students who worked in the industry. Having clear arrangements with the employer that gives students enough time to explore their research topic independently and with the necessary depths [*sic*] is critical. (Reihlen)

I try to accept PhD students with the aspiration to want to be an academic at a good place, which ultimately means to publish well. After a couple of years in the process, these students should "kick on" and want to work on manuscripts. My style is not to haul them in and force this, but rather is to leave the door ajar. Students should take ownership of matters and the opportunity to use a co-author who has the experience to guide the crafting of one or more manuscripts. Probably, if a student is not kicking on in this way it is a bad sign …

The best students are the ones who can manage the transition seamlessly into being staff members. Good students know their literature, are strong methodologically, and can write. But because they wanted to be academics throughout their PhD journey, they have learnt broadly about the profession. As such, there is no hiatus in their research when they take their first job. This said, sometimes such students get a first job that involves too much teaching emphasis. They should know how to protect their margins if this is the case. In sum, positive stories tend to involve students who mature quickly as professionals. (Robson)

I expect PhD students learn to become … independent scholars/researchers. My best students will have at least two manuscripts accepted while doing their PhD research. (Brodie)

Also, many collaborators reflected positively on students who showed an ability to work independently, and to take an idea and run with it:

My PhD students, the ones who opt to work for me, happen to be more independent and do not like too much of hand holding. In turn, I like to treat them as adults and not mollycoddle them. I respect their crazy ideas and help them develop their own ideas. Some of my students still come back after several years and ask me to work with them. I can think of three students in the last five years who asked if I would work with them, and would I give them a topic that they can work on. I turned around and said that is a bad idea. I asked them what they were interested in. When they started talking, I could see that they were not sure to start with but became very excited. I asked them to tell me a story. In turn, I just doodle and give back drawings of crazy models. They took those crazy drawings and ran with it. We went back and forth, and eventually they all ended up getting a publication in *Industrial Marketing Management*. (Paswan)

My first PhD student had some negative experiences with other faculty and ended up with me, as last resort. I took the student reluctantly, but he ended up being great, out of sheer determination. The student was not the best trained initially, but in the end was able to learn by doing and became fairly successful. (Luna)

My latest PhD student is a very positive and also unusual example. She worked for five years in the industry, in the end as a senior product manager for a large multinational company. She started her PhD program with a scholarship, which paid only a fraction of her former salary. By blending her curiosity in science with her industry background, she became a great and very valuable person of my research team. She finished her PhD with a *Journal of Management Studies* publication (as first author), won the best PhD paper award from the Research Methods Division of the Academy of Management and is now shortlisted for the EGOS [European Group for Organizational Studies] best PhD thesis award in 2020. She will now continue her academic career at Leuphana. (Reihlen)

Characteristics of Less Capable PhD Students

What about the cases where the PhD student's experience was not as positive? Are there signs that can be recognized early, and is there anything that can be done by the PhD supervisor? Typical problem areas include lack of effective collaboration, difficulties with English as a second language, or an inability to maintain focus after a promising start, sometimes because of personal reasons:

It is not so much the case that the collaboration deteriorates. It is more likely that the collaboration never really fired on all cylinders in the first instance – it did not kick on. A PhD student needs to be good at each step of the way. I am not familiar with a case where the literature review, conceptualization, and fieldwork were accomplished with aplomb, and then the work deteriorated. Usually, the signs are there. This said, sometimes you get a student who is absolutely brilliant at specific aspects of a study. Probably, such a student has real value as a member of a high-quality publishing team that includes complementary colleagues, although not in terms of producing sole-authored work. (Robson)

We have international PhD students who have English as a second language. Learning to write well for these students is challenging. (Brodie)

The main challenge is that PhD students may lose focus throughout their years as students. Five years is a long time for an adult person, and life has a way of derailing initial plans. Divorces, abusive relationships, deaths, all kinds of things can happen. The result is that the investment we put into a student may not pay off with a good placement in the end. That is totally outside of our control, though. (Luna)

One of my PhD students started on an externally funded research project. He was very ambitious, skilled, and well socially embedded in our research team. A first manuscript was successfully published, and it looked like that things would continue that way. Yet, in his private life things radically changed (I keep it here in abstract terms), and this disrupted his PhD program. For three years, we met regularly, yet more for counselling than research guidance meetings. Unfortunately, the research has not advanced and is likely to be terminated soon. It started out as a very promising research program with a highly talented person, and then life took a wrong turn, and we could not set the program on the right track again. (Reihlen)

A PhD student who had a lot of promise ended up dropping the ball and would disappear for long periods of time. He did not accept suggestions very well, and ended up not publishing any of his thesis work. He claims he ended up hating his thesis topic, which probably had something to do with his lack of follow through. (Luna)

I have had a PhD student who did all right while in the program. However, after graduation and getting his first job, he fell into the trap of "I will do research because I have to." This led to that person getting into a tight spot in his three-year evaluation. Thankfully, he woke up, reached out to me, and we were able to salvage the situation. That particular student will probably not be a stellar researcher, but he will probably be fine. Such people are adults and must find their own place in life that they are comfortable with. My role is to help them find that place in life. (Paswan)

Procrastination, perfectionism, occasional inability to deal with life's pressures, and other human failures can also inflict damage on a PhD student's progress. If the PhD supervisor can recognize such issues early and take action, perhaps the student can get back on track:

A common mistake is to wait too long to start a research program. These days, it seems like most of the PhD students see the need to hit the floor running and get started on research during their first year, but it is hard to get the students up to speed on the literature and methods fast enough, unless they come to us with some research background. As a result, we really try to admit new students only if they have previous research backgrounds. (Luna)

Serving both in the capacity of the department's PhD representative and as PhD supervisor for numerous PhD students, I have experienced many types of students. The procrastinator, the blame others, the perfectionist, and the realist types. At times, you come across a PhD student who possesses several of these types (excluding the realist type), which makes it next to impossible for the interaction, as well as the PhD research to end on a positive note. Each type requires very different strategies from the supervisor. Yet, in spite of extensive efforts by supervisors, I have yet to see any successful outcomes from the "blame others" type. The next in line are the procrastinator, the perfectionist, and the realist in terms of being successful. I have experienced successful outcomes in all of these cases, but with an inclining likelihood toward the realist students (who realistically assess their chances for fulfilling the requirements and finishing up). I have personally experienced all four types, and it does feel uphill when one recognizes too late in the process what one is up against as supervisor requiring having to make an assessment of whether to proceed or consider it sunk costs. In addition, there are some students who, when under pressure, experience sudden mental black outs, depression, borderline personality, etc. and require professional psychological intervention to get back on track. (Ringberg)

Characteristics of Good PhD Supervisors

So what is a good PhD supervisor? Certainly, it is not a one-size-fits-all position, as some PhD students may thrive under one supervisor and be a very poor match for another. Audhesh Paswan addresses this point, noting that some students will require more guidance, while others will be fine with a lighter touch. He implies that it is up to us to recognize and adapt to these differences:

In the last 5–10 years, I do not think the expectations of our PhD students have changed. I still feel that they expect us to mentor them in both research and teaching. The level and type of mentoring desired may differ from person to person. Some may expect a lot of hand holding, while others like to be gently guided and nudged, and not taken by hand through every corner. (Paswan)

Peter Naudé provides details on the kind of guidance the PhD supervisor needs to provide, including academic guidance, network building, and emotional support, noting that this work can be a major time commitment. He also stresses the need to challenge the PhD student to keep them on the right path and make progress:

> A good PhD supervisor should provide conceptual and methodological guidance and advisement; offer guidance in terms of the process (e.g., where to start, what to focus on, how to move on to the empirical sections of the PhD research, literature review, and conceptual grounding); open up for networking opportunists (putting the student in touch with experts in terms of the topic, as well as methodologies); open up for networking and relationship-building opportunities with other students; respond to the students' questions; and, finally, directing the students to the appropriate resources … It is a time-consuming exercise. Do not think you can do it on a half-time basis. You have to be committed to the process. You have to offer regular contact and availability, as well as emotional support … A supervisor should not be afraid to challenge students, for example in terms of their rate of progress. (Naudé)

Peter Naudé shared some of the feedback he has received over the years from PhD students he supervised. The comments showed that he had provided value in many different ways, for which students were very appreciative. These include:

- Being a mentor: providing support and help beyond expectation.
- Knowledge of the subject: asking challenging questions and giving direction.
- Networking: introducing academic colleagues, encouraging presentation at conferences, which provided experience and aided in further development of research ideas.
- Getting published: helping in the preparation of manuscripts for submission and through-out the review process.
- Attention: Always giving full attention, being available for in-person or Skype meetings, traveling for face-to-face meetings with students who were studying abroad; quick turna-round time for feedback.
- Creativity: Always encouraging of student creativity, avoiding judgmental comments, letting the student decide on research direction.
- Encouragement: Providing positive commentary, but being ready to correct when necessary.
- Gatekeeping: Helping the student through administrative issues, such as arranging for a work-abroad opportunity, cutting red tape on behalf of the student.
- Collaboration: Being more of a collaborator than manager; developing ideas jointly and encouraging research direction.
- Reliability: Showing total commitment to the student, providing timely feedback and reliable advice.
- Innovativeness: Ready to identify innovative frameworks or theories that the students might be able to integrate into their work, while not diminishing the students' own creative contribution.
- The right amount of guidance: An experienced researcher might be too passionate about their chosen subject and oversteer the student's research; this temptation is avoided and guidance is offered which is sensitive to the student's interests and passions.
- Coaching: Sound advice on the selection of external examiners, and suggestions on how to prepare for the thesis defense and not be intimidated.

PUBLISHING AND TEACHING

During their program, PhD students develop essential skills in conducting research, academic writing and publishing, and effective teaching. In this section, our contributors offer their thoughts on the role of the PhD supervisor in developing publication skills, while ensuring that the PhD program provides opportunity to grow as an effective communicator in the classroom.

Monograph versus Publishable Articles

Once the PhD thesis is defended successfully (and sometimes even before that), the PhD student has to convert the research into one or more publishable manuscripts. PhD supervisors can play a major role in helping their students get their work published in the best possible (journal) outlets. As Matthew Robson explains, this supervisory task may be particularly challenging in a more traditional setting, where the student is expected to produce one large piece of research, as opposed to the newer trend of requiring three chapters, which are meant to be distinct research manuscripts:

> Cardiff Business School seems to be a typical UK place in how it treats its PhD students and program. Students ultimately are tasked with producing one large document, rather than a set of individual manuscripts. This has pros and cons. The pro is that such a magnum opus type PhD can really advance the state of the art – it is amazing what a student can learn and achieve with the time and a liberal word count. The downside is that it is difficult to then turn such a piece of work into publications. Students are not developing skills to write in the most succinct and efficient way possible, and they are not focusing on how to craft publishable manuscripts. Going from 80 000 words down to 6000 words is a tall order even for experienced academics. I like the three-/four-manuscript PhD model that some other academic systems follow. Still, this can raise issues with a lack of thematic focus. The storyline that is meant to unite the manuscripts commonly does not hold up. (Robson)

In today's academic work environment, the expectations of graduating PhD students are higher than ever. The supervisor's role is even more critical in this environment: they need to set up realistic expectations, and also help the student establish a strong track record upon graduation that leaves the student poised for future publishing success:

> Modern PhD students face the depressing realization that (1) they must publish to get a good job that gives them the academic freedom to continue as active researchers, and (2) scholarly journal space is at a premium, as review funnels have become clogged with increasing submissions from all parts of the world. To get a job, a student now needs an early publication, coupled with medium-term work that shows a quality trajectory. For early career researchers, the learning never really stops. It is no longer the case that you can do good PhD research and be set for the next five years. (Robson)

> Expectations keep increasing. The timeline has accelerated because of the need to start projects early on. We expect PhD students to have two–three essays (three is the normal expectation). We also hope they will have at least a publication or a manuscript in advanced review at a top journal. (Luna)

Article publication and job placement, ultimately, are intertwined. The PhD students are under time constraints to complete their thesis and publish articles, develop teaching skills, and meet their responsibilities in their personal lives. PhD supervisors can only do so much, but they can provide opportunities for their students to develop their skills, and eventually create and communicate knowledge themselves. Hans Baumgartner and Audhesh Paswan offer their thoughts on this point:

> I think the main challenge these days is to find a good job in academia. This means that you have to start working on publications as soon as you join a PhD program, so you have publications by the time you go on the market. I do not think that necessarily is a good thing because PhD students do not have the time to take courses and read widely. (Baumgartner)

> We would like our PhD students to become future change agents through knowledge creation and transfer, and, even more important, capability developers. Accordingly, we expect our students, at least in the area of marketing to have (a) at least one journal article and (b) taught a couple of classes by the time they go into the job market. (Paswan)

Building Teaching Skills

While much of the supervisor's time is taken up in providing research and writing guidance, many universities provide opportunities for PhD students not only to teach, but also to develop their teaching skills through seminars or courses in pedagogy. Initiatives of this type ensure that the students have built up the required capabilities and are ready to take on teaching duties:

> The teaching capability enhancement part is taken care of through our teaching seminars and the Teaching Assistantship/Fellowship assignments. The research expectation is taken care of in our research tools seminars, as well as seminars that focus on major and/or minor areas. For example, in my business-to-business seminar, one assignment is to have PhD students develop a publishable quality manuscript, and most students do eventually end up with either a conference or a journal article with a focus on business-to-business marketing. Several of my students have published in *Industrial Marketing Management* because of this initiative. This also boosts a student's confidence. I also encourage the students in my seminar to volunteer for reviewing for a journal and/or a conference. (Paswan)

> At CBS, we require that full-time employed PhD students (who are paid as research assistants) contribute with 624 hours of teaching, advising (e.g., of master's theses), and/or co-examiner (oral/written). The students are not (as of yet) required to take a course in pedagogics and thus often have to do "the best they can". Most often, it goes quite well, although at times the students end up dreading the experience, which can be quite intimidating when standing in front of 100+ undergraduate students in a big auditorium. Teaching academic material is demanding, as it requires the ability to go beyond the textbook material to make the material come alive with other examples while providing additional academic depth. It is a sink or swim experience, but surprisingly many students survive the process and do quite well (based on teaching ratings). It is not an ideal situation, but with so many other chores at hand, as well as serving their dues (financially to CBS), it is probably the best set-up. I had similar experiences when I was a PhD student at Penn State where I taught undergraduate courses. (Ringberg)

REFLECTIONS ON THE SUPERVISION

In this section, we gather some of our contributors' overall reflections on the supervision process. How can we assess the contribution to knowledge made by our PhD students? How should one handle the student who is not planning a traditional academic career? And what are the long-term benefits of taking on supervisory responsibility?

Contributions of a PhD Thesis

Once the PhD thesis has been defended, how can its contribution to knowledge be measured? John Nicholson suggests a novel way for the PhD student to assess the type(s) of radical or incremental contribution that has been made. This technique can be used to enumerate the expected contributions in the introductory section, then to close the circle in the concluding section to show how these contributions have been achieved:

> One of the key measures of whether a thesis is awarded is the affirmation that a contribution to knowledge has been made. (For a comprehensive framework for writing contribution sections in journals, see Nicholson et al., 2018). However, I believe we should number contribution claims in the same way that we number objectives and questions. Why do we leave contributions vague when these are the essential measures of a PhD thesis' quality? For example, a grid could be placed in introduction sections relative to the two main contribution types, that is, incremental (gap-spotting) and revelatory (assumption challenging). In an introduction, and in a simple table, the PhD student could number each contribution, stating in which section of the literature review the gap is exposed or the assumption identified; then where the thesis' material fills that gap, or challenges that assumption; and, finally, that this table is returned to in the conclusions to complete the loop. These leaves an examiner few places to go in terms of the communication of the thesis' contribution, leaving only its substance to be challenged. (Nicholson)

John Nicholson also reminds PhD supervisors that one should not discount publications in non-traditional targets, such as trade journals, especially when working with experienced professionals. For this category of PhD students, a publication that is widely read by practitioners in their field may be viewed as just as impactful (if not more so) than a publication in an A-journal. In fact, the experienced professional's objective in entering the PhD program may be to return to industry with newfound understanding and knowledge. A good supervisor is receptive to these different goals and will be willing to adapt to them:

> PhD supervisors should accept that the ambitions of experienced professionals may not be the same as those of a career academic. An engaged supervisor should accept that impact in such students' community of practice may be a greater drive than publishing in highly ranked journals and building citations. Engaged supervisors should not see publications in trade journals as "wasting" good material. Equally, engaged supervisors should not see their role as assimilating a practitioner into academia where the student may wish to return to practice as a better practitioner. (Nicholson)

To Supervise or Not to Supervise

As a final topic, our contributors weighed in on the responsibilities of the PhD supervisor, and what one is "getting into" when agreeing to serve as a PhD thesis committee chairperson or member. The job is time-consuming and is perhaps not for everybody. However, it can be very rewarding for those who want to see their graduates make a real difference in the academic community. A further benefit is that some will become co-authors, possibly for years to come:

> I expect my students to go on to become research active scholars. Simply, I expect "to bump into them on the conference circuit". This is my base expectation, and I have not changed it over the years. Our responsibility is to leave something behind. This can be taken as advancing knowledge through publishing, but also it involves building the academy. Hence, I have supervised 17 students to completion thus far, which is a high number for someone with just over two decades of academic experience. There are professors who do very little supervision, viewing this as a distraction from

their core business of publishing few, good manuscripts with other senior academics and professing generally. I won't criticize that approach too much. Each to their own. (Robson)

Although I have served on the committees of many PhD students over the years, I have only been the main advisor for a relatively small number. Over the last 20 years or so, I have increasingly become interested in methodological issues related to survey research, and we do not have a lot of students who are interested in this topic and it is probably not a good topic for students if they want to find a tenure-track position. Almost all the students that I have worked with have exceeded my expectations, and I have worked with most of them long after they left Penn State. (Baumgartner)

Those who undertake PhD supervision need to be aware of the time commitment and level of bureaucracy, which can vary by university or host country. They should be aware of the bureaucratic requirements, which can be quite strict:

PhD advising at CBS represents less of supervision and more of a collegial process during which the supervisors are rewarded with hours (max 30 per semester) by the PhD students based on their active contribution to the PhD process. Obviously, supervisors do not take on students due to the additional hours (which count toward their own 840 hours of yearly obligations), but the opportunity to develop a productive collaboration that benefits both the student's and the supervisor's publication records. The students have the upper hand in terms of deciding whether they will change advisor during the process, whether they will change topic of the PhD thesis, etc. In fact, I have seen students whose salary has been financed by a grant attainted by a faculty, request and get another faculty person and keep the salary part of the grant, to the great frustration of the grant holder. That is part of Danish law. We have had several students who have changed supervisor mid-stream, but we try to amend the situation such that any manuscripts the supervisor has contributed to will include the supervisor as one of the authors. This is not an ideal situation for the supervisor. On the other hand, the student could end up with a supervisor (who might have been recommended by the department when accepted into the program) who is a bad fit, in which case the department's PhD representative and head of department will try to find another person. The collaboration between the supervisors and the PhD students is both based on a legal arrangement (Danish law) and a moral arrangement, which involves a fair give-and-take by all parties involved. Most of times, it goes quite well, but at times, a resolution might require quite some work and involve multiple administrative processes and time. (Ringberg)

CONCLUSION

After having considered the comments of our contributors, this chapter's co-authors took the time to reflect on their own experiences as PhD supervisors, and our role in guiding our students and responding to their requirements.

Reflections by Torsten Ringberg

As a PhD supervisor, I expect that PhD students are critical thinkers who also are interested, curious and willing to put in the time it takes to produce academic work, and last, but not least, willing to entertain advice I provide on their research path going forward. It is quite discouraging to spend time and effort guiding students with very relevant advice, only to realize that they either did not grasp the depth of the advice, or that they still want to go ahead with their idea without structure or hope of any contribution to the literature. That said, I expect students to engage critically with what I say, and of course appreciate if they constructively revise and further improve such advice.

It can be discouraging when students "think they know best" and continue down the path against advice without being able to substantiate any academic support for their plan. It has only happened once with a colleague who decided that they were not able or willing to provide the necessary support this student apparently needed. It turned out that the next supervisor had the same problem and also ended up opting out, still without the student recognizing this being their issue. I have very much enjoyed the collaboration and back-and-forth discussions with students about their research, which often turned in to a shared publication of articles and even books.

I do expect to be a co-author of my student's manuscript when submitted to a journal, provided of course that I have contributed to the overall content at a level similar to when I engage in collaborative research projects with other colleagues.

In one case, I entered as supervisor after the previous supervisor left. Here, I only helped change the format and structure from a three-manuscript submission to a monograph. In this case, I did not contribute to the content, only to the structural changes, and did not co-author later work based on the thesis.

On a more foundational level, I expect the students to have sufficient maturity to be in charge of their PhD process, so I do not have to be the controlling (i.e., supervising) force that requests ongoing meetings and deliveries beyond the semi-annually requirements, although in some cases it has been necessary. More broadly, I try to be compassionate when needed, as well as have patience. I would rather err on this side than being too authoritarian or rigid, as I think, ultimately speaking, part of the PhD process requires the students to be responsible for reaching the end goal. This is probably very different from the German model!

That said, it is not easy to determine how good a student is from the onset, and it can lead to a situation where neither I, as the supervisor, nor the student benefits much from the entire PhD process. Thus, it might be useful with more rigorous admission processes to save everyone from only later finding out that achievement of a PhD is not realistic for the student. In the United States many universities rely extensively on graduate admission tests (e.g., GRE, SAT or GMAT), which I believe have been shown to correlate the best among a range of other predictive variables (e.g., GPA, motivation letter, research proposal, etc.) with the potential for successful completion.

More generally, I find it intriguing and inspiring to interact with the vast majority of my students with whom I often engage in quite close academic collaborations. In some cases, it has led to long-lasting academic collaborations and friendships.

What students expect from me varies depending on their particular training, personality and research topics. Most of the students I have worked with appreciated my active engagement in helping them refine and develop their research topics, and also me being part of two of their three thesis manuscripts (the third has to be single-authored). They typically have cherished our ongoing and more informal interaction, in contrast to more strictly "planned ahead" interactions (although some personality types and perhaps younger students might benefit from more structure). The students also appreciate being shown compassion/sensitivity during stressful times. We have all been there, and it is only human to feel out of sorts during a PhD process, and they may request some personal advice on how to handle such situations.

Reflections by Adam Lindgreen

I believe that PhD students need to be curious, critical and creative (Lindgreen et al., 2001). Although PhD supervisors have gone through a PhD program themselves and subsequently published in academic journals, students soon should know more about the intricacies of their chosen topic than their supervisor. In contrast, the supervisors should be able to provide guidance that is more general in nature: for example, suggestions on how to identify original and courageous ideas; how to collaborate with practitioners; and how to undertake cross-disciplinary research. If the students need to apply for research funding, the supervisors can also provide sound advice from their own research-funding experience. Similarly, because the supervisors have a past record of publishing in academic journals, they are able to guide the student on how to develop a conceptual framework, to write up the methodology, to present and discuss research findings and, generally, to frame a manuscript.

In addition to these three personality characteristics, students should demonstrate independence, energy and determination. Equally important is that the students have self-discipline, persistency and organizational skills. The supervisors already have a PhD degree whereas the students do not. Thus, students need to mobilize all their energy and determination, make the best of all their intelligence, knowledge and skills, and ultimately find their "wow factor" that will enable them to go through three to five years of incredible hard work.

When supervisors find a student (or vice versa) with the above personality characteristics, the building blocks are in place for a fruitful research collaboration, because experience (in research and supervision) has been paired up with creativity, energy and determination. What could be better than to have highly motivated students who write up, for example, their thoughts on an original and courageous idea and outline possible avenues for future research on that idea? Such shared documents between supervisors and their students allow them to meet as equals early on in the PhD program. Often, the research collaboration between a supervisor and a student continues long after the student has graduated! And in some cases, a former supervision turns into a friendship.

Reflections by C. Anthony Di Benedetto

The PhD student enters the program as a graduate student, and is familiar with graduate student activities (attending classes, writing manuscripts and taking exams). The first couple of semesters in the PhD program will be familiar ground. By the time of the thesis defense, however, students have transitioned into a junior researcher, capable of identifying a research topic, conducting the research and publishing the results. The graduate student skills may get the student to the ABD (all-but-dissertation) stage, and no further. One of the roles of the supervisor, and indeed the entire PhD program, is to manage this transition so that the student acquires the skills to succeed as a career academic. Different schools do this differently, but at Temple's Fox School and many others, the student will be assigned to a mentor when entering the PhD program. This assignment is based on general student areas of interest, and as the student progresses, it may become clear that another mentor's research interests are a closer match, in which case the student can change. (Often, the student will not switch, and the mentor becomes the thesis supervisor. But from Day 1, the students will have someone they can work and share ideas with.) Working with the mentor, the student begins roughing out a research progress report in the first year, gradually getting this into the form of a required research proposal. This process eases the transition from term-paper-writing graduate student to independent-thinking researcher.

As my colleagues pointed out earlier, PhD programs attract both conventional students and experienced professionals, and these two groups are in many ways mirror images of each other. Conventional students are knowledgeable and excited about conceptual models and analytical techniques, but lack much business experience; experienced professionals can formulate a realistic practical problem easily, based on their years of experience, but may have difficulty creating a satisfactory conceptual model. The supervisor needs to recognize the individual strengths, be aware of where the weaknesses will appear, and be prepared to help the student overcome weaknesses. In working with students with 20 years of senior management experience, I start almost immediately with helping them build a sound conceptual model. Often, they will build a model that is really more like a ten-year research agenda, and the challenge is to get them to focus on the part that will make a good academic contribution and will become the basis of the thesis. The rest can come later!

Finally, one needs to be very sensitive to individual differences in work style. Our collaborators spoke of the need to find a balance between too much and not enough supervision, and that has been my experience. Some students thrive when left alone, with a rough idea of what research to look up, and will do most of the work on time with the occasional check-in with the supervisor. Others will make no progress in this environment. The supervisor may need to give some students explicit, monthly deadlines for every step of the PhD research, and hold the student to those deadlines. The constant pressure, which is unnecessary and even distracting for some, might be a requirement for others to meet deadlines and ultimately pass.

ACKNOWLEDGMENTS

This chapter first appeared as an editorial in *Industrial Marketing Management* (Di Benedetto et al., 2020). We would like to thank Hans Baumgartner (Penn State's Smeal College of Business), Rod Brodie (University of Auckland's Business School), David Luna (University of Central Florida's College of Business), Peter Naudé (Manchester Metropolitan University's Business School), John Nicholson (University of Huddersfield's Business School), Laura Peracchio (University of Wisconsin-Milwaukee's Lubar School of Business), Audhesh Paswan (University of North Texas's G. Brint Ryan College of Business), Ken Peattie (Cardiff University's Business School), Markus Reihlen (Leuphana Universität Lüneburg), and Matthew Robson (Cardiff University's Business School) for contributing with their reflections.

REFERENCES

Di Benedetto, C.A., Lindgreen, A., and Ringberg, T. (2020). How to guide your PhD students. *Industrial Marketing Management*, *93*, 1–10.

Kelly, S., Nicholson, J.D., Johnston, P., Duty, D., and Brennan, R. (2020). Experienced professionals and doctoral study: a performative agenda. *Industrial Marketing Management*. https://doi.org/10.1016/j.indmarman.2020.02.018.

Lindgreen, A., Vallaster, C., and Vanhamme, J. (2001). Reflections on the PhD process: the experiences of three survivors. *Marketing Review*, *1*(4), 505–529.

Midgley, G., Nicholson, J.D., and Brennan, R. (2017). Dealing with challenges to methodological pluralism: the paradigm problem, psychological resistance and cultural barriers. *Industrial Marketing Management, 62,* 150–159.

Nicholson, J.D., LaPlaca, P., Al-Abdin, A., Breese, R., and Khan, Z. (2018). What do introduction sections tell us about the intent of scholarly work: a contribution on contributions. *Industrial Marketing Management, 73,* 206–219.

PART VII

BRIDGING TEACHING, RESEARCH AND PRACTICE

23. How to translate research into teaching

Adam Lindgreen, C. Anthony Di Benedetto, Roderick J. Brodie and Peter Naudé

INTRODUCTION

At any business school worth its salt, one of the most important goals is to foster an environment of successful academic research. This is especially true at research-intensive business schools where a core of solid, productive researchers leads to recognition and ranking among the top business schools. The *Financial Times'* Business School Rankings and *Bloomberg Business Week*'s Best B-Schools Ranking are among the most well known. A select number of business schools, about 1 percent in total, are triple accredited, with accreditations from the Association to Advance Collegiate Schools of Business (AACSB), the Association of MBAs (AMBA) and the European Quality Improvement System (EQUIS). This scholarly recognition attracts not only undergraduate and postgraduate students, who want to achieve their full potential by acquiring the necessary capabilities and skills to manage and accelerate their career in business, but also PhD students eager to establish careers in a strong research environment.

Business schools have long had their research quality assessed. For example, in the United Kingdom (UK), the impact assessment evaluation of higher education institutions' research is the Research Excellence Framework (REF), which is the successor to the Research Assessment Exercise (RAE). These impact assessment evaluations provide benchmarking information according to which UK business schools (and other higher education institutions) are ranked (see, for example, the *Guardian* and *Times Higher Education*). Highly ranked business schools (i.e., schools that are conducting world-leading research in terms of originality, significance and rigor) use this information unashamedly when seeking to attract the best talent, be it researchers or students.

With the RAEs/REFs putting much emphasis on higher education institutions' research, there has been an increasing realization that it also is important to evaluate institutions' teaching. The UK government introduced a Teaching Excellence and Student Outcomes Framework (TEF) in 2017. Although participation in the exercise is voluntary, most UK colleges and universities have chosen to participate. An institution with gold status delivers consistently outstanding teaching, learning and outcomes for its students. At research-intensive business schools, the aim of the research strategy therefore should be to conduct demonstrably impactful research that influences society, can be deployed usefully in developing education, and can be communicated to and used by practitioners. Fulfilling this aim starts with publishing research with a high impact.

Business school leaders would like to attract and keep the top research talent in order to stay competitive, attract high-potential students and recruit the most promising young faculty. To accomplish these objectives, a successful research environment for its business academic researchers needs to be established so that these researchers can produce a sustainable research stream. In a recent editorial published in Industrial Marketing Management (Lindgreen et al., 2020), we examined important antecedents including business school research strategy, leadership and governance, and from these we developed a set of conditions that are related to long-term success of research programs in academic business institutions. As detailed illustrations, we elaborated the experiences of two active research institutions—the Industrial Marketing and Purchasing (IMP) Group and the Contemporary Marketing Practices (CMP) Group — and discussed how each of these groups has implemented the conditions for success. We concluded the editorial with general observations on the environmental conditions most conducive to sustainable business school research, and presented implications regarding the role of the journal editor as a gatekeeper.

Building on this editorial, we now examine how business schools contribute to education by translating their great research into great teaching for graduate business-to-business marketing classes (including MBA programs with such classes). To achieve this goal, this chapter is organized as follows. First, we present some of the most recent findings on teaching excellence, which pertain to business instructors as well as to academics in general. Next, we explore the specific opportunities and responsibilities facing the business-to-business marketing academic. We then discuss the process by which business-to-business marketing academics can transform our research in meaningful ways and deliver value to our practitioner audience in the classroom.

WHAT DOES GREAT TEACHING MEAN?

While it may be impossible to pin down the details, one can argue that great teachers facilitate the co-creation of learning with their students and thereby provide value. To understand this concept, one can apply the principles of service-dominant (S-D) logic (Vargo and Lusch, 2004), with the instructor playing the role of the "supplier" and the student as the "customer." According to S-D logic premises, the student is a co-creator of value, and the instructor does not deliver value, but can offer value propositions (for a detailed discussion of this topic, see Chalcraft and Lynch, 2011). The S-D viewpoint stresses the nature of the exchange between supplier and customer; or, in this case, instructor–student and even student–student interaction. The student is not a passive receiver of value from the instructor, since the instructor does not deliver value unidirectionally. Rather, the instructor's value proposition potentially can be converted to value, which is co-created by both instructor and student (Ballantyne et al., 2011; Vargo and Lusch, 2008). Suppliers know this, and willingly invite customers to participate in the development of the value proposition (Vargo and Lusch, 2008). To ensure a long-term relationship between supplier and customer, each must offer satisfactory value to the other, sometimes referred to as reciprocal value propositions (Ballantyne and Varey, 2006). Working jointly, the supplier and customer can integrate their resources to co-create value, which can then be used by the customer to generate value in specific applications, or "value-in-use" (Vargo and Lusch, 2004).

The parallel to the business-to-business marketing education scenario is clear. As service providers, instructors who provide the greatest value to students provide the requisite resources to students, who bring with them their own skills, capabilities and initiative, such that together instructors and students can co-create value. This value can then be exploited to co-create value-in-use, which allows students to achieve their potential (Chalcraft and Lynch, 2011).

Once their resources have been developed, students will then be able to enact the value-in-use through time and in different applications into the future. To achieve this co-creation of learning, the traditional unidirectional, instructor-to-student learning process will not be enough. Great teaching ideally facilitates learning processes in three different directions to encourage co-creation of learning: instructor-to-student, student-to-instructor and student-to-student (as actors all participate in the creation of value and all benefit from reciprocal value propositions).

Several actions can be undertaken to facilitate these three learning processes. First and perhaps most traditionally, instructors guide students, drawing on their academic and practical knowledge. This, of course, can be done well, or not well; and a later section will discuss the translation process from great research and practical experience into great teaching. Students can also interact with the instructor, applying and developing new ideas based on their own practical experience, under the guidance of the instructor, translating the lesson learned in the specific context to a resource that provides value-in-use in the future. A later section will explore how instructors can effectively use cases and other classroom tools to accomplish this translation process. Finally, students can interact with each other, sharing and developing their new ideas drawn from experience. While synergy and reciprocal value creation can be produced from all of these processes, it is this last one that might be the most fruitful if managed well. As will be discussed later, a typical graduate business-to-business marketing class will include students of different backgrounds and levels of experience. This, of course, can be viewed as a challenge by the instructor, but is really an opportunity for students with differing backgrounds to apply their knowledge in possibly unexpected ways.

Great teaching also recognizes the power of the available technology, and uses it to advantage. Both instructor and student have access to a wealth of knowledge about business-to-business practices and management, as well as strategy applications of all types. The challenge is to develop processes so that these resources can be used sensibly and efficiently to create value. Most business schools have moved to a platform such as Canvas, Brightspace, or the like, which offer diverse ways for instructors and students to interact: discussion boards, video lectures, access to media, in-class polling, breakout groups, online quizzes, and so on. Needless to say, many business schools are offering online versions of their classes, as well as conventional on-site classes, and these platforms are critical to the effective functioning of online programs. All of these tools can be used profitably to improve the classroom experience, and indeed to facilitate all three directions of learning processes discussed above.

Whether teaching online or on-site, the instructor can benefit from the flipped classroom format (Green, 2015; Jarvis et al., 2014). Using this format, the traditional "lecture in class, assignments outside of class" structure is flipped: video lectures and discussion boards are assigned as class work, to stimulate student-to-student and student-to-instructor interaction. Class time is then used for intensive discussions, case analyses, group work, and so on. That is, the flipped classroom can be used effectively to facilitate learning processes in all three directions, and encourage the co-creation of value, which is central to S-D logic, as applied in the classroom (Jarvis et al., 2014). The instructors then can further personalize the course to bring their own perspective or even personality into the course. This can be done in many ways, limited only by the imagination of the instructors: constantly scanning for and posting current articles illustrative of course material and encouraging students to do the same (for example, by adding to discussion boards), adding weekly announcements including thought-provoking websites, humorous but relevant videos or YouTube clips, and so on. There are many relevant articles in publications such as *Business Horizons, California Management Review, Harvard*

Business Review and *Sloan Management Journal* that can be added to the weekly readings, or online reports about recent company successes or failures. Adding these, and periodically updating them, provides a wealth of information to the students that shows the relevance of course material in real situations and helps to further the co-creation of value.

In addition to facilitating student–instructor and student–student interaction, the online class platform permits online group project work. Especially in an online class where students are recruited from miles away or even from different countries, the virtual meeting room facilitated by the online platform may be the only realistic way to meet. Students therefore have to get used to using technology as a substitute for travel when doing their group projects, which is a skill they will put to good use when they are working for multinational corporations that want to reduce their carbon dioxide (CO_2) footprint or are under price pressure to cut back on international travel, and therefore turn to virtual meetings.

The above discussion, of course, assumes an ideal context for instruction. It should also be noted that, at times, some adjustments will need to be made, as conditions may not permit easy transmission of information in all directions. A very large class (100 or more students) poses major challenges. Whether on-site or online, it is unrealistic to expect a free-flowing class discussion which includes all students. Even if class discussions go well, there will be dozens of students who did not participate and/or may feel left out. There are a few adjustments that may overcome some of the challenges: hiring several course assistants, or organizing small discussion breakout groups to encourage student–student communication. The assistants will need to be well trained and dependable, though, as otherwise the classroom experience will be compromised. Also, for anyone who has taught globally, or has had a class with a high percentage of international students, the challenges of effective student-to-instructor or student-to-student information flow are well known. In China and some other East Asian cultures, students are often very reluctant to participate in class, in spite of good English skills in many cases. When teaching in Japan, one of the authors used mandatory short presentations by individuals or student pairs, just to ensure that everyone does speak at least a couple of times during the semester! (This works especially well if there are support staff who can help students with accurate translations in good business English for their PowerPoint slides.) Even teaching a mixed group of European students reveals national differences regarding willingness to participate enthusiastically in class discussions.

WHAT DOES GREAT TEACHING IN BUSINESS-TO-BUSINESS MARKETING MEAN?

The previous section explored teaching in general from the perspective of value creation; here we examine the issues and challenges when applying these concepts specifically to the effective teaching of business-to-business marketing.

An obvious starting point is to know the students: their academic level and their level of experience and preparedness. Usually, basic marketing is a prerequisite for business-to-business marketing, and students at graduate level will have taken at least one marketing principles course. Therefore, the instructor can focus the business-to-business marketing course on how it adds to existing knowledge. A relevant question may be: how do basic marketing principles, such as research, customer behavior, segmentation or integrated marketing communications, apply in business-to-business marketing? A classroom group assignment might be to take a business-to-business market, segment it, select a target and a positioning strategy, and make marketing mix recommendations for the targeted customer groups. The instructor may also ask whether the basic principles do indeed apply, or whether we need new principles adapted to the business-to-business context.

Depending on student level, there is the possibility of prior relevant work experience, and the amounts of work experience can vary greatly. In a traditional MSc program, students typically come directly from their undergraduate program. In an executive MBA program, in contrast, students often have ten or more years of managerial experience, and some may be senior marketing executives at business-to-business companies. Others may come with a medical or engineering background and will have little or any interaction with marketing people on the job. The disparity therefore poses a real challenge for the instructor, but also presents an opportunity for student–student interaction. By focusing classroom time on cases, relevant online media reports or hands-on projects, and requiring group project work and discussion board participation outside of class for project work, students can be put into interactive situations. Ideally, the ones with the strongest marketing backgrounds can take a lead role and mentor those for whom the material is quite new. Real-world examples that the instructor or the students themselves find are an ideal basis for teaching and should be stressed in discussion board posts.

The instructor can insist on hands-on projects based on real issues faced by real companies, and in a graduate class can require that students work on current projects (sometimes within their own companies). This may not always work out, and the instructor may need to provide a "plan B" project, such as to report on a major company of the student's own choosing and search online for relevant background material. But, on project presentation day, it is always enjoyable for senior managers from the companies to come and listen to the presentations, ask questions and give feedback.

The instructor must always keep in mind what students will expect of a business-to-business marketing course. Business-to-business marketing is usually taken by marketing majors, some of whom have significant experience. They will not want to hear about about market segmentation or marketing programs yet again, unless the instructor can show successfully how the familiar concepts apply in a business-to-business setting. The students will find the content much more relevant if the instructor uses a business-to-business context with which they are familiar: a focus on the buyer–seller interaction, customer relationships and external network partners. Recent cases of good or not-so-good practice can be very effective here. In addition, students are unlikely to be interested in elegant academic theories, so the instructor needs to think carefully about translation of current research for relevance; we will take up this discussion below. Most importantly, students will want takeaways that they can apply right away; first and foremost to their class projects, perhaps, but especially in the workplace.

One useful technique to achieve relevant takeaways is to make term papers as applied as possible. The term paper could be based around a business-to-business marketing principle, as in: "Using the business-to-business segmentation concept as described in class, discuss how you might effectively segment the market served by your company" or, for executives, "Consider the organizational buying models discussed in your text and describe the buying process within your buying center, outlining how you resolved conflicts in a recent purchase situation." To make the assignment even more realistic, one can use a "boss test" grading structure: the instructor, playing the role of work supervisor, provides grades on a three-point scale:

- This is brilliant. I did not realize how much value you could add to our company. I am promoting you immediately. I am really glad you are doing this program. The program is clearly adding value to you and to our company (high pass/distinction).
- This is OK, but all you have done is to describe what we already know/do. I need to know what we need to do differently and why (low pass).
- You have not fully appreciated just what we do and why. I fear we are wasting our time and money sending you on this program (fail).

Taken together, the last two sections illustrate that there is no one clear answer to the question of what makes a great teacher. Rather, it is better to accept the principle of equifinality in teaching: there are many different routes to becoming a great teacher. Much of this will depend on the audience and their level of academic knowledge and practical experience. However, it will also depend on the individual instructors: to recognize their own strengths and to develop a style that works, rather than trying to copy anyone else. The next section addresses the issue of translating the best research into great teaching: the challenge of making relevant the work that we do as academic researchers.

TRANSLATING GREAT RESEARCH INTO GREAT TEACHING

At the outset, we recognize that great research must be presented in ways that add value to students. According to the S-D logic, we as instructors can only make value propositions, not create value ourselves. As is the case for any service provider, we need to understand customer needs such that we can develop the best value proposition for our customers (i.e., students) so that we can co-create value. The esoteric theories in and of themselves are not of interest to students. Instructors need to be able to pick the ones that potentially add the most value, and find a way to demonstrate their relevance to students so they will see the value in use.

A gifted teacher knows how to bridge the gap between academic research and practice. If our research is motivated by real, practical, managerial problems, the translation process is facilitated, since the academic contributions are at the same time relevant solutions for decision-makers. Luckily for us, much of our work in business-to-business marketing is like this. We study practically relevant problems, and our findings can substantially improve managerial decision-making. As business-to-business marketing researchers, we are also fortunate in that our target journals (*Industrial Marketing Management* and other top marketing journals) require statements of managerial implications. These publications ensure that the published articles have some managerial relevance.

Having said this, one must still note that the value-adding process is by no means easy in all cases. Many of the great academic marketing articles, published in the highest-ranked marketing journals (*Journal of Marketing, Journal of Consumer Psychology, Journal of Marketing Research, Journal of Retailing, Journal of Service Research, Journal of the Academy of Marketing Science, Marketing Science*; and also in *Industrial Marketing Management*, the top business-to-business marketing management journal) require substantial analytical skills on the part of the reader. It is safe to assume that the majority of MSc and MBA students do not have these skills. The answer is not necessarily to cut out all of the math. To simply present the results without justifying how the conclusions were reached trivializes the issue, probably oversimplifies the results, and ultimately frustrates the students. This translation process therefore is hard work.

Keeping in mind that students want answers, the instructor can use the available tools to demonstrate the relevance of academic research to practical decision problems. Many business-to-business marketing classes are designed around the use of large Harvard-style cases, which allow for in-depth discussion of complicated situations without a single clear answer. The instructor can stimulate deep group discussion, encouraging the use of conceptual models brought into class and/or application of textbook principles. One way this can be done is by using the set of questions that accompanies most cases in the corresponding teaching note: break the class into groups (this works on-site, as well as with online virtual groups) and allow each group some class time to address one of the questions and then present their findings to the class. After a healthy discussion and student-generated recommendations to the company, the instructor can reveal what the company actually did (the epilogue is frequently included in the teaching note). The class can conclude with a discussion of whether the students agree with the company's actions and what the long-term consequences of the actions taken were.

Especially when teaching postgraduate students or mid-career executives, there is always the question of relevance of cases. One might use, for example, a case about LEGO to illustrate the changing role of innovation of a company in transformation, or discuss Fitbit to develop strategies for sustaining a significant competitive advantage in a maturing market. It is important to remind students that the cases are chosen to illustrate specific concepts, and that the settings (in this case, the toy industry and the wearable technology industry) are just the context. This is an effective strategy to avoid the occasional question of relevance, such as "Why am I studying a toy company? I work in pharmaceutical management." To go a step further, the instructor can ask students to submit a report of at least one or two takeaways from the case with direct relevance to their own company or that can be implemented immediately.

The contemporary marketing practices (CMP)-based case study approach can be used effectively to ensure the relevance of academic research. A characteristic of CMP is the emphasis on active discussion with executive students, through research-led teaching and teaching-informed research. CMP researchers are typically experienced teachers of executive programs. CMP research efforts are designed to be integrated with teaching activities, to achieve a continuous cycle that connects research and learning. The CMP-based approach is characterized by using case studies drawing on the students' work environments and action research, as well as ongoing feedback both to and from the classroom. This leads to what Little et al. (2008) refer to as a "zone of mutuality" between research and teaching. They state (p. 126):

> While purpose and form of cases for research or teaching are very distinct, this does not necessarily imply these two endeavors are mutually exclusive. Rather, they can be seen as complementary activities and may even draw from the same source material. Both require a purposive and systematic approach. Both require the application of creativity in arriving at conclusions and in developing new knowledge or testing and exercising current knowledge about management practice or management theory. Whilst academic capability is required in both forms of case development, they differ fundamentally in their purpose and approach to theory: either a methodology to build or test theory in a rigorous manner, or a pedagogical technique that illustrates theory by adopting a narrative approach intrinsic to which is student engagement and participation. In addition, different quality criteria apply: case research is required to be rigorous and valid, whilst a teaching case must deliver against

the teaching objectives. Internal consistency, face validity, acceptability and comprehensibility for students are of primary importance.

Central to the idea of living case studies is the notion of "theories-in-use," a term used by Cornelissen (2002), which draws from Schön's (1983) notion of reflective practitioners and the work on the interface of theory and practice by Argyris and Schön (1974) and Zaltman et al. (1982). The living case study technique recognizes that practitioners and practical knowledge can play an important role in the theorizing process and the way managers use theory. The practices and experiences of previous actions of executive students can lead to expertise that offers important insight for theory development. Nevertheless, the process by which practitioners absorb understandings means that theory development may have subtle differences, and that therefore indirect and formal processes are required to theorize with practitioners (Nenonen et al., 2017). While the living case study approach was developed when teaching part-time executive students, the approach has been adapted to other types of student settings; graduate students may have work experience and hence can reflect on theories-in-use.

The evolution of CMP research has lessons for all academics wishing to make their own personal research meaningful to practitioners. At this point, however, action research-based articles are relatively poorly represented in the academic journals, so there is much room for growth and improvement. As discussed by Nenonen et al. (2017) and Brodie et al. (2017), abductive reasoning plays a central role in the collaborative processes when theorizing with practitioners. This is because most accounts of theorizing with practitioners use abduction – explicitly or implicitly – as the main mode of inference. For example, Nenonen et al. (2017) explore the use of abductive reasoning when theorizing with practitioners. They articulate a theorizing process that integrates general theoretic perspectives and contextual research to develop mid-range theory. The process is based on the principles of pragmatism and abductive reasoning, which have their origins in the 1950s when the management sciences were being established. This provides philosophical foundations of the living case study research.

Another important consideration when using living case studies is to develop a research design, which leads to knowledge that is meaningful to practitioners. As outlined by Little et al. (2006), attention needs to be given to understanding the differences between academics and practitioners. These differences, summarized in Table 23.1, are profound and must be understood and addressed to alleviate problems in communication between the two groups. As shown in the table, academics and practitioners differ greatly in terms of their overall career goals (publication versus personal and organizational performance), how to achieve these goals (conceptual breakthrough versus proprietary solutions), kind of knowledge sought (why versus how), even the kind of language used in communication (scientific versus business-oriented). The differences between the two groups are noticeable in a classroom of senior-management graduate students with years of experience in writing business reports, but who are new to academic writing. One of the authors of this chapter teaches in a DBA program whose students average 15 years of management or entrepreneurial experience. An anecdote from this program reveals much about the gap between the two groups. One student commented at the end of a semester that he thought his DBA class was going to be easy: he only had to write two papers that semester, and he was used to writing a paper every week at work! He admitted that he had no idea how much more difficult it would be to write a scholarly paper (such as a progress report on his academic research), as compared to writing a weekly report for his boss. As shown in Table 23.1, practitioners are in "action mode," seeking solutions to their organization's problems and used to writing business reports; it is a major change in direction to adopt an academic's "reflection mode" and to write research papers in an academic style.

Table 23.1   *Differences between academics and practitioners*

Issue	Academics	Practitioners
Goal	Publication	Personal performance, organizational performance
Means of achieving goals	Conceptual breakthrough	Proprietary problem solutions
Most valuable resources	Data, idea, insights	Time, energy
Time horizon	Medium to long term	Short to medium term
Key sources of frustration	Data not delivered or available	Time-consuming tasks
Knowledge sought	Why?	How?
Language	Academic/scientific	Organizational/business
Confidentiality	Not an issue	An important issue
Most common mode	Reflection	Action

Source: Adapted from Little et al. (2006, Table 2).

Also important is an understanding of the way practitioners use theory. Of particular importance is the research by Cornelissen and Lock (2005) and Åge (2014), who examined how and why practitioners use conceptual devices in business-to-business research. The research shows that practitioners, through translating research into their specific context, can find a new spectrum of research usage in their organization, but can also contribute to research in an interactive and creative way. A distinction is made between three ways in which practitioners use theory. The first is instrumental use, implying that practitioners use research to directly solve a problem. Much of the discussion in marketing regarding the use of research is based on this perspective on direct and instrumental use (e.g., Deshpande and Zaltman, 1982). In contrast to instrumental use, there is conceptual use, where concepts and theories are used to influence practitioners' thinking, but are not applied directly. Here "ideas, problem definitions, and interpretive schemes [are viewed] as a set of intellectual tools available to the practitioner in understanding and anticipating real-world phenomena" (Cornelissen, 2000, p. 319). Conceptual devices also offer practitioners considerable scope and flexibility, and play a key role in learning from work experience. Finally, Åge (2014) discusses symbolic use. This is where the use of concept and scientific research is deliberately taken out of context and used by practitioners, and is used for its symbolic value to legitimate the actions of the practitioner. Brownlie and Saren (1997, p. 150) elaborated upon this more "partisan" method of science, arguing that "Marketing managers are typically very adept at using this conceptual vocabulary to provide interviewers with persuasive accounts of their activities as marketing managers. In that sense they are authors too."

Åge's research suggests that:

> Contrary to what extant literature suggests ... research that is abstract in nature has inherently greater possibilities for managerial relevance compared to other research, due to its potential for flexible and dynamic interpretations. The present study also suggests that researchers are not simply the producers of research for managers to passively consume or reject. Instead, B2B [business-to-business] research can benefit from encountering the messiness and chaos of the managers' worlds. (Åge, 2014, p. 440)

This stream of research suggests that conceptual and symbolic, as well as instrumental use of research, can all be used by the business-to-business marketing academic to translate business research into effective teaching, though it is probably fair to say that we still rely greatly on instrumental use. Case studies derived from research can be adapted into teaching cases as a way to incorporate learning from work experience into the classroom. Especially in a class of senior executives with varying backgrounds, "messy" (to use Åge's term) teaching cases will take students out of their comfort zones and encourage student-to-student learning, stimulate communication and add more value to the classroom experience.

In conclusion, the CMP experience shows that case studies developed for teaching purposes and case studies developed for research purposes are not mutually exclusive. The needs of both students and researchers can be met contemporaneously if the research and learning projects are designed and implemented effectively. The value to students is created through the provision of an engaging "living" learning experience, enabling engagement in and application of theory, thereby creating enhanced understanding and greater perceived value. Using the living case study method, managers' tacit knowledge and experience can be accessed and used inductively. As committed teachers, we should always look for alternative ways to create and construct knowledge. The CMP approach has provided this group of instructors with a means of creating "requisite variety" (Weick, 2007); that is, has provided a rich basis of knowledge on which to construct theoretical frameworks that acknowledge the complexity and multi-dimensional nature of CMP. The living case approach provides a rich "zone of mutuality" whereby the needs of both learners and researchers can be met.

CONCLUSION

Business-to-business marketing academics can learn much from current trends in higher education to increase the value proposition to their students. As educators, we are service providers; the literature on service-dominant logic has been applied to the academic context, yielding insights on how we can encourage the co-creation of value. Since many of us teach in environments with their own peculiarities (MBA or MSc students, mid-career or senior professional students, occasionally large class sizes, online classes, and international classes, among others), we must often make adjustments or workarounds to adapt the ideal academic service encounter to fit the setting.

Furthermore, as business-to-business marketing academics, we potentially have an advantage in the classroom. Like many of our colleagues in the business school, our own academic research is very much driven by real-world problems faced by decision-makers. Our research is inherently practical; many times, our next research project is stimulated by a discussion with senior managers about the challenges they are currently facing. Ideally, we should be able to take our academic research, make some positioning adjustments to it, and deliver a presentation to a group of senior executives who will find value in it.

Despite these advantages, it is still not necessarily smooth sailing ahead, and we need to understand the nature of the gap between academics and practitioners so that we can recognize the slipping points and overcome them. Our goals do not match those of the practitioner community. In our publish-or-perish world, publications are the currency; this is quite foreign to most practitioners. We write in an academic style designed to please reviewers and editors, and to demonstrate our theoretical contribution to the extant literature; these are issues which are not of concern to a practitioner writing a report for senior management or for stakeholders. Even our definitions of what a "report" is can differ wildly. Furthermore, no matter how relevant the findings may be to practitioners, we must demonstrate analytical rigor and may use statistical jargon that will bog down any decision manager looking for a quick and practical answer. For all of these reasons, we need to be aware of the translation process between our research and potential classroom application. While not prescribing it as a one-size-fits-all strategy, we note the success that the CMP Group has had with its "living" learning experience, in which practitioners' knowledge and experience are used inductively. Using such a case study method, students can apply and engage in theory, increasing their understanding and the co-creation of value. This technique helps us to incorporate more conceptual and symbolic use of our research, as well as to complement instrumental use of research, which is more prevalent in business schools.

ACKNOWLEDGMENTS

This chapter first appeared as an editorial in *Industrial Marketing Management* (Lindgreen et al., 2020).

REFERENCES

Argyris, C., and Schön, D.A. (1974). *Theory in Practice: Increasing Professional Effectiveness*. San Francisco, CA: Jossey-Bass.

Åge, L.-J. (2014). How and why managers use conceptual devices in B2B research. *Journal of Business and Industrial Marketing, 29*(7/8), pp. 633–641.

Ballantyne, D., and Varey, R.J. (2006). Creating value-in-use through marketing interaction: the exchange logic of relating communicating and knowing. *Marketing Theory, 6*(3), pp. 335–348.

Ballantyne, D., Williams, J., and Aitkin, R. (2011). Introduction to service-dominant logic: from propositions to practice. *Industrial Marketing Management, 40*(2), pp. 179–180.

Brodie, R.J., Nenonen, S., Peters, L.D., and Storbacka, K. (2017). Theorizing with managers to bridge the theory-praxis gap: foundations for a research tradition. *European Journal of Marketing, 51*(7/8), pp. 1173–1177.

Brownlie, D., and Saren, M. (1997). Beyond the one-dimensional marketing manager: the discourse of theory, practice and relevance. *International Journal of Research in Marketing, 14*(2), pp. 147–161.

Chalcraft, D., and J. Lynch (2011). Value propositions in higher education: an S-D logic view. *Proceedings of the 44th Academy of Marketing Conference*, Liverpool, UK.

Cornelissen, J.P. (2000). Toward an understanding of the use of academic theories in public relations practice. *Public Relations Review, 26*(3), pp. 315–326.

Cornelissen, J.P. (2002). Academic and practitioner theories of marketing. *Marketing Theory, 2*(1), pp. 133–143.

Cornelissen, J.P., and Lock, A.R. (2005). The use of marketing theory: constructs, research propositions, and managerial implications. *Marketing Theory, 5*(2), pp. 165–184.

Deshpande, R., and Zaltman, G. (1982). Factors affecting the use of marketing research information: a path analysis. *Journal of Marketing Research, 19*(1), pp. 14–31.

Green, T. (2015). Flipped classrooms: an agenda for innovative marketing education in the digital era. *Marketing Education Review, 25*(3), pp. 179–191.

Jarvis, W., Halvorson, W., Sadeque, S., and Johnston, S. (2014). A large class engagement (LCE) model based on service-dominant logic (SDL) and flipped classrooms. *Education Research and Perspectives, 41*(1), pp. 1–24.

Lindgreen, A., Di Benedetto, C.A., Brodie, R.J., and Naudé, P. (2020). "Editorial: How to translate great research into great teaching," *Industrial Marketing Management*, *85*, pp. 1–6.

Little, V., Brookes, R., and Palmer, R. (2008). "Research-informed teaching and teaching-informed research: The Contemporary Marketing Practices (CMP) living case study approach to understanding marketing practice," *Journal of Business and Industrial Marketing*, *23*(2), pp. 124–134.

Little, V., Motion, J., and Brodie, R.J. (2006). Advancing understanding: the contribution of multi-method action research-based approaches to knowledge creation. *International Journal of Learning and Change*, *1*(2), pp. 217–28.

Nenonen, S., Brodie, R.J, Storbacka, K., and Peters, L.D. (2017). Theorizing with managers: increasing academic knowledge as well as practical relevance. *European Journal of Marketing*, *51*(7/8), pp. 1130–1152.

Schön, D.A. (1983). *The Reflective Practitioner: How Professionals Think in Action*. New York: Basic Books.

Vargo, S., and Lusch, R. (2004). Evolving to a new dominant logic for marketing. *Journal of Marketing*, *68*(1), pp. 1–17.

Vargo, S., and Lusch, R. (2008). Service-dominant logic: continuing the evolution. *Journal of the Academy of Marketing Science*, *36*(1), pp. 1–10.

Weick, K. (2007). The generative properties of richness. *Academy of Management Journal*, *50*(1), pp. 14–19.

Zaltman, G., LeMasters, K., and Heffring, M. (1982). *Theory Construction in Marketing: Some Thoughts on Thinking*. New York: John Wiley & Sons.

24. Work-integrated education: improving placement pedagogy and practice

Rachael Hains-Wesson, Leela Cejnar, Kaiying Ji, Maryam Shahbazi and Maria Luksich

Increasingly, business school graduates are expected to evidence their employability skills for job-readiness (Bennett 2018), with industry desiring business schools to provide high-quality, work-related approaches for teaching employability skills that emphasize professional behavior and personal branding outcomes (Jackson 2013, 2015). Work-integrated learning (WIL) placement programs are one way to meet industry and labor market requirements. According to the Australian Student Experience Survey (2019), WIL placement programs support students to measure and evidence employability skills, which are highly valued by industry (Australian Student Experience Survey 2019; Bosco and Ferns 2014; Jackson 2015; Zegwaard and Rowe 2019). Additionally, other WIL models, such as industry-based projects, service-learning, work-based and cooperative education, volunteering, fieldwork, project-based learning, business practicums and simulations (Brewer et al. 2020; Cooper et al. 2010; Rowe and Zegwaard 2017; Zegwaard and Rowe 2019) also increase students' employability skills and development (Hains-Wesson and Ji 2020a). However, placements are still the most popular WIL type for improving students' job-readiness (Brewer et al. 2020; Work Integrated Learning in Universities: Final Report, 2019). In light of this, we chose to evaluate a high-quality and well-known business school placement program to explore how best to improve practice for future iterations. The following research questions guided the investigation:

1. What are the key elements of a placement program at an Australian university business school?
2. What are the key limitations of a placement program at an Australian university business school?

The study was also timely, due to the recent release of the Australian Student Experience Survey (2019), which emphasized that nationally undergraduate business students were not rating their employability skill development as a positive learning experience (78 percent between 2018 and 2019), showing a much lower rate in comparison with other disciplines (80–89 percent). We also discovered that many employers (30 percent) were finding business graduates' generic employability skills – such as communication, team working and problem-solving – were not being as developed as they would preferred (Archer and Davison 2008; Australian Employer Satisfaction Survey 2019). We therefore anticipated that this study would not only assist us to answer the research questions, but also contribute to the employability skill and work-integrated learning research areas.

WORK-INTEGRATED LEARNING (WIL)

To assist with evaluating a high-quality WIL placement offering, we defined WIL as "an educational approach that uses relevant work-based experiences to allow students to integrate theory with the meaningful practice of work as an intentional component of the curriculum" (Defining Work-Integrated Learning n.d.). We also drew from the employability literature to include the following key criteria to help us ascertain what a high-quality placement experience included, which were: (1) authentic assessments that measured students' employability skill development (i.e., mirroring or closely aligned to industry practice); (2) students undertaking meaningful work in an industry that aligned to their degree; and (3) the integration of reflective learning and practice for employability learning (Brown 2010; Cooper et al. 2010; Purdie et al. 2013; Rowe and Zegwaard 2017).

EMPLOYABILITY

Critical to defining and offering high-quality work-integrated learning is that students are also taught and assessed on employability skills, transferring knowledge and skills across diverse contexts (Jackson 2015; Jackson et al. 2019). Students require psychological empowerment and self-confidence building when undertaking placements (Drysdale et al. 2012; Subramaniam and Freudenberg 2007). Therefore, defining what "employability" means to different people can be difficult, especially when the term is continually evolving due to the unknown workplace of the future (Zegwaard and Rowe 2019) or the aftermath of COVID-19. In terms of this study we therefore termed employability as a learning and teaching framework that focuses on students "having the requisite skills to obtain or create work" (Smith et al. 2018, p. 18) and to "find work" (Jackson 2015, p. 10). Additionally, employability skills are best defined as non-technical skills that prepare students for the 21st century unknown workforce (Binkley et al. 2012). For instance, in the literature, employability skills have been identified to include: creativity, critical thinking, problem-solving, metacognition, communication, collaboration, information literacy, technology literacy, citizenship and social responsibility, to name just a few (Kaider et al. 2017; Hains-Wesson and Ji (2020b). Other employability skills are time management, conflict management, cultural awareness, responsibility, etiquette and good manners, courtesy, self-esteem, sociability, integrity/honesty, empathy and work ethic (Schulz 2008), as well as self-management, lifelong learning, and ability to demonstrate initiative and enterprise (Bowman 2010).

CONTEXT

Program Design

The placement program was purposefully designed to equip students with developing employability skills, such as inventiveness, agility and interpersonal communication skills for job-readiness. The program was offered in two formats: (1) as a ten-week part-time, in-semester program for local, unpaid placement; or (2) as a six-week full-time, intensive and unpaid placement. The placement experience was completed locally in Sydney, Australia or internationally, such as in China, the United States of America (USA), South America or Europe. Each placement afforded students with an opportunity to work as an intern in corporate, not-for-profit, non-government, small to medium-sized enterprises or with larger organizations and start-ups. The placement curriculum included employability skill development via self-reflection assessments as part of the pre-placement, during-placement and post-placement workshops (Billett 2019). The industry host supervisors were not involved in the marking of students' assessments, as this role was conducted by a designated Work-Integrated Learning Unit Coordinator. Host supervisors' roles provided students with appropriate mentorship, supervision and meaningful work that related to a student's career interests and degree. The program met the required Australian Fair Work Act (2009) (Cth) and policy requirements. The offering was worth six credit points that went towards a student's degree. Each student's placement was approved by the business school's Work-Integrated Learning Placement Manager through an industry agreement with respective hosts. Students were invited to sign the placement agreement and intellectual property disclaimer form, stipulating the organization's intern expectations and responsibilities. The agreement outlined students' expected work tasks and activities. For instance, students were expected to arrive (or login remotely due to COVID-19 work requirements) to work on time, be willing to engage with colleagues via a positive, flexible mindset and undergo appropriate supervision. Students were expected to complete a set amount of administration tasks, complete industry orientation, and meet occupational and health safety requirements, while completing the placement.

Student Selection

Students undertook a competitive application process. The program had prerequisites for entry that included the completion of a minimum of 48 credit points of business school units (i.e., one year of study) and a minimum 60 percent weighted average mark (WAM). To apply for a placement, students were asked to complete three key phases. First, students underwent an online application and conducted a video (self-to-camera) interview. In the video interview, students were required to explain why they wanted to complete the placement and what skills they brought to the host organization and why. The self-video interview required students to answer questions that highlighted their behavioral and motivational responses to set employability questions. Students' responses were assessed using the following criteria: (1) suitability to the placement and host partnership; (2) motivation for desiring a placement and why; and (3) evidencing presentation skills for completing a placement experience. Shortlisted students fulfilled a face-to-face (or online), group work activity, which included a written task. This formed the second phase of the selection process. The final selection phase was concluded at an assessment centre (face-to-face or online), which mirrored graduate recruitment practices and was conducted with a panel consisting of career experts, WIL educators and industry representatives. The overall selection process for the placement selection was highly competitive, with approximately 400 students applying per year with a 30 percent success rate. Students who were unsuccessful were offered a detailed e-mail as to why, offering advice on how to improve employability through career development activities as well as to undertake alternative WIL programs, such as industry, group-based business practicums.

Learning Framework

The placement framework concentrated on students' reflective learning and practice, oral presentation skill development and report writing, and purposely linked theory to practice. This was achieved by students undertaking the following learning components: (1) a pre-placement workshop; (2) a midway check-in and catch-up workshop; (3) a health and safety milestone check; (4) performance objectives in consultation with the host supervisor; (5) an individual digital presentation; (6) reflective practice assignments; and (7) an end-of-program debriefing workshop.

Assessment

Students were expected to draft and complete workplace performance objectives, in consultation with the WIL Unit Coordinator and host supervisor. The performance objectives were then refined by the host supervisor before sign-off was completed. Students also undertook a number of short reflective essays, which invited critical self-reflection on students' personal and professional development during the placement as well as post-placement. Students delivered a five-minute, digital, individual presentation, which focused on summarizing their placement experience, presenting oral communication skills, reconciling performance objectives and learning outcomes for augmenting personal and professional growth. These tasks enable students to deeply and critically reflect on their placement experience holistically.

METHODOLOGY AND METHODS

We used a case study methodology and employed a mixed-methods approach that included the collection of participants' responses through an online survey about their placement program experience. We chose a case study methodology along with mixed-methods because this type of methodology and this approach are ideal for researchers who desire to analyse multiple data instruments for eliciting differing opinions (Eisenhardt 1989; Flyvbjerg 2004). Furthermore, the mixed-methods approach enabled us to understand and explore the phenomenon from different perspectives (Kember et al. 2017). To adhere to an accepted mixed-methods undertaking, we ensured that we documented, recorded and analysed the data as a collective research team for validity. This decision was an important one and is a key criterion for using survey instruments via a case study methodology (Hains-Wesson 2017; Hains-Wesson and Appleby 2017). The research project received ethics clearance, with all data being rendered anonymous (SHR Project 2019/040).

Survey Instruments

The online placement experience survey was administered to students and industry partners who had taken part in the program from 2017 to 2019. The survey questions included direct and indirect questions, with each question being designed to elicit students' and industry's responses, to aid in answering the research questions.

Data Analysis

A probability sampling method was instigated with a modest number of student responses (N = 768) and host supervisors (N = 272). The participants included those who had taken part in the placement program in a local context (i.e., Sydney, Australia) and an international context (i.e., China, USA, Chile, and Paris). Table 24.1 presents the distribution by location of participants who took part in the study.

Table 24.1   Participants' information by destination

Years 2017–19	Destination	No. of students	No. of hosts
	Chile	14	0
	China	155	89
	Local	457	75
	Paris	42	22
	USA	100	86
Total		768	272

RESULTS

In this section, we pay close attention to the student survey results, which centered on pre-, during and post- the placement program before illustrating the key findings ascertained from the host supervisors' responses.

Selection Experience

Students were first asked to rate their experience of the student selection process. We used a Likert scale of 1–5, with 1 being not challenging at all, and 5 being extremely challenging. We present the overall results for this section of the program in Table 24.2, where the data shows that the majority of students intimated that the online application, interview and group activity were more challenging than the written task.

Table 24.2   Students' selection experience

Activities	Count	Average	Std. Dev
Online application and interview	762	3.36	0.93
Group activity	686	3.42	0.89
Written task	690	2.86	0.87

Online application and interview

Students explained that the online application and video interview process was difficult to navigate because of the nature of being placed "on the spot" for the interview request. Students said that they found it "difficult to think on-the-spot" (N = 9), "it is awkward when talking in front of a computer and to a camera" (N = 15), and "time constraints added to nervousness"

($N = 8$). A number of students mentioned that they felt they lacked interview experience ($N = 7$) and practical work experience ($N = 4$), which made the process even more challenging for them.

Group activity
Students advised that they found the face-to-face (or online), graduate recruitment-like, group activity most challenging, because it was conducted via a panel of experts, and it felt similar to what would occur in the workplace. For instance, students ($N = 6$) felt that their teamwork skills, communication skills and leadership skills were highly tested, feeling challenged by the group activity. A few students ($N = 7$) also indicated that they were uncomfortable when invited to collaborate with their peers (and in front of the panel), who they had only just met. They felt challenged intellectually and practically by this request, because they were "competing with very talented students, which makes it difficult to stand out."

Assessment Experience

We asked students how they perceived the curriculum-based elements of the placement program, which were interconnected to their placement experience, such as the set assignments. We used a Likert scale to rate students' responses, where 1 meant strongly disagree, and where 5 meant strongly agree. We present the overall results of the evaluation section for this part of the program in Table 24.3.

Table 24.3   Students' responses to the curriculum-based elements

Placement program components	Count	Average	Std. Dev.
The pre-placement workshop	759	3.78	0.84
The placement experience	768	4.45	0.71
Midway check-in and catch-up session	587	3.74	0.93
Reflective presentation and assessments	767	3.75	0.96
Debrief session	701	3.45	0.91

The results indicated that the placement experience was considered by students as being the most relevant component of the program, with an average score of 4.45, reflecting agree and strongly agree responses to these survey questions. The remaining curriculum-based components were rated closely together, but with an average score ranging between 3.45 and 3.78. The debrief workshop was considered the least relevant element of the program, which aligns with other research conducted in this area (Billett 2019). For instance, only recently has an emphasis been placed on the benefits of "bringing the learning back" for business discipline placement experiences for enhancing employability outcomes (Hains-Wesson and Ji, 2020a).

Pre-placement workshop
The results from this part of the online survey showed 38 out of 71 students believed that the pre-placement workshop helped them to prepare for the placement, set realistic expectations, set learning goals, and allowed participants to understand how to prepare for and utilize the experience prior to commencing the placement. Students rated the pre-placement workshop highly, especially when they felt that their placement experience may not have gone according

to plan, because they were able to self-intervene, improving their placement activities. For instance, some students mentioned in the online survey that the pre-placement workshop clarified how to negotiate difficult conversations with their host supervisor' ($N = 8$), refreshed their employability knowledge around the importance of non-technical skills in the workplace ($N = 7$), prepared them for becoming a professional colleague, and supported their development for increasing self-efficacy and interpersonal communication skills when dealing with unknowns ($N = 4$). A number of students ($N = 8$) also recommended that the pre-placement workshop provided them with the opportunity to connect with other students in the program, enhancing well-being. A few students ($N = 12$) mentioned that the content of the pre-placement workshop was too broad or basic. Finally, a minority of students ($N = 3$) expressed that the timing of the workshop was too early, because the pre-placement workshop materials were largely forgotten by the time the placement started.

Placement experience
A total average of 4.22, Std. Dev. 0.83 was ascertained for students' perspectives about their overall satisfaction with the placement program when working in industry. This result remained the same, no matter where a placement occurred (i.e., locally or internationally). Overall, 87.2 percent ($N = 464$) of students indicated that they were very satisfied or satisfied with the placement experience, with only a minority of students (4.5 percent, $N = 24$) indicating dissatisfaction. When students commented on why their placement experience was negative, they said that this was often due to their perceptions of being mismatched with the organization's culture, lack of relevant work tasks, or limited work experience connection to their degree. When students were invited to reflect on their overall experience, 36.6 percent ($N = 131$) of participants rated the placement experience as outstanding, with 47.2 percent ($N = 169$) rating it as good. It is important to note that when answering this question, students were asked to also compare their placement experience to other units of study at the business school and university. The majority of students (88.3 percent, $N = 671$) agreed or strongly agreed that participating in the placement experience would assist them in sourcing and securing a job in the future, especially when they compared this experience with other non-WIL units of study at the university, with only 4.1 percent ($N = 31$) of students disagreeing or strongly disagreeing with this statement. A total average of 4.16, Std. Dev. 0.82, which equated to 90.3 percent ($N = 690$) of participants, proposed that they would recommend the placement experience to their peers; with 9 percent ($N = 7$) suggesting that they would not. Those participants who suggested that they would not recommend the program to others said that the program did not meet their expectations for undertaking meaningful work that related to their degree or career interests.

Overall, when students were invited to provide an explanation to the survey question: "The placement experience will assist me in getting a job in the future," a total of 361 valid responses were received. Students either agreed or strongly agreed with this statement, with a total of 196 students (54.3 percent) mentioning that the placement experience provided them with practical skill development for improving their employability. Seventy-seven participants (21.3 percent) considered that they had gained relevant employability proficiencies. For instance, a number of students mentioned that they not only acquired technical skills such as Excel and industry-specific software, but also non-technical skills such as communication, time management, problem-solving, research, critical thinking and interpersonal skills. Some students considered professionalism and a positive attitude, such as being hard-working, eager to learn and being resilient were also top differentiators when positioning oneself in a competitive job market. Sixty-seven students (18.6 percent) acknowledged the value of these compe-tences: "without participating in a placement experience, I would never have the opportunity to work in such a big firm and meet such incredible colleagues."

Midway check-in and catch up session
Some students ($N = 24$) considered that it was beneficial to meet with peers undertaking the program, learning and sharing their experiences midway through the respective placements. Those students who found the midway check-in and catch-up session most useful were students who had encountered challenges in the workplace ($N = 7$). For instance, students believed that the catch-up session helped them to discuss workplace issues, investigate possible solutions, and strategize with peers and the WIL Unit Coordinator. Students also emphasized that the catch-up workshop aided in clarifying the requirements of the assessments ($N = 35$), such as reflective learning expectations. Particular students ($N=10$) expressed that they felt more time was needed for the catch-up workshop to hear from their peers, discussing in more detail students' challenging incidents.

Reflective assessment
A number of students ($N = 73$) claimed that the reflective assessments, in general, allowed them the opportunity to critically reflect and analyse their placement experience while also improving work practice for the future. For example, one student commented on this particu-lar discovery by stating, "this is an important process to get the most out of the placement experience," and "it makes you look back and gauge how far you have come." Many students ($N = 73$) suggested that they found the reflective assessments a way to provide them with the opportunity to think about work examples and scenarios to use in future interviews, adding these examples to resumes. However, some students ($N = 15$) complained about the high focus on reflective assessments and being weighted too heavily for the WIL unit for final grades. Students expressed this point of view further, by stating that they desired assessments to be centred on the practical know-how of the placement and from their host supervisors' perspec-tives. Students indicated that host supervisors should be given the option to provide grading of the assessments ($N = 15$).

Debrief session
A number of students ($N = 22$) stated that the debrief session was a great opportunity to further reflect on the placement encounter as well as to capitalize on the skills gained for their future careers. Other students also acknowledged the value of strategies acquired in the debrief work-shop for utilizing the placement experience as an opportunity to update their LinkedIn profile ($N = 4$), curriculum vitae (CV) ($N = 2$), future job applications, or to prepare for interviews ($N = 4$). However, some students ($N = 7$) commented negatively about the reflective component that formed a part of the debrief workshop, because they felt that it served the same purpose as the reflective assessments during the placement experience. Therefore, they noted that the content overlapped with the pre-placement workshop and was "a waste of my time." Students ($N = 9$) noted that it would be more beneficial if the debrief workshop was held before the due date of major reflective assessment, because the workshop largely guided students on how to reflect on their placement experiences. Additionally, students ($N = 22$) pointed out that the debrief workshop allowed them to articulate their overall placement experience to their peers and receive feedback. Participants, therefore, implied that they acquired useful business

insights about their respective industry placement upon reflecting on the experience, and once it had been completed ($N = 9$). For instance, one student mentioned, "I have a more holistic perspective on my career, which is incredible. This is a fantastic initiative and would recommend all students to apply because of this."

Hosts' Perspectives

The results from the hosts' online survey showed that the majority of participants ($N = 153$, 96.2 percent) considered supervising students' placement experiences as extremely beneficial or beneficial to their company for acquiring potential graduates. Only one host considered it as unbeneficial, with no explanation or comment as to why. Overall, the results implied that a total average of 4.42, Std. Dev. 0.59 of informants found that the placement was beneficial to their organization. For instance, 71 participants (72.4 percent) stated that having students from the business school was extremely important or important to their recruitment strategy, because this kept them informed about graduate potential, providing them with a competitive edge to recruiting the best candidates. Only a few (8.1 percent) hosts believed it was unimportant or not important, with no further comment explaining why. This particular point equated to a total average of 3.76, Std. Dev. 0.84, with almost all (99 percent) hosts claiming that they would like to take part in the program in the future.

Host participants (with a total of 49 valid responses) suggested that they would like to see the following enhancements made. First, an increase in the length of the placement program; that is, five days per week for six weeks, or three days per week for ten weeks, was not ascertained as being long enough. For instance, host supervisors mentioned, "students can gain only a basic understanding of our industry and business in six weeks, and just as they are warmed up, the program is due to finish." Second, host participants advised that they would like the business school to provide students with the option to extend the placement, "if there was a mutual agreement and without needing to pay students." Third, eight hosts (16.3 percent) said that they "would love to be more involved in the student recruitment process, such as being offered the information of potential candidates, interviewing them, and selecting the most suited interns." The host supervisors (50 percent) also emphasized that they would like to be able to spend more time with interns to introduce them to industry-specific orientation information (before students begin their placements), because they valued contributing to students' well-being and organizational cultural acceptance.

DISCUSSION

We investigated how to improve a large, high-quality, well-known Australian University Business School's placement program. To achieve this, we undertook an evaluation research project through a case study methodology, using a mixed-methods approach to analyze a set of qualitative and quantitative data that was gathered from online survey instruments. We invited students and host supervisors who had participated in the business school's placement program, between 2017 and 2019, to complete the online post-placement experience survey. We collected 768 student responses and 272 host responses. The results showed that the placement program was satisfying for the majority of participants, with most students suggesting that the placement experience was a highlight of their university degree, further assisting them to gain graduate employment. Other participants mentioned ($N = 9$, 2.5 percent) that the placement experience helped them to clarify their career goals and boosted their self-confidence ($N = 9$, 2.5 percent). A total average of 4.29, Std. Dev. 0.80 of students suggested that the placement experience was beneficial in securing future paid work, whereas those students who said that they were not satisfied with their placement experience focused on the following: (1) a lack of relevance to their degree; (2) receiving little or inadequate supervision; and (3) needing to complete basic administration tasks while on placement instead of meaningful work that was linked to their degree. Lastly, a number of students felt that there was not enough time to discuss workplace problems during the midway catch-up and debrief workshops, noting that they struggled with the reflective assessments, lacking intrinsic motivation to complete these.

The hosts' responses also illustrated that they found their involvement in the program to be highly beneficial for their company, and saw that this was an important future recruitment process. However, hosts also desired to be more involved with understanding students' assessment requirements as well as supporting the matching of students to their organization's needs. Additionally, host organizations expressed that they desired student placements to be for a longer period of time and without payment. Hosts felt that the longer a placement experience was for, "the better business students would then increase their employability skill development."

RECOMMENDATIONS

The findings from our evaluation study have influenced the development of the following set of recommendations. It is also important to note that the following recommendations are not exhaustive; however, they have been established through an evidence-based approach, which focused on answering the study's research questions. Therefore, the recommendations are most aligned to a business school's WIL context for unpaid placements in Australia, and as part of a business education curriculum:

1. Clearly articulate (pre-, during- and post-placement) to students why:
   a. the placement program is unpaid, working more closely with the Fair Work Act 2009 (Cth) (government organizations) to meet the non-entitlement for payment and that placements must be part of an educational program;
   b. host supervisors are not able to contribute to the grading of students' assessments; that is, not able to guarantee a similar practice experience for all students.
2. Introduce an online community of practice, via the post-midway check-in and catch-up sessions, to enable industry to take part in discussing challenges and issues on an ongoing basis as well as showcase success stories with peers and the WIL Unit Coordinator.
3. Provide an online resource (pre-placement):
   a. in consultation with students and industry partners, that focuses on how students can navigate a placement opportunity when "things go wrong," such as a misalignment to the area of their degree;
   b. for when students are not given purposeful work to complete or when there is a lack of effective supervision;
   c. provide clarity (pre-, during- and post-placement): through additional online, just-in-time resources and learning activities for students and industry partners

that focus on the importance of reflective learning for evidencing self-efficacy, self-conception and perception of self for job-readiness.

4. Provide engaging, fun, post-learning sessions that include the opportunity for students to bring a draft of their final assessment for peer review.

5. Provide additional and relevant training for WIL Unit coordinators and in consultation with students and industry partners for improving pre-placement, midway check-ins and debrief sessions for enhancing the design and delivery of the WIL placement curriculum.

CONCLUSION

The results of the study revealed that placement programs are one of the most beneficial experiences students and hosts believe will improve employability and job-readiness for a complex employment market. However, placement programs are also highly problematic to get right, especially when trying to meet multiple stakeholders' requirements, global pandemic disruption, and government mandates and policy. For instance, there are always several variables, opinions, needs and expectations to continually consider, including effective and engaging pre-, during- and post-placement learning requirements for improving students' employability outcomes. This is further a challenge when, in particular, how to best design and deliver placement curriculum for business education has been modestly articulated (Billett 2015; Kaider and Hains-Wesson 2016; Hains-Wesson and Ji 2020a; Jackson 2015).

Additionally, due to the current global pandemic disruption, meeting multiple stakeholders' needs is therefore more imperative than ever. It is vital that WIL placement teams continue to evaluate established placement programs through an evidence-based approach, and before incorporating key recommendations for improving practice. This, in turn, will allow for proactive measures to take place for the quality of the entire employability educational experience for business education in Australia and beyond.

LIMITATIONS

This study concentrated on one local and international placement WIL program at an Australian university business school. We did not compare our results with nor validate results for other settings. Nor did we compare the similarities or differences between local and international placements or other types of WIL programs at different universities.

FUTURE DIRECTIONS

It would be advantageous to expand upon this investigation to include different demographic, economic, cultural, and global pandemic factors for placement programs. Additionally, undertaking a comparison study that includes other placement types, such as micro-placements, online placements and group-based placements, that occur in different disciplines, locally and internationally, would be advantageous. This in turn, would aid in widening the employability, WIL literature and labor market research areas for job-readiness.

REFERENCES

Archer, Will and Jess Davison (2008), "Graduate employability," Council for Industry and Higher Education, London.

Australian Student Experience Survey (2019), https://www.qilt.edu.au/qilt-surveys/student-experience. Canberra, Australia.

Australian Employer Satisfaction Survey (2019), https://www.qilt.edu.au/qilt-surveys/employer-satisfaction. Canberra, Australia.

Bennett, Dawn (2018), "Embedding employABILITY thinking across higher education," Department of Education and Training. Canberra, Australia.

Billett, Stephen (2015), *Integrating Practice-based Experience into Higher Education*. Dordrecht: Springer.

Billett, Stephen (2019), "Augmenting post-practicum experiences: purposes and practices," in Stephen Billett (ed.), *Augmenting Health and Social Care Students' Clinical Learning Experiences*. Cham: Springer, 3–25.

Binkley, Marilyn, Ola Erstad, Joan Herman, Senta Raizen, Martin Ripley, et al. (2012), "Defining twenty-first century skills," in P. Griffin, B. McGaw and E. Care (eds), *Assessment and Teaching of 21st Century Skills*. Dordrecht: Springer, 17–66.

Bosco, Anna Maria and Sonia Ferns (2014), "Embedding of authentic assessment in work-integrated learning curriculum," *Asia-Pacific Journal of Cooperative Education*, 15(4), 281–290.

Bowman, Kaye (2010), "Background paper for the AQF Council on generic skills." http://www.aqf.edu.au/Portals/ 0/Documents/Generic%20skills%20background%20paper %20FINAL.pdf.

Brewer, Margo, Sonia Ferns, Sally Lewis, Jeri Childers and Leoni Russell (2020), "Interdisciplinary project-based work-integrated learning: the Australian good practice guide," Australian Technology Network.

Brown, Natalie (2010), "WIL [ling] to share: an institutional conversation to guide policy and practice in work-integrated learning," *Higher Education Research and Development*, 29(5), 507–518.

Cooper, Lesley, Janice Orrell and Margaret Bowden (2010), *Work Integrated Learning: A Guide to Effective Practice*. London: Routledge.

"Defining work-integated learning" (n.d.), *International Journal of Work-Integrated Learning*. https://www.ijwil.org/defining-wil.

Drysdale, Maureen, Lisa J. Ward, Kristina Johansson, Elena Zaitseva and Sheri Dressler (2012), "Comparing the Attributes of Students in Cooperative Education or Work-Integrated Learning Programs in Four Countries," Australian Collaborative Education Network 2012 Conference, 29 October – 2 November, Geelong, Melbourne, Australia. (Unpublished.)

Eisenhardt, Kathleen M. (1989), "Building theories from case study research," *Academy of Management Review*, 14(4), 532–550.

Flyvbjerg, Bent (2004), "Five misunderstandings about case-study research," *Qualitative Inquiry*, 12(2), 219–245.

Hains-Wesson, Rachael (2017), "Why aren't we talking? Third-party providers and mobility programs," *Higher Education Research and Development*, 36(4), 866–869. doi:10.1080/07294360.2017.1284033.

Hains-Wesson, Rachael and Mary Appleby (2017), "A perspective on third-party providers and study tour programs: a mixed method study," *Issues in Educational Research*, 27(3), 435–452.

Hains-Wesson, Rachael and Kaiying Ji (2020a), "Students' perceptions of an interdisciplinary global study tour: uncovering inexplicit employability skills," *Higher Education Research and Development*, (39)4, 657–671. https://doi.org/10.1080/07294360.2019.1695752.

Hains-Wesson, Rachael and Kaiying Ji (2020b), "Developing self-confidence: students' perceptions of post-practicum project teamwork," in Stephen Billett (ed.), *Enriching Higher Education Students' Learning Through Post-Work Placement Interventions*. Cham: Springer.

Jackson, Denise (2013), "The contribution of work-integrated learning to undergraduate employability skill outcomes," *Asia-Pacific Journal of Cooperative Education*, 14(2), 99–115.

Jackson, Denise (2015), "Employability skill development in work-integrated learning: Barriers and best practice," *Studies in Higher Education*, 40(2), 350–367. doi:10.1080/03075079.2013.842221.

Jackson, Denise, Jenny Fleming and Anna Rowe (2019), "Enabling the transfer of skills and knowledge across classroom and work contexts," *Vocations and Learning*, 12(3), 459–478.

Kaider, F. and Hains-Wesson, R. (2016). "Enhancing courses for employability," Report, Australian Collaborative Education Network, Victoria, Australia. https://acen.edu.au/wp-content/uploads/2015/09/Enhancing-Courses-for-Employability.pdf?x83956.

Kaider, Friederika, Rachael Hains-Wesson and Karen Young (2017), "Practical typology of authentic WIL learning activities and assessments," *Asia-Pacific Journal of Cooperative Education*, Special Issue, 18(2), 153–165. http://www.apjce.org/files/APJCE_18_2_153_165.pdf.

Kember, David, Celina Hong, Vickie W.K. Yau and Shun Amaly Ho (2017), "Mechanisms for promoting the development of cognitive, social and affective graduate attributes," *Higher Education*, 74(5), 799–814.

Purdie, Fiona, Lisa Ward, Tina McAdie, Nigel King and Maureen Drysdale (2013), "Are work-integrated learning (WIL) students better equipped psychologically for work post-graduation than their non-work-integrated learning peers? Some initial findings from a UK university," *Asia-Pacific Journal of Cooperative Education*, 14(2), 117–125.

Rowe, Anna D. and Karsten E. Zegwaard (2017), "Developing graduate employability skills and attributes: curriculum enhancement through work-integrated learning," *Asia-Pacific Journal of Cooperative Education*, Special Issue, 18(2), 87–99.

Schulz, Bernd (2008), "The importance of soft skills: education beyond academic knowledge," *Nawa Journal of Communication*, 2(1), 146–154.

Smith, Martin, Kenton Bell, Dawn Bennett and Alan McAlpine (2018), "Employability in a global context: evolving policy and practice in employability, work integrated learning, and career development learning," Wollongong, Australia: Graduate Careers Australia.

Subramaniam, Nava and Brett Freudenberg (2007), "Preparing accounting students for success in the professional environment: enhancing self-efficacy through a work integrated learning programme," *Asia-Pacific Journal of Cooperative Education*, 8(1), 77–92.

"Work Integrated Learning in Universities: Final Report" (2019), Deakin, Australian Capital Territory. Retrieved from https://internationaleducation.gov.au/International-network/Australia/InternationalStrategy/EGIProjects/Documents/WIL%20in%20universities%20-%20final%20report%20April%202019.pdf

Zegwaard, Karsten E. and Anna D. Rowe (2019), "Informed curriculum and advancing innovative practices in work-integrated learning," *International Journal of Work-Integrated Learning*, Special Issue, 20(4), 323–334.

25. On the busyness of business schools: harnessing synergy in research, teaching and engagement

Sandra Seno-Alday

> "To be is to do" – Socrates.
> "To do is to be" – Jean-Paul Sartre.
> "Do be do be do" – Frank Sinatra.
> (Vonnegut 1982)

ON BUSYNESS

I came to the world of business and management scholarship to escape busyness. In my past corporate life, I was busy. In my past consulting life, I was busy. In my past entrepreneur life, I was busy. I finally got tired of being constantly busy, so I completed a PhD to retire to what I envisioned would be a sedate scholarly life, only to find myself ... busy. Busier than ever.

The busyness of business scholarship was like no other. Every day was a workout requiring me to pivot rapidly across three different parts of my brain. Marching into my classroom, I had to harness my teaching brain to foster learning effectively (or suffer the dread student evaluation). Dashing out of my classroom and pushing past the fog of fatigue, I had to summon my research brain to publish that stubborn paper (or perish before getting even a whiff of what I thought was retirement). And sprinting into that conference room, I had to channel my engagement brain to serve the wider university community and persuade grant funding bodies to feed the future of my research (or risk depriving myself of retirement altogether).

The endless bustle of the business school got me thinking about how the best and most prolific business and management thinkers found the time to think.

Thinking was supposed to be at the core of a scholar's being. But if Socrates argues that soul (one's being) is expressed through action (one's doing) (Cooper 2007; Yu 2005), and if Sartre suggests that pursuits (one's doing) are a reflection of character (one's being) (Webber 2009), then why did I feel that all of what I was doing was a huge distraction from being?

In the end, it was my fledgling researcher self, struggling to make sense of the absurdity of it all, that helped set me on the path of pulling myself out of the downward spiral of busyness. The scholar in me finally found the sense and the energy to do what a good scholar was supposed to do when confronted with a confusing, curious or frustrating phenomenon: take to the literature to find some answers.

My objective was to unpack the seeming doing–being dichotomy that was causing me significant stress. Taking a Socratic step back to examine my scholarly life, I first looked outside myself to focus on the context of business schools and higher education. Looking outward, I sought to comprehend the factors at play in order to understand the doing that was making it very busy. I found myself in a turbulent world of powerful, dynamic forces pulling in different directions and competing for urgent attention.

And then I looked inward, reflecting on the fundamental purpose of universities and business schools. Reconnecting with the purpose of higher education helped me remember the reasons for being and becoming a scholar. I found that focusing on purpose was key in making sense of the seeming madness and in keeping anchored in the turbulence.

Finally, in top business journals, I searched for evidence of how other business and management scholars have managed to live out their being in the midst of all that doing. I found that the doing–being dichotomy was, in fact, false: the path to sanity lay in recognizing and harnessing the endless possibilities of the doing–being synergy.

ON ALL THAT DOING

Why was I so busy? My first stop was to try to pin down the drivers of the busyness. To do this, I hunted through the *Academy of Management Learning and Education* (AMLE) journal and the *Financial Times* 50 (FT 50) journals to learn what I could about what was going on in universities and business schools. AMLE is the main publication vehicle of the Academy of Management for scholarly work on management teaching and learning, and the top management education journal on major journal ranking lists in the world (Harzing 2020). The FT 50 have been identified by the *Financial Times* as the most critical journals contributing to the research rank in the much-coveted FT rankings for business schools (Ormans 2016). Collectively, these journals are the key influencers of business and management thought, education, practice and policy around the world.

What I learned from the influencers gave me a sense of troubled relief. I was not alone in the maelstrom. Most, if not all, of us in the academy were indeed very busy. Here is what I found about all the doing that was making us all so busy.

Teaching More

We have more students than ever. The sheer (and increasing) number of students in universities (Delavande and Zafar 2019) has created an environment of "mass education" (Degl'Innocenti et al. 2019), which means that we are teaching more. It does not matter whether we are teaching more students or more hours (or both). Having more students simply equates to more work.

Having a global population of 7 billion-and-counting should be enough to explain why there are more students in our classrooms. But United Nations data[1] shows otherwise. On the one hand, global population grew at a compound annual growth rate (CAGR) of around 1 percent between 2005 and 2017. On the other hand, the number of students enrolled in tertiary education in the same period grew at a CAGR of around 4 percent. What is going on here? What has propelled the popularity of universities for student numbers to skyrocket at four times faster than the world population?

Scholars have highlighted a combination of social, policy and regulatory, and economic factors that have made higher education institutions very attractive places (Delavande and Zafar 2019). On the policy front, the 1990s appears to have been a watershed decade. For example, the United Kingdom[2] in 1992 granted university status to teaching institutions focused on developing skills immediately relevant to industry (for example, polytechnics, vocational education and training institutions) (Degl'Innocenti et al. 2019).

This and similar higher education policy reforms in Europe,[3] the United States[4] and other countries tell us that governments have literally been ushering students to seats in our lecture halls. Governments want more students to undertake higher education degrees, and have made university education more accessible to more students. Policies have strengthened the link between human capital development and economic development, highlighting the strategic role of university teaching in national development. This has made us popular. Very popular.

Our popularity, unfortunately, does not always come down to our awesome and inspiring teaching (although many of us are awesome and inspiring teachers). Our popularity is better explained by our students' assumption that university attendance is strongly related to employability and a future earnings premium (Degl'Innocenti et al. 2019; Delavande and Zafar 2019). Greater access to higher education, accompanied by prospects of better employability, future financial gains, and career or entrepreneurial success, have boosted the social desirability of higher education degrees, thus motivating legions of students around the world to troop into our classrooms (Delavande and Zafar 2019; Fortin 2006; Millan et al. 2014).

Alongside these policy reforms and social trends, more of the world has become more affluent too. Global economic growth led by the internationalization of businesses from both developed and emerging economies has increased the demand for university degrees among globally mobile students. This has not only further increased the number of students in our classrooms, but has also increased diversity significantly (Hardy and Tolhurst 2014; Zhang et al. 2016). That has tricky implications.

Teaching Differently

With more students comes greater diversity (Guri-Rosenblit et al. 2007; Mercer-Mapstone and Bovill 2020). While having different kinds of students makes classes interesting, it also comes with the challenge of employing new pedagogical approaches. Teaching five students from relatively homogeneous backgrounds is necessarily different from teaching classes of 20, 60, 300 or 1800 students from a wide range of cultural, linguistic, epistemological and other backgrounds (Hardy and Tolhurst 2014; Zhang et al. 2016). We are having to learn new ways of teaching and evaluating student learning outcomes, given the changing classroom conditions.

Classroom size and diversity have not been the only factors that have been leading us to teach differently. In line with policies focused on the relevance of a university education to the job market, there has also been increased pressure from employers for universities to develop workforce-ready graduates (Bedwell et al. 2014; Rubin and Dierdorff 2009, 2011). This has required constant review of curricula and continuous redevelopment of teaching and learning approaches to ensure that graduate learning outcomes meet the rapidly changing demands of the global workplace (Bagley et al. 2020; Bunch 2020; Harker et al. 2016).

The combined pressures from government, employers and students to produce job-ready graduates have led universities to collaborate more closely with industry to come up with non-traditional educational approaches (Borah et al. 2019; Paton et al. 2014). New pedagogies and models of teaching have been designed to bring industry and the workplace into the classroom, and vice-versa. These collaborative models include curriculum-embedded internships (Narayanan et al. 2010), problem-based learning (Ungaretti et al. 2015), case and business plan competitions (Kwong et al. 2012) and work-integrated learning (Bowen and Drysdale 2017).

Needless to say, the constant and rapid redevelopment of curricula and pedagogies to ensure the employability of greater numbers of students in an increasingly diverse higher education environment is a lot of work.

Racing to the Top

With the increased demand for higher education (from students, employers and governments) has come a rise in the number of universities and other higher education providers to meet this demand, thus intensifying competition in the sector (Alajoutsijärvi et al. 2018).

This has led to pressures for universities to explicitly differentiate themselves in unique ways. For example, in addition to public universities, there has been significant growth in private universities and not-for-profit universities with specific religious or doctrinal foundations (Delavande and Zafar 2019). This has signaled a wider range of choice for university students (Delavande and Zafar 2019).

The extensive options available to globally mobile students have raised the importance of university ranking as an indicator of quality and competitiveness (Collet and Vives 2013). The methodologies and criteria applied by the major world university rankings are varied, but typically include employability or employer reputation, research output and impact, and the teaching and learning environment (Chan 2020; QS World University Rankings 2020; THE World University Rankings 2020).

Graduate employability and employer reputation account for a significant component of the *Financial Times* rankings, where employment and career-related criteria (for example, employment within three months of degree completion, salary, salary increase, and others) account for around 50 percent of a business school's rank (Chan 2020). The Times Higher Education (THE) World University Rankings, however, are heavily skewed towards research. In these rankings, research output and research impact (measured by citations and technology transfer to industry) account for more than 60 percent of a university's rank (THE World University Rankings 2020).

If universities want to raise their profile and their reputation, then they need to be placed as close as possible to the top across several rankings. And if different rankings employ different criteria, then a higher education institution that seeks to be globally competitive would need to ensure high levels of performance across all the major criteria of graduate employability, teaching and learning, and research.

Churning out Innovative Research

Research volume, citations and technology transfer are important criteria in major university rankings: we need to research more (to address volume), research differently (to attract citations) and research with relevance (to enable technology transfer). The pressures of research are essentially the same as the pressures of teaching.

The challenge of producing more research is that it does not simply involve churning out papers. It requires publishing in top journals, which we know is difficult and getting increasingly so (Adler and Harzing 2009; Certo et al. 2010). Journal ranking matters because top journals attract the most citations (which is what makes them top journals in the first place), and citations matter in university rankings.

As if the pressure for research volume were not stressful enough, there is further pressure to ensure research relevance: that is, our scholarship needs to be grounded in practice and also needs to have potential to make a positive impact on practice (Bapuji and Beamish 2019; McGahan 2007; Singhal et al. 2014).

And as if the responsibility to effectively communicate and disseminate findings to influence practice were not difficult enough (Peng and Dess 2010; Van de Ven and Johnson 2006), there has been increased pressure for universities to monetize research (Barr et al. 2009; Pisano 2006). This "third mission" requires universities to generate income by commercializing research through industry partnerships (Chai and Shih 2016; Degl'Innocenti et al. 2019; Horner et al. 2019). At times, this has required universities to have equity holdings in spinoffs (Feldman et al. 2002; Muscio et al. 2016). The pressure to monetize research clearly introduces another dimension to achieving research competitiveness, making universities not only research and teaching but also entrepreneurial institutions (Feldman et al. 2002).

It is easy to comprehend that research matters in stretching the boundaries of knowledge and in influencing practice. But how many prospective students really care about research output and impact in university rankings? Studies have found that while students are unlikely to break rankings down into individual components in order to inform their higher education choices, they do associate overall business school and university ranking with better employability prospects (Ruigrok et al. 2017). There is also evidence that research performance does have some positive effects on business programs and students (Mitra and Golder 2008; O'Brien et al. 2010).

While rankings may be blunt and imperfect measures of worth, we can be certain that ranking matters in establishing and reinforcing university and business school reputation. And reputation matters significantly to students, employers, governments and grant funding agencies.

Stressing Out

All this busyness has been making scholarly life hectic and stressful. Despite having to manage time across teaching, research and engagement accountabilities, these three areas of performance are valued very differently. The publish-or-perish dictum that governs decisions on tenure and promotion has led to the overwhelming weight of research and publication output above all else (De Rond and Miller 2005). Despite rewards that may exist for good teaching and good external engagement, our "research career capital" remains far more important to achieve not only the higher-order concerns of scholarly legitimacy and credibility but also the basic concerns around career stability (Bedeian 1996; Ryazanova and McNamara 2019).

But publishing in top-ranked journals is getting increasingly tough, and the deadline imposed by universities on academics to get published in order to get tenure or promotion compounds academic stress (De Rond and Miller 2005). That it is difficult to cope with these pressures is an understatement. Sadly, some of us have not been coping very well.

For many, the default response has been to treat research and teaching as a zero-sum game: that is, time spent on teaching is necessarily time spent away from research (Loyd et al. 2005). This could mean simply teaching at the barest possible minimum in terms of both quantity and quality. This can clearly have a negative impact on the student experience. Or this could involve negotiating for a "reasonable" teaching load (Ryazanova and McNamara 2019). But what is reasonable? And who is to say that what is reasonable for one is reasonable for all?

There has also been evidence of increased scientific misconduct among some scholars. These include plagiarism (Lewis et al. 2011) and other forms of questionable ethical research practices (Butler et al. 2017; Cox et al. 2018; Hall and Martin 2019; Honig et al. 2014). There also have been situations where scholars attempt to "game" the system of research performance measurement (Graf et al. 2019).

Some coping mechanisms at the institutional level also leave much to be desired. One response designed to alleviate the pressure to teach and to ensure that no precious time is taken away from research has been to increase the number of part-time or sessional faculty with heavy teaching loads and with little or no security of tenure (Shulman 2019). Sure, hiring part-time staff may contribute to helping ease teaching load in the here-and-now. This approach also helps in managing the variable resources required to match the ebbs and flows of student numbers. But this does not necessarily ease the pressure of having to update teaching and learning techniques to address the needs of rapidly changing student cohorts. And it does not necessarily help in maintaining a high level of teaching quality that meets the expectations of students and employers required to stay at the top of those rankings (Shulman 2019). In fact, the reality of having a large number of colleagues with no security of tenure is that stress does not go away: it instead intensifies and permeates across the entire institution, making business schools and universities tightly wound, anxious places (Kraimer et al. 2019).

The stress is further compounded by the increased "managerialism" in universities (Sousa et al. 2010). While this has been found to result in some positive gains, this has also in some cases led to a short-term, opportunistic research outlook (rather than a longer-term outlook focused on boundary-breaking creativity, innovation and quality) (Alvesson and Sandberg 2013; Sousa et al. 2010). Alas, in the end, it is our scholarship in our own field of inquiry that suffers from our stress.

Pausing: Business Education in the Time of COVID-19

And then there are the Black Swans: catastrophic events that have a low probability of occurrence, but that appear to be completely predictable with the perfect vision of hindsight (Taleb 2007). As I write this in mid-2020, I breathlessly watch the world spinning as it grapples with containing the novel coronavirus COVID-19.

With no available vaccine or cure, national borders have closed, entire cities have gone into lockdown, and organizations have had to either close down or rapidly create a remote workforce infrastructure in order to stem the spread of the virus (Hale et al. 2020; Lau et al. 2020). The COVID-19 crisis has taken governance and management down paths and up against challenges that some observers say have not been seen since the 1918 flu pandemic (Gates 2020; Gössling et al. 2020; Hale et al. 2020).

Universities have had to shut down campuses and move to online teaching platforms practically overnight (Crawford et al. 2020). This has added yet another pressure to teaching, requiring educators around the world to teach differently and ramp up efforts to bring online teaching and learning skills up to speed with the changed conditions (Bao 2020). Institutions have also had to review syllabi and grading or assessment regimes in acknowledgment of the steep adjustment challenges faced by everyone across the board (Assunção Flores and Gago 2020; Sahu 2020).

Students have had to make difficult adjustments as well (Peters et al. 2020). Exchange students have been sent home. With national borders closed, international students have had to stay home and reconsider their overseas education plans (Sahu 2020). Other students have reported significant concerns about their university experience and have, or are intending to, put their studies on hold. The data continues to be fuzzy at the moment, but the cold fact is that enrollments have already begun to reflect decreased student numbers (Rumbley 2020).

Falling enrollments and the currently unfolding global economic fallout signal an important opportunity to revisit not only teaching and learning approaches but also, more fundamentally, higher education operating and financial models. The ongoing process of reflection and taking stock will have significant implications on the way we research, teach and engage with the rest of the world.

The emergence of the novel coronavirus has underscored the dynamism of the environment within which universities and organizations need to function. And the national and organizational responses to the crisis raise questions about what we know and do not know about the world and how we engage with it.

Rankings aside, therefore, there is urgent pressure to push the boundaries of management and business thinking, because our field hurtles forward faster than the time it takes to publish a high-quality journal article. Not only do we need to understand and inform the constantly shifting challenges of business and organizational management, but we also need to prepare the future workforce and leaders of the very businesses and organizations we investigate. Is this all sustainable? How can we as scholars cope?

ON REMEMBERING BEING

In the midst of that bleak news, the good news was that I was getting a bit of clarity. It took a lot of courage to look into the faces of my (our) three-headed teaching–research–engagement demon of busyness. We have all been very busy because the context within which higher education institutions operate has become increasingly dynamic over time. Our major stakeholders — students, governments, organizations — demand much from us. And because their own contexts have likewise become increasingly volatile, then what they require from us rapidly changes as well. We must accept that if the businesses, organizations and managers that are the focus of our scholarship need to be agile to survive and compete, then so must we.

How can we cope with busyness while remaining productive and agile business scholars?

On further reading and reflection, I came to the conclusion that the key to making sense of it all and to paving the way forward was to go back to what lies at the core of a university: knowledge. If a university exists to create knowledge through research, share this knowledge through teaching, and apply this knowledge through engagement, then the university is the ultimate "knowledge organization" (Bennet and Bennet 2004).

When I viewed things this way, then I was able to focus less on what appeared to be disjointed research-teaching-engagement activities. I was instead able to comprehend their logical and coherent linking. In coming to internalize their interdependent relationship and remembering the purpose of scholarship, I was finally able to see the faint markings of a path towards sanity.

Mastering the method to the madness required viewing teaching and engagement as opportunities to do research and co-create knowledge (Loyd et al., 2005; Van de Ven and Johnson, 2006) and, conversely, undertaking research with a view to communicating and transferring knowledge to students and practitioners (Steffens et al., 2014; Van de Ven and Johnson, 2006).

This sounded like a sensible way out, but was it feasible? I wanted to know whether there were scholars out there who were successful at finding synergy in teaching, research and engagement.

ON THE FALSE DICHOTOMY

I went back to the FT 50 journals and did a search of articles published in 2019. I went on a hunt for evidence of synergy in teaching, research and engagement activities. I wanted to know if this synergy could be harnessed to publish successfully in top journals, or if this was all just a myth. To find publications that drew on teaching and/or engagement within these disciplinary journals, I performed a search using the keywords "student" or "classroom" and "university." I ended up with 82 articles whose abstracts I analyzed. As I combed through the abstracts, I felt my spirits lift a little bit. I unexpectedly began to feel the stirrings of hope.

I was able to distill four strategies by which our colleagues in the academy have been able to move past the doing–being dichotomy, capitalize on research–teaching–engagement interconnectedness, and harness the doing–being synergy.

Strategy 1: Draw on Student Data to Make Disciplinary Contributions

Around 30 percent of the papers I found used student data to tackle research questions about business and management. And there it was: the first trick was to recognize the fact that our students are not just students. Our teaching does not take us away from our research. It brings us closer to it.

Our large and diverse student population are also consumers. They consume a vast range of products and services from around the world. We have significant opportunity to deepen our understanding of consumer behavior right inside our classrooms (see e.g., Craig et al. 2019; Vredeveld and Coulter 2019; Winterich et al. 2019).

Our students are also current managers with significant industry experience, undertaking MBAs or other postgraduate programs. We have direct access to managers and executives who can help us gain rich insights into management thinking and behavior (see e.g., Fleischman et al. 2019; Johnson et al. 2019). We have the benefit of walking with current and future entrepreneurs as they go on the journey of building, creating and growing their enterprises (see e.g., Ebbers and Wijnberg 2019; Kaandorp et al. 2019; Krishnan and Wang 2019). The opportunities to conduct longitudinal studies of entrepreneurs and their enterprises are unparalleled.

Of course, we have the benefit of access to future managers and leaders. We are in an exceptional position to investigate their motivations, thought processes and behavior (see e.g., Cartabuke et al. 2020; Mihelič and Culiberg 2019). We also have the privilege of having them in our classrooms at a unique stage in their development, journeying with them as they go through their individual process of becoming (Barnett 2009).

Needless to say, our students also comprise the current and future workforce. We have unique opportunities to investigate the psyche and motivations of human capital (see e.g., Ferris et al. 2019; Robinson et al. 2019; Samek 2019; Schlegel and Mortillaro 2019). And we are also able to explore the dynamics of teams (see e.g., Aggarwal and Woolley 2019; Lount Jr et al. 2019; Maloney et al. 2019).

Finally, our students give us opportunities to gather data to test our statistical methods and models (see e.g., Gillen et al. 2019; Jochmans and Weidner 2019).

Strategy 2: Draw on Student and Industry Data to Make Disciplinary Contributions

A much smaller number of papers (around 9 percent of the sample) employ student data to tackle questions about management and business (as in the case of Strategy 1), but with the big difference of also drawing on industry data.

The second trick was to recognize that our students can function as an excellent control or comparator group. We have exceptional opportunity to validate classroom experiments and simulations with industry or workplace data (see e.g., Baur et al. 2020; Hussain et al. 2019; Parker et al. 2019). We can also undertake comparative or replication studies to test our hypotheses across samples and contexts (see e.g., Daniels and Zlatev 2019; Hu et al. 2019). We need only to turn to our classrooms to take advantage of the opportunities available to us to create methodologically interesting studies.

It occurred to me that this strategy presented a good approach to bridging the perceived teaching–research–engagement divide. Judging from the small number of papers in the sample, this underscores an important opportunity for us to do more of it.

Strategy 3: Draw on Student Data to Make Management Education Contributions

A further 30 percent of the papers draw on student data to make contributions to business and management education. These contributions focus on the drivers, processes and impact of our efforts to develop managers. It surprised me to discover that these top disciplinary journals published papers with contributions to management education. It was then that I realized that management education papers were not after all within the exclusive purview of management education journals.

This discovery brought our purpose as scholars into sharper relief for me. The third trick was to always remember that we do not only create knowledge by making disciplinary contributions to business and management. We are also responsible for effectively communicating and transferring knowledge to future and current managers of businesses and organizations. And we must never forget that the communication and transfer of knowledge begins in our classrooms.

We are called to reflect on what we teach our students, and whether what we teach continues to be relevant under changing business conditions (see e.g., Dierksmeier 2020; Moosmayer et al. 2019). We are in a great position to understand who our students are. In investigating these managers-in-training and understanding how they think, perceive and behave, we gain insight into the kinds of individuals who aspire to be managers and leaders (see e.g., James et al. 2019).

We also need to reflect on how we teach our students and to understand their learning processes. If we are to effectively transfer the knowledge we create, then we must pay close attention to our teaching approaches. As organizations, technologies and students change, so must our knowledge communication and knowledge transfer strategies and techniques change (see e.g., Hull et al. 2019). We need to constantly examine whether our conventional teaching approaches are appropriate for developing new ways of thinking and leading (see e.g., Garcia-Rosell 2019; Reficco et al. 2019). We likewise need to investigate how we can employ new methods to foster new learning (see e.g., Azmat et al. 2019; Hamington 2019). Consistent with the need for external engagement, there are significant opportunities to explore how co-designing learning experiences with industry stakeholders can help facilitate the knowledge transfer process (see e.g., Borah et al. 2019).

Finally, we are best positioned to evaluate the impact of our teaching on the learning and development of the current and future managers in our classrooms (see e.g., Burnette et al. 2019; Høgdal et al. 2019; Yang et al. 2019). We have the benefit of witnessing and documenting the transformational processes of management education (see e.g., Meier and Carroll 2019; Mladenovic et al. 2019; Tomlin et al. 2021; Walker et al. 2019). And we can allow ourselves a distinctive glimpse into how our teaching influences career decisions (see e.g., Hayter and Parker 2019), managers' values and ideologies (see e.g., Delis et al. 2019; Racko 2019), and indeed future strategic management decision-making (see e.g., Jung and Shin 2019).

Strategy 4: Turn Our Lenses Onto Ourselves

The final surprise for me was the discovery that around 30 percent of the papers in the sample rose to the challenge of turning our theoretical lenses onto ourselves (Starkey and Tempest 2005). The final trick was to recognize that business schools and universities are themselves organizations: highly complex, knowledge-based institutions that operate within a unique context and conditions.

Like all organizations, universities need to perform a range of management functions that need to be designed in efficient and effective ways. Our own workplaces, therefore, give us significant scope to explore questions on operations management (see e.g., Cire et al. 2019). Higher education institutions are heavily dependent on talent and human resources, and present an interesting context to investigate questions on human resource management, including issues on compensation (see e.g., Shulman 2019), training and career development (see e.g., Shibayama 2019), and performance management (see e.g., Broström 2019; Graddy-Reed et al. 2019). The unique higher education context also fosters distinct organizational cultures and organizational dynamics that present rich opportunities for study (see e.g., Sapir 2019).

Business schools and universities are accountable to a range of internal and external stakeholders. We face increasing challenges of managing and making the most of these complex relationship networks while meeting diverse and at times competing stakeholder demands and expectations. We operate in a most interesting environment within which we can investigate issues of organizational performance and stakeholder management (see e.g., Degl'Innocenti et al. 2019; Dionne et al. 2019; Horner et al. 2019).

As knowledge producers working in knowledge- and innovation-based organizations, we are in an exceptional position to uncover the processes of knowledge creation, communication and transfer. These include gaining insight into how knowledge flows (see e.g., Solomon et al. 2019), and how collaboration can lead to innovation (see e.g., Lee and Miozzo 2019). And of course, we are also in a position to uncover the nature and drivers of behavior that can ultimately have a negative impact on us and the knowledge that we create (see e.g., Graf et al. 2019; Hall and Martin 2019; Pfleegor et al. 2019; Radaelli et al. 2019; Seeber et al. 2019).

We operate in an industry like no other, and this gives us considerable opportunity to explore questions on industry dynamics, change and sustainability. These include issues on how students go about university selection (see e.g., Delavande and Zafar 2019; Fack et al. 2019) and the implications of these decision criteria and processes on how we remain competitive (see e.g., Kodeih et al. 2019). There are also much broader issues of how we can ensure financial sustainability (see e.g., Dougal et al. 2019), and of our impact on individuals, the economy and society (see e.g., Abbott et al. 2019; Célérier and Vallée 2019; Mueller and Yannelis 2019).

Our industry and our organizations are among the most complex and unique in the world. We must recognize the remarkable opportunity we have to reflect on ourselves and learn more about what and how we do things. Not only can other organizations benefit from our insights, but we can also better ourselves in the process.

ON BEING BY DOING

It was heartening to find that I was not having a pipe dream.

It was unfortunate for me to belatedly realize that I chose to retire into an insanely busy life. But it was fortunate that I was able to step back to comprehend the busyness, achieve clarity and gain perspective. Better late than never.

I saw that we were all busy not least because our industry is constantly under tremendous pressure to make sense of the turbulence of business and management. On top of the whirlwind of our own sensemaking, we also have to offer managers and policy-makers the tools to deal with the turbulence. We are the storm chasers of the social sciences.

I reconnected with the scholarly purpose of knowledge creation, communication and transfer. And came to understand that the teaching–research–engagement trifecta was not a zero-sum race, but a positive-sum game. Teaching does not only involve communicating what we know from past research. It also offers significant opportunity to test what we know by undertaking wide-ranging and interesting research with our students and industry partners. Our research cannot be divorced from the reality of the managers at the forefront of dealing with business turbulence. Our engagement thus offers us opportunities not just to transfer what we know, but also to test what we think we know and to discover what we do not yet know.

There are ways to take advantage of synergy in teaching, research and engagement. There are scholars out there who are successfully doing it. There is strong evidence that highly influential business and management journals welcome it. With the right perspective, we can ride the storm of our busyness.

It seems that Socrates and Sartre (and Sinatra) were really on to something:

To be is to embrace what we do;

To immerse in what we do is to seize opportunities to be;

And in harnessing the doing-being synergy, we, too, can do be do be do.

NOTES

1. http://data.un.org/.
2. http://www.legislation.gov.uk/ukpga/1992/13/contents.
3. http://ehea.info/page-sorbonne-declaration-1998.
4. https://www2.ed.gov/policy/highered/leg/hea98/index.html.

REFERENCES

Abbott, B., Gallipoli, G., Meghir, C., and Violante, G.L. (2019). Education policy and intergenerational transfers in equilibrium. *Journal of Political Economy*, 127(6), 2569–2624.

Adler, N.J., and Harzing, A.W. (2009). When knowledge wins: Transcending the sense and nonsense of academic rankings. *Academy of Management Learning and Education*, 8(1), 72–95.

Aggarwal, I., and Woolley, A.W. (2019). Team creativity, cognition, and cognitive style diversity. *Management Science*, 65(4), 1586–1599.

Alajoutsijärvi, K., Kettunen, K., and Sohlo, S. (2018). Shaking the status quo: Business accreditation and positional competition. *Academy of Management Learning and Education*, 17(2), 203–225.

Alvesson, M., and Sandberg, J. (2013). Has management studies lost its way? Ideas for more imaginative and innovative research. *Journal of Management Studies*, 50(1), 128-152.

Assunção Flores, M., and Gago, M. (2020). Teacher education in times of COVID-19 pandemic in Portugal: National, institutional and pedagogical responses. *Journal of Education for Teaching*, 46(4), 507–516.

Azmat, G., Bagues, M., Cabrales, A., and Iriberri, N. (2019). What you don't know … can't hurt you? A natural field experiment on relative performance feedback in higher education. *Management Science*, 65(8), 3714–3736.

Bagley, C.E., Sulkowski, A.J., Nelson, J.S., Waddock, S., and Shrivastava, P. (2020). A path to developing more insightful business school graduates: A systems-based, experiential approach to integrating law, strategy, and sustainability. *Academy of Management Learning and Education*, 19(4), 541–568.

Bao, W. (2020). COVID-19 and online teaching in higher education: A case study of Peking University. *Human Behavior and Emerging Technologies*, 2(2), 113–115.

Bapuji, H., and Beamish, P.W. (2019). Impacting practice through IB scholarship: Toy recalls and the product safety crisis. *Journal of International Business Studies*, 50(9), 1636–1643.

Barnett, R. (2009). Knowing and becoming in the higher education curriculum. *Studies in Higher Education*, 34(4), 429–440.

Barr, S.H., Baker, T.E.D., Markham, S.K., and Kingon, A.I. (2009). Bridging the valley of death: Lessons learned from 14 years of commercialization of technology education. *Academy of Management Learning and Education*, 8(3), 370–388.

Baur, C., Soucek, R., Kühnen, U., and Baumeister, R.F. (2020). Unable to resist the temptation to tell the truth or to lie for the organization? Identification makes the difference. *Journal of Business Ethics*, 167(4), 643–662.

Bedeian, A.G. (1996). Lessons learned along the way: Twelve suggestions for optimizing career success. In P.J. Frost and M.S. Taylor (eds), *Rhythms of Academic Life: Personal Accounts of Careers in Academia* (pp. 3–9). Thousand Oaks, CA: SAGE.

Bedwell, W.L., Fiore, S.M., and Salas, E. (2014). Developing the future workforce: An approach for integrating interpersonal skills into the MBA classroom. *Academy of Management Learning and Education*, 13(2), 171–186.

Bennet, D., and Bennet, A. (2004). The rise of the knowledge organization. In C.W. Holsapple (ed.), *Handbook on Knowledge Management 1* (pp. 5–20). Berlin, Heidelberg: Springer.

Borah, D., Malik, K., and Massini, S. (2019). Are engineering graduates ready for R&D jobs in emerging countries? Teaching-focused industry-academia collaboration strategies. *Research Policy*, 48(9), 103837.

Bowen, T., and Drysdale, M.T. (2017). *Work-Integrated Learning in the 21st Century*. Bingley: Emerald Publishing.

Broström, A. (2019). Academic breeding grounds: Home department conditions and early career performance of academic researchers. *Research Policy*, 48(7), 1647–1665.

Bunch, K.J. (2020). The state of undergraduate business education: A perfect storm or climate change? *Academy of Management Learning and Education*, 19(1), 81–98.

Burnette, J.L., Pollack, J.M., Forsyth, R.B., Hoyt, C.L., Babij, A.D., et al. (2019). A growth mindset intervention: Enhancing students' entrepreneurial self-efficacy and career development. *Entrepreneurship Theory and Practice*, 1042258719864293.

Butler, N., Delaney, H., and Spoelstra, S. (2017). The gray zone: Questionable research practices in the business school. *Academy of Management Learning and Education*, 16(1), 94–109.

Cartabuke, M., Westerman, J.W., Bergman, J.Z., Whitaker, B.G., Westerman, J., and Beekun, R.I. (2020). Empathy as an antecedent of social justice attitudes and perceptions. *Journal of Business Ethics*, 157(3), 605–615.

Célérier, C., and Vallée, B. (2019). Returns to talent and the finance wage premium. *Review of Financial Studies*, 32(10), 4005–4040.

Certo, S.T., Sirmon, D.G., and Brymer, R.A. (2010). Competition and scholarly productivity in management: Investigating changes in scholarship from 1988 to 2008. *Academy of Management Learning and Education*, 9(4), 591–606.

Chai, S., and Shih, W. (2016). Bridging science and technology through academic–industry partnerships. *Research Policy*, 45(1), 148–158.

Chan, W.K. (2020). Financial Times Global MBA 2020 ranking: Methodology and key. *Financial Times*. https://www.ft.com/content/8bb6737c-35ed-11ea-a6d3-9a26f8c3cba4. Accessed 27 March 2020.

Cire, A.A., Diamant, A., Yunes, T., and Carrasco, A. (2019). A network-based formulation for scheduling clinical rotations. *Production and Operations Management*, 28(5), 1186–1205.

Collet, F., and Vives, L. (2013). From preeminence to prominence: The fall of US business schools and the rise of European and Asian business schools in the Financial Times Global MBA Rankings. *Academy of Management Learning and Education*, 12(4), 540–563.

Cooper, J.M. (2007). Socrates and philosophy as a way of life. In D. Scott (ed.), *Maieusis: Essays in Ancient Philosophy in Honour of Myles Burnyeat* (pp. 20–43). Oxford: Oxford University Press.

Cox, A., Craig, R., and Tourish, D. (2018). Retraction statements and research malpractice in economics. *Research Policy*, 47(5), 924–935.

Craig, K., Thatcher, J.B., and Grover, V. (2019). The IT identity threat: A conceptual definition and operational measure. *Journal of Management Information Systems*, 36(1), 259–288.

Crawford, J., Butler-Henderson, K., Rudolph, J., and Glowatz, M. (2020). COVID-19: 20 countries' higher education intra-period digital pedagogy responses. *Journal of Applied Teaching and Learning* (JALT), 3(1), 1-20.

Daniels, D.P., and Zlatev, J.J. (2019). Choice architects reveal a bias toward positivity and certainty. *Organizational Behavior and Human Decision Processes*, 151, 132-149.

De Rond, M., and Miller, A.N. (2005). Publish or perish: Bane or boon of academic life? *Journal of Management Inquiry*, 14(4), 321-329.

Degl'Innocenti, M., Matousek, R., and Tzeremes, N.G. (2019). The interconnections of academic research and universities' "third mission": Evidence from the UK. *Research Policy*, 48(9), 103793.

Delavande, A., and Zafar, B. (2019). University choice: The role of expected earnings, nonpecuniary outcomes, and financial constraints. *Journal of Political Economy*, 127(5), 2343-2393.

Delis, M.D., Hasan, I., and Iosifidi, M. (2019). On the effect of business and economic university education on political ideology: An empirical note. *Journal of Business Ethics*, 155(3), 809-822.

Dierksmeier, C. (2020). From Jensen to Jensen: Mechanistic management education or humanistic management learning? *Journal of Business Ethics*, 166(1), 73-87.

Dionne, K.E., Mailhot, C., and Langley, A. (2019). Modeling the evaluation process in a public controversy. *Organization Studies*, 40(5), 651-679.

Dougal, C., Gao, P., Mayew, W.J., and Parsons, C.A. (2019). What's in a (school) name? Racial discrimination in higher education bond markets. *Journal of Financial Economics*, 134(3), 570-590.

Ebbers, J.J., and Wijnberg, N.M. (2019). The co-evolution of social networks and selection system orientations as core constituents of institutional logics of future entrepreneurs at school. *Journal of Business Venturing*, 34(3), 558-577.

Fack, G., Grenet, J., and He, Y. (2019). Beyond truth-telling: Preference estimation with centralized school choice and college admissions. *American Economic Review*, 109(4), 1486-1529.

Feldman, M., Feller, I., Bercovitz, J., and Burton, R. (2002). Equity and the technology transfer strategies of American research universities. *Management Science*, 48(1), 105-121.

Ferris, D.L., Fatimah, S., Yan, M., Liang, L.H., Lian, H., and Brown, D.J. (2019). Being sensitive to positives has its negatives: An approach/avoidance perspective on reactivity to ostracism. *Organizational Behavior and Human Decision Processes*, 152, 138-149.

Fleischman, G.M., Johnson, E.N., Walker, K.B., and Valentine, S.R. (2019). Ethics versus outcomes: Managerial responses to incentive-driven and goal-induced employee behavior. *Journal of Business Ethics*, 158(4), 951-967.

Fortin, N.M. (2006). Higher-education policies and the college wage premium: Cross-state evidence from the 1990s. *American Economic Review*, 96(4), 959-987.

García-Rosell, J.C. (2019). A discursive perspective on corporate social responsibility education: A story co-creation exercise. *Journal of Business Ethics*, 154(4), 1019-1032.

Gates, B. (2020). Responding to Covid-19—a once-in-a-century pandemic? *New England Journal of Medicine*, 382(18), 1677-1679.

Gillen, B., Snowberg, E., and Yariv, L. (2019). Experimenting with measurement error: Techniques with applications to the Caltech cohort study. *Journal of Political Economy*, 127(4), 1826-1863.

Gössling, S., Scott, D., and Hall, C.M. (2020). Pandemics, tourism and global change: A rapid assessment of COVID-19. *Journal of Sustainable Tourism*, 29(1), 1-20.

Graddy-Reed, A., Lanahan, L., and Eyer, J. (2019). Gender discrepancies in publication productivity of high-performing life science graduate students. *Research Policy*, 48(9), 103838.

Graf, L., Wendler, W.S., Stumpf-Wollersheim, J., and Welpe, I.M. (2019). Wanting more, getting less: Gaming performance measurement as a form of deviant workplace behavior. *Journal of Business Ethics*, 157(3), 753-773.

Guri-Rosenblit, S., Šebková, H., and Teichler, U. (2007). Massification and diversity of higher education systems: Interplay of complex dimensions. *Higher Education Policy*, 20(4), 373-389.

Hale, T., Petherick, A., Phillips, T., and Webster, S. (2020). Variation in government responses to COVID-19. Blavatnik School of Government Working Paper, 31.

Hall, J., and Martin, B.R. (2019). Towards a taxonomy of research misconduct: The case of business school research. *Research Policy*, 48(2), 414-427.

Hamington, M. (2019). Integrating care ethics and design thinking. *Journal of Business Ethics*, 155(1), 91-103.

Hardy, C., and Tolhurst, D. (2014). Epistemological beliefs and cultural diversity matters in management education and learning: A critical review and future directions. *Academy of Management Learning and Education*, 13(2), 265-289.

Harker, M.J., Caemmerer, B., and Hynes, N. (2016). Management education by the French Grandes Ecoles de Commerce: Past, present, and an uncertain future. *Academy of Management Learning and Education*, 15(3), 549-568.

Harzing, A-W. (2020). Journal Quality List, Sixty-sixth edition. https://harzing.com/resources/journal -quality-list. Accessed 20 March 2020.

Hayter, C.S., and Parker, M.A. (2019). Factors that influence the transition of university postdocs to non-academic scientific careers: An exploratory study. *Research Policy*, 48(3), 556-570.

Honig, B., Lampel, J., Siegel, D., and Drnevich, P. (2014). Ethics in the production and dissemination of management research: Institutional failure or individual fallibility?. *Journal of Management Studies*, 51(1), 118-142.

Horner, S., Jayawarna, D., Giordano, B., and Jones, O. (2019). Strategic choice in universities: Managerial agency and effective technology transfer. *Research Policy*, 48(5), 1297-1309.

Høgdal, C., Rasche, A., Schoeneborn, D., and Scotti, L. (2019). Exploring student perceptions of the hidden curriculum in responsible management education. *Journal of Business Ethics*, 168(1), 1-21.

Hu, J., Zhang, Z., Jiang, K., and Chen, W. (2019). Getting ahead, getting along, and getting prosocial: Examining extraversion facets, peer reactions, and leadership emergence. *Journal of Applied Psychology*, 104(11), 1369-1386.

Hull, D.M., Lowry, P.B., Gaskin, J.E., and Mirkovski, K. (2019). A storyteller's guide to problem-based learning for information systems management education. *Information Systems Journal*, 29(5), 1040-1057.

Hussain, I., Shu, R., Tangirala, S., and Ekkirala, S. (2019). The voice bystander effect: How information redundancy inhibits employee voice. *Academy of Management Journal*, 62(3), 828-849.

James, M.X., Miller, G.J., and Wyckoff, T.W. (2019). Comprehending the cultural causes of English writing plagiarism in Chinese students at a Western-style university. *Journal of Business Ethics*, 154(3), 631-642.

Jochmans, K., and Weidner, M. (2019). Fixed-effect regressions on network data. *Econometrica*, 87(5), 1543-1560.

Johnson, E.N., Kidwell, L.A., Lowe, D.J., and Reckers, P.M. (2019). Who follows the unethical leader? The association between followers' personal characteristics and intentions to comply in committing organizational fraud. *Journal of Business Ethics*, 154(1), 181-193.

Jung, J., and Shin, T. (2019). Learning not to diversify: The transformation of graduate business education and the decline of diversifying acquisitions. *Administrative Science Quarterly*, 64(2), 337-369.

Kaandorp, M., Van Burg, E., and Karlsson, T. (2019). Initial networking processes of student entrepreneurs: The role of action and evaluation. *Entrepreneurship Theory and Practice*, 1042258719834019.

Kodeih, F., Bouchikhi, H., and Gauthier, V. (2019). Competing through categorization: Product-and audience-centric strategies in an evolving categorical structure. *Organization Studies*, 40(7), 995-1023.

Kraimer, M.L., Greco, L., Seibert, S.E., and Sargent, L.D. (2019). An investigation of academic career success: The new tempo of academic life. *Academy of Management Learning and Education*, 18(2), 128-152.

Krishnan, K., and Wang, P. (2019). The cost of financing education: Can student debt hinder entrepreneurship?. *Management Science*, 65(10), 4522-4554.

Kwong, C.C., Thompson, P., and Cheung, C.W. (2012). The effectiveness of social business plan competitions in developing social and civic awareness and participation. *Academy of Management Learning and Education*, 11(3), 324-348.

Lau, H., Khosrawipour, V., Kocbach, P., Mikolajczyk, A., Schubert, J., et al. (2020). The positive impact of lockdown in Wuhan on containing the COVID-19 outbreak in China. *Journal of Travel Medicine*, 27(3), taaa037.

Lee, H.F., and Miozzo, M. (2019). Which types of knowledge-intensive business services firms collaborate with universities for innovation?. *Research Policy*, 48(7), 1633-1646.

Lewis, B.R., Duchac, J.E., and Beets, S.D. (2011). An academic publisher's response to plagiarism. *Journal of Business Ethics*, 102(3), 489-506.

Lount Jr, R.B., Doyle, S.P., Brion, S., and Pettit, N.C. (2019). Only when others are watching: The contingent efforts of high status group members. *Management Science*, 65(7), 3382-3397.

Loyd, D.L., Kern, M.C., and Thompson, L. (2005). Classroom research: Bridging the ivory divide. *Academy of Management Learning and Education*, 4(1), 8-21.

Maloney, M.M., Shah, P.P., Zellmer-Bruhn, M., and Jones, S.L. (2019). The lasting benefits of teams: Tie vitality after teams disband. *Organization Science*, 30(2), 260-279.

McGahan, A.M. (2007). Academic research that matters to managers: On zebras, dogs, lemmings, hammers, and turnips. *Academy of Management Journal*, 50(4), 748-753.

Meier, F., and Carroll, B. (2019). Making up leaders: Reconfiguring the executive student through profiling, texts and conversations in a leadership development programme. *Human Relations*, 0018726719858132.

Mercer-Mapstone, L., and Bovill, C. (2020). Equity and diversity in institutional approaches to student–staff partnership schemes in higher education. *Studies in Higher Education*, 45(12), 2541-2557.

Mihelič, K.K., and Culiberg, B. (2019). Reaping the fruits of another's labor: The role of moral meaningfulness, mindfulness, and motivation in social loafing. *Journal of Business Ethics*, 160(3), 713-727.

Millan, J.M., Congregado, E., Roman, C., Van Praag, M., and Van Stel, A. (2014). The value of an educated population for an individual's entrepreneurship success. *Journal of Business Venturing*, 29 (5), 612-632.

Mitra, D., and Golder, P.N. (2008). Does academic research help or hurt MBA programs? *Journal of Marketing*, 72(5), 31-49.

Mladenovic, R., Martinov-Bennie, N., and Bell, A. (2019). Business students' insights into their development of ethical decision-making. *Journal of Business Ethics*, 155(1), 275-287.

Moosmayer, D.C., Waddock, S., Wang, L., Hühn, M.P., Dierksmeier, C., and Gohl, C. (2019). Leaving the road to Abilene: A pragmatic approach to addressing the normative paradox of responsible management education. *Journal of Business Ethics*, 157(4), 913-932.

Mueller, H.M., and Yannelis, C. (2019). The rise in student loan defaults. *Journal of Financial Economics*, 131(1), 1-19.

Muscio, A., Quaglione, D., and Ramaciotti, L. (2016). The effects of university rules on spinoff creation: The case of academia in Italy. *Research Policy*, 45(7), 1386-1396.

Narayanan, V.K., Olk, P.M., and Fukami, C.V. (2010). Determinants of internship effectiveness: An exploratory model. *Academy of Management Learning and Education*, 9(1), 61-80.

O'Brien, J.P., Drnevich, P.L., Crook, T.R., and Armstrong, C.E. (2010). Does business school research add economic value for students? *Academy of Management Learning and Education*, 9(4), 638-651.

Ormans, L. (2016). 50 Journals used in FT Research Rank. *Financial Times*, https://www.ft.com/content/3405a512-5cbb-11e1-8f1f-00144feabdc0. Accessed 20 March 2020.

Parker, S.K., Andrei, D.M., and Van den Broeck, A. (2019). Poor work design begets poor work design: Capacity and willingness antecedents of individual work design behavior. *Journal of Applied Psychology*, 104(7), 907-928.

Paton, S., Chia, R., and Burt, G. (2014). Relevance or 'relevate'? How university business schools can add value through reflexively learning from strategic partnerships with business. *Management Learning*, 45(3), 267-288.

Peters, M.A., Wang, H., Ogunniran, M.O., Huang, Y., Green, B., et al. (2020). China's internationalized higher education during Covid-19: Collective student autoethnography. *Postdigital Science and Education*, 2(3), 968-988.

Pisano, G.P. (2006). Can science be a business? Lessons from biotech. *Harvard Business Review*, 84(10), 114-124.

Peng, M.W., and Dess, G.G. (2010). In the spirit of scholarship. *Academy of Management Learning and Education*, 9(2), 282-298.

Pfleegor, A.G., Katz, M., and Bowers, M.T. (2019). Publish, perish, or salami slice? Authorship ethics in an emerging field. *Journal of Business Ethics*, 156(1), 189-208.

QS World University Rankings (2020). *QS World University Rankings Methodology.* https://www.topuniversities.com/qs-world-university-rankings/methodology. Accessed 27 March 2020.

Racko, G. (2019). The values of economics. *Journal of Business Ethics*, 154(1), 35-48.

Radaelli, G., Guerci, M., Cabras, F., and Dalla Chiesa, N. (2019). How are professionals recruited by external agents in misconduct projects? The infiltration of organized crime in a university. *Human Relations*, 72(9), 1407-1435.

Reficco, E., Jaén, M.H., and Trujillo, C. (2019). Beyond knowledge: A study of Latin American business schools' efforts to deliver a value-based education. *Journal of Business Ethics*, 156(3), 857-874.

Robinson, C.D., Gallus, J., Lee, M.G., and Rogers, T. (2019). The demotivating effect (and unintended message) of awards. *Organizational Behavior and Human Decision Processes*, 163, 51-64.

Rubin, R.S., and Dierdorff, E.C. (2009). How relevant is the MBA? Assessing the alignment of required curricula and required managerial competencies. *Academy of Management Learning and Education*, 8(2), 208-224.

Rubin, R.S., and Dierdorff, E.C. (2011). On the road to Abilene: Time to manage agreement about MBA curricular relevance. *Academy of Management Learning and Education*, 10(1), 148-161.

Ruigrok, W., Gratwohl, M., and Ruppert, A. (2017). Rankings, information asymmetry and mobility: An empirical study on students' ranking perceptions. *Academy of Management Proceedings* 2017(1), 15399.

Rumbley, L.E. (2020). *Coping with COVID-19: International Higher Education in Europe.* European Association for International Education.

Ryazanova, O., and McNamara, P. (2019). Choices and consequences: Impact of mobility on research-career capital and promotion in business schools. *Academy of Management Learning and Education*, 18(2), 186-212.

Sahu, P. (2020). Closure of universities due to Coronavirus Disease 2019 (COVID-19): Impact on education and mental health of students and academic staff. *Cureus*, 12(4). doi: 10.7759/cureus.7541.

Samek, A. (2019). Gender differences in job entry decisions: A university-wide field experiment. *Management Science*, 65(7), 3272-3281.

Sapir, A. (2019). Mythologizing the story of a scientific invention: Constructing the legitimacy of research commercialization. *Organization Studies*, 0170840618814575.

Schlegel, K., and Mortillaro, M. (2019). The Geneva Emotional Competence Test (GECo): An ability measure of workplace emotional intelligence. *Journal of Applied Psychology*, 104(4), 559.

Seeber, M., Cattaneo, M., Meoli, M., and Malighetti, P. (2019). Self-citations as strategic response to the use of metrics for career decisions. *Research Policy*, 48(2), 478-491.

Shibayama, S. (2019). Sustainable development of science and scientists: Academic training in life science labs. *Research Policy*, 48(3), 676-692.

Shulman, S. (2019). The costs and benefits of adjunct justice: A critique of Brennan and Magness. *Journal of Business Ethics*, 155(1), 163-171.

Singhal, K., Sodhi, M.S., and Tang, C.S. (2014). POMS initiatives for promoting practice-driven research and research-influenced practice. *Production and Operations Management*, 23(5), 725-727.

Solomon, G.E., Youtie, J., Carley, S., and Porter, A.L. (2019). What people learn about how people learn: An analysis of citation behavior and the multidisciplinary flow of knowledge. *Research Policy*, 48(9), 103835.

Sousa, C.A., de Nijs, W.F., and Hendriks, P.H. (2010). Secrets of the beehive: Performance management in university research organizations. *Human Relations*, 63(9), 1439-1460.

Starkey, K., and Tempest, S. (2005). The future of the business school: Knowledge challenges and opportunities. *Human Relations*, 58(1), 61-82.

Steffens, P.R., Weeks, C.S., Davidsson, P., and Isaak, L. (2014). Shouting from the ivory tower: A marketing approach to improve communication of academic research to entrepreneurs. *Entrepreneurship Theory and Practice*, 38(2), 399-426.

Taleb, N.N. (2007). *The Black Swan: The Impact of the Highly Improbable* (2nd edn). New York: Random House.

THE World University Rankings (2020). THE World University Rankings 2020: methodology. https://www.timeshighereducation.com/world-university-rankings/world-university-rankings-2020 -methodology. Accessed 27 March 2020.

Tomlin, K.A., Metzger, M.L., and Bradley-Geist, J. (2021). Removing the blinders: Increasing students' awareness of self-perception biases and real-world ethical challenges through an educational intervention. *Journal of Business Ethics*, 169(4), 731–746.

Ungaretti, T., Thompson, K.R., Miller, A., and Peterson, T.O. (2015). Problem-based learning: Lessons from medical education and challenges for management education. *Academy of Management Learning and Education*, 14(2), 173-186.

Van de Ven, A.H., and Johnson, P.E. (2006). Knowledge for theory and practice. *Academy of Management Review*, 31(4), 802-821.

Vonnegut, K. (1982). *Deadeye Dick*. New York: Random House.

Vredeveld, A.J., and Coulter, R.A. (2019). Cultural experiential goal pursuit, cultural brand engagement, and culturally authentic experiences: Sojourners in America. *Journal of the Academy of Marketing Science*, 47(2), 274-290.

Walker, K., Dyck, B., Zhang, Z., and Starke, F. (2019). The use of praxis in the classroom to facilitate student transformation. *Journal of Business Ethics*, 157(1), 199-216.

Webber, J. (2009). *The Existentialism of Jean-Paul Sartre*. New York: Routledge.

Winterich, K.P., Nenkov, G.Y., and Gonzales, G.E. (2019). Knowing what it makes: How product transformation salience increases recycling. *Journal of Marketing*, 83(4), 21-37.

Yang, H., Carmon, Z., Ariely, D., and Norton, M.I. (2019). The feeling of not knowing it all. *Journal of Consumer Psychology*, 29(3), 455-462.

Yu, J. (2005). The beginning of ethics: Confucius and Socrates. *Asian Philosophy*, 15(2), 173-189.

Zhang, M.M., Xia, J., Fan, D., and Zhu, J.C. (2016). Managing student diversity in business education: Incorporating campus diversity into the curriculum to foster inclusion and academic success of international students. *Academy of Management Learning and Education*, 15(2), 366-380.

Index